SENTENCING AND PENAL POLICY

LAW IN CONTEXT

Editors: Robert Stevens (Haverford College, Pennsylvania),
William Twining (University College, London) and
Christopher McCrudden (Lincoln College, Oxford)

Sentencing and Penal Policy

ANDREW ASHWORTH

Fellow of Worcester College and Acting Director of the Centre for
Criminological Research, University of Oxford

WEIDENFELD AND NICOLSON
London

George Weidenfeld & Nicolson Ltd
91 Clapham High Street, London sw4 7ta

ISBN 0 297 78236 3   cased
ISBN 0 297 78241 X   paperback
Photoset by Deltatype, Ellesmere Port
Printed by Butler & Tanner Ltd., Frome and
London

CONTENTS

CASES AND STATUTES

CASES

STATUTES

PREFACE

Recent years have seen a resurgence of serious interest in the theory and practice of sentencing. In the second half of the nineteenth century there was lively public debate about the proper principles of sentencing, with magistrates and judges writing articles and pamphlets, debating not merely broad theories of punishment but also 'middle-range' issues such as the sentencing of persistent offenders. In the second half of the twentieth century, discussion has taken a rather different form. There has been renewed philosophical debate about the justifications for punishment and the aims of sentencing, but this has not (with a few exceptions) been extended to a discussion of the range of practical sentencing problems which arise daily in the courts. There has been a growing academic interest in the principles of sentencing as laid down by the Court of Appeal when dealing with appeals against sentence, but this has largely been unaccompanied by any case-by-case or principle-by-principle examination of the assumptions behind those decisions. There has been some empirical research into sentencing, but this cannot be said to have penetrated far into the complex processes which appear to be involved in this kind of decision-making. There has also been a substantial increase in the number of government statements about penal policy, probably resulting from the fact that the numbers sent to prison now considerably outstrip the accommodation provided, and the use of custodial sentences by the courts has been the focus of considerable public discussion. This last facet of contemporary concern has led the senior judiciary in the Court of Appeal to urge sentencers to reduce the level of sentences for certain types of offence, but they have continued staunchly to defend the discretion of the courts to select the sentence for each case from among a wide range of alternatives, with a minimum of statutory restriction.

The aim of this book is to place sentencing in the context of penal policy, to explore some of these neglected issues, and to examine the assumptions which underlie prevailing patterns of thought. For this, it is necessary to begin with a general overview of the sentencing system (Chapter 1). This is followed by an examination of the conceptions of judicial independence which play such a predominant part in English thinking on the subject (Chapter 2), and a discussion of the relationships between sentencing and criminal law reform, sentencing and the decisions which precede it in the criminal process, and then sentencing and the decisions of penal policy which lead the legislature to provide the courts with new penal measures (Chapter 3). Many modern approaches to sentencing, whether in theory or in practice, invoke the idea of proportionality. For some, it is the central element in determining the amount of punishment; for others, proportionality is regarded as setting an upper limit to the severity of punishments. However, the implications of references to proportionality are rarely subjected to detailed consideration, and some other principles which might refine it or conflict with it tend to be neglected. Chapter 4 explores the notion of culpability, considering the ideas of seriousness of offence and culpability of offender which form integral parts of the concept of proportionality. The next chapters focus upon some of the practical problems of sentencing and some general principles which have been laid down by the courts – the problem of persistent offenders (Chapter 5), the approach to sentencing multiple offenders (Chapter 6), the principles of equality of impact and equality before the law (Chapter 7), and the various symbolic and self-reinforcing elements in sentencing practice (Chapter 8). Here, as throughout the book, the emphasis is less upon the legal minutiae of the decided cases or the general 'aims of punishment' than upon theories of the middle range – examining critically some of the maxims and general principles which are invoked by sentencers in particular kinds of case. Chapter 9 considers the courts' use of custodial sentences, exploring the justifications for imposing imprisonment and for choosing certain lengths of sentence. Chapter 10 discusses the criteria for imposing the various non-custodial measures. In Chapter 11 the various relationships between sentencing and other parts of the criminal process are drawn together, in the context of suggested procedural changes which might improve those relationships.

No attempt is made to survey all the relevant decisions of the courts or all the known studies; the aim is rather to draw upon selected materials in order to provide a structure for critical evaluation of the practice and principles of sentencing. Although no book on this topic could be written without making assumptions of social philosophy, the emphasis here lies upon middle-range issues which have to be resolved whatever the general philosophical approach, and which often seem to be resolved independently of any 'master theory' of punishment. There are no separate chapters on such topics as victims and compensation, the sentencing of 'dangerous' offenders, the sentencing of young offenders or the disposal of mentally disordered offenders; nor is there an attempt to describe the ranges of sentences for particular offences, as in Dr Thomas's *Principles of Sentencing*. The aim is to examine, for the benefit of those studying sentencing, criminology or penology, what might be termed 'general principles of sentencing', in their context of penal policy.

I have incurred many debts of gratitude during the period of writing. Shortly after it was agreed that I should write this book, I had the good fortune to be invited by the late Sir Rupert Cross to join him in preparing the third edition of his book on the *English Sentencing System*. The few months of our collaboration in that work stimulated me greatly, and the fact that that book sets out the legal details of the various orders on conviction available to English courts makes it unnecessary to repeat them in this book. Shortly after finishing work on the third edition of Cross, I was invited to direct a research project into sentencing in the Crown Court, being carried out by a team of four researchers at the Centre for Criminological Research in the University of Oxford. In the event, that research came to an abrupt end after only one year, when the Lord Chief Justice, Lord Lane, refused his permission for the project to proceed beyond a 'pilot study'. That decision effectively prevents access to systematic knowledge about the approach to sentencing of those who pass sentence in the courts which deal with our most serious crimes. Despite the tragedy of that decision, I must record that the year which I spent working with the four researchers on that project was one of great pleasure and profit for me: my outlook on sentencing was enriched by our lengthy discussions.

I owe thanks to all members of the Centre for Criminological Research for their support and for their helpful comments on aspects of my work. Several other friends have kindly read chapters or parts of the book in draft, but I am reluctant to implicate them by listing their names here. I must, however, single out Martin Wasik of Manchester University for special thanks, since he read and

commented on most of the chapters in draft. I have certainly
benefited greatly from his criticisms and suggestions, but he is not to
be implicated in the way the book has been written. I ceased to
collect new material after the end of September 1982, but I have
been able to incorporate some more recent developments and I have
treated the Criminal Justice Act 1982 as being in force – in fact, most
of its provisions come into force on 24 May, 1983.

Andrew Ashworth
Oxford, March 1983

I

An introduction to sentencing

1 Courts and crimes

Although some common law crimes remain, most of the offences which make up English criminal law were created by statute and have a statutory maximum penalty. For the purposes of trial, offences have since the Criminal Law Act 1977 been divided into three categories – offences triable only on indictment, offences triable only summarily, and offences triable either way. Relatively few offences are triable only on indictment (i.e. at the Crown Court); a large mass of less serious offences are triable only summarily (i.e. in magistrates' courts); most of the offences with which this book is concerned are triable either way, which means that they will be tried in a magistrates' court unless the prosecution, the defendant or the magistrates wish to have the case tried at Crown Court.

The Crown Court sits with a High Court judge, Circuit Judge or Recorder, with a jury. There are three levels of Crown Court centre: first-tier centres, where both criminal and civil cases are tried and which High Court judges and Circuit Judges attend; second-tier centres, attended by High Court judges and Circuit Judges but dealing only with criminal cases; and third-tier centres, attended by Circuit Judges and dealing only with criminal cases. England and Wales are divided into circuits, and each circuit has a number of court centres in each category. Recorders and assistant Recorders, who are part-time judges and spend the rest of the time practising as barristers or solicitors, may sit at a court centre of any level, but there are restrictions on the kind of case they may deal with. These restrictions are expressed through the division of criminal offences into four classes, according to their gravity. Class 1 offences (including murder and treason) may only be tried by a High Court judge; class 2 offences (including manslaughter, rape, abortion, and incest or unlawful sexual intercourse with a girl under 13) may only be tried by a High Court judge unless the presiding judge of the circuit authorizes a case to be tried by a Circuit Judge or Recorder; class 3 offences form a residual category and are normally tried by a High Court judge but may be tried by a Circuit Judge or Recorder; and class 4 includes most offences which are triable either way (including serious woundings and robbery), and such cases may be tried either by a Circuit Judge or by a Recorder. A person who has been convicted and sentenced at Crown Court may appeal against sentence to the Court of Appeal (Criminal Division), but he must first seek leave to appeal from that Court. Applications for leave to appeal are considered by a single High Court judge. If the appeal is heard, the Court of Appeal has the power to substitute any sentence or order which is no more severe than the sentence imposed at Crown Court.

Where a person is tried summarily, either for a summary offence or for an offence triable either way, he will appear at a local magistrates' court. Each county is divided into a number of petty sessional areas, each of which has a magistrates' court which sits as frequently as business justifies. The bench of magistrates which deals with the case may number between two and seven magistrates, but in practice most benches sit with three magistrates. The exception is in certain large conurbations, where stipendiary magistrates also sit. A stipendiary magistrate is a full-time appointee, with at least 10 years' standing as a barrister or solicitor, and in court he has the same powers as two lay magistrates. The powers of magistrates' courts are more limited than those of the Crown Court: not only are they limited by the maximum penalty laid down by statute for each offence, but they are also limited to 6 months' imprisonment in respect of any one offence (or a maximum of 12 months by way of consecutive sentences for two or more offences) and to a fine of £1,000 for most offences, together with a compensation order of no more than £400. If the magistrates form the view that their sentencing powers are not adequate to deal with a person whom they have convicted of an offence triable either way,[1] they may commit him to the Crown Court for sentence. A person who has been sentenced in a magistrates' court may appeal against sentence to the Crown Court. The appeal takes the form of a complete re-hearing of the case, before a Circuit Judge or Recorder and two lay magistrates, and the Crown Court has the power to pass any sentence which the magistrates' court could have imposed, whether that sentence be more or less severe than the sentence which the magistrates' court actually did pass in the case.

Summary offences are little discussed in this book. The main concern is with indictable offences, which include offences triable only on indictment at the Crown Court and all offences 'triable either way', whether in fact they are tried at the Crown Court or in magistrates' courts. Almost all the statistics quoted refer to indictable offences.

2 The available sentences

Few would dispute that the most lenient course which an English court can take after conviction is to order an *absolute discharge*. The power is granted by section 7 of the Powers of Criminal Courts Act 1973, and for most purposes the conviction does not count against the offender in future. Formally the court must be satisfied that it is 'inexpedient to inflict punishment' and that a probation order is 'not appropriate'. In practice the power is not greatly used – it accounted for a mere 1 per cent of indictable cases in magistrates' courts and a negligible percentage of cases in the Crown Court in 1981 – and its use seems to vary inversely to the extent to which the local police force uses formal cautions. Thus it has been found that 'certain urban [police] forces have a deliberate policy of cautioning as few adult indictable offenders as possible, with the result that large numbers of minor offenders are sent to court', and the number of discharges (absolute and conditional) in that area is unusually high.[2] A court will generally reserve the absolute discharge for a case where there is very little moral guilt in the offence, where mitigating factors are overwhelmingly strong, where an offence was committed by the offender some years earlier against a different social and personal background,[3] or in other cases where it is thought inexpedient to punish, and indeed in some cases where the court thinks it wrong that a prosecution should have been brought.

The power to grant a *conditional discharge* is also to be found in section 7 of the 1973 Act, and the condition is that the offender must commit no offence within the period, of not more than three years, specified by the court. If he is convicted of an offence committed during the specified period, he is liable to be sentenced for the original offence as well. The court imposing a conditional discharge must be satisfied that it is 'inexpedient to inflict punishment' and that a probation order is 'not appropriate'. These requirements have a little more bite in this context: a court which wants to inflict a moderate fine combined with a conditional discharge for a period of two or three years cannot do so, because the fine is 'punishment' and cannot therefore be imposed in a case where a conditional discharge is imposed; and in forming the view that probation is not appropriate, the court must in theory be satisfied that the offender can keep out of trouble for the period of the discharge without the need for support from the probation service. Otherwise a probation order would be appropriate, and since it is open to the court on breach of a probation order to impose a sentence for the original offence, the kind of standing threat implicit in a conditional discharge is present in a probation order too. Conditional discharges account for a significant proportion of sentences in indictable cases – 13 per cent in magistrates' courts and 4 per cent in the Crown Court in 1981 – and may be used in a wide variety of circumstances. At one extreme there is the case which is not quite so venial as to warrant an absolute discharge; at the other, the case of an offender who is unable to pay a substantial fine for a fairly serious offence, who should not be given a suspended sentence for that reason alone, and who is therefore conditionally discharged.

The *fine* is by far the most-used penal measure in English courts, being the sentence imposed for almost all summary offences and accounting for no less than 52 per cent of indictable offenders sentenced in magistrates' courts and 11 per cent in the Crown Court in 1981. The maximum fine for some offences is fixed by statute,[3a] and for others is left at large. Magistrates' courts are generally unable to impose a fine of more than £1,000, but most fines are well below this limit. Some guidance on the level of fines for motoring offences is given by the Magistrates' Association's 'Suggested Basic Penalties for Road Traffic Offences', although research has shown that local benches accept the Association's suggestion that they may wish to vary the level of fines for their area.[4] There is also evidence of lists of recommended penalties for other offences at some courts,[5] but in general it seems that both magistrates and judges are left without much substantial guidance on levels of fines. One factor which courts probably do take into account, however, is any profit which the offender made from the offence, since it is widely agreed that one purpose of the financial penalty is to deprive him of any ill-gotten gains. Apart from that, it is a clear principle that the court must adjust the fine in accordance with the offender's means. This principle is discussed in detail in Chapter 7: where the court finds that the offender is unable to afford a fine sufficiently high to mark the gravity of the offence, it may be driven to impose an alternative sentence, and in general the Court of Appeal has maintained that this should not be more severe than a fine would have been[6] (a suspended sentence, for example). Courts must also have regard to the totality of the financial burden imposed on the offender: section 67 of the Criminal Justice Act 1982 now provides that compensation orders should be accorded priority over fines, and there is also the question of payment of costs. Where it seems likely that an offender will experience difficulty in so organizing his finances as to pay the fine, the court may impose a Money Payment Supervision Order,[7] which usually places the offender under the supervision of a probation officer for this purpose. The court which imposes a fine may give the offender time to pay, and may agree to payment by instalment over a considerable period of time. Often, however, these details are either agreed with or altered by the fines and fees office of the local magistrates' court; that office will also control the pace at which enforcement procedures are mobilized against a fine defaulter.[8] Courts have the power to commit to prison an offender who wilfully defaults on his payment.

One measure which has tended to decline in proportionate use is the *probation order*: whereas over one-fifth of adults convicted of indictable offences were put on probation in 1938, the proportion declined to 5 per cent in 1978, although its use has recently increased for young adults (from 7 per cent in 1978 to 8 per cent in 1981). The essence of a probation order is that the court places the offender under the supervision of a probation officer for a specified period, between 6 months and 3 years. The offender must consent to this, and the court makes the order 'instead of sentencing him', so that if he breaches the order or re-offends whilst it is in force, he is liable to be sentenced for the original offence. The court may, where appropriate, require the probationer to reside in a hostel, or to undergo mental treatment, or to attend at an approved day centre, or to fulfil certain other conditions. The idea of placing an offender on probation will often originate in the social enquiry report, and the evidence suggests that positive recommendations for probation are taken up in the majority of cases.[9]

The probation order is not, as is sometimes assumed, a measure for first offenders: it is used more as a response to the perceived needs of the offender, as where his offending appears related to some serious personal or domestic circumstances, and it is sometimes used even for persistent offenders who have experienced custodial sentences. The probation service has a wide variety of tasks, including the preparation of social enquiry reports for the courts and the supervision of those released from custody on parole or on compulsory after-care. The supervision of probationers usually takes the form of periodic interviews at the probation office and discussions at the probationer's home, and may involve group activities. As with the fine, there are variations in the way in which the conditions of orders are actually enforced: probation officers may overlook a small number of technical breaches of the order, but sometimes an officer fails to initiate breach proceedings until there have been repeated breaches of the order. There are several restrictions on the combination of a probation order with other penal measures, as we shall see later, but it is permissible to combine probation with a compensation order, and to place an offender on probation for one offence and to fine him for another.

Courts now have a power of *deferment of sentence*, under section 1 of the Powers of Criminal Courts Act 1973. Sentence upon an offender may be deferred, with his consent, for up to six months for the purpose of enabling the court to have regard (a) to his conduct after conviction, such as making reparation for the offence, or (b) to any change in his circumstances. The power tends to be used when there is the distinct prospect of some impending change in the offender's circumstances which might affect his subsequent behaviour. At the end of the period of deferment, the court will then pass sentence for the original offence in the light of the offender's behaviour in the meantime.

In the last ten years the *community service order* has been added to the list of available measures, beginning on an experimental basis in six probation areas and then being gradually extended to all courts since 1975. Section 14 of the Powers of Criminal Courts Act 1973 provides that a court may make a community service order of between 40 and 240 hours for any imprisonable offence, provided that the offender consents to the order and that the court is satisfied, after considering a report from a probation officer, that the offender is suitable and work is available. The community service order has rapidly established a significant place in the alternatives for young adult offenders, aged 17 to 20, being given to 11 per cent of such offenders in 1981; for all indictable offenders it was given in 5 per cent of cases in magistrates' courts and 8 per cent of cases in the Crown Court. Nonetheless, there are two fundamental ambiguities in the community service order which loom large in practice: one is that its purpose and effect are unclear, since the order may be viewed as retributive (by making the offender work hard in his leisure time), rehabilitative (by bringing him into contact with public-spirited voluntary workers and with disadvantaged members of the community), or reparative (by requiring him to give something back to the society whose rules he has broken); the second ambiguity is whether the community service order is properly viewed as an alternative to an immediate custodial sentence or as simply a further variety of non-custodial measure. At present, it seems that both ambiguities flourish in practice, with sentencers and probation officers viewing the order in different ways; some are quite content with this position, so long as the order is relatively well used. The range of tasks which offenders are required to perform is wide, from constructing children's playgrounds to clearing canals, and from assisting the mentally handicapped to repairing toys. The community service order is conditional: if there is a breach, either by conviction of a further offence or by failure to observe the conditions of the order, the court may revoke the order and deal with the offender for the original offence – in addition to sentencing him for any further offence. In that sense, community service holds the same kind of threat as a conditional discharge, although community service orders must be completed within one year and are usually completed more quickly than that.

The *suspended sentence* has been available to English courts since 1967: a court may now suspend any sentence of 2 years' imprisonment or less, for a period of between one and two years. Suspended sentences were imposed on 12 per cent of adult male indictable offenders and 4 per cent of young adult males in 1981, but the Criminal Justice Act 1982 has now made the suspended sentence unavailable for young adult offenders. In principle, a court ought only to impose a suspended sentence when it would, in the absence of that measure, have imposed an immediate custodial sentence (section 22(2) Powers of Criminal Courts Act); and it should not impose a longer sentence when suspending than it would have imposed if the sentence had been immediate.[10] If the offender is convicted of another imprisonable offence committed during the operational period of the suspended sentence, the court should activate the suspended sentence consecutively to the sentence for the new offence, unless it is of the opinion that this would be 'unjust' in view of all the circumstances (e.g. the facts of both offences). Suspended sentences were given to 5 per cent of indictable offenders in magistrates' courts and 16 per cent in the Crown Court in 1981. Just over a quarter of suspended sentences are breached, and in about three-quarters of these cases the court activates the suspended sentence in full.

The sentence of *immediate imprisonment* is the most severe measure for adults now known to English law. Life imprisonment is the mandatory sentence for murder. Life is also the maximum sentence for a number of other serious offences, such as manslaughter, rape, robbery and arson, and in practice it is imposed upon about 150 offenders each year who are regarded as particularly dangerous. All other custodial sentences are determinate, and are subject to the statutory maximum penalty for the particular offence – such as 14 years for burglary and for handling, 10 years for theft and for criminal damage, and 5 years for assault occasioning actual bodily harm and for malicious wounding. These maxima were created at different times against different social backgrounds, and in no way form a rational scale of comparative gravity. Beneath these statutory maxima the courts are guided by common practice and by the judgments of the Court of Appeal. The proportionate use of immediate imprisonment has begun to increase again, after a decline in the mid-1970s: thus it stood at 18 per cent in 1981 compared with 15 per cent in 1974 for adult male indictable offenders. Magistrates sentenced 5 per cent of indictable offenders to immediate imprisonment in 1981, whereas the figure for the Crown Court was 36 per cent. Offenders serving sentences of over 18 months are eligible for parole after 12 months or one-third of their sentence (whichever is longer), and in 1981 almost two-thirds of released prisoners who were eligible for parole were in fact released on parole, with an average period on licence of about 9 months each.

A new form of prison sentence for adults is the *partly suspended sentence*, introduced in March 1982 by bringing into force Section 47 of the Criminal Law Act 1977, and subsequently amended by section 30 of the Criminal Justice Act 1982. The court may order that any prison sentence of between 3 months and 2 years must be served in part and part held in suspense. The total sentence may be said to mark the gravity of the offence, and the court may make some allowance for mitigating factors (although not as much allowance as is required before fully suspending the sentence) by reducing the proportion to be served immediately, which may be up to three-quarters of the sentence but in no case less than 28 days. The remainder is then held in suspense, and may be activated if the offender is convicted of an imprisonable offence committed during the whole term of the original sentence.[11]

For young adult offenders, aged 17 and under 21, imprisonment is technically not available and there are two forms of custodial sentence – detention centres and youth custody. The *detention centre* order was formerly an order to spend between 3 and 6 months (less remission) in the relatively disciplined regime of a senior detention centre: the Criminal Justice Act 1982 has now reduced the length of the order to between 3 weeks and 4 months, as specified by the court. In 1980 the Government introduced a much brisker 'short, sharp shock' regime into a limited number of detention centres. *Youth custody* was introduced by the Criminal Justice Act 1982 to replace the sentences of borstal training and imprisonment for young adult offenders. Whereas borstal was an indeterminate sentence of between 6 months and 2 years, the duration of youth custody is fixed by the court (with remission and parole as for adult imprisonment). Sentences of 18 months or less youth custody are served in 'training establishments', the regime of which is 'modelled on the best of the borstal system'.[12]

Neither the suspended sentence nor the partly suspended sentence is available for young adult offenders, but there are 14 senior *attendance centres* to which young adult offenders may be sent by the courts. The attendance centre order requires the offender to spend between 12 and 36 hours (as specified by the court) at a nearby centre, where there is physical training and a choice of short courses on such subjects as motor repairing.

This book is principally concerned with offenders aged 17 and over, and therefore no mention is made here of the various powers available to the courts when dealing with juveniles. The details of other orders which criminal courts can make upon adult and young adult offenders may be found in the leading textbooks.[13] In this book, there are chapters on custodial sentencing (Chapter 9) and on non-custodial sentencing (Chapter 10).

Table 1 Serious offences recorded by the police by offence group (in thousands)

Offence group	1970	1971	1972	1973	1974	1975	1976	1977	1978	1979	1980	1981
Violence against the person	41.1	47.0	52.4	61.3	63.8	71.0	77.7	82.2	87.1	95.0	97.2	100.2
Sexual offences	24.2	23.6	23.5	25.7	24.7	23.7	22.2	21.3	22.4	21.8	21.1	19.4
Burglary	431.4	451.5	438.7	393.2	483.8	521.9	515.5	604.1	565.7	549.1	622.6	723.2
Robbery	6.3	7.5	8.9	7.3	8.7	11.3	11.6	13.7	13.1	12.5	15.0	20.3
Theft and handling stolen goods	952.6	1,003.7	1,009.5	998.9	1,189.9	1,267.7	1,285.7	1,487.5	1,441.3	1,416.1	1,463.5	1,603.2
Fraud and forgery	89.5	99.8	108.4	110.7	117.2	123.1	119.9	120.6	122.2	118.0	105.2	106.7
Criminal damage	17.9	27.0	41.9	52.8	67.1	78.5	93.0	123.9	140.5	160.5	191.8	217.2
Other serious offences	5.4	5.6	6.9	7.8	8.2	8.4	10.1	9.7	3.5	3.7	4.1	4.1
Total	1,568.4	1,665.7	1,690.2	1,657.7	1,963.4	2,105.6	2,135.7	2,463.0	2,395.8	2,376.7	2,520.6	2,794.2

Table 2 Percentage clear-up rates for serious offences recorded by the police by offence group

Offence group	1970	1971	1972	1973	1974	1975	1976	1977	1978	1979	1980	1981
Violence against the person	82	82	81	82	80	81	79	79	77	77	77	75
Sexual offences	76	76	77	78	78	78	77	77	76	75	74	73
Burglary	36	37	37	37	34	34	34	31	32	31	31	30
Robbery	42	42	43	46	40	40	33	28	30	31	29	25
Theft and handling stolen goods	43	43	43	43	42	41	41	40	40	40	39	38
Fraud and forgery	82	83	83	82	82	84	81	82	84	82	75	70
Criminal damage	39	34	37	39	38	37	35	30	30	30	28	27
Other serious offences	94	92	94	93	91	92	93	94	92	90	91	88
Total	45	45	46	47	44	44	43	41	42	41	40	38

3 The general statistical background

Some 2.8 million 'serious offences' were recorded by the police in 1981: this may be compared with the 1.6 million indictable offences recorded in 1970, since the categories of indictable and 'serious' offences are broadly similar and the changes in recording procedures in the intervening years have only a minor effect on the comparison. (If offences of criminal damage to the value of £20 and under are included, the 1981 total becomes nearly 3 million.) Table 1[14] shows how the annual total of serious offences recorded by the police has increased during the last decade: the average increase is around 5 per cent per annum.

The proportion of these offences 'cleared up' by the police decreased slightly during the decade, varying from 45 to 47 per cent in the early 1970s and then falling to around 40 per cent in the last three years, as Table 2 shows.[15] In round terms, about 1 million of the 2.8 million serious offences recorded by the police in 1981 were cleared up. This does not imply that in all these cases a conviction was obtained or a police caution administered, for the 'cleared up' category also includes such offences as those traced to children under 10 and those 'taken into consideration' on other charges. The clear-up rate varies from offence to offence, as Table 2 also demonstrates. About three-quarters of offences of violence and sexual offences were cleared up in 1981, largely because the victim could usually identify the offender and was often previously known to him or her; in contrast, the proportion of burglaries and robberies cleared up has dwindled to less than one-third.

Of the one million serious offences cleared up in 1981, some 567,000 resulted in either a finding of guilt for an indictable offence or a police caution for an indictable offence. The figure includes about 104,000 cautions, of which some 85 per cent were given to children and young persons under the age of 17. Among the 463,000 persons found guilty of indictable offences by the courts, the distribution of age-groups and sex is set out in Table 3. The ratio of convictions for indictable offences was therefore about 6 males to 1 female.

When we turn to consider the types of indictable offences of which these persons were found guilty, we find that they were predominantly offences of theft and handling, followed by burglary and then offences of violence. Table 4[17] shows the pattern of convictions for indictable offences during the last decade. If these figures are

Table 3 Convictions for indictable offences, 1981

Age	Males	Females
10–13	15,100	1,800
14–16	62,300	7,500
17–20	113,900	14,600
21 and over	206,600	41,600
Totals[16]	397,900	65,500

Table 4 Offenders found guilty at all courts, by type of offence (in thousands)

All offenders Indictable offences	1970	1971	1972	1973	1974	1975	1976	1977	1978	1977	1978	1979	1980	1981
Violence against the person	23.4	26.3	28.2	33.0	33.2	36.3	38.4	38.7	40.0	42.6	44.4	48.5	52.3	50.8
Sexual offences	6.7	6.8	6.5	7.2	7.2	6.8	6.6	6.2	6.5	7.0	7.5	7.4	8.0	6.9
Burglary	68.1	65.4	60.9	54.4	64.1	69.3	67.8	70.4	69.4	70.1	69.0	59.1	68.1	76.4
Robbery	2.6	3.0	3.4	3.2	2.8	3.5	3.6	3.2	3.4	3.2	3.4	3.2	3.5	4.1
Theft and handling stolen goods	199.2	193.5	189.0	180.9	204.1	218.7	225.9	236.6	233.8	233.8	226.3	220.6	233.6	232.2
Fraud and forgery	15.9	16.6	17.5	16.1	17.7	19.6	21.4	21.0	20.1	20.8	19.9	20.9	24.9	25.7
Criminal damage	21.5	23.8	26.8	33.2	36.3	38.5	40.8	42.1	45.0	8.9	9.5	9.2	11.4	11.8
Other (excluding motoring offences)	3.9	4.4	5.5	6.5	6.5	7.0	8.8	8.4	4.0	15.0	16.2	21.6	27.9	29.0
Motoring offences	1.5	1.9	2.2	3.0	3.2	2.8	2.3	2.1	1.8	24.2	20.3	21.8	25.7	27.7
Total	342.7	341.7	340.0	337.4	374.9	402.5	415.5	428.7	424.1	425.5	416.5	412.3	455.4	464.6

compared with the figures in Table 1, we can see that offences of burglary recorded by the police increased by nearly 50 per cent between 1970 and 1980, whilst the number of persons convicted of burglary was virtually the same, at about 68,100 in both 1970 and 1980 (although 1981 shows an unprecedented increase). The earlier stability of the number of convictions may be attributed partly to the fall in the clear-up rate for burglary, from 36 per cent in 1970 to 31 per cent in 1980 (see Table 2). The more striking fall in the clear-up rate for robberies, from 42 per cent to 25 per cent in ten years, has likewise meant that the doubling of recorded robberies has not been matched by a correspondingly large increase in the number of persons convicted of robbery (see Table 4). For the purposes of this book the number of convictions each year is the crucial figure, since it shows the number of persons the courts have to sentence.

How do the courts use their sentencing powers? The information for the last decade is probably best presented in separate tables for adult offenders and for young adults aged 17 and under 21. Dealing with adults, Table 5[18] shows that for adult males, the proportionate use of immediate imprisonment has begun to increase after a decline in the mid-1970s, and that the rise of community service orders has been accompanied by a decline, not in probation orders, but in fines, suspended sentences and discharges. For young adult males, the position is in some ways similar, as Table 6[19] shows, with the rise of community service orders being accompanied by a decline in the proportionate use of fines and suspended sentences. However, a striking feature is the doubling of the proportion of young adult males sentenced to immediate terms of imprisonment, and the proportionate decline of sentences to detention centre and borstal. As we have seen, the effect of the Criminal Justice Act 1982 is to combine borstal and imprisonment for young adult offenders into a new sentence of youth custody.

What is the effect of these sentencing patterns upon the custodial population? Table 7 shows the average daily population of prisons, borstals and detention centres for the years 1971 to 1981.[20] When these figures are compared with Table 4, it quickly becomes clear that the average population in custody would form a comparatively smaller proportion of those convicted of indictable offenders in 1971 than in 1980, as Table 8 shows. Indeed, the comparison is all the more striking when it is noted that there were only 2,749 untried prisoners in the 1971 daily average custodial population, whereas the 1980 total

Table 5 Percentage of persons aged 21 and over sentenced for indictable offences by sex and type of sentence or order

Sex and Year	Total	Absolute or conditional discharge	Probation order	Fine	Community service order	Imprisonment		Otherwise dealt with
						Suspended	Immediate	
Males								
1971	100	9	7	51	—	14	18	—
1972	100	9	7	52	—	14	18	—
1973	100	9	7	55	—	12	16	2
1974	100	9	6	56	—	12	15	—
1975	100	9	6	55	1	13	16	—
1976	100	9	5	53	2	13	16	—
1977	100	9	5	53	2	12	17	—
1978	100	8	5	53	3	12	17	—
1977	100	8	5	55	2	13	16	—
1978	100	7	4	54	3	13	17	—
1979	100	7	5	54	3	12	17	—
1980	100	7	5	52	4	12	17	—
1981	100	8	6	49	5	12	18	—
Females								
1971	100	20	15	56	—	5	3	—
1972	100	20	15	57	—	5	2	—
1973	100	20	15	56	—	5	3	—
1974	100	21	14	58	—	5	2	—
1975	100	21	13	58	1	5	3	—
1976	100	20	12	57	—	6	3	—
1977	100	20	12	57	—	6	3	—
1978	100	19	12	56	1	6	4	—
1977	100	19	12	58	—	6	3	—
1978	100	19	12	57	—	6	4	—
1979	100	18	13	55	—	7	4	—
1980	100	18	15	53	2	7	4	—
1981	100	20	16	49	2	7	5	—

Table 6 Percentage of persons aged 17 and under 21 sentenced for indictable offences by sex and type of sentence or order

Sex and year	Total	Absolute or conditional discharge	Probation order	Fine	Community service order	Detention centre order	Borstal training	Imprisonment		Otherwise dealt with
								Suspended	Immediate	
Males										
1971	100	8	12	54	—	8	8	3	3	3
1972	100	8	12	55	—	8	7	4	3	2
1973	100	8	11	59	—	6	7	3	3	3
1974	100	7	10	60	1	6	7	3	3	2
1975	100	8	9	59	2	6	7	4	4	2
1976	100	8	8	57	4	6	7	4	5	2
1977	100	8	7	57	5	6	6	4	5	2
1978	100	7	6	57	6	6	6	4	5	2
1977	100	7	7	56	6	6	7	4	5	2
1978	100	6	7	55	7	6	7	5	6	2
1979	100	6	7	54	7	6	6	5	6	2
1980	100	7	8	51	9	6	6	4	6	2
1981	100	7	8	48	11	6	6	4	7	2
Females										
1971	100	20	28	46	—	—	3	2	1	1
1972	100	20	26	48	—	—	2	3	1	1
1973	100	19	24	51	—	—	2	2	1	2
1974	100	19	23	52	—	—	2	2	1	1
1975	100	20	22	51	1	—	3	2	1	1
1976	100	20	20	51	1	—	2	3	1	1
1977	100	20	19	52	2	—	2	3	2	1
1978	100	18	18	53	2	—	2	4	2	1
1977	100	20	19	52	2	—	2	3	3	2
1978	100	17	18	54	2	—	2	4	2	2
1979	100	17	19	52	2	—	2	4	2	2
1980	100	17	20	50	3	—	2	4	2	2
1981	100	19	21	47	4	—	2	4	2	2

includes some 4,904 untried prisoners. The average daily population of convicted prisoners has therefore shown only a small increase during the last decade. In part this may be attributed to the effect of the parole system in reducing the effective length of some of the longer sentences handed down by the courts. The parole system began cautiously in 1968, so that only about a quarter of those released from prison who were eligible for parole were in fact released on parole in 1969. However, by 1980 and 1981 the percentages had risen to 60 per cent and 63.6 per cent respectively, and the average length of parole licence granted was almost 9 months.[21] The wider use of parole could not be said to be the sole cause of the relative stability of the custodial population (by comparison with the increasing number of convictions for indictable offences): the number of sentences of 18 months and over has not increased in step with the number of indictable offences but has remained relatively stable. Although Tables 5 and 6 point to a proportionate increase in the imposition of custodial sentences, this increase has been chiefly in short sentences. There has been a decline in the average length of sentences for males, from 12.1 months in 1970 to 10.3 months in 1981. The pattern of custodial sentences for adult males is illustrated by Table 9, which shows the receptions of adult males into prison.[22] This shows that, whilst sentences of 18 months and over have remained relatively stable, the number of shorter sentences has increased at a rate beyond the annual increase in convictions – sentences of up to 3 months increasing by around 130 per cent in 10 years. However, this fashion for using very short sentences has not caused a correspondingly great increase in the average daily custodial population (since it would take 6 persons sentenced to 3 months, thus serving only 2 months each, to increase the average daily population by 1).

4 The aims of sentencing

Criticism of sentencing practices has often dwelt on the issue of effectiveness, and that term can only be used meaningfully in the context of effectively achieving a given aim. It is therefore necessary to give a brief introduction to some of the aims and concepts relevant to English sentencing.

The general justifying aim of sentencing is probably a modified version of what might be termed *modern retributivism*: punishment of those who break the criminal law is justified so as to restore the

Table 7 Average Daily Custodial Population, 1971–81, by sex of offenders

	1971	1972	1973	1974	1975	1976	1977	1978	1979	1980	1981
Male	38,673	37,348	35,747	35,823	38,601	40,161	40,212	40,409	40,762	40,748	41,904
Female	1,035	980	1,027	1,044	1,219	1,282	1,358	1,387	1,458	1,516	1,407
Total	39,798	38,328	37,774	36,867	39,820	41,443	41,570	41,796	42,220	42,264	43,311

Table 8 Average custodial population compared with number of indictable convictions

	1971	1980	Percentage increase
Indictable convictions	341,700	455,400	+30%
Average custodial population	39,708	42,264	+7%

Table 9 Receptions under sentence of immediate imprisonment: by length of sentence, 1971–81, adult males aged 21 and over

Length of sentence	1971	1972	1973	1974	1975	1976	1977	1978	1979	1980	1981
Imprisonment (total)	29,641	27,392	23,607	24,487	27,353	29,089	29,564	29,999	31,023	32,130	36,368
Up to 3 months	4,222	3,758	3,121	3,333	4,008	4,701	5,563	5,713	6,314	7,112	9,777
Over 3 months and up to 6 months	6,410	5,624	4,866	5,114	5,409	5,870	6,187	6,440	7,126	7,142	8,003
Over 6 months and under 18 months	12,273	11,097	6,759	7,044	7,934	8,258	8,402	8,404	8,445	8,749	9,435
18 months			2,363	2,470	2,632	2,492	2,526	2,455	2,177	2,296	2,242
Over 18 months and up to 4 years	5,732	5,872	5,485	5,499	6,224	6,457	5,714	5,818	5,745	5,633	5,684
Over 4 years and up to 10 years	877	918	873	842	964	1,097	991	988	1,032	982	1,043
Over 10 years	46	51	45	53	59	83	51	48	57	54	52
Life	81	72	95	132	123	131	130	133	127	162	132

balance which the offence disturbed. It is unfair that an offender should gain an advantage over law-abiding people through contravening a prohibition when they have denied themselves that indulgence. It is unfair that the offender should be allowed to 'get away with' that advantage, and it is therefore right that he should be subjected to a disadvantage so as to cancel out (at least symbolically)[23] his ill-gotten gain. This description of modern retributivism is not moralistic, whereas some sentencers would probably subscribe to a moralistic version whereby criminal conduct is assumed to be morally wrong and punishment is thought justifiable in order to counter-balance (in a symbolic sense) that moral wrong.[24] Leaving aside the moralistic version, however, it can be argued that a modern retributivist justification which sees punishment primarily in terms of a disadvantage to 'cancel out' the advantage gained by the crime is closely bound up with the idea of having social rules:

> No society which purported to be just would allow knowingly any of its members to break the laws with impunity. To allow the offender to get away with impunity would undermine the point of having rules in the first place; it may engender a sense of unfairness in the law-abiding members of the community and so undermine the general attitude that the law is to be obeyed. The offender for his part does not have good grounds for feeling unfairly treated if the community respond to his breaking the law in some way which is to his disadvantage.[25]

The fact of his having broken the law may justify singling out a person for punishment, but the justification for inflicting punishment upon him seems to some extent instrumental. Punishment is not only permissible but desirable; it is not merely inherent in the idea of law but also socially necessary in order to maintain laws. Society has an interest in crime control – that is, in ensuring that its laws are duly obeyed – and this provides a justification for taking punitive measures against those who have broken the law. Thus, on this modified version of modern retributivism, punishment is justified not merely because it is deserved but also because it contributes towards crime control.

Punishment, however, generally involves the infliction of some deprivation upon a member of society. Since it is generally accepted that it is wrong to inflict harm or deprivation upon members of society (indeed, much of the criminal law is concerned with that), it seems right that the State ought to inflict the minimum punishment consistent with its aims. Crimes themselves inflict misery on victims, but the State ought to avoid adding to the overall misery in society except to the extent that this may be necessary to attain other aims. This may be called the principle of *parsimony* in punishment.[26] Sentencers and others subscribe to this principle with varying degrees of commitment, and its main effect is to act as a limiting factor upon the amount of punishment inflicted. The principle commands strong support among those concerned with economies and the control of public expenditure, but at root it is a principle of humanity. In this respect it has similar origins to the *humanitarian* principle, whereby society ought to avoid inhumane punishments even if they are believed to be particularly appropriate or specially effective. It is this principle which leads to a rejection of amputation of limbs and, for many people, of capital and corporal punishment.

If crime control forms part of the justification for inflicting punishment, it is important to consider the various forms it may take. Some may be more enthusiastically pursued than others; some may be more open to objections than others. The prevention of crime may, of course, be pursued by a range of methods other than the sentences imposed upon convicted offenders, and indeed the principle of parsimony enjoins this,[27] but crime control through sentencing is our present concern. One approach is *individual prevention*, which involves preventing this offender from committing further offences after he has experienced the sentence imposed by the court. Individual prevention may be brought about by measures which deter the individual from committing further offences or by measures which reform or rehabilitate him. A second approach to crime control is the aim of *incapacitation*, which involves protecting the public from the depredations of an offender during the currency of his sentence by substantially reducing his opportunity to commit offences for that period. Permanent incapacitation is practically possible, by means of amputation of limbs or capital punishment, but the humanitarian principle is taken to rule this out and imprisonment is the most completely incapacitative sentence available. It will be observed that whereas individual prevention is concerned with the after-effects of a sentence, incapacitation is concerned with the preventive effect of a sentence whilst it is in force. Thirdly, there is *general prevention*, which is the aim of deterring others from committing offences. General prevention may be pursued on at least three different levels: there is short-term general deterrence, which it is sometimes sought to achieve by passing an 'exemplary' sentence on one or a few offenders in an attempt to deter others from committing this particular kind of crime; then there is standing general deterrence against particular types of crime, which involves maintaining a high level of sentences for certain types of crime in order to provide a standing deterrent against committing them; and lastly there is long-term general deterrence, which involves maintaining general sentencing levels so as to provide a sufficient set of disincentives to lawbreaking in general and to reinforce social attitudes against lawbreaking. Some of those who subscribe to 'denunciation' as an aim of sentencing probably do so in the belief, not that denouncing crime publicly by means of a condign sentence is good in itself, but that it is justified because it contributes to upholding general respect for the law and obedience to it.[28]

Even this bare statement of the various approaches to crime control suggests that pursuit of any one approach may well conflict with pursuit of another, and the possibility of conflicts becomes greater when the limiting principle of parsimony is taken into account. Wherever there is a conflict, it can only be resolved if there is some ranking, weighting or priority of the various aims; and conflicts can only be consistently resolved if there is an agreed order of priority. The conflicts arise most poignantly at the stage of deciding how much punishment.[29] On what principles should the levels of severity in sentencing be set? If the fundamental justification for inflicting State punishment is not merely that it is deserved but also that it contributes towards crime control, then one might say that the level of punishment should be as much as is deserved and as much as contributes towards crime control. There are recognized social and moral differences in the gravity of offences, and it is fitting that these differences should be broadly reflected by relatively severe sentences in serious cases and less severe sentences in less serious cases. Additionally, if the principle of parsimony is accepted, then the level of punishment should be no more than is deserved and no more than is necessary for purposes of crime control. It is here, however, that the deepest conflict becomes apparent: it is possible that the deserved punishment differs from the punishment needed to ensure maximum prevention. Where the individually preventive sentence is thought to be less severe than the deserved sentence, the principle of parsimony would favour the less severe sentence, unless it could be shown that the imposition of these lower sentences adversely affected general prevention by lowering the long-term general deterrent effect of the law.

The problems are more difficult when the preventive sentence would be more severe than the deserved sentence, for the principle of parsimony now exerts its weight upon the other side of the scales. The tendency of those who subscribe to modern retributivism and to liberal political philosophy is to accord priority to the deserved sentence: the individual offender, they argue, has a right not to be subjected to a more severe punishment than he deserves for the offence he has committed, and that right cannot be overridden by a general policy of protecting society from the risk presented by certain offenders. However, some concede that the right not to be punished more severely than is deserved may be overridden in extreme cases where the danger to the liberty of other members of society is very great or 'vivid'.[30] Where a modern retributivist would allow the right to receive no more than proportionate punishment to be overridden by the urgent need to protect the rights of other members of society to be free from harm, he would require the circumstances to be defined clearly and narrowly (i.e. what characteristics of the offence, the offender and his record) and the basis for predicting his future behaviour to be satisfactorily established.[31] Again, where it is believed that a more severe sentence than is proportionate would have a greater individual preventive effect (for example, by enabling a full course of treatment for addiction), the reply of the modern retributivist would be that the offender should receive no more than the proportionate sentence, and that any subsequent treatment 'for his own good' should be on a voluntary basis. Again, where it is believed that there are strong preventive reasons for imposing a more severe sentence than deserved in order to act as a short-term general deterrent, modern retributivists would insist that the individual's right to receive no more than proportionate punishment should prevail. This is probably one respect in which many sentencers disagree with modern retributivists: the latter point to the lack of evidence for general deterrent effects except in carefully controlled situations, the former often seem to believe that general deterrence can work and therefore ought to be pursued where a particular type of crime becomes prevalent.[32]

Two further points about conflicting aims might be made. First, most of the observations on conflicting aims of punishment have been made in relation to particular sentences, but there are also questions about the general level of punishment. Levels of punishment for certain crimes might be raised in an attempt to incapacitate a significant proportion of offenders and thereby to achieve an improvement in crime control, but this would conflict with an offender's right to receive no more than a proportionate punishment and would be unacceptable to modern retributivists. Levels of punishment should also, if long-term general deterrence is to be achieved, be sufficient to reinforce social attitudes against offending; since there is little knowledge about the working of this species of prevention, it is difficult to tell in what circumstances it might conflict with other aims, but one source of conflict might be where sentences become so low that they are thought to depreciate the seriousness of lawbreaking. A second point, closely connected with the last, is that pursuit of the various preventive aims depends to some extent on whether there are effective means of achieving them. Insofar as we lack reliable evidence of preventive effects, then the limiting force of proportionality becomes much keener.

There remains the question of how the level of penalties should be set. The general principle is that sentences should be proportionate to the seriousness of the case, and certain modern theorists refer, as we have seen, to a right not to be subjected to more than proportionate punishment. In order to achieve proportionality, there must be settled criteria of the seriousness of cases; there must be an agreed ranking of the severity of the available sentences; and there must be acceptance of a certain relationship between cases and sentences. The last point raises the problem of how high or low the general level of sentences ought to be pitched. There is a theoretical relationship here with 'modern retributivism' as described above, for the level of punishment must be such as to make some contribution to the maintenance of law and order and to crime control. The precise nature of the relationship must remain vague, however, because modern retributivism does not specify (nor, indeed, do most preventive theories) how much contribution sentences should make towards crime control – draconian penalties might be more effective, but unacceptable for humanitarian or other reasons, whereas a slightly more severe penalty system might be no more effective in preventing crime than the existing one, and indeed a lower level might not be significantly less effective than the existing one. The conceptions held by sentencers and perhaps by policy-makers about public opinion are likely to be influential when changes in the level of sentences are considered, but how accurate those conceptions are remains to be examined.

This brief discussion of the philosophy of punishment as it relates to English sentencing practice has not tackled the many major problems which arise, not merely in determining what should be the principal aim of State punishment, but also in resolving the inevitable conflicts between the various approaches and subsidiary and limiting principles which command some acceptance. Some of the problems are tackled in the relevant chapters below – for instance, the question of desert and culpability (Chapter 4), the question of desert and principles of equality (Chapter 7), the justification for short-term general deterrence and for standing general deterrents against certain kinds of offence (Chapter 9), and the question of individual prevention (Chapter 10). It is hoped that this introduction provides a broad context into which to weave those particular discussions.

5 The effectiveness of sentences

In discussions of sentencing and of penal policy, questions are often asked and assertions made about the effectiveness of sentences. It has usually been assumed that effectiveness concerns the success of a particular kind of sentence in preventing offenders from re-offending. However, that is to take a narrow view of effectiveness. Not only is it true that sentencers may use the available measures in a way which is inconsistent with the pursuit of maximum effectiveness, but it is true at a more fundamental level that simple talk of effectiveness is often loose. A sentence can only be effective in achieving a given aim. There is no warrant for assuming that preventing individuals from being reconvicted either is or should be the principal aim of sentencing. In the foregoing section we considered some of the justifications for punishment and the aims of sentencing; in this section we examine in a brief introductory fashion the available evidence on the effectiveness of sentences in achieving each of those aims. Some of the arguments are pursued further in later chapters.

(a) Counter-balancing the crime

How effective are English sentences in restoring the balance of advantages or cancelling out the commission of crimes? This is a crucial question if it is accepted that modern retributivism supplies both a justification for singling out offenders and a justification for inflicting proportionate punishment upon them. Since the notion of

State punishment as 'cancelling out' or 'counter-balancing' the crime is a symbolic one, it is not readily apparent how effectiveness should be assessed. One question may be whether offenders regard sentences as counter-balancing their crimes, but a more prominent question is whether the public regards sentences as an adequate counter-balance. Does the public regard the differences (relativities) between sentences for crimes of varying gravity as appropriate? Does the public regard general sentencing levels as appropriate? Is it felt that the sentences imposed by the courts make an inadequate contribution to the prevention of crime? There are few surveys of public opinion on these questions, and it is essential to enquire how the opinions expressed by members of the public are formed. It is too easy to state that public views of acceptability and appropriateness should be the benchmark without considering the formation of these views.

Individuals in their homes, pubs and clubs may express strong views about sentencing or about law and order; groups in their campaigns may also express views. The first major problem is how to identify a general view or a majority view. The opinions of particular groups cannot be taken as representative of wider society; what appears in newspapers and television is equally unlikely to be representative; indeed there exists no satisfactory mechanism for making people's opinions known on matters such as these, except for the referendum of voters. It therefore follows that those who claim, as some magistrates and judges do, that they are well aware of public opinion on a particular issue cannot substantiate their claims. They may know what individuals in their social circle are saying, and they may hear opinions as they travel on public transport and go about their daily business. But their contacts are likely to be few in number and unsystematic, and may have no connection at all with certain sections of society. Even where a judge or magistrate is absolutely sure about the range of people he consults – say, even if there were a perfectly designed and meticulously executed public opinion poll – there is the even more serious problem of imperfect information and understanding. People in general are imperfectly informed: their information is often limited to a minuscule proportion of the cases dealt with and sentences meted out, even then they may lack an appreciation of the full facts on which the court bases its sentence, and often the cases about which they do hear are atypical. This is because the cases and the information about them are often selected by the press and television. They tend to select cases which are atypical –

which is often the reason why they 'make news' – and this leaves members of the public with little opportunity to form rounded and reliable opinions about sentencing or about the crime rate. They may, morever, have an imperfect understanding of the problems of sentencers and the ways in which they try to solve them. And conceptions about the crime rate are highly unlikely to be objective in any sense. The Floud Committee refer to Lord Ashby's despairing view of public opinion, that 'there is no rationality in the arithmetic of perception' and that views seem to be formed on a puzzling basis so that 'five people killed in one road accident makes a much greater impact – and will be included in a [news] bulletin – than five people killed in five different accidents'.[33] His mistrust of the way in which public perceptions of risk are formed surely applies equally to public perceptions of the crime rate and sentencing. Some insight into the formation of these public perceptions is provided by Maguire's research on burglary.[34]

Although there have been some surveys of public opinion on sentencing,[35] it would be unsafe to rely on their results in the light of the deficiencies of information and understanding suggested in the foregoing paragraph. There is little helpful research on the quesiton of whether offenders (or particular types of offender) believe that 'crime pays'. Even if it could be ascertained that this was the general opinion among offenders, it might owe as much to the low risk of detection as to sentencing levels which were thought to be an insufficient counterweight to offending. It seems, therefore, that it would be hard for the modern retributivist to find reliable empirical evidence on which to base any judgment of whether English sentencing is an appropriate counter-balance to crime. Public opinion, even if taken at face value, might be unambiguous only in ruling out certain extremes of disproportion.

(b) **Individual prevention**
How effective are English sentences in preventing individuals from being reconvicted? A preliminary point is that, since it is not known how frequently the courts pursue this as their main aim in imposing a particular sentence, any figures which might be produced may be worse than if courts consistently pursued individual prevention. In other words, if a majority of sentences are simply passed on a proportionality principle, any statistics are likely to measure the preventive effect of proportional sentences rather than the preventive

effect of sentences selected in order to achieve prevention. On the other hand, there are undoubtedly some cases in which the court (often at the instigation of the social enquiry report) selects a measure with a view to individual prevention. And, more generally, any statistics about the comparative efficacy of the various sentences in preventing reconviction might justify the inference that sentencing levels could be lowered without producing a significant increase in offending, which could be of some importance in setting the general level of sentences.

Individual prevention may be achieved by means of deterring the offender from further lawbreaking or reforming his character so that he does not re-offend. Individual deterrence is associated with measures such as immediate custodial sentences, partly suspended sentences, suspended sentences, fines and perhaps conditional discharges; rehabilitation is associated with probation orders and measures for the mentally disordered. Community service orders are perhaps more likely to fall into the former category, but there is room for disagreement. Whichever approach is taken, preventing the individual from further lawbreaking is taken to be the aim. From this it would seem to follow that the test of effectiveness should be the extent to which, in a given period after sentence, each type of measure is followed by reconviction.

There are obvious difficulties in treating reconvictions as a measure of effectiveness. There is the causal question: we cannot assume that the presence or absence of reconvictions is attributable to the influence of the sentence upon the offender's behaviour, for there are so many influences in any individual's life (family, finances, employment, peer group and so on) that it is unsafe to assume that the sentence he received is the most powerful. The best one can hope for is that these other influences have a fairly even effect from one sentence to another. Then there is the incompleteness of reconvictions: not all offences are reported, and less than half of those which are reported are cleared up, so it is quite possible that some of those who appear 'successes' have in fact committed further offences without detection. Again, one hopes that these balance out. A further difficulty in regarding reconvictions as a satisfactory measure is that a sentence may be said to have some preventive effect if it causes an offender to commit crimes of a less serious nature, or to offend less frequently, or to make a real effort to change his way of life. Judges and magistrates would probably accept this qualification: after all, only three-quarters of suspended sentences are activated on conviction for a fresh offence committed during the operational period, so that in one quarter of cases the second offence is not thought sufficiently serious, and the Court of Appeal has occasionally approved the making of a second probation order where an offence has been committed during an existing order.[36] Sentencers, then, do not invariably take the view that 'all is lost' when an individual re-offends whilst his previous sentence is still in force; they too are willing to consider the circumstances. However, there have been few attempts to devise a more sensitive test of the relative effectiveness of penal measures so as to take account of differences in the seriousness or frequency of offending,[37] and one obvious difficulty is that of devising an acceptable scale of the relative seriousness of offences. In general, therefore, the available research treats any conviction during the follow-up period as a failure in the preventive effect of the sentence, and must therefore be interpreted subject to the many qualifications outlined in this paragraph.

Ideally, information about the preventive efficacy of the available sentences would come from a reasonably up-to-date follow-up of a sufficiently large number of offenders during a period of two or three years after sentence, and making sufficient allowance for the influence of other factors which are known to affect the probability of reconviction. Few comparisons on this scale have been attempted. The well-known study by Hammond, presented in 1964 in an Appendix to the first edition of the sentencer's handbook, *The Sentence of the Court*, is now out of date and was convincingly attacked for its failure to allow for certain factors which might affect the probability of reconviction.[38] No subsequent research has attempted a comparison of all available measures which avoids this problem. However, Walker, Farrington and Tucker have recently used a slightly improved version of Hammond's methodology in re-working the data on the adult male members of a sample of offenders sentenced in 1971, and the results are present in Table 10.[39] The method is that of expectancy: the researchers take, say, first offenders given probation, then calculate the number of reconvictions one would expect from offenders who had committed offences of those kinds and had those numbers of previous convictions, and then express the actual number of reconvictions as a percentage of the expected number of reconvictions within the follow-up period (6 years in this study).[40] Thus, the further below 100 the percentage is, the more effective the

Table 10 Corrected actual and expected reconvictions of adult men in the Phillpotts-Lancucki sample (*in percentages*)

	Number of previous standard list convictions			
	None	One	Two, three or four	Five or more
Discharge	97 (19% of 113)	115 (50% of 24)	140 (90% of 20)	98 (85% of 13)
Fine or compensation	96 (19% of 578)	93 (41% of 181)	92 (61% of 221)	97 (84% of 77)
Probation	188 (38% of 36)	94 (46% of 26)	85 (54% of 48)	100 (88% of 24)
Suspended sentence	124 (27% of 60)	121 (56% of 64)	110 (73% of 112)	100 (88% of 59)
Immediate imprisonment	69 (15% of 47)	102 (51% of 49)	104 (69% of 148)	102 (90% of 169)
All disposals above	21% of 834	47% of 344	66% of 549	88% of 342

Note. Corrected actual reconvictions are shown as percentages of corrected expected reconvictions (see text). The numbers in brackets represent individuals at risk of reconviction, and the bracketed percentages are their corrected actual reconviction rates.

measure would appear; the further above 100, the less preventive effect it would appear to have.

At face value, Table 10 suggests that those with 5 or more previous convictions are extremely likely to be reconvicted, no matter which sentence they are given. First offenders are much more likely to be reconvicted if given a suspended sentence or probation order than if fined or imprisoned. Those with between 1 and 4 previous convictions are likely to do better when fined or put on probation than when conditionally discharged, given a suspended sentence or imprisoned. Financial measures performed better than expected throughout. It might be said, however, that the number of offenders in certain categories was so small as to turn slight variations in reconvictions into rather large percentage variations: one might therefore have reservations about accepting the percentages for probation, for the imprisonment of first and second offenders, and for the conditional discharge of those with more than one previous conviction. The sample was taken in 1971, so that measures such as the community service order and deferment of sentence are not included, the 6-month probation order was unavailable and it was still mandatory to suspend short prison sentences for certain types of offence and offender.

It is not, however, the sentence imposed which has the strongest association with reconviction but the number of previous convictions an offender has. This is made clear by the following table from the study by Phillpotts and Lancucki, from which Walker, Farrington and Tucker drew their data:

Table 11 Males convicted of standard list offences in January 1971: percentage reconvicted by age and number of previous convictions

Number of convictions prior to January 1971	Age in January 1971				
	All ages	10 and under 17	17 and under 21	21 and under 30	30 and over
0	29	50	34	21	18
1	54	73	57	50	37
2 to 4	70	83	74	65	63
5 or more	87	97	87	85	89
Total	50	63	56	49	38

If this table[41] is considered in conjunction with Table 10, it seems clear that a sentencer confronted with an offender of any age who has

5 or more previous convictions is unlikely to be able to find a measure which is more effective than any other, in terms of individual prevention. Indeed, almost nine out of every 10 such offenders will be reconvicted within 6 years, and almost all of those aged between 10 and 17. However, for first offenders and, to a lesser extent, for offenders with 1 to 4 previous convictions, choice of sentence does appear to affect the probability of reconviction: at least Table 10 suggests so for adult male offenders. Table 11 also shows that the probability of reconviction varies according to age: it seems clear that those under 21, and particularly those under 17, are more likely to be reconvicted than older offenders.

Even if the variations in age and number of previous convictions are taken into account when calculating such percentages, there are still drawbacks to the Hammond approach. Indeed, Walker, Farrington and Tucker recognize this when they lament the absence from their data of information as to whether or not each offender was employed, 'since Softley's findings[42] showed that being employed was associated with a higher likelihood of being fined and a lower likelihood of being [re]convicted.'[43] Another drawback is that no account is taken of the stability of the offender's home background, and whether he or she has a stable relationship with another person. Such factors may well influence a court in deciding upon sentence, and they have some association with the probability of reconviction. This may help to explain some of the relatively high reconviction rates for probation orders, just as the likelihood that courts tend to fine people who are employed and from a stable background might help to explain the relatively good results of financial measures.[44] Another possible drawback derives from the fact that, as mentioned above, sentencers will sometimes impose sentences for reasons other than individual prevention: for example, a sentencer might feel constrained by Court of Appeal decisions to impose a conditional discharge on an impecunious offender whom he might otherwise have fined or, if not, have given a suspended sentence.[45] The conclusion must therefore be that Table 10 cannot be taken at face value, and that we do not know to what extent other factors might increase or reduce the differences in reconviction rates following sentences.

Whilst attempts to assess the comparative effectiveness of all available sentences have been rare, there has been a much greater number of attempts to compare the efficacy of two sentences or of two types of one sentence. In broad terms, the findings are insufficient to establish the superior efficacy of one measure or type of measure over another. Brody reviewed the relevant English research and some American research and concluded that 'there is no evidence that longer custodial sentences produce better results than shorter sentences.'[46] He also found no reliable evidence that custodial sentences are followed by fewer or more reconvictions than non-custodial sentences. Brody's survey contains much criticism of the methodology of the various studies: apart from differences in the follow-up periods, he associates himself with general criticisms of the non-comparability of samples and inconsistencies in the standard of 'failure'.[47]

One approach which might well uncover some differences in the relative efficacy of sentences would be to examine 'interaction effects'. It seems likely that each kind of sentence or regime will have a different influence upon offenders with different personalities or backgrounds: for example, probation might be more effective with certain types of individual than with others, and community service orders likewise. Such differences are obscured by producing a single reconviction rate following each measure; in order to identify them, it would be necessary to obtain a wide range of data on each offender and then to test whether there are any significant differences in responsiveness. Few studies have attempted this, and one notable English exception (the IMPACT survey of the effects of intensive probation) found only one significant interaction effect out of the many tested – that probationers with moderate or high 'criminal tendencies' and average or few 'personal problems' were more likely to be reconvicted following intensive supervision than following normal probation.[48] To make use of findings such as these it would be necessary for offenders to undergo the necessary tests, and at present this is probably considered uneconomical of time and money.

(c) **Incapacitation**
This approach to prevention looks not to the effect upon the offender's conduct after the end of the sentence, but to the effect of the sentence during its currency. Leaving aside the extreme examples of capital punishment and amputation of limbs, what is known about the incapacitative effect of existing measures? Imprisonment and other custodial sentences (detention centres, youth custody) have an almost complete incapacitative effect for their duration, for escapes from penal institutions are few and short-lived (some 421 escapes and

1,364 cases of absconding in 1981, out of a prison population of 43,311). It would, however, be unsafe to draw the conclusion that this justifies the use of custodial sentences at the present rate. The point of incapacitation is surely to reduce the risk that members of society will become the victim of an offence, and research suggests that if the length of all custodial sentences were reduced by a nominal 6 months (i.e. 4 months of time actually served, allowing for remission), this reduction would produce only a slight increase in the risk of being a victim. Some of the difficulties of the calculation by Brody and Tarling that the number of convictions would increase by only 1.6 per cent per annum are discussed in Chapter 9;[49] it is sufficient here to note that the risk of being a victim would not necessarily show such a low increase as the total number of convictions, since that would depend on the volume of unreported and undetected crimes and the proportion of them committed by the imprisoned offenders.

A different incapacitative argument is that the protection of the public over a given period of time might be better ensured by a non-custodial measure than by a relatively short period of custody. Short custodial sentences provide little direct incapacitation – the public is 'given a rest' from the offender for only a few months, and then the offender is released back into the community, without any super-vision (unless he is under 21). Now the figures for 2-year probation orders show that 76 per cent of probationers complete them without breach or further conviction. So if this is compared with the probability that an offender who receives a prison term of, say, 6 months will be reconvicted within the same 2-year period, that may well be higher: although society is almost totally protected from him during his 4 months in custody, he is more likely than not to be reconvicted in the remaining 20 months of the 2 year period – a 2-year follow-up of all those released from prison in 1978 showed that 54 per cent of those released from 3–6 month sentences were reconvicted within 2 years.[50] The argument is therefore that the public might be no less well protected, or might even be better protected, if some of those given short custodial terms were placed on probation for 2 years. Some would vigorously protest that the characteristics of the offenders are likely to be different: those now receiving probation are likely to have fewer previous convictions, and will for this or other reasons be less likely to be reconvicted anyway, which is why the 'success rate' is comparatively high. There is no research which demonstrates this, and the difference may well be less than is believed

– insufficient to outweigh the argument, supported by the principle of parsimony, in favour of experimenting with the wider use of probation.

(d) **General deterrence**

Whatever form of general deterrence or general prevention is envisaged, the difficulties of conducting satisfactory research are formidable and, for the most part, criminologists have made greater progress towards identifying the conditions under which general deterrent effects might or might not be expected than towards actually demonstrating their effect in social situations. Some of the problems of assessing the effectiveness of long-term general deterrence were discussed in part (a). The other kinds of general prevention – short-term general deterrence and standing general deterrence –must operate, if at all, through the minds of potential offenders and thereby affect their conduct. Put broadly, the sentences of the courts must become known to those who contemplate offences, and must operate on their minds so as to persuade them to desist from committing the offences. The 'target group' is different, of course: for short-term general deterrence it consists of all those at a certain time and place who might think of committing this type of offence, and in standing general deterrence it consists of those who at any time contemplate the commission of the particular kind of offence. But the essential factor is the beliefs of the offender about the likely consequences of acting in a particular way – not the actual risks, but his beliefs about the risk.[51] In carefully contrived social situations, general deterrence has been shown to work. The clearest example was the introduction, in 1967, of the 'breathalyser' law for drunken driving, together with 1 year's mandatory disqualification from driving. The widespread publicity and the popular belief that there was a considerable risk of detection seem to have combined to reduce the incidence of that kind of offending. However, the research by Ross[52] also shows that after a few years the effect began to wear off: a strategy which was probably intended as a form of standing general deterrence had in fact operated as short-term general deterrence. More relevant to the imposition of sentences by the courts are the questions raised by exemplary sentences intended as short-term deterrents, and long sentences for crimes such as robbery which are intended as standing general deterrents. There is very little research of direct relevance to these issues, but, as will be discussed in some detail in Chapter 9, there has been sufficient criminological and philosophical enquiry to demonstrate the doubtfulness of many of the assumptions which appear to be made by sentencers.[53]

6 The sources of sentencing law

The principal sources of English sentencing law are twofold: legislation and judicial decisions. Academic writings might also be said to be a source, in a broad sense. The leading writer is Dr D. A. Thomas of Cambridge University, whose work falls into two distinct categories – first, his book on *The Principles of Sentencing*, with editions in 1970 and 1979, and his new cumulative encyclopaedia of *Current Sentencing Practice*, all of which collate the guidance laid down by the Court of Appeal on sentencing, with little evaluative comment; and secondly, his commentaries on cases reported in the *Criminal Law Review*, which provide a critical analysis of the reasoning in sentencing decisions and suggest ways in which the law should be developed. In the first category there is also Mr B. T. Harris's *Criminal Jurisdiction of Magistrates*,[54] which relates Court of Appeal decisions to the problems of magistrates' courts; and in the second category there is Sir Rupert Cross's *English Sentencing System*.[55] The academic writings in the second category are a source of law in the sense that sentencers, advocates and magistrates' clerks may pay attention to them, but they are not formally a source in the sense of being cited in court as authority (save on rare occasions). Nevertheless, sentencing law is relatively young and underdeveloped and, just as academic writers are cited with increasing frequency in appellate decisions on criminal law, it will surely not be long before judges and advocates openly recognize that academic writers can make a contribution to the rational development of this branch of the law.[55a]

(a) Legislation

Statutes passed by Parliament establish the framework of English sentencing law, as is evident from sections 1 and 2 of this chapter. Statute lays down the terms of the orders which a criminal court may make after conviction, and imposes restrictions on the making of orders in certain cases and upon the combination of certain orders with others (for instance, a suspended sentence may not be imposed on the same occasion as probation). Statute also lays down the limits of the powers of magistrates' courts. All these statutory provisions have to be interpreted by the courts, and some of the cases which go to the Court of Appeal raise a particular point of statutory interpretation (about the extent of the courts' powers) rather than any general issue of principle (as to how courts should exercise their powers). The powers of the court are also circumscribed according to the offence of which the defendant is convicted: legislation attaches a maximum penalty to almost every criminal offence.

The role of legislation as a source of English sentencing law is therefore essentially one of providing powers and laying down the outer limits of their use. It is unusual for legislation to go further than this, although there are some broad attempts to shape the courts' approach to sentencing certain classes of offender in section 20 of the Powers of Criminal Courts Act 1973 (the first prison sentence on an adult) and in section 1 (4) of the Criminal Justice Act 1982 (a custodial sentence for a young adult) and, exceptionally, a requirement that a court must disqualify from driving for at least one year any person convicted of drunken driving unless there are 'special reasons' for not doing so.[56] Apart from these and a few other scattered provisions, choice of sentence is left by English law to the discretion of the court.

(b) **Judicial decisions**
Since the creation of the Court of Criminal Appeal in 1907 it has been possible for an offender to appeal against sentence. The Court formerly had the power to increase sentence on appeal, but this was abolished in 1966 and, by section 11(3) of the Criminal Appeal Act 1968, the Court must ensure that the appellant is not more severely dealt with on appeal than he was dealt with in the court below. Two principles had been established by the Court at a very early stage: that the statutory maximum sentence should be reserved for the worst possible case,[57] and that the Court would only alter a sentence if it was 'wrong in principle'.[58] However, the development of detailed principles to guide the courts in their use of the wide discretion left by Parliament was slow until more extensive reporting of sentencing decisions began in the *Criminal Law Review* in 1954, the Streatfeild Report in 1961 created greater awareness of the problems of sentencing, Professor Rupert Cross took the unusual step of devoting his inaugural lecture in 1965 to sentencing principles, and Dr Thomas began the writings which culminated in the publication in 1970 of the first edition of his *Principles of Sentencing*. That book drew on many

unreported, as well as the reported, decisions of the Court of Appeal and was, at the very least, influential in creating an atmosphere in which the detailed principles of sentencing came to be taken more seriously.

If the principles of sentencing are regarded as underdeveloped, this can no longer be attributed to the under-reporting of appellate decisions: in addition to the *Criminal Law Review*, there is now a regular series of law reports devoted exclusively to sentencing decisions, the *Criminal Appeal Reports (Sentencing)*. One might therefore think that the principles of sentencing are undergoing rapid growth in the true tradition of the common law, a case-by-case development by the judges in reported decisions. However, there are three major differences – in the use of precedents, in the limited coverage of appellate decisions, and in the limited control over decisions at trial level.

First, the value and use of previous decisions differ from most other areas of law. It is, of course, a moot point whether sentencing decisions do establish rules of law: decisions on points of law and statutory interpretation clearly do, but our principal concern here is with appellate guidance on how to exercise the wide discretion left to sentencers by the legislature. Here there are few judicially created *rules* of sentencing, but some judgments of the Court of Appeal are clearly intended to lay down *principles* which sentencers are expected to follow. In this context, the difference between rules and principles may be thus expressed: rules prescribe a course which must be taken unless there is an applicable exception, whereas principles indicate a course which ought *ceteris paribus* to be followed, although the court may find that one principle is outweighed by another in a particular case. In the light of modern jurisprudential writing, there is much more that could be said about the legal nature of different kinds of proposition about sentencing. For present purposes, it is sufficient to examine how closely the use of previous decisions approximates to that in other areas of law. In legal theory, one decision of an appellate court such as the Court of Appeal sets a precedent which ought to be followed not only by lower courts (i.e. the Crown Court and magistrates' courts) but also by the Court of Appeal itself in subsequent cases, unless the precedent can be 'distinguished' (i.e. regarded as not binding in the later case because its facts are materially different) or is overruled by a 'full' Court of Appeal consisting of 5 judges rather than 3.[59] The fact that the Court of

Appeal has thought it necessary to assemble a Court of 5 judges to overrule a previous decision on sentencing principles, together with the occasional citing of precedents by the Court, leads Thomas to conclude that

the Court takes the view that while its decisions on the proper exercise of sentencing discretion do not create law, they are intended to be binding on and followed by judges of the Crown Court and, where they are applicable, magistrates exercising summary jurisdiction.[60]

In jurisprudential terms it might be disputed whether decisions which are intended to be binding and are generally treated as binding can nevertheless be said not to 'create law'. Of more immediate relevance is the question whether the Court's use of its own precedents on sentencing really does attain the level of consistency implied by Thomas. Very few of the judgments of the Court of Appeal collected in the *Criminal Appeal Reports (Sentencing)* contain even one reference to another decision of the Court, and there appear to be different strengths of precedent authority in sentencing. Most sentencing decisions of the Court are delivered in *ex tempore* judgments, after hearing argument only on behalf of the appellant. On some days the 3 judges who are sitting in the Court of Appeal may divide the cases among them, each delivering the judgment on one appeal whilst the others are perusing the papers relating to other appeals in which they will have to deliver the judgment of the Court. This is not to suggest that these decisions are not thoroughly discussed by the members of the Court, but it does afford some explanation of why judges are sometimes reluctant to attribute weight to the precise words spoken during the judgment on an earlier appeal. On the other hand, there are some judgments which have evidently been more fully prepared, and which contain either a review of some previous decisions or a statement of policy or principle which is intended to be authoritative. Thus, the statements of policy by the Lord Chief Justice in such 'landmark' judgments as *Begum Bibi*[61] and *Clarke*[62] must have been much more carefully prepared than the texts of most sentencing judgments, and accordingly have a much higher status as individual precedents.

If one cannot always regard the particular words used in an appellate judgment as authoritative, can one rely on the outcome of the appeal as an authoritative indication of the sentence appropriate in that type of case? To some extent, this depends on how one characterizes the concept of the 'type of case', for there are often many factors in each case whose interplay has an effect on the ultimate sentence, and it is usually more helpful to consider a line of decisions before, say, relating custodial sentences of a certain length to offences of a particular kind. One should therefore seek what French lawyers call a *jurisprudence constante* – a line of decisions establishing a consistent principle.[63] Moreover, in some judgments the Court might describe a sentence as 'not a day too long', perhaps implying that an even longer sentence would have been appropriate; in other judgments the Court reduces a custodial sentence so as to allow the offender's release the following day, suggesting that the appropriate sentence would have been even shorter than the offender has actually served and might not have been a custodial sentence at all. It is fairly rare for the Court to quash a custodial sentence and state that the offender should in the first place have received a non-custodial sentence: the decisions in which the Court has replaced substantial custodial sentences with probation orders form a small and atypical group, but there are a few recent examples of more general application (such as the decision in *Brown*, quashing the sentence of a young man who had already spent some 3 months in borstal and stating that a community service order would have been appropriate).[64] There may be some reluctance to take this course, since it may leave the offender with a strong sense of grievance and may cause some embarrassment to the trial judge. It is a much easier course for the Court to take when the offender has been granted bail pending the appeal.[65] In sum, therefore, it is generally unwise to treat the outcome of a particular appeal as establishing a norm for sentences in that type of case.

These two weaknesses in appellate decisions on sentencing – that they are usually *ex tempore* and that the Court's order may not reflect its view of the appropriate sentence – may provide part of the explanation why they are rarely cited by advocates or by the Court of Appeal in its judgments. However, it is also true that many appellate judgments on matters of criminal law and evidence are delivered *ex tempore* (although after argument by both sides, and usually with less pressure of numbers of appeals to be dealt with). Two further factors in relation to sentencing appeals may be the force of tradition and the fear of misuse. The tradition is that advocates in their speeches in mitigation of sentence do not refer to appellate decisions, and it may indeed embrace the Court of Appeal's reluctance to cite its own previous decisions. Indeed, it is not many years since the Court of

Appeal rebuked counsel for the appellant for attempting to bring relevant precedents to the Court's attention:

> Counsel had sought to refer the Court to other cases of importation of cannabis but it had declined to have them put before it. Keeping sentences in step was a matter for judges, not counsel. Cases could not be allowed to generate an argument on what had happened in other cases.[66]

These extraordinary propositions, in a Court presided over by the then Lord Chief Justice, Lord Widgery, are evidence of a tradition into which many judges and advocates have been schooled, and which continues to exert an influence.[67] If the principles of sentencing are to develop in a consistent manner, the Court must exploit its own rich progeny, by increasing its own citation of precedents and encouraging advocates to make proper reference to relevant precedents, as it has occasionally done.[68] But here we meet a further factor – fear that the precedents will be misused. The sheer volume of reported decisions is daunting, and indiscriminate citation could lengthen proceedings both at trial and on appeal without any corresponding benefit. What is needed is instruction on the proper use of sentencing precedents as part of the training of barristers and solicitors.[69] Improving the training should help to ensure that the use of precedents is selective, relevant and helpful to the courts. English law has developed through the citation and analysis, by advocates and judges, of precedents. Without this, the principles of sentencing will remain underdeveloped.

The second respect in which appellate decisions on sentencing differ from those relating to other branches of law is that their scope is somewhat confined by the limitations on appeals. Only the offender may appeal, the Court of Appeal may not increase the severity of a sentence even if it thinks a higher sentence appropriate, and there is no provision for the Attorney-General to refer cases to the Court for a ruling (as he may do on points of criminal law).[70] There may be good reasons for these limitations – a hard-pressed appeals system should give priority to defence appeals, and if the Court were empowered to increase an appellant's sentence, genuine appeals might be deterred and appellants' expectations cruelly reversed[71] – but the limitations lead to a lop-sided set of precedents. The Court hears appeals only against sentences which are thought by the offender to be too severe, with the result that there are myriad precedents on the aggravating features of serious offences but very few decisions at all on non-custodial sentences or the least serious kinds of manslaughter, rape and robbery. It is hardly too much to say that the more frequent the type of case, the less appellate guidance there is likely to be. Precedents on serious woundings, robberies and rapes abound; precedents on everyday assaults, theft and damage are hard to find and – because the sentence which gave rise to the appeal was probably abnormally high in the first place – afford little guidance to the magistrates' court or third-tier Crown Court.

What, then, is the scope of the Court of Appeal's decisions? Four categories may be put forward:

(i)   lengths of prison sentence for types of offence;
(ii)   the decision whether or not to impose a custodial sentence;
(iii) general principles of aggravation and mitigation;
(iv)   general questions of sentencing policy.

The strengths of the English Court of Appeal lie in the relatively sophisticated case-law on long prison sentences for relatively serious offences (i) and, to a small but increasing extent, in declarations of general sentencing policy such as that contained in *Begum Bibi*[72] (iv). There may be some doubt about whether the statements of general policy in *Begum Bibi* are technically binding, since in strict legal theory they might be regarded as mere *obiter dicta* which are not part of the decision on the point raised in the case; in their context, however, they were clearly intended to be binding and will doubtless be thus treated. Several principles of aggravation and mitigation (iii) are also fairly well developed, although others (such as the approach to persistent offenders) remain in a rather vague and unsatisfactory state. The weaknesses of the Court of Appeal's precedents lie in the dearth of guidance on the question of whether to impose a custodial sentence or not (ii) and, as mentioned above, the paucity of precedents in the whole range of non-custodial sentences and everyday offences. Considerable advances in the range and style of guidance have been made since Lord Lane became Lord Chief Justice in 1980, and the occasional use of 'guideline judgments' to set out sentencing levels for a whole range of manifestations of a particular crime (i) such as rape or drug offences[73] is a welcome development. However, realistic guidance for magistrates' courts and third-tier Crown Courts requires an intimate knowledge of their practical problems, which the Court of Appeal probably does not possess.

This leads on to the third major difference between appellate decisions on sentencing and those on other branches of law: there seems to be a gap between the level of sentences generally approved by the Court of Appeal and the level generally imposed in the courts below, suggesting a lack of coherence between the principles enunciated by the Court and those applied at trial level. Some judges interviewed in the Oxford pilot study expressed a scepticism towards Court of Appeal judgments which bordered on contempt. The root of these feelings was that the Court is thought to be out of touch with the problems which face sentencers every day, and so accustomed to dealing with lengthy prison sentences that it cannot 'adjust its sights', as it were, so as to deal realistically with less serious cases. The suggestion that the Court of Appeal is out of touch might appear extraordinary: it is as if a democrat were to criticize the public for being out of touch with what members of parliament want, for one might think that it is the business of judges and magistrates to keep in step with the Court of Appeal and not *vice versa*. Yet there is evidence that, in the case of sentencing appeals, the allegation has some foundation. Lawton LJ's reference to 18 months' imprisonment as a proper sentence for a first offence of residential burglary is a prime example,[74] since only one-third of residential burglars receive any form of custodial sentence, and the vast majority of those are for less than 18 months.

Lest that be dismissed as a single instance, a more compelling example is provided by *McCann*,[75] one of the cases which the specially constituted Court of Appeal (Lord Lane CJ, Lawton LJ and Shaw LJ) dealt with on the same day as *Begum Bibi* in an attempt to demonstrate how sentences for 'run-of-the-mill' offences might be reduced. Here Lord Lane CJ referred to the case as 'a comparatively trivial type of burglary' – it was a rather feeble attempt to break into a shop, by a man with only one distant previous conviction – yet came to the conclusion 'that nine months' imprisonment would be appropriate in place of the two years which he originally received'. Again, less than one-third of those who break into commercial premises receive custodial sentences, and 9 months is more than any magistrates' court can impose. If the explanation for this *faux pas* by an appellate court anxious to provide guidance which would reduce sentencing levels lies, not in ignorance of sentencing practice for non-serious offences, but rather in a reluctance to declare that the offender had spent some or all of his time in prison unnecessarily (he had apparently spent 6 months there), then that is a further indictment of the Court's self-imposed restraints. The more general point, however, is that many judges and other observers believe that there is a gap between the sentencing levels of the Court of Appeal and trial courts. If that is so, then guidance of the kind offered in the *Begum Bibi* may be effective ('reduce your sentences for these kinds of crime') but when it is illustrated by decisions such as *McCann* it becomes baffling, for courts are being requested to reduce their sentences to a level which is above the level they already impose. In this situation, is the Court of Appeal rather clumsily asking them to reduce the level of their sentences further, or asking them to increase the level of their sentences by using words such as 'reduce' and 'lower'? The answer, as we know, is the former; but clumsiness is no merit in a Court which has undertaken the duty 'to lay down principles and guidelines to assist sentencers of all grades in the application of the discretion which the imposition of sentence requires'.[76]

In sum, judicial decisions on sentencing have not yet developed as a source of law to the same extent as the Court of Appeal's decisions on almost all other matters. Not all appellate decisions on sentencing have the same binding force as precedents. Fully binding according to normal legal principles are decisions on the interpretation of statutes such as the Powers of Criminal Courts Act. Policy decisions which are obviously intended to be binding, such as *Begum Bibi*, will invariably be treated as binding; so will those relatively infrequent judgments in which the Court of Appeal formally overrules a previous decision.[77] Otherwise, it may require a line of decisions (a *jurisprudence constante*) either to establish a particular principle, such as the 'clang of the prison gates' principle for a fairly serious offence committed by a person of good character,[78] or to establish a range of sentences for a particular type of crime. In practice, the position is complicated by the failure of the Court to refer regularly to its own previous decisions. This leads to regrettable inconsistency, since there is a number of issues on which contradictory precedents may be found.[79] The Court can only properly fulfil its role in providing guidance for sentencers if there is regular citation of relevant precedents at every stage of the sentencing process.

7 The stages of decision-making in sentencing

Many of those who study sentencing are content to use, as a starting point, the stages described by Thomas. First, there is the primary decision, which lies between 'what is conveniently, if inelegantly, known as a tariff sentence and a sentence based on the needs of the offender as an individual.' Once this decision has been taken, 'the sentencer must apply the appropriate body of principle to determine the precise form of the sentence or measure he will adopt.'[80] This is the secondary decision. Where the sentencer decides that the gravity of the offence makes it necessary to impose what Thomas calls a 'tariff sentence', the secondary decision requires him first to identify the normal range of sentences for crimes of that kind, secondly to place this particular offence at an appropriate level within that range (according to whether it is an offence of low, medium or high gravity), and thirdly to make any allowance for mitigating factors by reducing the sentence. If, on the other hand, the sentencer decides that the perceived needs of the offender rather than the gravity of the offence should determine the sentence, and thus to pass what Thomas calls an 'individualized measure', he will usually be able to make the order which (on the information presented to the court) seems to meet those needs – a medical disposal, a probation order, or perhaps deferment.

These are the bare essentials of the framework which Thomas puts forward to characterize sentencing in the Crown Court, based on his extensive study of appellate sentencing judgments. The model seems chiefly concerned with custodial sentences and cases in which probation is used instead of a custodial sentence. Since only 50 per cent of those sentenced in the Crown Court receive immediate custodial sentences, and only a further 6 per cent are put on probation (many of those orders in cases where an immediate custodial sentence was probably unlikely), it is important to consider how the other half of Crown Court sentencing, and indeed sentencing in magistrates' courts, can be brought into the framework. Fines, community service orders and suspended sentences could hardly be regarded as 'individualized measures', and so the question is whether they can be regarded as 'tariff sentences' at the bottom of the scale. How easily could the three stages in decision-making which Thomas so aptly applies to determining the length of custodial sentences be applied to non-custodial sentencing?

First, the normal range of sentences for the offence must be identified. Thomas tends to look to the Court of Appeal's decisions for this, but we have seen that the Court of Appeal may approve levels of sentence above those which prevail in the courts. Moreover, there is very little appellate guidance on non-custodial sentences. The normal range for relatively modest offences which rarely attract a custodial sentence can therefore only be identified by someone who possesses a thorough knowledge of sentencing practice in less serious cases. That knowledge, where it is believed to be possessed, is likely to be either incomplete or localized. At this essential stage, then the 'appropriate body of principle' to which Thomas refers may not exist.

Secondly, the sentencer must place the offence within that normal range according to its relative gravity. If it has been possible to identify a normal range, then the Court of Appeal's decisions on matters of general principle should give some assistance at this stage – was there violence or not? was the offence premeditated or not? was it provoked or not? was there a breach of trust or not? and so on. But, for non-custodial sentences, this second stage involves an extra decision which is not necessary in custodial sentencing: there is a choice among types of non-custodial measure. Can the measures be ranked in order of severity, as we rank lengths of custodial sentence? There is no authoritative ranking, but the result of a small experiment by Kapardis and Farrington[81] was to suggest the following 'Sentencing Severity Scale' for magistrates:

Final score	Sentence	Mean score in pilot study
1	Absolute discharge	9.9
2	Bound over for 1 year	23.2
3	Conditional discharge for 1 year	24.9
4	Fined £10	26.0
5	Fined £40	38.3
	Sentence deferred for 6 months	47.0
6	Probation for 2 years	47.5
7	Fined £100	53.2
8	Community service 60 hours	58.2
9	6 months prison suspended for 2 years	64.2
10	6 months prison	77.5
11	Committed to crown court	76.1

It is not known how widely this ranking would be accepted among magistrates or among judges in the Crown Court. The difference in the scale between a £40 fine and a £100 fine illustrates that each measure has its own internal range of severity (e.g. long and short community service orders), and so it is probable that the scale would be much more complex if a fuller range of alternatives had been considered. In the absence of authoritative guidance or of more broadly based research, however, the scale is a useful starting point.

If the sentencer reaches the third stage, he must then make allowance for any mitigating factors. This may also be dependent on a ranking of non-custodial measures, in the sense that he may wish to impose a measure less severe than he would otherwise have imposed. The Court of Appeal's judgments afford some general guidance on the mitigating effect of such factors as pleading guilty, family responsibilities, old age, etc., and one particularly important factor will be the offender's previous record. As we shall see in Chapter 5, it often appears that the more sentences an offender has received, the more likely he is to be treated more severely and, ultimately, to receive a custodial sentence.

The absence of identifiable 'normal ranges' for non-serious offences, and the absence of a settled ranking of non-custodial measures, makes it difficult to apply the secondary decision in Thomas's framework to non-custodial measures, which account for almost half the sentences in the Crown Court and almost all in magistrates' courts. The judgments in *O'Keefe*[82] and *Clarke*[83] suggest an alternative framework which requires sentencers to go through the following process of elimination:

- is an absolute discharge appropriate?
- is a conditional discharge appropriate?
- is this a proper case for a probation order?
- is a fine appropriate?
- is a short community service order appropriate?

If all those questions are answered in the negative, the next question is: is this a case for a custodial sentence?

If it is, then the court must ask itself whether it can make a long community service order as an equivalent to a custodial sentence, or whether it can suspend the whole sentence.

If it feels unable to take either course, then the court must decide what is the shortest sentence it can impose.

This process of elimination may prove to be a useful addition to the framework put forward by Thomas: in cases where there has been a primary decision in favour of a 'tariff' sentence, the process of elimination might effectively replace the first and second stages of the secondary decision for cases of low and moderate seriousness. It has the additional merit of coinciding with the policy of reducing the use of custodial sentences, by requiring the sentencer to consider each non-custodial alternative (although this consideration might be no more than peremptory if the sentencer forms the view that the offence 'calls for' immediate imprisonment). However, it is merely a possible framework – it assumes a particular ranking of the severity of non-custodial measures which has not been authoritatively established –and as such says nothing about the criteria which should inform each of the decisions. Moreover, the framework begins with the primary decision between what Thomas calls 'tariff' and 'individualized' measures, and appellate decisions do not provide a full specification of the principles on which probation should be preferred to custody. Frameworks of this kind can only accurately reflect, or have an influence upon, the approach to sentencing decisions if sentencers have reasonably clear and full guidance as to the proper principles on which to take each decision: insofar as the guidance is unclear or incomplete, there remains room for individual preferences and local variations.

8 The factors in decision-making

Having considered the formal stages in the mental process of determining sentence, we must now give some consideration to the various factors which may have a bearing upon the way in which sentencing decisions are taken. Referring back to Table 11, it will be seen that there is some measure of likeness in the decisions, inasmuch as a custodial sentence becomes more probable as the number of previous convictions increases. That general impression does, however, mask considerable variations from court to court – as the studies of sentencing in magistrates' courts show[84] – and leaves open the question of what factors actually influence sentencers in their decision-making. Since these are human decisions, it must be borne in mind that what matters is not the guidance laid down by the Court of Appeal or the advice of the Clerk to the Justices but, in all cases, how these various sources of guidance strike the sentencer. It is essential to consider the principles, policies and assumptions on which sentencers actually act, and not simply to assume that all guidance given to sentencers is followed in precisely the intended manner. What factors might be supposed to enter or influence a sentencer's thought processes when he is deciding on the sentence in a particular case?

I   View of the Facts of the Case
II   Views on the Principles of Sentencing:
       (a) views on the gravity of the offence;
       (b) views on the aims, effectiveness and relative severity of
            each type of sentence, deriving to some extent from the
            sentencer's experience of sentencing;
       (c) views on the general principles of sentencing;
       (d) views on the relative weight of mitigating factors.
III   Views on Crime and Punishment:
       (a) views on the philosophy of punishment;
       (b) views on the causes of crime and the attitudes of offenders;
       (c) views on the role of the sentencer and the function of the
            court in passing sentence.
IV   Demographic Features of Sentencers:
       (a) age;
       (b) social class;
       (c) occupation;
       (d) urban or rural background;
       (e) race;
       (f) sex;
       (g) religion;
       (h) political allegiance.

It will be observed that groups I, II and III are expressed so as to
emphasize that it is what the sentencer thinks about the data
presented to him – his 'views' or the various factors – which are
relevant, not the actual content or intended purport of each source of
guidance. This is equally true in relation to the information and
argument presented to the sentencer, a matter discussed later in this
section.

   What is the relevance of the fourth group of factors to an
explanation of sentencing? It seems inherently likely that every one of
us projects into our daily decisions certain aspects of our personality
which are traceable to demographic features of the kind listed. It
would be wrong of a sentencer knowingly to allow a particular bias to
influence a sentencing decision, and many of those who sit in the
courts (especially judges) maintain that they become accustomed to
preventing their own personal preferences and personality from
influencing their decisions. There is no evidence of how successful
sentencers are in this enterprise of prevention, and there remains the

possibility of unknown bias – a tendency to view matters from a particular perspective or to select certain kinds of information, which the sentencer himself does not realize. Avoiding bias might be relatively easy where an obvious matter such as politics or religion is concerned. It might also be possible where there is a racial difference between sentencer and offender, in view of the legislation and public discussion of racial discrimination in the last two decades: indeed, a recent study suggests that there is no evidence of bias against racial minorities in English sentencing practice.[85] The possibility of age discrimination has been less widely discussed, and is probably worth close examination. Most sentencers are at least one generation older than most offenders, and in some cases may be two generations older, and they may fail to understand the context or meaning of certain offences committed by young people. Hood, for example, found that the age of magistrates was related to the size of the fine imposed in his dangerous driving cases, with older magistrates being relatively severe in two of the cases involving young drivers and relatively lenient in the three cases involving older drivers, as compared with the fines imposed by their younger colleagues.[86] It is at least possible that many sentencers fail to understand the 'younger generation' and characterize as wanton vandalism or as unprovoked viciousness some behaviour which might have explanations other than the sheer wickedness to which they attribute it. In his study, Hogarth found a relationship between specific beliefs and the age of the sentencer, with older magistrates having some tendency to minimize sociological explanations of crime and generally to be more offence-oriented than offender-oriented in their approach to sentencing.[87]

This leads to the question of how the demographic features in group IV influence sentencing policy. What should be made of Cohen's finding that 76 per cent of those appointed as High Court judges and 67 per cent of those appointed as Circuit Judges during 1980–82 had attended public schools, and that 88 per cent of the former and 57 per cent of the latter had studied at Oxford or Cambridge?[88] One might paint with a broad brush and suggest that an identified characteristic (high social class) may lead to particular views on the causes of crime (IIIb) and to particular views on the gravity of offences (IIa); or one might seek more detailed relationships, suggesting that high social class (with or without a certain political allegiance) leads the sentencer, for instance, to take a more serious view of social security frauds and a less serious view of tax evasion. Hood was, however, unable to find that magistrates' attributes exerted more than a limited effect on sentencing practice.[89] The fourth group of factors, then, raises a number of hypotheses about the influence of demographic features on sentencing practice which have not yet been fully tested in England, although Hogarth's Canadian study found a number of significant relationships between the social background of magistrates and their attitudes and beliefs. The strongest relationship he found was in fact with the degree of urbanization of the community in which the magistrate lived,[90] with urban magistrates being generally more punitive. If demographic features have an influence, then it may well be exerted without the sentencer's knowledge. If it is exerted with the sentencer's knowledge, he may feel it necessary to draw upon his own principles in the absence of proper guidance on the exercise of his wide sentencing discretion. He will, however, be using his own beliefs as a basis for views in groups III and II, which we now go on to consider.

Turning to the factors in group III, it seems inherently likely that in a sentencing system which does not give complete guidance on the exercise of sentencing discretion, the views of sentencers on these matters are likely to influence their approach to sentencing. To some extent, the views in group III will be the product of the demographic features in group IV; but with some individuals this will not be the case, and with others a more powerful source will be the bench which a magistrate joins. Thus Hood found that members of the same bench, determining a sentence at home without consulting colleagues, were still 'more likely to do something similar to their colleagues than we would expect by chance', and he found 'evidence that certain assumptions about penal policy are shared by magistrates on the same bench.'[91] Whereas magistrates may be subject to the influence of a legally qualified clerk, the judge in the Crown Court is a more isolated figure. Judges occasionally discuss sentencing difficulties with colleagues and attend judicial seminars, but they seem more likely to have confidence in their own experience than magistrates do.

It seems inherently likely that a sentencer's view of the philosophy of punishment – of the relative importance or applicability of general deterrence, rehabilitation, denunciation, retribution and other aims – will have some effect on his approach to sentencing, and this is borne out by the available research.[92] The same might be said of sentencers' views about the causes of crime, and their willingness to accept that some offences proceed as much, or more, from circumstances of social deprivation as from greed or wickedness. Relevant here are sentencers' views of what might loosely be termed the 'attitudes of offenders'. There has been little systematic investigation of sentencers' beliefs about the ways in which offenders typically think and about the factors which might enter an offender's mind when he commits a crime, yet it seems likely that such beliefs have some effect on sentencing practice. For example, one magistrate has expressed his belief that offenders tend to know that they rarely risk a custodial sentence for their first few crimes, and tend to think that they are bound to be given a suspended sentence before receiving the first immediate sentence of imprisonment.[93] One magistrate's assertion gives no impression of how widely this view is held – although it has an affinity with the thinking behind the 'nip in the bud' theory of sentencing[94] – but it could clearly affect the way in which a sentencer approaches his task: the magistrate in question was using his belief to advocate a greater willingness to use a short custodial sentence earlier in an offender's career. Lastly, sentencers' views on the function of the court in passing sentence may also influence their approach. Hogarth, for example, found that most of his Canadian magistrates felt that public opinion is punitive and that it is right to take this into account when sentencing.[95] If sentencers do feel that it is important, especially when passing sentence for crimes which give rise to public concern, to have regard to public opinion (or, to be more precise, to what they believe public opinion to be), this may lead them to pass a slightly different sentence than they might otherwise have imposed.

Turning to the factors in group II, one might expect that principles of sentencing would be closely related to the sentencers' views on the philosophy of punishment. However, there is some evidence from Lemon's study[96] that magistrates' views on crime and punishment do not determine their sentencing practices. This finding may provide support for the argument that definite guidance on the principles of sentencing can exert an independent effect on sentencing behaviour, and that personal views may have greater scope when there is less authoritative guidance for the sentencer.

There is considerable scope for any variation in sentencers' views on the relative gravity of offences to affect sentencing practice. The criminal law itself rarely indicates the factors which it regards as making an offence more or less serious, and the absence of a rational structure of maximum penalties means that it is not often safe to infer from the statutory maxima that one class of offence should be regarded as more grave than another. Hood's research included an exercise in which a group of magistrates were asked to rank in order of gravity a number of offences; the results showed some overall similarity, although there were differences of opinion on the ranking of assault and of possessing an offensive weapon.[97] However, exercises of this kind are conceptually difficult to participate in and to interpret, for the subject is asked to 'imagine a typical case of each offence when making comparisons', which leaves it possible that different subjects regard different types of case as typical. Moreover, Hood's research also suggested that disparities in sentencing become wider as the case becomes clearly atypical. Indeed, on the basis of his study of magistrates' handling of sentencing exercises, he concluded that there is 'general support for an explanation of sentencing which sees differences in the way magistrates perceive and categorize offences as an important factor in producing disparate sentences.'[98] On the other hand, Hood regarded this merely as one important factor; he did not suggest that there is a simple relationship between regarding an offence as relatively grave and imposing a more severe sentence than colleagues, for there are other influential factors.

Some of these would be found in group II(b), sentencers' views of the aims, effectiveness and relative severity of each type of sentence. At a crude level, it is possible that some magistrates who regarded an offence as particularly serious would seek a relatively severe sentence and would impose a suspended sentence; other magistrates who regarded a similar offence as not particularly serious would impose 120 hours' community service. Who is to say which offender is more severely treated? Some sentencers might regard community service orders as demanding and thus quite severe, whilst others may regard them as 'a joke'.[99] Some sentencers might regard suspended sentences as a sharp and powerful deterrent, whilst others may regard them as a 'let-off'. Some sentencers may regard probation as a 'waste of time' on the ground that it is 'ineffective', whilst others may have some confidence in the ability of local probation officers to deal with difficult cases. There exists little systematic information about sentencers' view on these matters, but discussions with judges and magistrates tend to support the finding of the Oxford pilot study that sentencers have different opinions of the available measures. These opinions may derive from different views on crime and punishment or on the causes of crime, or they may have been formed in the light of experience. The sentencer is likely to bring to each case his own 'knowledge', based on his experience of sentencing, of its problems and of its 'results'. Similarly, there is the question of the way in which a sentencer regards the available measures: does he see them as forming a kind of 'penal ladder', with absolute discharges on the bottom rung and immediate imprisonment on the top rung and the other measures ranged between?[100] Or does he reject the analogy of a ladder and argue that certain measures are appropriate for some types of offence and offender and not for others? Are there some cases in which he allows himself to be drawn towards a particular sentence by the social enquiry report or the speech in mitigation? If the answer is that most sentencers use each approach to some extent, this – combined with probable differences in opinions about the relative severity and effectiveness of the measures – suggests that there is once again considerable scope for variations. There is little authoritative guidance on these questions, so that a sentencer could not easily maintain that he is following the correct approach.

Similar points could be raised in relation to views on the general principles of sentencing (II(c)) and views on the relative weight of mitigating factors (II(d)). There is some general appellate guidance on general principles, but there remains scope for different views on such crucial questions as the proper approach to sentencing a persistent offender who commits crimes of low or moderate gravity. There is also appellate guidance on factors which may and may not mitigate, but that guidance is clearest in cases which focus on one factor alone and the sentencer has his greatest need of guidance in cases where there are combined and conflicting factors, with elements of mitigation and aggravation. Hood found that where complicating factors were introduced into his motoring cases, such as where damage or injury resulted from a piece of bad driving or where the driver had previous convictions, 'there are large differences in the way these differences are acted upon.'[101] And Diamond has argued, on the basis of her American research, that 'when both aggravating and mitigating factors are present . . . there is evidence for greater disagreement among judges.'[102]

The only factor in group I is the sentencer's view of the facts of the case. It is often said by sentencers that no two cases are the same, and indeed this statement is often used as an argument against attempts to structure or confine the sentencing discretion too rigidly. Its relevance for present purposes is that, from the range of facts presented to the court, the judge or magistrate is likely to select certain features as particularly important. Each sentencer will bring to the case his own 'knowledge', accumulated through the experience of dealing with other cases, and his own opinions. Moreover, some sentencers may place a different interpretation on what they hear in court according to their view of the defendant's 'attitude', his appearance, or the line of defence he adopts. There is no evidence as to whether these factors do lead to different views of the facts and hence to different sentences; but the Oxford pilot study raised the possibility that different judges' perceptions of what occurred in court had some influence on their characterization of the case, and since judges are human this does not seem inherently improbable. Whether the effect of these differences is a minor or a significant factor in judicial sentencing practice is a matter for empirical study.

The discussion of factors in groups I, II and III has laid emphasis on the sentencer's *views* on certain matters, as distinct from the formal rules and principles laid down for sentencers. If these factors were to be used as the basis for a model of decision-making in sentencing,[103] then account would also have to be taken of the effect of information and opinion presented to sentencers in some cases. Thus the sentencer's view of the facts of the case may not only be influenced, as suggested here, by his impression of the defendant's manner and his line of defence, but also by the facts which are selected for him by the prosecution in cases where there is a guilty plea. The prosecution may present a description of the facts which, either deliberately or unwittingly, lays emphasis on certain factors and not on others. Unless the defence challenge the prosecution's version of the facts – in which event there may be some argument and some evidence heard – the 'raw data' which reach the sentencer have already been subject to a process of selection over which the sentencer has no control. In many cases the sentencer is likely to hear an advocate's speech in mitigation, on behalf of the defendant, and this might lead him to alter his view of such factors as the relative gravity of this particular offence (II(a)), or of the relevance of the offender's record (II(c)), or the strength of the mitigating factors (II(d)). In cases where there is a social enquiry report, this will usually express an opinion on the effect of one or more measures on this offender's future conduct (II(b)) and may provide information which leads the sentencer to re-assess the strength of the mitigation. As with the principles of sentencing laid down by the Court of Appeal, however, it is not the *actual* opinions and information conveyed by reports and submissions to the court which lead to some alteration in the sentence which might otherwise have been imposed, but rather the sentencer's *views* of what he reads and hears. To give two crude examples, a sentencer may be more likely to pay heed to a report from a probation officer he knows and respects than to a report from an unknown or less respected officer; and a sentencer may be more receptive to a speech in mitigation which manifests 'realism' than one which does not.[104] To some extent, probation officers and advocates may appreciate this and adapt their presentation so as to exert the maximum effect upon the court, but that in no way weakens – indeed it virtually concedes –the argument that it is the sentencer's view of the information and opinions which matters.

These, then, are the factors which might be supposed to enter or influence a sentencer's thought processes when he is deciding on the sentence in a particular case. They have been ranged from I to IV for the purpose of exposition: it is suggested that this reflects the directness of their influence, so that factors in groups I and II might be expected to exert the most direct influence on the sentence imposed. There exists a considerable amount of authoritative guid-ance on the factors in group II, mostly in the form of decisions of the Court of Appeal, but they may be less significant than the views which are actually held by most of those who pass sentence in English courts. There is no basis for assuming that most sentencers con-scientiously follow appellate guidance for most of the time: that guidance may not be fully known, it may sometimes be regarded as inappropriate to the problems which confront most sentencers in magistrates' courts and third-tier Crown Courts, and it is in any event incomplete. Where guidance is lacking, or where the guidance provided is regarded as inappropriate, the sentence may be in-fluenced by the opinions of the individual sentencer, often stemming from factors in groups III and IV. There is, however, no systematic evidence on which one can base any assertion about the degree to which the principles of sentencing laid down by the Court of Appeal or principles and opinions derived from personal or local sources predominate in sentencing practice.

This attempt to describe the range of factors which may influence sentencing decisions has placed simplicity of exposition above explanatory force. Even if the factors discussed here are the principal determinants of sentencing decisions, they probably interact in a complex way which is difficult to ascertain. There is a need for well-conceived empirical research on many aspects of sentencing, but whether it could be expected to produce a reasonably complete *explanation* of sentencing practice is not clear. If, however, it seems likely that many of the factors here discussed do have an influence on sentencing practice, that supplies an argument for more guidance on sentencing principles. It is surely in the absence of clear guidance that the sentencer's own views are likely to have their greatest influence.

9 An outline of government penal policy

Although the English tradition is for the legislature to provide the penal measures and for the courts to decide in their discretion how to use them, governments have in recent years made it clear how they would like to see certain types of measure used by the courts. In 1977 the Home Office published A Review of Criminal Justice Policy 1976, a unique document which outlined official policy on a wide range of penal matters, many of which had direct implications for sentencers. Since 1979 the Conservative Government has clearly attempted to shape penal policy in particular directions, a goal which (as government ministers have expressly recognized in their speeches) requires the co-operation of the courts in sentencing policy. Three major concerns have manifested themselves in recent government statements – controlling the custodial population, increasing the use of non-custodial measures, and sharpening the focus of the criminal justice system. Each may be considered briefly in turn.

The policy of controlling the prison population appears to be the result of a crisis of economics and planning on the one hand, and a shift in penal thinking on the other hand. The general economic restraints on public expenditure have been felt in the penal system, and the fall in the custodial population in the early 1970s (see Table 7, above) led to the abandonment of plans for substantial prison building. The custodial population increased rapidly in the late 1970s, with the result that insufficient custodial places are available, overcrowding is high, and the fabric of many penal institutions is literally crumbling. Although the present government has announced a programme of prison building,[105] this is both expensive and unlikely to add significantly to the number of prison places available (since some buildings are coming to the end of their useful life). The shift in penal thinking has consisted of a growth of the belief that custodial sentences have no greater reformative or individually preventive effect than non-custodial sentences, a belief which indicates shorter and fewer custodial sentences. The policy of reducing the effective length of custodial sentences has been pursued by maintaining a relatively high parole rate (almost two-thirds of eligible prisoners are released on parole) for those serving more than 18 months, and for those serving sentences of up to 2 years the Government has introduced the partly suspended sentence and has commended the Lord Chief Justice's guidelines in *Begum Bibi*[106] to sentencers.[107]

The policy of fostering the greater use of non-custodial measures is also born of a combination of economic and penological considerations. Non-custodial measures are generally cheaper than custodial sentences and are therefore favoured by the Home Office on economic grounds, and research suggests that they may be no less effective in terms of reconvictions. Indeed, the Home Secretary has urged sentencers to consider the benefit of a 2 year probation order in cases where they are minded to impose a short custodial sentence.[108] Whatever the justification, however, the Government's view is said to be that 'unless there are clearly overriding public interest considerations pointing in the opposite direction, non-custodial disposals should be preferred.'[109]

The third major concern – sharpening the focus of the criminal justice system – has received rather less public attention. The Government has stated its concern that as many drunks, mentally disordered and persistent petty offenders as possible should be kept out of the criminal justice system by the wider provision and use of treatment centres, hospitals and hostels.[110] There have also been many statements which urge the courts to concentrate on the violent offender and to reserve the more serious penalties for him.[111] But there have also been exhortations from the Attorney-General urging changes in practice and procedure:[112] charges should be restricted (especially in fraud cases) to the 'real villains', rather than attempting to catch all the fringe men; counsel should keep cross-examinations as short as possible; trial judges should avoid summings-up which continue for seven or eight days. Disclosure of the prosecution case to the defence is being urged on a wider scale,[113] and pre-trial reviews are being developed.

Since these policies have been advanced in public speeches and urged upon sentencers by a Conservative Government, there might appear to be an inconsistency between the strong advocacy of a reduction in the prison population and the 'law and order' policies which are usually associated with the Conservative party. The apparent inconsistency has not gone unnoticed within the party, as Mr Whitelaw discovered at the party's annual conference in 1981 when his speech as Home Secretary was badly received. However, the party's 1979 manifesto drew a distinction between the 'real thugs' and 'hardened criminals' on the one hand, and many less serious offenders for whom custodial sentences are regarded as unnecessary on the other hand.[114] This 'bifurcated' policy has been maintained in speeches by ministers, when they have made it clear that they advocate no softening of the approach to dealing with 'violent offenders'. However, the introduction of 'experimental' regimes of 'short, sharp, shock' at some detention centres, the introduction of shorter detention centre orders and the strengthening of courts' powers for dealing with juvenile offenders combine to cast some doubt on the degree of any bifurcation. Ministers' speeches have sometimes offered direct advice to sentencers,[115] but the present Government has rarely attempted to use legislative means of restricting the wide discretion which sentencers now enjoy. In this they have deferred to the principle of judicial independence, to which we now turn.

2

Judicial independence and discretion in sentencing

The prevailing English approach, as we have seen, is for the legislature to set maximum penalties for each crime and to limit the sentencing powers of migistrates, and then to leave the courts with a large sentencing discretion. In consequence, the courts have considerable *de facto* power to shape sentencing policy. Is it constitutionally appropriate that they should possess this power? Is it practically wise that they should be left with so much discretion, or are there satisfactory means by which the legislature could confine or structure it?

1 The principle of judicial independence

Writers on the British Constitution have generally regarded it as axiomatic that the judiciary should be independent from the legislature and from the executive. Judges often have to determine the balance between the individual and the State, and should therefore be in a position to administer the law without fear or favour. The independence of the judiciary is supported by a number of constitutional rules and conventions, so that (for example) High Court judges may not be dismissed except by a formal parliamentary procedure.[1] The characteristic judicial function is that of applying and developing legal rules in order to decide individual cases. It is often assumed that sentencing is also a characteristic judicial function, but this is by no means self-evident. Thus, in discussing the separation of powers, one leading work on constitutional law states that 'Other tasks (for example the sentencing of criminals) are

arguably not essential judicial functions, although they are traditionally the work of judges.'[2]

In recent years the idea of judicial independence has acquired a
particular connotation in the field of sentencing. In the late 1970s a
succession of official committees considered ways of furthering
various elements of penal policy described in the last chapter; each of
them considered the potentiality of changes in sentencing practice,
and each of them clearly felt inhibited from recommending changes
by 'the principle of judicial independence'. No coherent statement of
the principle has yet appeared, but from the way in which the
principle has been used one can deduce the following propositions:
'There is a principle of judicial independence; attempts by the
executive arm of government to influence sentencing policy are
unconstitutional; attempts by the legislature to interfere with the
sentencing discretion of the courts are, even if not strictly unconstitutional, bound to result in both practical confusion and injustice to
defendants; the development of sentencing policy should therefore be
left to the wisdom of the courts, under the guidance of the Court of
Appeal, and intervention by other bodies can only worsen the
situation.' Behind these propositions lies a network of assumptions
about the proper relationship between the legislation, the judiciary
and the executive in matters of sentencing. These assumptions may
fruitfully be examined through a series of questions.

(a) **Is legislative curtailment of judicial sentencing discretion unconstitutional?**

In the tradition of Blackstone and Dicey, the constitutional lawyer
Jennings identified three characteristics of the courts in the English
system:[3]

(i)   'their subordination to the legislature';
(ii)   'their independence of administrative authorities';
(iii)   'the methods of the courts' (by which he meant the openness of
         their proceedings, the right to be represented, and other
         features of 'natural justice').

The answer to question (a) is contained in his first proposition: the
courts are subordinate to the legislature, and they are therefore
constitutionally bound to apply statutes duly enacted by Parliament.
'The doctrine of the separation of powers does not prevent Parliament
from making laws relating to the exercise of judicial power by
properly constituted courts', as Menzies J has put it. What appears to

be a different interpretation of the constitutional position has been advanced by Lord Hailsham, however. He regards it as fundamental that the judiciary should have the decision whether or not to deprive an offender of his liberty.

> The Judiciary is essential because it has to decide whether a man is to lose his liberty which is the fundamental right of the English citizen since Magna Carta, and the Judiciary stands between the citizen and the Government who wants to prosecute him through the executive arm, in this case the Attorney General or whoever is prosecuting. The Judiciary stands between them and says, 'No, not until you have had a fair trial in front of a judge and jury and not unless you are sentenced to a loss of liberty by one of us.' I regard that as essential to liberty.[4]

It is doubtful whether these *ex tempore* remarks should be treated strictly as a denial of Parliament's power, for example, to lay down mandatory or minimum sentences. The remarks are probably better viewed as a traditional and pragmatic justification of the practice of leaving the widest sentencing discretion to judges. The strict relationship between legislature and courts appears from the Australian case of *Palling* v. *Corfield*,[5] where a defendant challenged the validity of a statutory provision which *required* the court to impose a particular sentence on conviction for a specified offence. Barwick CJ gave an account of the constitutional position which applies equally well, perhaps *a fortiori*, to England.

> Ordinarily the court with the duty of imposing punishment has a discretion as to the extent of the punishment to be imposed; and sometimes a discretion whether any punishment at all should be imposed. It is both unusual and in general, in my opinion, undesirable that the court should not have a discretion in the imposition of sentences, for circumstances alter cases and it is a traditional function of a court of justice to endeavour to make the punishment appropriate to the circumstances as well as to the nature of the crime. But whether or not such a discretion shall be given to the court in relation to a statutory offence is for the decision of the Parliament. It cannot be denied that there are circumstances which may warrant the imposition on the court of a duty to impose specific punishment. If Parliament chooses to deny the court such a discretion, and to impose such a duty, as I have mentioned the court must obey the statute in this respect assuming its validity in other respects. It is not, in my opinion, a breach of the Constitution not to confide any discretion to the court as to the penalty to be imposed.[6]

Attempts by the English legislature to 'interfere with' the sentencing discretion, such as the restrictions formerly imposed by section 3 of the Criminal Justice Act 1961 (young adult offenders) and by the

Criminal Justice Act 1967 (mandatory suspension of certain prison sentences), were attacked as unpractical and unwise, but there was no suggestion that they were unconstitutional. It might be argued that in imposing such restrictions the legislature was fulfilling its natural role in policy-making, for on principle questions of social policy, such as are inevitably involved in sentencing policy, ought to be primarily for the legislature to resolve. The judicial role is to apply to the individual case the general rules laid down by parliament – a process which may conveniently be termed 'individuation'. That this is the proper judicial role is rarely questioned in other contexts: in the criminal law itself, questions of policy are determined by Parliament and the results expressed in statutory rules; in family law the same applies, as it does in every other field of law. The process of individuation is in practice not merely a question of rule-application: there is some, often a great deal of, interpretation to be done before a statutory rule can be applied in particular cases, and in this respect the role of the courts is unavoidably creative. Yet this creative role ought to be exercised within, and to the furtherance of, the policies implicit in the legislation.

There is, of course, room for the argument that the actual distribution of functions between the legislature and the judiciary ought to be arranged in the most effective manner. Even if it is correct in principle that the legislature should prescribe the policies and the courts should implement them when dealing with individual cases, it might be found that this is not the most effective means of achieving certain policies. This is one interpretation of the present distribution of functions in England. The principle was clearly stated by Sir James Fitzjames Stephen: if the judiciary were to take upon themselves the task of formulating principles of sentencing, 'they would be assuming a power which the constitution does not give them.'[7] In fact, the legislature in the nineteenth century progressively removed the minimum sentences which had previously so restricted the courts, leaving it open to the judiciary to assume the very power which Stephen maintained they ought not in principle to possess. As the Advisory Council on the Penal System put it:

> While, within the bounds laid down by Parliament, the courts have an absolute discretion to decide the most appropriate sentence in every individual case, sentencing policy is determined largely, if not exclusively, by the decisions of the Court of Appeal.[8]

This is not to imply that the courts are to blame for this usurpation. On the contrary, it is inevitable that a court which gives reasoned judgments on appeals against sentence will draw upon broad principles. If no such principles are laid down, they will surely develop over a period of time. This is how the courts developed the English common law over the centuries, and it is also how they have developed principles of sentencing since the creation of an appeal court in 1907. In those branches of the criminal law on which Parliament has not yet legislated, for instance most of the law of murder and manslaughter, the courts continue to develop the common law by judicial decisions; and this is what the courts are doing in developing principles of sentencing. By comparison, Parliament's desultory forays into sentencing policy have been rather insignificant and not conspicuously successful. The mandatory disqualification from driving of persons convicted of drunken driving is perhaps the most successful of the legislative provisions on sentencing; paradoxically, some of the provisions which accord most closely with the current official policy of reducing the prison population – e.g. the 'restrictions' on imposing a custodial sentence upon any person who has not previously served a prison sentence –are phrased in such broad terms that it is difficult to see what practical influence they exert upon the courts.[9]

It is thus fair to say that in England the legislature has *de facto* delegated a large part of its policy-making function on sentencing to the judiciary. The principle of judicial independence has undoubtedly played its part in this neglect, but more pragmatic considerations (such as the difficulty of legislating successfully in this sphere, particularly if the judges proved to be inimical to the notion of detailed legislation on sentencing) must also have exerted an influence. However, so accustomed has the judiciary become to wielding the power which results from this wide discretion that in 1981 senior judges successfully dissuaded the Government from introducing legislation which would have permitted the automatic release of prisoners under supervision after serving one-third of their sentences. In its description of the proposed scheme the Home Office had mentioned the possibility that judges might try to counteract its effects by imposing higher sentences,[10] but it was denied that the judges had even implied such sabotage when communicating their opposition to the proposal.[11] In principle, there is no constitutional bar to legislation on any aspect of sentencing, and the courts should loyally apply any statutes which are passed.

(b) **Are executive attempts to influence the judiciary unconstitutional?**

We have seen that the second of the three characteristics of the English courts identified by Jennings is 'their independence of administrative authorities'.[12] The courts should not be subject to criticism or influence by members of the executive. It would surely be unconstitutional for the Government to 'pack' the bench with sentencers of a particular persuasion, or to attempt to exert influence over the sentence to be passed in a particular case, and Home Secretaries have traditionally declined to comment on sentences in particular cases. Executive review of sentences after they have been passed by the courts has long been a subject of controversy, but the debate has focused rather upon the way in which executive review should be carried out[13] than upon the constitutionality of such provisions as release upon parole or conditional release. The Government will generally only exercise its prerogative of mercy, in order to release someone sentenced to imprisonment, if new facts have come to light since he was sentenced or if there are overwhelming compassionate reasons: political sympathy with the motives behind the offence has been held insufficient.[14] Moreover, as is often pointed out in this context, the position of the Lord Chancellor under the British Constitution goes against any notion of a strict separation of powers, for he is a member of the Government, head of the judiciary and sits upon the woolsack in the House of Lords. In their judicial capacity Lord Chancellors have from time to time offered advice on sentencing to the magistracy; to what extent they might do the same for the judiciary has not been tested.

The prevailing understanding of the relationship between the executive and the judiciary was expressed thus in the report of the House of Commons Expenditure Committee:

> The starting point of our discussion must be recognition of the constitutional position of the judiciary as independent of the executive arm of the government and the legislature. This means that it would not be appropriate for the Home Office to tell the judges what to do, even if the result of judicial activity were to threaten the breakdown of the prison system, which is very nearly what has occurred.[15]

This suggests that the proper role of the executive is to service the courts, providing facilities and information and ensuring that (subject to the exercise of executive review, through the parole system or the prerogative of mercy) the sentence of the court is duly carried out. In effect, the principle of judicial independence outlined at the beginning of this chapter seems to operate as a taboo, leading to the avoidance of direct recommendations on sentencing policy.

In their report, the Expenditure Committee were investigating 'The Reduction of Pressure on the Prison System'. Their report considered alternatives to custodial sentences and possible new alternatives to prison, and also reviewed 'Sentencing Policy and Sentencing Length'. Consistently with several other committee reports of the time, the Expenditure Committee stressed the import-ance of reserving custodial penalties only for those 'whose behaviour seriously menaces society and threatens personal safety', and of not imprisoning those who are young enough to 'grow out' of their criminal behaviour or whose offences are more of a nuisance than a menace (para. 237). But when they came to the implementation of this policy, the inhibiting effect of the taboo showed itself:

> It is the courts who decide into which of the various categories described the offender fits, in the light of his offence and his previous behaviour. The Sub-Committee firmly believe in the principle of judicial independence and accept its consequence in terms of our recommendations. At the same time we feel more could be done to *acquaint* the courts at all levels with reliable information about the availability of accommodation in custodial insti-tutions, which we feel might *help* them in making their decisions. We also believe that relevant *information* about the alternatives to imprisonment should also be *supplied* to the courts . . . [16]

The words italicized here show the practical limitations imposed by the principle: the executive may strive to provide all sentencers with the maximum information about alternatives to custodial sentences, but it must not tell the courts what to do. The report does, however, accept the importance of *persuading* the courts to impose shorter sentences of imprisonment, and adds:

> It is our view that for a small but significant proportion of cases which come before the courts there can be no clearcut reasons for choosing imprisonment for deterrent, retributive, containment or rehabilitative reasons. We wish the courts to be more aware of these considerations, and to choose for cases which fall within this margin, non-custodial rather than custodial sentences. [17]

The practical implications of 'wishing the courts to be more aware . . .' remain obscure: in effect, this is a policy recommendation without much hint of how it might be implemented, save by 'informing' the courts of the Committee's reasoning. The Home

Office itself has been more bold. It ensured that a copy of the Advisory Council's interim report on *The Length of Prison Sentences* was sent to every judge and every bench of magistrates in the country. The report argued that imprisonment should no longer be seen as reformative, and that research findings show that long custodial sentences are no more effective than short ones; and it followed this with some direct advice to sentencers.

Given, however, that there is no reason to suppose that longer sentences have a greater impact upon the prisoner than shorter ones, the general rule which we *advocate* for all courts to follow is to stop at the point where a sentence has been decided upon and consider whether a shorter one would not do just as well.[18]

We think that the time has come when the courts should be *invited* to make their contribution towards a solution of this problem [sc. overcrowding in prisons].[19]

Although the effect of the taboo is apparent from the deferential tone of a later remark – 'we are encouraged to believe that the judges who sit in the Court of Appeal, Criminal Division, will be sympathetic to our overall approach'[20] (para. 18) – this interim report and the Home Office's action in distributing it to all sentencers assume a more active role for the executive than merely 'servicing' the courts. Indeed, during 1980 and 1981 there were several suggestions that the Government might be considering legislation which might restrict the sentencing discretion of the courts in order to reduce the prison population, but the approach of government ministers in their speeches was to suggest that the reduction could be effected by the courts themselves. The Home Secretary declared the Government's belief that 'through the exercise of judicial discretion it should be possible to bring about a significant reduction in the general level of sentences'[21] and in view of the great difficulties presented by the drafting of any effective legislation this form of executive exhortation may prove to be the furthest extent of government influence.

(c) Might judicial study courses breach the principle?

In 1975 a joint working party was appointed by the Home Secretary, the Lord Chancellor and the Lord Chief Justice '(i) to review the machinery for disseminating information about the penal system and matters related to the treatment of offenders; (ii) to review the scope and content of training, and the methods whereby it is provided; and to make recommendations.' In 1976 this committee, known as the Bridge Committee, produced a working paper under the title *Working Party on Judicial Training and Information*. Now it appears that the reference to 'training' (although it was clearly suggested by the committee's terms of reference) drew from the judiciary 'a widely felt and strongly voiced objection' – with the effect that the term was dropped from the committee's final report, entitled *Judicial Studies and Information*.

It is said that 'training' implies that there are 'trainers' who can train people to be judges, and so long as this concept is capable of influencing the thought of those concerned with the provision of 'judicial training' this must, despite all protestations to the contrary, represent a threat to judicial independence.[22]

The Bridge report took pains to emphasize that the 'indoctrination' or 'conditioning' of newly appointed judges was never intended, yet in deference to the objections it abandoned the term 'judicial training' in favour of the more neutral 'judicial studies'. Yet there is much more at stake here than a simple matter of terminology. Despite the change of nomenclature, the report notes, 'some would still argue that any proposal for officially sponsored and organised programmes of instruction for judges is objectionable;' and one of the grounds for that argument would be that the proposed courses of study 'would tend to promote an "official line" which judges would be expected to follow'.[23] The response of the report to the argument was, interestingly, neither one of acceptance nor one of rejection: the report observed that the dangers are 'exaggerated' and that the recommendations should be 'sufficient to safeguard against them'. The reader of these passages in the Bridge report can hardly fail to discern the strong undercurrents of a struggle between a powerful and defensive cohort of the judiciary and the innovating forces of the working party and (probably) the Home Office. Some crucial points of principle are not examined at all, perhaps for prudential (some would say, political) reasons. What is so objectionable about promoting an 'official line' on sentencing which judges would be expected to follow? Is there not an important distinction here between an 'official line' sanctioned by the legislature, which (as argued earlier) the judiciary ought constitutionally to follow, and a 'line' developed by 'officials' (i.e. by members of the executive), to which there might well be a good constitutional objection? On this point, Lord Devlin expresses the judicial view when he argues that the

Home Office merely has one set of interests (predominantly the reduction of the prison population), and that it would not be right to allow that single concern to dominate judicial studies.[24]

Again, in their working paper, the working party considered the content of the proposed judicial study courses and remarked that 'there could be no question of any training programme seeking to impart a particular philosophy of sentencing in this highly controversial field.' Of course as a method of study and instruction it is often effective to raise questions about the assumptions and half-formed maxims upon which we all tend to proceed. Yet the English judiciary has always prided itself on the success of its efforts to ensure consistency in sentencing principles. It is hard to conceive of a study course on judicial sentencing which would not involve reference to and reverence for the principles of sentencing which the Court of Appeal has developed. At present those principles are surely central to the task which the Bridge report had in mind. Moreover those principles do embody 'a particular philosophy of sentencing', even if they do not supply a *complete* philosophy of sentencing, and one function of a course of study must surely be to reveal rather than to conceal this. Did the Bridge Committee think it desirable to have a diversity of sentencing philosophies among judges – a position more extreme even than the broadest principle of judicial independence? As Lord Devlin rightly asserts,[25] it surely saw the study courses as promoting the principles developed by the Court of Appeal, in which case the relation of those principles to the various 'philosophies of punishment' ought to be exposed. It would be naïve in the extreme to suppose that the principles do not involve value judgments, even if it is fashionable to regard those value judgments as uncontroversial.[26]

(d) Asserting independence

The vigour with which some judges jealously guarded judicial independence against the supposed assault of the Bridge Committee's working paper and its use of the term 'training' is a clear indication of the strength of feeling in the judiciary about 'interference' by either the executive or the legislature in sentencing matters; and there is little doubt that the strength of this feeling is well known not only in government circles but also in the committees who make recommendations on sentencing (as is illustrated by their deference to judicial discretion). The opposition to parliamentary interference is probably based less on constitutional principle than on beliefs about practicality: legislation could never adequately deal with the many and varied types of case which come before the courts, and would therefore impair the flexibility which is essential to a just and effective sentencing system. This line of argument contains a number of further assumptions. On the practical point there is the assumption that no method of statutory regulation could deal successfully with the range of cases, an assumption based on experience of the English legislature's desultory forays into sentencing. That experience is not a sound basis for the general proposition that all attempts at legislative regulation are likely to be unsuccessful. More important are the assumptions which underlie the use of such terms as 'just', 'effective' and 'successful' in this context, since the criteria on which such terms rest are far more controversial than is often admitted. Most important of all is the assumption that it is proper for judges to pursue their own ideology of sentencing, even in the face of legislative attempts to shape sentencing policy in other directions.

2 Techniques of regulating discretion

The sentencing process has to be applied not only to a very large number of individuals but also to the variations in response to the sentence, often unpredictable, which may be exhibited by any one individual. The process has to be applied to offenders ranging in character from the determined, committed criminal, who is intelligent and in full possession of his faculties, to those of low-grade intelligence, the immature, the inadequate, and those addicted to drink or drugs. The practice has to be applied to the old lag and to the first offender, to the elderly and to children.[27]

It is clear from this passage why James LJ felt that statutory regulation would be inferior to maximum judicial discretion. It is as much the power to mitigate and to 'individualize' sentences as the ability to impose long sentences which leads the judiciary to argue for maximum discretion. Thus when in the nineteenth century the statutes which established minimum periods of penal servitude were progressively repealed, Ruggles-Brise (the Prison Commissioner) referred to judicial sentencing discretion as 'the most sacred principle of English criminal law'.[28] But when we discuss discretion, two important distinctions should be noticed. One is the distinction between variations to reflect the circumstances of a particular case and variations to reflect the sentencer's own preferences. The purpose of discretion is certainly to allow the sentencer to select the sentence which he believes to be most appropriate in the individual case, considering both the facts of the case and any reports on the offender's character. The purpose of discretion is surely not to enable individual judges and magistrates to pursue personal sentencing preferences. Whether a system of sentencing can successfully promote the former whilst controlling the latter may depend on the strength of collegiate pressures among sentencers and the operation of the appeal system; the English appeal system, which often only corrects errors of principle in sentencing and in any event only corrects errors of severity and not errors of leniency, is perhaps not the most fit instrument for this purpose. A second distinction is that between choosing which policy to apply and choosing how best to implement a given policy in an individual case. It may be strongly argued that it is essential to preserve a judicial discretion to individuate a given policy by applying it to a particular case, and it might be found that for some classes of case the courts must in effect be left to select the appropriate approach – because of the difficulty of laying down criteria in some areas of sentencing. But the principal arguments in favour of discretion merely support discretion to select the appropriate way of implementing the given policy in a particular case, not a discretion to select the policies to be applied.

Let us turn now to consider a number of possible means of regulating sentencing. It would be possible to go into much greater detail, in view of the different approaches taken in different jurisdictions, but the discussion will focus upon past and possible English experience.

(a) Forms of judicial self-regulation
In the English context it is perhaps wise to begin by considering three methods by which sentencers can, so to speak, police themselves according to their own rules.

(i) *Appellate review* A sentencing system in which the legislature merely sets the maximum penalties for offences may allow appellate review, and in deciding appeals the appellate court will develop principles of sentencing which will then carry the force of the appellate court's rulings. Thus in England the Court of Appeal's pronouncements on sentencing are judicial precedents of that court, and are in theory binding on all those who pass sentence in lower courts (i.e. the Crown Court and the magistrates' courts). A system which relies on appellate decisions for the development of sentencing policy and sentencing principles may be said to have the advantage of flexibility and adaptability which are usually incompatible with statutory regulation, together with the advantage that since the principles are made *by* the judges *for* the judges they are more likely to commend themselves to sentencers than principles imposed *ab extra* by Parliament or by an independent Sentencing Commission. In constitutional terms this is an extraordinary point to have to make, since courts are clearly bound to apply legislative enactments; but it was also argued that the individuation of statutory provisions inevitably leaves the judges some latitude in interpretation, and if they disagree with the policy of a particular provision it is possible for them to interpret it consistently with their own policies and not the policies implicit in the legislation. Where there is a strong judiciary imbued with high notions of judicial independence, this is a practical point in favour of judicial self-regulation. The disadvantages of appellate review depend to a large extent on the precise system adopted. If (as in England) only the defendant is allowed to appeal against sentence, the appeal court will tend to hear only cases in which the sentence was allegedly too severe. In consequence, as mentioned in Chapter 1, the court's principles might be patchy (covering serious crimes and high sentences in great detail, but saying little about run-of-the-mill offences) and the court's pronouncements might be viewed as somewhat unreal by the sentencer whose everyday fare consists of routine thefts, petty burglaries, assaults and minor damage. In the English system it may be said that few of the Court of Appeal's decisions have a direct bearing on sentencing in magistrates' courts; many of them, moreover, are not directly relevant to what a considerable number of Crown Court judges are dealing with from day to day. One means of remedying this would be for the appeal court to deliver judgments which travel beyond the point raised by a particular case and suggest a sentencing structure for a range of variations of the crime committed in that case. Such 'guideline' judgments, used sparingly in England,[29] run the risk of being treated as mere *obiter dicta* – that is, as pronouncements unnecessary to the decision of the court and therefore not binding upon lower courts. And as a practical point the effectiveness of any system of appellate review will depend on the relationship between the volume of appeals and the availability of judges: a court which is inundated with appeals and which (for whatever reasons) cannot call upon more judges will of necessity be more constrained in the development of wider principles of sentencing than a court which has a favourable ratio of judges to appeals.

(ii) *Normal maximum sentences* An alternative to self-regulation by means of an appellate system would be for the legislature to prescribe a set of normal maximum sentences for all offences, based upon the practices of the courts. In 1978 the Advisory Council on the Penal System proposed some such system. The essence would be that one could calculate for each offence a level beneath which 90 per cent of all sentences fell, and this limit could then be regarded as the normal maximum sentence. The Advisory Council acknowledged that it would be necessary for the court to be empowered to exceed the normal maximum sentence in exceptional cases, and made provision for that.[30] It would be possible for the legislature to enact a set of normal maximum penalties, either directly in a statute or (since this device is more flexible) in a statutory instrument which might be altered by compliance with a certain procedure; but the Advisory Council proposed that in the first instance the judges should be left to operate such a system by means of ordinary appellate control and the consent of the sentencers themselves.

If what we propose finds acceptance with the judiciary, it would be perfectly possible for the courts, under the direction of the Court of Appeal (Criminal Divison), to work for an experimental period to new maxima calculated as we suggested. During this period it would be possible to assess whether the 90% cut-off did cover the majority of ordinary cases, what criteria the judges were applying to exceed the new maxima, and whether reference to the new maxima was having the effect we would expect of reducing the average length of prison sentences.[31]

If the approach of self-regulation were thus chosen, then the advantages would be that the system of normal maximum penalties should afford more realistic guidance as to sentencing levels than a study of the decisions of the Court of Appeal would yield under present conditions. Sentencers would have a more realistic view of the level of sentence for most such offences; they would not be at risk of being misled by the high sentences sometimes approved by the Court of Appeal in dealing with the somewhat atypical class of cases which tend to result in appeals. Against this, however, it could be argued that a system of normal maximum penalties promises no improvement at all in the qualitative regulation of sentencing: in other words, maximum sentences help to set the ceiling but do not deal at all with questions of the factors which should be recognized as aggravating or mitigating certain types of offence, within the gross limits set by normal maxima. The Court of Appeal would be left to develop principles on those matters, with the disadvantages described in the foregoing section.

(iii) *Guidelines or basic penalties* The question of sentencing guidelines has provoked much discussion in recent years, particularly in the United States[32] and Australia.[33] For present purposes, it is sufficient to explain that the guidelines approach sets out a whole network of sentences according to several variations in each type of crime. The sentencer will then be faced with a matrix, rather in the form of a road mileage chart, and by identifying the particular variation of the offence he is dealing with and the record of the offender he has before him, he will find the guidelines indicate a certain sentence. He is at liberty to depart from this sentence if he regards it as inappropriate to the particular circumstances of the case, but he should record his reasons for doing so. Two general questions are, how are the guidelines originally formulated? and by what means are they enforced? If we are considering guidelines as a means of judicial self-regulation, then it would be quite possible for the guidelines to be agreed by members of the judiciary (perhaps a small committee of judges, acting on the basis of sentencing levels identified for them by a group of researchers, drawing on Court of Appeal decisions and empirical investigation). It would be equally possible for the guidelines to be enforced by the judges themselves, not merely through Court of Appeal decisions but, more practically and more effectively, through monitoring of sentencing decisions carried out by, say, a team of researchers in the Lord Chancellor's office, and resulting in periodic meetings of Crown Court judges to consider emergent trends, and so forth. By these means it would be possible to ensure both that the guidelines system was sufficiently flexible to retain judicial respect and approval, and that sentencers who frequently departed from the guidelines without sufficient reason could be identified and then approached by a senior judge.

The advantages of sentencing guidelines are that they can attain a much more complete coverage of sentencing decisions than Court of

Appeal judgments under the existing English system; that if they were accompanied by periodic reconsideration and (if necessary) revision of the norms, this would encourage meaningful discussion; and that they offer (so long as accompanied by regular monitoring of sentencing practice) a particularly effective way of fostering consistency. One disadvantage which sentencers might feel is that guidelines would be too rigid and inflexible: however, that is surely appearance rather than reality, for it is always possible for a judge to depart from the guidelines if he feels that the present case has features which serve to distinguish it from the closest category in the guidelines. The disadvantage of inflexibility would be much more real if a statutory approach to guidelines were adopted: the judicial approach to statutes tends to be much more technical and legalistic than their approach to other written sources of guidance. A set of extra-statutory guidelines might well refer to categories of offence by such terms as 'serious violence', 'medium violence', 'premeditated', and so forth. Terms of this kind might be broadly and sensibly construed in that context: if they appeared in a statute, then it is likely that the prevailing method of legal training would lead both advocates and judges to subject them to the kind of minute analysis which would greatly impair their effectiveness as guidelines. This is a pessimistic view, but it arises out of the dilemma which faces those who would prefer to rely upon statutory rather than judicial guidelines – whether to re-draft the whole criminal law so as to make absolutely clear the dividing lines between classes and variations of offence, or whether to opt for broad statutory language which runs the risk of destructive interpretation in the courts.

(b) **Forms of statutory restriction**
We now turn to consider eight forms of statutory restriction which might be placed on sentencing for particular offences or in respect of particular kinds of offender. They are considered in the context of a system which has statutory maximum sentences (whether in the conventional style, or 'normal maxima' along the lines proposed by the Advisory Council on the Penal System) and which has appellate review. All eight forms have been employed at one time or another in English statutes.

(i) *Mandatory sentences* In England there is only one possible sentence for murder: life imprisonment is now the mandatory sentence for that offence. Some jurisdictions in the United States use mandatory sentences more widely: one example is the mandatory 1-year prison sentence prescribed by the New York gun laws,[34] and certain states have 'habitual offender statutes' which prescribe a mandatory sentence for an offender with a particular kind of criminal record. One reason for prescribing mandatory sentences is the heightened deterrent effect which they are supposed to achieve (members of the public know that if they are caught and convicted, the sentence is bound to follow); from the courts' point of view, it can be claimed that mandatory sentences leave sentencers with no opportunity to show leniency towards certain offenders and ensures perfect consistency by leaving no opportunity for waywardness. Against this, it would be argued that the increased deterrence resulting from mandatory sentences cannot compensate for the injustice which courts are required to inflict on certain offenders whose sentences ought, out of 'justice', to be mitigated; and that mandatory sentences do not remove inconsistency but merely shift it to another (and probably less visible) stage in the criminal process. For instance, the decision to prosecute would become crucial, as would the judge's power to dismiss a case, the jury's so-called liberty to return a perverse verdict, and any opportunities for plea negotiation which might emerge.

(ii) *Mandatory or minimum sentences with a 'special reasons' exception* This is the model used in England for cases of drunken driving. The court is required to disqualify the offender from driving for a minimum period of 12 months, unless it finds 'special reasons' for not doing so. Once again, the deterrent effect of this approach is claimed to be one major advantage. From the sentencing point of view it could be said to foster consistency whilst allowing some scope for recognition of mitigating circumstances; and in England there is the marked advantage that the existence of 'special reasons' is treated as a question of law,[35] so that the prosecution has a right of appeal against the magistrates' finding of special reasons in a particular case. Whether the interpretation given to 'special reasons' makes sufficient allowance for mitigating factors is likely to be a point of controversy: there may be some sentencers who argue that the reasons allowed are too narrow, so that the statute purchases consistency at too high a cost to individual justice. The more narrowly the exception is interpreted, the more will be the attention focused on other stages in the criminal process – not merely other areas of discretion, as mentioned above, but also (as has occurred with the English law on drunken driving) on the legal technicalities which must be established before conviction.

(iii) *Mandatory sentences with an 'unjust to do so' exception*   In England a court which convicts an offender of an offence which he committed during the operational period of a suspended sentence must activate that suspended sentence unless it takes the view that it would be unjust to do so: Powers of Criminal Courts Act 1973, section 23(1). This kind of provision is a somewhat diluted form of the mandatory sentence. To what extent the supposed deterrent effect of a completely mandatory sentence is lost by a formula which allows the court some measure of latitude, although only upon reasons stated,[36] is a matter of conjecture; but there are those who strongly believe that offenders' perceptions of the seriousness of a suspended sentence would be significantly impaired if they knew that courts had a complete discretion whether or not to activate the suspended sentence on the occasion of a subsequent conviction. One advantage of this form of statutory restriction is that it makes the legislature's policy clear (to the extent that the sentence should be activated unless there is a good and strong reason for not doing so, although it leaves unspecified the circumstances in which courts might decline to activate), whilst allowing the courts that degree of flexibility which they regard as essential to the doing of justice. However, the disadvantage is the absence of appellate control in a system which makes little allowance for prosecution appeals.

(iv) *Mandatory sentences with stated exceptions*   Another variation on the theme of mandatory sentences with some limited relaxation is the statutory formula which lists a number of exceptions. This was the approach adopted in the Criminal Justice Act of 1967, when an attempt was made to require courts to suspend sentences of imprisonment of 6 months and under, but subject to various exceptions in respect of violent offenders, persistent offenders, and so on. This approach affords fairly clear guidance on policy. On the other hand, the broader the exceptions, the more room there is for courts to introduce their own policies, to the possible detriment of the legislative policies implicit in the statute. This approach is not directed at potential lawbreakers but at the courts themselves: it is solely a device to shape sentencing policy. Indeed, from the point of view of the potential lawbreaker whose case falls outside the exceptions, such a provision might have been seen as weakening the deterrent effect of the law: he knew he was unlikely to receive an immediate (as opposed to a suspended) prison sentence for a crime of medium-low gravity!

(v) *Prohibited ranges of sentence* The prohibited sentence or range of sentences shares many of the features of the mandatory sentence. However, it is directed principally at the courts rather than at potential lawbreakers, and its aim is generally to enforce a particular pattern of sentencing. One English example was section 3 of the Criminal Justice Act 1961, which formerly prohibited courts from imposing on an offender aged between 17 and 21 any sentence of imprisonment which was longer than 6 months and shorter than 3 years. There was a circumscribed exception to this prohibition, where the offender had previously been to prison or to borstal. The policy of this provision formed part of a general scheme for young adult offenders. The advantage of a prohibition is that it is peremptory – certain forms of sentence are simply unlawful – unless exceptions are allowed, in which case the width of the exceptions determines the tightness of the constraint. The disadvantage of prohibited sentences is that, if sentencers resent the prohibitions, they may attempt to circumvent them and thereby distort sentencing practice. For example, English law does not allow a suspended sentence super-vision order to be made unless the sentence which is suspended is longer than 6 months: if a judge in the Crown Court would like to impose such an order, he may impose a 7-month sentence, in order to evade the prohibition. Again, if a judge believed that a young adult offender ought to go to prison because 'borstal would do him no good', and if 6 months' imprisonment was regarded as too short, he would have had to impose a sentence of 3 years' imprisonment. The Court of Appeal did lay down from time to time that it was improper for a judge to pass a longer sentence than he would otherwise have done, solely in order to evade the prohibition.[37] But it seems likely, especially in view of the congested nature of the English appeal system, that this was done on some occasions without appellate correction. To that extent the policy of the prohibition will be subverted.

(vi) *'No other method appropriate'* Several English statutes have en-joined sentencers to impose a particular sentence on a certain type of offender only if no other method is, in the opinion of the court, appropriate. This device was originally used in 1948 to restrain the sentencing of offenders under 21 to imprisonment, and there appears to have been an immediate effect.[38] It now also applies to the sentencing to imprisonment of any offender who has not previously served a prison sentence: Powers of Criminal Courts Act 1973, section 20. This statutory approach seeks to enforce a particular pattern of reasoning rather than a particular sentence: it respects judicial discretion in sentencing matters, indicates a particular policy and leaves the courts to implement it to the extent that they believe desirable. It has been said that the 'restriction' (as it is termed by the optimistic marginal note to section 20) is virtually ineffective.[39] The same might be said of section 22(2) of the 1973 Act, which enjoins courts to impose a suspended sentence only when an immediate prison sentence would have been imposed if the power to suspend had been unavailable. A more promising approach to the structuring of judicial discretion is embodied in section 1(4) of the Criminal Justice Act 1982, which sets out three heads of justification for forming the opinion that no other method of dealing with a young adult offender (apart from a custodial sentence) is appropriate. At least this should lead the sentencer to direct his mind towards each of the three justifications – seriousness of offence, protection of the public, and the inability or unwillingness of the offender to respond to non-custodial measures.[40] The real test will be whether the Court of Appeal, through its judgments, is able to make the requirements more specific and develop more detailed guidance for each head of justification. Otherwise, if the words of the section remain at the level of generality, the impact of the section on sentencing practice is likely to be slight.

(vii) *Broader statutory formulae* English legislation employs a number of looser terms: a probation order may be made when the court is 'of the opinion that, having regard to the circumstances, including the nature of the offence and the character of the offender, it is expedient to do so' (section 2 of the 1973 Act); the court may grant a discharge to an offender if it is 'of opinion, having regard to the circumstances including the nature of the offence and the character of the offender, that it is inexpedient to inflict punishment and that a probation order is not appropriate' (section 7). It is difficult to believe that these terms exert any effect at all upon sentencing practice. Perhaps more meaningful would be a provision which permitted a court to impose a certain kind of sentence only if this was considered 'necessary for the protection of the public from serious harm', as the Advisory Council recommended with reference to 'exceptional sentences' going beyond the normal maxima which they proposed.[41] Such a formula indicates the policy of the legislature in general terms, but leaves the court with almost unlimited flexibility in the extent to which they pursue that policy. Much will depend on the effectiveness of the appeal system in allowing the Court of Appeal to establish clearer and more precise principles and to enforce those principles. In the latter respect, the Advisory Council did propose that any person subjected to an exceptional sentence should have a right to apply directly to the Court of Appeal for leave to appeal, and that there should be an entitlement to legal aid for such applications.[42] This kind of procedural provision is surely essential to the effective structuring and control of sentencing discretion in a particularly sensitive area: it is only shortage of resources (in terms of the decision not to increase expenditure so as to provide sufficient judical manpower to ensure that all appeals against prison sentences are heard in this way) and perhaps a shortage of persons suitable for judicial appointment which reserves this procedure for limited classes of case. But without such procedures, general references in statutes are unlikely to exert much effect on sentencing practice.

(viii) *Judicial prescriptions* Although this section of the chapter is concerned with forms of statutory restriction on sentencing discretion, it is worthwhile to draw a comparison briefly with two methods of judicial self-regulation. It was mentioned in Chapter 1 that the Court of Appeal has experimented with two types of prescription: first came the 'guideline judgment', which purports to deal with a range of variations on the offence actually involved in the particular case and to suggest levels of sentence appropriate to them; secondly there is the type of judgment delivered in *Begum Bibi*,[43] which sought to refer generally to sentencing levels for different classes and types of offence. The two kinds of judgment have different functions – the former being concerned with relativities within a particular offence-category, the latter concentrating on relativities between offence-categories and on what one might call 'across-the-board' sentencing levels – but they are, as presently used in England, attempts at partial structuring of the sentencing discretion. Compared with the other types of partial structuring which have been considered in this section, they have the great advantage of being prescribed *by* judges *for* judges: the method of communication is more favourable to sensible interpretation, since judges may well construe judicial precedents more meaningfully than statutes, and the prescriptions carry the authority of senior judges. It may appear more likely that they are informed by the same ideology as that of the judges who actually pass sentences. On the other hand, the apparent precision of this form of prescription might fail in its objective if the Court of Appeal is insufficiently in touch with the realities of Crown Court sentencing. If there is indeed a 'gap' between the level of sentences upheld by the Court of Appeal and the levels generally adopted in most Crown Courts, let alone magistrates' courts, a purported reduction in the level of sentences advocated by the Court of Appeal may have little effect on day-to-day sentencing practice because the sentencers will perceive the judgment merely as overdue recognition of what happens in the 'real life' of everyday sentencing. Judicial self-regulation is therefore a tool to be carefully prepared before use. Moreover, if the ideology of appellate judges differs from the prevailing ideology of trial judges, a principal advantage of this approach is lost.

(c) **Forms of statutory regulation**
Having considered methods by which the judges can for themselves regulate the use of their sentencing discretion, and having then considered some of the means by which legislatures may restrict the use of discretion in certain spheres, we now come to methods of statutory regulation – means by which the legislature takes over more or less of the discretion which is usually vested in the judges. Three forms of statutory regulation will be considered, in ascending order of constraint.

(i) *Normal maximum penalties* In part a (ii) of this section we considered the Advisory Council's proposal for a system of normal maximum penalties, which the court might only exceed if the criteria for an 'exceptional sentence' were satisfied. The Advisory Council recommended that at first such a system should be operated by the judges themselves.[44] But it would be possible to embody the system in statutory form at the outset. This might be regarded as having the advantage that the legislature would be declaring sentencing policy, although on the Advisory Council's approach the level of the normal maximum penalties would be constructed on the basis of the practice of the courts. However, several disadvantages might be anticipated in the English context. The system would be less flexible if put into statutory form, and the judges could not simply revise a normal maximum which they found, in the light of experience, was widely considered to be too high or (more likely, perhaps) too low. Parliamentary interference would be more likely, in the sense that a bill passing through Parliament might be subjected to amendments which altered aspects of the penalty structure for reasons which were political, transitory or simply misconceived. Moreover, it is likely that the Advisory Council recommended that the judges should first operate the system for themselves as a means of gaining acceptance for this new form of sentencing regulation. The Advisory Council's recommendation might therefore have been founded on a hard-headed realism about the likelihood of judicial resistance, coupled with the knowledge that if the judges regard a statute as both unwise and an unwarranted interference they might subject it to a kind of destructive interpretation which might subvert its aims.

(ii) *Statutory or other extra-judicial guidelines* In part a(iii) of this section we considered the general notion of sentencing guidelines. Such guidelines can be drawn up, implemented and revised by a number of alternative methods. We have considered them as a form of judicial self-regulation. If the guidelines were embodied in statutory form, then there would be all the disadvantages mentioned in the above discussion of statutory normal maximum penalties, notably the possibility of judicial resistance to a system of guidelines which for some reason they did not accept. It would be particularly difficult to draw up guidelines so that they might be put into statutory form, and the intricate parliamentary bill which would result from that would be prey to all kinds of small amendments which might impair the whole scheme. An alternative, which would restore some of the flexibility lost through legislative enactment, would be for the guidelines to be drawn up by a specially constituted and independent Sentencing Council. This is the approach proposed by the Australian Law Reform Commission. Their survey of judicial and magisterial opinion revealed widespread opposition to the idea of legislative principles and guidelines for the imposition of prison sentences,[45] and so they suggested that the principles and guidelines should be drawn up by an independent Sentencing Council of

Australia, consisting of 5 judges and 4 others. The membership of that tribunal may be seen as an attempt to win the acceptance of the judiciary whilst at the same time allowing other influences to flow into the process of policy-making for sentencing.

(iii) *Presumptive sentences* The most complete and restrictive form of legislative control currently in use in some American states is the presumptive sentence. The legislature lists sub-categories or bands of each kinds of offence and assigns to each sub-category a presumptive sentence. The court has a limited discretion, inasmuch as it may impose the presumptive sentence itself, an aggravated sentence or a mitigated sentence (also specified in the statute). By these means a tight control is exercised over judicial discretion. The idiosyncrasies of particular judges, whether they proceed from deliberate policy differences or simply from ignorance of the norm, are virtually eliminated. Presumptive sentencing might also have a deterrent effect on potential lawbreakers, inasmuch as they know (within a small range) what sentence they will receive on conviction, and they know that there is little opportunity to persuade the court to act differently. The great disadvantage of this system is that it drives discretion out of the sentencing stage into other stages, such as the discretion to prosecute, the choice of charge and the negotiation over plea. Unless these stages in the criminal process are controlled to an equal extent, the anticipated effect of presumptive sentencing might be reduced. A great practical barrier to this approach is that it requires re-drafting of the entire criminal law: in order to specify the sub-categories of offences with sufficient precision, there must really be a reconsideration of the form and style of the criminal code. This is not a matter which can be successfully accomplished in a short time.[46]

3 The form of the criminal law

It follows from the previous section that the form of the criminal law has a close relationship to the form of the sentencing system. The criminal law itself is fundamental to sentencing in an obvious sense: there can be no sentence unless the offender is convicted of an offence, and if the reach of the criminal law is reduced there will be correspondingly fewer cases to be sentenced. Inasmuch as criminal law reform leads to a reduction or enlargement of the scope of the criminal law, it will have some effect (the precise extent being determined by prosecution policy if a new offence is created) on the volume of sentencing. There has been little significant decriminalization in recent years, although parts I and II of the Criminal Law Act 1977 (which tightened the law on conspiracy and on squatting) may have had some effect. In a procedural sense it is relevant inasmuch as the form of the law determines whether particular issues are decided by the jury as questions of fact relating to the defendant's liability, or by the judge at the sentencing stage. If an issue (such as the victim's age in a sexual offence, or the existence of provocation in an offence of violence) appears as an element in the definition of the offence, it will have to be determined by the jury in a contested Crown Court trial. If it does not appear in the definition of the offence, the prosecution are not required to bring evidence on the point in order to establish the defendant's liability, and the matter does not become a live issue until the sentencing stage. Apart from that procedural point, there is the substantive question of drawing distinctions between types and degrees of offence. As we shall see below, the way in which the law defines the various offences can be an indication to sentencers of the gravity with which the legislature views certain forms of criminality. A further matter which has always been thought to be a question of criminal law reform (as distinct from penal reform) is that of setting the maximum penalty for a new offence. In the reforms of the last twenty years, such as the Theft Act 1968 and the Criminal Damage Act 1971, the setting of maximum penalties has been regarded as a question for the law reform body, and those bodies have generally proceeded on the basis that the maximum should be high enough to cater for the worst conceivable case which could fall within the offence as defined. When the Advisory Council on the Penal System reported in 1978 on the general question of maximum penalties, the problems of this piecemeal and traditional approach were laid bare.[47] It is an approach which leaves to sentencers the widest discretion, and in that sense it consigns the whole of sentencing practice to what one may describe as 'the common law' – in other words, to judicial discretion subject to the establishment of precedents by the Court of Appeal and the appellate review which that implies. The report of the Advisory Council showed that there can be different approaches to the question of attaching penalties to offences, such as lower 'normal maximum' sentences, which are less of an abdication than the traditional approach. The point is carried further by reflecting on some of the American approaches briefly described earlier in this chapter. Where a legislature decides either to enact presumptive sentences or to enact sentencing guidelines, that approach to sentencing *requires* a much more detailed approach to the form and structure of the criminal law: it requires the legislature to draw fine distinctions between types and degrees of what might otherwise be regarded as a single offence, and to do so in order to attach to each type and degree of the offence either a presumptive sentence or a 'band' of sentences. Those approaches to sentencing therefore compel a much more detailed approach to the definition of criminal offences. Ten or more forms of burglary, differentiated according to such matters as the kind of building, whether it was occupied at the time, and the amount stolen, would replace the single offence of burglary. By contrast, the general English approach to formulating the criminal law has few direct implications for sentencing, since it maximizes discretion by defining offences broadly and by attaching high maximum penalties. But it remains important to examine the choices which are being made.

Let us begin by describing some salient features of recent changes in English criminal law. Before 1968 the law of theft and related offences consisted of a mass of intertwining and overlapping offences: there were various offences of stealing; what we now know as burglary was divided into separate offences of housebreaking, office-breaking and so forth; there were three offences covering the field which we now know as blackmail, and so on. The Criminal Law Revision Committee considered the law and recommended the simplification which is now to be found in the Theft Act 1968. The changes were from groups of narrowly defined offences to single broad offences, and the aim was to avoid technical distinctions whilst continuing to draw broad distinctions between stealing, swindling and handling stolen goods. A similar but more radical exercise was carried out by the Law Commission when they came to report on offences of damage to property. Their recommendation was to sweep away the mass of distinctions embodied in the Malicious Damage Act 1861, mostly distinctions according to the type of property damaged, and to replace all those offences with a single general crime, now enacted in the Criminal Damage Act 1971, section 1(1): 'A person who without lawful excuse destroys or damages any property belonging to another, intending to destroy or damage any such property or being reckless as to whether any such property would be destroyed or damaged, shall be guilty of an offence.' The 1861 Act had not only drawn distinctions between kinds of property damaged but had also attached different maximum penalties to the offence, thus giving some indication of the legislature's view (in mid-Victorian times) of the relative seriousness of damaging certain kinds of property. The Law Commission eschewed that approach on the argument that[48]

distinctions based upon the nature of the property or its situation, or upon the means used to destroy or damage it, or upon the circumstances in which it was destroyed or damaged, should not affect the basic nature of the offence. This is the philosophy underlying the Theft Act and we are convinced that it is right. Such features as the means used or their consequences are subsidiary matters relevant, if at all, in regard to sentence.

The logical consequence of this approach, so far as sentencing is concerned, is the setting of a maximum penalty which is 'high enough for the worst cases' and which would 'leave a wide discretion to the courts'. The alternative would have been 'to lay down scales related to particular aggravating features,' but the Criminal Law Revision Committee argued against this in its report on theft:[49]

Since the seriousness of an offence always depends on a combination of factors, it is in general misleading to single out certain factors for the purpose of providing maximum penalties. Moreover the simplification of the law which is obviously desirable could not be achieved unless the present policy of graded maximum penalties were for the most part abandoned.

That approach was also followed by the Law Commission in their report on offences of damage to property, and it seems to have become the modern orthodoxy in criminal law reform. Thus in their report on *Offences against the Person*, the Criminal Law Revision Committee followed this approach, recommending that the 'catalogue of offences in the Act of 1861' should be replaced by offences which 'group criminal acts according to a small number of important characteristics so that the issue will be whether the acts fall within the mischief against which the criminal law is aimed rather than whether they relate to one of a series of special relationships.'[50] It is to be noted, however, that none of the committees has gone on to discuss sentencing policy in relation to the broad offences recommended. Probably this is understandable in view of the strong principle of judicial independence on sentencing matters. Yet it seems naïve for a committee to recommend the replacement of an intricate set of distinctions by a broad offence, and not to appreciate that sentencers will have to draw distinctions of some kinds when dealing with the various manifestations of crime which fall within the new offence. Some reasoned discussion of factors which might aggravate and mitigate offences within the broad category would certainly contribute towards the development of the principled sentencing policy which is essential if the trend towards broader categories of offence is not to result in broader disparities in the significance attributed by different sentencers to essentially the same factors. A committee which is considering the range of conduct covered by an offence is in a good position to make some contribution towards the necessary debate on matters such as these.

This tendency to move towards fewer, broader offences and away from 'catalogues' of separate offences has not, however, been universal. Whilst it characterizes the reforms carried out in the realms of theft and criminal damage, and the reforms proposed for offences against the person and (tentatively) for sexual offences,[51] a different approach has been adopted in some fields of criminal law which are more politically sensitive. Thus the various offences concerned with occupation of premises owned by another, and particularly the crime of conspiracy to trespass, were revised so as to ensure that the circumstances in which a squatter is liable for a criminal offence are stated with a much greater degree of certainty and clarity. The offence of conspiracy was until 1977 as broad an offence as a prosecution might wish to have, and it fulfilled all the criteria laid down by the Law Commission and the Criminal Law Revision Committee in the quotations above. The great difficulty was that its boundaries were so uncertain that it could be used oppressively, and in particular it could be brought as a charge in circumstances where no one could be clear beforehand whether or not the conduct was criminal. Occasionally we tolerate an unduly wide offence (a rather different example of this would be the crime of unlawful sexual intercourse with a girl under 16) where experience shows that prosecutors only bring charges in 'bad' cases. This was not thought to be the case with the crime of conspiracy in the early 1970s, which is why the Law Commission were asked to review the law as a matter of urgency. But the point at issue in these areas is rather different from the difficulties inherent in the former law of theft and criminal damage. The problem with conspiracy at common law was that the boundaries of the law were uncertain: it was not the technicality but the vagueness of the law which caused misgivings.

What is to be said, in relation to sentencing, either in favour or against the use of broad offences in criminal law? Considerations in favour of broadly defined offences are (i) that they reduce the scope for technical legal argument and appeals, and increase the likelihood of guilty pleas, thereby lessening the load on the criminal justice system; (ii) that they create fewer problems of use and interpretation for policemen, prosecutors, magistrates, juries and citizens. Considerations which tell against broad offences are (a) that they fail to mark all distinctions which might be regarded socially as relevant to a fair appraisal of the person's offence; (b) that they fail to indicate both to the public and to sentencers the factors which are regarded as making an offence particularly serious or less serious; (c) that by removing distinctions they ensure that certain questions of fact relevant to sentence are determined not by the jury but by the judge alone at the sentencing stage; and (d) that by removing certain distinctions from the legal definition to the sentencing stage they make it more difficult for the defendant to challenge the way in which the court treats those distinctions. It is worth considering these advantages and disadvantages in a little more detail.

In favour of broadly defined offences Little further needs to be said about the effect on the criminal justice system of broadly defined rather than technically differentiated offences. Any reform which seems likely to save court time is viewed with enthusiasm in the present climate, as the outline of current penal concerns showed.[52] Broadly defined offences reduce the scope for lawyers to argue that the defendant's conduct falls into one category rather than another; for the same reason they increase the likelihood of guilty pleas, since the broad definition of an offence greatly reduces the number of factors over which there could be argument at the stage of criminal liability and relegates them – if that is not too pejorative a term – to the sentencing stage. Another major argument is that broadly defined offences are easier for non-lawyers to work with. The Criminal Law Revision Committee used this argument when making recommendations for a new law on non-fatal injuries. In the first place they proposed an offence of causing serious injury with intent to cause serious injury, which would be underpinned by an offence of causing serious injury recklessly (the second offence carrying a maximum penalty of 5 years' imprisonment, the first carrying life imprisonment). But when they came to consider lesser offences of causing injury (as distinct from causing *serious* injury), they declined to recommend distinct offences for the two mental states, and proposed a single offence of causing injury either with intent to cause injury or recklessly. Their explanation was that the distinction between causing injury with intent and recklessly 'is not an easy distinction for the police, magistrates and juries to make'.[53] Although the Committee's position may appear inconsistent, inasmuch as they require the police and juries to draw that very distinction in cases of *serious* injury, it might be defended by saying that in cases of serious injury it is more important for the distinction between the two mental states to be argued about in open court, whereas in cases of injury which are not serious the point is less significant. But the upshot of the Committee's argument in favour of the broader definition in cases of causing injury is that the point ceases to be an issue at the stage of criminal liability, although it is still an issue at the sentencing stage and in a Crown Court trial the judge may need to hear further evidence on the matter.[54]

Against broadly defined offences The first argument is that broadly defined offences fail to mark all the distinctions which might socially be regarded as relevant to a fair appraisal of the nature and degree of a person's wrongdoing. For convenience, the Criminal Damage Act 1971 lumps together all kinds of damage to all forms of property. The Law Commission even suggested that damage by fire should be covered by the general definitions, but Parliament felt that people really do (and rightly) regard arson as a separate type of offence and so provided that it should be labelled separately. Some might go further and argue that arson of a building is more serious than and quite different from burning someone else's chattels, but that distinction is now submerged in the general offence. Again, it is possible as a matter of legal draftsmanship to create a single offence which covers theft and deception, or which covers theft and handling stolen goods; but the Criminal Law Revision Committee recommended that the law should continue to draw these distinctions because people see a real difference between stealing and swindling or receiving, and the Theft Act 1968 so provides. But that Act did ride roughshod over other distinctions which continue to have relevance to social judgments and to sentencing. Burglars of houses tend to be viewed and treated differently from burglars of other premises such as shops and offices, but they now fall within the same offence. Traditional 'receivers' of stolen goods tend to be viewed and treated differently from those who merely help to move stolen goods, but they now fall within the same offence. In many instances, therefore, English criminal law has opted for an approach which sacrifices accurate labelling of each offence to procedural simplicity and expedition. This sacrifice may also be relevant at stages in the penal process other than sentencing: wherever offenders are categorized according to the nature of their offence, it is possible that the label may come to be taken at face value whereas a more detailed set of labels might produce different judgments of the individual. The broader the categories of offence, the less informative is an offender's criminal record.

A second argument is that broadly defined offences fail to fulfil the declaratory purpose of the criminal law. That purpose is to declare to the public and to the courts that certain kinds of offence are viewed as particularly heinous. Declarations are much clearer if they draw distinctions based on the degree of harm caused, the defendant's mental state, the method used to perpetrate the offence, and the status of the victim or the defendant. If such distinctions do not appear on the face of the statute and are left to be reflected by the sentencing practice of the courts, it is arguable that an opportunity to make a clear and open statement about the law's priorities and concerns is being lost. Some may doubt whether the law loses a deterrent effect in this way: it might be argued (with what force it is hard to speculate) that those who contemplate committing offences largely know what factors tend to aggravate and mitigate offences, or that to enshrine them in a statute would not ensure that they became much more widely known. Should the law provide that the offence becomes more serious (either in its label or in the maximum penalty or both) if a weapon is used or carried? There are crimes, such as aggravated burglary, where this approach has been taken, but generally it is not the English approach and a separate offence concerned with offensive weapons or firearms is charged if it is thought necessary. Yet the carrying of firearms is often thought important for categorizing offenders.[55] Again, English law has opted for general offences of assault but the Criminal Law Revision Committee, whilst proposing the abolition of many aggravated assaults concerned with magistrates and clergymen, recommends the retention of assaulting a police officer as a separate offence. This clearly has a declaratory purpose vis-à-vis both the police and those who are tempted to attack them. However, assaults *by* policemen are traditionally viewed seriously as well,[56] but there is no special offence to mark that. Another example could be drawn from sexual offences: the offence of unlawful sexual intercourse with a girl under 16 lays down a broad prohibition which is actually enforced in a much more selective manner. Where the age of the boy is close to that of the girl, the offence is rarely prosecuted at all. By contrast, where the man has a special responsibility for the girl (e.g. schoolteacher, choirmaster), the offence is regarded as particularly serious. In England this point is left to the sentencing discretion of the courts. Other countries do have some special offences, but when the Policy Advisory Committee on Sexual Offences raised this issue with the Criminal Law Revision Committee, they were told that it would be impossible to produce a complete list of the status relationships which ought to aggravate the offence, and that even if it were possible 'it would be so long and detailed as to be totally out of place in criminal legislation on sexual matters, where the guiding principles are clarity, certainty and brevity.' A broadly drafted special offence covering status relationships and material inducements would also be out of place, since it could 'cause serious problems of application for those concerned with the administration of justice'.[57] It therefore appeared that the only solution consistent both with the English legislative tradition and with the need to expedite court proceedings would be to retain one general offence, and leave these matters to the sentencing stage. Obviously the decisions which have to be taken at that stage are similar to decisions which would have to be taken in open court if the matter were embodied in legislation (by way of a special offence) but it is now for the sentencer to determine whether the relationship was such that it should aggravate the offence. Again, some people (including some sentencers) regard it as significant if the girl initiated the offence of unlawful sexual intercourse. The Canadian Criminal Code provides that a defendant may be acquitted if the evidence does not show that, as between him and the girl, he was wholly or chiefly to blame. The prevailing English view is 'that this matter too is best left . . . to the discretion of the police in prosecuting and of the court in sentencing'.[58] This avoids time-consuming and embarrassing discussion in open court, but it also leaves considerable scope for the infiltration of varying opinions into the criminal process. English law does mark one distinction: where the girl is under 13, it is regarded as a separate offence and carries a much higher maximum sentence (life imprisonment, instead of 2 years' imprisonment). The argument would presumably be that society regards such offences as particularly grave;[59] but the same might be said of some of the other variations we have briefly considered.

The general tendency of English criminal law to leave variations in culpability to the sentencing stage also means that there is less control over the way in which courts evaluate aggravating and mitigating factors, and correspondingly less assurance for the defendant that due consideration will be given to each factor. For example, if a factor (such as intent) is an element in the definition of the offence, the judge must explain to the jury in a contested case what 'intent' means in law, and if he errs an appeal may be brought. Again, if a factor (such as provocation) is not merely a matter to be taken into account when sentencing but constitutes a 'defence', which the defendant may raise in order to reduce his crime from one category (e.g. grievous bodily harm) to a lower category (e.g. unlawful wounding), then the judge will have to direct the jury about the meaning and scope of that defence. He will then have the benefit of a jury verdict on the issue, and of hearing evidence on the issue in open court. Moreover, there are a number of elements of the defence which can be evaluated differently by different judges: the significance of apparent planning, as by preparing a weapon for use, and the effect of what might be called 'cumulative provocation' (a course of provocative conduct by the victim towards the defendant over a considerable period of time). If provocation were a distinct defence to a crime of violence (which it is only for the crime of murder, in English law), the significance of matters such as these would soon be tested on appeal, because appeal on points of law is as of right, and there would then be greater uniformity in summings-up to juries, and when the judge came to pass sentence he would have a clear indication of the importance he ought to attribute to the major factors in the defence. So long as provocation is not a distinct defence those matters can be fudged, and neither judges nor defendants know what the significance of such factors ought to be.[60]

These problems could be alleviated if the relevant principles of sentencing were clearer and more extensive. If the principles were clear, if judges had to explain each sentence in terms of those principles, and if appeals stood a greater chance of being heard, then the individual might be as well protected as he would if the relevant factors were set down as part of the definition of an offence or defence. Yet even in this context it is proper to employ the conditional, 'might'. There is a further difficulty: if an aggravating or mitigating factor is part of the definition of an offence or defence, this means that in a contested Crown Court trial the jury have to decide whether or not the required elements are present in each case; but if aggravating and mitigating factors do not form part of the legal definition, neither side needs to argue the point at the trial and the question will be raised only at the sentencing stage. How are disputed questions of fact settled at this stage? Is there room for a dispute on the facts where the defendant pleads guilty to the offence with which he is charged, but wishes to establish that he committed the offence in a less serious manner than the prosecution allege? We saw earlier that the Criminal Law Revision Committee has proposed that the three principal non-fatal offences against the person should be:

– causing serious injury with intent to cause serious injury;
– causing serious injury recklessly;
– causing injury with intent to cause injury or recklessly.

It would appear logical to have separated the last-mentioned offence into two, distinguishing the reckless offence from the offence 'with intent', particularly since the Committee acknowledged that a major reason for drawing that very distinction in cases of serious injury was that there was a significant 'moral distinction' between intent and recklessness. They recommended against drawing the distinction in cases of injury so as to make the administration of the law easier for police, magistrates and juries. From the point of view of fact-finding, the recommendation seems hardly to help magistrates (who ought to draw the distinction anyway if they are to take proper account of the 'moral distinction' in their sentencing) and may well make matters more difficult for a Crown Court judge in a contested trial, since he does not have the benefit of a jury finding on the point. If we accept the Committee's argument that the matter is unnecessarily complicated for the jury, what can the judge do to determine the presence or absence of intent? The answer to this question is explored in the next section of the chapter.

4 The factual basis for sentence

The foregoing discussion establishes that the form taken by the criminal law determines the precise elements which the prosecution must prove (or the defendant admit). Some offences may be so narrowly defined that the verdict or plea of guilty provides the sentencer with all the facts which he needs for the purposes of sentencing. Other offences, however, are defined more broadly, with the result that the verdict or plea of guilty does not establish all the facts necessary as a basis for sentence. How is the sentencer to ascertain these facts? If the process of determining these facts involves neither admission by the defendant nor a full trial of the issue, can the court be satisfied of their accuracy? Is the defendant adequately protected from the possibility of being sentenced on a factual basis which has not been soundly established? These and other related questions can arise in a number of different situations. The more important situations are now discussed in turn.

(a) Interpreting a jury verdict

The general principle is that the judge must base his sentence on a version of the facts which is consistent with the verdict. Where the verdict is ambiguous on a crucial issue, such as the degree of the offender's participation in the offence or the mental attitude of the offender, it is not open to the judge to ask the jury for a special verdict[61] and he must therefore base his sentence on the less serious of the versions put to the court.[62] Ambiguities in verdicts are inevitable so long as English law contains broadly defined offences such as manslaughter, but in some cases the difficulty can and should be avoided by charging the defendant separately with a firearms offence or with assaulting a police officer (since the possession of firearms and the element of assault on a law enforcement officer are crucial issues for sentencing).[63]

(b) Interpreting a guilty plea

Even where the offender pleads guilty, the factual basis for sentence may not be clear, if the prosecution state the facts in one way and the speech in mitigation states them in another way. The first duty of the sentencer is to resolve the dispute: it appears that he may require the issue to be resolved by directing a trial on a not guilty plea,[64] but the proper course will usually be for the sentencer to invite the parties to call evidence, with a view to determining the issue of fact himself.[65] Where the sentencer fails to take this course, he should not base his sentence on the more serious of two versions of the offence, and the Court of Appeal will substitute a sentence based on the less serious version.[66] If the proper procedures are followed, it appears that it is open to the court to sentence an offender on the basis of an aggravating factor which could have been the subject of a separate charge, if it can be said that the failure to add that charge does not imply an acceptance that the aggravating factor was not present. The Court of Appeal's decisions are not, however, entirely consistent[67] and in principle a defendant should be charged with the separate offence and should thus have the opportunity to plead guilty or not guilty, electing for a trial if he disputes the additional allegation.

(c) Specimen counts

It should be axiomatic that an offender ought to be sentenced only for offences which he has admitted or which have been proved against him. If he asks the court to take into consideration further offences, he will be treated as admitting those offences and will be sentenced on that basis: the House of Lords has laid down the proper procedure in such cases.[68] Occasionally, where the prosecution alleges a course of offending during which numerous crimes were committed by the defendant, it will bring 'specimen' charges, relating to only a few of the alleged crimes. If the defendant is convicted on these charges and then asks the court to take into consideration the numerous other offences, he can accordingly be sentenced on that basis. If he is convicted on the specimen counts but continues to dispute the prosecution's allegations of a course of offending, it is established that the court should pass sentence only for the offences proved.[69] The Court of Appeal has departed from this principle, however, in a case where the defendants were convicted on some of the specimen counts and acquitted on others, approving a sentence which took account of the wider course of offending alleged by the prosecution.[70] The decision is contrary to principle, and ought not to be followed.

(d) Procedure and evidence

Where the sentencer has to resolve a factual issue in order to provide a proper basis for sentence, what procedure should he adopt, and what standards should be applied to the evidence? The procedure should clearly involve the hearing of evidence on both sides; it is also desirable that the defence should be given notice of any allegations which the prosecution are to make, and indeed that the prosecution should be informed if mitigation based on a particular version of the facts (not accepted by the prosecution) is to be put forward. One approach would be to require the prosecution to provide the defence with the summary of facts which it is proposed to state in court, and to require the defence to signify objection if they do not accept that version and yet plead guilty to the offence as charged. These preliminaries ought to be developed if these post-conviction hearings are to be placed on a sound footing. At present, as we have seen, there is ample authority in favour of such a hearing where there is a disputed issue of fact after a guilty plea.

What kind of evidence ought to be admissible? It has been decided that the sentencer should disregard evidence arising from the trial of a co-defendant,[71] and should disregard allegations made by a co-defendant during a joint trial,[72] although the judge could presumably hear further evidence on these issues. What he must not do is to base himself on these claims unless evidence is called and the defendant is given the opportunity to rebut them. There are conflicting decisions of the Court of Appeal on the propriety of basing sentence on admissions made by the defendant to the police during questioning:[73] the better view is surely that, as in relation to specimen counts and offences taken into consideration, no person should be sentenced for an offence which he has not admitted to the court. The sentencer should not simply accept what the defendant may have said to the police, under entirely different circumstances.

It seems established that the evidence adduced at post-conviction hearings should be first-hand and not hearsay,[74] and that the sentencer should not base the sentence on allegations from a victim which are uncorroborated in respect of certain points of difference.[75] There have been statements that the defendant should be given the benefit of the doubt in determinations of the factual basis for sentence,[76] but in principle it should be clearly stated that allegations which tend to aggravate the offence must be proved beyond reasonable doubt (which is the standard applicable to the offence itself).

(e) **Establishing the factual basis for sentence**[77]
It is abundantly clear that many issues which may have a significant effect on sentence – which may make the difference between a non-custodial and a custodial sentence, or between a short and a long custodial sentence – are not resolved by the verdict of the jury in a Crown Court trial or by a plea of guilty. Altering the definitions of criminal offences, so as to produce a large number of narrowly defined offences, could remove many of these ambiguities; but, as Dr Thomas has argued:

No system of substantive law can be so detailed that the responsibility for making findings of fact relevant to sentence can be entirely removed from the sentencing process; it is a question of getting the right issues in the right place. Issues which are frequently the subject of a contest, which can be categorised as 'either/or' issues and which are of critical importance to sentence, should so far as is possible be incorporated in the substantive definition of the offence. This will mean that the potential offender will have advance notice that the offence is aggravated by the presence of such a feature, and the person accused will have adequate opportunity to dispute the issue if he chooses. Questions which are rarely disputed, or raise issues of degree, such as provocation, are probably best left out of the trial of guilt for determination in the sentencing process.[78]

One might dispute details of this – for instance, provocation is an issue which is often integral to the evaluation of a violent crime, and it may raise factual issues – but the general points remain. Greater specificity in the criminal law is the first step, but there will inevitably remain some issues of aggravation and mitigation which the sentencer will have to determine himself.

Clear and fair rules for post-conviction hearings must therefore be devised as soon as possible. The leading principle is that the post-conviction hearing should have no less concern with accurate fact-finding and with fairness to the defendant than the criminal trial itself. The consequences for the defendant may be considerable, and he should be given the same protection as at the criminal trial. The Crown also has an interest in accurate fact-finding at this stage.[79] There should be provision for due notice of disputed issues, a fair opportunity to raise them and to lead evidence in rebuttal, the rules of evidence should apply, and the criminal burden and standard of proof should be required before a person is sentenced on the basis of a fact which he disputes. We should insist on these safeguards, even if they will probably lengthen post-conviction hearings and will thus reduce the extent to which guilty pleas contribute to the smooth running of the criminal justice system.[80]

Even when a satisfactory procedure is devised, it should not be used in inappropriate cases. The proper ambit of a post-conviction hearing is to determine factual issues left in doubt by a verdict or guilty plea. It is surely wrong to use such hearings to determine the presence or absence of an aggravating factor which could have been the subject of a separate charge. It is certainly wrong to use such hearings to determine whether or not the defendant has committed further offences with which he has not been separately charged, and which he does not ask the court to take into consideration: the decision in *Robinson*,[81] which did provide for such issues to be resolved at a post-conviction hearing, should not be followed. These last two points confirm the role of prosecution policy in these matters. If it were etablished as a principle that the prosecution should charge as a separate offence any aggravating factor which fulfilled the definition of another offence,[82] this would obviate many of the problems which have given rise to the appellate decisions discussed in this section.

5 Conclusions

Two questions were posed at the beginning of this chapter. First, is it constitutionally appropriate that the judges should possess such great power to shape sentencing policy? The answer is that in principle the formulation of general policy should be for the legislature and its implementation and individuation for the judiciary. However, there is no constitutional inappropriateness in the legislature delegating its policy-making function to the judiciary: what is inappropriate is any assumption that this function is by right that of the judiciary, for there is no constitutional bar to legislation on any aspect of sentencing policy. This leads to the second question: is it practically wise to leave the courts with such wide discretion, or are there satisfactory means by which the legislature could confine or structure it? A clear answer can only be given after the full range of sentencing problems considered in this book has been examined. In this chapter we have given brief consideration to the various legislative and other techniques which are available, and it has been observed that English law has tended (with a few exceptions) to adopt the least restrictive techniques, with the result that beneath the statutory maxima the sentencing discretion of the courts is broad and unstructured by legislation. Sentencers would doubtless defend this as necessary, so as to allow them the flexibility to do justice on the particular facts of each case. The import of this justification depends, as we shall see in later chapters, on the criterion of 'justice' adopted. We have also considered the extent to which the form of the criminal law imposes restrictions on judicial discretion: we saw in section 3 that recent statutes tend to leave the widest discretion, but the Misuse of Drugs Act 1971 shows that another approach is possible. That Act provides separate offences of possession, possession with intent to supply, and supply; it also divides controlled drugs into classes A, B and C, and prescribes different levels of maximum sentences. The latter approach imposes more structure upon the sentencing discretion. That approach is also more helpful in establishing the factual basis for sentence, as we saw in section 4. However, it is unlikely in the short term that English law will move substantially towards the narrower definition of criminal offences, and it is therefore imperative to devise fair and clear rules for the conduct of post-conviction hearings. Otherwise, there is the risk that the level and even the form of an offender's sentence may be determined by the sentencer's view of facts which have not been properly established.

3
Penal policy and sentencing policy

We have seen that, under existing conventions, penal policy is for the Government and sentencing policy is for the courts. This has been made possible by the high maximum penalties provided by the criminal law, and the separation has gained strength from the principle of judicial independence. There is now some evidence that the separation is being challenged: government ministers have with increasing frequency addressed remarks to sentencers, and the judges have declared that they are taking account of the gross overcrowding in the prisons. In this chapter we look further into the relationship between penal policy and sentencing policy, considering the allocation of responsibility for matters of criminal justice, the extent to which policies and practices at other stages in the criminal process can have an effect on the sentencing practices of the courts, and the process by which penal policy comes to be formulated. In particular, attention is focused on the formation and implementation of penal policy in the last ten years, to discover the extent to which sentencing practices and policies have been taken into account. The conclusion is that those who have formulated penal policy have until recently had too little regard to sentencing, and that a means must be found to achieve greater co-ordination of policy in the criminal justice system.

1 Official responsibilities for criminal justice policy

In some countries, responsibility for matters of criminal justice policy is brought together under a Minister of Justice. In England, responsibility has long been shared among different authorities. At one level there are three government ministers – the Home Secretary, the Attorney-General and the Lord Chancellor. Each of these has direct or indirect responsibility for part of the criminal justice system. The widest spread of responsibilities falls to the Home Office, which has three departments concerned with criminal justice:

Criminal Department This has a general responsibility for overseeing the administration of criminal justice. It does not deal with the appointment of judges or with the Crown Court (which falls to the Lord Chancellor's Department), but it does exercise a supervisory role over magistrates' courts and controls a proportion of their financial grant. The Department has direct responsibility for the scope and content of the criminal law. It examines the reports of the Criminal Law Revision Committee, together with any reports of the Law Commission and of *ad hoc* committees which relate to criminal law, and it decides whether and in what form legislation should be brought forward. Formerly there was a separate department of the Home Office which was indirectly responsible for the Probation and After-Care Service, but this function now falls to the Probation and After-Care Division of the Criminal Department. It controls a substantial proportion of the budget of the probation service, organizes training and maintains an inspectorate. In theory, Chief Probation Officers are accountable to local Probation and After-Care Committees, and the Home Secretary has only indirect responsibility. In practice, through appointments, inspections and the issue of circulars, there is a considerable amount of Home Office control.

Prison Department This has direct responsibility for the running of the prison service. Despite the appointment in 1980 of a Chief Inspector of Prisons, who operates independently of the Prison Department and reports directly to the Home Secretary, this remains the only law enforcement function which is directly under government control.

Police Department This maintains an inspectorate of constabulary, provides certain facilities on a national basis (such as forensic science laboratories), and influences a substantial proportion of the police budget. Beyond that, there are 43 police forces and the theory is that a chief constable's duty is

to enforce the law of the land. He must take steps so to post his men that crimes may be detected; and that honest citizens may go about their affairs in peace. He must decide whether or not suspected persons are to be prosecuted; and, if need be, bring the prosecution or see that it is brought. But in all these things he is not the servant of anyone, save of the law itself. No Minister of the Crown can tell him that he must, or must not, keep observation on this place or that; or that he must, or must not, prosecute this man or that one. Nor can any police authority tell him so. The responsibility for law enforcement lies on him. He is answerable to the law and to the law alone.[1]

A chief constable cannot be required to take particular decisions in particular cases, but at the more general level of formulating policy for prosecution and for policing he may be subject to judicial review and, in practice, is subject to considerable control from the Home Office. The Home Secretary is the police authority for the Metropolitan Police, and he is able to exert considerable influence over other forces, through his power to dismiss a chief constable,[2] through inspections and meetings, and through his power to make regulations for conditions of service in the police.

It therefore emerges that the prisons are the only agency of law enforcement for which the Home Secretary has direct responsibility. His other responsibilities vary, both in theory and in practice, and correspondingly there are varying degrees of autonomy which local chief officers (especially chief constables) may use to pursue particular policies. These variations might be reduced if the recommendations of the Royal Commission on Criminal Procedure were enacted:[3] the police would then retain only the discretion whether or not to initiate a prosecution (the Home Secretary would issue guidelines for this), and the decision whether or not to continue a prosecution initiated by the police would be in the hands of Crown prosecutors (for whom the Attorney-General would probably have overall responsibility).

The Home Office also contains a number of smaller departments, such as the Scientific Research and Development Branch, the Statistical Department and the Research and Planning Unit, which both service the larger departments and conduct their own enquiries. Between 1974 and 1981 there was a Crime Policy Planning Unit, charged with the co-ordination and promotion of medium and long term planning for all aspects of criminal justice. In 1980 the then head of the Crime Policy Planning Unit wrote of the difficulties of policy planning in this field:

The Home Secretary is not a free agent with liberty to transform things as he pleases: he operates within strict constitutional boundaries and is hemmed in too by resource considerations which inhibit flexibility. Above and beyond these political verities are obstacles peculiar to the social policy environment: defective and fragile measures of actual behaviour; lack of certainty in interpreting observable phenomena; a shortage of effective instruments for State intervention; and inherent and perpetual volatility in and between all the moving parts as society itself changes. This means that obtaining lasting consent to agreed objectives is especially difficult, even if objectives of more than rudimentary precision can be designed.[4]

These are undoubtedly real difficulties, especially for a planning unit within the Home Office, and they have not been diminished by the subsequent absorption of the CPPU within a new Research and Planning Unit, which superseded the Home Office Research Unit in 1981. The Research and Planning Unit continues to undertake its own research into the operation of the criminal justice system and to fund and support research by outside agencies, but its work is now 'more closely associated with the formulation and monitoring of policy.'[5] This is to some extent an acknowledgement and accentuation of a growing tendency in publications in the series of Home Office Research Studies to conclude with positive suggestions on policy matters.[6]

Turning away from the Home Office to the law officers of the Crown, the principal responsibilities of the Attorney General in matters of criminal justice are to supervise the Director of Public Prosecutions, to take the decision to prosecute in cases of a political nature, and to refer to the Court of Appeal any point of law which is felt to have been interpreted inconsistently or wrongly by trial courts.[7] The independence and impartiality of the Attorney-General are frequently emphasized, and it has been said that he should 'absolutely decline to receive orders from the Prime Minister or Cabinet or anyone else that he shall prosecute.'[8] The Director of Public Prosecutions acts under the general superintendence of the Attorney-General, and has the principal functions of deciding whether to prosecute for certain offences, undertaking prosecutions for certain serious or politically sensitive offences, and advising government departments and chief constables on prosecution policy. There is a list of offences for which the Director of Public Prosecutions has the duty to consider and undertake prosecutions, and a list of other types of offence which have to be reported to his office. However, these lists are comparatively short[9] and it is the Director's advisory function which is most significant. The Director may offer advice to prosecutors either on request or upon his own initiative. The organization of the prosecution system is under review, and it is possible that the Director of Public Prosecutions will be called upon to perform a more central role in the future.[10]

The Lord Chancellor's Department administers the Crown Court and has responsibility for the appointment and training of magistrates, and the Lord Chancellor is *ex officio* President of the Magistrates' Association.

The very diversity of departmental responsibilities makes co-ordination of policy difficult, and clearly the independence enjoyed by some agencies increases the problems of fashioning an integrated criminal justice policy. Whatever the policy initiatives within the Home Office, the fact remains that the Home Secretary cannot exert sufficient executive control over certain vital aspects of the system. For example, 'Constitutional considerations put policy-making in the areas of prosecution and sentencing remote from the influence of central government, save through changes in law.'[11]

Legislative change brings its own difficulties. Even when it is regarded as a practically and politically appropriate approach to a problem,[12] the Home Office has to make a case for a particular bill to be included in the Government's legislative programme. There *are* changes which can be accomplished within the existing legislative framework – examples in recent years would be changes in the organization of the prisons, reducing the minimum period of a probation order to 6 months, changing bail policies (which was effected by a 1975 circular, before the Bail Act 1976) – but these are inevitably limited in scope by the autonomy of the courts and of chief constables. Whether there is a strong case for introducing a new body to discuss and formulate criminal justice policy as a whole, or for bringing the various responsibilities together under a single government department (such as a Ministry of Justice), is considered at the end of this chapter. First, it is necessary to look in greater detail at those elements of practice and policy which have a bearing on sentencing.

2 Convicted offenders and the criminal process

In debates on the overcrowding in prisons, it has sometimes been assumed or stated that the prison problem is caused by the sentencing policies of the courts. That, however, is to neglect the influence of the number of serious offenders convicted each year. Even with a stable sentencing policy, variations in the flow of persons convicted by the courts will affect the gross numbers of offenders assigned by the courts to the various penal agencies, such as the prisons and the probation service. Where do these variations come from? One obvious answer is 'the crime rate'. As the 'crime rate' increases, so sentencers have to deal with more and more offenders. If they do not alter their sentencing practice, more offenders will be sent to prison. But the answer is too simple and too sweeping: we must examine the idea of an increase in the 'crime rate', and then look at the ways by which any such increase might filter through to sentencers.[13]

There is, to be accurate, no such thing as 'the crime rate'. A number of ways of measuring the amount of crime in a particular jurisdiction offer themselves, but all have drawbacks. From the sentencer's point of view, what immediately strikes him is the number of persons convicted; especially, how that varies (and usually increases) over periods of time. Can the number of offenders convicted by the courts be taken as an objective measure of the crime rate? It cannot. The number convicted by the courts is a product of too many variable factors in the criminal process. For example, any change in the number of offenders caught could result in more convictions even if the actual number of offences committed remained constant. This is a good reason for scepticism about broad references to 'crime rates' and 'crime waves', until it is proved that an increase in the numbers convicted reflects a true increase in the number of offences actually committed. Could that be proved? Can we tell how many offences are actually committed?

The best that the official criminal statistics can offer is the annual total of crimes recorded by the police. It will be recalled that Table 1, 'Serious Offences Recorded by the Police',[14] shows trends in reported offences – particularly, large increases in recorded offences of criminal damage, robbery and less serious violence against the person, and very small changes in more serious offences against the person and sexual offences. Much could be written about the apparent trends in recorded offences of each category, but the point of general import-ance is that statistics about *recorded* offences – even if they are more representative of the true crime rate than detected offences or offences resulting in a conviction – lead us to enquire into the means by which an offence comes to be recorded.

In order to treat the statistics of recorded offences as a reliable indicator of trends in crime, we would need to be sure that there is a constant relationship between the number of offences recorded each year and the number of offences actually committed each year. In other words, we can only take these apparent trends at face value if we know that a similar proportion of all offences actually committed is reported to the police and recorded by them each year. To be sure of that relationship, we would need to know how many offences actually are committed each year. If the official statistics cannot tell us, how can we find out? Attempts have been made to estimate the number of unreported offences (often called the 'dark figure' of crime) by asking groups of people to divulge in confidence how many offences each has committed during a specified period of time (these are called 'self-report studies'), or alternatively by asking people to state in confidence the number of crimes of which they have been a victim during a specified period (these are called 'victimization studies'). By comparing the figures with the number of recorded crimes over the same period, and taking account of police recording practices, an estimate of the proportion of crimes unrecorded can be made. Studies of both kinds raise theoretical and practical difficulties, quite apart from the obvious problem of ensuring truthfulness and accuracy.[15] Nevertheless, it is noteworthy that most such surveys suggest that the dark figure of unreported crime is several times greater than the number of crimes reported: the recent British Crime Survey estimated that there may be 4 to 5 times as many unrecorded as recorded crimes.[16]

This uncertainty about the number of offences actually committed means that there is little basis for assuming that variations in the number of offences recorded by the police indicate an actual increase in offending. There might be changes in reporting habits: a decline in social tolerance of minor violence and damage might lead to greater reporting of those kinds of offence, and the advent of the telephone might simplify reporting, with the result that an increase in the numbers of recorded offences might to some extent reflect an increase in the public's willingness and ability to report them. About three-quarters of offences which come to the notice of the police are reported to them by members of the public rather than 'discovered' by the police themselves,[17] and so there can be no doubt that the figures upon which offences recorded by the police are based are vulnerable to changes in the reporting habits of the public. As for the offences which the police discover for themselves, these will be affected by levels, styles and targets of policing. A great increase in the number of recorded offences of possession of drugs, homosexual importuning or possession of obscene articles for gain might be produced simply by a police 'drive' against those types of offence. The discovery of many of these so-called 'victimless' crimes, in which there is rarely anyone with sufficiently direct interest to make a complaint to the police, is largely a function of the degree of police activity, and may therefore bear little relation to variations in the actual rate of offending.

Once a crime has come to the notice of the police, that does not ensure that it will appear in the criminal statistics. A number of incidents which are initially recorded as crimes may subsequently be 'no-crimed' (i.e. removed from the records before they are sent to the Home Office) if there is doubt about the initial classification or for other reasons. About 3 per cent of incidents initially recorded as crimes are subsequently 'no-crimed', but the percentage varies according to the police area: Coleman and Bottomley found a rate of 6 per cent in one northern city,[18] whereas McCabe and Sutcliffe found that in Oxford the 'no-crime' rate was also 6 per cent, whilst in Salford it was only 2 per cent.[19] The classification of an incident which is recorded may also be a point on which discretion is exercised: for example, McCabe and Sutcliffe found that in Salford many domestic disturbances which should strictly have been recorded as offences against the person were recorded and treated as offences of simple drunkenness, and Chatterton has argued that the police will sometimes refrain from recording violent incidents either in the hope of bringing about a reconciliation or in the belief that justice has been done.[20] Thus local police practices of 'no-criming' and of dealing with particular kinds of incident may to some extent be regarded as a conscious filter into and out of the criminal process. Police methods of dealing with domestic violence in particular may well keep a number of fairly serious cases out of the criminal process.

Of those offences which are recorded as known to the police, less than half are 'cleared up' each year. An offence is treated as 'cleared up' not only if a person is convicted but also if the offence is 'taken into consideration' by the court on conviction for another offence, if the offence is believed to have been committed by a child under the age of criminal responsibility, and in a number of other cases where the police believe they have sufficient evidence against a person but he cannot for some reason be prosecuted.[21] The clear-up rate has increased slightly in recent years, and this could bring an increase in the number of offenders convicted by the courts without reflecting any increase in the number of offences actually committed. The clear-up rate varies from offence to offence. In crimes of violence the clear-up rate has always been high, partly because the offender is often known to the victim. The clear-up rate for most property offences is low (partly, perhaps, because the identity of the offender is usually not known to the victim), but for such an offence as shoplifting the clear-up rate may be almost 100 per cent – reflecting not the ease of detection but rather the fact that a loss of stock is unlikely to be regarded as a case of theft unless the offender is caught and reported, and if he is caught and reported the offence will invariably be treated as 'cleared up'.

Even if an offence is cleared up, we have seen that it follows from the definition of 'cleared up' that the suspected offender will not necessarily be prosecuted in every case. Apart from those cases which are cleared up by being attributed to children below the age of criminal responsibility, there is in most other cases a discretion in the police whether to prosecute, to caution or to take no further action. The cautioning rate (i.e. the percentage of all offenders cautioned or prosecuted who are cautioned) varies quite widely from one police force to another and from one offence to another. As a generalization, urban police forces tend to caution extremely few adult offenders for indictable offences, whereas rural forces seem more willing to do so. The converse of this is, of course, that prosecution policies also vary. These variations are largely the result of different forces adopting different policies, but to some extent they reflect the different kinds of offence reported to the police in different parts of the country.[22] Inasmuch as property offenders are more likely to be cautioned than violent offenders, who are highly likely to be prosecuted, the courts may receive the impression that there are proportionately more violent offences and fewer property offences than is in fact the case. Moreover, changes in prosecution and cautioning policy in a police area will have obvious consequences for the number of persons brought before the courts. The Royal Commission on Criminal Procedure has recommended that the police should retain the discretion whether to initiate a prosecution, to caution or to take no further action; it has also recommended that the Home Secretary should draft guidelines on prosecution and cautioning policy. Under the Royal Commission's scheme, the decision whether or not to withdraw a prosecution initiated by the police will be transferred to the Crown prosecutor.[23]

Whilst the discussion of offences recorded and cleared up has so far concentrated on the role of the police, it is important to appreciate that as many as one-quarter of all prosecutions of adults for non-motoring offences are not initiated by the police. Government agencies such as the Inland Revenue and the Department of Health and Social Security, local authorities, retail stores and (to a very small extent) private individuals bring these prosecutions. Although research into the workings of the relevant organs of central and local government is at an early stage, the evidence so far suggests that there are considerable variations in policy from one agency to another and even from one area to another.[24] It is perfectly understandable that many of these agencies see their primary task as one of securing compliance rather than initiating prosecutions, and therefore regard prosecution as a last resort in trying to bring about compliance. But it does mean, not only that any slight change in prosecution policy might appear to the courts as a substantial variation in the 'crime rate', but more significantly that the extreme reluctance of certain agencies to bring prosecutions (notably the Inland Revenue's reluctance to prosecute for tax evasion) combines with the general readiness of the police and others to prosecute for property offences of small value to produce a rather distorted view of patterns of offending in our society. This is not an imbalance which the courts can be expected to redress: it is an issue of prosecution policy.

Those offenders who come before the courts for sentence are therefore not merely a small but a selected sample of all those who commit criminal offences. There are also ways in which the court's perception of offences and offenders might be coloured by the way in which a case is presented. Thus, the charge selected by the prosecution may well influence the court's view of the seriousness of the offence. Particularly where there is a guilty plea, the court will hear only a prosecution summary of the facts, and it may rely (consciously or subconsciously) upon the prosecution's choice of offence-category to inform its general view of the seriousness of the offence. There is some empirical evidence for this in Shea's experiments with magistrates, which suggested that many of them viewed the same case of bad driving as more serious if the police had charged dangerous driving than if they had charged careless driving.[25] This kind of reasoning might equally apply to cases of theft or robbery, to cases of grievous bodily harm or unlawful wounding,[26] and in other situations where prosecutors have a choice between charges.

Lord Devlin has said that as a general principle prosecutors should bring the most serious charge that is fairly supported by the evidence they expect to be given:[27] if the prosecution over-charge, the court is there to classify the offence correctly, whereas if the prosecution under-charge the error cannot be rectified since the court cannot convict of a more serious offence. The rationale behind this principle is probably that a citizen has a right to have the seriousness of his offence determined in open court by magistrates or by a jury. Reality is far from this, however. About two-thirds of defendants in the Crown Court plead guilty, and nine out of every ten defendants in the magistrates' courts do so.[28] Thus in the vast majority of cases the defendant's offence is classified by his own plea of guilty. But the decision to plead may itself be a significant filter, particularly when the defendant first enters a plea of not guilty and decides to change his plea to guilty at a late stage. This late change of plea might be prompted by a number of events. The defendant may be advised by his legal representatives that by pleading guilty he is likely to receive a substantially lower sentence, or even a different type of sentence (e.g. a suspended rather than an immediate prison sentence), and that the case against him is strong.[29] Alternatively, there might be a discussion between prosecution and defence lawyers leading to one of these two results:

   a defendant charged with a number of offences may decide to plead guilty to some of them, in exchange for the prosecution offering no evidence against him on the outstanding charges;

   a defendant charged with an offence which can in law be reduced to a lesser offence (e.g. grievous bodily harm reduced to unlawful wounding, attempted murder reduced to grievous bodily harm) may plead guilty to the lesser offence, and the prosecution may then drop the higher charge.

Plea negotiations take place on a wider scale than this, and it is not claimed that all those who agree to 'bargains' of this kind are in fact guilty of the more serious offence charged or the larger number of offences charged. Some of them will be, however, and to that extent cases of late change of plea may distort the court's perception of the seriousness of the offender's lawbreaking. Another source of distortion, which is probably rather small in its practical effect, is that juries may acquit a defendant or convict him of a lesser charge because they think he should be sentenced more leniently than they think he is likely to be sentenced. Cornish has argued that juries probably do acquit in some cases simply because they believe that the offender ought not to be punished for what he has done;[30] and the Oxford Jury Project provides some empirical evidence that juries occasionally take account of what they believe to be the likely consequence of conviction.[31]

The conclusion to be drawn from this brief survey of 'Convicted Offenders and the Criminal Process' is that the people who come before the courts for sentence differ both quantitatively and qualitatively from the total number of people known (or strongly believed) to have committed offences. They differ quantitatively in that some known or believed offences are not even recorded, others which are recorded do not result in prosecution, others which are prosecuted do not result in a conviction despite a sufficiency of evidence. They differ qualitatively in that reporting and recording behaviour, prosecution policy, choice of charge and plea negotiations inevitably produce for the courts a sample of cases which have already passed through various filters, notably those applied by the police or other enforcement agency in the decision to prosecute. Indeed, sentenced offenders may differ even more widely from all those who actually commit offences than they evidently differ from those who are *known* to have committed offences. The implications of this for the role of sentencing policy in the criminal justice system emerge from Baldock's pertinent remarks about attempts to reduce the prison population:

> Prisons stand at the end of an elaborate process of selection by the public, police, courts and judges. Consequently, relatively small changes at any point in this process can have an amplified impact on the prison system. It is a mistake to seek the causes and remedies for the growth of the prison population by looking only at the very late stage of these processes, sentences of imprisonment. This is the tail end of the story and, as most of the attempts to 'reform' or counteract sentencing policy have shown, it is a tail which cannot easily be made to wag the dog.[32]

The link between penal policy and sentencing policy should be neither overestimated nor minimized. Many penal policies or criminal justice policies cannot be put into practice without co-operation from the courts at the sentencing stage, but on the other hand the ability of the courts to respond to the crises of resources and facilities within the penal system is limited, and the question whether this ought to be the principal determinant of their sentencing policy is debatable.

If the aim is to reduce the input of the penal system, at least four methods should be considered – decriminalization, non-prosecution, changes in sentencing policy, and administrative measures. De-criminalization has been viewed cautiously in England, on the argument that the criminal sanction might thereby be removed from some forms of conduct which ought to remain punishable. The tendency has been to consider the application of the criminal sanction in discrete spheres, so that the decriminalization of street soliciting is considered in the context of the law of prostitution and the question of decriminalizing certain credit card offences has not fallen for consideration at all. What is required is a thorough study of the possibilities of decriminalization as a technique for focusing the criminal justice system upon the more heinous acts.

As for prosecution policy, it is arguable that the panoply of court proceedings is not necessary in order to deal adequately with certain kinds of offenders: they can and should be dealt with by less formal and less drastic methods, such as the police caution or even, in some cases, the taking of no action at all. As a mechanism this seems justifiable: it reserves court proceedings for the worst types of case, and does not risk bringing the law into disrepute by taking to court trivial cases or relatively blameless offenders. Of course it is important that these classes be properly defined, and that there be safeguards against abuse of discretion: the suggestion of the Royal Commission on Criminal Procedure that guidelines for the exercise of this discretion be drawn up is worthy and long overdue, and the recommendation of the Australian Law Reform Commission[33] to the effect that prosecution policy and sentencing policy should be overseen by a single agency points up the need for co-ordination in society's response to lawbreaking.

The possibility of using changes in sentencing policy to bring about a reduction in pressure on the penal system, particularly the prison system, has been raised frequently in recent years. In a sense, it is said, the courts are responsible for the size of the prison population, since it is a direct result of their sentencing policies and could be altered by a change in those policies. Indeed, it might be possible to devise a method by which courts were restricted to so many units of custody (e.g. weeks or months of custody) each year, or each month, and within that limit had to decide how to allocate the units among offenders. A quota system of this kind, adjusted to the capacity of the prisons, might be an economist's dream – a practical response to the lament that

> when the judiciary have taken their decisions and come to consider sentencing, they become part of society pre-empting resources from the taxpayer for expenditure on the particular person. The difficulty seems to me to be that the considerations which they apply to that bear no relationship to the availability of the resources . . .[34]

This was the view of one member of the House of Commons' Expenditure Committee, and was countered by the chairman's remark on the same subject: 'I do not think the Committee would wish to come to the conclusion that we ought to adjust our criminal law or criminal sentencing to the size of the prisons.'[35]

The chairman's view is to be preferred. Sentencing by the courts is more than a tap by which to regulate the flow of offenders into our custodial institutions. Sentencing involves a public statement about an offender and an offence. It is a purposive activity, relating to the offence for which the offender has been convicted, the characteristics of the offender, and the aims of sentencing. It is not, and cannot be justified as, a mere response to economic constraints or planning failures. Economism may help to indicate which groups of offenders are taking the largest slice of expenditure (for example, that the prison problem cannot be properly tackled unless attention is paid to the large mass of property offenders with three or more previous convictions), and it may force the urgent reconsideration of priorities and justifications for sentencing policy. It therefore has its benefits. But it is surely incompatible with the nature and function of sentencing that it should be regulated by reference to whether a wing of one prison has collapsed, or whether the sewerage system of another prison has become inoperative. If there are crises of safety and humanity within the penal system, so that prison conditions have to be alleviated locally, there may be a justification for obtaining relief by using administrative measures (such as the power taken by the Home Secretary in the Criminal Justice Act 1982, section 32, to release selected classes of prisoner before the end of their sentences). But in a system to which proportionality is central, seasonal variations in sentencing policy according to the problems of the prison service are difficult to justify.

Morover, as has been demonstrated in this section of the chapter, the sentencing practices of the courts are to a considerable extent a response to the nature and volume of offenders convicted, which in turn derive from the numbers prosecuted, which in turn derive from the numbers detected, which in turn are affected by the numbers reported and recorded. If the courts were to pursue a constant sentencing policy, then the prison population would be increased – because the actual number of serious offenders detected and convicted increases from year to year. Therefore, to use sentencing as the primary regulator for the input of the prisons would require the courts to respond not merely to the problems of the Prison Department but also to the vagaries of reporting habits and prosecution policy. Enough has surely been said at this stage to indicate that, whilst economic restraint and social priorities should lead us to conduct a detailed reconsideration of sentencing policy – to which this book is intended as a contribution – sentencing has distinct social functions which make it inappropriate for use as a mere tap by which to regulate the pressure upon the penal system. If it is decided that pressure must be reduced, the problem must be tackled by a range of measures, from crime prevention to prosecution policy and even executive release.

3 The formation of penal policy

Penal policy is that part of criminal justice policy which determines the measures which should be available to the courts and the precise form they should take. The single theme which dominates the last ten to fifteen years is that of reducing the prison population (or, at least, keeping increases to a minimum). In legislative terms this has meant providing the courts with a number of new measures which they might use in sentencing offenders. By increasing the alternatives to immediate custodial sentences, it has been hoped to exert some influence over the number of occasions on which the courts resort to immediate custody. At a glance, the policy may appear to have succeeded: whilst the number of offenders convicted of indictable offences has risen from 242,000 in 1967 to 455,000 in 1980, the average daily population of convicted offenders in Prison Service establishments stood at 35,831 in 1980 compared with 29,913 in 1967. Of course there is more to the problem of prisons than dealing with sentenced prisoners: those remanded in custody pending trial. But the perceived need to control the number of persons given immediate custodial sentences has influenced most of the major changes in the penal system in the last 20 years – suspended sentences, parole, community service, day training centres, detoxification centres, and the recent movement (not embodied in legislation) towards fewer and shorter custodial sentences – although it has not always held sway, as the White Paper on *Young Offenders*[36] and the Criminal Justice Act 1982 show. In order to lay a proper foundation for considering penal policy in the last 10 years, it is necessary first to describe penal change in the previous 5-year period, in which the Criminal Justice Acts of 1967 and 1972 were particularly significant.

(a) Penal change 1967–72

The 1967 Act introduced the suspended sentence and parole. The decision to introduce the suspended sentence had somewhat unusual antecedents. The measure had been rejected twice by the Advisory Council on the Treatment of Offenders, in 1952 and 1957; yet support for it was re-kindled in the 1960s, it was proposed by policy groups within both the Labour and the Conservative parties, and a number of those who gave evidence to the abortive Royal Commission on the Penal System, which sat from 1964 to 1966, favoured its introduction. The Government in 1967 commended it to Parliament as an alternative to an immediate custodial sentence: it would enable the court to mark the gravity of the offence without sending the offender straight to prison. There is little doubt that the popularity of the suspended sentence with the Government of the time was strongly connected with their desire 'to find ways of emptying the prisons'.[37] There was equally little doubt that much of the wider support for the suspended sentence derived from the belief that it would be a useful addition to the range of non-custodial penalties – a non-custodial measure with particular bite, which would carry individual deterrence to its furthest extreme without actually imposing a custodial term straight away. Rather than simply saying to the offender, 'Next time it will be prison', the court could impose a sentence which explicitly carried that threat with it. Yet neither this view of the suspended sentence nor the Government's view was clearly located in a theory about its likely effect on the sentencing patterns of the courts or the behaviour patterns of those who might be subjected to the measure. The government spokesmen clearly intended the courts to use it as an alternative to immediate custody, but did they really believe that this would happen? They took considerable pains to ensure that courts did suspend short sentences, by introducing (for the first time in English sentencing legislation) an elaborate frame-

work of mandatory suspension of prison sentences of 6 months and
under, with a number of exceptions to allow the courts to impose an
immediate prison sentence of 6 months or less upon such groups as
violent offenders and those who had been to prison before. But the
1967 Act included no provision designed to ensure that courts used
the sentence only in cases where an immediate custodial sentence
would otherwise have been passed: such a requirement was subsequently declared by the Court of Appeal in *O'Keefe*[38] and is now
embodied in section 22(2) of the Powers of Criminal Courts Act 1973.
The Government's preoccupation in 1967 was with the probable
under-use of suspended sentences, and not with their over-use –
despite the evidence that much of its support from sentencers (as from
the Conservative opposition) derived from its usefulness as a non-
custodial sentence with added bite. Moreover, the precise steps by
which a court should decide on a suspended sentence and fix its length
were tackled neither by the legislation nor by clear instructions to the
courts. Even if the Government's view were followed and the court
only considered a suspended sentence when it had already decided
that a custodial sentence was called for, how was its length to be
calculated? It seems that in theory mitigating factors govern the
length of the sentence and govern the decision to suspend. If they are
not thus given weight twice, the alternative is that where the court
decides to reflect mitigating factors by suspending, it should not also
reduce the length of the prison sentence. In other words, were the
offender sent immediately to prison he would receive a very short
sentence, but since he is being given the benefit of suspension the
sentence should be for 6 or 9 months. This difficulty has been inherent
in the suspended sentence ever since it was introduced, and Bottoms
has shown how magistrates' courts seem to lengthen the term when
suspending a sentence whereas the Crown Courts appear not to do
so.[39] The difficulty may well increase, in view of the recent trend
towards very short sentences of immediate imprisonment, unless the
courts take great pains to fix the length of imprisonment as if the
sentence were to be served immediately. The lessons to be learned
from the experience of introducing the suspended sentence are
manifold. Indisputably they show the close relationship between
penal policy and sentencing policy, as well as illustrating the need to
envisage the place which a new penal measure should occupy in the
court's sentencing practice and to devise measures for ensuring that
courts use it accordingly.

Just as the Government of the day appears to have failed to examine the possible effect of the suspended sentence on established sentencing patterns, so they also appear not to have thought about types of offender for whom the sentence might be particularly appropriate or inappropriate. Should the first prison sentence be suspended (if within the legal limit of 2 years' imprisonment)? Should suspended sentences ever be used for those who have been to prison before? Could they be useful for the non-serious recidivist? Would they be more appropriate for offenders who were perceived as having no social or psychological problems? The Advisory Council, in their 1952 and 1957 reports,[40] relied on what we would now call 'treatment ideology' in their rejection of the suspended sentence. They took the view that by and large offenders need support and treatment, and that the probation order provides the proper framework for this. If the suspended sentence were made available to the courts, it might be imposed in cases where probation might be more suited to the offender's needs; and, if activation of the suspended sentence were to be mandatory on conviction of a further offence during the operational period, that would prevent the court from looking at the particular circumstances of offence and offender. Moreover, if mandatory activation were not to accompany the suspended sentence, what would be its advantage over other conditional sentences such as probation and conditional discharge? The Advisory Council's attitude, then, was firmly embedded in a rehabilitative approach. No trace of that approach is to be found in the suspended sentence as enacted (although the suspended sentence supervision order, introduced in 1972, allows an element of supervision where the sentence which is suspended exceeds 6 months). The general assumption behind the suspended sentence seems to be that offenders are capable of responding to direct threats, and are able to choose (without the benefit of supervision or advice) between keeping out of trouble during the operational period of the suspended sentence or committing a further offence. The views of the 1967 legislation and the Advisory Council in the 1950s are much too sweeping and indiscriminate: attention ought to have been devoted to the identification of those for whom probation or a suspended sentence might be particularly appropriate; in other words, to the practical sentencing relationship between probation and suspended sentences.

Although parole shares with the suspended sentence the aim of reducing the prison population, the element of supervision on licence shows that it also had a rehabilitative rationale. Parole was introduced by the Criminal Justice Act 1967; like the suspended sentence, it had not been recommended by an official committee. The idea was put forward in a 1965 White Paper on *The Adult Offender*, and it emerged from the parliamentary debates that a number of different beliefs and hopes lay behind its introduction. One important belief, fundamentally rehabilitative in nature, was that 'a considerable number of long-term prisoners reach a recognisable peak in their training at which they may respond to generous treatment, but after which, if kept in prison, they may go downhill'.[41] A second belief was based on probabilities of reconviction. It was thought that, if proper regard was had to a prisoner's record, to any remarks of the court on sentencing him and to his likely circumstances on release, certain prisoners could be released on licence without significantly reducing the amount of public protection offered by the prison system. In short, some prisoners were being kept in prison longer than was necessary to prevent reconviction. To some extent this view may have been connected with 'a growing recognition of discrepancies in the length of prison sentences imposed by the courts',[42] which may have encouraged the idea that parole could perform a levelling function. But the policy of releasing prisoners on parole seems to be grounded in conceptions quite different from those which influence sentencing. Courts may impose sentences for reasons of general deterrence, retribution or simple proportionality without thereby implying that it would be dangerous to the public to release the prisoner at any time before the expiry of his sentence (less remission). The decision to release on parole depends largely on the perceived likelihood of the offender re-offending if released on licence, although it is fair to say that from the outset the parole decision has taken account of factors which clearly are related to sentencing – such as the gravity and notoriety of the prisoner's offence, and any remarks of the judge on passing sentence.

In practice the parole system has changed considerably. The rehabilitative notion of a 'peak in training' has been supplanted by statistical calculations of risk, based on factors in a prisoner's personal and criminal record.[43] The relation of parole to custodial sentencing is discussed in some detail in Chapter 9; it is sufficient here to note that a primary reason for its introduction was to reduce the custodial population, and that its effect was small in the early days but is now quite substantial, inasmuch as the proportion of released prisoners eligible for parole who are actually released on parole has increased to nearly 64 per cent in 1981.

Community service orders were introduced by the Criminal Justice Act 1972 and, after initially being restricted to six 'experimental' areas, were gradually introduced into all parts of the country during 1975 and 1976. Unlike suspended sentences and parole, community service orders did result from the deliberations of an official committee. The Advisory Council on the Penal System proposed in their 1970 report on *Non-Custodial and Semi-Custodial Penalties* (known as the Wootton report, after the chairperson of the subcommittee which prepared the proposals) that community service orders ought to be introduced. The idea of community service quickly became attractive to a wide spectrum of politicians and administrators, and indeed it was partly its chameleon-like attributes which led the Advisory Council to recommend it.

> The proposition that some offenders should be required to undertake community service should appeal to different varieties of penal philosophy. To some, it would be simply a more constructive and cheaper alternative to imprisonment; by others it would be seen as introducing into the penal system a new dimension with an emphasis on reparation to the community; others again would regard it as giving effect to the old adage that the punishment should fit the crime; while still others would stress the value of bringing offenders into close touch with those members of the community who are most in need of help and support.[44]

This passage establishes rather too much. Not only does it show how people of different penological persuasions might feel attracted to the community service order, but it also shows that courts could use it in different ways – in particular, that they could use it as an alternative to imprisonment or for other sentencing purposes. The Government was less equivocal on this point: by increasing the maximum number of hours which a court might order from 120 to 240 they evinced an intention that community service should be taken seriously as an alternative to custodial sentences.[45] But the Government did not say that it should be used *only* as an alternative to imprisonment, and therefore seems to have accepted the Advisory Council's view that it could usefully be ordered on a wider basis.

Now this might explain and excuse the failure to incorporate into the 1972 Act a requirement similar to the provision which declares policy in relation to suspended sentences. A court should only impose a suspended sentence where it would (if there were no power to suspend) have imposed an immediate custodial term. The absence of such a requirement for community service orders suggests they were never seen merely as an alternative to custody, whereas suspended sentences were. Nonetheless, no attempt was made either by the Advisory Council or by the Government to suggest how the community service order might fit into the courts' sentencing practices. How should it relate to probation and to the suspended sentence, to the fine and to immediate imprisonment? Community service may well have been a 'good idea' but on many levels it was also a vague idea. It stands as a prime example of the failure of those concerned with penal policy-making to pay sufficient attention to the sentencing implications of what they do.

Fourthly, brief mention should be made of the power to defer sentence, also introduced by the Criminal Justice Act 1972. The reasoning behind this innovation was largely rehabilitative: deferment was seen as having the 'merit of involving sentencers in the reformative effect of the criminal process', and also of involving the offender himself 'in making a positive contribution to his own reformation without cost to the public.' Thus 'if the offender has shown by his conduct [following deferment] that he genuinely intends to try to make a fresh start, the court can more readily gauge the right penalty for his offence'.[46] The existing law did in effect allow courts to defer sentence in certain circumstances, but the legislation provides a general power to defer sentence for up to 6 months 'for the purpose of enabling the court to have regard, in determining his sentence, to his conduct after conviction (including, where appropriate, the making by him of reparation for his offence) or to any change in his circumstances.'[47] The Advisory Council did discuss the kinds of case in which it thought deferment might be a useful option for the court, and it stated the view that deferment might be used in some cases where probation or a conditional discharge would otherwise be given. But the Advisory Council came down against 'tying the hands of the sentencers' by specifying in the legislation cases where deferment would be permitted. It is therefore fair to say that the Advisory Council did consider the place which deferment might be expected to take in the courts' sentencing practice.

(b) Penal change 1967–72: a critique

There were other new measures in the period between 1967 and 1972. Day training centres were introduced by the 1972 Act to deal with a particular group of offenders with particular problems, but their contribution to the penal system has been numerically small because only four centres have been opened. The 1972 Act also gave the police the power to escort a person who appears drunk to a detoxification centre; again, the impact of this provision has been limited. Of the measures we have briefly considered, deferment of sentence alone appears not to have been motivated by a desire to control the size of the prison population. From another point of view, the suspended sentence alone has no direct rehabilitative pretensions; parole, community service and deferment all have some element of rehabilitation in their aims.

What are the lessons of penal change in this period? In particular, what are the implications for the relationship between penal policy and sentencing policy?

In his masterly analysis of penal change in the period 1967–72. Roger Hood[48] identifies at least four major failings in the approach which had been taken: (i) a failure to argue for the proposed new measures on the basis of existing penological and criminological knowledge; (ii) a failure to analyse and explain why the existing penal measures were thought to require changes or additions; (iii) a failure to predict and to plan how each new measure might affect existing patterns of sentencing by the courts; and (iv) an undue concentration on the ideological and political appeal of certain proposed measures.

The fourth point clearly cannot stand alone. There may be much to be said in favour of new measures which are able to command widespread ideological support from the general public, from sentencers and even from offenders. The danger lies in allowing this ideological attraction to obscure the penological and sentencing difficulties which might prevent a new measure from achieving its declared aims. Those dangers are particularly great when, as with the suspended sentence, the ideological support is based upon a different conception of its use than is the Government's introduction of the measure. If the Government had attended to the fact that some of the support for the suspended sentence did have its basis in the idea that it would be a useful addition to the range of non-custodial measures, then it might have given greater priority in the 1967 Act to attempting to prevent the over-use, as well as the under-use, of the new measure.

Hood's major point is the first one: the theoretical basis of the proposed new measures was generally weak, and the proposals were not grounded in a thorough analysis of criminological and penological knowledge. In the 1950s the Advisory Council had rejected the suspended sentence on the basis that it made little contribution to rehabilitation and might indeed lead the courts to pass fewer rehabilitative sentences. But in the 1960s there was little analysis of the likely effectiveness of the 'individual deterrent' which many saw in the suspended sentence. Again, the rehabilitative effect of the community service order was expected to come through offenders working alongside volunteers and coming into contact with others less fortunate than themselves: but there was no detailed analysis of the process by which rehabilitation of the offender would come about, no examination of the psychological and other processes which might be expected to take place. These criticisms are fair up to a point. But it is questionable whether they should be regarded as conclusive. In order to withstand the kind of theoretical scrutiny implicit in Hood's criticisms, the Advisory Council would be expected to hold a consistent and fairly exhaustive theory of human behaviour, its motivation and the effect of certain measures on particular types of personality. 'Where, one may ask, is that "body of criminological and penological knowledge" to which Hood so lightly refers, which would enable anybody to predict with confidence the reaction of different classes of offenders to new forms of treatment?'[49] Even if one concedes that the Advisory Council could not fairly be expected to unfold a grand theory of human behaviour, however, they should at least have gone as far as they could in exploring the assumptions on which the new measure was based. If they expected a particular kind of response to a particular measure, ought they not to have made this clear – and, perhaps, have gone on to state what kind of personality might be most likely to respond to such behavioural cues? They ought also to have examined whether particular measures could be expected to achieve the desired ends without changes in the social system. If crime (or at least known and detected offending) is to some extent a function of the social organization of a particular country, then this will affect the probability that a new penal measure will achieve the aims of its promoters.

A wide range of factors are believed to be causally related to known offending ('causes of crime'), and there can be little doubt that the form of the social system does at least determine the nature of some lawbreaking. Hood has written of

the political hypocrisy of using the criminal justice system as a therapeutic tool to control social behaviour and ... the inherent conservatism of a therapeutic system, when what is required is not just a challenge to the deviant's conception of his social world as unjust, depriving and uncaring but major changes in a re-allocation of social resources to education, housing, hospitals, mental health and community development. A society which values its light entertainers above its teachers, which puts economic consumption above the values of equity, will produce much crime. It should not scapegoat those who in this system are unable to feel a sense of security, identity and personal worth.[50]

This passage makes a number of assumptions about the causes of crime, or at least about the causes of forms of lawbreaking in modern British society, but its writer is not led inexorably to the view that the utmost effort must be directed at removing what are seen as causes. Instead he argues that 'if [society] wants freedom to exploit and freedom to change then it must extend some tolerance to the deviance this produces and not pretend that its systems of sanctions are not ultimately and inextricably bound up in the web of social values and interests.'

Thus, a firm view about the major causes of lawbreaking does not necessarily lead to a particular view about the appropriate penal measures. It may be desirable for those who propose new penal measures to attempt to spell out the assumptions which underlie their views about how the measures are to operate in practice; but the process does not necessarily work in reverse, and those who subscribe to certain causal theories do not find themselves constrained to adopt penal measures of particular kinds. This last point can be reinforced by reference to our ability to predict which offenders are likely to re-offend: such factors as age, marital status and number of previous convictions are quite strong predictors of reconviction in general, and to a considerable extent they apply irrespective of the sentence passed on the offender. Alternatively, it might be argued that the heightened form of individual deterrence embodied in the suspended sentence might be effective when applied even to those who are regarded as being in need of supervision (because of social or psychological difficulties); in other words, the individual deterrent does not necessarily presuppose a rationalistic model of offenders but may even have some effect on those given to 'crisis' offending. Indeed, deterrent stratagems do not attempt to tackle any underlying cause of offending.

What is this notion of 'cause'? If we say that the 'cause' resides in the offender's failure to adjust to the social system which is the 'cause' of this misalignment – the offender or the social system? If we 'treat' the offender, we are attempting to bring him into harmony with a social system and to show him how to cope with it. If we decide that the fault lies in the social system, then political action (possibly of a radical and fundamental nature) is required. If we take a middle line, acknowledging some element of fault in the social system but shrinking from the revolutionary upheavals which might be necessary in order to change it, the path is 'to extend tolerance' and, in Hood's words, not to 'scapegoat' offenders. But what implications does that have for the devising of new penal measures or, indeed, for penal change in general? Hood stated in 1974 that 'the new approach addresses itself directly to the moral evaluations of the judges and the way they interpret the gravity or dangerousness of various offences'[51] – itself an important task, to which this book aims to make a modest contribution, but not a view which has more than general relevance to detailed questions of prescribing penalties for offenders and selecting offenders for penalties.

Hood's second criticism of the 1967 to 1972 reforms is that they were not preceded by 'a convincing analysis of why the methods already available had failed or needed re-inforcing'.[52] Although written in relation to community service orders, the following observations are apposite to any proposal which is seen as an alternative to prison:

one would have expected to see an analysis of the extent to which imprisonment is used, for what purpose and for what type of offence and offender, a discussion of why the alternative penalties were not used and a justification of the proposed alternatives both from the standpoint of satisfying the courts that their sentencing aim when formerly using imprisonment could still be achieved, and that the 'measures' being advocated appeared to be at least not less effective than imprisonment and to have a different effect upon offenders than the range of non-custodial measures already available.[53]

This is a healthy prescription for well-founded proposals for change. It does not appear how closely the Advisory Council followed this approach, if at all. Part of the difficulty may, however, rest in respect for the principle of judicial independence. It was shown in the previous chapter that many committees charged with making recommendations for penal reform have faltered on this point: there is a boundary beyond which they feel unable to tread, for fear of violating some constitutional convention. On the other hand, we must not be over-anxious to reach for this explanation in the present context. The Advisory Council on the Penal System did contain judicial members (although the subcommittee chaired by Lady Wootton, which prepared the proposals on *Non-Custodial and Semi-Custodial Penalties*, did not); and the Council's handling of the deferred sentence shows that they did feel able to make proposals squarely within the area which might be regarded as the judicial preserve. What is called for, on this approach, is an analysis of the reasons of sentencers for choosing certain sentences rather than others, of the occasions on which they feel constrained by the lack of a penalty they deem appropriate, and of the types of offence, criminal record and previous sentences of offenders currently receiving certain sentences.

What Hood's second point seems to indicate, then, apart from the need for a great deal of long-term research, is that at least such committees should take careful notice of what sentencers themselves see as the gaps in the existing measures and what they would like to have available. By tying proposals closely to sentencers' own perceptions of the problem, it is more likely that the policy behind legislative changes will be faithfully reflected by changes in practice. On the other hand, it could operate as a serious restriction unless it were combined with the more vigorous and assertive method of telling courts where a particular measure would be expected to fit into the penal armoury: exactly what existing sentences it would displace and why. That detail might be helpful to courts; but it would require committees (and the Advisory Council no longer exists) to work in a more painstaking and detailed way. Penal change has been limited in effect because the preparatory work has been limited in scope.

This takes us on to a third point – the failure of either reform committees or parliament to locate the new measure clearly within the established sentencing patterns of the courts. If a new measure is designed to fulfil a particular purpose, it seems self-defeating if no attempt is made to tie it to that purpose. The self-effacing nature of the Advisory Council's remark when proposing the introduction of community service is startling. 'We have not attempted to categorise precisely the types of offender for whom community service might be appropriate, nor do we think it possible to predict what use might be made by the courts of this new form of sentence.'[54] The term 'predict' in this context is extraordinary: reform committees should offer *guidance* based on their own enquiries and discussions. Unless they are content merely to toss a new measure to the courts and see how it is used, it is surely desirable to draw up guidelines which explain the aims of the new measure, the types of offender for whom it is thought most suitable, and the types and range of sentence which it would be expected to displace. The Home Office Guide for the Courts to the Criminal Justice Act 1972 stated: 'The Government has aimed at providing a power which the courts and the public will see as a viable alternative to shorter custodial penalties.'[55] This clearly evinces the Government's intention in introducing community service orders. The idea of a 'Guide for the Courts' to explain the new legislation was an excellent one. But there was no detail in the guidance given. An alternative to which shorter custodial penalties? – to them all? to the first custodial penalty? to anyone who had not yet experienced community service? only to offenders with particular characteristics? Again, the guidance was equivocal as to whether all community service orders were to be regarded as alternatives to short terms of imprisonment; this might be plausible in relation to the higher numbers of hours, but much less plausible for 40, 80 or even 100 hours. So it would have been helpful if there could have been some indication of the relationship of number of hours' community service to number of weeks' or months' imprisonment, etc. One exception to these deficiencies of policy implementation is deferment of sentence: its narrow purpose was always fairly clear, although certain difficulties have developed,[56] for which the only remedy under present arrangements (with a largely quiescent legislature) is judicial decision on appeal. In general it is fair to say that, not only are courts not supplied with detailed guidance which indicates the Government's view of the group of offences or offenders for which a new measure is likely to be most suitable, but also that committees which recommend such measures rarely enter into details of such groups.

(c) **Penal change 1973–81**
This most recent period in English penal history has seen modest but significant changes, brought about by methods and inspired by beliefs which differ from those which have gone before. Statutory change has been almost nonexistent: the Criminal Law Act 1977 did make provision for a new measure called the partly suspended sentence, but that was not brought into force until March 1982. The parole system was extended in 1975, following the issue of new guidelines by the Home Secretary, so that now over 60 per cent of parolable prisoners released each year are released on parole. Community service orders were made available to courts in all areas

during 1975 and 1976, after the initial 'experimental' period, and in 1981 they accounted for some 8 per cent of those sentenced at Crown Court. In 1978 the minimum period for a probation order was reduced from 1 year to 6 months, but these shorter orders are used relatively rarely. The Conservative Government has since 1979 greatly increased the number of junior and senior attendance centres, thus effectively adding a further available sentence for young offenders in some areas. To a large extent, therefore, the courts have been using the same range of sentences since the Criminal Justice Act of 1972.

Reference back to Tables 5 and 6 in Chapter 1[57] will demonstrate that, despite the insignificance of legislative change in this period, there have been substantial changes in sentencing practice since 1974. In that year, the use of imprisonment (both immediate and suspended) was at its lowest proportionate level and the fine at its highest level. Since then, the fine has taken a smaller share, as has probation, and the corresponding increases have been in immediate sentences of imprisonment and in community service orders. The relation of these changes to any waning of the 'rehabilitative ideal' is problematic, partly because of the penological ambiguity of community service (which some see as a rehabilitative measure), partly because the expectations of sentencers in passing sentences of imprisonment may have undergone a change. Thus it was argued in the early 1960s that any prison sentence should be sufficiently long to allow the prison authorities time to influence the offender's attitudes and habits. This was the penological wisdom of the day, and sentencers were urged, at the early sentencing seminars and conferences, to adopt this approach. Now, however,

Against the backcloth of a pessimistic conclusion about the reformative potential of prison, deterrence and the need to protect the public have become the principal justifications for the penalty of imprisonment and few now would claim, as they might have done twenty years ago, that the principal role of prison is to reform.[58]

Two things heralded the change. The first was the set of findings that the reconviction rates which follow longer terms of imprisonment are no better than those which follow short terms of imprisonment – which seems to suggest that neither the reformative nor the individual deterrent effect of imprisonment increases with the length of incarceration. The methodology of many of these studies has, however, been convincingly criticized,[59] and it is more accurate simply to state that there is no reliable evidence that longer custodial sentences have a greater individual preventive effect than shorter custodial sentences.

The second thing to have changed since the 1960s is that there is now greater awareness of and emphasis on the detrimental effects of imprisonment upon inmates.

All sentences, save the shortest, follow a familiar pattern; most prisoners settle down to the routine and become inured to the attendant hardships and deprivations of prison life. Prolonged and repeated imprisonment is destructive of family relationships, and by encouraging the prisoner's identification with the attitudes of the prison community increases his alienation from normal society. In addition, long-term institutionalisation is all too likely to destroy a prisoner's capacity for individual responsibility and to increase the problems he must face when he returns to society. Likewise society, by labelling the prisoner a convict and thereby socially and personally handicapping him on his return to the community, alienates itself from offenders.[60]

Indeed, so prominent had this reasoning become that in the *Review of Criminal Justice Policy 1976* it was listed as the second of three major policy assumptions 'that the institutionalisation of offenders can itself be harmful.'

Now, evidence of the detrimental effects of institutionalization had been available for some time, and the cynic might ask whether it was not revived to give criminological support to an objective which had assumed importance for other reasons. The mid-1970s saw the resurgence of economic arguments for reducing the numbers held in custody. Parole and suspended sentences were seen by the Government in 1967 as means of emptying the prisons, and in the mid-1970s the reduction of the prison population assumed a still more central role in official penal policy. Thus Brody observed that:

A noticeable trend has been a readiness to justify non-custodial sentences in preference to imprisonment or incarceration, on the grounds that they cost very much less to implement, and decrease at the same time the risk of psychological and practical harm to the offender. As 'softer' sentences have apparently no worse effect on recidivism and still offer the chance of less tangible if as yet unknown advantages, they are seen as preferable by all schools of thought except perhaps the retributivist.[61]

Likewise in his Presidential Address to the Magistrates' Association in 1976 Lord Elwyn-Jones, as Lord Chancellor, put the case for shorter prison sentences on grounds of deterrence and the absence in prison sentences of a reformative effect, and then added:

Imprisonment is a costly way of dealing with offenders. It costs well over £3,000 to keep one man in prison for twelve months. At present we are in a situation where we cannot find more money and more staff for more prisoners, or even for better prisons. Our only hope of improvements in the prisons is by getting the population down so there is less over-crowding and less pressure on staff. A more sparing use of imprisonment, through shorter sentences, could be one way of achieving this.[62]

The figure quoted by Lord Elwyn-Jones would now be much higher, but the point was one frequently made to sentencers at that time. Some sentencers reacted against the economic argument, resenting the financial approach on the ground that the task of the courts was to protect society and to deal fairly with offenders, and arguing that the Government ought to ensure that the facilities necessary to carry out these purposes were available. Implicit in this sort of reaction is a criticism of the Government's expenditure priorities, which locates the debate squarely within the political arena.

The emphasis placed on economic considerations by those ex-horting sentencers to change their practices was probably unwise. If persuasion were the aim, then the argument might have been better put on grounds of the avoidance of detrimental side-effects and the effectiveness of penal measures, although it is true to say that at that time there was no evidence to show whether shorter and fewer custodial sentences would or would not lead to an increase in the conviction and reconviction rates. The introduction of economy as a distinct reason – rather than one of the benefits flowing from the desired change in policy – may well have unbalanced the argument and led to resistance to a policy which might have received a greater welcome if put forward in a different way. Nonetheless the economic argument continues to be heard in certain quarters.[63]

At the beginning of the 1980s the major thrust of Government penal policy continues to be the effectiveness of certain measures. Thus, the first of two pieces of research reported in Home Office Research Study no. 64, *Taking Offenders Out of Circulation*, calculates the effect on the conviction rate of certain changes in the use of imprisonment. The authors estimate that if remission on prison sentences were increased from one-third to one-half, the overall annual rate of criminal convictions would increase by 1.2 per cent; they estimate that if all sentences of imprisonment were reduced by 6 months (i.e. by 4 months actually served), the annual increase in conviction would be 1.6 per cent. Now these calculations depend on official statistics and, as we saw earlier in the chapter, they do not tell the whole story about patterns in lawbreaking. On the basis of this research, the authors suggest that 'modest reductions in the lengths of prison sentences awarded, or in the length of time served by each offender, would not lead to a large number of additional convictions but would significantly decrease the size of the prison population'.[64] This is to put the claim too high: quite apart from the possibility that the general level of sentences has a general deterrent effect on potential offenders as well as offenders, there is the difficulty that the offenders who are reconvicted may have been responsible for many other crimes which remain unattributed or even reported. The authors acknowledge this possibility by saying that 'no analysis of the preventive effects of imprisonment can be entirely convincing in the absence of notable information about the real extent of crime and responsibility for it', and they continue by detailing the precise information which is necessary.[65] There is a tendency for the findings of research to be quoted without the qualifications. The lay-out of this Research Study, with the serious qualifications upon the research methodology separated spatially from the 'findings' (and not even mentioned when the findings are summarized in the Conclusions), may lead some to believe that there is now a firm basis for asserting that shorter terms of imprisonment are not likely to cause a significant number more reconvictions than longer terms of imprisonment; yet until there has been an effort to compare like with like – to see whether those given substantial terms of imprisonment would re-offend more frequently than they do, if they were given shorter terms – the proper basis for the assertion is absent, and the policy to which the research is said to point must remain one of hope rather than confident expectation.

Another theme among government spokesmen is that probation should be more widely used because of its 'holding effect'. The Home Secretary, Mr Whitelaw, pointed out in May 1980 that some 77 per cent of probation orders are successfully completed. Although the proportion is slightly lower for 3-year orders, some three-quarters of 2-year probation orders ensure 2 years 'free of trouble'.[66] A custodial sentence of 6 months, say, would ensure 4 months of complete public protection (since escapes from custody are extremely rare) but would leave the offender unsupervised for the remainder of the 2-year period which is relevant for purposes of comparison. Since some 57 per cent of those serving prison sentences of 3 to 6 months are reconvicted within a 2-year period,[67] the inferiority of imprisonment in this sense is said to be established.

But these examples betoken a distinct shift in the criteria for evaluating the effectiveness of penal measures. Previously the general criterion was known reconvictions of the offender during a stated follow-up period (usually 2 years). The emphasis now seems to be upon known reconviction or other breach of a court order *during the currency of that order*. Moreover, whereas the effectiveness studies of the 1960s attempted to provide a measure of comparative effectiveness by means of elaborate techniques, the references to a 'holding effect' are open to the obvious charge that a probation order would hardly be as effective in holding for 2 years some of the types of offender who are sent to prison. In the absence of any attempt to estimate the comparative 'holding effect' of various sentences, there is surely little basis for the implication that if offenders now sentenced to immediate or to suspended imprisonment were placed on probation their reconviction rates during the 2 years from the imposition of the sentence would not be significantly different. Indeed, it might be argued that the apparently strong 'holding effect' of the probation order in recent years derives from the very selectivity of its recommendation by probation officers and use by courts, although that argument would depend on whether probation officers do select, and are capable of selecting, offenders for whom probation is likely to 'succeed'.[68]

Another use of the concept of effectiveness which has emerged is in relation to the individual deterrent effect of the first prison sentence. It has been widely asserted that the first prison sentence should be short, because the maximum deterrent effect is achieved after a few weeks. The reasoning appears to be that prisons have a traumatic initial impact, but that after a few weeks a prisoner might begin to grow accustomed to the environment; the first sentence should therefore be sufficiently short to ensure that the adverse initial impact is felt, but not long enough to weaken that impact by allowing the offender to come to terms with prison. This has been called the 'clang of the prison gates' principle,[69] and in a sense it involves the attainment of an individual deterrent goal by what are considered as humanitarian means. If one grants that the sentence of imprisonment is thought to be 'necessary' and 'unavoidable', then it is humane to make it as short as possible, and if the short sentence has an increased deterrent effect too, that is a further reason in its favour. The increased deterrent effect has not been demonstrated by research, but it is supported by an intuitive feeling of common sense. The practical difficulty is that, once the great deterrent effect of a short prison sentence comes to be accepted in the lore of sentencers, it might result in the imposition of short prison sentences where otherwise the offender might not have been sent to prison (or at least the sentence might have been suspended). Recent statistics suggest that this might well have happened.[70]

The approach described in the previous paragraphs has been advocated only in relation to what have become known as 'run of the mill' offences. Serious offenders have always been exempted. Thus the Advisory Council recognized that:

There are certain offenders who present a serious threat to society and from whom society finds it necessary to seek protection. We do not deal in this report with the lengthy sentences passed by the courts in cases such as armed robbery or serious crimes of violence. There is a clear distinction to be drawn between crimes of that kind and the offences committed by the majority of those who enter our prison system.[71]

In the same vein, the *Review of Criminal Justice Policy 1976* declared that a principal preoccupation of policy was 'to protect society from the dangerous offence and offender, with particular reference to crimes of violence and crimes of particular concern, e.g. the production and supply of dangerous drugs'; and the primary policy aimed at this goal was 'the increase in penalties for firearms offences and for the production and supply of drugs'.[72] That reference was to raising the maximum penalties by statute,[73] but clearly it was intended, at the very least, to endorse the passing of substantial prison sentences for such crimes. This dualism of policy was clearly set out in the Conservative Party Manifesto for the 1979 General Election: 'For violent criminals and thugs really tough sentences are essential. But in other cases long prison sentences are not always the best deterrent. So we want to see a wider variety of sentence available to the courts.'[74] A number of ministerial speeches during 1980 and 1981 made it clear that the dualism remains. In his widely reported speech to the Leicestershire Magistrates in February 1981, the Home Secretary generally advocated a 'move towards shorter sentences', but he added that 'This does not imply in the slightest that the courts should not deal firmly with violent offenders. I have always made it clear that the case for shorter and fewer prison sentences does not apply to them.'[75]

In this passage, Mr Whitelaw spoke of '*the case* for shorter and fewer prison sentences', and this points to another respect in which penal policy-making has changed during the period since 1972. The way in which penal policy is formulated and promulgated has changed, and one can even discern different influences during the period 1973 to 1978, and the period 1979 to 1981. In the earlier period the Advisory Council on the Penal System assumed a much more assertive role than it had hitherto thought appropriate. The 1975 report on *Young Adult Offenders* does not fall into this category, but the interim report of 1977 on *The Length of Prison Sentences* and the final report in 1978 on *Sentences of Imprisonment: a Review of Maximum Penalties* clearly do. Several passages from the 1977 report have already been quoted, and its direct orientation towards policy-making is clear from the following: 'the general rule which we advocate for all courts to follow is to stop at the point where a sentence has been decided upon and consider whether a shorter one would not do just as well.'[76] And the interrogatory form of another passage barely conceals its policy recommendations:

. . . at this juncture we wish merely to pose a few simple questions. Are there not cases of two years' imprisonment where 18 months, or 15 or even less, might safely be passed, and sentences of twelve months when six months would do just as well? And for the offender going to prison for the first time, should not even a shorter sentence suffice? Are not many suspended sentences longer than the sentence would have been if it had been immediate, and, in many such cases, does not the eventual activation of the suspended sentence without any reduction in its length create a situation where the total sentence is too long?[77]

The Advisory Council's function was to advise the Home Secretary on such matters as he referred to them. On this occasion they took it upon themselves to offer direct advice to sentencers, and the Home Secretary evidently approved of this since he directed that a copy of the report be sent to each judge and each magistrates' court in the country. Similar advice and exhortations are to be found in Lord Elwyn-Jones's Presidential Address to the Magistrates' Association in 1976, and in the *Review of Criminal Justice Policy 1976*, and it was evident that the earlier process of parliamentary debate (sometimes preceded by a committee report) followed by legislation was no longer seen as the way to engineer penal change. The committee reports of this period made few proposals relating to sentencing practice: for example, the Expenditure Committee of the House of Commons paid detailed attention to plans for relieving the prisons of the mentally disordered, alcoholics, defaulters on fines or maintenance payments, and the so-called 'inadequate' offenders.

The use of the Advisory Council as a vehicle for formulating and
promulgating government penal policy passed away in 1979 with the
demise of that body. In its place rose government ministers and the
Lord Chief Justice, a combination peculiarly appropriate to the kinds
of change which were thought necessary – changes in sentencing
practice rather than legislative structure. The Government's
approach was set out in a succession of speeches by ministers, and by
the paragraph of the 1980 White Paper in which they 'particularly
commended to the courts and the public' the following conclusion of
the Expenditure Committee two years earlier:

> In many cases where there is a real choice available to the court between a
> longer sentence and a shorter one, or between a short sentence and some
> alternative means of disposing of the case, the court should bear in mind the
> general experience and the scientific evidence we have mentioned and
> consider whether the balance should not be tipped in favour of a shorter
> sentence or not to use imprisonment. . . . The question we have to ask, in the
> light of all the evidence cited, is whether in this country we should maintain
> the level of sentencing which has been customary and indeed whether it is
> necessary to do so in order to prevent or reduce crime.[78]

In a series of major speeches by Home Office ministers, culminating
perhaps in the Home Secretary's speech to the Leicestershire
Magistrates, the elements of government penal policy were spelt out:
long custodial sentences should be reserved for the violent, the
dangerous and those from whom the public need protection; other
prison sentences should be reduced in length; non-custodial
measures, especially probation, should be more widely used; and
executive means of releasing medium-term prisoners at an earlier
stage should be developed. The last-mentioned plank of government
policy was set out in the *Review of Parole 1981*, where a system of
automatic early release under supervision was proposed, but that
proposal was subsequently retracted in favour of the introduction of
the partly suspended sentence.[79]

Perhaps the most important development in the latest phase of
penal policy, from 1979 to 1981, is the willingness of the Lord Chief
Justice, Lord Lane, to be publicly associated with many causes which
seem close to the Government's concern. This is not to say that judges
had hitherto proceeded in ignorance of official penal policy and
thought: in his judgment in *Sargeant*,[80] Lawton LJ argued in favour of
the more selective use of individual deterrents and against the use of
general deterrents, and also recognized that prisons could no longer

be seen as rehabilitative institutions. But this was an isolated decision, and cannot be compared (in terms of the development of penal policy) with the significance of two strong declarations by a newly appointed Lord Chief Justice, sitting in a Court of Appeal which included two senior Lords Justices of Appeal. In fact the decisions in *Upton* and *Begum Bibi* marked two significant advances. The first was to recognize expressly the relevance of prison over-crowding to the use of prison sentences by the courts: 'Sentencing judges should appreciate that overcrowding in many of the penal establishments in this country is such that a prison sentence, however short, is a very unpleasant experience indeed for the inmates.'[81]

This is not an economic argument which points to the high cost of imprisonment; it is a humanitarian argument which draws attention to the increased unpleasantness of imprisonment which has resulted from the expenditure restrictions. Economic factors may therefore be the ultimate cause of the change of policy, but the primary reason for advocating a more sparing use of imprisonment is that the sentence itself has become more arduous. The second and, both actually and potentially, more significant step taken in *Begum Bibi*[82] was to specify the kinds of offence for which the level of sentences might be lowered and to distinguish them from certain other types of offences for which sentencing levels should remain unchanged. The exercise, it is true, was a limited one. The method is one which could and should be more widely used in order to give guidance about critical decisions in sentencing – for example, identifying offences which 'call for' imprisonment notwithstanding the good character of the offender. That apart, it is arguable that the consequences of *Begum Bibi* (and of the 10 other decisions made by the Court of Appeal at about the same time, and reported with *Begum Bibi*) have been disappointing. The spirit of those decisions often seems to have been absent from more recent Court of Appeal pronouncements.

(d) Penal change 1973–81: a critique

The main characteristic of penal change in 1967–72 was the introduction of new measures for the courts to use in the sentencing of offenders, although the advent of parole was also significant. The main characteristic of penal change in 1973–81 was the orchestration of changes in the sentencing practices of the courts, although the more liberal granting of parole (following the 1975 initiative) was also significant. Whether the changes in sentencing practice have been either as swift or as far-reaching as their proponents hoped may be doubted. The judiciary has become more involved in the formulation of policy than hitherto, and this has helped to ensure that policies have become more detailed and therefore more directly applicable to sentencing practice, thus removing one of the major difficulties of penal reform in 1967–72. But the later period shows how much further it is still necessary to go.

There remains no clear guidance on how the non-custodial sentences relate to one another and to the suspended sentence. The remarks made in *O'Keefe*[83] are rather general and out of date, and the spate of decisions in 1982 on such matters as the suitability of offenders for community service orders and the proper use of the partly suspended sentence,[84] whilst they should be welcomed as far as they go, serve mainly to indicate that guidance of this detailed nature *can* be formulated yet so rarely has been formulated by the Court of Appeal. Thus, the crucial question about criteria for the first custodial sentence has not been tackled as a whole, although it seems little less susceptible to guidance than the matters discussed in *Begum Bibi*. Moreover, the general principles of sentencing have been neglected, and the proper approach to dealing with such groups as persistent offenders, female offenders, multiple offenders has not been considered in general – despite the fact that they are hardly less important to sentence length than the nature of the offence.

Part of the blame for the failure of penal policy to develop even further in the direction of detailed prescriptions about the criteria for sentencing must be laid with the Advisory Council on the Penal System. The reference from the Home Secretary which led to their 1978 report on maximum penalties began thus: 'to consider the general structure and level of maximum sentences of imprisonment available to the courts; to assess how far they represent a valid guide to sentencing practice.' They took the view that the existing structure of maximum penalties did not at all represent a valid guide to sentencing practice. Yet they remained wedded to the notion that maximum penalties adjusted to the nature of the offence would be the best guide, and so proposed a system of 'normal maximum penalties' which varied according to the offence. Their report, whilst bursting with fascinating historical detail, failed to consider the ingredients of sentencing. They failed to analyse the practices and principles of sentencing first, and only then to look at the role of the maximum sentence for each offence. In consequence there is hardly a reference in the report to 'general principles'. A few remarks were devoted to multiple offenders and the use of consecutive and concurrent sentences.[85] That awkward section of the report should surely have alerted the Advisory Council to the need to consider the relationship of maximum penalties – even their own 'normal maximum sentences' – to such matters as intentionality, age, previous record, circumstances leading to the offence, and so on. Of course these matters were not within the Advisory Council's terms of reference, and therefore could not be examined in detail. What the Advisory Council should have done was to emphasize their significance for sentencing levels and to press for a further inquiry into their formulation and application. That inquiry would probably not have been a task which the Advisory Council would have relished, since they sought to avoid controversial value judgements in their *Maximum Penalties* report and could hardly have done so when it came to general principles. If guidance on sentencing is to be developed, that must be the way forward.

4 Blueprints for penal change

From this discussion of the workings of the criminal justice system and the making of penal policy, it clearly emerges that the processes are haphazard and tend to lack co-ordination. To some extent this may be the result of respect for the independence of the judiciary and of chief constables; to a large extent it may be the product of a failure to appreciate the steps which must be taken if declared policies are to be put successfully into practice. New measures which have been introduced have not been properly grounded in either penal theory or sentencing practice, with the result that no guidance has been given to the courts on the types of offence and offender for whom the measures might be appropriate – a natural result of the failure on the part of those introducing the new measure to locate it within existing sentencing practice. Guidance could not be given because the groundwork necessary to generate that guidance had not been carried out. The lack of empirical knowledge about sentencing practices might in part have been remedied by proper co-ordination in devising the measures and in planning their implementation, but this has not usually taken place.

It is clear, not only from the period 1979–1981 but also from 1967 onwards, that the introduction of new forms of sentence will only achieve the policy objectives of their proponents if close attention is paid to their integration into sentencing practice. In blunt terms, the courts can make or break a new penal measure. This indicates the desirability of providing guidelines for sentencers, once it has been decided exactly how the new measure ought to fit into sentencing practice. The great difficulty is that there exists no systematic knowledge about sentencing practice. The Lord Chief Justice saw fit in 1981 to refuse permission for one detailed study of sentencing in the Crown Court to take place,[86] thereby not only depriving members of society of knowledge with which to evaluate the sentencing practice of the judges but also depriving policy-makers of the necessary empirical basis for formulating penal policy. The crucial part to be played by knowledge of sentencing practices is plain if we consider in broad terms the formal requirements of successful penal policy-making.

(1) Identify the need for change:

this will be related to the preoccupations of the policy-makers, who may wish to see changes in a particular direction. There should then be consultation with the judiciary and magistracy, so as to assess the potentiality for change. Are existing measures working unsatisfactorily? If so, does the solution in practice lie in the introduction of a new measure or in some changes in the way in which existing measures are used?

(2) If a new measure is indicated, then:

(a) select or construct a measure which appears to fulfil the need which has been identified. This might well involve an analysis of the prison population (using data such as those of the survey of the South East prison population in 1972[87], in order to identify the types of offender who are now sentenced to imprisonment, or it may require a study of the characteristics of a major group of offenders such as burglars. Much will depend on the aim of the change, but the important point is to consider information about the types of offence and offender for whom the new measure might properly be used.

(b) Identify the relationship of the new measure to existing measures: which sentences would the new measure displace? Would its introduction have direct or indirect effects on other aspects of sentencing practice? Would the courts see it as a realistic alternative to the sentences which it displaces?

(c) Steer the courts towards the desired use of the new measure: based on a prediction of how the new measure would fit into the sentencing pattern of the courts, this stage would involve consideration of the various ways of inducing conformity. This is a general topic which has already been discussed briefly:[88] in the present context, what is essential is that detailed guidance be available for sentencers. Without that, *any* method of steering the courts towards a particular approach is likely to be unsuccessful since there will be no clear signposts.

(3) If a change in existing practice, without the introduction of a new measure, is indicated, then:

(a) Identify the nature of the change required and the cases it would affect: this would involve a detailed study of sentencing practice. As in 2(a) above, it would be important to gather details of the groups of offender for whom the new approach might be suitable, and to assess the effect of any change on sentencing patterns in general. Very few studies of sentencing practice exist, and one of the most detailed (Home Office Research Study no. 54 on sentencing for sexual offences) considers the problem from the point of view of offences rather than the characteristics of offenders. Both aspects of sentencing, together with the aims and character-istics of the available penal measures, need to be covered if any change is to be securely based on a realistic view of practice.

(b) Steer the courts towards the desired change of approach: this would include the elements mentioned in paragraph 2(c) above, but it is especially important to consider fresh methods of providing guidance to the courts, perhaps by way of Practice Directions from the Court of Appeal presided over by the Lord Chief Justice.[89]

An approach which adopted these formal steps would be more likely to achieve the translation of policy into practice than the existing haphazard processes. However, it is also evident from section 2 of this chapter that sentencing is merely one part of the criminal process, and that a small change at one stage of that process may have repercussions at other stages. It therefore follows that co-ordination of policy, from prosecution through to parole (including procedural issues such as expediting criminal trials), is essential if the criminal justice system is to be shaped so as to achieve agreed policy objectives. It has sometimes been argued that this indicates the need for a Ministry of Justice, which would bring together in one government department all the various responsibilities (outlined in section 1 of this chapter) for parts of the criminal justice system. The Lord Chancellor, Lord Hailsham, has stated that he 'would not desire to have either the prosecuting process or the penal treatment process under his responsibility' because they are incompatible with the judicial function, for which he now has responsibility.[90] It is difficult to assess the strength of this argument. The Lord Chancellor seems to fear that the independence and impartiality of the judiciary would be put in danger by such a change, but that does not follow. The degree of control over such groups as the judiciary or chief constables might or might not be changed: that is a separate issue. No such change would be necessitated by the creation of a Ministry of Justice. Perhaps the real reason is a fear of undue political control over the process of law enforcement: if the various responsibilities were brought together within a single ministry, it would be easier for political influence to be exerted upon the criminal justice system than it is with the existing fragmentation of responsibilities.

The case in favour of a Ministry of Justice is not crucial to the argument here. What is most important is that a far wider range of groups within the criminal justice system are brought into the formal process of the creation and implementation of penal policy. With the demise of the Advisory Council on the Penal System, the position is that the introduction of new penal measures is a matter for the Home Office and its implementation for the courts. What is needed is a body which will bring together all the relevant groups – police, probation officers, prison authorities, magistrates, judges, and so on – to discuss the form of penal policy and its implementation. The present Government has rejected one similar proposal – that of the House of Commons Home Affairs Committee, for the establishment of a National Criminal Policy Committee charged with the planning of criminal justice policy.[91] It is indeed important that new committees should not lightly be proposed. But there are two strong reasons why a committee is needed which could discuss and make proposals on penal policy. First, on principle, it is wrong to regard the parts of the criminal process as independent, and to pursue policies at one stage in the criminal process which counteract practice at another stage. Co-ordination of policy makes elementary sense. Secondly, on a pragmatic level, proposed changes in the criminal justice system some-times draw opposition from particular groups (such as the police, or probation officers, or the judiciary) which may be based on purely sectional arguments. This is not to suggest that the mere creation of a committee will put an end to 'criminal justice syndicalism', by which particular groups attempt to advance their own working interests by opposing changes. However, there is a positive merit in bringing representatives of the various groups into the very process of formulating policy. Representation of this kind might bring both influence and information about the problems of others and of the system as a whole.

4
Constructing culpability

I **Introduction**

Many observations, both *about* sentencing and *by* sentencers, are based on the assumption that there exists a rough scale of the relative gravity of criminal offences. In all the spheres of social life in which some kind of punishment is imposed, we tend to feel that there is a moral distinction between those transgressions which are serious and others which are much less serious. In the criminal courts, sentencers not only publicly draw distinctions of that kind among the myriad manifestations of criminality with which they have to deal, but also prescribe a sentence in each case. If 'modern retributivism' is regarded as the principal aim of sentencing, proportionality is of central importance;[1] moreover, many of those who regard the prevention of crime as the principal aim of sentencing accept proportionality as a limiting principle, maintaining that no sentence should be disproportionate to the seriousness of the case. However, the concept of the 'seriousness' of a case is not simply a matter of assessing the gravity of the offence. As the Streatfeild Committee recognized in 1961, 'in every sentence the offender's culpability has to be taken into account.'[2] It may therefore be postulated that the idea of the seriousness of a case is composed of two elements – the gravity of the offence, and the responsibility of the offender – and that the sentencer should assess both in the process of constructing culpability.

Let us, as a first step, explore further the notion of proportionality inherent in the proposition that sentences should be proportionate to the seriousness of the case. At a crude level, most people would probably 'admit or even insist that greater wickedness should aggravate, and less wickedness should mitigate, the severity of punishment.[3] This yields the general principle that 'moral differences between offences should be reflected in the gradation of legal penalties', which, argues Hart, can be supported on two main grounds:

There are many reasons why we might wish the legal gradation of the seriousness of crimes, expressed in its scale of punishments, not to conflict with common estimates of their comparative wickedness. One reason is that such a conflict is undesirable on simple utilitarian grounds: it might either confuse moral judgments or bring the law into disrepute, or both. Another reason is that principles of justice or fairness between different offenders require morally distinguishable offences to be treated differently and morally similar offences to be treated alike.[4]

The first reason is not a moral proposition: it relates to the symbolic elements in sentencing, albeit in the negative sense that gross departures from what appears to be 'public opinion' might undermine what may be termed the symbiotic relationship between sentencing policy and the social system.[5] Hart's second reason amounts to the suggestion that certain 'principles of justice or fairness between different offenders' exist and properly exercise influence on sentencing policy. Yet Hart warns elsewhere of the dangers of assuming that 'a single homogeneous social morality' prevails in this country.[6] There is a plurality of moral standpoints, and there are bound to be differences of opinion on the relative seriousness of such offences as the importation of cannabis, tax evasion, shoplifting, and so forth. Moreover it is highly unlikely that any of these moral doctrines include principles which are sufficiently detailed to yield answers to the kinds of question (such as the relative gravity of pickpocketing and shoplifting, burglary and blackmail, or the relative effect on culpability of financial hardship or previous convictions for offences of a different kind) with which sentencers have to deal with every day. Attempts to develop a relatively cohesive moral code which answers questions of this kind were made by eighteenth-century masters such as Beccaria, Bentham and Paley, but have since fallen out of fashion. Without some framework of agreed categories, relativities and priorities, it is difficult to see how the principle of fairness which requires like cases to be treated alike could have practical application.

Whilst few writers since the eighteenth century have approached the problem of the relative seriousness of criminal offences in a systematic way, there have been notable attempts to explore the justifications behind some of the divisions between offences. Edward Cox's *Principles of Punishment* in 1877 attended to the assumptions behind some of the relativities in sentencing, and Sir Rupert Cross's *English Sentencing System* (which first appeared in 1971) discusses the justifications for some of the major principles of sentencing and divisions between offences. Judicial forays into the realms of justifying relativities have been restricted to small parts of the whole system. Perhaps the most notable came in *Turner*,[7] where Lawton LJ sought to relate sentencing levels for several very serious offences to the effective length of sentence for murder. The next most serious group of offences after murder, held Lawton LJ, comprises 'such crimes as the Great Train robbery, bad cases of espionage, cases of horrid violence' (of which torture was the example), bomb outrages, terrorism and political kidnapping. The only justification advanced for this selection was that these offences 'may endanger the state'. This is hardly a sufficiently specific criterion for use in distinguishing offences, although it is possible to extrapolate from it. Thus it would probably be argued that these offences strike directly at the existing social order. That assumption is likely to be well founded in most cases of terrorism, political kidnapping and espionage. The category of 'horrid violence' is more closely linked with the crime of murder itself, as a direct and calculated attack on the physical integrity and dignity of members of society.[8] The second most serious category of offences after murder was said to include those bank robberies which are well organized and involve firearms. The large amount of money typically involved in such cases contributes to their gravity, but what places them in this specially high category is the planned and calculated assault on part of the social system, and the elements of professionalism and dedication to taking advantage of the system. These elements not only confirm that the offenders had ample realization of what they were doing, but they also set the offenders unequivocally against the existing social order in a way that less deliberative lawbreaking does not.

These attempts to extrapolate from the terse justifications offered in Lawton LJ's judgment illustrate the small distance that the English judges have gone towards articulating the reasons for the relativities between offences. Even the so-called 'guideline' judgments, in which the Court of Appeal (with Lord Lane CJ presiding) has considered the appropriate sentences for a whole range of manifestations of a certain offence, are predominantly descriptive and tend not to enter into the justifications for the distinctions they propose.[9] Thus in their published judgments the courts have not provided sufficient justificatory reasoning from which to construct even the skeleton of a systematic pattern of reasoned relativities between the most frequent types of case. Any attempt to remedy this deficiency must struggle against the restrictiveness of established patterns of thought and expression. Almost all discourse on the subject seems to assume that the gravity of the offence is of greater moral significance than the characteristics of the offender. Newspapers tend to print headlines such as 'Rapist gets only 18 months' rather than 'First offender of exemplary previous character imprisoned for 18 months'. Those who complain about inconsistency or disparities in sentencing invariably seem to assume that the standard should be set according to the gravity of the offence, so that the proper comparison is between two rapists rather than two first offenders. In *Doing Justice* the American writer von Hirsch states that ' "seriousness" depends both on the harm done (or risked) by the act and on the degree of the actor's culpability',[10] but goes on to insist that the seriousness of the offence is far more important than the characteristics of the individual offender.

> Imposing only a slight penalty for a serious offence treats the offender as less blameworthy than he deserves. Understating the blame depreciates the values that are involved: disproportionately lenient punishment for murder implies that human life – the victim's life – is not worthy of much concern; excessively mild penalties for official corruption denigrate the importance of an equitable political process. The commensurability principle, in our view, bars disproportionate leniency as well as disproportionate severity.'[11]

This view leans heavily on a particular conception of the symbolic function of sentencing, and the first sentence betrays the assumption that a 'serious offence' is defined without regard to the characteristics of the individual offender. Now this is an assumption which, in view of the symbolism involved in sentencing, is not to be lightly dismissed. Findings from those concerned in the administration of juvenile justice, where Parliament has strongly indicated that courts must consider the characteristics of each individual offender, show the continuing influence of patterns of thought based on the gravity of the offence: Priestley, Fears and Fuller report the unwillingness of the police to deal differently with individual members of a group of young offenders who commit offences together,[12] and in their survey of the opinions of children and parents Morris and Giller found a strong expectation that courts would adjust the disposition to the seriousness of the offence, and found considerable scepticism about the relevance and propriety of looking at wider matters.[13] Conceptions of fairness and consistency evidently tend to revolve round the nature and gravity of the offence, and this constitutes a natural restraint upon the free consideration of the relative seriousness of different types of case.

A further difficulty in the task of exploring the justifications for regarding some types of case as more serious than others derives from the vast range of offences in English criminal law. All that can be attained here is an examination of some of the more important conceptions about the gravity of offences and conceptions about the responsibility of offenders. As Bentham remarked when introducing the lengthy discussion of the 'division of offences' in his *Principles of Morals and Legislation*:

> Complete success, then, is, as yet at least, unattainable. But an attempt, though imperfect, may have its use; and, at the worst, it may accelerate the arrival of that perfect system, the possession of which will be the happiness of some maturer age. Gross ignorance describes no difficulties; imperfect knowledge finds them out, and struggles with them: it must be perfect knowledge that overcomes them.[14]

There is every indication that both sentencers and people in general will continue to make judgments about the relative seriousness of different cases, and the time has surely come for a determined exploration of the moral and other assumptions behind those judgments – an enterprise which will serve some purpose even if its errors provoke others to suggest sounder justifications. Hood has pointed to the wide range of moral questions which underlie sentencing practices.

> What weight should be given to harm done? to previous record? to poor environment? to cultural differences in the interpretation of challenges to personal status or integrity? to marital stress or inadequate income? Which offences should be regarded as the most socially injurious? Have we placed traffic offences in their right order compared with most petty thefts and common-or-garden assaults?[15]

After resolving questions of this kind, the next step which ought to be taken from the point of view of sentencers would be to select a sentence which matches both the features of the case and prevailing sentencing policy. In this part of the book however, the emphasis lies upon the kind of questions posed by Hood. He argues that only 'by forcing judges to evaluate social behaviour' and 'to articulate the moral judgments on which their sentence is passed' can we expect to make progress towards a clear appreciation of the principles and preferences upon which our sentencing system is based. English judges have ventured only a short distance along this path: the task here is to pursue the issues further. The discussion is inevitably abstract to a considerable extent. It begins with a fairly detailed examination of offences of violence. We then turn to the personal responsibility of the offender, considering the way in which that contributes to estimations of the seriousness of a case. The discussion is then extended to property offences, and some of the thorny questions of proportionality as between violent and property offences are broached. Finally, some general principles relating to factors which aggravate offences are explored.

2 **Offences of violence**

(a) **Introduction**
It has been said to be part of the very definition of 'law' that the state should have a monopoly of the legitimate use of force:

> The development of the law from primitive beginnings to its present stage in the modern state displays . . . a tendency which is common to all legal orders. It is the tendency gradually and increasingly to prohibit the use of physical force from man to man. Use of force is prohibited by making it the condition for a sanction. But the sanction itself is a use of force . . . Gradually, however, the principle is recognized that every use of physical force is prohibited unless – and this is a limitation of the principle – it is especially authorized as a reaction against a socially detrimental fact attributable to the legal community. In this case, the legal order determines exhaustively the conditions under which (and the men by whom) physical force may be used . . . Then we are confronted with a monopoly of force of the legal community.[16]

The great Austrian jurist Kelsen put this forward as a historical fact and as a matter of definition: that the legal order claims a monopoly of the legitimate use of force is an element in the definition of law, and 'if from the existing social orders designated as law the element of coercion were to disappear – as predicted by Marx's socialism –then these social orders would indeed fundamentally change their character.'[17] To what extent a complex society could survive without rules limiting the use of force remains a matter for speculation and some scepticism. Indeed, one might argue that the reason why societies have invariably had rules of certain kinds is linked with certain natural features of human beings. Of these rules

the most important for social life are those that restrict the use of violence in killing or inflicting bodily harm. The basic character of such rules may be brought out in a question: If there were not these rules what point could there be for beings such as ourselves in having rules of any other kind? The force of this rhetorical question rests on the fact that men are both occasionally prone to, and normally vulnerable to, bodily attack.[18]

It is these facts, human vulnerability and the occasional proneness to violence, which have led to the virtually universal rules restricting the use of force. The vulnerability of human beings to physical attack is therefore one factor which shapes social organization and has led virtually every society to create rules restricting the use of force. Another fact is the propensity of most people to feel the urge to use force in certain circumstances – an urge which some, but not all, succeed in repressing or channelling lawfully. A further fact is that some members of society may believe that the use of force is their only means of redressing what they perceive as an unfair social imbalance. This kind of belief is not necessarily inconsistent with support for democracy as a method of government, because such support can be and often is combined with an insistence that certain principles and certain 'human rights' be respected; but the question of justifying the use of force in an attempt to vindicate principles or rights which are violated raises serious difficulties which will not be explored here. It is rare for courts to be confronted with allegations of unfairness in the social system or political violation of human rights as the express motivation for an offence, and it is unlikely that they would excuse or mitigate violence on this account. It is more likely that they would regard it as part of their symbolic function to use the sentencing process as a means of publicly denouncing a challenge to the social system.[19]

If it is agreed, then, that prohibitions on the use of force may fairly be regarded as fundamental to modern legal systems, we must briefly consider the contours of violence from the social point of view. The term 'violence' has a condemnatory ring, whereas 'the use of force' is more neutral and people use force in a whole range of everyday situations without attracting social censure or legal sanction. Consider this example:

A few days ago I witnessed an incident where someone was hit in the face by another person who was much bigger and stronger. The blow was powerful enough to cause the assaulted person's nose to bleed, yet there was a policeman standing within a few feet of the incident who must have seen it but who took no action.[20]

From these bare facts one might think it extraordinary that the event was not thought worthy of the policeman's intervention. But if one adds a description of the social context of the violence, judgments tend to change:

As it happens, however, there is more to it in this case. The incident occurred on the pavement alongside a busy main road, and the assailant, an adult, had called out to the victim, a child, 'Keep away from the road and hold Mummy's hand.' The child had paid no attention and had in fact nearly been knocked down by a passing car. The agitated mother seized the child, roughly pulled her to safety and hit her across the face, causing the nosebleed.[21]

The context now makes the use of force understandable in social terms. The law permits a parent to use reasonable force in the correction of his or her child; whilst one might argue that this mother was probably acting impulsively in outrage rather than meting out measured punishment, and one might doubt whether strictly the force was reasonable, there would be little social or legal interest in even bringing a prosecution under circumstances of this kind. There has in recent years been a re-awakening of interest in domestic violence, much of which has no colour of legal justification and goes well beyond the bounds indicated even by the loose phraseology of the law ('reasonable force'). But the point here is that English law does allow the use of some force for disciplinary purposes by persons who are not formally agents of the state.

Another setting in which the law permits the use of force is self-defence, the defence of one's property or the prevention of crime. Once again, in legal theory the requirement that the force be 'reasonable' is designed to keep a sense of proportion between the amount of force which is lawful and the gravity of the harm thereby averted. Another reason which the law accepts as a justification for the infliction of force is where the victim consents. This does not apply where the harm inflicted amounts to death or serious injury, but there are major exceptions to this. Medical operations may well inflict or risk inflicting serious injury, but this is generally thought to be justified; and the law condones the infliction of varying degrees of force during sport (e.g. boxing, rugby, cricket). In relation to both surgery and sport the limits of the law are unclear, but that is unimportant in the present discussion. What these rules and exceptions show is that not all force against others is outlawed: indeed in some situations people enjoy using force against one another and are allowed to do so. Thus the idea of 'monopoly of force' must be read subject to certain legal and social qualifications, and a more precise approach would be to assert that physical force is restricted to certain situations and relationships defined by the State. Moreover that aspect of the human condition most closely connected with laws against violence is human vulnerability, and human vulnerability is more open to attack from 'accidental' deaths and injuries than from the kinds of conduct covered by most modern criminal codes. A road accident, unsafe machinery at work, an electrical fault in the home, a strike by ambulance drivers – each of these may have just as great an effect on life and limb as the deliberate and unjustified use of force against another.

(b) Evaluating violence: the criminal law

Not all violence is equally heinous. People generally draw distinctions between serious cases and less serious cases in their everyday judgments about the use of force. Sentencers have to act upon (if not articulate) criteria of aggravation and mitigation. What are these criteria, and what are their justifications? We begin by considering the criteria disclosed by the criminal law itself. The main offences can most clearly be presented in tabular form (as below).

From this table, which, even though fairly intricate, does not cover every legal detail, it can be seen that the principal criteria for the legal categorization of offences are twofold – the amount of harm done, and the mental attitude of the offender towards the doing of harm. The actual infliction of the harm intended is not always necessary: where an offender clearly had the intention to inflict violence but failed in his endeavour to do so, he can usually be charged with attempting to commit the offence intended. The crime of attempted murder is included in the table as an example of this possibility; attempts to commit other offences against the person may also be charged in appropriate cases. It is also noteworthy that the offence of voluntary manslaughter is not distinguished from the others either by the amount of harm done or the mental attitude of the offender. The alternative grounds are diminished responsibility or provocation, and

Table of principal offences against the person

Category of offence	Degree of harm	Mental attitude
Murder	death	intent to kill; *or* knowledge that death is probable to result; *or* intent to cause really serious harm; *or* knowledge that really serious harm is probable to result.
Voluntary manslaughter	death	any of the mental attitudes required for murder, and *either* provocation *or* diminished responsibility
Involuntary manslaughter	death	gross negligence *or* intent to commit a crime likely to result in harm
Attempted murder	(none necessary)	intent to kill
'Grievous bodily harm'	really serious injury or wounding	intent to do grievous bodily harm
Unlawful wounding	a wound or really serious injury	foresight that some physical harm might result
Assault occasioning actual bodily harm	actual bodily harm	intention or recklessness as to assault
Common assault	apprehension of violence	intentionally or recklessly causing fear of unlawful violence

they are discussed later.[22]

Apart from the principal offences listed above, there are various other crimes whose rationale is wholly or partly the prevention of bodily harm. The preventive function is manifest in offences concerned with the possession of firearms and offensive weapons, where the law aims to bite even before the offender has had the opportunity (or even formed the intention) to use the weapon against another. The same may be said of the offence of behaviour likely to cause a breach of the peace. The preventive function is perhaps less manifest in such crimes as drunken driving and speeding, although in both instances the prevention of death and injury ranks high among the justifications for penalizing such conduct. The offences of reckless driving and careless driving likewise have a preventive function, inasmuch as they penalize departures from the standards of safe driving set forth in the Highway Code; the same may be said, albeit in a more indirect fashion, of offences against the vehicle safety regulations. Further, by means of such statutes as the Health and Safety at Work Act 1974, the Consumer Safety Act 1978 and the Safety of Sports Grounds Act 1975, the ambit of the criminal law has been extended to more activities which threaten to cause injury. Many now acknowledge that the criminal sanction may properly be used to impose a higher standard of care on those whose activities (especially when they are conducted for profit) risk causing harm to others. Crimes of this last kind differ from many motoring offences in that their perpetrators may not realize the risk which they are creating, and they are often defined as crimes of negligence. This means that no mental attitude is required of the offender and the offence may therefore be regarded as less serious, since a negligent action is one in which the actor neither chose to produce nor chose to risk producing the harm, but merely failed to attain what the law regards as a reasonable standard of care. The criminal law also contains a few offences of 'strict liability' in this sphere. These are offences whose requirements are fulfilled by a particular course of conduct without the need for proof of any mental attitude on the part of the perpetrator; if it is shown that the offender was inadvertent to the significance of his conduct, and not even negligent about it, then very little moral guilt attaches to the offence.

From this discussion it emerges that the law employs a fourfold classification of the mental elements of offences: intention, recklessness, negligence and strict liability. How relevant are these to the sentencer in his task of evaluating the gravity of different offences? If the law specifies recklessness or even negligence as the threshold of criminal liability for a particular type of offence, must not the sentencer enquire further so as to discover whether the offence was in fact intentional – which might well justify him in taking a more serious view of it?

(c) Behind the 'Mens Rea'

The two mental attitudes of greatest significance in the law are intention and recklessness, and either one of them amounts to what lawyers term '*mens rea*', loosely translated as 'the guilty mind'. Neither intention nor recklessness means quite what it may appear to mean, but for present purposes it is unnecessary to enter into the refinements.[23] We can say that a person is treated as having intended a certain harm if he tried to cause it or if he realized that it was bound to follow from his actions. No such confidence can be shown in the legal definition of recklessness. As an element of *mens rea* at common law, it means that the defendant realized that there was a risk that his conduct would cause the prohibited consequences and nevertheless went on to take the risk. However, the House of Lords held in *Caldwell* (1981)[24] that where a statutory offence is defined so as to include recklessness, the definition is satisfied if the defendant would have realized the risk of causing the proscribed consequences if he had thought about it. This new concept of recklessness, which has been applied to criminal damage and rape, moves away from the idea of *mens rea* as the actual mental attitude of the defendant at the time of his conduct, towards a more 'objective' conception of guilt. However, the fundamental issues which this raises will not be pursued here.

The distinction between intention and recklessness is undoubtedly of some importance to the evaluation of culpability. The law chooses to rely on the distinction, in some instances to the extent of determining the category of offence on this basis (as with the difference between wounding with intent to cause grievous bodily harm and unlawful wounding), but moral reasoning is not constrained in that way. Contrast, for example, a case where someone deliberately sets out to fire an air pistol at another with a case where someone impulsively fires an air pistol across a busy street, realizing the risk that injury might result. We might wish to say that the former case is more serious than the latter, but the gravamen of the distinction may lie as much in the difference between planned offending and impulsive behaviour as in the distinction between intention and recklessness. In fact, the legal concept of intention is apt to cover far too wide a range of mental attitudes to be of great use in the moral evaluation of conduct. An offender may be found to have intention, for legal purposes, if he planned an offence meticulously with full appreciation of the physical and legal consequences, or if he deliberated before causing the harm, or if he suddenly decided to respond violently to a situation, or even if he struck out in what may be described as a 'split second reaction' without really thinking at all. If for the merest moment he realized what he was doing to his victim, then he would probably satisfy the legal test of intention.

English law ignores these distinctions and classifies all those mental states as 'intent'. The distinction which it often does draw is that between intention and recklessness, but recklessness too can exist in many and varied forms. For example, at the most obvious level, there can be cases where the risk is a high one and cases where the risk is low, and there can be risks taken in the heat of the moment and risks carefully calculated in advance; after the decision in *Caldwell*, risks which could have been foreseen also fall to be considered. Once again, there is a wide gulf in culpability between a high risk which has been deliberately taken and a relatively low risk taken on the spur of the moment, but in law they both fall within the same category. Nothing said here amounts to a denial of the qualitative difference between most cases of intention and most cases of recklessness: the point is that when it comes to quantifying culpability, some cases of recklessness may be treated as more serious than some cases of intention, and the sentencer also has to draw moral distinctions between kinds of intention. The approximate grading of culpability according to various mental attitudes might be sketched thus:

Table of mental attitudes

'Intention'	'Recklessness'	
planned	calculated risk	
deliberate	deliberate risk	
sudden	sudden risk	high risk
'spur of the moment'	'spur of the moment' risk	
impulse	(under *Caldwell*) a risk which could have been foreseen if thought about	low risk

This is merely a sketch: the shadings of culpability are great, and the 'definite moral and psychological difference' between intentional and reckless offending[25] is merely a small part of the whole. In cases of recklessness, there may be further shadings according to the magnitude of the risk that the offender believed he was taking. In crimes for which intention alone is sufficient (such as wounding with intent), the judge's evaluation of the offence as impulsive or premeditated is of great significance for sentencing purposes.[26] The reason for drawing distinctions of this kind is that the offender who plans his offence is not only coolly defying the law but is going to some lengths to ensure that he succeeds and, sometimes, that he is not detected. He clearly and unequivocally places his interests above the constraints imposed by society on him and all others. As Bentham put it, the longer the offender continued under the influence of antisocial motives, the more convincing is the evidence that he has rejected social motives.[27] Deliberate offending suggests the lapse of sufficient time for the offender to consider the ramifications of what he proposes to do, whereas the sudden or impulsive offence on the spur of the moment seems more to amount to a failure to restrain a strong reaction to a situation. Impulsive reactions are generally the least blameworthy kind of intentional act, inasmuch as there has hardly been a decision to take advantage of the self-restraint of others. However, where an offender has a history of violent reactions and knows the kinds of situation which arouse his temper, one may regard him as more culpable.[28]

Comparing the Table of Mental Attitudes with the earlier Table of Principal Offences against the Person, it is evident that a planned offence within a lower category might well be regarded as more heinous than an impulsive offence in a higher category. The appellate decisions show this may occur with, for example, a planned assault occasioning actual bodily harm and even an impulsive wounding with intent.[29] Thus behind the legal concept of *mens rea* lies a whole range of mental attitudes which, although irrelevant to the legal categorization of the offence, are central to its evaluation for the purposes of sentence.

Indeed, this argument may be taken further by contending, with Hadden, that the court should 'be required to assess the extent to which the offender's action was planned, impulsive or unintended, and in addition whether he had been culpably reckless, all with respect to the particular result. This would not add appreciably to the complexity of the decision to be made, and could in many cases ease the very great difficulty which the jury must face in fitting an obviously impulsive killing into the existing legal conception of intentionality.'[30] Some would argue that the complexity of trials *would* thereby be increased. But, to set against that argument, there is the moral point that if it is these distinctions rather than the difference between intent and recklessness which in reality govern severity of sentence, a defendant has the right to have them determined according to the strictest legal procedure rather than by the judge alone after conviction.[31]

(d) 'Actus Reus' and 'Mens Rea'

It is a general principle of modern English criminal law that the *mens rea* must correspond with the *actus reus*, or, in plainer words, the required mental attitude must be shown to have been directed at the kind and degree of harm specified in the offence. We may call this 'the subjective principle', and a good example of it is provided by the offence of assault: it must be proved that the defendant intended to assault the victim or was reckless as to assaulting him. But the bulk of the offences set out in the table do not accord with this principle: murder can be committed even where there is neither intent nor recklessness as to causing death, assault occasioning actual bodily harm can be committed even if the offender did not foresee the possibility of causing bodily harm, and so on. The Criminal Law Revision Committee has proposed that the more gross departures from the subjective principle should be removed from the law. It recommended, for example, that a mental attitude directed only at the causing of grievous bodily harm should no longer be sufficient for conviction of murder when the victim dies; the offence should be manslaughter and no more. The present offence of involuntary manslaughter should be abolished, because where a person intends only to commit an assault but his act unforeseeably causes death 'the offender's fault falls too far short of the unlucky result' to justify a manslaughter conviction.[32] Presumably the offender should then be convicted only of the assault he intended to inflict. But the sentencing problem would remain: should an offender who causes more harm than he contemplated be sentenced on account of the 'unlucky result'?

Although the Court of Appeal is occasionally tempted to hold that he should, the general current of decisions favours sentencing him on the basis of what he contemplated or knowingly risked at the time.[33] This is an application of the 'subjective principle of sentencing', whereby an offender should be sentenced on the basis of what he intended to do or knowingly risked doing. Its corollary is that where an offender intended to inflict more harm than he succeeded in inflicting, he should be sentenced on the basis of what he tried to do. As the Court of Appeal said when dismissing an argument for mitigation on the basis that a burglar did not take anything away, 'we think that was bad luck rather than good management on the part of the appellant.'[34] The justification of the principle[35] is that an offender ought only to be held responsible for that which he chose to bring about, or at least chose to risk. It is sometimes difficult to be sure about the degree of injury which the offender intended to inflict. As Cox put it, rather quaintly, in 1877, 'In ordinary assaults the blow is rarely aimed at any particular part of the person. When a stab, for instance, is given, accident usually determines where it shall alight and what obstacles may arrest its progress.'[36] On the other hand, cases of this kind might be encompassed by the fullest statement of the subjective principle, which is that an offender may rightly be held responsible if he knowingly risks causing a certain degree of harm. Even if a blow is not aimed at a particular part, the offender may realize the risk that it will hit one of a number of parts of the body in the general area of the strike. On the other hand, where the injury suffered by the victim is greater than ought reasonably to have been foreseen – or, in precise legal terms, greater than the offender actually thought he was risking – he ought not to be held responsible for the excess over what he intended. Cox put the point thus:

> On the one side, the crime is not diminished because accidentally no great injury has been done by that which might equally have caused death; on the other side, the extent of the wound is no proof that injury to that extent was designed.[37]

Of course, there may be a tendency to impose a higher sentence where an offender intends an assault and causes death without foreseeing the possibility – should not the very fact of death resulting from his criminal behaviour be marked by at least some augmentation of sentence? Emotive considerations there may be in favour of this course, but in logical terms it flows not from the subjective principle but from the wide view that anyone who sets out to commit a crime must answer for all the consequences which result, however unexpected they may be. English law has been trying, from the seventeenth century onwards, to break away from that view and to move towards the subjective principle (although the widening of 'recklessness' in *Caldwell* goes against that principle). It would be extraordinary and unfitting if the judges should, in the exercise of their sentencing discretion, restore the substance of that discarded and draconian doctrine.[38]

One reason why the law itself has not moved more quickly and more unequivocally towards the subjective principle is precisely *because* the courts can give practical effect to prevailing moral doctrines in their sentencing. On this view it matters little whether a person who intends an assault and actually causes death is convicted of manslaughter, because the sentence of the court can reflect the fact that the death was an unforeseeable and unlucky result, and the court can explain the matter when passing sentence. Equally it could be said to matter little if the wide range of possible offences of damage to property are reduced to a single broad offence with a high maximum penalty, as occurred in the Criminal Damage Act 1971, because again the courts can adequately reflect the various shadings of gravity and culpability in the sentences they pass.[39] It is not in every sphere that the criminal law has opted for the broadest possible offences: crimes of violence might in theory be reduced to a single offence of causing personal harm to another, leaving the courts to mark the variations in the degree of harm (from death to a mere scratch) and in mental attitudes with the sentences they passed, but the Criminal Law Revision Committee has proposed that we should retain a set of distinct offence-labels which would differentiate between murder, manslaughter, serious injury, injury and assault.[40] In this way the law itself can perform part of the expressive or labelling function which in other respects is left to the observations of the court on passing sentence, it can structure the discretion of the courts, and it can ensure that an offender's record more accurately characterizes his previous crimes.

For so long as the law does contain offences for which the necessary *mens rea* does not correspond to the harm caused, and indeed for so long as the law eschews distinctions between mental attitudes other than that between intention and recklessness, sentencers must shoulder a heavy burden in the evaluation of culpability. In doing this they will act on certain assumptions and certain definitions, and the argument here is that the general approach should be based on the subjective principle of sentencing, combined with the view that the gravity of a crime increases with the amount of time for deliberation before the offence, save in cases where an impulsive attacker knows from experience that he is likely to react violently in given situations. However, it will also be argued below that this subjective approach should be extended in certain circumstances.

(e) **Elements of justification**
We have mentioned that the law permits self-defence, defence of property, the prevention of crime and parental discipline as complete defences of criminal liability for the use of force in certain circumstances, usually rather vaguely delineated by the concept of reasonableness. Just as the basis of social life might be threatened if there were no general prohibition on the use of force, so the survival of each individual might be at the mercy of anyone unless a right to use force in self-defence were recognized. Just as the law determines the circumstances in which the use of force is a criminal offence, so (and indeed as part of the same exercise) it determines the circumstances in which some violence is permissible. The law generally uses the concept of 'reasonableness' to mark the boundaries of permissibility, and this concept effectively leaves the decision in the hands of the court in each case. Supposing, however, that a defendant is convicted of an offence of violence in a case where he meant to teach a lesson to

an obvious malefactor (e.g. a persistent trespasser on his land) but went beyond the boundaries of permissible force, how should the court approach the matter on sentence? The use of force in such a case is invariably intentional, and may even be deliberate or planned (on the scale suggested above); but should the fact that the offender believed he was acting with moral or even legal justification be treated as reducing the seriousness of the crime? Members of extreme political or religious groups sometimes claim a moral or social justification for using force, but their cases might be distinguished on the ground that their beliefs are incompatible with the prevailing social order whereas the 'vigilante' is acting on an unlawfully exaggerated version of the socially accepted principle that force may be used where reasonable and necessary in self-defence or the prevention of crime. Indeed, it might be said that generally the courts look more benignly upon motives for offending which are loosely compatible with the prevailing social order than upon those which challenge it. Determinations of what factors should mitigate and what factors should aggravate will naturally tend to be made according to principles which are consistent with the courts' views of maintaining the legal system and its institutions.

This leads to questions of the 'protection' of those whose task is the enforcement of the law. Should sentencers treat the fact that the force was used against a law enforcement officer as an aggravating factor? The law itself indicates that such cases ought to be singled out for separate and more severe treatment. Assaulting a constable in the execution of his duty is a separate offence (although by an anomaly it carries a lower rather than a higher maximum penalty than common assault). However, there is an indictable offence of assault with intent to resist arrest which carries a maximum of 2 years' imprisonment; inflicting grievous bodily harm or wounding with intent to resist arrest is an offence which carries life imprisonment, even though on the strict words of the provision it appears that the prosecution need not establish that there was an intent to wound or to cause grievous bodily harm; and it may be recalled that when the Homicide Act 1957 marked out certain kinds of murder as 'capital murders' three of the categories were the murder of a police officer, the murder of a prison officer and a murder committed whilst resisting arrest. In their recent review of the law, the Criminal Law Revision Committee regarded it as important that the courts should continue to impose higher sentences on those who use violence against the police.

. . . there is some danger that if the offence of assaulting a constable were abolished the special protection afforded by the courts at present to the police might be eroded. Moreover, it is advantageous that a court when sentencing should be clearly apprised of the fact that a previous assault committed by the defendant was upon a police officer. Furthermore, if assault on a police officer is likely to be treated as a matter deserving of imprisonment, then in our opinion it should be proved that the police officer was acting in the execution of his duty and that the defendant knew that he was assaulting a police officer or was reckless as to whether his victim was a police officer.[41]

This passage raises at least three important points for the present discussion. The last point is an example of what was earlier described as an extension of the subjective principle; the extension is that where the defendant is proved to have known that the victim of his violence was or might be a police officer,[42] it is right to regard his offence as more serious than if he lacked that knowledge. It is a general social proposition that violence against those enforcing the law is regarded as particularly grave, and offenders are therefore rightly taken to understand this.

Another point raised by the quotation from the report of the Criminal Law Revision Committee is that many regard the more severe sentences imposed in these cases as constituting 'protection' of the police. That relies on the deterrent reasoning that the higher penalties commonly imposed for violence against police officers are widely known and actually exert an effect on individuals who find themselves in situations where there is a choice between violence or quiet submission, to the extent that the higher penalties deter individuals from violence when the ordinary penalties would not. Whether this process occurs to any significant extent may be doubted. The retributive aim of sentencing may provide an independent justification for higher penalties which begs no factual questions about the marginal effect of general deterrence. This justification relies on the position of the police as the body who are charged by the State with the task of enforcing the laws. Indeed, Cox argued that assaults on the police should receive double the punishment of ordinary assaults, because of the defiance of the law and the injury to the public arising from the attempt to prevent officers from performing their public duty.[43] Earlier, the Criminal Law Commissioners had argued that such a rule is one which 'policy, or rather necessity, peremptorily requires' because it is 'essential to the very existence of law as an imperative rule of conduct'.[44] Submission of citizens to lawful authority is an important part of social order: assaulting a law enforcement officer is therefore morally worse than assaulting a private citizen, *ceteris paribus*, because of the implied rejection of the authority of the law itself.

This reasoning shows the importance of courts explaining the reasons for a particular sentence, particularly where the offender is not charged with one of the separate 'police' offences and is convicted of one of the general offences against the person. The symbolic or expressive function becomes all the more important in those cases where there is most unlikely to be a separate offence – such as where the violence is used against an official (not being a police officer) who is endeavouring lawfully to restrain the offender, or indeed against an ordinary member of the public who is exercising a power of arrest or who is assisting another to do so. Once again, if it is established that the offender knew that the victim was attempting to arrest him, there is justification for regarding the offence as aggravated.[45] The same rationale of submission to lawful authority applies. Citizens have a liberty to prevent crime and apprehend offenders whereas the police have a duty, but in either event resistance by the offender is a serious matter. There will be difficult cases, as where either a police officer or an ordinary citizen purports to exercise a power of arrest against an individual who is and knows himself to be completely innocent, and that individual resists violently. If in such a case the offender were convicted on the basis that he had used excessive force in the circumstances, the sentencer would have to take account of both of the offender's supposition that he was behaving rightly in resisting what he took to be an unwarranted incursion on his liberty, and of the general policy of marking public disapproval of those who use undue force against persons enforcing the law of the land. Such cases will be very few, and should not be magnified so as to obscure the general policy of disapproving of violence against the police.

The other side of the coin is violence committed *by* a person who has undertaken a public duty of enforcing the law. Society not only mandates such a person to uphold the law and permits him to use a reasonable amount of necessary force (in the name of the State) in order to do so, but society trusts him not to abuse that power. A deterrent rationale could be advanced for treating force unlawfully used by police officers as aggravated in the sense that sentences of increased severity are likely to deter them from exceeding their powers in this way. But a more solid justification, which again begs no factual questions about the marginal effect of general deterrence, is that such offences are more heinous because the officer abuses the position of authority which has been bestowed upon him. Thus in *Lewis* (1976)[46] a police officer with 24 years' service was convicted of assault occasioning bodily harm against a suspect, and, despite his excellent record and the fact that he was under the combined influence of alcohol and pain-killing drugs, the Court of Appeal upheld the sentence of 2 years' imprisonment in the public interest. Clearly it is the breach of trust which is being marked by the longer sentence: a police constable's oath includes the promise, made before a Justice of the Peace, to 'prevent all offences against the persons and properties of Her Majesty's subjects'. It is one thing to fail to prevent obvious and serious offences;[47] it is even more serious to commit the very kinds of offence that the officer has solemnly and publicly promised to prevent. To some extent the same considerations apply to others who have undertaken responsibilities for the welfare of individuals upon whom they subsequently use unlawful force.[48]

These arguments about the relative justifiability of different kinds of physical attack perpetrated by an offender of a certain status or upon a victim of a certain status may be generalized into the view that the 'legitimacy of the occasion' is a significant factor in the evaluation of violence. As Hadden wrote some years ago,

the illegitimacy of the occasion on which the injury was inflicted may often outweigh the considerations raised in dealing with the mental element in isolation: an impulsive killing in the course of a robbery might be thought to be more serious than a planned and premeditated murder in an impossible domestic situation.[49]

This passage reminds us of a consideration which must be kept in view throughout the present discussion, which is that we are taking in isolation a number of factors which will usually appear in clusters and which may require the sentencer to consider their relative weight and the priority of the relevant principles. The 'legitimacy of the occasion' is therefore put forward merely as one possible factor which, other things being equal, will affect the gravity with which an offence is viewed. Where, for example, violence is used in the heat of the moment by an offender in resisting arrest, does the illegitimacy of the occasion outweigh the impulsivity of the offender's conduct? In other words, can we say whether the aggravating and mitigating factors balance one another out, or whether one is normally more powerful than the other? It might be argued that it is fruitless to debate abstract questions of this kind. Yet that response abandons the inquiry at the very stage which is likely to be crucial for the individual sentencer. If no guidance is given on questions of priority such as this, there is a real danger that different sentencers may place different weight on essentially the same factors. Some will give priority to the illegitimacy of the occasion, others will allow it to be overridden by the mitigating effect of the impulsive nature of the offender's conduct. The suggestion here is that although impulsivity or 'heat of the moment' recklessness should be accorded some mitigating effect, neither should outweigh the duty to submit without violence to the lawful authority of a police officer. This is put forward not as an absolute but as a general proposition, which should guide the sentencer's approach unless there are other factors in the case. It is not uncontroversial: it rests on the value judgment that attacks on police officers are so direct a challenge to the social order that the aggravating effect of such an attack should outweigh all but the most appealing set of mitigating circumstances, and that it is important to mark this by regarding it as an aggravated form of the offence, justifying a more severe sentence than the assault itself (if committed on not such an 'illegitimate' occasion) would have warranted. A practical drawback to this view is that from time to time the police are known to exceed their powers, and also that the offence of assaulting a constable may be used as a 'resource charge' in a somewhat technical way so as to justify arresting a person who was not showing deference to the police officer. It is highly likely that some such cases occur; when they do occur, the individual is in a poor position to authenticate his version of events and a court may well believe the police officer. There is no English study of the circumstances in which offences of assaulting a police officer come to be charged, and so there is no basis for asserting that 'doubtful' cases form a majority or minority of police assaults coming before the courts. The assumption here is that they form such a small minority that it remains right to take a serious view of such cases, even though it is difficult for a defendant to establish that the case against him has been 'trumped up'. To adopt this approach is to trample hard upon the rights of those who have been wrongly charged but cannot prove it; but that is no more uncomfortable than a failure to mark the general aggravating effect of committing an offence against someone who was enforcing the law.

Returning to the quotation from Hadden, his example of the illegitimacy of the occasion was killing in the course of robbery. The

Homicide Act 1957 retained as a form of capital murder (until 1965) 'any murder done in the course or furtherance of theft', and this included burglaries and robberies. It is unclear in logical terms why the distinction should be drawn between murders in the course of acquisitive crimes and murders in the course of other crimes such as rape or arson. One possible deterrent rationale is that acquisitive crimes are more likely than rapes or arsons to be committed by professional criminals, who might be expected to calculate the advantages and disadvantages of using force. As for a retributive rationale, it is difficult to see why these occasions for the use of violence ought to attract heavier penalties. They are not mitigated cases, it is true, but there are no special duties which warrant an aggravated sentence. There will in any event be an element in the sentence for each offence (the crime which he was committing, and the violence he used in the course or furtherance of it), and that ensures that such an offender is, *ceteris paribus*, treated more severely than the offender who commits the same offence of violence without the wider criminal context. If that is all that the 'illegitimacy' of the occasion adds in this instance, then the point is a fair one.

Another type of case which might be generalized as an 'illegitimate occasion' is where violence is used against a young child. Such offences may be viewed as aggravated forms of violence because (a) adults have a duty towards children, particularly those to whom they are parent or guardian, which gives them a special responsibility, and (b) children are less able to defend themselves than adults and it is, *ceteris paribus*, morally worse to use violence against a defenceless person than against someone who has a real opportunity to make some defence or escape. Another point which is raised in this context, although it is not unique to violence against children, is that an incident of domestic violence may often have been preceded by a course of ill-treatment which had not previously come to light. Often these previous occasions of violence are neither the subject of distinct charges nor taken into consideration as offences admitted by the offender, and it is therefore on sentence for the current offence that the previous conduct comes into the reckoning.[49a] The Court of Appeal decisions suggest a threefold grading of offences according to their context:[50]

- a course of persistent ill-treatment
- a single outburst of repeated blows
- a single blow

The justification for treating such cases differently runs parallel to the justification for treating planned offences as more serious than impulsive crimes. Probably few cases of violence against children could be described as planned, but the argument is that a long course of ill-treatment suggests that at the very least the offender had some opportunity to find another way out of the domestic situation which allegedly led to the violence, and for that reason such cases are morally worse than cases involving a single incident. The distinction between a single incident which involves repeated blows and a single incident with one blow is perhaps less persuasive, for in many cases of repeated blows the offender's story is that he completely lost self-control or 'went berserk'. If that is accepted, then it would seem unfair to hold him fully responsible for the extent of the violence inflicted after loss of self-control, although it can be argued that he should not have lost control at all towards a child, or at least not to the extent he did. These arguments will be taken up when discussing provocation.[51] The infliction of a single blow, in a momentary fit of temper or frustration, is an indication less of wickedness than of a failure to control the natural urges to which we are all subject. The duty to control such urges when in charge of a young child remains primary, but a less censorious view of the offence may then be taken.

Cases of this kind raise, once again, formidable problems of priority. Many cases of violence against children are characterized by such normally mitigating factors as lack of sleep, exasperation, overcrowded or otherwise constricting domestic circumstances, and depression; but on many occasions the Court of Appeal has held that these factors should not be allowed the substantial mitigating effect they might have in other types of case.[52] The Court's reason for this is 'the need to mark public revulsion' against this type of offence. Certainly the symbolic function of sentencing is much to the fore in these cases. There is a separate offence of wilfully assaulting or neglecting a child, contrary to section 1 of the Children and Young Persons Act 1933, but it has a relatively low maximum penalty (2 years' imprisonment), which is insufficient for the more gross forms of violence. It is therefore common to charge one of the general offences against the person, and this leaves it to the court to state clearly the relevance to sentencing of the fact that the victim was a young child. The 'public revulsion' to which the courts refer can be rationalized on the ground that the parental duty towards a child is so central to social organization, and the child's ability to determine its own fate and to defend itself is so negligible, that the duty should be regarded as overriding all but the most powerful of mitigating factors. The question of priority, then, should once again be decided generally in favour of the duty towards young children.

If part of the rationale for regarding violence against children as aggravated offences is that children are less able to defend themselves, then this supplies a reason for regarding offences against disabled victims, against the elderly and (perhaps) women as more serious than offences committed by one man upon another. Arguments based on the unequal position of offender and victim are also relevant to the question of the methods of inflicting harm, to which we now turn.

(f) Methods of inflicting harm

The method which the offender employs in the infliction of violence may have a significant bearing on the gravity of his offence. Some might argue that where a firearm is used or carried in another crime the severity of the sentence should be increased for reasons of general deterrence. However, it may be questioned whether such a policy has the marginal deterrent effect which is claimed,[53] and it is sounder to consider the various moral reasons for treating weapons as aggravating factors. One reason why the *carrying* (as distinct from the *use*) of a weapon may be regarded as an aggravating factor is that it can usually be inferred that the offender contemplated the use of violence and had prepared himself for it. In the nineteenth century Cox recognized that there were a number of factors which a sentencer ought to consider 'for the purpose of resolving whether and to what extent there was deliberation in the use of the weapon'.

> How came it into the hands of the defendant? Had he been using it for some lawful purpose? Was it in his hand at the moment of the assault? Or was it snatched up as it lay near? Or was it taken from some other place of deposit? Was the possession of it prompted by any supposed requirement for defence, or was it purely aggressive?[54]

Thus, unless there is a credible story of self-protection against an anticipated attack, the *carrying* of a weapon will usually give rise to the inference of planning and premeditation. Where the weapon was used although it had not been previously carried, other inferences may be drawn according to the circumstances.

Quite how the law should take account of this factor of aggravation, in a procedural sense, is open to dispute. There are separate offences for the carrying of firearms and the carrying of offensive weapons, although the maximum penalty for offensive weapons stands at 2 years' imprisonment: one approach would be invariably to charge both the offence of violence committed and the crime of possessing a firearm or offensive weapon, and then to impose a separate and consecutive sentence for the latter offence; another approach is merely to charge the offence of violence committed, and to regard the carrying of the firearm or offensive weapon as an aggravating factor in that offence. So long as the sentencer mentioned the significance of the weapon in explaining his sentence, the only difference would be that the offender's criminal record might not reveal the offender's possession of a firearm or other weapon (which might be material to sentencing in later cases) and that the symbolic function of the court might be less adequately fulfilled if there is no separate conviction for a distinctly labelled offence of possessing a firearm or offensive weapon.

The total sentence should be the same whichever approach is taken, but the separate charge, conviction and sentence is preferable on a number of grounds, and is now favoured by the Court of Appeal.[55]

A second reason why the carrying of a weapon should be regarded as an aggravating factor, quite apart from the inference of deliberation, is that a weapon may make it more likely that injury (indeed, serious injury) will result from a violent encounter. Clearly this is the case with a firearm: a single shot can be fatal, and this supplies a strong reason for regarding the carrying of firearms as specially blameworthy (and, on the deterrent view, for an increased penalty in the hope of discouraging offenders from arming themselves). This can be conjoined with a third reason, which is that if one person has a firearm the other is placed at a great disadvantage in the encounter. In the seventeenth and eighteenth centuries, there was much law on the doctrine of 'change medley', whereby a killing might be reduced from murder to manslaughter if it occurred in the course of a sudden fight between two persons who were more or less evenly armed. Modern law no longer shows indulgence towards fights of that kind (although it does excuse violence inflicted in the course of sports such as boxing according to the Queensberry rules), but the moral view that offences where there is a disparity of weapons should be viewed as more serious than offences where the parties fight on even terms surely survives. It was argued above that the defenceless position of a young child was one reason for regarding violence against children as aggravated; that was extended to cover the disabled and the elderly; the same point applies, surely to the use of firearms. However, where both parties have firearms the third rationale for treating such cases as aggravated does not apply, for the parties are on even terms. The second rationale – the inherent likelihood of death or serious injury – then predominates.

Is there a convincing reason why we should regard cases involving firearms as more serious than poisoning, for example? The Homicide Act 1957 retained capital punishment for murders 'by shooting or by causing an explosion': other categories of murder (such as murders of police or prison officers) were also retained as capital, but shooting or causing an explosion were the only *methods* of killing which were to attract the ultimate sanction. The Home Secretary argued that these methods were selected in order to deter professional criminals from carrying weapons and to discourage indiscriminate murders. Neither reason was sufficient to support the particular provision. Knives and many other weapons fell outside it, and poisoning can be indiscriminate but was excluded. This led to the retort that the Government had singled out 'noisy' murders, and the following address to a person convicted of capital murder was put forward in jest:[56]

> You are not only a murderer but a noisy murderer. You upset people. You not only commit one of the wickedest offences a human being can commit, but you needs must go and make a noise about it, and very probably the Home Secretary will have to answer questions about you in the House of Commons. If you show disregard of public decency to the extent that you not only murder people but do it in a noisy fashion, you must expect to be put to death.

The lampooning of the 1957 Act should put us on guard against too simplistic an approach to classification. In general it is fair to say that firearms can be more lethal than other weapons or methods, that they put the victim at a greater disadvantage, and that often their use (where there is forearmament) is evidence of premeditation. Yet on each of these counts, poisoning remains difficult to distinguish – a strong poison can be lethal and indiscriminate, the victim is at the very great disadvantage that he does not realize his life is being threatened, and poisoning probably justifies an inference of premeditation in as many situations as does the use of a firearm. One distinguishing feature is that firearms tend to put victims in a terrible state of fear, whereas poisoning may not do so, but enough has surely been said to justify the view that poisoning itself should generally be treated as an aggravating factor when evaluating the seriousness of an offence against the person. It is true that other methods – such as strangulation, asphyxiation, kicking, punching, butting and perhaps the use of an instrument found close at hand (and not brought with a view to use) – may occasionally justify an inference of premeditation or another aggravating feature; it is equally true that a factor which might normally be treated as an aggravating feature may not be so regarded in a particular case – as, for instance, where a farmer who lawfully possesses a shotgun turns it against another person with whom he is arguing: anyone with a firearms certificate has a duty to take great care and not to abuse the special liberty granted to him, but even then his offence is less serious than one involving an unlawfully possessed firearm. But, by and large, there are sufficient grounds for drawing distinctions on the basis of the method used to effect the crime, so long as the underlying criteria remain in view – planning and premeditation, inherent likelihood of serious harm, disparity between the offender and victim.

(g) **Provocation**

It has traditionally been thought that provocation is *par excellence* a factor which should go in mitigation of sentence rather than justifying a reduction in the category of the offence. Provocation is allowed as a defence to murder in English law, reducing the crime to 'voluntary manslaughter', because of the mandatory penalty for murder. Its extension to other crimes against the person, as a defence which would justify a reduction in the class of offence, was mooted by the Criminal Law Revision Committee but quietly dropped in its final report.[57] Juries have been known to treat provocation as a complete defence to lesser crimes, despite judicial directions to the contrary, but usually the issue of provocation is first raised at the sentencing stage. The sentencer then has to decide whether, and if so to what extent, the provocation should be regarded as a mitigating factor.

Two factors seem important in the evaluation of the provocation received – the relative strength of the provocation itself, and the degree to which the retaliation was sudden and impulsive. The criteria of strength of provocation are difficult to state. At one extreme, it is clear that where an individual returns home to find his or her spouse in bed with someone else that is generally regarded as strong provocation which will substantially mitigate an impulsive wounding or even homicide; it is also clear that a man who bullies other members of his family provides strong provocation. In this kind of case, the mitigation of sentence is some recognition of the value (e.g. physical security or marital fidelity) which the provoker was violating and which the offender may be seen as upholding (albeit by an excessive show of violence). At the other extreme, it is unlikely whether calling someone a name would in ordinary circumstances be treated as provocation for more than a slight assault, although in particular circumstances (such as a history of verbal taunting) it might do. A more intractable difficulty arises in cases where the provocation is alleged to have been 'cumulative', so that the final provoking act may appear trivial if viewed in isolation but takes on a different character in the context of a course of previous conduct. Should the sentencer take account of the whole course of conduct in assessing the strength of the provocation received by the offender? If so, should the provocative course of conduct be regarded as weakening the provocation on the argument that the offender had ample time to come to terms with it and to take other (non-violent) measures, or as weakening his resistance to stress on the argument that he was progressively tormented and eventually his self-restraint gave way? The answer given to this question by each sentencer will be crucial to his sentencing decision. Yet the Court of Appeal seem unclear on the question, having adopted each argument in different cases,[58] despite the fact that it is extremely rare to find a case of manslaughter upon provocation in which the provocation was *not* to some extent cumulative.

The question goes to the very heart of provocation as a mitigating factor. Does provocation primarily mitigate because of the understandable nature of the offender's violent response to a wrong done either to him or to someone close to him? If so, the enormity of that wrong will largely determine the strength of the provocation. Or does provocation primarily mitigate because it excuses the offender's behaviour on the basis that he reacted in an uncontrolled manner to something which he regarded (and others would not necessarily regard) as provocation? If so, it is the degree to which the offender lost control over his actions which will determine the strength of the provocation. In ordinary language, it is the difference between 'he was *provoked*' and '*he* was provoked'. In fact most cases involve both factors to an extent, but that leaves a question of priority to be decided in those cases where the factors are not evenly balanced. Is the man who totally loses his self-control and causes grievous bodily harm to another as a result merely of being derided as a 'Yorkshire peasant' to be regarded, *ceteris paribus*, as equally worthy of mitigation as the person who impulsively causes grievous bodily harm to a man whom he surprises in a state of undress in his own bedroom? What if the insult was one which had peculiar significance for this offender because of his race or religion? Before approaching these questions, it is worthwhile to consider the second question in provocation cases – was the retaliation sudden and impulsive?

It is the elements of suddenness and impulsivity which serve to distinguish provocation as a mitigating factor from revenge, which may be treated as an aggravating factor because it is usually accompanied by planning and premeditation. Swift and impulsive retaliation is far less blameworthy than the deliberate fetching and even the purchasing of a weapon, which suggests time for reflection. If the retaliation is made on the spur of the moment, then it is less a considered breach of the law than a momentary failure to control natural passions which were understandably aroused (but ought to have been controlled). In cases where there was strong provocation but where the offender appears to have taken his time in retaliating, then, subject to any evidence about his personality which suggests that he is of the type who stores up anger rather than giving vent to it immediately,[59] the case should be regarded as close to a case of revenge. Some of the cases in which verdicts of manslaughter upon provocation have been returned come extremely close to being revenge murders.

Is provocation primarily a ground for mitigation based on the degree to which the offender himself was provoked to lose his self-control, or is it based on the extent to which the events which provoked the offender would be regarded by most people as provocative? It is suggested that in principle it ought to be the latter. Where the individual offender's reaction was more a function of his own psychological or other condition than of the objective strength of the provocation, the case ought to be regarded as one for personal mitigation (on grounds of mental disturbance, for example) and not as a case of provocation. This approach has the advantage that the courts may then stipulate roughly what they are and what they are not willing to accept as provocation. This is likely to be important in cases where the 'illegitimacy of the occasion' is great. Thus it is probable that most of those involved in violence against children are in some sense provoked; but the law may effectively rule out that ground of mitigation in such cases, imposing on parents and others the primary duty of retaining self-control in dealing with children. The offender will be left to argue for mitigation on personal grounds, but without the aid of provocation as a distinct doctrine. The same might apply in cases of violence against the police: doubtless some of the offenders were provoked, in the sense that they were caused to lose their self-control, but society might imply a primary duty to retain control if the police are merely attempting a lawful arrest.

Some have argued that too great an indulgence is shown towards cases of violence preceded by provocation. Can it ever be right to pass a relatively slight sentence (such as a conditional discharge or suspended sentence) where life has been intentionally taken, albeit under strong provocation? Cox argued that in cases of this kind courts cannot be content merely 'to apportion the punishment to the degree of moral guilt involved in the particular offence', and he argued strongly for a deterrent approach even in cases where there had been provocation, because crimes of violence

are more noxious to the community by the terror and distrust they occasion, by their dangerous tendency to incite irregularly constructed minds to imitation and the dissolution of society itself that would result from extensive following of the example.[60]

Cox's argument assumes that if cases of provocation were punished more harshly this might have some general effect on the number of such crimes and upon the amount of violence in general; others, even among the utilitarian theorists, might tend towards the view that mitigation in cases of provocation does not cause significant loss to the deterrent effect of the law. But quite apart from arguments about deterrence, Cox's view is a poignant reminder that even the most extreme provocation must be viewed in the light of the harm which the offender then went on to inflict. If the prohibition of violence really is regarded as so central to the existence of society, this is a strong reason for taking a more restrictive view of the mitigating effect of provocation in cases of violence. Inasmuch as sentencers take a broader view, they choose to give greater weight to the mitigating effect of loss of self-control, particularly when that loss of self-control was an understandable response to a situation which the offender regarded as a wrong to him. In a sense the courts are accepting the values of hypothetical 'reasonable men' rather than reasonable values in according this mitigation – for some would argue that to find another man in the act of adultery with one's wife is not the 'highest' provocation, a notion which derives from the idea of a married woman as her husband's possession. So long as the mitigation is based on understandable rather than reasonable loss of self-control, these points need not be argued.

(h) Intoxication

What is the effect of intoxication on the moral gravity of offences of violence? The question brings into play a series of distinctions no less complicated than those found in other areas. An obvious variable is the degree of intoxication: not only may a given quantity of intoxicants have varying effects on different individuals, but the degree of intoxication progressively weakens self-control, so that the completely intoxicated offender presents a different problem from the offender who is merely 'tipsy'. Alongside these individual differences must be ranged certain general social propositions: each individual probably has some idea of the amount of intoxicants he or she can consume without losing control, and everyone is surely aware of the disinhibiting effects of intoxication.

How does the offence of someone who is completely intoxicated compare with an intentional or reckless infliction of the same harm? Since (for legal purposes at least) complete intoxication is defined in terms of the absence of intent, knowledge or recklessness, the offences stand at opposite ends of the spectrum of mental attitudes. Complete intoxication negatives any choice to cause or to risk causing the harm which ensued. Although there is therefore no direct link between the harm done and the offender's mental direction and control, the two 'general social propositions' articulated above combine to impose some responsibility upon the offender. The degree of fault is not necessarily reflected by the nature and degree of the harm caused. The offender's real fault lies in allowing himself to become so intoxicated that he could not control and direct his actions, thereby creating the risk that harm would result. When an offender is being blamed for knowingly creating a risk, it becomes important to enquire about the magnitude of the risk, and the justifications for taking it. We have no statistical evidence of the proportion of those people who become completely intoxicated who subsequently act violently, or indeed who subsequently commit any kind of criminal act, but the proportion would probably be very low. There may be some social justification for the moderate use of alcohol, as a means of inducing relaxation in those who are unduly tense, but that hardly extends to complete intoxication. It might therefore be argued that total intoxication has no social value, and that any amount of danger arising from this degree of intoxication is too great. The further question whether the law ought not to prohibit intoxication and regard it as a serious offence does not concern us here. Our concern is to assess the gravity of an offence committed by someone who was completely intoxicated.

A pragmatic solution would be to sentence the offender on the basis that he knowingly risked causing the harm – to sentence him as a reckless offender, even though it cannot be established that he was actually reckless.[61] It is difficult, if not impossible, for a court to determine whether he really was so intoxicated that he did not realize what he was doing and could not control his actions. This solution proceeds on the footing that either he was not so completely intoxicated or, if he was, that he ought to be restrained for a considerable period on preventive grounds. But the preventive argument raises questions about the likelihood of his making the same mistake again: the argument in favour of passing a preventive sentence upon an offender whose intoxication has more than once led him into crime is far stronger than that in favour of passing a substantial sentence upon an offender for his first conviction under these circumstances. Even if his first intoxicated crime was man-slaughter, a court which was satisfied that he was completely intoxicated at the time of the offence can logically only sentence him for his fault in becoming intoxicated, not in relation to the degree of harm actually caused. It was presumably this style of reasoning which led the Butler Committee to recommend that the first conviction for their proposed offences of 'dangerous intoxication'[62] should have a maximum penalty of only one year's imprisonment, whatever harm had been caused. The gravity with which we view the first intoxicated offence of violence depends on beliefs about the culpability of complete intoxication, not upon an assessment of the harm actually done.

Complete intoxication is more culpable in itself, yet has greater effect on a person's knowledge of and control over his actions, than partial intoxication. Where the offender was partially intoxicated, had some knowledge and control of what he was doing, but nevertheless offended in a way that he would probably not have done whilst sober, his responsibility is perhaps closest to the impulsive offender. He realizes what he is doing, he could control himself, but his inhibitions more readily give way as a result of the intoxication.

Once again, it is fair to distinguish between the offender who knows from past experience of the likelihood of his behaving in this way, and the offender for whom the offence is out of character.

The upshot of this argument is that intoxication is in general neither an aggravating nor a mitigating factor, and the main reason for this is that the ordinary mitigating effect of weakened self-control and less appreciation of the situation is counterbalanced by the aggravating effect of the general social propositions about the use of intoxicants.

3. Culpability and personal responsibility

In the discussion of offences of violence it was argued that the legal concept of *mens rea* is not an adequate tool for the moral evaluation of culpability, and that we ought instead to consider a range of mental attitudes which constitute a scale of responsibility. Attending to these mental attitudes shares the same justification as the legal doctrine of *mens rea*, and this is what we shall call the subjective principle. Its essence is that a person should only be held responsible for an offence if and to the extent that he chose to commit it, believed he was committing it or knowingly risked committing it. It is therefore his choosing which ought to govern both the existence and the extent of his responsibility. The subjective principle therefore serves as a principle of criminal liability, prescribing what ought (in general)[63] to be a minimum condition of liability for any offence, and, as a principle of sentencing, prescribing the degree of an offender's responsibility for what did or did not follow from his action.

The subjective principle can be said to serve both as an exculpatory and as an inculpatory principle. What it does, in effect, is to reduce the role of chance in the determination of personal responsibility. Thus where the offender intends a mere assault upon his victim and unexpectedly causes death, the subjective principle prescribes that his responsibility should extend only so far as he knew that he was creating a certain risk. Where death follows unexpectedly, his 'fault falls too far short of the unlucky result'[64] and he ought only to be held responsible to the degree that he intended or knowingly risked causing harm to the victim. In other words, in this example he should be held responsible for an assault and nothing more. The subjective principle also operates to diminish the role of chance in a case where an offender shoots to kill his victim and misses. In this type of case the offender intends to cause harm and fails, but where that failure is a matter of chance he might properly be held responsible to the degree that he intended causing harm. His liability will be for an attempted crime, rather than a completed crime, but in moral terms the extent of his responsibility is rightly governed by the extent of the harm which he chose and tried to cause.

It would, however, be short-sighted and erroneous to lay such emphasis on the element of choice if there were substantial doubt about the capacity of individuals to control their actions. To hold a person responsible for an action which he could not avoid or 'could not help' clearly runs counter to the spirit of the subjective principle, even if the situation was such that the individual could foresee what was going to happen and thus literally satisfied that principle. Where an action lies beyond the individual's control, he should not be held responsible for it. Or, to cast this into a wider principle of moral responsibility, 'one cannot be more culpable or estimable for anything than one is for that fraction of it which is under one's control.'[65] To the extent that one's behaviour is governed by factors outside one's control, there should be no responsibility.

The debate then moves to the concept of 'control'. What does it mean in this context? Hart has argued that it is wrong to place primary emphasis on the element of choice, as represented by intention, knowledge and recklessness. These mental attitudes are not in themselves as important as another factor:

> What is crucial is that those whom we punish should have had, when they acted, the normal capacities, physical and mental, for doing what the law requires and abstaining from what it forbids, and a fair opportunity to exercise these capacities.[66]

On this view, having the normal capacities and a fair opportunity to exercise them is sufficient as a *ground* of moral responsibility. As a *measure* of moral responsibility (which is our principal concern in sentencing contexts) it might be argued on this view that responsibility may be reduced in circumstances where the offender 'had, owing to some external cause, lost the power of [normal] control'.[67] Hart's reference here is to cases where an offender was provoked by another and as a result lost his self-control ('external cause'). In the absence of any such 'external' explanation for a failure of control, and in the absence of any other obvious deprivation of control (Hart instances 'paralysis, reflex action, coercion, insanity'), are we entitled to assume that the offender did have control over the actions which he knew he was doing?

At one level we are. A possible barrier is the doctrine of determinism, which in its strongest form insists that individuals lack freedom of choice and that all actions are predetermined by causes outside the individual's control. But Kenny has demonstrated that no convincing reason has yet been produced to establish that determinism is either true or false, and that even if we accept certain forms of physiological determinism we need not abandon the commonsense view that in most matters we have some choice whether to act or refrain from acting.[68] Moreover the law is not necessarily wrong to focus its enquiries, when determining the existence of grounds for criminal liability, upon what Hart calls the 'psychological elements' and what have here been called the mental attitudes. Criticisms along these lines have been made, often in relation to the legal definition of insanity (which takes account only of cognitive factors and not of the power of control over actions). But the intellect and the will are merely abstractions which we tend to use in analysing and evaluating behaviour: they are not separate compartments of any known phenomenon (the mind, too, is an abstraction), and we can surely follow Kenny in arguing that intellect and will are closely related in human action and that 'an investigation of an agent's ability to understand what he is doing . . . is not something distinct from, and irrelevant to, an inquiry into the effectiveness of his will.'[69]

However, to adopt Kenny's defence of the law's concentration on cognitive tests of responsibility is not to conclude the debate about the concept of control: hence the qualification 'at one level', with which the preceding paragraph began. There are at least two important respects in which the principle that 'one cannot be more culpable or estimable for anything than one is for that fraction of it which is under one's control' might be invoked to sever the assumed connection between cognizance and control. There are cases which are often said to involve *loss* of self-control, such as provocation cases. There is also a more general question about the relevance of psychological and social factors which shape each individual's character.

Many offences, particularly those involving violence, take place against a background of stress, argument and provoking events. Individuals are subjected to a variety of pressures in everyday situations, and on some occasions the pressure overcomes the restraints which have been developed to curb aggressive impulses towards others. Cases of provocation involve an event, often a series of events, giving rise to some loss of self-control by the offender and the commission of a crime under provocation. There are degrees of loss of self-control, just as there are degrees of provocation. One may partly lose self-control, momentarily lose one's head, or totally go berserk; and provoking events may be described as trivial, serious or overwhelming. So far as criminal liability is concerned, even the most overwhelming provocation followed by complete loss of self-control does not amount to an excuse, save in the narrow circumstances of a murder charge, which may be reduced to manslaughter on this account. The general rule is that if the defendant knew what he was doing (i.e. had *mens rea*, even for a fleeting moment of time), he should be found guilty of the offence which resulted. But when we turn from the *grounds* of responsibility to the question of the *measure* of responsibility, loss of self-control becomes an important matter. Lawyers have frequently justified their failure to take account of provocation in relation to criminal liability by pointing out that its effect can be adequately reflected at the sentencing stage. But in what way should this be done? It is a commonplace that some individuals are endowed with weaker controls than others: there are some who lose their temper readily, others whose stoicism shades into apparent emotionlessness. If the law sets a general and unbending standard of self-control, and punishes simply for failure to attain it, it will be carrying to excess Kenny's general view that an enquiry into the offender's knowledge and foresight affords strong inferences about the freedom of his actions. There are surely occasions when the emotions are so aroused that they overwhelm the normal directive force of the intellect. Even those who take the rather strict view that it is a person's choice whether or not he allows himself to lose control must admit that the particular actions *after* loss of control cannot individually be traced to any choice: if there is true loss of self-control, each action is not chosen in the normal way. Many would doubt whether it can really be said that people are able to choose whether they lose self-control in the first place. On this point the difference in individual personalities is relevant. Those who are endowed with weak controls might find themselves unable to resist the urge to respond to what most others would consider to be a relatively trivial provocation. Those endowed with what is sometimes termed an 'intra-punitive' personality might allow a series of provocations to build up anger and resentment, so that they lose control at a later stage than many other people but their loss of control may be triggered by what appears to be a relatively trivial event. Each of these possibilities strikes a chord of familiarity; yet each of them begs important questions about the individual's ability to do otherwise. Are they really exceptions to Kenny's generalization about the intellect and the will? Are people 'endowed' with personalities which they cannot change or control? How can we ever tell whether a person could have resisted the violent urge but failed to exert any self-control, or whether he was absolutely incapable of doing so? Why could it not be said that the receipt of grave provocation deprives the individual of a fair opportunity to exercise his capacity for self-control in the same way that an accident or mistake is taken to do? Hart's answer to the last question is that 'though the accused's capacity for self-control was not absent its exercise was a matter of abnormal difficulty.'[70] This is to maintain, as the Court of Appeal has insisted in some provocation cases, that 'there is in every human being a residual capacity for self-control'[71] and that it ought to be exercised at all times.

It is unnecessary to examine here whether extreme provocation ought in law to take away the grounds of responsibility – to be a 'defence', in the same way as mistake or duress. Difficult enough is the question of the extent to which provocation should affect the measure of responsibility. As we saw when discussing offences of violence, there are several major issues still unresolved: does provocation mitigate primarily because of the understandable nature of the offender's response to a wrong done to him, or because it led the offender to act in an uncontrolled fashion? How should cumulative provocation be evaluated? Is it morally justifiable to insist that people simply ought not to allow themselves to be provoked by children or by policemen? Indecision on these moral issues cannot be concealed by simple references to the court's discretion in sentencing.

The relationship between responsibility and an individual's control over his actions also raises a more general question about the relevance of the psychological and social factors which shape each individual's character. The answer to this question can be approached by considering the table below constructed from Professor West's study, *Who Becomes Deviant?*[72]
The figures show the percentage of boys with each characteristic who were subsequently detected in lawbreaking. It might be tempting to argue that an individual with a known delinquent sibling has less

Group	% of class 'delinquent'	% of remaining boys 'delinquent'
Lowest income ('poor')	33	17
Large family (5 or more children)	32	17
Criminal parent	36	16
Known delinquent sibling	45	15
Bad parental behaviour	32	16
Parental separation before boy aged 10	39	19
Teachers' ratings of boys 'most troublesome' at age 8	38	12

chance of avoiding detection than one without a known delinquent sibling. Even allowing for the possibility that such an offender may be more likely to be detected and subjected to official action (because the family is 'known'), can any inferences about culpability be drawn? Is there reason to argue that the behaviour and circumstances which constitute the offence were less under his control? It would be difficult, because of the fact that more of those with delinquent siblings were *not* detected in delinquency (55 per cent) than were (45 per cent). That hurdle might be overcome by taking a cluster of characteristics: West's study suggested that half of the boys with 3 or more of 5 adversities (low family income, large family size, parental criminality, low intelligence and poor parental behaviour) became delinquent. Since these characteristics suggest that the boys had from an early age been subject to influences which were not conducive to law-abidance, there is some basis for the argument that they should be treated as less culpable than those who have had the benefit of more benign influences. But we must immediately spell out the limitations of this view. As West himself stated, 'a statistical correlation does not necessarily imply a direct causal link, and the statistical importance of these five background factors does not mean that they were the essential causes of delinquency.'[73] On the other hand, it is true to say that the statistics do point to explanations which accord with much modern criminological theory. Again, even if we grant the causal relationship, that does not mean that such individuals cannot respond to deterrent sanctions: the operation of deterrence is independent of estimations of moral responsibility, and it might well be possible to deter such people, although the amount of punishment necessary to achieve that purpose might be very high if their natural restraints and self-control were very low. Nor does it necessarily mean that such persons are unable to develop sufficient self-restraint for lawful behaviour: it places them in a group for whom law-abidance might be abnormally difficult, but it makes it no easier in an individual case to distinguish those who do from those who do not experience this difficulty.

Environmental factors and differences in social learning are, however, neither necessary nor always sufficient explanations of behaviour which is to some extent beyond the offender's control. Apparently similar environmental conditions and similar techniques of social learning may have different effects on various kinds of personality. There is evidence that certain personality traits have an hereditary basis (emotionality, and extraversion/introversion), and these traits may go a considerable way to explaining the differential impact of environment or conditioning upon individuals. Again, individuals may react in different ways to the structure of the social system. Some may feel that the fruits and symbols of 'success' (money, cars, electrical goods and other material possessions) are worth obtaining but that the system unfairly restricts the legitimate means to do so. If the system is capable of arousing this mixture of feelings of jealousy and injustice, individuals may well feel a pressure to obtain the symbols of success by illegitimate means; and this could be seen as something which reduces the offender's control over the circumstances and hence the degree of his responsibility, inasmuch as this particular source of pressure would not exist in a fairer system. A somewhat similar argument can be constructed against those social arrangements which create opportunities for lawbreaking and neglect precautions which are known and available. The creation of opportunities may be designed so as to create optimal conditions for trade and commerce (as in the design of 'walk-round' stores and supermarkets): in doing this, the opportunities for crime are also increased, and the precautions taken may not be sufficient to eliminate that increase. There is a growing body of knowledge about the effect on crime rates of different designs of buildings and public service vehicles, for example, because some leave greater opportunities for unobservable behaviour than others;[74] inasmuch as we fail to adopt known techniques of crime reduction, we increase the temptations to lawbreaking and thereby risk reducing an individual's control over the circumstances which lead to an offence. A similar point has been made recently by Lord Lane CJ, when he quoted with approval the observation of a probation officer in a social inquiry report that 'it is time in my opinion that the London Clearing Banks attempted to make credit cards less open to abuse with the possible introduction of photographs on the card', and added that credit cards 'provide a great temptation to people who are minded to commit fraud.'[75] Thus there are certain types of offence, of which theft from shops and credit card frauds are two, whose frequency is largely the result of the opportunities and temptations provided by commercial developments, and the failure to take greater precautions. If these commercial developments are permitted without insisting on greater precautions, it is surely unfair to take severe measures against those who succumb to the mounting temptation.

These considerations apply generally to categories of offence, and not to categories of offender. There are many who would argue against treating an *offender* differently because of his family background, his psychological make-up or environmental considerations. Some of these would dispute the inferences on which such approaches are founded (i.e. that a person from a particular family background was less in control of the circumstances which led to the offence), and would argue that the effect of such factors is usually minimal and is insufficient to deprive the offender of full responsibility. Some of the sceptics would not dispute the effect of these social and psychological factors, but would argue that we lack the ability to determine the extent to which the various influences operated in an individual case, so that a general concession in favour of those subject to these influences would inevitably involve a concession also to the few 'wicked' offenders in the group who could conform to the law but choose not to do so. Other sceptics, whilst acknowledging the social and psychological influences, would exclude them on the ground that their inclusion would import all kinds of value judgments about individuals, the effect of which would probably be less fair than failure to take account of them at all. All these sceptical views argue against the attempt to import such factors into the evaluation of culpability, whilst not disputing their general causal relevance to culpability. As for society's 'responsibility' for facilitating certain kinds of offence, this raises the general issue of the level of penalties. Some hardliners might argue that greater opportunities do not reduce the culpability of those who succumb to the temptation, for they should not yield; and to this they might add that, as society progresses, higher standards of self-control come to be expected of its members. A more sympathetic and (probably) more realistic approach would be to admit that any society which tolerates developments which are known to risk greater crime is giving priority to some other value over the prevention of crime, and that therefore it ought to moderate its response to those who fall to the temptations held out by these developments.

4 Property offences and proportionality

We now return from questions of personal responsibility to consider some of the problems involved in assessing the gravity of property offences, together with the problem of relating the social and moral gravity of property offences to that of offences of violence.

English law generally divides its offences against the person according to the magnitude of the harm done, not the method used; whereas its property offences are generally divided according to the method used, not the magnitude of the harm. Yet there is no doubt that the value of the property obtained is an important element in assessing the gravity of a property offence. Discussing the point in connection with the issue of which offences of dishonesty ought to carry the right to elect for Crown Court trial, the James Committee maintained that by and large the monetary value of the property is a fair indicator of the gravity of the offence, but they accepted that this might not always be so:[76]

> The circumstances in which an offence was committed or the character-istics of the offender may sometimes make an offence more serious than the value of the goods alone might suggest. Examples of this are the particularly mean theft from an old or disabled person; theft by a person in a position of trust; theft of an article of little intrinsic value, such as a key or cheque-book, which is intended for use, or which is capable of use, in connection with a more serious offence (with which there may not be sufficient evidence to charge the defendant if his plans are not sufficiently advanced at the time of arrest); and theft of an article of small value which the thief believes to be worth much more, for example, where imitation pearls are stolen by mistake for real pearls or where an empty wallet is stolen which the thief has reason to believe contains a lot of money.

This statement is pregnant with question-begging assumptions. Why are thefts from the old or disabled particularly 'mean'? In the discussion of violence it was argued that crimes against defenceless victims are morally worse than other crimes which do not share that feature, and this would apply to crimes against the old and disabled.

But there may be other assumptions. Are such crimes thought 'mean' because the old and disabled are more likely than others to be poor? If so, this advances the poverty of the victim as a distinct factor in aggravation of a property crime (and, on the subjective principle, the offender must be shown to have known or suspected that the victim was poor); and it assumes that old age and disablement are reliable indicators of poverty, which may or may not be true. Or are such crimes thought 'mean' because the old and disabled are more likely to be affected by shock? This rests on the factual question of whether they are more susceptible to shock;[77] and then, taking the subjective principle seriously, there is the question whether a person should be sentenced on this basis if he was unaware of this greater susceptibility. These are all matters which should be examined before classifying a particular offence as 'mean'.

Thefts by persons in a position of trust are discussed later. Thefts of property either intended for use or capable of use for a more serious offence raise the problem of establishing a factual basis for sentence. If a further charge of possession 'with intent' results in a conviction, he can be sentenced for that. If there is no such conviction, care must be taken to establish any further intention of the offender on which sentence will be based.[78] On the substantive issue, however, it is surely right to increase a sentence where this ulterior purpose is established, for the property offence charged is also an early stage towards a greater crime.

The last category mentioned in the quotation from the James Committee indicates their adoption, in part at least, of the subjective principle.[79] It is consistent with the principle that if an offender is proved to have believed that the property was far more valuable than it actually was, he should be sentenced on the basis of that belief.

When they went on to discuss exceptions to the proposition that the gravity of property offences turns largely on the value of the property, the James Committee referred to some further types of theft which 'tend to be more serious than thefts which do not contain those particular aggravating features'[80]: thefts committed jointly with another (which perhaps create greater fear and alarm, put the victim at a greater disadvantage, and reduce the probability that the enterprise will not be carried through); and thefts of documents (the true significance of which might not be reflected by their monetary value as paper). Only in relation to a third group, however, did the James Committee make an exception to the monetary limit (£20) beneath which they proposed to make Crown Court trial unavailable.[81]

Theft from the person, particularly pick-pocketing, however, seems to us to fall into a different category. It is generally regarded as a particularly offensive and frightening type of theft, in some ways akin to robbery and burglary in its invasion of a person's privacy; the amount stolen bears little or no relation to the 'criminality' of the offence because the pick-pocket cannot know the amount until he completes the theft; and the offence tends to be committed by gangs, which often operate on a semi-professional basis.

Now the combination of these factors clearly would render theft from the person more serious than, for example, theft from a shop or stall – so long as it is fair to assume that the offender knew of the greater fear and alarm generated by this kind of offence. Less readily acceptable is the suggestion that the amount stolen has scant bearing on the gravity of pickpocketing because the offender cannot know the amount until he completes the theft. This factual proposition may be true in a narrow sense; but cannot the same uncertainty be found in many thefts, burglaries and robberies? Some robberies are so highly organized that everything is known about the target; others are impulsive, and involve the seizing of a purse, bag or wallet with unknown contents. The burglar and the shoplifter, admittedly, can usually see what they are taking. Yet it may be argued that the pickpocket, too, may have particular hopes and expectations when he approaches certain victims, judging them according to their appearance and any specific evidence. The implication of the James Committee's approach is that it is proper to regard all pickpocketing as more serious because of the uncertainty involved: whilst that may have been a fair argument for the purposes of determining mode of trial for the whole group of offences, it is surely less persuasive as a general reason for viewing this type of theft more seriously. The Committee's reference to pickpocketing as more serious because it tends to be committed by gangs which often operate on a semi-professional basis would equally not amount to a reason for treating all offences of pickpocketing as more serious: those offences which actually involved gangs of this kind could be so treated, but the reason for that would then be a general principle about offences committed by groups or offences committed by 'semi-professionals'.[82]

One theme which emerges from this discussion is the propriety of holding offenders responsible for what we may call the 'secondary consequences'[83] of the crimes they commit. In other words, is it fair to view an offence more seriously because it is the type of offence which might result in great psychological harm to the victim? The question is a poignant one in relation to rape: how many rapists consider the possible psychological and emotional effects of being the victim of that offence? But we have seen that the question is raised in property crimes too. Pickpocketing is regarded as a 'particularly offensive and frightening type of theft'; residential burglary is likewise viewed as much more serious than burglary of commercial premises, because of the distress and alarm which is likely to be felt by the householder.[84] The three examples of rape, pickpocketing and burglary may well have a common feature, in that they are all liable to be perceived by the victim as invasions of his or her private and personal world. But what is the significance of this feature for sentencing? If it can be shown that the offender knew about the probability of consequences of this kind, it must surely be fair to hold him responsible on that account. He might acquire this knowledge through previous offences, or remarks made by sentencers on previous occasions. If he has this knowledge, it should not be relevant whether or not the feared consequences actually ensue in the particular case: this is a matter of chance, rather like the James Committee's example of stealing imitation pearls by mistake for real pearls or like the intending killer who shoots and misses, which should not intrude into sentencing.

There is also the question of the degree of probability. Although this is a relatively neglected area for research, there has been a recent resurgence of research interest in the psychological effects of crime (and fear of crime).[85] The general finding is that people's fears are exaggerated, being based on the (relatively rare) serious cases. For example, Maguire's study of the effects of burglary[86] suggests that very few victims come face to face with the burglar (some 4 per cent in his study), thus raising questions about the risk of violence resulting from burglary; and his study also shows, more pertinently to the present inquiry, that victims with certain characteristics are much more likely to suffer lasting psychological consequences than others. If, for example, we take Maguire's broad conclusion that women who have been separated from their husbands by death or divorce are an especially vulnerable group for lasting psychological consequences, how ought this to be translated to a general factor in sentencing for burglary? Ought we to treat all burglaries as more serious because of the risk that a minority of victims will suffer really serious psychological consequences? Or should we treat burglaries of women who live alone as much more serious? If we incline towards the latter conclusion, on the basis that it would be unfair to judge the seriousness of all burglaries according to the effects of a minority of them, would we still be satisfied that a burglary of the premises of a woman living alone should be treated as particularly serious when the offender had no reason to believe, when he burgled the house, that it belonged to a woman living alone?

The core of this discussion lies in the propriety of assuming that offenders have certain general knowledge. This is something which sentencers are generally prepared to do when the question of intoxication is raised:[87] one of the reasons for holding intoxicated harmdoers liable for the harm done and for not treating drink as a mitigating factor is that members of society are properly taken to know about the effects of too much drink. They may not know the precise effect it will have on their own actions, and the harm or damage which is likely to result, but it is fair to hold them liable because they ought not to have taken the risk in the first place. The same might be said of burglary: every burglar ought to know that there is a considerable risk of causing psychological harm to the victim (as well as the material loss – or, indeed, at a time when insurance of household contents is becoming widespread, instead of material loss), and he ought also to know that there is a small risk of meeting the householder face to face and of a violent encounter resulting. There is no justification for his taking either of these risks, and so he ought to be held liable on the basis of their existence. This line of argument could, however, lead to great severity. We saw earlier that the result of the argument in intoxication cases would logically be to hold all persons who become intoxicated liable for the offence which they risk committing, even if the risk fails to materialize; there is no social justification for doing so, because the risk is probably a low one and the use of alcohol may have some social value, and of course because punishment should be meted out as sparingly as possible. That line of argument is much weaker in burglary cases: whilst the general proposition that punishment should be used as sparingly as possible remains, it could not be said that there is any social value in the committing of burglaries, and Maguire's research shows that over one-quarter of victims of residential burglary suffer quite serious shock as a result of the offence and that the lives of some two-thirds of victims are affected for a period of weeks following the burglary. It may therefore be argued that the risk of causing psychological effects is significantly greater in residential burglary than where a person renders himself totally intoxicated, and that this founds a stronger case for regarding residential burglary as being generally a more serious offence – even in those cases where the risk of 'secondary consequences' does not materialize.[88]

Another general issue in property offences which is raised by the example of pickpocketing is whether we can support the general proposition that offences against the property of individuals are more serious than offences against companies. There are immediate difficulties with this: many trading concerns are run by one person or a small group of persons, and their feelings towards the shop or workshop concerned may be just as personal as the feelings of a householder towards his possessions. But as a general proposition there are three major reasons for regarding offences against larger companies, such as Woolworth and Marks and Spencer, as less serious than an offence involving the same amount of property but committed against an individual victim. First, an individual's possessions are more likely to have a personal ('sentimental') value to him which is additional to, and may indeed be more important to him than, the economic value. This personal attachment to possessions is far more likely to be found where the victim is an individual than where the victim is a company, especially since those who sell goods rarely have an attachment to any particular item of stock. Thus the theft of an individual's wrist-watch (which, perhaps, was a present from a member of the family) may properly be viewed as more serious than the theft of such an article from a jeweller's shop. Secondly, thefts from individuals are more likely to cause fear and alarm than thefts from companies: even if the property taken is money, to which there is no personal attachment, an individual is perhaps more likely to experience psychological consequences than the directors of a company. Thirdly, companies would generally be better able than individuals to afford and to off-set any loss through theft. It is true that some individuals may be so rich that they hardly notice the economic effect of a burglary (although they may feel the personal and psychological effects no less); equally it must be conceded that some companies may be operating on such a close margin of profitability and survival that, for example, the need to charge higher prices in order to off-set losses through shoplifting might significantly impair their economic position. But as a general proposition it may be maintained that the larger stores and supermarkets are better able to defray the costs of theft than is a small shop or an individual. There is considerable complexity to this argument, since an individual may be insured against a particular form of loss. Once insurance is brought into the calculations, the indirect secondary consequences of offences become hard to calculate: shoplifting leads to higher prices for all, burglary leads to higher insurance premiums for household contents, and so forth. It is therefore suggested that the most powerful considerations remain the first and second: the degree of personal attachment, which can lead to direct psychological consequences, serves to distinguish offences against individual victims from those against corporate victims.

Having considered the general proposition that offences against individuals are more serious than those against corporate victims, we now return to the general question of the relative seriousness of property offences. It was observed above that, whereas there is a clear hierarchy of offences against the person, based on the degree of harm and the degree of responsibility, property offences are divided according to the method used to obtain the property. Is there any sure way of deciding whether one method is to be viewed as more serious than another? If we hold constant the value of the property obtained –say, £250 in cash – and consider theft, burglary, handling, deception and robbery, we might start by arguing that robbery may generally be the most serious offence inasmuch as it involves violence (or the fear of violence). It is true that some robberies involve minimal force and are also impulsive offences, but there are others which show planning, physical force and indeed a degree of professionalism. These are factors which generally aggravate. Burglary cases, as argued above, typically involve some degree of psychological harm to the victim, and in some cases a considerable amount of harm; this may justify treating them as more serious than the run of thefts and handlings, although in general they should be regarded as less serious than robbery because there is rarely any form of intention to inflict personal harm upon the victim (which, in robbery cases, there is). As between deception, theft and handling there is intrinsically little to choose. Can we really say that obtaining by a trick or deception is more serious than simply taking goods? Can we really maintain that it is morally worse to arrange for the disposal of stolen goods than it is actually to steal them? There may well be some strong grounds for inferring that cases of deception involve an element of deliberation, if not planning, which marks them as calculated acts of lawbreaking.

Acts which amount to handling stolen goods, however, may be calculated or done on the spur of the moment. It is often argued that handling should be treated more severely than theft because if there were no handlers there would be fewer thieves: that argument could indeed be extended so as to justify treating handlers more severely than burglars and some robbers, on the basis that they would be unable to prosper in the absence of handlers who would exchange their loot for money. Arguments of this kind have a far stronger application to the professional handler than to the casual or occasional receiver, but it must be recognized that they are essentially deterrent arguments which are not supported by any increased moral heinousness in the offences concerned. Handling does not generally involve force, fear or fraud. It is therefore suggested that handling should not, of itself, be viewed as any more serious than theft; but, since there is a general principle that offences by 'professionals' should be visited with greater severity, it might be appropriate to view the handling as more serious where there was satisfactory evidence of professionalism.[89]

Further questions of the relative gravity of property offences are raised by what might be termed 'economic crime': offences committed through companies, or those committed against companies by those involved in them. The sums of money which these offences involve are often great – far beyond the returns of ordinary thefts, burglaries and deceptions – and Levi's analysis of sentences for 'long firm fraud' shows that the size of the fraud was the strongest determinant of sentence.[90] Discussion of the relative gravity of the various types of economic crime is handicapped by the dearth of systematic information about the forms which it takes, the circumstances in which offences are typically committed, and upon whom the losses fall. Levi's study of 'long firm fraud'[91] provides information about one particular type of economic crime, but the myriad varieties of commercial fraud to which Leigh alludes in his study of legal controls[92] show how complex the subject is.

5 Ranking types of offence

Making sense, at a general level, of the aggravating and mitigating features of property offences is a difficult and abstract enterprise, but it is necessary because inasmuch as sentencing practice purports to be based on proportionality it proceeds on certain assumptions about the relative seriousness of property offences. The difficulties of comparison become even greater when the relationship of property offences to offences against the person is considered. How can one possibly range along the same continuum offences which are essentially fish from different kettles? Sentencers have to do so, insofar as proportionality is an element in sentencing, and other members of society do so when they express different degrees of disapproval towards various kinds of offending. There have been attempts to measure how sentencers rank the various types of offence[93] and attempts to measure how people in general rate the relative gravity of criminal offences. The best-known approach is the scale developed by Sellin and Wolfgang,[94] and an improved version of their methodology was applied by Sparks, Genn and Dodd to some 500 citizens of London ten years ago. The results are presented in Table 12.[95] The authors remark that the ranking was 'agreeably rational' and that there was, as most other researchers have found, a 'broad concordance between the mean scores given by our sample and the seriousness attached by the law[96] to various kinds of crimes.'[97] Comforting as this may be, the generality of this kind of survey raises difficulties if the results are to be used to inform a discussion of the relative gravity of criminal offences. Such surveys, for example, neither examine the network of assumptions and beliefs which underlie the approach of subjects to the task of ranking, nor deal with the effect of factors such as premeditation and suddenness upon the ranking. On the first point, the authors lament that the sale of marijuana to a 15-year-old received a higher score, on average, than rape, and they suggest that this might have 'resulted from a general ignorance among our sample as to the nature of marijuana.'[98] This directly raises the issue of the assumptions upon which the answers were founded. Might not the same lament be made about the relatively low ranking of burglaries, which seems to neglect the psychological effects of that crime? What, for example, might be the effect upon the ranking of the kind of stereotyping postulated by Maguire in his discussion of attitudes to the sentencing of burglars?[99] The utility of attitude surveys or rankings of offence-seriousness for the examination of the proper relativities between types of offence (whatever their uses for other criminological purposes) is therefore a matter which must be approached with caution.

As for the effect of factors such as premeditation and suddenness upon the ranking, this is probably of great importance in current

Table 12

	Mean score	S.D.	Rank of mean score
Attack with blunt weapon causing death	10.67	0.90	1
Attack with knife causing death	10.64	1.01	2
Rape and beating, serious injuries	10.12	1.15	3
Attack with knife, serious injuries	9.52	1.51	4
Rape, no other injuries inflicted	8.98	2.03	6
Assault on police officer-serious injury	8.84	2.01	8
Attack, blunt weapon – minor injury	8.02	2.06	10
Assault on police officer – minor injury	7.79	2.32	12
Attack with fists – minor injury	6.71	2.37	18
Robbery of £25 + serious injury	8.96	1.81	7
Robbery of £25 + minor injuries	8.00	2.09	11
Robbery of £25 with no injuries	7.34	2.21	15
Burglary + assault, nothing stolen	7.53	2.17	13
Burglary + theft of £10 cash	5.42	2.60	27
Burglary + theft of £10 in property	5.35	2.49	29
Burglary – nothing taken	5.03	2.45	30
Obtaining £1,000 by fraud	7.37	2.72	14
Obtaining £100 by forged cheques	6.60	2.66	19
Embezzlement of £100	6.57	2.65	20
Theft of £100 property from car	6.49	2.47	21
Theft of £100 materials from work	6.25	2.53	22
Theft of £10 from wallet	6.10	2.61	23
Theft of £10 by employee from shop till	5.40	2.65	28
Theft of £10 property from car	4.94	2.36	31
Theft of £10 materials from work	4.91	2.55	32
Theft of goods worth £10 from shop	4.83	2.47	33
Reckless driving causing injury	8.58	2.02	9
Reckless driving £100 property damage	6.83	2.46	17
Sale of marijuana to person aged 15	9.13	2.41	5
Sale of marijuana to adult	7.08	3.45	16
Causing £50 damage to private property	6.04	2.53	24
Causing £50 damage to public property	5.47	2.51	26
Buying property known to be stolen	5.73	2.95	25

Source: Sparks, Genn and Dodd (1977), p. 184.

sentencing practice. If we compare a planned offence of criminal deception (such as obtaining goods from a shop by changing the price-label on them and paying a much lower price) with an impulsive assault as a result of an argument between neighbours, it appears that the deceiver could go to prison,[100] whereas an assault occasioning actual bodily harm could result in a fine or even a conditional discharge. Does this necessarily mean that the law is setting a higher value on property (indeed, upon the property of a company) than upon an individual's physical integrity? The sentence might be thus interpreted by those who looked solely or primarily at the title of the offence. A moral justification of the different seriousness of the two offences might, however, point to the significance of the different mental attitudes. The deceiver deliberately set out to break the law; he planned the way in which he was to secure an advantage for which others had to pay. By contrast, the assaulter lost his temper, and cannot be said to have set himself against the law in the same way as the deceiver. One might argue that he ought to have learnt sufficient self-control to deal with the situation, and that he has at the very least neglected a social duty in failing to develop sufficient control over his temper. In that way one could argue that a person who was provoked into using physical force really ought to be treated more seriously than someone who merely swindles a victim out of a few pounds, however deliberately. Thus, it might be claimed that since physical security is more central to social life than security of property, there is a 'fundamental social ranking' of classes of crime, and sentencing should ensure that even crimes of violence which are sudden and impulsive are regarded as more serious than deliberate property crimes not involving enormous losses. Some would justify this by arguing that 'the harm caused by major offences against property will be confined to institutions or, in any case, will take the form of compensatable financial loss.'[101] But quite apart from these empirical assumptions it can be maintained, as the Floud Committee concluded, that 'harms to the person are *sui generis* and enjoy special moral status.'[102]

If it is possible to speak of a 'fundamental social ranking' of offences which places the infliction of force above others, then there are still further awkward questions to be discussed. Consider the wide range of preparatory and preventive offences, whose purpose is to safeguard physical integrity. A large part of the justification of many motoring offences must be their contribution to physical safety – drunken driving, reckless driving and careless driving are obvious examples, but the same considerations lie behind offences such as exceeding the speed limit and infringing the 'construction and use' regulations. A car-owner's failure to examine the vehicle's tyres and to replace a worn tyre may represent a greater threat to social values than the deliberate theft of a bottle of whisky from an off-licence, since the car-owner places life and limb in danger. If it were shown that he knew about the worn tyre and continued to drive his car without replacing it, is he not more culpable than the whisky thief? Again, there is now a wide range of statutes (Health and Safety at Work Act 1974,

Consumer Safety Act 1978, Safety of Sports Grounds Act 1975) which impose standards of safety upon employers, manufacturers and the owners of sports stadia, and which create various criminal offences. If it were shown that an employer, manufacturer, etc. knew that he was failing to meet his statutory obligations, is he not more culpable than the whisky thief, for the same reason that he creates a danger to life and limb? Arguments of this kind apply less strongly where the motorist, employer or manufacturer is merely negligent: he fails to consider the regulations or to carry out the checks which they enjoin. Even accepting that negligence may be a proper *ground* for criminal liability, because people may properly be blamed for failing to apply their minds in situations where there is a social and legal duty to do so, it does not follow that the negligent offender is culpable *to the same degree* as the intentional or reckless offender. Indeed, since he does not consciously choose to cause or to risk harm to others, the degree of his responsibility is generally on a lower plane. Many of the preventive offences in this area may be committed by negligence, whereas almost all property offences require intention or recklessness. Brutish as the question is, we must ask whether a negligent failure to attain statutory standards of safety ought to be ranked as morally worse or not so blameworthy as the deliberate stealing of, say, a bottle of whisky.

Progress towards answering the brutish question may be made through four arguments: (i) the deliberate thief chooses to set himself against the law whereas the negligent offender cannot be said to do so (it would be otherwise if it could be shown that, although the offence merely requires negligence, the offender was recklessly or even intentionally flouting the regulations); (ii) if physical safety is ranked so high among social values, then a failure to acquaint oneself with and to fulfil the duties laid upon a person who carries on a particular activity (such as running a factory or driving a car) ought to be regarded as serious: (iii) however, the preventive offences with which we are here concerned lie relatively remote from the actual causing of harm – their purpose is to reduce the risk of danger, and although that purpose is firmly linked to the social value of preserving physical safety, they come much lower down the moral scale than the man who attempts to cause harm to another (e.g. by throwing a brick) or the man who prepares himself to cause harm to another (e.g. by arming himself with a weapon); and (iv) there may be a distinction inasmuch as it is accepted that the factory-owner has some social justification for his activities (providing goods which are desired or even necessary, and providing employment), whereas the property thief has not. This last argument is open to serious doubt: it can be strongly contended that employers should have due regard for the health and safety of their employees and of others who may be affected by their operations.[103]

What is therefore required is a finer appreciation of the relation of these preventive offences to the social prohibition on violence. Lawyers are apt to refer broadly to 'regulatory' offences, a classification which encompasses the kind of preventive offences considered above; but there is a substantial and significant moral difference between offences whose purpose is safety and the many others (such as failing to obtain a television licence) whose purpose is to enforce certain social obligations unrelated to physical safety. Sentencers have been urged to take a more realistic approach to preventive offences.

I would draw your attention to one particular area in which adequate penalties still do not seem to be imposed. There has been much concern about the generally low sentences in cases involving health risks and risks of injury to employed persons ... Most prosecutions are brought only in the more flagrant cases, either subsequent to a serious accident or where there is a clear risk to life or danger to health. When one looks at the heavy fines which are often imposed on private individuals convicted of motoring offences, there seems to be something out of balance when such small monetary penalties are imposed on those limited companies who are found guilty of risking the lives and health of their employees.[104]

This advice by Lord Elwyn-Jones to magistrates shows that there is some awareness of the inequities of this aspect of sentencing, but if traditional modes of thinking about offences of this kind are to be radically altered a bolder initiative from both the courts and Parliament is needed. The maximum penalties provided by Parliament for these preventive offences are relatively low, when compared with the inchoate and completed offences against the person; and the enforcement of this branch of law is left to specialist groups (such as the Health and Safety Executive) whose policies are far more sparing of the legal sanction than the policy of the police in cases of relatively minor theft, damage and even assaults. This is not to maintain that there should necessarily be more assiduous prosecution and severer penalties for these preventive offences, for it might be thought that more sparing prosecution and lower penalties for minor property offences would be a more appropriate solution. But at least there should be a reappraisal of the gravity with which small thefts and breaches of the various safety regulations are viewed.

6 Some general principles

During the course of discussing offences of violence and offences against property we have encountered a number of general principles, mostly relating to aggravating factors. Indeed, it could be argued that general principles of this kind play a much larger part in the construction of culpability than is commonly recognized, since they either explicitly determine or implicitly inform many judgments about the relative seriousness of offences falling within a single legal category. It is therefore proposed in this section to discuss some of the general principles which have not been examined in detail. Offences against persons in authority have been discussed fairly fully,[105] as have offences committed against the defenceless.[106] The principles examined here relate to (a) breach of trust, (b) ease of commission, (c) offences committed by groups, (d) organized crime, and (e) temptation.

(a) Breach of trust

Where an offence involves a breach of trust, this is generally treated as an aggravating factor. Its powerful influence is shown by the degree to which it outweighs factors which would normally go in mitigation. Indeed, there is the paradox that some of the strongest factors in mitigation (unblemished career, model citizen, good employment record) are often present in these cases and yet do not tell greatly in the offender's favour. The reason is that positions of trust are not normally given to individuals unless they have unblemished references, and so the offence may be seen as a betrayal of those very characteristics. Society operates in certain spheres largely on the basis of trust, and one of the burdens of a position of trust is an undertaking of incorruptibility. The individual who puts himself forward as trustworthy, is trusted by others and then takes advantage of his power for his own personal ends can be said to offend in two ways – not only does he commit the crime charged (be it theft, false accounting or a sexual offence), but in addition he breaches the trust placed in him by society and by the victims of the particular offence. However, it must be borne in mind that there is another and independent reason why offences of this kind are often viewed as particularly grave: they are usually deliberate, and often involve systematic offending over a considerable period of time, and so may possess strong aggravating features apart from the breach of trust.

It can also be argued that the higher the social position, the higher the standards of honesty which go with it. Thus the taking of £100 by a senior civil servant with financial responsibilities is a worse offence than a similar taking by a lowly DHSS clerk. The standards, however, must be those relevant to the position of trust concerned: we are speaking of the revenue officer who embezzles rather than indecently exposing himself, or of the accountant who falsifies rather than driving recklessly, so that it is not merely a question of *social* position but rather of the particular obligations and expectations which go with each office of trust. Thus policemen abuse their position of trust if they commit any crime, since the office of a constable is to prevent crime;[107] postmen abuse their position if they steal from the mail, since the security of the mail is in their hands; court officials abuse their position if they divert funds which are under their control, since the court's control of funds must be utterly safe; and schoolteachers abuse their position if they have unlawful intercourse with pupils in their charge, since they have some responsibility for the moral welfare of their pupils.

Similar arguments apply to persons who are not public employees but members of a trusted profession. Professional people, such as solicitors and accountants, 'trade upon their honesty. They sell their trustworthiness.'[108] As the Court of Appeal has put it: 'If people cannot deal with solicitors in absolute reliance upon their honesty, the business of the country would be, seriously affected in all sorts of ways.'[109] The same reasoning presumably underlies the Inland Revenue's readiness to bring prosecutions against accountants who are found to have made false declarations for taxation purposes, which contrasts with their extreme reluctance to bring prosecutions against almost all other taxpayers.[110] Undoubtedly there is a symbolic element in the rather stringent attitude of the courts towards this kind of offence: severe sentences are seen as upholding the value placed upon the proper fulfilment of trust. That value is linked to the proper functioning of society: it is neither desirable nor possible for every relationship to be policed by agents of law enforcement, and much of social life therefore has to be based upon trust. To undertake a public or professional position is to promise to fulfil that trust, even in the face of provocation and temptation. As the Court of Appeal remarked in one case:

It was said by counsel that the relationship had begun as a result of some kind of approach from the young girl. But this is a known hazard of a school master who teaches young girls, that some kind of affection will develop on the part of the girl, and it is part of the task of a school master in such circumstances to be on his guard that a relationship of an undesirable and unlawful nature does not grow out of such affection.[111]

Breaches of trust are viewed as grave because they may tend to weaken the essential social network of trust, and because the offender falls down on one of the primary social duties attaching to his position.

We have spoken of public employees and of professional persons. Do the same arguments apply to others who may be trusted in the ordinary course of business? Are the company bookkeeper who embezzles or the parcels delivery driver who steals packages to be treated in the same way as the accountant or the postman? Cox thought that their offences were not so serious, remarking that 'All of us are obliged to trust more or less to the honesty of ordinary bailees in ordinary matters, and we count upon a certain amount of risk in doing so and guard ourselves accordingly.'[112] The reasoning here is probably that one makes individual judgments about the reliability of traders, and that in the commercial world one adopts a rather more guarded approach in one's earliest dealings with a particular trader: every public official or professional person should be capable of trust, however, by virtue of his office. Of course there are marginal cases (what should be the view taken of gas board officials who steal from houses in which they are carrying out repairs?), but in broad terms it is surely right to regard breaches of trust by public officials and professionals more seriously than defalcations in the ordinary course of business.

A further type of case is where the person voluntarily undertakes a position of trust in relation to others – for example, the treasurer of a club or fund, or a scoutmaster or choirmaster. If the treasurer is trusted with considerable sums of money by others on a voluntary basis, is his offence worse than if he had stolen goods to that value? If a scoutmaster or choirmaster is convicted of offences of indecency with children in his charge, are those offences worse than similar offences with children for whom he had no responsibility at all? The answer must surely be that the offences are morally worse, inasmuch as a person who voluntarily undertakes this kind of responsibility might fairly be said to represent that he will not abuse the power which he is given, but that they are not morally as bad as breaches of trust by those who occupy public or professional positions. In those cases where a person very clearly and explicitly obtains a position by representations about his fitness for that position, a much more serious view may once again be taken. Thus, where a person puts himself forward for election as a councillor, for example, that implies a representation about his honesty; and if corruption in local government is traced to such individuals, they are rightly viewed as having offended as badly as those who hold paid public office. Local government operates on a network of relationships of trust, which public accountability can never expect fully to penetrate.

Finally, the importance accorded by the courts to the element of breach of trust may be illustrated by reference to the Court of Appeal's decision in the unusual case of *Lindley*.[113] The offender had unlawful sexual intercourse with his stepdaughter and another girl staying at the house, both of them aged 14. The Court took the view, in upholding concurrent sentences of 18 months' imprisonment (the maximum is 2 years), that 'the essential feature of this case' was that on the night in question 'he was responsible for both of them'. The mitigating factors in the case were powerful: the offender was elderly, of previous good character, had been depressed on the night in question because of the impending death of his sister-in-law, had readily confessed and pleaded guilty, and the offences were truly unpremeditated and isolated. In fact the offences were committed after he had taken considerable drink, although the Court regarded that as an aggravating factor. Intoxication apart, however, the Court's view was that the offender's failure to fulfil his responsibility (which was more akin to parental responsibility, and therefore incest, than to breach of a public or professional trust) was such as to outweigh this formidable array of mitigating factors.

(b) **Ease of commission**

It has been suggested from time to time that the ease with which an offence can be committed is an aggravating factor.[114] It is unlikely that this argument will be raised in many cases, but it has some application to cases of breach of trust (in that positions of trust are rarely supervised closely) and to cases where there is temptation. The ease with which certain kinds of fraud can be committed has sometimes been taken as a justification for increasing sentence: on what basis can this be defended? The only answer seems to be a deterrent one: the courts must increase the severity of sentences so as to deter offenders and potential offenders from taking advantage of the relatively easy opportunities for crime. But there are two strong grounds for scepticism about this approach. First, it begs questions about the individual and general deterrent efficacy of severer sentences in this kind of case.[115] Are the courts satisfied that the severer sentences really would result in a diminution in the number of such offences, and that the greater severity is morally justified? If not, then (in Bentham's words) the aggravation of sentence is 'so much misery in waste'. Secondly, there appears to be no suggestion that an offence is morally worse if it is easier to commit. Indeed, the reasoning here would seem to be similar to that on the effect of temptation. If the opportunity to offend presents itself so conveniently, this holds out a temptation to the individual and his succumbing is a less conclusive indication of bad character than if he had offended under different circumstances. Moreover it was argued earlier that inasmuch as certain social arrangements do offer new and easy opportunities for offending, society bears some responsibility for failing to adopt the most rigorous safeguards and ought therefore to treat those who seize the new opportunities with understanding and moderation.

(c) Offences committed by groups

An individual's offence may be regarded as more serious if he committed it as part of a group or gang of offenders. One reason which has already been given is that such offences place the individual victim at a far greater disadvantage, and tend to cause greater fear and alarm. Rape by a gang has generally been treated as more serious than rape by a single offender,[116] and the greater terror inspired in the victim provides an obvious justification for that (moreover the terror could hardly escape the notice of each individual member of the group). Another reason may be that the group's activities were a form of organized crime (discussed separately in section (d), below). But it could be argued that in some circumstances the commission of offences in groups does not aggravate the offence of each member: it is well recognized that fringe members of a group and those who have been 'led astray' should receive lesser sentences, and it can be argued that where a group forms spontaneously (as in some football hooliganism or street fights) the emotionalism and contagious 'crowd effect' might properly be regarded as a factor which mitigates an offender's responsibility.[117] It could be maintained, however, that this is an occasion upon which there is a social duty to retain self-control.

(d) **Organized crime**

Well-organized groups of offenders constitute a particular source of danger to society. Many of their offences possess the aggravating features of a group offence, but in addition the elements of planning and preparation take organized crime to the most serious end of the scale of moral attitudes. In some cases it may be difficult to obtain sufficient evidence that an offender's activities did form part of organized crime. But where the evidence is plain, there can be no doubt that organized crime is among the most calculated forms of defiance of the law and is rightly viewed as an aggravated form of offending.

(e) **Temptation and other mitigating factors**

As a postscript and a counterbalance to this discussion of aggravating factors, it is worthwhile to indicate some of the factors which might place an offence at the lower end of the scale of gravity, irrespective of the personal characteristics of the offender. Obviously the absence of aggravating factors will have some such effect, and we have already seen that certain mental attitudes (impulsivity, for example) place an offence in a less serious light. Where there is an offence committed by a group, it is proper to regard some members of the group as more culpable than others. If it is clear that one member was the 'ringleader', initiating plans and encouraging their execution, he will rightly be regarded as more culpable than someone on the periphery or 'outer circle' of a conspiracy, whose part is relatively small.

Three distinct mitigating factors are partial justification, provocation and temptation. In offences of violence we saw that elements of justification may be present where the offender overreacts to an unlawful challenge, as by beating a trespasser severely when in law he merely had the right to remove him forcibly from land. The element of justification distinguishes the offender from someone whose undertaking was entirely unlawful: it is a case of lawful motives taken to an unlawful excess. The same might be said of an offender who steals from his employer at a time when he is owed a considerable sum in payment for work done: the fact of the debt cannot justify the theft, but may suggest that the offender's motivation was not criminal in the fullest sense. The effect of provocation was also considered in connection with offences of violence, although it is present in other kinds of offence such as criminal damage. Its mitigating effect stems partly from the impulsivity or loss of self-control which characterizes the offender's actions, and which serves to place the offence at the lower end of the scale of mental attitudes, and partly from the element of 'partial justification' for the offender's response.[118]

Is it right to regard an offence committed after an offender succumbs to temptation as morally less bad than an offence committed without temptation? Most people accept that it is, and the reason is well expressed in the first part of the following quotation from Bentham, although in the second part he goes on to doubt whether it should lead to a reduced punishment.

> Authors of celebrity . . . have said, that the greatness of the temptation is a reason for lessening the punishment; because it lessens the fault; because the more powerful the seduction, the less reason there is for concluding that the offender is depraved . . . This may all be very true, and yet afford no reason for departing from the rule. That it may prove effectual, the punishment must be more dreaded than the profit of the crime desired. Besides, an inefficacious punishment is doubly mischievous; – mischievous to the public, since it permits the crime to be committed, – mischievous to the delinquent, since the punishment inflicted upon him is just so much misery in waste.[119]

Bentham was therefore in no doubt that the conflict between the moral significance of temptation, as revealing a less depraved character, and the necessity for effective punishments should be resolved in favour of the latter. But it is just these wide divergences of utilitarianism from morality which have led many to abandon the deterrent approach to punishment. In general, the existence of temptation diminishes the gravity of an offence because it furnishes an explanation of why the offence was committed which does not imply great wickedness on the part of the offender: it leaves open the possibility that the strong temptation was such as to overwhelm reasonably normal controls.

Does this apply equally in cases of breach of trust? There is an argument here that persons occupying such positions ought to possess or to develop stronger controls which are sufficient to withstand the temptations which naturally accompany the trust which others place in them. The existence of temptation is part and parcel of positions of trust, just as previous good character is a natural precondition of occupying such a position, and anyone who undertakes such a position has the additional obligations which go with it. It is therefore suggested that temptation should not mitigate offences of breach of trust.

7 Conclusions

We have seen that in speaking of crime, criminals and sentencing the general practice seems to be to make judgments about offences rather than offenders, and to regard consistency as a standard which is tied to the gravity of offences. An attempt has been made here, however, not only to explore the assumptions and justifications which lie behind common judgments of the serousness of offences, but also to examine other major components in the construction of culpability. What conclusions may be drawn?

The discussion has extended only so far as offences of violence and some property offences, but even in these limited areas it has proved difficult to grapple with the problems at a theoretical level. At the very least, it has been shown that behind the case-by-case pragmatism of English sentencers there must lie a reservoir of assumptions and judgments about morality, society, public acceptance and deterrence – a reservoir from which sentencers inevitably draw when considering and weighing the various factors in a particular case. It is possible to construct a justification for the imposition of a more severe sentence on a person who obtains a small amount by deception or by shoplifting, than upon a person who commits a wounding: the justification would rely heavily on the element of planning or deliberation in the property offences, as compared with the impulsivity (and perhaps provocation) in the offence of violence. But to allow such a justification to stand raises questions about the moral and social evaluation of different kinds of harm (e.g. to the person, and to property), and that evaluation may in turn rest upon ingrained social attitudes which seem resistant to rational reappraisal. Thus the traditional ordering of penalties implicit in what some have loosely termed the 'tariff' may well reflect an insufficient emphasis on personal safety, inasmuch as there is a failure to attend to dangers from the whole range of preventable or controllable sources, and an over-emphasis on invasions of property rights which, though deliberate, are of relatively less social significance. It may also neglect the fact that in some respects the very organization of social life generates opportunities and temptations to crime.

It might be said that a principal function of the courts is to reflect general social attitudes when determining the relativities among types of offence. Whether that is either possible or desirable may be disputed: there is certainly a need to review the relativities which are embodied in sentencing practice and to examine the assumptions which underlie them. The Advisory Council on the Penal System shied away from an ordering of maximum penalties which would attempt to reflect a fresh overall ranking, partly on the view that agreement for political purposes would be difficult to achieve and would probably be an unattractive and illogical compromise if achieved.

Even were we able to agree among ourselves about the precise relativity of different offences (and agreement could probably only be achieved by wholesale compromise, submerging each of our individual judgments and proving satisfactory to no-one), we felt sure that the judges, the legislators and the public at large would all take different views, both from ourselves and among themselves. . . .

They also claimed that to base new norms 'upon the contemporary practice of the courts' would be an approach which would 'eschew all fresh and controversial value judgments'.[120] Yet it must be true that one reason why the value judgments underlying sentencing practice are 'uncontroversial' is that they are not widely known and have rarely been searchingly explored; and that an accepted reason for discouraging such an exploration has been the 'particular case' argument – that criticism is usually misplaced because each case turns on a unique combination of factors, and those factors are invariably misreported or partially reported. Once it is appreciated that the uniqueness of the particular case still requires the sentencer to select certain factors which are relevant to sentence and to attribute degrees of importance to them, and that these activities inevitably involve abstract judgments, the importance of exploring the assumptions on which sentencers act is established.

Discussions about moral and social preferences should also be informed by more empirical research into the circumstances in which various offences come to be charged, the effects of those offences upon the victims (what have here been called the 'secondary consequences'), and if possible the motivation of those who commit such offences. There has not been a great deal of research of this kind, but research such as Levi's study of long firm fraud and Maguire's study of burglary[121] would be most helpful in informing the moral and social debate about the relative seriousness of types of offence.

A further set of moral arguments concern the personal responsibility of offenders. An offender who deliberately plans his offence is regarded as more culpable than the impulsive offender, but there are also deeper questions of the effect on individual responsibility of various personality traits and social influences. Should we maintain the hard line that anyone who is not mentally disordered is capable of conforming to law, and that those who find law-abidance more difficult than others simply have to try harder? Or should we allow those personal difficulties as a mitigating factor? The most accurate reflection of moral responsibility, it was argued above, might be achieved by allowing personal difficulties to mitigate to some extent; that allowance would inevitably bring leniency in some cases where the offender could have controlled himself but did not. It is virtually impossible to determine whether or not a person is capable of developing sufficient self-control or of exerting it on a particular occasion, and in practice the choice lies between allowing substantial mitigation for all those with unfavourable psychological or environmental backgrounds (thereby showing leniency towards the wicked and self-indulgent among them as well as the genuinely trapped), and giving no concession except in the rare cases where there is clear and cogent evidence of acute personal difficulties.

Allowing such factors to mitigate and not entirely to excuse reflects the view that almost all people know what the law is and are capable of so arranging their lives as to conform with it. It has been argued above that it is also fair to presume knowledge of what we called 'general social propositions' – that offences against law enforcement officers are particularly serious, that offences against children are similarly viewed, that intoxication may lead to a weakening of self-control, and possibly that burglaries of women living alone may cause greater distress to the victim. In principle these general social propositions should only be applied in cases where the offender either knew or risked the existence of the 'basic fact' of the proposition. Where the law itself designates an aggravating factor as part of the definition of an offence, it must be proved that the defendant had *mens rea* (i.e. knowledge or recklessness) as to the aggravating circumstance. From the moral point of view the same should apply to aggravating factors in sentencing. Thus, unless the offender knew that his victim was or might be a police officer or (as the case may be) a citizen making a physical intervention purely for the purpose of enforcing the law, there is no justification for invoking the general social proposition and treating the offence as aggravated. Some might regard this as over-refined, but the answer to that allegation is that it is vital to establish what would be ideal in theory so that we may properly evaluate what is desirable and possible in practice. Some might argue that the general social propositions travel too far beyond prevailing social attitudes, and that may be a fair reproach in the present circumstances. The Floud Committee discussed the psychological effects of crime and commented that 'an insensitive public is inclined to set them aside or, at least, to discount their significance in comparison with physical harm.'[122] This strengthens the case for a thorough review of relativities among offences, considering the assumptions which inform popular attitudes and any systematic knowledge which we have about certain kinds of offending.

The modern tendency in criminal law reform towards creating fewer and broader offences has resulted in a greater number of factors in aggravation being left exclusively to the sentencing stage. This legal sleight-of-hand reduces the moral significance of such factors not one whit: in the absence of legal divisions there are fewer signposts for the sentencer, but he is still expected to take the factors into account. We have discussed possible justifications for some of the leading aggravating factors, and have related them to the general scheme of sentencing for offences of violence. The thorny problem of conflicts between aggravating and mitigating factors was also raised, a problem which of course occurs in addition to the questions of the ranking of offences according to their seriousness, of the measure of personal responsibility, and of the criteria of aggravation. If, for example, there is an impulsive offence in breach of trust, what should be the relative moral importance of the (favourable) mental attitude and the (unfavourable) breach of trust? Again, if there is a provoked and impulsive attack on a policeman, what should be the relative moral importance of the (favourable) mental attitude and provocation and the (unfavourable) challenge to law enforcement? These are *par excellence* matters on which sentencers will differ and on which some priorities ought to be established at a general level. To claim that each case is different is true but not telling, for we have seen that a sentencer is bound in his own reasoning to attribute different importance to factors of one kind or another.

Culpability, then, is concerned not only with the gravity of the type of offence – the factor which probably has the greatest influence upon popular judgments – but also with the personal responsibility of the offender and with the interplay of aggravating and mitigating factors. That interplay has not been fully explored, since there has been little reference to the effect of the offender's criminal record (if any), the number of offences of which he is convicted, his personal circumstances, etc. These are considered in the chapters which follow. In this chapter we have identified various factors which call for deeper and more sustained analysis than has been possible within the present confines. There can be little doubt about the sophistication of the distinctions to which an analysis of the moral foundations of sentencing policy leads; and the injunction contained in Bentham's 'rule 13' on proportionality – 'For simplicity's sake, small proportions may be neglected'[123] – seems as strange yet welcome as it did in its original context.

5
Punishing persistence

The sentence of the court is passed not merely for an offence but also on an offender. The concept of proportionality does not require that the sentence is set solely according to the seriousness of the case: the offender's record is properly taken into account, so that the first offender is sentenced more leniently than the persistent offender. Once an offender has been convicted five or more times, the probability of his reconviction within the next 6 years is almost 9 out of 10 (as Table 11 in Chapter 1 shows). It is therefore not surprising that persistent offenders have been the subject of special legislative measures in the past, as section 1 of this chapter describes. Apart from such special measures, the principle of English sentencing is that a persistent offender gradually loses all claim to mitigation, but ought not to receive a sentence above the 'ceiling' set by reference to the gravity of his most recent offence. However, the elasticity of these ceilings is such that English sentencing practice goes some way towards cumulative sentencing for persistent offenders, and the justifications for this are examined in section 3. The justifications for dealing differently with certain classes of persistent offender are discussed in section 6, and in section 7 the problems of sentencing those persistent offenders who breach conditional sentences are discussed. First, however, the history of special legislative measures for persistent offenders will be sketched.

1 Historical introduction

The history of English measures aimed specifically at persistent offenders seems universally to be acknowledged to be a history of persistent failure. The judges have had sufficient discretion, for the last hundred years at least, to allow them to pass fairly long sentences on recidivists without invoking any special powers or imposing a special sentence. But penal reformers and governments have invariably felt that no major set of penal reforms would be complete without a special measure aimed at persistent offenders. The Gladstone Committee in 1895 argued in favour of a special measure against persistent thieves and robbers, who would otherwise serve a succession of fairly short sentences and therefore return frequently to prey on the community. The Committee's proposals led, after much debate,[1] to the Prevention of Crime Act 1908. This empowered a court to impose, upon an offender with three previous felony convictions since the age of 16, a sentence of preventive detention of between 5 and 10 years, *in addition to* the normal sentence for the offence (a so-called 'double track' system). The Act was aimed at 'persistent and wilful dishonesty of a serious character – such as burglary, housebreaking, coining, larceny from the person, robbery with violence and the like,'[2] but its aims were soon revised when Winston Churchill became Home Secretary. He took the view that the Act, as it was being administered, concentrated unduly on mere repetition in lawbreaking, and he exposed the minor nature of some of the offences which had led to the imposition of preventive detention. He issued a new circular which declared that 'mere pilfering, unaccompanied by any serious aggravation, can never justify proceedings under the Act', and propounded the general test of whether the nature of the crime was 'such as to indicate that the offender is not merely a nuisance but a serious danger to society.'[3] The aim of preventive detention thus became that of 'protecting society from the worst class of professional criminal:' in fact the courts often found their ordinary sentencing powers sufficient in such cases, and so the use of preventive detention declined.

The double track system established by the 1908 Act, always vulnerable to the criticism that it is unjust to sentence a person twice for his crimes, was abandoned in 1948. In its place the Criminal Justice Act 1948 introduced two new sentences. Corrective training was a sentence intended to offer between 2 and 4 years' training to the recidivist aged under 30, whilst a new form of preventive detention for recidivists over 30 could be imposed for between 5 and 14 years 'for the protection of the public'. This version of preventive detention was instead of, and not in addition to, the sentence for the particular crime. The Dove-Wilson Committee, upon whose 1932 report these measures were based, had envisaged that this kind of preventive detention would be suitable principally for 'professional criminals who deliberately make a living by preying on the public', but that it might also be used for 'those who practise thefts or frauds on a comparatively small scale – the victims usually being poor people on whom the loss of a small sum may inflict a more serious injury than the loss of valuable property on persons of means.'[4]

This seems to set a lower threshold than the Churchill circular of 1911, and it was the Government's intention that the 1948 Act should 'cover the relatively trivial offender'.[5] The judges soon found themselves passing sentences of preventive detention on offenders whose records, whilst showing persistence, were not serious. But in the late 1950s the judges increasingly set their face against this, and indeed in 1962 the Lord Chief Justice issued a Practice Direction to restrict the use of preventive detention.[6] Following a gloomy report from the Advisory Council on the Treatment of Offenders,[7] and two other studies which demonstrated the triviality of the offences generally committed by many of those receiving long terms of preventive detention,[8] preventive detention became little used and was abandoned in 1967. Corrective training had also faded out of sentencing practice, since the 'training' regime now differed little from the regime of most prisoners.

The next measure to be introduced was the extended sentence: the Criminal Justice Act 1967 empowered a court to extend a sentence beyond the normal length or (in limited circumstances) beyond the statutory maximum where it apprehended the need, in view of the offender's record, to protect the public. The White Paper of 1965 proposed the extended sentence for those offenders who are a 'real menace to society' and not for the persistent perpetrator of lesser offences.[9] But a parliamentary amendment which would have at least required the court to have regard to the gravity of the last offence was not accepted by the Government. Once again the courts soon found themselves using the extended sentence for persistent offenders who could hardly be described as real menaces to society, and its use has rapidly declined almost to vanishing point.

This brief historical survey reveals two major recurrent difficulties. First, legislation on persistent offenders has generally been framed in broad terms, leaving in the early stages chief constables and the

Home Secretary and in later years the judiciary to determine the actual scope and incidence of specially protective sentences. Secondly, and more fundamentally, there has been little agreement about the group or groups of offenders who should be the target of the protective sentences: the term 'professional criminal' has frequently been used, but in 1948 Parliament (following the Dove-Wilson Committee) treated this as covering all persistent acquisitive offenders whereas Churchill in 1910 and the Government in 1967 sought to identify smaller groups of 'real menaces'. The questions of policy which underlie this disagreement now tend to be little discussed in England, and the focus of penological debate has shifted to the issue of sentencing 'dangerous offenders', briefly discussed in section 6(i) below. However, despite the obsolescence of the only special measure now provided for persistent offenders, the courts deal with persistent offenders every day and the questions of policy confront them. How do they, and how should they, deal with such cases?

2 The general principle: progressive loss of mitigation

The general principle is that with each subsequent conviction an offender progressively loses the mitigation which he had as a first offender; but, on the other hand, no matter how long his record of previous convictions, this 'will not justify the imposition of a term of imprisonment in excess of the permissible ceiling for the facts of the immediate offence.'[10] The gravity of his present offence sets the ceiling for the sentence and, although a long criminal record loses him mitigation, it should not be allowed to operate as an aggravating factor. The proper approach is for the court to determine the sentence appropriate for the offence, and then to consider whether it can extend some leniency to the offender, having regard to his record.[11] If the record is bad, it probably cannot. Thus in *Connelly*[12] a man with a substantial record of offences of dishonesty and several previous custodial sentences had been convicted of stealing two letters from the hall table of a house. The sentence of 5 years' imprisonment was obviously based on his previous record rather than upon the facts of the present offence, and the Court of Criminal Appeal, holding that the sentence 'must bear some relation to the gravity of the offence', reduced it to 18 months.

The theory of progressive loss of mitigation does, of course, mean that at the end of the day the persistent offender will receive a more

severe sentence than the first offender. As Lord Donovan put it,
'judges have always (and I think rightly) felt themselves entitled to
deal with a persistent offender by increasing the sentence which they
would have passed if he were not.'[13] So long as the idea of a ceiling is
kept firmly in mind, there is a distinction between progressive loss of
mitigation on the one hand and aggravation on the other. Yet it must
be conceded – and the point will be developed later in the chapter –
that the principle of progressive loss of mitigation may involve too
many loose notions to serve as a useful guide. How much mitigation
must be lost? At what rate should it be lost as the persistent offender
accumulates convictions? Is there, indeed, a notional sentence for
each offence which can fairly be called a ceiling? Moreover, it is
arguable that the progressive loss of mitigation might not be
appropriate to all persistent offenders. There are obvious reasons for
showing leniency towards the first offender, even though the term
'first offender' is rightly taken to include persons whose first *conviction*
this is, they having been convicted of a number of offences which had
been committed before they were caught. When a person receives his
first conviction and sentence, this is the first time he has personally
been given an authoritative warning about lawbreaking: we say that
he 'deserves' a second chance, we visit him with 'less than the full
weight of disapprobation' and give him the opportunity to attend,
reflect as a moral agent and then try to conform to the law.[14] Again, a
first offence may fairly be seen as an isolated lapse (unless there is
evidence to the contrary);[15] further offences become less and less
explicable on those grounds. On the argument of individual prevention, leniency for first offenders may also be supported by
reference to Table 11 above, which shows that only 29 per cent of first
offenders are reconvicted within 6 years. This may be taken to suggest
that one experience of prosecution, court appearance, conviction and
sentence is enough for most offenders and that the sentence of the
court need not be particularly harsh. However, all these reasons in
favour of lenient treatment for first offenders do not compel the
conclusion that persistent offenders must in all cases be treated with
progressive severity. The seriousness of their offending, their motivation and their response to penal measures may differ: thus, for
example, with some of them (such as 'persistent petty offenders')[16] it
would be unfair to assume that the degree of moral blameworthiness
increases with the number of convictions.

Against the theory of progressive loss of mitigation is the argument that it is unjust to punish a man twice for his crimes or (as is more frequently the case) to increase the punishment for one offence on the basis of previous crimes for which he has already served a sentence. This was an objection against the 'double track' system introduced by the 1908 Act, and it has been re-stated in a modern context: 'the fundamentals of sentencing policy are that a man must be sentenced for the offence he has committed and not for his record'.[17] In its strongest form this might amount to a denial of the idea of progressive loss of mitigation, because its implication is either that on each subsequent conviction the offender must be treated as a first offender, or that there should be a 'flat rate' of penalties for offences – a rate which could not be varied on account of the offender's previous record and character, whether it was good or bad. Any tying of penalties to offences alone neglects an important aspect of culpability – the responsibility of the offender. In general, as argued in the last paragraph, persistent offenders are more blameworthy because they have lost all trace of the normal mitigating circumstances – they know the law only too well, they know what they can expect if caught offending, and it is no isolated lapse. Indeed, where the court imposes a conditional sentence (such as a suspended sentence or conditional discharge) the consequences of further lawbreaking are fairly clearly brought to the offender's attention.[18] It is not that to flout the law three times is necessarily more than three times as harmful to society –indeed, from the point of view of society and of the victims the damage is the same whether the offences are committed by one person or by three separate persons. It is that the individual offender is generally more blameworthy on the third occasion than he was on the first. The principle, as the Dove-Wilson Committee put it, is that 'of relating the sentence to the offender rather than the offence'.[19]

It must be borne in mind that as an offender receives more convictions, so the deleterious effects upon him are likely to increase. A person with a substantial record may be more likely to be visited by the police when they are investigating offences of a particular kind; perhaps prosecutors will accept less compelling evidence against a 'known' offender than they would against someone with an un-blemished record; juries and magistrates often realize, from the way in which the defence advocate avoids reference to the accused's character, that they are dealing with a person who has a criminal record;[20] and even in times of fuller employment than the present, it may be more difficult for a person with several previous convictions to explain his past satisfactorily to a prospective employer. Moreover, inasmuch as imprisonment forms part of the law's response to persistent offending, it is a double-edged sword. It ensures that society is temporarily protected from the offender, but from the fact that many persistent offenders do return to prison time after time

the inference is that present methods not only fail to check the criminal propensities of such people, but may actually cause progressive deterioration by habituating the offenders to prison conditions which weaken rather than strengthen their characters.[21]

Custodial sentences of progressive severity, even within a 'ceiling' set by reference to the gravity of the offence, call for cogent social justifications. These justifications will be considered in connection with the more vigorous 'cumulative' approach to sentencing recidivists.

3 Cumulative sentencing

One approach to the sentencing of persistent offenders is to maintain that the sentence should be made more severe on each conviction; this will here be called the 'cumulative principle'. To an extent there is a similarity between the cumulative principle and the principle of progressive loss of mitigation, and some of the arguments considered below might be accepted by those who support progressive loss of mitigation. Inasmuch as both principles tend to lead to longer sentences for persistent offenders, they have some justifications in common. Where the cumulative principle differs from progressive loss of mitigation, however, is that it does not incorporate the same notion of a ceiling, set by reference to the gravity of the most recent offence. The ceiling is supposed to ensure that, when all mitigation has been lost by an offender, his sentences (assuming that he commits crimes of roughly the same gravity) cannot become any more severe. But under the cumulative principle, certainly in its most vigorous forms, there is no limit to the escalation of penalties other than the statutory maximum for the offence.

The second half of the nineteenth century saw a continuing debate about the proper approach to sentencing persistent offenders.[22] On the one side stood those who favoured a steeply cumulative principle, such as the renowned Gloucestershire magistrate Barwick Lloyd Baker.[23] On the other side stood Francis Hopwood, Recorder of Liverpool in the late 1880s and early 1890s, who was just as vocal as

Baker but who strenuously opposed heavy penalties for petty recidivists. The Lord Chief Justice at that time, Lord Coleridge, appears to have had greater sympathy with Hopwood's approach since he maintained that he would inflict punishment only 'for the particular offence for which the prisoner is being tried before me'. But even the Lord Chief Justice went on to admit that some of his colleagues had 'different guiding thoughts'.[24]

The debate has subsided in modern times, with the principle of progressive loss of mitigation being repeatedly endorsed by the Court of Criminal Appeal and now the Court of Appeal. But sentencing decisions have never been noted for their consistency, and there are occasional reincarnations of the cumulative principle. Thus in *Leadley* (1977)[25] the offender had pleaded guilty to the theft of 2 bottles of liqueur (valued at £10) from a supermarket. He had 12 previous convictions for offences of dishonesty, and had received fines, probation, borstal and several terms of 1 month or 3 months' imprisonment, some suspended. On this occasion he was sentenced to 2 years' imprisonment by the Crown Court. The Court of Appeal's judgment endorsed the cumulative principle,[26] and, although it did reduce the sentence to 15 months, that still exceeds a realistic ceiling for such a minor offence of dishonesty. Again, in *Gilbertson* (1980)[27] a woman of 59 was convicted of theft of goods worth £1.61 from Boots and food valued at £7 from Marks and Spencer. She had 14 previous convictions for similar offences, and had experienced several probation orders, a suspended sentence and short sentences of immediate imprisonment. In the Crown Court she was sentenced to two consecutive terms of 12 months' imprisonment. The Court of Appeal reduced the sentence, but only to 12 months in total (by making the sentences concurrent), and they endorsed the correctness of the approach taken in the Crown Court: 'One thing is certain, that if she goes on committing offences, the periods of imprisonment which will be imposed on her, merely to protect the shopkeepers, will become longer and longer.' If these observations accurately represent the Court's opinion, then they embody both a re-statement of the cumulative principle and a direct contradiction of the principle of progressive loss of mitigation. It therefore cannot be said that the creation of the Court of Criminal Appeal in 1907 has put an end to major differences of principle of the kind which attracted such an amount of public discussion towards the end of the last century.

By what arguments can the cumulative approach to sentencing be supported? A number of alternative justifications are now considered in turn.

(a) Prevention through individual deterrence

Cumulative sentencing might be justified by reference to the aim of prevention through the method of individual deterrence. To impose upon a persistent offender a succession of 'lenient' sentences may be to 'lull him into a false sense of security',[28] and a substantial sentence may appear to be the only measure likely to break the melancholy sequence. The classical theory of individual deterrence is captured by Moberly in the following quotation. 'If whipping does not suppress theft, let it be turned into severe flogging; if this be not enough, add exposure to the pillory; and if this will not do, try capital punishment.'[29] This simple notion of increasing the sentence for each further conviction includes no reference to the gravity of the offences concerned, unless its proponent also holds that in some sense there is a ceiling, referable to the gravity of the offences concerned, beyond which it is not permissible to increase sentence. Some of the nineteenth-century advocates of this approach did not subscribe to any such idea of a 'ceiling', and there are reports of sentences of 10 years for stealing a garden fork, 12 years for stealing a piece of canvas, 10 years for stealing a shovel and 7 years for stealing a hen – all sentences passed upon persistent offenders whose previous crimes had been similarly modest.[30]

But individual deterrence can also be invoked to support a rather different approach, and this is what Lord Widgery had in mind in *Leadley*.

He had consistently received light sentences. If ever there was a way of teaching a man to be an habitual thief, it was to give him the same light sentence each time he committed an offence. He would get into the frame of mind that whatever he did he would receive the same sentence. After the second or third offence he should have been given a sentence that would make him sit up and then there might have been a chance of stopping him before he became an habitual criminal.[31]

This approach is evident from a number of judicial pronouncements, and it seems to combine individual deterrence with elements of reformation and humanity. The idea appears to be that it is better in the long term for an offender to serve a substantial sentence at a relatively early stage in his career than to serve a succession of short sentences of imprisonment interspersed with brief periods of liberty. Reasoning of this kind has been favoured in such disparate places as the annual reports of the Howard Association in the 1870s and 1880s, where a campaign for cumulative sentencing for persistent offenders was mounted,[32] and the speech of Lord Donovan in the House of Lords decision in *Ottewell's* case in 1968, where he remarked that to increase the sentence for a recidivist is 'in the offender's own interest.'[33] It is also evident in the 'nip in the bud' theory, which is being advanced as an argument for imposing a detention centre order upon a young offender relatively early in his criminal career.[34]

It is wise to be sceptical when increased severity is justified, even in part, on paternalistic grounds. In what sense is it 'better' for the offender to receive a substantial sentence at an early age? Presumably the argument is that a substantial sentence is more likely to prevent the offender (either by individual deterrence or perhaps through reform) from persisting in a life of crime, and that law-abidance is a more welcome state than lawbreaking. Is there any evidence that a substantial period of incarceration is more likely than a shorter period to prevent the offender from breaking the law for a given number of years after release? On the contrary, the general findings have consistently shown that the length of imprisonment has little or no effect on the rate of re-offending. Those who take the approach of individual deterrence might well reply, undaunted, that their particular hypothesis has not been tested – that the effect of an unusually severe sentence 'after the second or third offence' (to take Lord Widgery's suggestion) has not been tested because it has not in recent years formed part of regular sentencing practice. A similarly stern doctrine did obtain in Gloucestershire in the latter part of the nineteenth century, under the influence of Barwick Lloyd Baker, whose scheme was that the third felony conviction should be met with a sentence of 7 years' penal servitude, and the fourth conviction with penal servitude for life 'or for some such long term as shall enable him to be released on ticket-of-leave but kept for the greater part of his life under surveillance.'[35] Baker also campaigned for the power to pass cumulative sentences upon habitual misdemeanants, since many summary offences could not be punished cumulatively, and it was argued that longer sentences would reduce the incidence of petty offences by some 60,000 a year.[36] But to test a hypothesis such as Lord Widgery's would be difficult: presumably the severe sentences have to be given to all indictable offenders with three previous convictions. This would have a considerable effect on the prison population;[37] longer custodial sentences have more deleterious side-effects than shorter ones (making the inmate more acquainted with the ways and thoughts of other offenders and straining his links with the outside world), and, most importantly, would condemn to a lengthy custodial sentence many offenders who might otherwise not receive a custodial sentence at all and might nevertheless cease to re-offend. Unless sentencers really maintain that they can distinguish those offenders with three previous convictions who are likely to commit further offences from those who are not, it would be morally and socially catastrophic to subject the hypothesis of individual deterrence to proper testing.

Individual deterrence is therefore not a persuasive reason for cumulative sentencing, particularly where it leads to the imposition of a substantial custodial sentence at a relatively early stage in the offender's career. That would probably bring two major dis-advantages – notably the social and psychological effects of prolonged incarceration, and the subjection to such incarceration of some who would not commit further offences anyway – which should be taken to outweigh the mere possibility of an improved reconviction rate for some. However, even if individual prevention were an acceptable aim, it would not follow that cumulative sentencing for persistent offenders is appropriate. First, the strength of the preventive rationale must surely depend upon the magnitude of the harm which it is sought to prevent. If the crimes which an offender is repeatedly committing are of a relatively minor nature, it is right to ask whether this justifies the use of such severe sanctions as imprisonment, especially if it is no more likely that prison will cause a cessation of offending than that any other measure will. Thus in *Leadley*[38] the conviction was for theft of 2 bottles of Cointreau, and the offender had previously served 13 prison sentences for such crimes as theft of a sack, theft of sweets, going equipped for burglary and being a reputed thief. Does it really matter, to quote Lord Widgery's example from that case, that an offender gets into the frame of mind that every time he is prosecuted and convicted for shoplifting goods worth £10 or £20 he is likely to receive 1 or 2 months' imprisonment? Prevention should not be pursued blindly, without regard to what it is sought to prevent. Cumulative sentencing loses the sense of proportion between crime and punishment which a 'ceiling' principle, with progressive loss of mitigation, ought to preserve. Secondly, cumulative sentencing may not in all cases be the most efficacious means of individual prevention. If it were possible to classify persistent offenders more closely,[39] we could then consider whether there are any groups whose persistence is not a deliberate choice but is the result of other factors, or whether there are groups for whom other preventive strategies might be more fruitful.

(b) Prevention through general deterrence

An alternative argument would be that cumulative sentencing exerts a preventive effect through general deterrence. To maintain that cumulative sentencing could be expected to operate in this way would be to assert that persistent offenders take notice of the penalties imposed on others and that this is instrumental in dissuading them from further lawbreaking, and also that first offenders (on seeing the sentences imposed on persistent offenders) would be influenced towards abstention from crime. Reasoning of this kind has not formed a large part of the justifications for cumulative sentencing: most have preferred to rely upon individual deterrence as the principal method. Moreover, the element of deliberation and calculation which is necessary if general deterrence is to exert an effect cannot be assumed in all kinds of persistent offender;[40] and, where it can be assumed, the probability of detection may be an equally important factor.

(c) Prevention through incapacitation

One justification which is frequently heard is that persistent offenders should receive longer and longer sentences because each conviction shows that society needs more protection from them. We have seen that one of the expectations from cumulative sentencing for minor offences such as poaching, drunkenness and common assault in the 1870s was that some 60,000 fewer such offences would be committed each year: Baker argued that in view of their total number, petty offences were 'more pernicious to the good of the nation than thefts and higher crimes', and this was advanced as a reason for removing petty recidivists from circulation for longer periods and thereby reducing the overall incidence of such offences.[41] In 1901, during the protracted debate which followed the Gladstone Report, senior officials in the Home Office clearly took the view that 'professional' thieves ought also to be subjected to cumulative sentencing so as to achieve an incapacitative effect. Radzinowicz and Hood report the opinion that

> Three or five years' penal servitude for the inveterate thief, who thereafter would be released to prey upon the community, was an unacceptable burden for the police in their struggle to protect society. The senior officials believed that, in the case of larcenies from the person or other thefts by criminals 'making a living' by dishonesty, the amount stolen was of minor importance. When a thief had already received a sentence of 12 months or more, 'it would be logical to prevent him preying on society for a prolonged period', for example, five or seven years. If, afterwards, the thief was convicted again and 'could not show that he had ever made an effort to make an honest living', ten years, or even the maximum of fourteen, would be justifiable in the interests of society.[42]

Even supposing that those who make a living by criminal dishonesty could be accurately identified, would incapacitative sentences of this length be justified? There appears to be no question of a ceiling set by reference to the gravity of the offence: the amount stolen was of minor importance. From what would society be protected? The answer appears to be, minor depredations which are a source of annoyance but not of great loss. With incapacitation as with individual prevention, a sense of proportion must surely be preserved. What are the values of a society which uses its most severe punishment for offences of low or moderate gravity, simply because they are committed repeatedly? Even if prevention is accepted as a proper policy, it is essential to keep the harms prevented in their proper social context. Moreover, the various studies of the incapacitative effects of imprisoning persistent offenders suggest that it is necessary to go to considerable lengths of severity before achieving a noticeable effect.[43]

Incapacitative sentences of relatively modest lengths have also been advocated as a means of dealing with the persistent petty offender. In the recent Home Office survey, a substantial proportion of the magistrates who were consulted argued in favour of a term of imprisonment of a few months for these homeless offenders with drink problems, so as to protect the public and as a means of giving a rest to the police, courts and probation service who had to deal with them so frequently.[44] Although it is possible that a temporary removal from their natural environment might bring about a change in drinking habits, the meting out of prison sentences can only be seen as a negative and temporary expedient. On the basis of the offence(s) committed, there is rarely sufficient justification for using society's ultimate sanction. And even if regard were had to the offences they might commit in the future, the level of social danger would be comparatively low. Short terms of imprisonment in these cases have little incapacitative effect. The foremost policy should be to deal with the persistent petty offender in the community.[45]

(d) **Prevention through the elimination of alternatives**

A common justification for imposing upon a persistent offender either a first prison sentence or the first long prison sentence is that all other forms of sentence have been tried without success. In these circumstances, sentencers sometimes make remarks which suggest that they feel constrained to impose the sentence because everything else had been tried and has failed. Cumulative sentencing appears to be the only logical course to take. A clear example of this approach is provided by the evidence of the Justices' Clerks' Society to the House of Commons Home Affairs Committee. In enumerating the circumstances in which they thought imprisonment to be a justifiable sanction, this body, which has produced a number of thoughtful memoranda on sentencing, included cases of 'repeated offences, where every other course has proved futile.'[46] Similar reasoning may be found in some Court of Appeal decisions. For example in *Gilbertson*, the case of the woman shoplifter aged 59 which was cited earlier,[47] it was said that she had received every form of sentence but that 'nothing appears to have had any effect on her at all', and that it therefore appeared that there was nothing that could be done to prevent the appellant from shoplifting. This was treated as a justification for imposing a substantial prison sentence of 12 months, when on previous occasions she had received only a short sentence. A similar approach is taken by Norval Morris in *The Future of Imprisonment*. He too argues that one sufficient reason for imposing a sentence of imprisonment might be 'when all else practicable has been applied' to an offender on previous occasions. He explains that:

This *faute de mieux* criterion is also subject to a retributive maximum; no repetition of the entirely inconsequential act should lead to imprisonment. However, there must be a role for the residual penal sanction, imprisonment, if the lesser sanctions have been appropriately applied and contumaciously ignored and the offender comes yet again for punishment.'[48]

Why exactly 'must' there be a residual role for the severest forms of penal sanction in cases of this kind? There seems to be an assumption that the imperative 'must' follows from the fact that all other forms of sentence have been tried and have failed. The logic, however, is flawed. From the fact that other forms of sentence have failed to prevent reconviction it does not follow that a custodial sentence is more likely to prevent reconviction than, say, a further sentence of a kind already tried. That does not follow as a matter of logic. Nor is there any empirical evidence to support it, although that is largely because there has been no systematic research into whether imprisonment is more likely than other measures to prevent the reconviction of someone who has previously experienced all other penal measures.[49] Why should the sentencer not try a further probation order, or another community service order or (if there are means) a substantial fine? The sentencer might protest that this takes no account of the gravity of persistent offending itself, or that it allows an offender to make a mockery of the legal system: these arguments are discussed in the sub-sections below. The sentencer cannot, however, protest that more community service or probation is less likely to be effective than imprisonment. There might be factors in a particular case which point to that probability, but there is simply no basis for it as a general proposition.

Moroever, any argument for a custodial sentence or for a substantial custodial sentence on this ground ought to attain a high standard of proof. Custodial sentences are society's strongest weapon against offenders, and it is hardly sufficient to refer to imprisonment as a 'residual' sanction or to accept any *faute de mieux* argument as sufficient. The great social and personal deprivation entailed by custodial sentences calls for a more positive justification; *faute de mieux* is a negative consideration, advanced in a somewhat resigned tone which demonstrates little concern for the destructiveness or the ultimacy of the custodial sanction.[50] The inadequacy of *faute de mieux* as an argument standing alone can easily be demonstrated. The motorist who is repeatedly convicted of exceeding the speed limit will be disqualified from driving, but we regard that as the strongest appropriate sanction for that crime. He might be disqualified from driving on more than one occasion, after a whole string of speeding convictions, but there is no call for imprisonment in such a case even though the ordinary penal approach of fines and disqualification has not 'succeeded'. How can we justify the unavailability of imprisonment in such a case? The justification must take the form that the offence itself, no matter how persistently committed, is not so serious as to make a custodial sentence appropriate. Of course the example is not perfect, since such motoring cases may offer a lengthy period of disqualification from driving as a kind of incapacitative sentence, but the point about imprisonment nevertheless stands. A number of summary offences which are non-imprisonable may be brought within similar reasoning: the persistent litter-dropper, puller of communication cords on railway trains, or television licence evader is simply not considered to present such a serious social problem as to make a custodial sentence appropriate.

The argument of Norval Morris in *The Future of Imprisonment* does not neglect this question of proportionality. He limits his *faute de mieux* proposition by adding that imprisonment should not be imposed in cases in which it 'would be seen by current mores as undeserved (excessive) in relation to the last crime or series of crimes.'[51] Current mores could, it is true, provide guidance about cases which are regarded as very minor such as speeding, litter-dropping and the evasion of television licences; but it is doubtful whether there exists anything worthy of the name 'current mores' which would help to resolve the many difficult issues on the borderline of imprisonability and non-imprisonability. Nor is the legislature always helpful, in England at least. Some offences are not imprisonable at all, and in respect of them a decision has been taken. But there are many more which carry the sanction of imprisonment, as almost every new statute demonstrates. A small study of statutes receiving the royal assent in 1979 revealed large numbers of offences which might be punished with imprisonment, most of them attached to statutes regulating business activities.[52] The study is not mentioned for the purpose of doubting whether imprisonment may properly be used as a sanction for misconduct in business: that remains an open question. The point is that imprisonable offences are each year enacted and re-enacted in multitudes, without any sign of systematic consideration of the proper limits to the use of imprisonment. It is therefore unsafe to infer from the fact that Parliament had provided imprisonment as a penalty that a custodial sentence is justified for persistent commission of the offence: the matter may never have been considered, or at least not for many years and therefore against a different background of penal thought.

In recent years, Parliament has often set a high maximum penalty for an offence which has a wide range of degrees of seriousness, theft being an obvious example.[53] There is a statutory maximum sentence of 10 years' imprisonment for any theft, and one consequence is that there are no statutory indications that imprisonment is considered inappropriate, 'undeserved' or 'excessive' for persistent thefts of property which has a small value. It is by no means easy to justify the view that repeated thefts of milk bottles or thefts of small amounts from shops or stalls are in a different category of heinousness from failure to purchase a television licence. The single statutory maximum for all forms of theft makes it very easy for a sentencer to reason that, if all other forms of sentence have 'failed', imprisonment is the only course left to take. However, Parliament's provision of imprisonment as a maximum penalty is rarely in itself a sufficient link in a chain of reasoning which leads to the imposition of a custodial sentence upon a persistent offender. Parliament provides a maximum penalty of imprisonment for a variety of reasons; offences usually vary considerably within the category to which that maximum applies; therefore the fact that a crime is imprisonable is no argument for imposing imprisonment in a particular case, even where the offender has previous convictions.

The conclusion is that the failure of all other forms of sentence is no reason for imposing a custodial sentence on a persistent offender. There is no foundation for it in empirical terms, since there is no evidence that a custodial sentence is more likely to be effective for such offenders than a further non-custodial sentence. In moral terms it often shows scant regard for the significant difference between custodial and non-custodial sentences, a difference which should require more than a *faute de mieux* argument to justify imprisonment, and it neglects the importance of preserving proportionality between the enormity of the offender's lawbreaking and the severity of society's response to it.

(e) Cumulative sentencing as just deserts

The justifications hitherto considered have relied upon the prevention of crime as the aim of cumulative sentencing. Quite apart from prevention, however, it might be argued that an offender's sentence ought to be made more severe with each conviction because he deserves greater punishment for repeated lawbreaking. Reference was made earlier to the oft-quoted maxim that a man should not be punished twice for his crimes; against that, it was argued that repeated offending increases the seriousness of each successive offence. It is not that the offence intrinsically is more serious, in terms of being more harmful: the additional gravity stems from that other component of the seriousness of a case, the responsibility of the offender. In general – subject to what is said below about different types of persistent offender – the offender with more than one or two previous convictions is more culpable than others, inasmuch as he has received a personal warning through his conviction and yet has chosen to commit further offences, there is no question of an isolated lapse into lawbreaking and (as von Hirsch argues) the ascription of culpability can be made with greater confidence on each successive conviction.[54]

Some have argued that modern retributivism or 'just deserts' as a theory of punishment cannot support higher sentences for persistent offenders, and that the reasoning employed is covertly preventive.[55] That would be true only if modern retributivism took the gravity of the offence as its sole reference point, whereas the responsibility of the offender is also a determinant. The Dove-Wilson Committee in 1932 may have gone too far when they stated that the principle to be applied is that of 'relating the sentence to the offender rather than to the offence'.[56] It is better to join von Hirsch in arguing that 'punishment is . . . neither exclusively act-directed nor exclusively person-directed: it involves condemning the person for having committed wrongful behaviour.'[57] It is therefore necessary to take account of any other proved criminal conduct of this offender, and to extend leniency to the first offender. Lowering the sentence for a first offender

is not a matter of muting one's response because one thinks it unlikely that the actor will do it again. (Were that the logic, some first offenders would get the benefit of the scaled-down condemnation and other first offenders would not – depending on the perceived likelihood of repetition; and that likelihood would, in turn, depend on a variety of facts about the actor, such as his apparent strength of character and the incentives he has to repeat the conduct.) Forecasts of this kind are precisely what is ruled out by the notion of the actor's deserving another chance. Rather than trying to foretell which actors will and will not do it again, the idea is that every actor is entitled to some scaling down of the disapproval directed toward him for the first act, and is so entitled as a moral agent presumed capable of responding responsibly to others' adverse judgment of his conduct.'[58]

However, this argument loses its force as the offender accumulates convictions, so that 'after a limited number of repetitions the plea will have been spent entirely, and the offender will get his full measure.'[59]

This, however, is where the importance of the gravity of the offence must be reasserted. On a preventive theory, the probability that an offender with so many previous convictions will commit a further offence might lead to cumulative sentencing, whereas a properly circumscribed theory of modern retributivism or just deserts should draw a line according to the gravity of the crimes. 'If, after that, the actor commits further repetitions, he should not get any severer a response.'[60] It is this sense of proportion which distinguishes retributive theories, as von Hirsch explained:

> Repetition affects one of the components of seriousness – culpability – but the other component, the harmfulness of the conduct, is more important still. Repetition of an offence that does comparatively little harm cannot justly be made the occasion for severe punishment.[61]

This clearly means that persistent minor offending should lead to persistent minor sentencing, and presupposes some notion of a ceiling set according to the gravity of the type of crime concerned. More difficult would be the offender with a record of fairly serious offences who commits a relatively minor crime. The better reasoning is surely that he should be sentenced on the basis of his most recent crime, and that the effect of his criminal record should only be felt within the limits of the sentence appropriate to the most recent crime.

The application of the just deserts approach to persistent offenders thus depends in practice on two considerations: first, is it possible to estimate the extent to which a previous criminal record of a particular kind does increase the culpability of a particular offender? The answer to this depends to some extent upon whether one is prepared to draw distinctions among types of persistent offender, along the lines suggested in section 6 below. Secondly, can the notion of a 'ceiling' be made convincing both in theory and in practice? The answer to this question is sought in section 5 below.

(f) Cumulative sentencing to maintain respect for the law

It could be argued that to give an offender the same sentence on each subsequent conviction for the same kind of offence is to bring the law into disrepute. If sentences are not increased for persistent offenders, this would 'risk the criminal justice system forfeiting its credibility' and 'risk the offender regarding it as a huge joke.'[62] For a court to give sentences of 1 or 2 months' imprisonment time after time to a persistent shoplifter of goods low in value is to invite the contempt of the public and of the offender.

One assumption underlying this view is that the public expect persistent offenders to receive increasingly harsh penalties. Now it may be true that most people have the idea that first offenders should be treated leniently and persistent offenders more severely, but the intricacies of the discussion in this chapter surely establish that that is too vague a notion upon which to build a rounded approach to the sentencing of recidivists. It may be unwise to ignore a clear up-swelling of public opinion. It would be still more foolish to give way to a partial view which neglects the wider problems of an ordered sentencing system. Some might express the view that successive sentences of 1 or 2 months' imprisonment show no effort to prevent the man from re-offending: that raises a variety of questions about prevention which have been encountered in the foregoing discussion. Others may argue that the court is failing to protect the public from this offender, but that too raises questions about the justification for imposing a disproportionately long sentence in order to protect victims from this particular kind of depredation. The appeal to public opinion leads to consideration of the very questions which have been discussed above.

As for offenders, would they regard it as a 'huge joke' and therefore as no disincentive at all if the courts merely gave them the same sentence after they had committed the offence four or five times? Why should a person who repeatedly receives short prison sentences for stealing goods valued at £20 or £30 consider it to be a matter of ridicule that this conduct 'merely' attracts a sentence of that length? Does the joke derive from the sentence itself, or from the low probability of detection? If it really is the sentence which is the object of ridicule, should the law concern itself that certain individuals regard the risk of 2 months' imprisonment as a 'good bargain' in return for relatively minor thefts? If the point of the joke is that the courts should really take more severe measures, why is that thought appropriate? Once this question is asked, one or more of the justifications canvassed in this part of the chapter is likely to be advanced.

4 The effect of a 'gap'

It is right that the significance attributed to previous convictions ought to decline with the passage of time. A person who makes the effort to abide by the law ought not to be unduly held back by convictions recorded against his name some years previously, particularly when those convictions occurred either at a time when his personality might reasonably be thought to have been maturing or in a social context which was markedly different from the present context (e.g. before marriage, or when living in a different milieu). The principle is recognized by the Rehabilitation of Offenders Act 1974, which provides that certain convictions become 'spent' for general social purposes after a number of years. A corollary of this is that where a person has a number of previous convictions, but has survived for a number of years since his last conviction without further recorded crime, he should be given credit for that if he is subsequently reconvicted. The principle is well-established,[63] and the Court of Appeal recently applied it when sentencing for grievous bodily harm a man of 35 with two previous convictions many years earlier: 'In our judgment his previous record for violence when he was in his late teens and mid-twenties should have been left out of account in deciding what action to take.'[64]

From a gap in an offender's record it is fair to draw inferences which counterbalance the usual inferences from persistent offending. The gap suggests that the offender is no longer committed to a life of crime, that he has made some effort to turn away from lawbreaking and that he is capable of doing so. The offender should be sentenced as he now is, not as he formerly was. Some of those involved in enforcing the law might dispute these inferences in particular cases, expressing themselves as 'pretty sure' that the offender has been constantly involved in crime and has simply not been caught. However great the suspicion that this is so, and even if offenders gain an advantage from this presumption, it would be utterly wrong for the sentencer to do other than act upon the view that the offender has been law-abiding during the intervening years – unless the new convictions relate to acts done over a number of years, or the offender asks the court to take into consideration a number of other offences which have been committed in the period free from convictions. At present, English law also allows the prosecution, after conviction and before sentence, to make allegations of further lawbreaking which the offender may then seek to rebut.[65] However, unless a definite procedure of this kind is followed, the court would be wrong to act upon nuances and inferences which have no basis in evidence before the court. A gap in offending should generally be treated as evidence of temporary law-abidance, and due credit should therefore be given.

5 The notion of a ceiling

Not all those who subscribe to the cumulative approach to sentencing persistent offenders would support an infinite escalation of penalties. Many – even some of those whose guiding principle is individual deterrence – might accept that there is a time when 'enough is enough', and a limit beyond which it would be wrong to increase the sentence for repeated offences of a particular kind, even if that limit is merely the statutory maximum for the offence.[66] By contrast, the principle of progressive loss of mitigation for persistent offenders inevitably imports the notion of a 'ceiling', and the difference between this principle and the cumulative approach depends to a large extent on the effectiveness of such a ceiling.

The principle of progressive loss of mitigation should ensure that an offender with a long record of previous convictions does not receive a sentence which lies beyond the normal range of sentences for the kind of offence of which he now stands convicted. Once he has lost all mitigation, his record should not have the effect of aggravating the sentence. For such a principle to work in practice, the extent of the normal range of sentences for each type of offence must be reasonably clear. It is difficult to tell whether in fact this is the case in the English sentencing system, simply *because* of the problem of sentencing persistent offenders. If the notion of a ceiling is only invoked in cases involving persistent offenders, the statement that a certain sentence is the ceiling for that kind of offence means only that it is the ceiling for that kind of offence when committed by a persistent offender. In fact the notion of a ceiling is used in a few other types of sentencing decision – notably cases where a court is minded to impose an 'exemplary' sentence[67] – but such cases are too rare to afford general guidance as to the level of the ceiling for a whole range of sentences and are, in any event, open to the same kind of critical enquiry: for what type of offence, in what circumstances and committed by what type of offender is a certain sentence the ceiling?

Suspicion that the notion of a ceiling is far more elastic than its pivotal position in the principle of progressive loss of mitigation might suggest is deepened when one considers leading Court of Appeal decisions. In the case of *Connelly*,[68] where the Court of Criminal Appeal reiterated the importance of the ceiling, the sentence of 5 years' imprisonment for stealing two letters from the hall table of a house was varied to 18 months. By what process of reasoning could it be said that 18 months' imprisonment would be a fair sentence for a minor theft of this kind? However bad the offender's record, the

particular offence is one which will always remain firmly at the foot of
the criminal calendar. The same argument applies to the example
given by the Dove-Wilson Committee in 1932 to illustrate the
principle of the ceiling.

> . . . the legal maximum sentence for larceny is five years' penal servitude, but
> the Recorder of London told us that for larceny of a bicycle he would never
> feel justified in giving a longer sentence than 12 or 15 months' imprisonment,
> no matter how often the offender had been previously convicted.[69]

After making due allowance for changes in penological fashion, it is
surely still fair to ask whether this level of punishment is not too high
for a relatively trivial crime. A more recent example is *Harrison*
(1979).[70] The offender had a substantial record of dishonesty
convictions, including a number of burglaries. On this occasion he
pleaded guilty to burglary, having broken into the house of an elderly
woman, leaving empty-handed when challenged by a neighbour. The
trial judge sentenced him to 5 years' imprisonment; the Court of
Appeal agreed that 'the public were entitled to be protected' from this
man but thought 5 years too long, and reduced the sentence to 3 years.
The commentary of Dr Thomas is loyal but pointed.

> A sentence of imprisonment must not exceed the level justified by the facts of
> the offence for which it is imposed, however bad the offender's record may
> be. . . . In the present case, the court treated the appellant as a person with no
> mitigation to offer, but proceeded on the basis that the longest sentence which
> would be justifiable for a single domestic burglary of the kind committed was
> three years.[71]

Thomas has argued that 'a sentence of three years will not
necessarily be considered excessive on the facts for a single burglary,
at least of a private home', but his examples concern offenders with
a record of burglary convictions. Indeed, when he discusses the types
of case in which sentences of between 3 and 5 years have been held
appropriate for burglary, he refers to cases 'where the offender is in his
mid-twenties or older, has committed several burglaries *and has a
significant record*.'[72] It is therefore clear that the ceiling for persistent
burglars is set not (or not merely) by reference to the gravity of the
offence but by reference to the offender's record.

The gravity of the burglary in *Harrison* should not be underestimated: there is always a danger in criticizing decisions on the basis
of a partial report of the facts and the judgment. The offence there was
against an elderly householder,[73] and the fact that the offender left
empty-handed was pure chance (since he would probably have stolen

property if he had not been disturbed). On the other hand, it is fair to enquire about the justification for regarding 3 years' imprisonment as part of the normal range of sentences for a single burglary. Even if we follow Thomas in arguing that 3 years is only part of the normal range in the sense that it is a sentence which can be given to an offender with a bad criminal record, there are further-reaching questions about its relation to sentences for other crimes. If 3 years' imprisonment is thought appropriate for a single residential burglary of the kind committed in *Harrison*, how are we to keep that sentence proportionate to the levels of sentence for more serious burglaries, for offences of wounding, for sexual offences, and so on? By setting the ceiling so high, the courts attribute considerable significance to persistence in offending. The idea that mitigation is being progressively lost appears somewhat further from the reality of the situation than the idea that previous record can aggravate an offence (within certain limits).

In their 1978 report on *Sentences of Imprisonment: a Review of Maximum Penalties*, the Advisory Council took the view that a firm ceiling ought to be fixed by reference to the gravity of the offence. They proposed that a 'normal maximum sentence' should be set for each crime, at a level which included some 90 per cent of sentences for that crime in the previous 3 years, and they made it absolutely clear that the length of an offender's record was not a reason for exceeding that normal maximum and imposing an 'exceptional sentence'.[74] It is true that one of their categories of exceptional sentence, confidently proclaimed by the Council but little discussed by commentators, was aimed at a type of professional (and therefore persistent) offender who committed 'extremely lucrative crimes':[75] that category is further discussed below. But they made it clear that the exceptional sentence was not concerned with 'mere persistence in crime': persistent offenders would have to be accommodated within the normal range of sentences for the offence concerned. The 'normal maximum' for theft and for burglary was set at 3 years' imprisonment. This would appear to indicate that a theft or burglary of modest proportions, and lacking substantial aggravating features, ought to have a lower ceiling than 3 years. If that is so, then sentences of the kind approved in *Harrison* and in the shoplifting case of *Reeves*[76] would be wrong in principle. The lower normal maximum sentence would have the effect of introducing greater realism into the notion of a ceiling.

It therefore emerges that this is one respect in which the Advisory Council were challenging sentencing practice rather than merely embodying it in their own approach. The value-judgments under-lying the difference in opinion are certainly not uncontroversial. If 3 years' imprisonment were to become the normal maximum sentence for burglary, a court would surely have to treat 3 years as the practical maximum for a bad residential burglary in which a substantial amount of property was stolen (although not enough to justify describing the burglary as 'extremely lucrative', and thus to qualify for the exceptional sentence). This would mean that a burglary such as *Harrison* might be expected to carry a working maximum or 'ceiling' of less than 3 years – otherwise the courts would be bereft of the means of signifying the proportionate gravity of different variants of the offence. Neither *Harrison* nor the other cases which Thomas cites for the proposition that 3 years' imprisonment forms part of the normal range of sentences for a single residential burglary could be decided in the same way under the Advisory Council's proposals. It is true that the Advisory Council do not appear to disagree with the prevailing principle of progressive loss of mitigation. In practice, however, the principle does not always operate as it ought to, since the notion of a ceiling is so elastic that it allows the rhetoric of progressive loss of mitigation to co-exist with heavy sentences upon persistent offenders convicted of relatively minor crimes. These problems were not subjected to principled argument in the Advisory Council's report.

6   Some special classes of persistent offender

It has been argued that there is in general insufficient justification for adopting a cumulative approach to the sentencing of persistent offenders, and that the leading approach should be tied to the concept of proportionality. However, even if that is the general principle, there may be certain classes of persistent offenders who are thought to justify special sentencing measures for the protection of society, and other classes who are thought more suitable for a different approach. In this section there is discussion of three special classes – dangerous offenders, professional criminals and petty persistent offenders – together with a reassertion of the general principle in respect of the residual group of persistent non-serious offenders.

(a) Dangerous offenders
The category of 'dangerous' offenders is essentially predictive in

nature: whilst the prediction of future offending may be one element in the sentencing of persistent offenders in general, it is the central element in proposals to deal in a distinct and usually more restrictive way with dangerous offenders. As soon as the concept of a dangerous offender is introduced, several questions of a fundamental nature press forward. Are we ever justified in taking measures more severe than is proportionate to the gravity of the offence committed, in an attempt to avert particularly harmful consequences, or is there a right to receive no more than a proportionate sentence? Can we identify with sufficient accuracy those offenders who present such a high degree of risk as to justify contemplating longer 'incapacitative' sentences? Is the probability of misidentification too high to justify taking any extra measures of protection against offenders believed to fall within a 'dangerous' category? Are indeterminate sentences ever justified, and if so, under what conditions?

It would be presumptuous, within the limited space available here, to offer comprehensive answers to these questions, which have recently been the subject of a wide-ranging inquiry and report by the Floud Committee[77] and of renewed debate among penologists.[78] In the general context of sentencing persistent offenders, however, the approach to sentencing 'dangerous' offenders has important implications. The resurgence of the debate appears to be connected with two concerns: the concern about the empirical basis for preventive sentencing, which has been accompanied by a return to prominence of retributive theories, and the concern about the restricted and possibly socially biased classes of harm against which preventive sentencing tends to have been directed. The latter draws attention to the fact that many sources of danger to the individual's physical safety are allowed to flourish with little social restriction, let alone criminal prosecution, and that if the aim is to reduce the probability that an individual will suffer death or injury, it would make more sense to take stronger preventive action against employers, manufacturers and perhaps motorists than to inflict severe sentences on offenders designated as 'dangerous'.[79] The former concern stems from the pessimistic conclusions of predictive research and has led to a reassertion of a retributive theory which incorporates a right not to be detained for a period longer than is proportionate to the offence committed.[80] The question then is whether this right should be regarded as absolute, or whether there are circumstances in which it might yield to the right of other citizens to be free from physical assault. If, for example, it could be predicted that a particular offender or offenders within a particular group would be highly likely to commit serious harm within some two years of release, would we be justified in imposing a longer term of detention?

Two questions then arise. First, what might count as sufficiently 'serious harm' to justify overriding the prima facie right not to receive a disproportionately severe sentence? The justification for taking incapacitative measures cannot be mere persistence in crime: it must be persistence in inflicting harm of a serious nature. The Advisory Council on the Penal System, in recommending an exceptional sentence which would be determinate but subject to no statutory maximum, suggested that any statutory provision should refer merely to the 'protection of the public from serious harm'.[81] They explained that 'serious harm' should be taken to include

serious physical injury; serious psychological effects of the kind which impair a person's enjoyment of life or capacity for functioning normally (for example, some sexual offences); exceptional personal hardship (for example, financial loss which markedly affects a person's way of life); and damage to the security of the State (for example, as a result of espionage) or to the general fabric of society.[82]

The Floud Committee took the view that if 'exceptional sentences' were introduced, these conditions must be refined; they rejected the vague notion of damage to the fabric of society, and wished to see greater specificity in the concepts of physical and psychological harm. Their formulation was

that grave harm shall be interpreted in this context as normally comprising the following categories: death; serious bodily injury; serious sexual assaults; severe or prolonged pain or mental distress; loss of or damage to property which results in severe personal hardship; damage to the environment which has serious adverse effects on public health or safety; serious damage to the security of the state.[83]

The Committee's approach has been criticized on the basis that it fails to go far enough towards specificity.[84] If we are to justify protective sentences beyond the normal length, it is imperative that the circumstances in which they may be lawfully imposed are clearly circumscribed. The difficulty is, however, that English criminal law is not ideally suited to this task. Some crimes are defined in terms which do imply a judgment of relative seriousness (murder, attempted murder, grievous bodily harm, rape): others are apt to span a wide range of culpability (such as manslaughter, arson and robbery) and therefore require some additional criterion, which is what the Committee try to supply through the adjective 'serious'. The term 'grave harm' is certainly too vague, but the existing structure of offences in English law offers no workable alternative form of classification.[85] Redrafting the criminal law might improve the position, but some of the vagueness – with the attendant possibilities of excessive use and political abuse – would probably remain.

The second question is, how accurately can we predict that an offender will commit dangerous offences? It is relatively easy to predict persistence in crime – almost 9 out of every 10 offenders with 5 or more previous convictions will be reconvicted within 6 years[86] –but it is far more difficult to predict the commission of a limited class of 'grave' crimes. Most projects appear to fail to reach even a 50 per cent success rate in prediction:[87] those which claim more seem to capture an unduly wide group.[88] It is doubtful whether there are many who would accept such low rates of prediction as sufficient justification for applying protective sentences to all members of the category concerned. Even adopting the Floud Committee's view that protective sentences might be regarded as a 'just distribution of certain risks of grave harm,'[89] the justice begins to wear thin when the best prediction that appears possible is that only a minority of offenders within a given group would cause grave harm if released at the end of an ordinary determinate sentence proportionate to the gravity of their last offence.

On the argument so far, it might be doubted whether there is a sufficiently strong case for introducing a protective sentence, and this indeed was the conclusion of the Floud Committee.[90] However, one protective sentence already exists. English judges have the power to award life imprisonment for certain serious crimes, and the criteria upon which they do so may be said to form a judgment of 'dangerousness':

(i)   the gravity of the offence(s) is such as to require a very long sentence;

(ii)   it appears, from the nature of his offence or his history, that the offender is unstable and likely to commit such offence in the future;

(iii)   if such offences are committed again, the consequences to others may be specially injurious, as in the case of sexual offences or crimes of violence.[91]

These criteria have been applied more restrictively in recent years,[92] but even in its more restricted form the life sentence raises at least two major problems. First, although it has been claimed that 'judges seem well able to include those who are ostensibly the most dangerous offenders, and prison authorities effectively to incapacitate them, for long periods',[93] it must also be recognized that 'the accuracy of their judgment must remain a little uncertain . . . because presumably no-one is prepared to risk testing the preventive effects of indeterminate sentences by releasing these people and seeing what happens.'[94]

It is difficult to know whether (in terms of accuracy of prediction) they use the life sentence too much or too little. It is equally difficult to know whether the Home Secretary detains lifers too long or releases them too early. The second problem is that the indeterminacy of the life sentence is now widely acknowledged to bring psychological effects which heighten states of anxiety and hopelessness in the prisoners.[95] Thus, there is not only the question whether the criteria for 'life' are sufficiently well focused to justify a protective sentence beyond the normal range, but also whether those criteria (or indeed any criteria) can supply sufficient justification for a wholly indeterminate sentence.

Apart from the indeterminate life sentence, the general principle of English sentencing is supposed to be that the court should not impose a longer-than-normal sentence on account of a prediction of dangerousness. The Floud Committee found, however, that there is considerable evidence of a covert protective element in English sentencing: 'it is clear that determinate sentences are being passed in greater length than they would otherwise have been because of an estimated likelihood that the offender will commit or repeat a serious offence'.[96]

The protective element is not always covert, for in two recent decisions the Court of Appeal has explicitly approved a long determinate sentence for protective reasons. In each case there were unusual features. In *Green*[97] the trial judge had imposed a sentence of 18 years' imprisonment upon a person convicted of unlawful sexual intercourse with a girl under 13, and it was not open to the Court of Appeal to replace it with a life sentence because that would be treated as a more severe sentence; and in *McAuliffe*[98] the crime was burglary with intent to rape, for which life imprisonment is not available, but the medical evidence of dangerousness was 'all one way' and the Court upheld a sentence of 10 years' imprisonment. Those who are satisfied that the judges use the sentence of life imprisonment in appropriate cases will presumably be equally satisfied with decisions of this kind, which could be said to constitute only technical breaches of the principle that determinate sentences should not be lengthened on protective grounds. However, the question of 'covert' protective sentencing remains unresolved: it is not known whether in these cases the judge acts upon medical evidence of the same quality as that received in cases which result in life imprisonment, or whether inferences are simply drawn from the type of offence and the offender's record. If the latter is the case, this is surely an infringement of the right to receive a sentence no longer than is proportionate to the seriousness of the case, and an infringement for which there seems insufficient justification.

In general, therefore, it seems that there is not a sufficiently strong case for imposing longer sentences on those who appear dangerous, since we cannot hope to identify groups of offenders among whom even half are likely to commit 'dangerous' offences. However, this is not to abjure the imposition of protective precautionary or incapacitative sentences completely. Even those who recognise the right not to be subjected to a disproportionately severe sentence may consistently accept that in certain extreme circumstances, if we were able to attain a sufficiently high rate of prediction, the right of citizens to be free from physical assault might take priority and thus justify a protective sentence.[99] There are many who assume that this justification is made out for sentences of life imprisonment in England, but there is little evidence as to whether the courts generally capture the 'dangerous' and not the 'non-dangerous' offenders.

(b) Professional criminals

How can we identify offenders as professional criminals? Those who are convicted of meticulously planning lucrative bank raids on more than one occasion would appear to satisfy almost any definition of the professional criminal. But what does the adjective 'professional' connote – that crime is the offender's principal source of income, or that it is a regular source of income, that he plans his offences so as to maximize profit and minimize the risk of detection, that he executes his offences with great skill, or merely that he frequently commits acquisitive offences?

The debate has a long history. When at the turn of this century the Gladstone Committee argued that the problem of persistent offenders should be a major target of penal policy, they referred generally to 'men and women who have taken to crime as a profession', and went on to specify

> a large class of habitual criminals not of the desperate order, who live by robbery and thieving and petty larceny, who run the risk of comparatively short sentences with comparative indifference. They make money rapidly by crime, they enjoy life after their fashion, and then on detection and conviction they serve their time quietly with the full determination to revert to crime when they come out. . . . The bulk of habitual criminals are of this class.[100]

It is clear that the Gladstone Committee included the petty persistent thief within this category, even though the amounts taken in many of these thefts were small and were, as Radzinowicz and Hood aptly remark, 'hardly in keeping with its image of a predatory class enjoying, for however short a time, the fruits of its crimes'.[101] The Committee's real target was persistence in crime; the gravity of the offences seemed to take second place. When in 1899 details of a case were sent to Ruggles-Brise, the Chairman of the Prison Commission, his response was in the same vein. The case concerned a man convicted on 15 occasions since 1871 for theft and damage, and his offences including stealing a book, a ham, and two pairs of shoes, for which he received 7, 5 and 3 years' penal servitude respectively. He had also experienced several terms of ordinary imprisonment of between 3 months and 2 years. The comment of Ruggles-Brise was that here was not a petty offender but a

> professional criminal . . . a danger to society. His . . . immediate offence may be trifling, e.g. the theft of a bootlace or a postage stamp, but his previous record . . . proves the absolute inefficiency of passing an ordinary sentence of imprisonment to meet the particular offence.[102]

In what sense is 'professional' used here? There is evidence of persistence, but little evidence that the offender could live by, or even greatly supplement his income by, the commission of such trivial offences as those of which he was repeatedly convicted. Perhaps the real reason for Ruggles-Brise's strong reaction emerges from the last sentence quoted. Appalled at the ineffectivenss of relatively short sentences of imprisonment, he regarded it as self-evident that more severe measures must be imposed. This is cumulative sentencing for reasons of individual deterrence: if 1 year proves ineffective try 2 years, if 2 years proves ineffective try 3 (or 4) years, and so on. It is an approach which penalizes persistence, with scant regard for the gravity of the offences themselves.

When the Prevention of Crime Act was enacted in 1908, after much debate about the correct approach to sentencing recidivists, it provided that before imposing a sentence of preventive detention for a prolonged period the court had to be satisfied, *inter alia*, that at the time of conviction the offender was 'leading a persistently dishonest or criminal life'. The circular sent to chief constables (who took the decision whether to invoke the Act against a particular offender) adopted a somewhat narrower view of professionalism than the Gladstone Committee.

> The crimes must be of a serious character – such as burglary, housebreaking, coining, larceny from the person, robbery with violence, and the like; there must be evidence that the dishonesty is persistent, and there must be good reason to believe that such dishonesty is part of the prisoner's ordinary mode of life, and is not due to drunkenness or destitution, or a mere aberration of intellect.[103]

Although the way in which the Act was used dismayed Churchill and led to the tightening described earlier,[104] it is significant that the guidance to chief constables did attempt to distinguish those for whom dishonesty was a chosen part of their ordinary way of life from others less able to make a free choice. Nevertheless, each of the offences listed in the circular could be committed by the taking of a relatively small sum of money, particularly larceny from the person and housebreaking; and, as a matter of interpretation, it is hard to see what the phrase 'part of the prisoner's ordinary mode of life' connotes, apart from the frequent commission of offences for which none of the explanations given (drunkenness, destitution or want of intellect) seemed appropriate.

The desultory attempts of later years to separate those persistent offenders who may be considered 'real menaces' from those who are 'mere social nuisances' came to little.[105] The courts have used a loose concept of professional crime in their ordinary sentencing practice, in order to justify particularly long sentences, but the concept was little used by the legislature or indeed in official proposals for penal policy until the report of the Advisory Council on the Penal System in 1978. We saw earlier that the Advisory Council adopted a strong but largely untrumpeted stance on persistent offenders, maintaining that the normal maximum sentence should not be exceeded merely because the offender had a long criminal record. However, the Advisory Council proposed that a court should be empowered to exceed the normal maximum and impose an exceptional sentence where it is considered 'necessary for the protection of the public against serious harm'.[106] The exceptional sentence was intended principally for those offenders who are broadly designated as 'dangerous', a category discussed in sub-section (i) above. But the sentence might also be used, the Advisory Council contemplated,

> to deal with offenders convicted of extremely lucrative crimes, if there were reason to think that the gains from such crimes were being regarded as sufficient recompense for serving shorter sentences. Such sentences . . . would in effect amount to the recognition of an exceptional category of robberies, frauds or similar offences.[107]

The Court of Appeal, too, has upheld exceptionally long sentences for offenders of this kind. In *Brewster*[108] (1980), Lawton LJ referred to 'professional criminals, who have long records, great skill as criminals and who from time to time make very valuable hauls'; he upheld a sentence of 10 years' imprisonment for a number of lucrative and daring burglaries. The justification for the long sentence was said to be incapacitation: 'to ensure that they [i.e. professional criminals of this kind] do not carry out raids on other people's houses for very substantial periods'.

One of the lessons of penal history is that it is difficult to draw satisfactorily the distinction between 'professional criminals' and other offenders. If there is to be a form of disproportionately long sentence for professional offenders, then the grounds for overriding the right not to be punished more than proportionately must be clearly argued. The formal justification would be to protect the right of citizens to be free from the depredations of these professionals, but there would need to be clear decisions on the seriousness of the crimes which justify this kind of protective sentencing, and the probability that they would continue to re-offend if given normal sentences. The Advisory Council's proposal for exceptional sentences in these cases was a step in that direction, but there is a dearth of knowledge about the characteristics, motivation, attitude towards sentencing and response to sentencing of individuals defined as 'professional criminals'. The literature is small, by comparison with that on 'dangerous' offenders,[109] and assumptions (especially the assumption that those identified as professional criminals are rational, calculating individuals who can choose whether to offend or not) are more prominent than evidence.

Quite apart from the question of a special protective sentence for professional criminals, however, the category is significant in general sentencing practice. Both on retributive grounds and on preventive reasoning, there is a case for giving more severe sentences to professional criminals. On retributive grounds they deserve more severe sentences than casual or inadequate persistent offenders, inasmuch as they deliberately and unequivocally set themselves against the criminal law. If individual prevention were the aim, sentences would be increased for those who persistently and calculatingly broke the law for profit, so as to make this style of lawbreaking a less attractive course than law-abidance, making the costs to the offender, in terms of sentence length, exceed the benefits, in terms of rewards from crime. Issues such as these are important in setting the level of custodial sentences for serious crimes, and this is discussed further in Chapter 9.[110] However, even the determination of whether a particular offender should be placed towards the top of the range (as a professional criminal) raises problems of evidence and of degree: if the point of the determination is to identify those who are rational, calculating offenders, it is not clear that inferences from the nature of the criminal record, the style of committing an offence or the equipment possessed[111] would always be reliable.

(c) **Persistent petty offenders**
This group is characterized by the comparatively trivial nature of the offending and the poor social ties of the offenders. The group has often been referred to as the 'inadequates', a term which at least directs attention to the fact that some of them lack basic social skills, have no permanent residence, no job, often have a drink problem, and tend to drift in and out of common lodging houses, prison and (where available) hostels. From the discussion of this group in the recent study of *Persistent Petty Offenders*,[112] it seems fair to say that the two leading characteristics of those falling within this group are that the offences are low in gravity, opportunistic and often related to the satisfaction of immediate desires for food and drink, and that the offenders typically betray a failure (often, an inability) to cope with the pressures and the conventions of modern social life. This is the barest sketch of this group of persistent offenders, but it is surely sufficient to demonstrate that the nature of the problem is more likely to be helplessness than wickedness. Some of this group, it is true, may have chosen to drop out of society; but it is likely that a great number more are the victims of a spiral of misfortune in which drink, marital or employment difficulties have played a large part.

If an analysis along these lines is correct, and the question remains one for further and more detailed enquiry, what policy is indicated? One approach is to argue that it is not a matter for the criminal justice system at all, and indeed that at present those who enforce the law do so selectively. As the author of the Home Office Research Study remarks:

. . . there is some evidence that there is an extreme group of homeless people who tend to be avoided by the police (and everyone else) because they are lice-ridden, dirty and smelly, and who therefore cease to get involved with the criminal justice system even though they continue to engage in behaviour for which others are arrested. Thus, persistence, in terms of numbers of recorded convictions cannot be taken as a measure of persistence in actual offending. The homeless poor may be persistently taken to court, and hence persistently returned to prison, because of a persistent failure to provide for them in any other way.[113]

This marks persistent petty offenders as a group for whom community and social services should assume responsibility. The Court of Appeal have from time to time adopted the same view, notably in the well-known case of *Clarke*[114] where (albeit in a slightly different factual context) they roundly stated that the courts should not be used as 'dustbins for the difficult' and varied a sentence of 18 months' imprisonment to a fine of £2. However, the Court has on other occasions accepted incapacitative sentencing for such offenders.

A second approach would be to argue that, since the courts are in fact confronted by cases of this kind, their duty is 'to give a rest to the police, courts and probation service who had to deal with them so frequently and to remove them from their environment as a necessary condition for them to change their drinking habits'.[115] This was the view of some magistrates interviewed as part of the Home Office study, which led them to impose short terms of imprisonment; other magistrates adopted the first approach and declined to use imprisonment in this way. Those who take the economic approach might well doubt the cost-effectiveness of imprisonment for this group. Those concerned to ensure proportionality would doubt the justification for imprisoning at all a group whose offending was of such a relatively minor nature.

A third approach would be to accept that the primary task lies with community provision of social services, but also to accept that in the short and medium term the courts and the penal system will have to deal with a number of offenders in this group. In these circumstances it might be thought most helpful to offer constructive treatment rather than the negative experience of imprisonment. Small steps in this direction have already been taken, in the form of detoxification centres, day training centres and day centres (which are not restricted to offenders). What is important, however, is that facilities of this kind should be offered to offenders within this group and not forced upon them: it is right to use persuasion, but wrong to use coercion and wrong to lengthen the period of social control so as to ensure a compulsory framework for treatment. Where treatment does take a long time, it should be voluntary and not sanctioned by the criminal law.

Each of the three approaches to the problems of this group accepts that there is no connection here between their persistence and wickedness. Their persistent lawbreaking is connected with a whole host of social and personal disadvantages which are a far cry from the cool calculation of profit which characterizes the professional offender and, although further enquiry is needed into the characteristics of this group and the most appropriate way of dealing with them, the classical model of crime and punishment is plainly inapplicable.

(d) Persistent non-serious offenders

An attempt has been made to identify three classes of persistent offender who might warrant a special approach in sentencing. Large numbers of persistent offenders fall into the residual category of 'persistent non-serious offenders': they do not qualify as sufficiently 'dangerous' or 'professional' to justify exceptionally severe measures, and are not petty offenders with personal or social problems. Most of this residual group will be recidivist thieves, burglars, swindlers and handlers of stolen goods, whose offences cannot be described as 'extremely lucrative'. To these offenders the general arguments outlined in part of this chapter should be applied. The leading principle should be proportionality, determined after discussing the relative harmfulness of criminal conduct along the lines of Chapter 4. Thus, no matter how persistent the small-time thief may be, his persistence should not result in his subjection to a sentence higher than a realistic ceiling proportionate to his latest offence.

7 Breach of conditional sentences

One aspect of the sentencing of persistent offenders to which the arguments discussed in this chapter might be applied is where courts have to deal with offenders who have committed a further crime during the operational period of a conditional sentence. Not all breaches of conditional sentences involve the commission of a further offence, but many do: all breaches of suspended sentences and of partly suspended sentences, some breaches of probation orders and community service orders, breach of conditional discharge and (itself an offence) breach of disqualification from driving. Those who place great emphasis on 'respect for the law' might regard these as especially heinous cases: the offender has not merely re-offended, he has done so in clear defiance of a court order and has, in a sense, betrayed the trust placed in him by the court or at least squandered an opportunity offered to him. Could these extra elements of defiance or squandering of opportunity justify a strongly punitive response to the new offence?

Those who view the new offence as a flouting of the court order may treat this as a signal to abandon all approaches other than individual deterrence. This is how a court is almost driven to view the new offence when the offender is subject to a suspended sentence: the court is obliged to activate the suspended sentence in full 'unless [it] is of opinion that it would be unjust to do so. . .'. Generally speaking, the Court of Appeal has tried to ensure that this exception is confined to cases where the new offence is relatively trivial.[116] Some three-quarters of breaches of suspended sentences are followed by the activation of the sentence; the sentence thus activated should generally run consecutively to the sentence for the new crime; and thus, to an extent, cumulative sentencing is institutionalized by the rules attending the suspended sentence. Furthermore, some two-thirds of suspended sentences are imposed by magistrates' courts, and there is evidence that magistrates' courts often give a longer term if they are suspending the sentence than they would if they were imposing immediate imprisonment,[117] a situation which might be exacerbated if sentences of immediate imprisonment become shorter and the lengths of suspended sentences are not adjusted accordingly. Thus the 'consecutive' principle and the tendency to impose a longer term if it is to be suspended may each, or in combination, produce the result that the offender in breach of a suspended sentence may serve a term longer than if he had been convicted on two separate occasions and given a genuine non-custodial penalty on the first occasion. The

Advisory Council recognized the point in their report on *The Length of Prison Sentences*, by means of this rhetorical question:

> Are not many suspended sentences longer than the sentence would have been if it had been immediate, and, in many such cases, does not the eventual activation of the suspended sentence without any reduction in its length create a situation where the total sentence is too long?[118]

Another consequence may be that the first prison sentence served by an offender, being composed perhaps of a fairly short term of immediate imprisonment for the second offence together with the activated suspended sentence for the first offence, is of medium length and goes beyond the very short first prison sentence which is often thought to be most appropriate these days (the 'clang of the prison gates' principle).[119]

Some sentencers might accept these points, and defend the suspended sentence on the basis that it carries a clear warning to the offender which he disregards at his peril. He knows exactly what is likely to happen if he is convicted of a further offence committed during the operational period of the suspended sentence, and he must adjust his behaviour accordingly or face the consequences. In von Hirsch's terms, this is to treat him as a responsible moral agent.[120] This defence of the suspended sentence assumes that it is invariably given only to offenders who are likely to be in full control of their behaviour (or, put another way, that all those offenders subjected to suspended sentences are in a position to determine whether they commit an offence during the operational period); it also assumes that any further offence may properly be taken to justify the activation of the suspended sentence. In a sense the two assumptions are closely related, for it is arguable that some offences are the product of an overwhelming combination of circumstances which lead a person to react under stress in a criminal way. Such behaviour is neither entirely under the offender's control nor necessarily a signal for a deterrent response. The protagonists of the suspended sentence may hold such a wholly rationalistic view of human behaviour that they would reject this out of hand; or, even if their view of behaviour is not entirely rationalistic, they may still maintain that almost all offenders are capable of responding to a clear and definite individual deterrent. This often leads to the argument that the suspended sentence of imprisonment has a specially powerful deterrent effect, over and above any deterrent effect exerted by, for example, the conditional discharge or probation, each of which carry the threat of an additional sentence for the first offence if a further offence is committed during their operational period. Against this, Bottoms argues that:

It is now well known that in general the penalty which is applied to a particular offender appears to make little or no difference to the subsequent likelihood of reconviction of that offender. There is no direct study which establishes that this is so for the suspended sentence as for other sentences, but equally there is no evidence to suggest the special efficacy of the suspended sentence. So it is reasonable to assume provisionally that this sentence has little, if any, 'special deterrent effect'.[121]

The question is whether it *is* reasonable to assume 'no effect' from 'no evidence'. There is surely a commonsense notion which suggests that the suspended sentence, with a specific term of imprisonment prescribed in case of breach, is much more likely to impress some offenders than the vague possibility of a custodial sentence on breach of a conditional discharge, probation order or community service order. It would be wrong to assert that this is necessarily so for all offenders; but even Bottoms acknowledges, in an indirect way,[122] that there may well be a group of offenders for whom the specific threat carried by the suspended sentence is more effective than the more vague threats inherent in other conditional sentences. Of course the courts use the suspended sentence more widely and more indiscriminately than this, probably in part for the very reason that no evidence has yet been produced which identifies the characteristics of offenders for whom the suspended sentence might be thought specially effective.

As for the assumption that the commission of any further imprisonable offence during the operational period is properly treated as a sufficient justification for activating the suspended sentence, this is largely a pragmatic matter. The whole idea of a special and individual deterrent would lose credibility if suspended sentences were not routinely activated in the majority of cases of breach, it is said. It is easy to ridicule an absolute rule of activation in full, by pointing out that an offence may be imprisonable yet trivial (such as minor damage or theft of a milk bottle), but the proviso that the court need not activate the suspended sentence if it appears 'unjust to do so' should cater for such exceptional cases. Indeed, the legislature has recently (in section 31 of the Criminal Justice Act 1982) enlarged the range of circumstances which a court may take into consideration when determining whether it would be 'unjust' to activate the suspended sentence in full. A court may now consider not merely circumstances arising *since* the suspended sentence was imposed, but also the circumstances *in which* it was imposed. This enables the court to consider the original offence and the new offence together, although it is still obliged to activate the suspended sentence in full unless to do so would be 'unjust'.

By contrast, it is possible for a court dealing with breach of any other conditional order to impose any sentence which could have been imposed for the first offence. This gives the second court a full opportunity to consider the two offences both individually and together. In fact, imprisonment is fairly widely used by the Crown Court in these circumstances, particularly when it is considered that not all breaches of other conditional sentences involve the commission of a further offence. Thus in 1980 the Crown Court sent some 65 per cent of those breaching community service orders immediately to prison, a figure which is very close to the 70 per cent of suspended sentences which were activated on breach by the Crown Court. In magistrates' courts only about a quarter of breaches of community service orders resulted in immediate imprisonment, compared with around 80 per cent of suspended sentences. The Crown Court imprisoned half of those breaching probation and a third of those breaching conditional discharges, whereas the figures for magistrates' courts were a quarter for probation and 12 per cent for conditional discharges. The element of flexibility means, however, that the second court may give only a nominal sentence for the first offence (such as 1 day's imprison-ment) or may indeed make a further order of the kind breached. In the case of *Crowley* (1971)[123] a young man with an institutional background had spent 12 months on a probation order before committing a further offence in a sudden outburst of temper. There was no doubt that 12 months without committing an offence represented a considerable improvement in the offender's way of life, but the second court felt bound to impose a prison sentence. The Court of Appeal took account of the reports on the offender's behaviour in recent months and substituted a further probation order, remarking that while

every court should be slow to make another probation order when one has been breached, and even slower still if there have been more than one breaches of that order . . . all cases must be viewed in the light of their particular facts.[124]

This decision illustrates the importance of flexibility for the second court (which is severely restricted where the offender is subject to a suspended sentence, even if it is combined with a supervision order) and it serves to reinforce the view that a breach of one order does not necessarily call for a more severe measure. The second offence must be viewed in terms of the offender's responsibility for it as well as its inherent gravity, and the choice of sentence made after consideration of response to the earlier court order. The decision in *Hyland* (1973)[125] bears similar features: after 18 months on a probation order the offender was convicted of possessing an offensive weapon, in circumstances where he was under threat of attack from a fellow lodger. He was, on breach, sentenced to 9 months' imprisonment for the first offence; the Court of Appeal substituted a fresh probation order, saying that imprisonment was not justified in view of the offender's positive response to probation and the facts of the later offence. Thomas adds that 'many similar cases can be found'.

Despite decisions of this kind, however, the notion that an offender who breaches a conditional order of the court ought generally to be visited with more severe penalties probably holds considerable influence in the minds of sentencers. Where there is no clear evidence to suggest that the second offence is a mere aberration which fails to reflect the offender's true response to the conditional order, it is likely that courts will be tempted to reason that the offender has failed to take advantage of the opportunity given to him by the first court and ought therefore to feel the full force of the law. One objection to the suspended sentence is that it institutionalizes just such reasoning. Bottoms has inveighed strongly against the suspended sentence for a whole range of reasons both theoretical and practical, maintaining that 'discounting the "special deterrent theory", it becomes plain that everything that can be achieved with the suspended sentence can be achieved equally well by the conditional discharge.'[126] The assertion that the conditional discharge can achieve everything which the suspended sentence can achieve might be acceptable at the level of pure logic if one does completely discount the 'special deterrent theory', but Bottoms acknowledges that in terms of penal policy the issues are more complex. There are at least three major dilemmas inherent in retaining the suspended sentence as part of sentencing policy to deal with persistent offenders.

First, the suspended sentence undoubtedly holds an attraction for the courts: it is the only available sentence which allows them to declare a period of imprisonment, whilst at the same time giving weight to considerations personal to the offender by allowing him (conditional) liberty. The dilemma is that it may hold too great an attraction for the courts, so that they use it not only for offenders who might otherwise have been sent immediately to prison but also for offenders who might otherwise have received a non-custodial sentence which did not oblige a court to activate and send the offender to prison for breach. Equally the Crown Court may impose suspended sentences with supervision orders upon offenders who might otherwise have received a simple probation order. The result is that some offenders who breach their suspended sentence may go to prison earlier and for longer periods than ought to be the case. Thus, whilst there is a case for preserving powers which the courts find useful, to do so carries the probability of a significant degree of misuse. The second dilemma has a similar source. What distinguishes the suspended sentence is that the court at the outset prescribes the penalty which will be imposed in the event of breach. Many think it would be futile if the second court were free to vary or to disregard the penalty prescribed by the first court; yet the result of restricting what the second court may do is that, even after s.31 of the 1982 Act, the court may be constrained to impose what it feels to be an inappropriate sentence for the two offences. This dilemma is inherent in the accepted notion of the suspended sentence. Would the 'special deterrent effect' of the sentence, if it exists, really be significantly impaired if the second court were permitted to impose for the first offence any penalty *up to the maximum* of the sentence suspended by the first court? A change of this kind would bestow much-needed flexibility on the court which deals with the breach, yet it is not known whether it would significantly reduce any individual deterrent effect. This is one of many related matters upon which there is insufficient basis in the research findings for any confident assertion. Some say that offenders are optimists, and that if the second court were not constrained to activate the sentence, the suspended sentence would lose its credibility. The third dilemma is that, for all its illogicalities and misapplications by the courts, it appears to make some contribution to penal policy inasmuch as it keeps out of prison some people who might otherwise go there. If the suspended sentence were abolished, there is the risk that sentencers might not view the remaining non-custodial penalties (such as community service orders, fines, probation and conditional discharges) as adequate to mark the gravity of some offences and so more offenders might receive immediate imprisonment. The dilemma here is that the suspended sentence probably makes some contribution to the policy of reducing the prison population, but not as great a contribution as it ought to.

Whether the partly suspended sentence[127] will bring similar problems of application, and what the effect of abolishing the suspended sentence for young adult offenders will be,[128] are both questions which will be answered in the years to come. For the present, it is sufficient to note that the flexibility which courts generally have in dealing with persistent offenders is absent where the offender is dealt with for breach of a suspended sentence and (to a lesser extent) for breach of a partly suspended sentence. This tends to draw the sentencer towards a form of cumulative sentencing, and away from a full consideration of the gravity of the offence and the responsibility of the offender. The other conditional sentences, apart from suspended sentences, leave room for this wider consideration, and thereby allow the court to take account of the circumstances of the later offences.

8 Conclusion

Cumulative sentencing is objectionable because it leads to sentences which are disproportionately severe when compared with the seriousness of the case. In general, a first offender should benefit from substantial mitigation, and this mitigation should gradually be lost when second, third or fourth convictions follow. That, however, is the general principle, and it is important to preserve a sensitivity towards the circumstances of each subsequent offence: the discussion of breaches of conditional sentences serves to demonstrate that progressive loss of mitigation should not inexorably be the result of repeated offending. If the general principle is to be effective in practice, there must be identifiable and realistic ceilings. The arguments in Chapter 4 about relativities between types of criminal offence must be pursued so as to produce a ranking which will then yield meaningful ceilings. The ceiling must be proportionate to the gravity of the offence, and must operate so as to prevent the occurrence of cumulative sentencing under the name of progressive loss of mitigation: in other words, the ceiling should not be set by reference to persistent offenders, otherwise the sentencer is punishing persistence to a disproportionate extent. We should be prepared to say that the persistent shoplifter of goods of low value simply should not receive a custodial sentence, however frequently he or she re-offends, because the offence is simply not serious enough. There may be grounds for limited exceptions to the proportionality principle for two classes of persistent offender, the 'dangerous' offender and the 'professional' criminal, as discussed in section 6(i) and (ii). Apart from these exceptions, however, the 'ceiling' principle should be put into practice much more rigorously than has yet taken place in England.

6
Multiple offenders

This chapter, like the last, deals with some of the problems posed by the sentencing of persistent offenders. Its focus, however, is upon offenders who come before the courts in a different context. In the last chapter the main concern was with the sentencing of recidivists – those who offend repeatedly, despite the fact that they have experienced criminal sanctions. The main concern in this chapter is with offenders who commit a number of offences before they are detected and convicted, so that the court has to sentence them on one occasion for several offences. Not all the offenders whom the courts have to sentence for several crimes could be described as 'persistent offenders', for in some cases the offender has been involved in a single incident which gives rise to a number of charges and convictions. But many 'multiple offenders', whom the courts have to sentence for more than one offence, are people who have been committing offences over a period of weeks, months or even years before they appear in court, and they then face a number of charges. The criminal record of such multiple offenders may vary: some of them will be recidivists too, having experienced a number of criminal sanctions in the past, whilst others will fall into that seemingly incongruous category of 'persistent first offenders' – those who, when they are convicted for the first time, are convicted of several offences which show that they are accustomed to lawbreaking, if not to the criminal process.

The focus of this chapter, then, will be on multiple offenders, some of whom will have been convicted of a number of offences arising from a single incident, but most of whom will have been convicted of offences committed at different times during the period before their court appearance. For any system of sentencing which places some emphasis on proportionality between the seriousness of the case and the severity of the sentence, multiple offenders give rise to difficulties both theoretical and practical. It is one thing to compare a residential burglary with a rape; it is quite another thing to draw comparisons of gravity between 2, 4 or 6 residential burglaries and a single rape. Before tackling these problems, however, the various procedural methods of dealing with multiple offenders must be briefly explained.

1 Charging the multiple offender

What approach should the police and prosecutors take when it emerges that a suspected offender may have committed more than one offence? A full answer to this question would import a mass of technical detail; for present purposes, a sketch of the three main avenues open to the prosecution should provide a sufficient basis for the remainder of the discussion.

(i) *Charge all offences* The straightforward approach is to charge all the offences of which the prosecution have prima facie evidence. This has the disadvantage that the indictment could be so long as to make it very difficult for the court to deal fairly and accurately with the various charges against the defendant. If he pleads not guilty, the task of a jury dealing with a lengthy indictment may be formidable and beyond what it is reasonable to expect of them. For this reason, it has long been accepted that the prosecution may, and indeed ought to, bring no charge in respect of relatively trivial incidents where the defendant already faces a number of more serious charges.[1] To some extent it remains in the prosecution's interest to bring a number of charges against a defendant, since they may then agree not to proceed with some of the charges in exchange for the defendant's agreement to plead guilty to the others. Where a defendant does plead guilty to some charges and it is consequently 'obvious to the prosecution that he [will] get a long sentence', it will probably be right for the prosecution to drop any further charges to which he pleads not guilty.[2] The prosecution should obtain the trial judge's consent not to proceed with certain counts in an indictment,[3] a requirement which suggests that the approach of charging all offences and then dropping some of the charges at the trial brings the exercise of discretion into the open and subjects it to judicial scrutiny. In practice, however, judges usually agree readily to this course; and there are strong arguments against 'overloading' the indictment in the first place.

(ii) *Charge specimen offences* Where the prosecution have evidence of a course of offending over a considerable period, usually but not necessarily against the same victim (e.g. incest with a particular child, theft from an employer), they may decide to charge only a few incidents as 'specimen counts'. The chosen 'specimen counts' should relate to the most serious of the alleged offences. This is obviously easier for the prosecution, since it spares them the burden of adducing evidence in relation to each one of a long series of offences. There may be certain problems at the sentencing stage, however, for it is axiomatic that an offender should not be sentenced on the basis of charges which either have not been proved against him or he has not asked the court to take into consideration (see below).[4]

(iii) *Offences taken into consideration* The police may invite a defendant to ask the court to take other offences into consideration when sentencing him for the crimes charged. The House of Lords has laid down that a defendant should be informed explicitly of each offence and asked to consent to the court taking each one into consideration when sentencing.[5] The offences thus taken into consideration do not rank as convictions, but the court is likely to increase the sentence in order to take account of them, and the procedure is a relatively informal and expeditious way of disposing of a long series of offences which are not especially serious in nature.

2 Concurrent sentences

At the outset, the limitations of any theoretical discussion of the sentencing of multiple offenders must be openly avowed. Because of the wide variety of combinations of offences in particular cases, and the equally wide variations in the time-span of the offending with which the court has to deal, it would be unwise to adopt too dogmatic an approach. Indeed Dr Thomas, after identifying two general principles, recognizes the existence of decisions 'which do not lend themselves to any generalisation.'[6] On the other hand, this wide variation in the circumstances in which courts may be confronted with the problem of sentencing a multiple offender should not be allowed to stifle the search for general principles. There can be no doubt, as the authorities cited in this chapter show, that courts do rely upon general principles when working out the appropriate sentence in these cases, and it is upon the general propositions that the discussion will focus.

Just as the straightforward approach to prosecuting is to bring a charge in respect of each offence of which there is prima facie evidence, so the straightforward approach to sentencing is to impose a sentence for each offence of which there is a conviction. The offender who is convicted of one crime receives one sentence; the offender who is convicted of three crimes receives three sentences, each one additional to the others. The logic of this approach, however, is far from perfect. It begins to appear less straightforward when it is realized that in certain instances the law may provide (and the prosecution charge) a number of offences where in theory one would suffice, and in other instances the law may provide (and the prosecution charge) one offence where it would be natural to think of two or three. For example, the offence of aggravated burglary contrary to section 10 of the Theft Act 1968 is apt to cover a case where a person commits burglary and has with him a firearm, an offensive weapon or an explosive; therefore it is unnecessary to charge such a person on one count with burglary and on a separate count with the offence of possessing a firearm, offensive weapon or explosive substance. The law provides a single offence, aggravated burglary, and the sentencer will naturally take account of both elements of the crime (the burglary and the possession offence) in his calculations. On the other hand, crimes such as manslaughter and robbery do not specify the use of a weapon; whilst it would be unusual to add a charge of possessing an offensive weapon to a charge of manslaughter or robbery (since the maximum penalty for offensive weapons is 2 years' imprisonment), prosecutors will often add a charge under the Firearms Act 1968 if the accused had a firearm with him.

Now from the point of view of calculating the total sentence, it should be immaterial whether a firearms charge is added in such a case or not. The sentencer has the facts before him, the maximum sentence for manslaughter or robbery is sufficiently high to allow him to take full account of any such aggravating factor, and it is highly unlikely that these features of the case would be overlooked. But there would be a choice as to how the sentence is expressed. If only manslaughter or robbery were charged, obviously there would be a single sentence. If there were an additional conviction under the

Firearms Act, the sentencer in theory has a choice: if he decides that, say, 7 years is the appropriate total sentence, he could express this in terms of two consecutive sentences (e.g. 5 years for robbery, 2 years for the firearm) or in terms of 2 concurrent sentences (e.g. 7 years for robbery, with 2 years concurrent for the firearm). The straight-forward approach cannot deal with this kind of problem, since it overlooks the vagaries of prosecutorial discretion and of the shape of English criminal law. In some fields of activity, the law provides several separate offences, in other fields a single encompassing crime. Merely to add a sentence for each conviction ignores these quirks of history and convention.

This is not necessarily to suggest that prosecutors in any way abuse the criminal process by, for example, adding a firearms charge to a principal charge of robbery or manslaughter when it is perfectly clear that the maximum sentence for the principal crime can accommodate any sentence the court might wish to pass. There are at least four independent reasons for adding a charge relating to firearms (or explosives). It ensures (i) that the user or carrier of firearms is clearly and separately labelled, in court, in public and in his criminal record, as an offender willing to resort to such means: if consistency can be attained among prosecutors and sentencers, then the form of a criminal record will become a reliable indicator of whether or not the offender is concerned with firearms, and this may assist in subsequent sentencing (and parole) decisions; (ii) that the defendant has a distinct opportunity to challenge the prosecution case on this ground; (iii) that if for some 'technical' reason he is acquitted on the principal charge, he may nevertheless be convicted on this ground; and (iv) in any event the firearms offence might relate to times and places other than those of the principal offence. The second point might be met by more rigorous fact-finding procedures before sentence, and the fourth by regarding this as a 'fringe' activity which does not justify cluttering the indictment where there are much more serious charges. But the first point may be considered important: the special heinousness of firearms offences should be marked, even if the principal charge is very serious in itself. If this is accepted, then the offender will be convicted of 2 crimes as a result of a single incident. This bare fact – whether he is convicted of two separate crimes, or the whole incident is brought under the umbrella of one crime – should have no influence on the total sentence, but there are procedural questions about the most appropriate approach.

(a) The idea of concurrence

Where a court has to pass sentence for two or more offences, the sentences might in theory be made concurrent or consecutive. Taking the question at the level of principle, what does the notion of concurrence imply? Its most obvious reference is temporal: offences committed concurrently ought to receive concurrent sentences. Of course, concurrence in time is not a precise concept: if one offence follows immediately upon another, or even rapidly upon another, one might be tempted to refer to them as occurring at the same time and to treat them as parts of the same incident. On the other hand, the longer an incident continues, the more serious it usually is; therefore, irrespective of the procedural issue of whether a continuing series of offences is thought to call for concurrent sentences (as the Court of Appeal has held in relation to a series of thefts from different shops, regarding them as forming part of a 'single shoplifting expedition')[7] or consecutive sentences, it is surely right that such a series of offences should be regarded *ceteris paribus* as a more serious manifestation of criminality than a single such offence and as justifying a greater total sentence.

Even where there is exact temporal concurrence, however, there might be other reasons for arguing that concurrent sentences would be inappropriate. Consider a case of burglary in which the offender enters the house, begins to steal items and to pack them into a bag, is surprised by the occupier and strikes the occupier in order to make good his escape. It would generally be said that the offence of violence was committed at the same time as the burglary (although in strict legal terms the burglary might have been committed at the time he entered the house).[8] In principle an offence of burglary accompanied by violence ought to be regarded as more serious than burglary without violence; the crime of burglary is not sufficiently broad to encompass all cases of violence;[9] therefore it could be both logically and morally appropriate to pass consecutive and not concurrent sentences. Although the offences were concurrent in point of time, they violated different kinds of legal prohibition (i.e. offences against property, offences against the person). The offender ought to be labelled both as a property offender and as a violent offender, and his criminality should be viewed more seriously than if he had committed the property offence alone. We may therefore conclude, at the level of principle, that the idea of concurrence combines proximity in time with proximity in type of offence.

(ii) The general principle

The English courts broadly follow the approach outlined above, so that where two or more offences are separately charged and they form part of a 'single transaction', the court should generally impose concurrent sentences. It is very difficult to construct a workable definition of a 'single transaction', but it may be said that the Court of Appeal has extended the concept considerably beyond what might be expected. Thus a series of offences of the same or similar type, committed against the same victim, may properly be regarded as parts of the same transaction unless they were committed over a fairly lengthy period of time.[10] On the other hand, the Court has recognized that concurrence in time is insufficient to justify concurrent sentences where the offences are of different kinds, upholding consecutive sentences where (for example) a person who has driven with an excess alcohol level then attempts to bribe a police officer to refrain from administering the breath test.[11] The same approach has been taken in cases of burglary accompanied by violence.[12] Interpreted in terms of proximity in time and proximity in type of offence, then, the 'single transaction' principle embodies the general approach.

(iii) Three possible exceptions

To this general principle there are three possible exceptions, each of them afflicted with some degree of uncertainty. The first concerns those situations in which two separate offences have been created and they deal with different stages in what many people would regard as the same transaction. Thus the offence of going equipped for burglary is distinct from the offence of burglary; in a strict sense the offences are separate in time, since the former is preparatory to the latter. Yet going equipped does not of itself render a burglary more serious, except inasmuch as it evidences premeditation. The real purpose of the offence is surely to penalize those who are detected whilst preparing to commit burglary, without the need to wait until the substantive crime has taken place. Yet in *Ferris* (1973)[13] the Court of Appeal held that, where an offender is convicted of both offences, it is right to impose consecutive sentences. 'Parliament has provided for two separate offences. It is one thing to commit a burglary; it is another to prepare oneself with equipment.' The reasoning is unconvincing: the 'going equipped' offence is clearly to be charged as a preliminary offence where the substantive crime is not committed, and the element of premeditation (as evidenced by the carrying of equipment) is not normally a sufficient justification for a separate sentence. There are authorities which go against *Ferris*,[14] and they are surely to be preferred from the point of view of principle. Where a burglary is accompanied by violence, it is surely right to mark the fact with consecutive sentences. Where a burglary is committed with tools which were brought deliberately rather than taken up impulsively, the fact is more appropriately reflected in the sentence passed for burglary. To add a further charge, conviction and sentence is to perpetrate needless duplication and complication.

In recent years the Court of Appeal has moved towards this view in cases involving firearms. It had long been thought axiomatic that where a firearms conviction accompanies a conviction for another offence (such as wounding or robbery), there should be a consecutive sentence on the firearms count. On this second possible exception, the leading authority for some years was probably *Faulkner* (1972):[15] the offender was seen on the roof of a warehouse and chased by the police, and was subsequently convicted of a number of offences including conspiracy to steal, assault occasioning actual bodily harm and offences contrary to the Firearms Act. He was sentenced to 3 years' imprisonment for the firearms offences and 3 years' consecutive for the other offences, and the Court of Appeal dismissed his appeal. The argument for the appellant was that the offences formed part of a single transaction and ought to attract concurrent sentences; the Court replied that if an offender carried a firearm with intent when pursuing a criminal enterprise, he ought to receive consecutive sentences to discourage such conduct. This deterrent reasoning gave way to arguments of administrative convenience and expedition in *Brown-Rampton* (1979)[16] and *Clarke and McGinn* (1981),[17] where the Court of Appeal maintained that an additional firearms count ought not to be charged and made the subject of a separate sentence; the apparent reason was the avoidance of 'confusing and unnecessary' complications in trials. However, in *French* (1982)[18] the Court of Appeal took the unusual step in a sentencing appeal of holding that *Brown-Rampton* and *Clarke and McGinn* had been decided *per incuriam*, without the decision in *Faulkner* being drawn to the Court's attention, and overruled them. The Court 'wholeheartedly agreed' that indictments should be kept as brief and as uncomplicated as possible, but pointed out the desirability of including a separate firearms count so that the defendant has the opportunity to dispute an issue on which he may subsequently be sentenced, and so that the judge has the jury's verdict on the issue. It is then proper for the judge to impose a consecutive sentence if there is a firearms conviction as well as a conviction for the substantive crime (in *French*, this was robbery), but he must ensure that 'the totality of the sentences is correct in all the circumstances of the case', so that the offender is 'not sentenced twice over for carrying a gun'. For the reasons given in section 2 of this chapter, the decision in *French* constitutes a welcome statement of principle.

The third exception concerns assaults on the police or upon others attempting to arrest the offender, and may not be a true exception. This is because, where a police officer is assaulted whilst trying to effect the arrest of someone who is in the course of committing another offence, the other offence may well be of a different type and committed against a different victim – each of which would take the case outside the concurrent principle in any event. Nonetheless, where a case involves an unwarranted attack on lawful authority this supplies an independent reason for imposing consecutive sentences.[19] As the Court of Appeal remarked in *Kastercum* (1972),[20] consecutive sentences are 'generally preferable to emphasise the gravity of assaulting the police as a means of escape.'

(d) The scope of the general principle
It has been emphasized that neither the general principle nor the three possible exceptions operate precisely, but the brief discussion shows that the choice of approach may have consequences for the offender and raise questions of policy. Lest the theoretical difficulties presented to the courts in some of these cases be overlooked, one more problem may be mentioned. Thomas cites a number of decisions as authority for the proposition that 'a sequence of offences involving a repetition of the same behaviour towards the same victim' may be regarded as a single transaction, and therefore sentenced concurrently.[21] Clearly this breaks away from the element of proximity in time which forms part of the idea of concurrence; but it derives some support from ordinary ways of thinking and speaking, since one might well say that offences of perjury committed on different days of a trial were part of a single transaction, or that instances of false accounting committed regularly over a period of weeks were in some sense part of a single transaction. However, Thomas places this proposition

alongside another proposition to the effect that a series of offences of the same kind committed against different victims ought to attract consecutive sentences. The question arises: should the identity of the victim have such a potentially large effect on the sentence imposed? In some cases it might indeed be less grave to commit further offences against the same victim than against a different victim – this might be the case with incest against a particular child, or with rape, but in both instances the point is arguable. Perhaps it could be said that in general the repetition of an offence against an 'established' victim requires less deliberation and evinces less wickedness than the selection of a new victim. Yet the overall effect on the length or severity of a sentence should surely be little. If all other factors are held constant – a given number of offences committed over a given period; the nature and circumstances of violence, or the amounts involved in theft or fraud, or the degree of sexual violation – it is hard to see why the mere fact that the offences were committed against the same victim or, as the case may be, against different victims should make a substantial difference to the seriousness of the case. It is equally hard to see why the probably slight difference in overall gravity should be reflected in a decision to impose concurrent rather than consecutive sentences.

3 **The totality principle**

It will be inferred from the previous section that consecutive sentences are proper where offences are not considered to form part of a 'single transaction' or where there is a reason of policy for imposing consecutive sentences even though the offences could be said to form part of a 'single transaction'. However, if a court imposes a separate and consecutive sentence for each such offence, a high total sentence could be reached. The same could happen if a sentence were increased incrementally for each offence taken into consideration. When drawing up their proposed scheme for a range of lower 'normal maximum' sentences, the Advisory Council on the Penal System expressed the fear that its effect 'might be eroded by an untrammelled approach to consecutive sentencing,'[22] and felt it necessary to draw up a set of 'ground rules' in order to ensure that an aggregated total of consecutive sentences did not go beyond the normal maximum for a single conviction of the most serious offence involved. How do the courts deal with the problem now?

(a) **Proportionality and totality**

The Court of Appeal itself has, over the years, developed a principle which is designed to limit the total sentence imposed in cases of multiple offences. The principle, which Thomas conveniently terms 'the totality principle', has been stated thus by the Court.

> When cases of multiplicity of offences come before the court, the court must not content itself by doing the arithmetic and passing the sentence which the arithmetic produces. It must look at the totality of the criminal behaviour and ask itself what is the appropriate sentence for all the offences.[23]

The application of such a principle would clearly produce what is in effect a discount for bulk offending. If the sentencer is expected to impose a sentence which is lower than the total which he has reached by a correct assessment of the gravity of each individual offence, then it follows that the offender will receive a lower total sentence than he would have received if he had been before the court on a number of separate occasions for the same number of offences. This is strikingly demonstrated in cases where an offender asks the court to take numerous other offences into consideration, although in those cases the discount might be justified as an incentive for the offender to own up and thereby to enable the crimes to be 'cleared up'. In most cases where a multiple offender is sentenced, however, the offender is being given a discount because his total sentence appears excessive, and that is because he managed to commit so many offences before being caught.

Implicit in the principle is a rather different sense of proportionality than that commonly used. The point is not whether one type of offence is *ceteris paribus* more heinous than another; it is a question of how a series of offences, sometimes all of the same kind and sometimes of different kinds, can be brought into a conceptual scheme which relates principally to single offences. The problem is illustrated by the Court of Appeal's remarks in *Holderness*, a case described by Thomas in the following terms.

> The appellant received sentences totalling four years' imprisonment for a variety of charges, primarily motoring offences. The Court stated that the sentencer had failed to 'take the step . . . of standing back and looking at the overall effect of the sentences,' and that if he had done so, 'he would have at once appreciated that he was imposing the kind of sentence which is imposed for really serious crime.' The sentence was reduced to

twenty-seven months.'[24]

The total sentence of 4 years passed by the trial judge was not impugned as an aggregate of the sentences appropriate for each individual crime. What the sentencer had failed to do was to consider that total sentence in relation to other crimes which would attract such long terms of imprisonment – a single rape or wounding would have to be fairly serious if it were to attract such a long sentence, as would a series of burglaries. It was argued above that some progress can be made towards criteria of proportionality between different types of offence, and certain parts of the criminal calendar were explored with that end in view.[25] We can give reasons why a single middle-range rape is *ceteris paribus* more serious than a single middle-range burglary or a single offence of driving whilst disqualified. But what reasons can be given for saying that a middle-range rape is or is not more serious than 4 burglaries or 9 cases of taking cars? Even if it is agreed that the comparison should be made between cases which are accepted to be middle-range burglaries or cases which are accepted to be middle-range takings of cars, it still seems implausible merely to 'do the arithmetic' and to rest content with that. 'Doing the arithmetic' might mean that the rape is given 4 years, that 4 burglaries at 9 months each amounts to 3 years, and that 9 offences of taking cars at 4 months each also amounts to 3 years. There is a feeling that any calculation which results in such a close approximation of sentence between a rape (4 years) and a moderate number of burglaries or of 'auto-thefts' (3 years) goes against common sense. This feeling may lead to assertions such as 'no number of offences of taking cars can be regarded as morally so heinous as a single middle-range rape', or 'no number of non-violent middle-range burglaries can be regarded as the moral equivalent of a single unprovoked serious wounding.' Yet assertions of this kind, even if acceptable, merely lay down limits rather than providing the hapless sentencer with guidance on the proper approach to such comparisons.

If we turn aside from the moral issue and enquire into popular judgments of the seriousness of a multiplicity of offences, the position is no clearer. Since Sellin and Wolfgang constructed their index of 'offence-seriousness' nearly twenty years ago there have been many criticisms of their methods and assumptions, and the issue of multiple offences provides a stern testing-ground.[26] An experiment by Pease and collaborators[27] suggested not merely that the popular conception of the relative severity of two rapes is not simply double that of one rape, but that two rapes might be regarded as *more than* twice as serious as one. This might differ according to the lapse of time between the two crimes, and whether they were committed against the same victim or separate victims. It clearly suggests that popular judgments of these matters are not straightforward.

Let us return to the moral issue by means of a further example. Thomas writes that

> In *McGready* the appellant was sentenced to three consecutive terms of two years' imprisonment for three offences of taking a vehicle without consent; the Court considered that although the sentences were properly made consecutive, the total of six years was 'excessive . . . the offences did not merit such a substantial term'.[28]

The sentence was reduced to 3 years, and the Court's reasoning seems to be that, however bad the offender's record, a sentence of 6 years is appropriate to relatively serious rapes, woundings and robberies and is hard to justify for a number of non-violent temporary deprivations of property. The sentence of 6 years' imprisonment, considered in terms of the sentencing system generally, is appropriate to a serious invasion of interests which are central to society and to the individual's liberty. Taking cars cannot be brought within this category: even if the case had concerned thefts of cars, and not merely temporarily taking them away from their owners, it would be difficult to place it in the same moral scales as physical or psychological harm. In the case of *McGready* it seemed to be accepted that 2 years was a perfectly proper sentence for a single taking of a car, and the overall sentence of 3 years suggests that the second and third offences were given much reduced sentences – perhaps an additional 8 months for the second, and an additional 4 months for the third. However, it would be very rare for 2 years' imprisonment to be thought appropriate for this kind of offence. Let us start with the notion that 1 year is appropriate for this kind of offender for this kind of offence –

1 offence	1 year
2 offences	18 months
3 offences	22 months
5 offences	25 months
10 offences	30 months
20 offences	36 months

still a very high penalty, but the example may be taken in order to illustrate a point. How is the court to calculate the sentence if more than one offence has been committed? The calculation presumably can be set out as has been done at the bottom of the previous page. This list is, of course, the product of imagination. But it illustrates how sentencers are expected to give a substantial and increasing discount for bulk offending, in order to preserve a notional proportionality. Some offenders appear before the courts with fifty or more offences to be taken into consideration; yet the strength of the feeling that we ought to distinguish the taker of cars from the rapist remains so great that the total sentence for the persistent taker of cars is depressed.

Before pursuing this argument further, a possible counter-argument must be considered. It is, quite simply, that by allowing such a large discount for bulk offending the courts may in effect be withdrawing from the person who has committed a single offence any disincentive to commit further offences. To put the matter more accurately, the more a person offends before he is caught, the less is the extra deterrent force of the law against each further offence. If second and subsequent offences were treated more or less in the manner outlined in the above list, there would indeed be some incremental sentence for the second and the third offences, but the difference between 12 and 13 offences would be slight and, perhaps, non existent. The same point was put in a different way in the Canadian case of *Chisholm*,[29] where the offender had committed 4 separate armed robberies and was sentenced to 7 years' imprisonment concurrent on each count. The prosecution appealed to the Ontario Court of Appeal, where Roach JA observed:

> If sentences were to be concurrent in such cases, that would almost be an inducement to a criminal not to refrain from crimes of the same sort or even of different sorts, committed at times closely related to one another. He would reason that, if he were not caught on the first one, any sentence he would get on the others would likely be concurrent, and his liberty not further restrained because of his committing these other offences.

The Court allowed the appeal and substituted consecutive sentences for the 4 robberies of 5, 2, 2 and 2 years respectively. The total sentence was thus effectively increased from 7 to 11 years. The Court's approach is to some extent consistent with the idea of a totality principle, inasmuch as the sentences for the second, third and fourth offences were lower than the sentence for the first. But there is no express reference to such a principle, nor is the sentence for third less than that for the second, and for the fourth less than for the third. The Court's 'inducement to bulk offending' argument appears to require the addition of a significant increment for each subsequent offence, so as to preserve the disincentive to further lawbreaking.

How far could such an approach be carried? What would have been the Court's approach in *Chisholm* if he had committed 8 robberies instead of 4? Would the Court have added 2 years for each subsequent robbery, reaching a total sentence of 19 years? That would certainly not be the English approach, as the judgment of Lawton LJ in the leading case of *Turner*[30] makes clear. The importance ascribed in this judgment to the idea of proportionality with other serious crimes has already been explained.[31] It was stated that a single organized and armed robbery of the *Turner* kind ought to attract a 15-year sentence; the principal offenders in *Turner* were convicted of 2 such offences; and so Lawton LJ posed the question:

What, if anything, should be added to the basic sentence of 15 years to cover the fact that they had committed more than one robbery? The Court is alive to the problems arising when men are kept in prison for very long periods of time. On the other hand it seems to the Court only just that those who are making a career of crime should receive more severe punishment than those who have been convicted of only one grave offence. We have come to the conclusion that something must be added to the basic sentence passed on those who have committed more than one robbery, but the maximum total sentence should not normally be more than 18 years. That is about the maximum sentence which should be passed for crimes which do not come into the category of offences on which we have put the description 'wholly abnormal'.[32]

This clearly amounts to a large discount for the second offence: if 15 years is accepted as the appropriate sentence for 1 such crime, simple arithmetic would produce a total of 30 years' imprisonment for 2 such crimes. On the *Turner* approach, the second offence attracts only an additional sentence of 3 years, which means 2 years with remission and possibly less if the offender is released on parole. Those who believe that 'professional criminals' take care not only to plan their offences but also to weigh the probable consequences of arrest and conviction may indeed view the *Turner* approach as offering an inducement to multiple offending where there ought to be a disincentive. On the other hand, the arguments relied on by Lawton LJ in *Turner* should not be overlooked: a system which is based on some concept of proportionality and which regards murder as the highest crime must take the sentence for murder as one of its principal points of reference; and prison sentences should not be lengthened indefinitely if we are to have due regard for the destructive effects which prolonged incarceration exerts upon a prisoner's personality. If proportionality with other serious offences such as manslaughter, spying, bombing, etc. is to be the major concern, then a series of several robberies of the *Turner* kind would be sentenced on a diminishing scale: 3 robberies would produce 20 years, 4 robberies 21 years, 5 robberies 21½ years and so on, with the sentencer remaining conscious of the need to preserve some proportion with the period to be served by a person who has committed murder without mitigating circumstances.

This, however, is not to concede the force of the deterrent argument. Is it not a gross exaggeration to suggest that the *Turner* approach offers an inducement to multiple offending, once a person has committed one offence? For each subsequent offence there is a risk of detection and, in the case of serious crime, the probability of a substantial sentence for the offence or offences already committed. Whether there would be a greater disincentive to each further crime if the courts rigorously adopted consecutive sentencing (without the restraining influence of the totality principle) is arguable, and depends on assumptions about the thinking and conduct of offenders which cannot be substantiated by evidence.

(b) The totality principle in operation

In his discussion of the totality principle, Thomas identifies two sub-rules which the Court of Appeal appears to use as a guide in this difficult area. The first is that

the aggregate sentence should not be longer than the upper limit of the normal bracket of sentences for the category of cases in which the most serious offence committed by the offender would be placed. This formulation would allow an aggregate sentence longer than the sentence which would be passed for the most serious offence if it stood alone, but would ensure that the sentence bore some recognizable relationship to the gravity of that offence.[33]

There have been exceptional cases in which even consecutive maximum sentences have been upheld, most notoriously *Blake*,[34] but the above proposition is advanced as the general rule. Why should the most serious of a group of offences spread, perhaps, over a period of months or years, be used as a benchmark for the total sentence? Why should that offence be plucked out of a sequence of lawbreaking and invested with overriding importance? If over a period of months an offender commits two residential burglaries, two commercial burglaries, an indecent assault and perhaps some shoplifting or taking of cars, why should the total sentence be constrained by the 'upper limit of the normal bracket of sentences' for residential burglaries of the kind committed? The offender's activities go well beyond and are unconnected with the two residential burglaries, and in logical terms the range of sentences for residential burglary[35] seems to bear little relation to the totality of the offender's law-breaking. The only justification for this sub-rule could be the pragmatic *tabula in naufragio*: without any point of reference the sentencer would be lost in a sea of conflicting considerations, and if sentences for multiple offending are to be integrated into a structure shaped mainly by conceptions of the relative gravity of single offences, this may be the simplest way of achieving it.

The Advisory Council on the Penal System proposed a system of 'normal maximum' sentences, set at the level of some 90 per cent of sentences for each crime in recent years, and expressed concern that sentences for multiple offenders should not exceed these normal maxima and intrude into the category of 'exceptional' sentences. The first of their three 'ground rules' for sentencing multiple offenders was therefore that:

> Sentences passed on the same occasion for a number of offences should not in total exceed the maximum that could have been imposed for the most serious of the offences, unless the criterion for exceeding the maximum is satisfied.[36]

No reasons were given for adopting this approach. It is undoubtedly simpler for sentencers, and it results in a more sparing use of punishment. An open question is whether it would fail to deter from further offending the offender who has already committed one or more undetected crimes. We do not know whether typically an offender who has already committed 5 undetected crimes would be deterred from committing further crimes if the sentences would necessarily be consecutive, whereas he would not be deterred if this kind of ground rule or totality principle were adopted.

The second sub-rule identified by Thomas is that the total sentence should not be such as to impose a crushing burden on an offender whose prospects are not hopeless – in effect, a last throwback to individualization. According to Thomas, this sub-rule operates so as to allow the sentencer to give some effect to mitigating factors in relation to the totality of the sentence, even though he has already taken them into account in calculating the penalty for each distinct offence. The decisions show that this sub-rule applies when an offender is sent to prison for the first time and, because of an accumulation of consecutive sentences, stands to receive a substantial term; and also where an offender has previously served one or more short prison sentences but has now received, because of consecutive sentences, a long term. The basis of the sub-rule therefore lies in general maxims of penal policy about the desirability of making the first custodial sentence a short one (the 'clang of the prison gate' maxim)[37] and the desirability of avoiding a 'jump' in the level of prison sentences imposed on a particular offender.[38] Neither maxim bears any relation to proportionality: they are limiting principles, whose rationale lies outside the present discussion.

(c) Exceptions to the principle

Brief mention should be made of exceptions to the totality principle, although they correspond to those exceptions which are generally made to limiting principles of sentencing in England. One exception would be where the court believes that there is an overriding need for general deterrence;[39] in such a case the total sentence produced by the elementary arithmetic of adding all the sentences for the various offences might be allowed to stand. Another exception would be where the court believes that a protective sentence is called for, because the offender is considered dangerous; thus in *Cunningham*[40] the court was unable to impose life imprisonment, since the offender had only committed attempted rape and not the completed offence of rape, and life imprisonment is not available for attempted rape, so the Court of Appeal upheld the maximum sentence for burglary with intent to rape (14 years) and a consecutive sentence of 1 year's imprisonment for an indecent assault on another occasion. The total of 15 years might well have been considered too high, had there not been the 'diagnosis' of dangerousness. These exceptions are, like many English principles of sentencing, so loosely stated as to be open to stretching in occasional cases. For example, in *Hayes*[41] the offender had entered a factory and stolen £25; had allowed himself to be carried in a stolen car; had broken into a school and stolen two cigarette lighters and a record-player; and had stolen a sweater from a clothes line. On conviction he asked for numerous other offences to be taken into consideration, some 28 being offences of taking a vehicle without the owner's consent, 7 theft and 2 burglary. He also had a number of previous convictions, and was described as bordering on subnormal intelligence. The trial judge had dealt with the case by imposing a sentence of 3 years for being carried in the stolen car, and 2 years consecutively for burglary, with the other sentences running concurrently. The Court of Appeal upheld the total of 5 years' imprisonment as appropriate to an offender who was a 'nuisance and menace'. However, it is unlikely that a strict application of the totality principle would have led the Court to uphold a sentence which is longer than most offenders convicted of rape or serious wounding would receive. In reality, therefore, the sentence was probably upheld as a protective measure against an offender who was thought to be a considerable nuisance in society. It is doubtful whether sentences of this kind can be justified, except in cases of 'dangerousness'.[42] However, where an offender stands convicted of 2 offences rather than 1, the notion that the choice between consecutive and concurrent sentences is fundamentally a matter of discretion may lead the court to impose a longer sentence than strictly it ought to.

(d) The mechanics of the totality principle

If a court decides that the totality of the sentences which would be appropriate for the number of offences taken individually is too great for the offences taken as a whole, the totality principle enjoins a reduction. The Court of Appeal has held that this reduction ought to be effected by making some or all of the sentences run concurrently, rather than reducing each sentence and allowing them to remain consecutive. The Court regards it as important to pass the appropriate sentence on each count, and to achieve a suitable total sentence by making some or all of the sentences run concurrently. The importance which the courts attach to the imposition of an appropriate sentence on each count is illustrated by *Tointon*.[43] The offender was convicted of an attempted rape which came close to the full offence, and indecent assault which consisted of approaching a woman from behind in an alleyway and putting his hand up her skirt. The judge imposed 6 years' imprisonment for the attempted rape and 2 years concurrent for the indecent assault. Whilst the Court of Appeal upheld the sentence of 6 years on the basis that the attempted rape was a comparatively bad offence, they decided to reduce the sentence for the indecent assault from 2 to 1 year. Since it was a concurrent sentence this reduction had no practical effect upon the time to be served by the offender. The justification was that the indecent assault was in itself not a particularly serious crime, and so the record should be set straight by reducing the relevant sentence from 2 years to 1. The Court recognized that this change was 'for the record', but nevertheless thought it worth making.

4 The problem of multiple offenders

Even at a general level, the principles evolved by the Court of Appeal for sentencing multiple offenders are complex and hedged about with restrictions and exceptions. Some sentencers might argue that there is so much variation between particular cases that general principles can provide nothing more than a starting point. The merits of a shared, reasoned starting point should not, however, be under-emphasized. The most widely accepted view seems to be that the ranking of offences in terms of relative gravity should not be eroded by 'an untramelled approach to consecutive sentencing'. The conceptions of proportionality used by the courts when comparing single crimes should remain the principal point of reference. Of course those conceptions have no absolute hold, even in respect of single offences –variations in the offender's responsibility and record may be taken into account, as may maxims of penal policy. But proportionality forms the bedrock of the English principles of sentencing. And that proportionality, as it is expressed numerically (at least for those crimes which often carry custodial sentences or which often carry fines) and as it is usually conceptualized, is based on single offences of different kinds.

On a logical basis it may appear difficult to escape the conclusion that there should be a noticeable increment in sentence for each conviction more than one, if not a simple cumulation of the appropriate sentences for each of the crimes. The result, however, would threaten to obliterate the notions of proportionality which underlie English sentencing practice. It can therefore be argued that the totality principle embodies an attempt to arrive at an acceptable compromise between the preservation of proportionality between classes of offence and the formal recognition that the offender is being sentenced for more than one crime – recognition which may be justified in terms of deterrent theory (it should not be thought that an offender who has already committed one or more crimes without detection can go on to commit further crimes with impunity) or in terms of a retributive theory which has strong links with popular notions of fairness: 'It cannot be right to say that, if over a period a man commits a large number of offences, in pursuance of a set policy or system, he should be treated no differently from a man who has committed only one offence.'[44]

As stated earlier, however, proportionality between classes of offence is not necessarily the primary consideration in sentencing, and the general principles for sentencing multiple offenders are subject to other policies. The totality principle may be neglected if the court holds that a protective sentence or a general deterrent sentence is necessary. The principle may be vigorously applied so as to reduce the length of sentence imposed upon a relatively young offender or an offender whose previous custodial experience has only been with very short sentences. And consecutive sentences might be imposed for the symbolic purpose of emphasizing the special gravity of offences committed in order to resist arrest by a police officer, or of making the point that offences committed whilst on bail for other charges will not go without effective punishment.[45] Each of these deviations from the totality principle calls for separate justification.[46]

Whilst the interaction of policies such as these goes some way towards explaining the reasoning of sentencers in cases of multiple offenders, they leave the fundamental question untouched: how can two or more offences of one kind be integrated into a system of proportionality based on single offences? Although the structure of proportionality can be expressed in numerical terms, it is impossible to devise a numerical formula to deal adequately with multiple offenders because the numbers of offences for which they fall to be sentenced vary so greatly. The number may be as many as ten, even more, in a single indictment; further offences taken into consideration might take the total number of crimes into hundreds. To preserve some approximate proportionality between classes of offence, whilst marking each offence for which an offender is being sentenced by some incremental addition to the total sentence, is virtually an impossible prescription. The practical consequence is that multiple offenders are under-sentenced, strictly speaking, inasmuch as they receive little or no sentence for their nth offence. For instance, there will be hardly any element in the sentence of an offender who admits 12 offences to distinguish it from the sentence he would have received for admitting 11 offences. In a sense, therefore, the courts are passing sentences upon offenders rather than sentencing for offences: a separate and consecutive offence for each offence might impose a crushing burden on the offender. Even this view is linked, however, to the concept of proportionality which stems from the relative gravity of this *type* of offence, no matter how many have been committed.

7
Two principles of equality

1 Introduction

It has been assumed in most of the discussion in this book that in general the sentencer's principal aim should be to impose a sentence proportionate to the seriousness of the case – seriousness in terms not only of the gravity of the offence but also of the culpability of the offender. Proportionality in this sense appears to play a large role in existing sentencing practice, it may be seen as safeguarding the individual by placing limits on the powers of the State over him and on his subjection to the predictions of 'experts', and it can claim a solid basis in moral theory and in popular conceptions of fairness. The last point can be illustrated by considering the consequences of neglecting altogether the idea of proportionality:

if we condemn all wrong acts equally without regard to how wrong each is, we invite serious troubles. In the first place, if right or wrong *tout court* were all that mattered, we would find the entire world divided starkly and simply into saints and sinners. Without greater and lesser punishment those who commit crimes would all be condemned simply as criminals; and since all would bear a stigma no different than that of the worst, all would be regarded as the worst. Under such a system we might also expect a deterioration of our moral sensibilities. Our sense of right and wrong is not unlike our sense of light and dark. If day or night alone mattered we should lose our ability to discriminate the flushes and shadows that fall between; and if only right or wrong mattered – never mind how wrong – we should be unable to perceive the moral world except in terms that are similarly stark.[1]

Making the moral point is not to overlook, let alone to dispose of, the formidable theoretical and practical problems of a sentencing system based on proportionality. There must be settled criteria of the seriousness of cases; there must be an agreed ranking of the severity of the available sentences; and there must be acceptance of a relationship between cases and sentences which is regarded as appropriate.

Settled criteria of the seriousness of cases are hard to come by. It is difficult enough to explore and to reconcile the various factors which may be considered relevant to an assessment of the gravity of offences, as the discussion of offences against the person and against property in Chapter 4 demonstrated. It is even more difficult to reach agreement on the factors by which culpability should be determined, as that chapter also showed.

To achieve an agreed ranking of the severity of available sentences is also a problematic exercise. It may be relatively easy to agree on certain kinds of penalty at the extremes – life imprisonment and an absolute discharge, for example, are clearly at opposite ends of the spectrum of severity. But a ranking of 50 hours' community service and a 2 year probation order might present greater difficulties, which would be increased by the interposition of a suspended sentence of, say, 6 months' imprisonment. It is one thing to rank types of sentence; it is quite another thing to formulate a ranking which can accommodate even broad variations in the quantum of each measure.

The whole enterprise of relating the seriousness of cases to the severity of penalties so as to achieve in practice a recognizable scale of proportionality brings in further difficulties. It is sometimes alleged that certain penalties can 'naturally' be tied to particular offences (e.g. capital punishment to murder, castration to rape), but this is often accompanied by a tendency to regard the harm actually caused by the offence as the proper index of its moral gravity, without reference to the culpability of the offender. The most satisfactory approach is to consider what sentences should be available to the courts in view of the types of case they have to deal with, and this requires serious examination of the justification for having an indeterminate sentence of imprisonment such as life imprisonment, and for having imprisonment available on a general scale or at all, and other fundamental issues of the penal system. It is then necessary to look again at the types of crime coming before the courts, because it does not follow that the most severe penalties we are prepared to contemplate are appropriate for the offences at the top of the criminal calendar, and more particularly because there can and should be keen debate about whether certain offences (e.g. thefts of small value) can ever justify a custodial sentence. Systems aspiring to proportionality are often the product of tradition and makeshift alteration, whereas proportionality in modern society ought to be arrived at by protracted and searching moral and political argument along the lines indicated above.

Some would argue against proportionality on the basis that the various stages – settling the criteria of seriousness, ranking the severity of sentences and proportioning penalties to cases – simply cannot be satisfactorily accomplished. It is true that many of those who have advocated a return to retributivism and adoption of a 'justice' model have failed to work out thoroughly the implications of the approach. Moreover the discussion in earlier chapters, sometimes intricate and rarefied, might be taken as a further demonstration of the great difficulty of this exercise. However, the process is vital because of the way in which concepts of proportion permeate moral judgments, and an approximate reflection of proportionality is to be preferred to the abandonment of all links. Those who argue that the inevitable frailty and approximateness of judgments of proportionality leads to injustices on the very definition which retributivists adopt go too far: even those retributivists who interpret proportionality as requiring an exact correspondence between seriousness of case and severity of penalty (i.e. commensurability) would reply that there are degrees of injustice, and that a slightly inaccurate estimation of desert is strongly preferable to an approach to sentencing which in no way aspired to proportionality and departed widely from it. Many retributivists would not accept a definition in terms of exact correspondence, because that sets the standard at an unrealistic and unnecessary level.

2 Towards equality of impact

The second stage in the calculation of proportionality is, it is suggested, the agreement of a ranking of available sentences in order of severity. It will readily be appreciated that the same penalty might have a radically different effect on various individuals. A fine of £100 may be a major burden to an offender with a low income and family commitments, whilst to the wealthy offender it may mean little more than the inconvenience of writing a cheque. Three months' imprisonment will probably cause greater hardship to an elderly offender who is suffering from Parkinson's disease than to a younger man in good health. To impose the same sentence on two offenders in such different personal circumstances strikes the chord of injustice: there is a feeling that it is unfair, because one offender is being hit much harder than the other. It is as if the rate of income tax were the same for all, instead of the graduated scale of taxation which has come to be widely accepted. The source of the feeling of injustice is, then, that individual differences will sometimes have the result that objectively similar sentences will have a subjectively variable effect on offenders. In order to avoid this, it would be necessary to travel outside proportionality and to adopt equality of impact as a principle, so as to take account of manifest differences between offenders which affect the degree of pain and deprivation caused to them by particular sentences. Bentham, as one might expect, essayed a catalogue and brief description of these 'circumstances influencing sensibility', but he warned that

> To search out the vast variety of exciting or moderating causes, by which the degree or bias of a man's sensibility may be influenced, to define the boundaries of each, to extricate them from the entanglements in which they are involved, to lay the effect of each article distinctly before the reader's eye, is, perhaps, if not absolutely the most difficult task, at least one of the most difficult tasks, within the compass of moral physiology. Disquisitions on this head can never be completely satisfactory without examples. To provide a sufficient collection of such examples, would be a work of great labour as well as nicety: history and biography would need to be ransacked: a vast course of reading would need to be travelled through on purpose. By such a process the present work would doubtless have been rendered more amusing; but in point of bulk, so enormous, that this single chapter would have been swelled into a considerable volume.[2]

Despite this warning, and despite the passage of two centuries since his ideas were formulated, it is still profitable to cast an eye over Bentham's list of 'circumstances influencing sensibility':

1. Health. 2. Strength. 3. Hardiness. 4. Bodily imperfection. 5. Quantity and quality of knowledge. 6. Strength of intellectual powers. 7. Firmness of mind. 8. Steadiness of mind. 9. Bent of inclination. 10. Moral sensibility. 11. Moral biases. 12. Religious sensibility. 13. Religious biases. 14. Sympathetic sensibility. 15. Sympathetic biases. 16. Antipathetic sensibility. 17. Antipathetic biases. 18. Insanity. 19. Habitual occupations. 20. Pecuniary circumstances. 21. Connexions in the way of sympathy. 22. Connexions in the way of antipathy. 23. Radical frame of body. 24. Radical frame of mind. 25. Sex. 26. Age. 27. Rank. 28. Education. 29. Climate. 30. Lineage. 31. Government. 32. Religious profession.[3]

We may content ourselves with the general impressions created by this list, and forego the explanations necessary for a proper appreci-ation of each of these circumstances. Their importance, according to Bentham, is that when the question of punishing a particular offender arises 'they will need to be attended to in estimating the force of the impression that will be made on him by any given punishment.'[4] In practice there would be problems in attending to some of the circumstances listed: 'either the existence cannot be ascertained, or the degree cannot be measured.'[5] Others, by contrast, apply in-discriminately to such general groups that the legislature can take account of them, as by providing special sentences for offenders in particular age-groups; and still others are present in varying degrees which a court can in each case assess and give effect to.

An example of the way in which a court might take account of the 'sensibilities' of a particular offender in an attempt to produce equality of impact is provided by *Varden*.[6] A man of 71 pleaded guilty to unlawful sexual intercourse with a girl aged 13. The girl was 'slightly mentally subnormal'; the offender was of low intelligence, was suffering from incipient senile dementia and had previously been of good character. The trial judge imposed a sentence of 8 months' imprisonment: normally the sentence would be closer to the statutory maximum of 2 years where the offender was a man of mature years and the victim a girl so young as 13, but the judge passed a lower sentence in view of the offender's mental condition, his advanced age and the fact that the sentence would probably be more unpleasant because it would have to be served in conditions of segregation under rule 43.[7] The Court of Appeal held that the judge had found a proper balance between 'the requirements of society' and 'the interests of the offender himself', and declined to reduce the sentence. The case combines two factors, each of which has independently been held to justify a reduction in the severity of a sentence. Advanced age has been accepted as a ground for imposing a shorter custodial sentence, on the basis that the hardship of prison life is greater for an elderly person.[8] Similar arguments are sometimes used to justify the non-prosecution of an elderly person against whom there is strong evidence of guilt. A report on prosecutions in Essex states that the police chose not to prosecute 88 per cent of old age pensioners against whom there was sufficient evidence of shoplifting, partly because of the mental and emotional distress which often surrounds or causes the offence, partly because elderly offenders have been known to over-react to being prosecuted and even to commit suicide.[9] Just as sentences for those of advanced years may be reduced, so also the youth of an offender is often treated as a reason for mitigation (indeed, legislation provides special sentences for offenders under 21), and this may derive partly from the belief that 'to spend part of one's youth in prison is worse than spending part of one's middle age there.'[10]

The second factor in *Varden* was the increased hardship of imprisonment for an offender who must serve his sentence in conditions of segregation under rule 43. Sex offenders, particularly those convicted of offences against children, are sometimes subject to ostracism and even violence from other prisoners and will therefore be segregated under rule 43 for their own protection. What this means in practice is that in training prisons they may have to endure a more solitary existence, whereas in local prisons they will be put in cells with other prisoners on rule 43, but inevitably with reduced opportunities to move freely round the prison. Rule 43 may also be used for prisoners who have given evidence for the Crown against other offenders, and the Court of Appeal has recognized that the greater pains of imprisonment for any offender on rule 43 justify some reduction in the severity of sentence.[11]

3 The principle of equal impact

The argument, then, is that whilst it is just to impose the same sentence on two equally culpable offenders for two equally grave offences, it is unjust to do so if the two offenders have such differing 'sensibilities' that the sentence would have a significantly different effect on each of them. The sentencer should take account of any relevant and significant differences, and should strive to achieve equality of impact. Bentham explained the principle thus:

Rule 6. It is further to be observed, that owing to the different manners and degrees in which persons under different circumstances are affected by the same exciting cause, a punishment which is the same in name will not always either really produce, or even so much as appear to others to produce, in two different persons the same degree of pain: therefore

That the quantity actually inflicted on each individual offender may correspond to the quantity intended for similar offenders in general, the several circumstances influencing sensibility ought always to be taken into account.[12]

We shall call this the principle of equal impact. To describe it as a principle is not to put it forward as an absolute moral prescription, for it will emerge from the ensuing discussion that other principles or policies may be given priority in certain circumstances. But in general the principle should lead a sentencer, for example, to reduce a fine for an offender of little means and to reduce a prison sentence for an offender whose expectation of life is short.[13]

One objection to the principle is that it enjoins the impossible. Thus Professor Walker has argued that the sentencer who adopts the principle 'can take this into account only in the crudest ways: for instance, by reducing a poor man's fine or an old man's prison term. He is in the position of having to adjust something he cannot measure.'[14] This is in the same vein as objections to the measurement of desert and proportion generally, and can be met with a similar answer. Some adjustment aimed at achieving equality of impact is better than none at all: the law has a maxim, *de minimis non curat lex* (the law takes no account of trivialities), and so an approximate measurement of equality of impact is acceptable even though a precise adjustment lies beyond human capability. Whether the courts can be sufficiently sensitive in their sentencing should at least not be prejudged until a wide range of applications of the principle has been reviewed.

A second objection is that the effect of the principle upon sentencing practice might be misunderstood by the public and by offenders. Because there is a crude assumption that offenders with similar records who commit similar offences ought to receive similar sentences, any departure from that kind of arithmetical consistency may be viewed as a disparity and as unjustified. Even offenders who lack the features which lead to reduction of sentence on this ground may feel hard done by. To adapt a passage from Gross:

> It is of course true that a man who has little or nothing to offer in his behalf may complain of a kind of cosmic injustice, and certainly of bad luck. But that is an objection against the way of the world and not against the human effort to avoid unnecessary suffering which the principle [of equal impact] represents.[15]

The problem, then, is partly one of explanation of the reasons for the apparently disparate sentences: offenders themselves must be told why certain cases attract specially low sentences, and so far as possible the public must be informed of the reasoning by which the court arrives at its sentence. One approach would be to announce the 'standard' sentence, and then the reduced sentence for the particular offender and the reason for the reduction. Could there be a problem arising from the public effect of any lower sentences to which the principle leads? Those who regard either denunciation or general deterrence as high among the functions or even the aims of the sentencing system may oppose any principle which could lead to a weakening of the denunciatory or deterrent effect of sentencing levels, seeing it as a licence to some (e.g. those too poor to pay fines) to offend with virtual impunity. Even on this view, an attempt to explain these unusually low sentences in terms of the principle of equal impact might help to restore any effect which the normal level of sentences has; but the basis for these general assertions about the effect on general deterrence or denunciation of a small proportion of aberrant sentences is doubtful.[16]

A third and more fundamental objection to the principle of equal impact is that offenders ought to be aware when they commit their crimes of any specially dire consequences for them of the due process of law. The clearest application of this counter-argument may be found in cases where offenders have claimed a reduction in sentence on account of the effect of the sentence on their family. Such a claim is not founded directly on the principle of equal impact but on an extension of it, since it is not the offender's 'sensibility' but that of his family which is being relied upon. The offender declares that he or she has young children to look after, or an ailing or dependent parent, or (in the case of a male offender) that his wife is just expecting a baby. The Court of Appeal has generally (although not invariably) answered this argument by saying that the offender ought to have thought about it before committing the offence: imprisonment is often a consequence of a serious offence, and imprisonment often causes hardship to the offender's family. The Court has reduced sentences out of mercy in a few extreme cases,[17] but in general this third objection to the principle of equal impact makes an important point for the sentencing of all but impulsive offenders.

4 Equality before the law

Equality before the law is one of the declared aspirations of most criminal justice systems. Its pursuit has led, for example, to the introduction of free or subsidized legal aid and advice, in order to reduce the effect on access to the law of unequal financial resources. The principle is that no person ought to suffer a disadvantage in the criminal process on account of his means, social background, race, religion, gender, colour or class; the quality of criminal justice should be the same irrespective of differences in these respects. The principle can be supported by those who are not committed to the view that there should be equality of income, drastic wealth taxes, etc., for it is well recognized that the quality of criminal justice ought to be uniformly high without reference to the personal or financial attributes of a particular defendant. As it stands, the principle embodies an ideal which few criminal justice systems, indeed few parts of any system, attain. A criminal justice system is only a small part of the wider social system, and to expect its processes even to neutralize the effect of deep-rooted social inequalities may be to expect too much. However, although the inequalities which the social system permits are almost bound to have some influence on the criminal justice system, sentencers should strive to counteract their effects.

In the context of sentencing, the principle of equality before the law enjoins the avoidance of patterns of disposal which have the effect of discriminating against groups or individuals for reasons connected with their social disadvantages. Indeed, this could ground a further objection against the principle of equal impact. Thus, a police officer or prosecutor may decline to prosecute for a 'student prank', on the basis that it would be wrong to jeopardize the career of a would-be professional person by registering a conviction for a momentary or trivial offence; the implication is that a person of similar age who was a manual worker or was unemployed might not benefit from a similar dispensation even if his offence was equally momentary or trivial – terms such as 'prank' or 'high spirits' might not be applied to his Friday night excesses. Again, the view might be taken that a 'respectable' person would respond sufficiently to a formal caution and that prosecution would be unnecessary. This approach has often been alleged to be the case with the handling of juvenile crime, there being suggestions of

a greater readiness by the police to hand out warnings and cautions to those who come from 'good homes', a greater unwillingness on the part of the courts to send middle-class children to institutions, a greater toleration for those forms of delinquency which are more typically associated with the middle-class, a greater ability by middle-class homes to 'contain' and 'deal' with their own delinquents.[18]

More directly, von Hirsch has argued that in an attempt to produce equality of impact a court might place a middle-class offender on probation and send a ghetto youth to prison, even though the cases were in other material respects comparable:

> More drastic measures thus come to be imposed chiefly on those of lower status who are deemed to have 'less to lose' – but only because they have lost so much already through their deprived social situation.[19]

A possible example of this might occur if a court imposed a lower-than-normal sentence upon an offender who had already, through the fact of being convicted, lost social esteem, employment prospects, pension rights and so on. By comparison with the humble offender with 'less to lose', the offender who had previously enjoyed social esteem or high position would be sentenced more leniently. It is, however, rare for the Court of Appeal to countenance this style of reasoning and more common for them to maintain that higher standards are expected of those who hold high positions, so that their punishment should certainly be no less.[20] Perhaps a more plausible example might be the use of the suspended sentence. There may be cases in which the decision to suspend a sentence of imprisonment rests on such factors as the offender's good employment record or his stable family background. This has led Professor Bottoms to argue that, insofar as there is a tendency to suspend, for persons of 'education and intelligence' and for 'white-collar' offenders, sentences of imprisonment which would otherwise be immediate, this amounts in practice to 'the suspension of terms of imprisonment for middle-class offenders' – which goes against the principle of equality before the law.[21] If such factors as good employment record, stable family background and exemplary previous character are used as criteria for suspending a custodial sentence, this will tend to favour the already advantaged members of society and to disfavour the disadvantaged. There is a further consideration: stability of employment record and family background might be associated with lower reconviction rates.[22] If so, there may be a stark choice between insisting on equality before the law (and thus leaving such factors out of account) and allowing such factors to lead to a reduction in sentence-length because the longer sentence is not necessary for preventive reasons (and thereby, in effect, introducing social inequality into sentencing).

Stark choices also arise on the related issue of community service orders for the unemployed. Some sentencers evidently believe that it is right to impose a longer community service order on an unemployed offender than would be imposed on an employed offender in a comparable case.[23] Whether this means that the appropriate length of an order is shortened for employed offenders or lengthened for the unemployed is not clear, but the latter could be defended as a fair application of the principle of equal impact: unemployed offenders have more leisure time, and so the community service order should be longer if it is to have the same impact as upon employed offenders (who have less spare time). The analogy is with increasing the size of a fine for a wealthy offender. Does the imposition of longer orders upon unemployed offenders violate the principle of equality before the law? It does so only if the unemployed offenders are in fact punished more severely, whereas the logic of applying the principle of equal impact is that the longer order merely goes towards the equalization of punishment, not greater effective severity.

A less disputable appliction of the principle of equality before the law is that a wealthy offender should not be allowed to 'buy his way out of prison', by being required to pay either a large fine or substantial compensation in a case where immediate imprisonment would have been considered appropriate for a less wealthy offender. The point was forcefully made in the well-known case of *Markwick* (1953),[24] where a wealthy member of a golf club had been fined £500 for stealing two shillings and sixpence from the club changing-room. In the Court of Criminal Appeal Lord Goddard CJ increased the sentence to two months' imprisonment, holding that in such a case a high fine

would give persons of means an opportunity of buying themselves out of being sent to prison . . . there should be no suggestion that there is one law for the rich and one for the poor.

The Court no longer has the power to increase sentences, but it has continued to make this point in relation to offenders who are in a position to pay substantial fines or sums in compensation.[25] The converse point is that an offender who lacks the means to pay an appropriate fine ought not to be subjected to a more severe sentence for that reason, and this is discussed below.[26] However, in cases where imprisonment is a probable outcome and where the offender is a person of considerable means, the defence advocate may sometimes construct his mitigation around the offender's ability to pay a substantial sum by way of fine or compensation, in the hope of persuading the sentencer to suspend any sentence of imprisonment and to make a financial order.[27] In principle this is a course which the sentencer should not take, because it results in a wealthy offender retaining his liberty in circumstances in which a poorer offender would lose his liberty.[28] Mitigation along these lines can be counter-productive, as where the sentencer imposes an immediate prison sentence and a substantial financial order.[29] Where a court accedes to the advocate's argument and imposes a suspended sentence combined with a substantial fine, problems may arise if it is subsequently discovered that the offender does not possess such considerable sums as the court was led to believe, and he appeals on the basis that the fines are much too high. If appeals on this basis were allowed to succeed, the result would be that a person who should probably have received an immediate sentence of imprisonment escapes with a suspended sentence and a much-moderated financial penalty; it is hardly surprising, then, that the Court of Appeal has taken to dismissing such appeals, thereby leaving the offender to be committed to prison for non-payment of the substantial fines.[30]

5 Equal impact and changing sensibilities

An offender's sensibilities, particularly in relation to a certain sentence, may undergo change during that sentence. Events may take place which could not have been foreseen at the time when sentence was originally passed. Thus, if it is accepted that imprisonment is a more painful sentence when it has to be served under rule 43 and that a judge should reflect this by reducing the sentence, it must surely also be accepted that if an offender is placed on rule 43 during the currency of his sentence this provides a prima facie reason for reducing the length of sentence. In respect of sentences of over 18 months the Parole Board can effect this, but for shorter sentences it cannot. The problem of changing sensibilities has arisen more frequently in the general context of an offender's reaction to prison life, and the Court of Appeal's approach to the problem has not been consistent. In *Brotherton*[31] that Court had received a 'very favourable' prison report, stating that the appellant had learnt his lesson and showed definite signs of remorse: the Court substantiallly reduced a sentence which they recognized as having been correct in principle. In *Skinner*[32] there was evidence that the appellant had suffered 'a great deal of mental trauma' in prison, and the Court reduced the sentence in order to allow for 'his subjective reaction to imprisonment during the

period he had already served.' In contrast stands the decision in
Kay[33], where there was clear evidence that a first offender sentenced
to 5 years for robbery was 'unable to come to terms with imprisonment,' 'suffered very sorely at the hands of his fellow prisoners' and
consequently had 'to be seen by a psychiatrist and to be supported by
medication.' The Court of Appeal held, however, that 'how a man
reacts to prison life is not a matter which should affect the principle of
the sentence,' and dismissed the appeal. Counsel's particular
argument in this case was that if Kay had been remanded in custody
before his trial (rather than released on bail), the trial judge would
have had evidence of his abnormal reaction to prison conditions.
Courts take account of age, infirmity and physical illness so as to
produce equality of impact; why should they not take account of an
extraordinary mental anguish produced by the experience of incarceration? In terms of authority, the three decisions cited here show
that this is one of many general issues on which the Court has failed to
evolve a consistent policy. As a matter of principle, acceptance of
equality of impact as a proper consideration in sentencing should lead
to acceptance of an abnormal reaction to imprisonment as a reason
for reducing the sentence. The third objection to the principle (that
offenders know their own circumstances) cannot be taken, because it
is not a personal circumstance which the offender should have known
about when he committed the offence. The second objection (public
misunderstanding of sentences) may be much weaker, since appellate
decisions are less widely reported than trials, and aims such as
denunciation and general deterrence are enhanced rather than
hindered by the pronouncement of high sentences at the trial and
their subsequent reduction in less well publicized circumstances. But
there is a whole host of institutional objections to the practice of
taking into consideration on appeal the offender's subjective reactions
to a sentence which was correct when passed: the practice encourages
speculative appeals, lodged at an early stage in the sentences when
the offender's reaction is not yet established; it divorces the considerations on appeal from the criteria applicable to the original sentence;
and in doing so it blurs the proper dividing line between the functions
of the Parole Board and the Court.[34] The Court is, in effect, assuming
the role of a Parole Board without the same amount of document-
ation. That, however, raises the question whether this is a matter
which should fall within the discretion of the Parole Board: some
might wish to argue that mitigation of sentence on this ground is a

matter, if not of right, then of just expectation, and certainly not a mere privilege to be withheld without reasons.

'Stale' offences raise other temporal difficulties. It is often said that stale offences should not even be brought to trial, years after the event, unless they are so serious that the public interest requires prosecution.[35] Indeed, there is a network of time limits applicable under English law to different offences – 6 months is the general limit for summary prosecution, and some indictable offences have short limits (such as 1 year for homosexual offences, under the Sexual Offences Act). However, there can be prosecutions for many stale serious offences, and the sentencer is then faced with the problem of imposing on the offender a sentence for something he did years before – his character may have changed in the meantime, he may have acquired different family circumstances, or the offence may have been committed against a social or emotional background which no longer obtains. It may appear unfair to subject the present person to the full force of the sentence for lawbreaking by his underdeveloped self: the offender may have become a 'different moral being', and should be sentenced as he now appears.[36] Thus in *Tierney*[37] some 18 months had elapsed between a burglary at a cricket club and the trial, part of the delay being due to the fact that the offender had spent some time in hospital after a road accident. In the meantime he had married and settled down; he had a good job, and his employer spoke well of him. The Court of Appeal held that the sentence of 9 months' imprisonment ought to have been suspended, because 'the just way to deal with the appellant is to deal with him as he is today and not as he was eighteen months previously.' Unfortunately delays of over a year between offence and conviction are not uncommon and the point raised in *Tierney* therefore has considerable practical importance. Cases which involve the prosecution of an offence committed a few years earlier, because either the offender or the offence has only just come to light, are much rarer and those which are then prosecuted tend to be crimes such as murder, manslaughter or robbery, which remain serious despite the lapse of time.

6 Financial penalties and equal impact

(a) Fines and means

Perhaps the most obvious and least contentious application of the principle of equal impact is to financial penalties, especially the fine. Section 35 of the Magistrates' Courts Act 1980 states:

In fixing the amount of a fine, a magistrates' court shall take into consideration among other things the means of the person on whom the fine is imposed so far as they appear or are known to the court.

The same principle is accepted in the Crown Court, and is generally understood to mean that courts should reduce the level of a fine where it appears that the offender's income is so low that a fine of the 'normal' amount would cause hardship to him. Some courts attempt to overcome the problem of the offender with a low income by extending the time allowed for payment: the fine is set by reference to the seriousness of the case, and the poorer offender is given longer to pay, by means of instalments stretching over a period of months. This is often advanced as the most reasonable of a range of solutions to the sentencing problem set by the offender of few means. One of the less acceptable solutions is to impose a suspended sentence of imprisonment when the court forms the view that the offender lacks the means to pay a fine which would sufficiently reflect the seriousness of the case: this is a solution which the Court of Appeal has condemned on some occasions and endorsed on others. Thus in *McGowan* (1975)[38] the Court held that it was wrong in principle to impose a suspended sentence of imprisonment where a fine would have been considered appropriate if the offender had had sufficient means, and the Court referred to the principle that a suspended sentence should not be imposed unless a sentence of immediate imprisonment would have been appropriate in the absence of the power to suspend (section 22(2) of the Powers of Criminal Courts Act 1973). But in *Myers* (1980)[39] the Court of Appeal upheld a suspended sentence of 1 month's imprisonment on a woman with two young children who was entirely supported by state benefits (£43 per week). The judge had arrived at the sentence by arguing that the offender lacked the means to pay a substantial fine, that a conditional discharge would not reflect his view of the gravity of the offence, and that probation was inappropriate; the Court of Appeal held that the sentence could not be criticized.[40] The reasoning in *Myers* is, however, open to two major criticisms: first, it flouts section 22(2) of the 1973 Act, to which the Court drew attention in *McGowan*; and secondly it results in the imposition of a more severe sentence[41] upon an offender for the sole reason that he is poor, an outcome which goes directly against the principle of equality before the law. Is the alternative of imposing a fine but extending the period for payment preferable? It is not clear on the authorities what should be the maximum length of repayment, but it is thought that a court should not make an order which requires repayments to go beyond 1 year.[42]

It is, however, open to question whether extending the period of repayments is a fair means of adjusting the fine for the poorer offender. The Advisory Council on the Penal System criticized this approach as inconsistent with the principle of equal impact, and they were surely right to do so.[43] The total fine should be adjusted according to the means of the offender, and this requires the court to consider his income in a case where there is no capital. If they take his income into account only for the purpose of calculating what instalments he could afford to pay and the length of time over which it would be reasonable to require him to pay, the effect would be to subject him to much greater punishment than the more wealthy offender who could settle the amount of the fine in a matter of days. Thus the expedient of extending the period over which the poorer offender may pay his fine is open, albeit less obviously, to the same objection as the expedient of imposing a suspended sentence upon him: it violates the principle of equality before the law.

The reason why sentencers feel themselves driven to use these expedients is not far to seek: they believe that it would be inappropriate to impose upon the poorer offender a fine small enough to reflect his lack of means, this belief is closely linked to their view of the seriousness of the case, and the belief derives ultimately from a crude conception of sentencing which ties the penalty to the gravity of the crime itself.[44] In other words, they think that a very small fine would hold the law up to ridicule, because it would be said that the fine was a paltry sentence for such a crime, and members of the public would think that the courts were not properly discharging their functions. No account is taken, in these beliefs and conceptions, of factors other than the gravity of the offence – such as the culpability of the offender, the principle of equal impact and the principle of equality before the law. These principles must be explained whenever a sentencer takes one or more of them into account, and the mass media should take greater care to state those reasons rather than trading on the apparent diversity of sentences passed. It should not, then, be for the sentencer to modify his approach to sentencing because the proper approach may be misunderstood; it is rather for him to explain matters so as to reduce the opportunity for misunderstanding.

One system which combines respect for the principle of equal impact with an element of public clarification is the 'day fine' system, used in Sweden and some other European countries. For this system the court must obtain information about the offender's annual income, together with information about his liabilities and any capital he may possess. In general the day fine is assessed at one-thousandth of his annual income. Once this calculation has been completed, the court can order him to pay so many day fines, the number being calculated according to the seriousness of the case. Thus the two factors, the seriousness of the case and the offender's means, are determined quite independently of each other, and both the number of day fines and the amount of each are announced in court.[45] Although sympathetic to the aims of the day fine system, the Advisory Council concluded that the introduction of such a system in England 'would present practical problems out of proportion to the advantage to be derived from it',[46] and successive governments have reiterated this view.[47] The practical problems are threefold: first, there is the difficulty of obtaining reliable information about means in this country, as compared with Sweden; secondly, the English system of maximum fines would require either a radical change or complete abolition; thirdly, the maximum fine which a magistrates' court may impose would have to be raised or abolished, since the actual level of fines would vary according to the wealth of the offender as well as the seriousness of the case. The second and third problems are not insuperable – indeed, the structure of maximum fines requires revision, despite the raising of maxima in the Criminal Justice Act 1982 – and the first may well be exaggerated. Day fines promote the principle of equal impact and ought to be introduced.

There would then be the question whether certain less serious classes of offence should be excluded from a 'day fine' system, as in Sweden. At present, many motoring offences are dealt with by magistrates' courts on a tariff approach, with the offender's means being allowed to affect the quantum of the fine in only a small proportion of cases. Indeed, the extension of a fixed penalty system from parking offences to a wider range of motoring offences has recently been recommended:[48] the offender would retain the opportunity to have his case brought before a court, but most offenders would agree to pay the fixed penalty. Systems of this kind make no allowance whatever for the means of offenders, and it may be argued that the anticipated penalties of £10 or £20 should be within the means of any offender. On the other hand, it remains true that even such apparently small amounts will have a far greater effect on the very poor than upon the wealthy, and we must be clear that any preference for fixed penalties, whether in court or out of court, sets simplicity and administrative convenience above individual justice.

(b) **The very rich and the very poor**

The uncomfortable relationship between the principle of equal impact and the idea that sentencing should be governed by the gravity of the offence is especially strained by the problem of fining the very rich. Most of the discussion of the principle of equal impact in this chapter has portrayed it as a vehicle for obtaining a measure of social justice for the financially disadvantaged. However, the principle ought to lead to higher fines for the rich as well as lower fines for the poor, and this is a result which many feel unable to accept. The point arose for decision in the well-known case of *Fairbairn* (1980),[49] where a railway employee had been convicted of theft of goods in transit to the value of some £700. In mitigation counsel had made the point that the offender was in a position to pay a substantial fine, since he owned two houses and one was free of encumbrances. Counsel's apparent attempt to obtain a suspended sentence was unsuccessful, since the judge imposed 9 months' imprisonment, but a fine of £7,500 was added. The Court of Appeal reduced the fine to £1,000, saying:

> In principle, the amount of the fine should be determined in relation to the gravity of the offence, and then – and only then – should the offender's means be considered to decide whether he has the capacity to pay such an amount. In this case the amount of the fine was over 10 times the value of the goods stolen, and in this Court's view that amount is out of scale in relation to the gravity of the offence of which he was convicted . . .

This seems to indicate that the gravity of the offence sets the 'ceiling' for the fine, with the offender's means justifying a reduction for the poor but not an increase for the rich. A similar approach was counselled by Lord Hailsham in a speech to Surrey magistrates:

> Should a poor man be made to pay less than the tariff if the tariff is too high for him? The answer is 'Yes'. He should not be made to suffer disproportionately because he is poor. Should a rich man be made to pay more because he is rich and therefore can pay more easily? . . . The answer is not 'Yes' because the controlling factor is the gravity of the offence.[50]

But Lord Hailsham thought that there was at least one qualification upon this view:

A rich man can be ordered to pay more than the 'Tariff' when there are circumstances of aggravation, notwithstanding that the controlling factor is the gravity of the offence, but because the gravity is aggravated and the defendant can afford to pay the fine.

As it stands, this is not a true qualification, however, since the size of the fine remains limited by the gravity of the offence. The rich man is paying more because his offence is regarded as more serious, not because he is rich.

The decision in *Fairbairn* accords with Thomas's longstanding view that it is 'inconsistent with basic tariff principles to impose a fine out of proportion to the offence on the grounds of the offender's wealth.'[51] The justification for this view is weak, and seems to rest largely on the idea that the sentence ought to be determined solely by the gravity of the offence. It may indeed be wrong to exceed the tariff in order to impose a higher sentence for general deterrent purposes, because that is to treat the individual as a pawn in social policy; it may also be wrong to exceed the tariff in an attempt to ensure a sufficiently lengthy period of treatment, because treatment ought to be voluntary and ought not to lead to disproportionate compulsory intervention. But neither of these familiar arguments against exceeding the tariff applies here. The point of exceeding it is to ensure that sentences make an equal impact on all offenders – that they penalize the rich as well as and as much as the poor. The principle of equal impact leads, in effect, to a denial that there should be a tariff of fines expressed in monetary terms. If there is a tariff, it should be expressed in units (such as day fines) which indicate the gravity of the offence separately from the means of the offender, for the correct approach is to assess each separately and a financial 'ceiling' set by reference to the gravity of the offence hampers this. A sentencer who fines a poor man £20 should be quite prepared to fine a wealthy offender £500 for the same offence, if his means are so great that this is the level of fine necessary to make the equivalent impact upon him. If he is not prepared to fine him £500, then he should equally not be prepared to fine the poor man £20, because £20 may mean a great sacrifice to a person who relies entirely on State assistance.

There is a fairly strong argument for saying that, not only is the 'ceiling' principle out of place in the calculation of fines, but that even a system of day fines would not succeed in achieving equality of impact. The point may be approached by considering the exasperated remarks of the judge in *Hanbury* (1979), who had to sentence for the offence of dangerous driving a man who was said to have gambled away some £500 in one night: 'I do not see what a fine can do. A fine to you means nothing. £500 down the drain in a couple of hours. It was just a joke – you go on to the next gambling club. What is £500? Nothing.'[52] The judge obviously felt that it would be improper to impose a fine which might be considered disproportionate to the offence (the 'ceiling' principle), and he therefore imposed a suspended sentence of imprisonment together with a fine of £500. Quashing the suspended sentence, the Court of Appeal observed: 'The judge there seems to be saying that because £500 means nothing to the man and because he cannot very well fine him much more than that, therefore a term of imprisonment seems necessary. That is false reasoning.' Clearly it would be wrong to penalize the wealthy offender by imposing a suspended sentence when a less wealthy offender would simply be fined. The only satisfactory escape from the judge's dilemma is to increase the fine of a wealthy offender just as courts reduce the fines of poorer offenders. But behind the judge's remarks in *Hanbury* lies the more subtle point that the arithmetical progression of the day fine approach ignores economic reality. A fine of £500 on an offender with £20,000 disposable income may have less impact than a fine of £50 on an offender with £2,000 disposable income, simply because in the former case the purchasing power of what remains is far greater in real terms. A fine which is proportionate to means may be less significant in effect where the offender starts from a position of considerable wealth, because he may have to forego little (or nothing) as a result of the financial deprivation. This is similar to the argument for progressive taxation of income.

To base a 'day fine' approach on a progressive rather than an arithmetical calculation would import even more difficulties of judgment into the process of fixing fines. But that is no justification for throwing the baby out with the bath water. It illustrates Walker's argument that in practice it will be virtually impossible to achieve equality of impact,[53] but it in no way weakens the reply that it is fairer to move some distance towards the principle of equal impact than to ignore it altogether.

(c) **Fine, tax or licence**

Even if it were possible to adjust the amount of fines so that they precisely achieved equality of impact upon a wide range of offenders, some would wish to argue against the use of financial penalties for certain classes of offender. The argument is that in some types of cases a fine constitutes nothing more than a tax levied on a course of unlawful conduct, or that the payment of fines amounts merely to a licence to break the particular law.[54] The argument was used in favour of retaining imprisonment for loitering and soliciting by prostitutes. Quite apart from the difficulty of ascertaining what the prostitute's income is, the contention was that prostitutes will continue soliciting so as to obtain the money to pay the fines. They will accept that from time to time they will have to pay fines; they will either allow for that in their charges to customers, or increase their soliciting whenever fines are imposed on them.[55] The same might be said against fining burglars, on the basis that an offender with a record of burglary may well commit further burglaries in order to raise the money to pay the fine. In both soliciting and burglary the risk of apprehension may be regarded as low, which certainly assists in tilting the balance towards further offending.

The 'tax' or 'licence' argument, then, is applied to crimes which are taken to be career crimes – committed for gain, repeatedly and (probably) as a way of life. It would be unusual to hear the argument used in relation to the impulsive and repeated offender, such as a man convicted of three or four assaults and breaches of the peace who had been fined on each occasion; it would hardly be said that the fines were merely a tax on his behaviour, a licence for self-indulgence. But perhaps it could be said that some persistent offenders would regard a few months' imprisonment as an occupational hazard – to be avoided so far as possible, but otherwise an accepted risk of a lucrative way of life.[56] The reason why some people do not regard fines as 'real sanctions' against prostitutes or short custodial terms as 'real sanctions' against burglars may well be that those sentences fail to turn the offenders away from their particular course of lawbreaking, the point being much stronger in the case of fines because they can be met from the proceeds of crime. On the question of definition, the argument cannot succeed because it would be extraordinary to restrict the definition of a sanction or punishment to those sentences which actually prevented offenders (or offenders of a particular kind) from re-offending: the definition must remain tied to general social attitudes, so that punishment connotes 'pain or other consequences normally considered unpleasant.'[57]

The significant feature of the argument is not so much the definition of a sanction or punishment as the relation of sentences to the persistent course of lawbreaking. Of the various reasons for increasing the punishment with persistence in offending which were considered in Chapter 5, there appears to be a particularly strong link with a cumulative approach based on deterrent reasoning: if a small fine fails to deter, try a larger one; if large fines fail to deter, try a suspended sentence; then comes a short term of imprisonment; then longer terms of imprisonment. Even on a retributive approach there appears to be some justification for increasing penalties, in proportion not to the actual comparative gravity of the offence but to the profits derived from it. This is an issue which will be further discussed in the section on deprivation of profits, below. In essence, the 'tax' or 'licence' argument is that sentences on those who offend persistently should be severe enough to deter them from further offences or, at least, to deprive them of the profits obtained from or as a result of their unlawful activity.

(d) Deprivation of profits

It seems unfair that a person who breaks the law should reap a financial advantage from doing so and should, despite being caught, prosecuted and convicted, be allowed to keep any part of that advantage. Where a victim suffers loss, it is unfair for the simple reason that the property taken is rightfully his; more generally, and where there is no victim or no identifiable victim, it is unjust on other members of society who adopt lawful means of obtaining satisfaction for their needs and desires. The crime gives the offender an unlawful advantage, and justice requires that the unlawful advantage be removed and the social balance restored.[58]

In order to remove the unfair advantage, a number of steps must be carefully taken by the court. For example, the profit which the offender has made from the offences proved or admitted must be calculated; the extent to which he still possesses those profits, or their proceeds, or sufficient other means to pay a commensurate financial penalty, must be ascertained; and then the court must assess the amount of penalty which will deprive him of the profit to the extent that he is capable of disgorging it. Then there is the question of the most appropriate financial order to use. Where a loss has been sustained by a victim of the offence, it is surely right that there should be a compensation order (or, in rare cases, a restitution order) in favour of the victim, provided that the usual conditions for making such an order are met.[59] Where the profit was made without causing loss to a victim or to identifiable victims, the offender should nonetheless be deprived of the profit: in such cases, the fine must be used for that purpose, as has been done in certain decisions concerning drug smuggling[60] and others concerning illegal escort agencies and massage parlours.[61] Then there is the problem of extracting the money from the offender: in recent years the criminal bankruptcy order has been introduced to deal with some of the more gross examples of hoarding the profits of crime, and an informal committee is reviewing the adequacy of the law on such matters.[62]

In principle, the exercise of depriving an offender of the profits of his illegal activities is distinct from and additional to the task of sentencing him for his crimes: the sentencer should first impose the sentence indicated by normal principles, and then consider the questions of deprivation of profits and compensation (having due regard to the effect of the principal sentence upon the offender's financial position). Those who accept deterrence as the aim of punishment would probably think it insufficient merely to restore the offender to his financial position before committing the crime, without any sanction aimed at deterring this offender from re-offending or others from imitating his actions: the prevention of future offences is a goal, quite apart from depriving of profit those who are caught and convicted.[63] Those who accept a retributive aim would probably distinguish between the breach of law involved in the offence and the profit which resulted, and would insist that he ought to be subjected to some disadvantage which symbolically cancels out the breach of law. In principle, therefore, and if the offender has sufficient means, there should be both sentence and deprivation of profit. If his means are insufficient to satisfy both, the law now states the court should give preference to the compensation order.[64]

7 Conclusions

Each of the principles considered in this chapter amounts to a derogation from the principle of proportionality which generally guides English sentencing practice. The statutory provision which requires a magistrates' court when imposing a fine to have regard to the means of the offender seems to yield a principle of equal impact: that penalties should be so adjusted as to inflict an equivalent amount of 'pain' (deprivation or suffering) upon offenders in different circumstances. The courts have not always followed the logic of this principle, for the Court of Appeal has held that the size of a fine should not be increased simply because the offender is extremely wealthy. The Court seems to rely on the 'ceiling' principle here, but it could be argued that increasing fines for the wealthy or lengthening community service for the unemployed does not involve the excessive punishment which the 'ceiling' principle aims to prevent. The logic of the principle of equal impact is that it equalizes the actual deprivation or suffering, so far as possible. The awkwardness of these and other examples certainly shows that other considerations may alter our approach as we move away from the central example of reducing fines for the poor.

One problem of the principle of equal impact is that it may produce an intricate sentencing structure. Bentham's list of 'circumstances influencing sensibility' illustrates this, and general assumptions about the effect of age and health may produce similar intricacy. In relation to age, Walker points out that

we might have quite complicated calculations, starting with the assumption that the normal sentence is appropriate for a man of, say, 25, and that the offender will live for three score years and ten (or indeed until the average age of death for an overweight heavy smoker, or whatever he is). A ready reckoner would then tell the sentencer how many months to deduct for a man of, say, 43. If this is regarded as reductio *ad absurdum*, why?[65]

The answer must be by way of confession and avoidance. A ready reckoner or even a computer programme for the effect of age on imprisonment does seem absurd, but only because it carries the principle of equal impact to lengths which would impose a disproportionate burden on sentencers, bearing in mind that it is only one of many considerations which should enter into their calculations. The argument in favour of the principle of equal impact is not weakened by the practical difficulty of taking it into account in other than fairly clear cases: it is surely acceptable in an imperfect world to take account of advanced years and of youth by reducing the sentence, whilst leaving it undisturbed for offenders in the intervening age-range, unless (perhaps) there is specific evidence of an abnormal reaction to imprisonment by an individual offender.

When the principle of equal impact is invoked, the decision is often based on assumptions about the typical reaction to the sentence of persons in a class to which the offender belongs (e.g. the elderly or the young) or of persons placed in the situation in which this offender finds himself (e.g. segregated in prison under rule 43); the decision is sometimes based on the reaction of the individual offender to the particular sentence, as in the contradictory cases on responses to imprisonment quoted above.[66] How soundly based are these general assumptions? It is unclear, for example, to what extent those segregated under rule 43 in *local* prisons do suffer more than other inmates; yet it is uncertain whether the courts take notice of any difference in the conditions between local and 'training' prisons. Again, evidence of remorse on the part of the offender is often treated as a justification for a reduction in sentence, and one reason for this may be the belief that less punishment is needed to make the same impact on a contrite offender than upon one who is not contrite. How can the court be satisfied that an offender is truly suffering remorse, rather than appearing to do so? This is a difficult question, and confidence in the answer is not improved by the frequent observations that pleading guilty is itself evidence of remorse.[67] Again, where an offender has suffered personal injury as a result of his offence or where a close relative has been killed or injured as a result of it, it is common to reduce the sentence on the assumption that a lesser penalty will have a sufficiently great impact upon him in his physical or psychological condition.[68] Indeed, in some such cases it is thought appropriate to refrain from bringing a prosecution.[69] This is acceptable as an application of the principle of equal impact, but raises different considerations if it is regarded as an exercise in 'moral accounting'.[70]

The second principle is 'equality before the law'. It is most easily stated and justified as a negative principle – that an offender should not be punished more severely on account of his race, religion, colour or class. This is not to propound a positive principle that all offenders should be sentenced without regard to personal factors: there are justifications for taking account of previous convictions, as explained in Chapter 5, and the English system has generally favoured leniency, separate sentences and even (for those under 17) separate proceedings for younger offenders, largely through a desire to minimize the harmful effects of the criminal process on their development. The principle, then, is essentially a negative or limiting consideration: its plainest application is that a wealthy offender should not be fined simply because he is in a position to pay a substantial sum, in circumstances in which a less wealthy offender would receive a more severe sentence, such as imprisonment. However, it seems possible that courts, whether at the suggestion of advocates or on their own motion, sometimes go against the principle by, for instance, suspend-ing sentences more readily for what may be called 'middle-class' offenders. The arguments are complex: it may be right and just that sentencers should take no account of social inequalities in sentencing, and it may be improper that sentencers should attempt to compensate for the wider social inequalities among the offenders who come before them, but is it not reasonable for the sentencer to take account of factors associated with a lower probability of reconviction? If a good work record or a supportive family are factors associated with lower reconviction rates, the sentencer might believe that there is some justification for reducing the sentence, yet might in effect be discriminating against those who through no fault of their own have been unemployed. Further difficulty is caused by the case of an offender who has lost his job as a result of the conviction. In a sense one could argue that in his psychological condition he requires less punishment in order to make the same impact as that upon an offender who has not suffered any such dire consequences. Again, the result is to treat the previously employed offender more leniently than the unemployed, and this seems contrary to the principle of equality before the law.

One way of resolving such conflicts between principles is to regard the ensuing difficulties as illustrating the unfairness wrought by traditional sentencing systems, and to argue for a 'justice' model which makes crude divisions between types of offence and offenders with certain criminal records and which ignores all other personal and social factors. Von Hirsch would thus contend that it is in general fairer to ignore issues of equal impact so as to ensure that there is no encroachment upon the equality before the law which the 'justice' model ensures. Only by excluding from consideration such personal and social factors can true equality before the law be achieved. Those who would wish to give effect to the principle of equal impact would argue that if employment status does result in a shorter community service order for the employed and a longer order for the unemployed offender, the unemployed offender may complain of what Cross terms 'a kind of cosmic injustice' and of the social injustice of being unemployed, but not of the sentencer's attempt to avoid unnecessary hardship.

A justice model of sentencing would, then, appear to lead to the demise of the principle of equal impact and, as von Hirsch accepts,[71] to the abandonment of financial penalties. If we are to keep financial

penalties, the inherent fairness of the principle of equal impact is hard
to resist. Indeed, as argued in section 6(a) above, fidelity to the
principle requires the introduction of a system based on the 'day fine'.
If we are to keep financial penalties, there is also a need to assert the
principle of equality before the law, so as to remove the unwarranted
social injustice which would arise if a rich offender were fined when a
poor offender would be imprisoned. Retaining financial penalties and
applying the two principles of equality, if only to the clearest cases,
must be accompanied by the clearer explanation of sentencing
decisions. What may appear to be a disparity between sentences must
be explained and justified by reference to the appropriate principle, so
that the offenders and the public have the reasons for the different
treatment. This is particularly important in the sentencing of co-
defendants: in his section on disparity of sentence[72] Thomas gives a
wide range of examples of disparity between co-defendants which can
be justified according to one sentencing principle or another, some of
which were not accepted and others probably not understood by the
co-defendant who received the more severe sentence. The English
system has a long way to go in ensuring that the moral distinctions
which it invokes are properly explained and declared to a wider
audience.

8
Symbolism, moral accounting and the smooth running of the system

1 Sentencing as symbolism

A court has only two means by which to convey, to those who hear and those who take note, the factors which have been taken into account in sentencing: the words spoken on passing sentence, and the terms of the sentence itself. In a small survey some years ago White found that it was comparatively rare for a magistrates' court to make observations on passing sentence (about one-quarter of the cases), whereas it was much more common in Quarter Sessions.[1] In her study in 1976 and 1977, Shapland found that observations were made on passing sentence in about half of the cases in magistrates' courts and in almost all the Crown Court cases.[1a] In another small study, Spreutels found that it was almost invariably the practice in the Crown Court for the sentencer to make observations on passing sentence:[2] his sample was taken from cases which reached the Court of Appeal, and that Court's task is particularly difficult if the Crown Court has given no explanation of how it arrived at the sentence imposed.

Would anything of value be lost if sentencing were performed by courts *in camera*, and the sentence communicated only to the offender himself and those involved in carrying it out? Some would argue that, even if the process of trial and conviction were open and publicized, so as to avoid 'secret justice', it would remain symbolically important that the sentence of the court be pronounced in public. However, that view is usually combined with the assumption, either implicit or explicit, that the symbolic effect of the sentence will operate on other members of society (both potential offenders and those who regard themselves as law-abiding) so as to strengthen their inhibitions against lawbreaking. In other words, the symbolism is not merely ritual but instrumental.[3]

On this view, the whole process of sentencing, especially when preceded by a trial (rather than a guilty plea) and particularly in the Crown Court, can be seen as a symbolic expression of society's denunciation of the offence, and as a re-affirmation of the law and its values. Many other decisions in the criminal process may have as much bearing on how the defendant is treated (the decision to prosecute, choice of charge, grant of parole, etc.), but most of them are taken in private without reasons being given. Sentencing is a public act, typically accompanied by some remarks (at least in the Crown Court) which give the opportunity for public pronouncements about this offender, his offence, and about law and order generally.

The sentence of the court, and any judicial observations which accompany it, is the authoritative medium for 'the expression of attitudes of resentment and indignation, and of judgments of disapproval and reprobation,' on the part 'of those "in whose name" the punishment is inflicted.'[4] Sentencing the offender is the conventional way of channelling and expressing society's condemnation of the offender's behaviour. Moreover, the reprobation or condemnation may be said to involve 'the state's marking its disapproval of the breaking of its laws by a punishment proportionate to the gravity of the offence.'[5] The element of proportionality points to another distinctively judicial function in sentencing – expressing the *degree* of social condemnation. By increasing or decreasing sentences to allow for certain aggravating and mitigating features – and, vitally, by declaring that this has been done – the court is able to mark the differing degrees of reprobation attaching to various offences which fall within the same legal category, and to mark other significant factors in the case.

If it is conceded that a major part of the courts' purpose in sentencing is to arrive at a sentence proportionate to the seriousness of the case, then in one sense the symbolic element in sentencing is inevitable. Proportionality, as we saw in Chapter 7, involves setting a level of sentences which both reflects the seriousness of this offence compared with others and is generally accepted as neither inappropriately severe or lenient. The level of sentences chosen can only be described as symbolic: there is no natural equivalence or commensurateness. The symbols may also become to some extent conventional: our courts have tended to use only certain lengths of custodial sentence – any examination will show sentences clustered round traditional lengths such as 3, 6, 9, 12, 18 months and, at a higher level, 3, 5 and 7 years.[6] The fact that the lengths of sentence are largely conventional may give some grounds for optimism about the possibility of change: if, for example, magistrates' courts were to announce their custodial sentences in terms of weeks and the Crown Court in terms of months, a general reduction in lengths might be effected without loss of the relativities between types of offence.

It is in relation to custodial sentences that the symbolic element in sentencing requires close scrutiny. This form of symbolism hurts. Solemn conviction of an offender in a public court, followed by words of condemnation from the judge, is itself symbolic. If the actual infliction of punishment is to be justified, particularly the imposition of custodial sentences, we must search for a strong reason. Durkheim maintained that the justification and necessity stemmed from the desirability of preserving the 'moral conscience' of society. He regarded punishment as an 'authentic act' which symbolically redressed the evil to society and re-affirmed the values inherent in the criminal law. 'Without this necessary satisfaction, what we call the moral conscience could not be conserved.'[7] In this justification there seems to be an element of general deterrence, probably long-term general deterrence:[8] the practice of regular state punishment serves to reinforce people's attitudes against lawbreaking. This may have similarities with some versions of 'modern retributivism', which justify punishment not merely because it is a fair response to lawbreaking but also instrumentally, in that punishment is supposed to contribute to crime control. The assumption seems to be that a certain level of sentences is needed in order to reinforce social values, to ensure that they do not wither away and to create the conditions in which they are transmitted from generation to generation; moreover, it is assumed that sentencers are able to interpret and weigh these social values. This, however, begs a whole range of questions about the effect of sentencing practices upon people's attitudes and behaviour. How much do people know about sentencing practice? As suggested in Chapter 1, the answer is probably that very little is known, and that knowledge is selectively acquired and only partly understood. There is room for considerable scepticism about a view which relies so heavily upon popular attitudes as a justification for substantial custodial sentences. Walker is right to accuse those who adhere to a denunciatory theory based on long-term general deterrence of 'a failure to take account of the facts of life.'[9] Even Walker's own tentative research finding that the degree of people's disapproval of offences can be influenced by the degree of disapproval expressed by others is, as he acknowledges, inconclusive because in real life members of society may have so little knowledge of the sentencing practices of the courts. It might be possible to avoid this counter-argument by postulating that long-term deterrence works in a much more indirect way, seeping into what Durkheim termed the 'moral conscience' through individuals who do have first-hand knowledge of the sentencing practices of the courts. But it seems more likely that the 'moral conscience' is shaped by myriad influences – newspapers, television, films, trades unions, golf clubs, recreation facilities provided by planners, unemployment, social opportunity, religion, and many others – of which the sentencing practices of the courts form a small and rather ineffectual part. It may be correct to assert, as does Hart, that 'the threat of legal punishment is required to create or maintain the voluntary practice of morality',[10] but that is to support some minimum level of legal sanctions rather than to prescribe a particular level.

The denunciatory theory is therefore insufficiently persuasive as a justification for inflicting punishment and (except in a minimum sense) as a justification for a given level of sanctions. However, even if we adopt the view that the denunciatory element is a socially useful by-product of pursuing other sentencing aims – a valuable *function* of sentencing, if not a sufficient aim – there are further questions. First, is it not self-defeating to take account of mitigating factors if a principal aim of sentencing is to symbolize society's disapproval of the offence, for the lower sentences which result may be regarded as inadequate condemnation of the crime? If the denunciatory element is regarded as part of modern retributivism, it is surely right that the sentences should take account of the circumstances of mitigation, for the 'moral conscience' must be responsive to more and less serious cases. To inflict the normal punishment on offenders with a strong claim to mitigation might have the effect of blunting rather than sharpening the moral conscience.[11] However, some might argue that substantial allowances for mitigation could bring sentences below the 'minimum level' thought to be necessary. Thus Walker contends that it is unsafe to argue that reducing sentences to allow for mitigation does not weaken the denunciatory effect:

> This would be true only if everyone who knew about the lighter penalty understood and agreed with the sentencer's reasons for choosing it. In real life it just does not happen that way: judges who deal with robbers, rapists and other serious offenders by means of suspended sentences, fines or probation provoke storms of protest from newspapers and readers who either were not told the reasons for such leniency or do not accept them.[12]

Is this 'real life'? Surely it is possible that a small number of cases, however well publicized, may be insufficient to affect deeply ingrained views about the degrees of right and wrong in criminal offences. It remains to be established that sentencing levels do have some connection with, and effect upon, the moral views of members of society; there is surely no empirical argument for or against the proposition that allowances for mitigation impair the law's denunciatory effect, and there is some reason to suggest that that effect (among the many other influences upon individuals) is not as great as is sometimes supposed.

The second question is whether denunciatory theories require the conviction and proportionate punishment of *every* known offender. Since the concern of those theories is that sentencing should produce certain effects among members of society, the question again returns to the empirical issue: would the failure to convict and sentence proportionately some known offenders weaken the general deterrent effect achieved by the punishment of the many? There is no clear evidence, but the relationship between sentencing practice and the 'moral conscience' seems to be so loose that there is certainly a possibility that the non-punishment of a few would have no effect on the moral conscience, even if the non-punishment of large numbers of convicted adults would. Thirdly, would the symbolic effect be impaired if the sentences declared in court were known not to be carried out in the form announced? This may explain why the probation order is (in some quarters) regarded as not having a significant symbolic effect, if it is believed that the declared supervision will be loose and fitful and that breaches of the order may be made with impunity (up to a certain extent). However, the principal problem is with custodial sentences. The sentence of life imprisonment is sometimes dismissed as 'only 9 years', often in a context which suggests that the speaker does not believe it to be as severe a sentence in fact as it is declared to be in court. Determinate sentences may now be believed to mean far less than the sentence of the court declares:

not only is one-third deducted from each sentence by way of remission, but there is the possibility of a further reduction in the effective length of sentences longer than 18 months through the operation of parole. There is, once again, no evidence of the effect (if any) of this gap between declared and actual sentence-lengths upon popular conceptions of proportionality or upon moral attitudes towards types of behaviour. Any effect would stem from the *believed* gap, rather than the actual gap. Some citizens might assume that parole is regularly granted to all prisoners serving over 18 months, so that sentences of 3 years are taken to mean 'only a year' and sentences of 6 years to mean 'only 2 years'. Other members of the public may not take account of either parole or remission, and may believe that 3 years means what it says. The further these arguments are taken, the more apparent becomes our ignorance about the degree to which sentencing practices influence the beliefs, attitudes and behaviour of members of society either in the short term or in the long term, and the more doubtful become the grounds for relying upon denunciation as a justification for imposing sentences of a given length.

To some extent the appeal system may assist with the symbolic effect of some sentences, since it enables the Court of Appeal some weeks or months after the pronouncement of sentence at the trial to reduce the sentence, and that reduction may receive less publicity than the original sentence. However, even the Court of Appeal is sometimes concerned about the possible loss of symbolic effect which might result from the reduction of a sentence.[13] A recent example is *Robinson*:

> This Court is acceding to that submission [based on the offender's good record as an employee and a father] by reducing the sentence from 15 months to eight months . . . But in so doing we are not seeking to encourage any other jilted lover to use violence towards his former lover or former spouse. This sentence is plainly justifiable, and the reduction is made solely out of mercy.[14]

Reducing sentences 'solely out of mercy' is thus believed to preserve the symbolic and general deterrent effects of the sentence whilst showing leniency to the particular offender. This suggests that sentencers believe that the 'moral conscience' or public attitudes to crime are affected by the sentence pronounced and not by the reasons given. Otherwise it would surely be proper to argue that sentencers may take account of factors affecting the individual's culpability, of the two principles of equality and of the offender's co-operation with the police, so long as the influence of those factors is clearly announced in court. In this way the court might achieve the desired symbolic effect by first pronouncing what the sentence would have been in the absence of mitigating factors, and then pronouncing the actual sentence after taking account of those other factors, which should be explained.

This, however, is to seek to exploit the symbolic *function* of sentencing. The justifications for punishing criminals, the justifications for mitigating and aggravating factors and the justifications for setting punishments at a particular level must be sought in retributive or preventive theories.[15] Denunciatory theories which are said to provide justifications of those kinds seem to lack a sound basis either in empirical evidence or in intelligent speculation, save for the possibility that there is a minimum level of sanctions beneath which large numbers of people would cease to take the criminal law seriously and that the authority of the law would be put in doubt. Sentencing as a public activity may have a legitimate function as a form of instrumental symbolism, reassuring the general public that legal values are being upheld and thereby tending to reinforce those values. But this will take the form of words spoken when imposing a sentence which is justified and calculated on other grounds, providing also the opportunity for the court to explain the other factors (apart from the gravity of the offence) which have been taken into account. We now turn to consider two of those factors – moral accounting, and upholding the system.

2 **Moral accounting**

On the theory of modern retributivism, sentences may be seen as 'cancelling out' the unfair advantage gained by the offender in committing the crime. The cancellation takes place only in a metaphorical or symbolic way, and is calculated by reference not solely to the gravity of the offence but also to the offender's culpability, his previous record, the principles of equality before the law and equality of impact, and other relevant principles. The accommodation of these other factors suggests that English sentencing has a loose connection with the notion of moral accounting: in other words, sentencing may be intended as a broader social judgment upon the offender, not dealing only with his offence and his probable reaction to the sentence, but considering them in the wider context of his contribution to society. Thus, where the court states that it is reducing the sentence which it would otherwise have passed, so as to take account of the offender's good war record, or of the fact that he has saved a child from drowning, it may be seen as to some extent 'settling the offender's moral account'. In the last chapter it was argued that sentencers may be justified in pursuing a principle of equality before the law by means of ensuring that sentences do not effectively discriminate against offenders of a certain social class, race, colour and so on, but that the principle neither requires nor justifies attempts to use sentencing to compensate for wider social inequalities. To what extent, if at all, should sentencers indulge in 'moral accounting'?

Quite apart from the spectacular cases, such as offenders who have saved a child from drowning, it is arguable that sentencers attempt to settle offender's moral accounts every day at a more mundane level. Many of the matters raised in mitigation and apparently taken into account by sentencers bear on the offender's general character, apart from the offence of which he stands convicted. Much is sometimes made of an offender's good employment record, or of his contribution to the community through voluntary work such as running a youth club. An example is provided by *Ingham*,[16] where the Court of Appeal observed:

> It seems also that this man shows some indications of social responsibility because he has done quite a lot of good voluntary work, and that is something which in a situation like this must stand him in good stead, since it shows that he has got inclinations to serve others rather than to prey upon them.

It is not always clear whether a court in these circumstances is indulging in pure moral accounting (i.e. that there are some positive contributions to society which should be weighed against the negative effect of the crime), or is adopting a kind of preventive reasoning (i.e. that his good deeds in the past make it less likely that he will re-offend, as compared with an offender who has no such record of contributions to society). The preventive reasoning is speculative, and it is thought that there is a measure of moral accounting in the calculations of many sentencers who allow positive factors in the offender's past (even a fine record in employment)[17] to mitigate the sentence for the offence.

The idea of moral accounting may therefore be said to underlie some of the practices of mitigation of sentence, particularly where a person's contribution to society (rather than the simple fact that he is a first offender and therefore of 'previous good character') tells in his favour. The issue is raised most poignantly by the spectacular cases:

> Men have had prison terms shortened because they have had good war records (a quarter of a century before!), have saved boys from drowning, or have given their sisters kidneys. This makes sense only if:
>   (a) offenders are being sentenced for their total moral worth rather than the offence of which they stand convicted;
> and (b) their moral worth can be calculated by moral book-keeping of this crude sort, in which spectacular behaviour counts more than unobtrusive decency.[18]

Point (b) has greater force than point (a). Courts have neither the evidence nor the training to evaluate an offender's 'total moral worth'; indeed, it is doubtful whether anyone could be said to have the training, especially since there are no agreed criteria of moral worth. Even the fullest speech in mitigation is likely to provide a court with evidence relating to only a fraction of the offender's life story, and there may be doubts about the reliability of such statements as are made.[19] It may be thought that, where the offender has committed a spectacular social act, the state of his moral account is much clearer; one could then argue that the existence of numerous other doubtful cases does not make it improper to take account of an act of heroism in a clear case. However, if the reason for taking account of the act of heroism does lie in moral accounting, then it would surely be as erroneous to consider that act as reflecting the state of his entire moral account as it would be to regard the crime as doing so – a court which conscientiously pursued this approach ought to seek evidence on the whole of his life, to find out just where the balance of his moral account lies. This exercise would be presumptuous and probably fruitless (although, again, it is only an accentuated form of some speeches in mitigation). If there is a justification for taking account of acts of heroism, it must surely be the pragmatic consideration that people who hear about the sentence might have a low opinion of the standard of criminal justice if the court were to ignore these (spectacular) contributions to society. There is no means of determining whether this is so – whether in fact people do expect courts to take account of such factors and would lose confidence in the courts if they ceased to do so – but if it is, this sense of 'fairness' may provide an answer to Walker's pointed statement that he has not come across a case 'in which a judge *increased* a man's sentence because he had evaded conscription, let a swimmer drown or refused his sister a kidney.'[20] However, the stronger answer to this point is that there is a difference between increasing and decreasing a sentence, if the principle of parsimony in punishment is accepted. A much higher standard of proof must be satisfied if it is proposed to justify an increase in the proportionate sentence rather than a decrease, and in view of the difficulties of evidence and evaluation on matters of moral or social 'worth' it would be rare that the case for such an increase could be made out.

Any element of moral accounting would be anathema to those who propound the 'justice' model of sentencing: allowing courts to take account of the background and life of the offender opens up considerable opportunities for bias to enter sentencing. This goes against the principle of equality before the law, and the only justification offered is that the public might lose respect for a criminal justice system which failed to take account of spectacular social acts. On the other hand, the information which the sentencer and the public are given about the offender may be incomplete and sometimes unreliable. Generally there is more information favourable to the offender (presented in mitigation, or in a social enquiry report) than adverse to him, since the police antecedents statement will rarely delve deeply into his past moral behaviour. The dangers of relying on the information typically presented to courts are discussed below.[21]

3 Upholding the system

A number of sentencing practices may be seen as upholding the criminal justice system, in a symbolic sense. Substantial sentences have been upheld for such offences as perjury and attempting to pervert the course of justice, even though the offender is of previous good character. In *Warne*[22] the Court of Appeal held that 'perjury is one of the most serious offences on the criminal calendar, because it wholly undermines the whole basis of the administration of justice', and similar observations were made about the attempt to persuade a prosecution witness not to give evidence in *Hill*.[23] In both cases it was held that a sentence of immediate imprisonment was appropriate. To some extent the reasoning behind these substantial sentences may rely on general deterrence, but it seems also that to a large extent it is a form of denunciation of those who interfere with the administration of criminal justice.

However, this symbolic re-assertion of the basis of criminal justice is not considered appropriate for offenders who perjure themselves in their defence. Such persons are not normally charged with perjury, and the principle is that the sentence for the offence of which they are convicted should not be increased because of the style of defence. Thus, where the defence which was run at the trial was said to consist of imputations upon the police or other prosecution witnesses[24] or simply of 'lie after lie after lie',[25] the Court of Appeal held that the sentences should be governed by the offences of which they are convicted. It is true that such offenders forfeit the mitigation which results from pleading guilty, but in principle that is forfeited even where the defence involves no imputations or lies.[26] It is also unclear whether it is general deterrence or denunciation which is uppermost in sentencing in cases of assaults on police officers and others engaged in enforcing the law. It has been seen that there are social justifications for imposing higher sentences for these assaults than for comparable assaults on ordinary citizens,[27] and one of the functions of these higher sentences may be symbolic. It may well be the case that sentencers regard it as important to make public observations which demonstrate support for those engaged in law enforcement, and to pass sentence accordingly. To some extent, again, these higher sentences may be aimed at general deterrence, but it is thought that the symbolic function of signifying support for the criminal justice system is also significant.

4 Ensuring the smooth running of the system

In a criminal justice system with a clear-up rate which is less than half of all offences recorded by the police and is falling, and with congestion in the courts which results in some long waiting periods before trial, it is understandable the sentence of the court may be used to offer incentives to offenders to assist the smooth running of the system. The sentence is not the only incentive which can be used – others would be complete immunity from prosecution, or early release on parole – but it is more easily apportioned than complete immunity and more widely available (and publicized) than parole. It has long been established that an offender who assists the police by giving information about other offenders should receive mitigation of sentence,[28] and in recent years there has been a succession of offenders who have 'turned Queen's evidence', not only to give information about other offenders but also to give evidence in court against them. Some of these so-called 'supergrasses' have been granted immunity from prosecution as a reward for their efforts. There have been other 'supergrasses' whose own criminal activities have been so serious that it was not felt proper to overlook them entirely, and they have received substantial mitigation of sentence.[29] The reason for this is, as Roskill LJ stated in _Lowe_,[30] that: 'Unless credit is given in such cases there is no encouragement for others to come forward and give information of invaluable assistance to society and the police which enables these criminals . . . to be brought to book.' Lowe's sentence should probably have been at least 18 years' imprisonment for the multitude of serious robberies in which he admitted involvement. The trial judge imposed a sentence of $11\frac{1}{2}$ years, taking account of Lowe's great assistance to the police, and the Court of Appeal further reduced it to 5 years in view of the fact that some 50 other offenders had been implicated by Lowe's evidence. Can this substantial reduction be justified? The justification must be pragmatic: the reduction provides an incentive to offenders to contribute to crime control (undoubtedly a primary goal of the criminal justice system), and insofar as that incentive has some effect it furnishes the police with a means of penetrating circles of serious criminals which might otherwise flourish undetected. Whether the incentives now offered are too great is a matter for debate. It is sometimes said that bargains have no place in the administration of criminal justice, but the substantial incentive for giving information about other offenders surely has the commercial flavour of a 'discount'.

Another well-established principle is that an offender ought to receive some mitigation of sentence for pleading guilty.[31] The predominant reason for this sentencing discount has never been clear: sometimes it is asserted that a guilty plea can be treated as evidence of contrition, sometimes it is simply said that guilty pleas should be encouraged because they contribute to the smooth running of the system and are therefore in the public interest. The 'contrition' rationale is open to serious doubt. There may be some cases where a court can be satisfied that· an offender is genuinely remorseful, especially if he owned up to the offence before he was detected;[32] but there must be many cases in which a sentencer simply cannot be sure whether there is genuine remorse, and the guilty plea may stem primarily from the realization that the evidence is likely to lead to a conviction in any event. It certainly seems odd to speak of contrition where there is a late change of plea or where the plea is only changed to guilty after some prosecution witnesses have given evidence, as in the leading case of *de Haan*;[33] on the other hand, it seems odd to suggest the discount for a guilty plea should be less if there was no possible defence to the charges anyway,[34] because that may also imply that contrition rather than saving public money is the major justification for this sentencing principle. The major justification surely lies in the contribution to the smooth running of the criminal justice system. If a significantly higher proportion of defendants were to plead not guilty than the one-fifth of those charged with indictable offences who now do so, the shortage of judicial manpower and of court buildings would mean that the system would be hard pressed. It is in the public interest that the guilty should have an incentive to plead to their offences rather than putting the prosecution to proof:

the court bears in mind that these kinds of criminal will do anything at their trial to try and evade verdicts of guilty. They often do so by making attacks on police officers and by trying to beguile a jury into believing that in some way they have been treated unfairly. Fortunately they seldom succeed, but in the course of failing they waste much public time and money. They should be encouraged, as far as it is possible to encourage criminals, to stop these sort of tactics. In this case they did not try to hoodwink the court in any way. They did not try to cause as much trouble as they could.[35]

This, then, makes a prima facie case for the discount for pleading guilty: some of the objections are considered below.

What should be the extent of the discount? Baldwin and McConville reported 'a spectrum of views' on this question:

Some judges regard a reduction of perhaps a quarter or a third of whatever sentence is to be imposed as a fair reward in most cases for a guilty plea; others view any mitigation of sentence as being solely conditional upon evidence of contrition on the part of the defendant, which is recognised as a fairly exceptional occurrence.[36]

This suggests not only that some sentencers fail to recognize and to act upon the pragmatic reason for offering a discount for pleading guilty, but also that the extent of the discount is uncertain. In *McPhee*[37] the Court of Appeal held that one-half was the appropriate discount for an offender who, unlike his co-defendant, had not 'put the public to the expense of a trial'. The proper sentences were 2 years' imprisonment for the co-defendant, and 1 year for this offender. However, in an earlier decision the present Lord Chief Justice seems to have acquiesced in discounts within the 20 to 30 per cent range,[38] and this seems both more appropriate and more usual[39] than 50 per cent. There is some evidence for the proposition that a guilty plea may make the difference between a custodial and a non-custodial sentence. Baldwin and McConville's research suggested that a plea of guilty, particularly where it is a late change of plea, may have this effect,[40] and the Court of Appeal has not clearly disavowed the practice. Whilst in *Tonks*[41] the Court held that an offender who pleaded not guilty and was convicted would have a legitimate sense of grievance if he received an immediate custodial sentence when his co-defendants who pleaded guilty received suspended sentences, that very practice was approved by a differently constituted Court of Appeal in *Hollyman*.[42]

Why is it assumed that the Court of Appeal should disavow the practice of reducing a custodial to a non-custodial sentence in return for a guilty plea? If there is indeed a prima facie case for offering an incentive to the guilty to plead guilty, does not that case become stronger as the incentive becomes greater? There are two major respects in which the discount for pleading guilty may produce injustice. First, an inevitable concomitant of the discount is that a person who pleads not guilty and is convicted receives a more severe sentence. In effect, this raises a disincentive against pleading not guilty even where there is an arguable point of law or a disputable question of degree. To protest that the sentence after a trial is the 'normal' sentence, and that the convicted offender is merely 'not favoured with a benefit' rather than actually penalized, is unhelpful, even if logically correct. There is in fact a difference between the two sentences which is attributable to the presence or absence of a guilty plea, so that pleading not guilty (unsuccessfully) costs more.

The possibility of injustice arises when this difference in sentences is considered from the point of view of the defendant. The existence of a significant discount for pleading guilty can exert considerable pressure towards a change of plea. Indeed, the purpose of the discount is precisely to act as this kind of inducement. The injustice arises when the pressure is so great – as where the likely difference is that between an immediate custodial sentence and a suspended sentence or non-custodial measure – as to induce a defendant to change his plea even though he believes that he is innocent, or that he has an arguable point of law or question of degree. The English courts have recognized this danger, and have taken steps to eliminate one source of pressure – the belief that the trial judge has stated his intention to impose a lower sentence if there is a plea of guilty. Thus in *Turner* the Court of Appeal laid down *inter alia* that: 'A statement that, on a plea of guilty, he would impose one sentence, but that, on a conviction following a plea of not guilty, he would impose a severer sentence is one which should never be made.'[43]

All that a judge may properly do is to indicate that, whatever the plea may be, the sentence will or will not take a particular form. Now it may be right to assume that the degree of pressure on the defendant would be greatest if he was led to believe that the judge himself had indicated that the sentences would differ according to the plea;[44] but there is evidence to confirm that the degree of pressure exerted by the advice of a defendant's legal representative may also be high.[45] The decision in *Turner* expressly preserved the liberty of counsel 'to give the accused his best advice, albeit in strong terms'. It is well known that guilty pleas tend to be rewarded with a discount in the sentence, and counsel will use his knowledge of the particular judge in framing his advice to the defendant. How much freedom of choice has a defendant whose counsel tells him that the prosecution case is fairly strong, and that there is a strong probability of a reduced sentence and even a non-custodial sentence if he changes his plea? It is at least possible that defendants will regard their legal representatives as 'experts' and will find their advice compelling; and it is also possible that counsel will not always be able to tell which defendants are really guilty and which are not, when determining what advice to give.[46] These observations do not imply criticism of counsel, who must give advice on the basis of sentencing practices as they are; rather, they call into question the very practice of offering a discount for a guilty plea.

There is also a further aspect, illustrated by the passage quoted above from Lawton LJ's judgment in *Davis*: the existence of the sentencing discount for guilty pleas is one disincentive to challenging the police evidence of an alleged confession which the defendant denies making or denies making in that form (the other disincentive is the provision that a defendant who makes such an allegation and then gives evidence himself may be cross-examined on his previous convictions).[47] It is possible that the sentencing discount does operate to discourage some defendants from trying to 'hoodwink the court', to use the words of Lawton LJ, but it is also possible that it makes it even more hazardous to make a proper challenge to a genuinely disputed confession.

Thus, although there are pragmatic arguments of an administrative and economic nature in favour of the discount for a guilty plea, there are grave dangers of injustice in its practical operation. Even if there were no involvement of either judges or legal representatives in the matter, the very fact that the discount is normally given is reasonably well known and may exert some influence upon those who maintain their innocence as well as upon those who are in fact guilty. To support the discount is therefore to endorse a dilution, for bureaucratic reasons, of rights which the criminal process is supposed to protect – the right to require the prosecution to prove guilt, the right to trial in open court, and most fundamentally the right not to be subjected to unfair pressure in determining how to plead to the charges.

It has long been established as a positive rule of English criminal law, that no statement by an accused is admissible in evidence against him unless it is shown by the prosecution to have been a voluntary statement, in the sense that it has been obtained from him either by fear of prejudice or hope of advantage exercised or held out by a person in authority.

That is Lord Sumner's classic statement,[48] which yields a right not to be subjected to such pressure when taking decisions in the criminal process. The discount for pleading guilty, when it is so great as 20 to 30 per cent of the 'normal' sentence, and particularly when it reduces a custodial sentence to a non-custodial sentence, considerably weakens that right.

What would be lost if the discount were prohibited? It is widely assumed that this would cause the rate of guilty pleas to decline, leading to congestion in the courts. Defendants would have nothing to lose by pleading not guilty, and their legal advisers might more readily advise in favour of a 'fight'. But these remain as assumptions: there is no evidence of what the effect would be, and it might well be marginal, with most defendants admitting their guilt and wishing to 'get the matter over and done with' in the least formal and most speedy manner. Alternatively, a modest discount with a maximum of, say, 10 per cent of the 'normal' sentence (not permitting the suspension or partial suspension of a sentence which would otherwise be immediate) might be sufficient to provide a small incentive without imposing undue pressure upon the innocent to plead guilty. That middle way, however, would still involve a dilution of fundamental rights. The proper course would be to consider abolishing the discount, at least on an experimental basis.

5 **Conclusions**

The principal argument of the first section of this chapter was that sentencing may serve a symbolic *function* but that denunciation is an insufficient *justification* for punishment. The symbolic, denunciatory or expressive function should therefore be seen as a by-product of sentencing, and no more. If one considers the various audiences at whom the sentencer may direct his remarks, they could be as many as fivefold:

(i)   the offender himself, and his offence;
(ii)   the victim, and the victim's family;
(iii)   potential imitators, either by warning of the serious view which courts take of this kind of offence or (where the particular sentence is mitigated to take account of this defendant's characteristics) by explaining that the offence would have attracted a heavier penalty if it had not been for these mitigating features;
(iv)   the public, by denouncing this kind of offence in particular or by making general remarks aimed at reassuring the public that the courts are striving to uphold law and order;
(v)   the police and other agents of law enforcement, by encouraging them in the performance of their duties.

The anticipated reactions of any one audience should not determine the level of sentences, but the existence of the various audiences supplies a reason for fuller and clearer explanation by courts of the sentences which they pass. One approach would be for the court to state what sentence would be appropriate for a crime of this gravity and then to explain any other factors which lead to a different (lower) sentence.

What might a victim and his family think of the criminal justice system if an apparently lenient sentence is imposed on someone whom they regard as a serious offender? Although research suggests that there is general satisfaction among victims with the level of sentences imposed on those who committed offences against them,[49] dissatisfaction might result from inadequate explanation of the sentence as much as from unduly low sentencing. Moreover, the specific concern of victims is as much with compensation, and that raises issues which are separate from sentencing. There are powerful arguments in favour of instituting an efficient system of compensation for those who suffer physical or psychological harm as a result of crimes committed against them, and in England the Criminal Injuries Compensation Board and the power of a criminal court to make a compensation order constitute significant advances in this direction.[50] The English system still falls short of an ideal scheme of compensation for criminal injuries, but it would be wrong to expect the courts to attempt to make up for any dissatisfaction among victims by increasing the level of sentences.

So far as potential imitators are concerned, this points to general deterrence as a justification for punishment and for a certain level of punishment. The arguments were discussed briefly in Chapter 1, and will be further examined in Chapter 9.

It was argued earlier in this chapter that beliefs about public attitudes to sentencing form an unsteady basis for arguments about the level of sanctions. There is a dearth of information about what public attitudes are, for what is written in the newspapers or widely agreed in a club may not represent the majority opinion. Moreover, the basis for any opinions which *are* widely held is equally uncertain: information about what the courts do may be incomplete, and understanding imperfect. Von Hirsch argues that:

> Imposing only a slight penalty for a serious offence treats the offender as less blameworthy than he deserves. Understating the blame depreciates the values that are involved: disproportionately lenient punishment for murder implies that human life – the victim's life – is not worthy of much concern; excessively mild penalties for official corruption denigrate the importance of an equitable political process.[51]

This is not necessarily so. A sentence which is properly explained may both uphold the sanctity of human life and respect a principle of fairness such as the principle of equal impact; again, it may both uphold the importance of an equitable political process and respect some other principle. Only a crude connection between gravity of offence and severity of sentence seems to preclude consideration of these other principles and factors. If their influence is clearly explained, a lower sentence should not necessarily depreciate the values which a particular law seeks to uphold.

Higher sentences might be supposed to improve police morale, for example, but that surely would not be a sufficient reason for inflicting greater punishment; other means of improving morale must be found. It is one thing for sentencers to use the sentencing process as an opportunity to make remarks which reassure the public and encourage the police; it is quite another thing for these functions of sentencing to be elevated to the status of aims and allowed to determine lengths of sentence.

We have also in this chapter considered the claims of moral accounting and maintenance of the administration of justice as factors to be taken into account in sentencing. It was argued that there is no justification for moral accounting even in the few clear cases of individuals who have made some spectacular contribution to the community. However, if there is factual substance in the argument that people would think the sentence unjust if no allowance were made, there might be a slender justification. Doubtless there is a considerable amount of 'moral accounting' in mitigation of sentences generally, and there are dangers in the incompleteness and un-reliability of information provided to courts, much of it based merely on the *ipse dixit* of the offender. Discounts for those who co-operate in crime control by giving information to the police or evidence in court against other accused persons may be justified on pragmatic grounds, even though some may argue that the incentives now offered are too generous. However, the discount for pleading guilty has more far-reaching effects in the criminal process. Essentially, it derogates from the fundamental right not to be subjected to unfair pressure when taking decisions in the criminal process, and derogation is excessive when the defendant is led to believe that his plea may make a major difference to the length of a custodial sentence or may make the difference between a custodial and a non-custodial sentence.

9
Custodial sentencing

1 Custodial sentences and the principle of parsimony

Imprisonment is now society's ultimate penalty – the most severe form of sentence which English society will contemplate. As a sentence it came to be regarded and used as a punishment for serious crimes only in the second and third quarters of the nineteenth century, partly as a result of the reduction in the number of offences which carried the death penalty and partly as a result of the decline in transportation of serious offenders to the colonies. Harsh forms of incarceration were tried – the separate system (involving solitary confinement for the first part of a sentence), the tread-wheel, hard labour – but were abandoned, and in 1895 the Gladstone Committee proclaimed deterrence and reform as the dual aims of imprisonment.[1] Those aims have coexisted uncomfortably in the years since then, and in the mid-twentieth century there was a resurgence of belief in the potentiality of prisons for reforming inmates, but in recent years that optimism has ebbed away. There is now widespread support for applying the principle of parsimony[2] to custodial sentences. This is sometimes expressed as the principle that custodial sentences should only be used as a last resort, but that formulation would permit the use of a custodial sentence simply because all other measures have 'failed'.[3] A preferable formulation is that custodial sentences should be used as sparingly as possible. There seem to be three main reasons for supporting this principle.

(a) Doubts about the reformative potential of penal institutions
There have always been doubts about this, and earlier in the century

Alexander Paterson, one of the most influential of Prison Commissioners, declared that 'it is impossible to train men for freedom in a condition of captivity'. The point has subsequently been recognized in several official documents, beginning with the statement in the 1959 White Paper that figures which record the reconviction rate of those discharged from prison must be treated with caution because 'it is not possible to say whether that result is because of their treatment in prison, or in spite of it, or whether it would have been the same if they had never come to prison.'[4] The same point was made in the 1969 White Paper,[5] and its 1977 successor was more forthright:

Experience in recent years has led increasingly to scepticism about the compatibility of rehabilitation in this traditional, paternalistic form with the practicalities of day-to-day life in custody. The coercion which is inherent in a custodial sentence and the very nature of 'total institutions' tends to direct the whole of the inmates' individual and group energies towards adjustment to the austerely unnatural conditions; towards alienation from authority; and thus towards rejection of any rehabilitative goals toward which the staff may be working.[6]

This did not lead to the abandonment of all rehabilitative claims for custodial sentences, for the 1977 document went on to advocate a less paternalistic and more 'man-to-man' approach, claiming that 'a steady if modest measure of reform has been achieved and is continued, through personal contact between individual prison officers and individual inmates.' The claim was not supported by evidence and will, like the May Committee's recommendation of a new concept of 'positive custody',[7] remain at the level of a fine hope which seems almost impossible to realize with the conditions and the priorities which exist. The conditions are those associated with the total institution and compounded, in the local prisons of England, by severe overcrowding; the main priority is security which, as it is now implemented, restricts the opportunities for regimes which might warrant the description 'rehabilitative'. Indeed, the failure of rehabilitative efforts in English prisons might be ascribed more to the fact that those efforts have usually been severely restricted by the perceived demands of security and of economy than to the rather specious logic of Paterson's dictum, which might be applied more or less to any form of training which does not take place 'on the job'. It is possible that there could be a rehabilitative total institution, but it is unlikely to become a reality in the present economic and penological climate. Whilst it is right to attempt constructive regimes in penal institutions, we cannot expect more than limited success in identifying which offenders might benefit from them and which might not, and it is important to ensure that no offender is unfairly treated as a result of these well-meant attempts. It is therefore wrong to lengthen an offender's sentence in an attempt to give the prison authorities sufficient time to rehabilitate him, and *a fortiori* wrong to lengthen all custodial sentences in the hope of rehabilitating a few.

(b) Beliefs in the deleterious effects of penal institutions

To the extent that prisoners are allowed to associate with one another, there is always the risk that, as Bentham put it, prison will be 'a school in which wickedness is taught by surer means than can ever be employed for the inculcation of virtue.' On this view, less experienced criminals may be 'contaminated' by the more experienced offenders, and techniques and ideas for further law-breaking will be spread. It is possible that the opposite might happen, and that contact with other prisoners will help to reform an inmate, but the former assumption seems the more likely. More recently, however, emphasis has been placed on other deleterious effects. The psychological effects of imprisonment are often great, stemming from the degradation of being stripped of one's possessions on entry to the institution and then forced to associate (even to share a small cell) with prisoners who may be thought aggressive and unpleasant, together with the various deprivations inherent in prison life, and the result may be deleterious to the offender's personality.[8] Thus there are influences and pressures at work during imprisonment which make it reasonable to conclude, as did Sir Rupert Cross, that 'the chances of deterioration in prison are at least as great as those of reform.'[9] This is no less likely to be the case with short custodial terms served in overcrowded conditions than with long terms, which may induce a sense of hopelessness and isolation. Cross was led to conclude that 'the main aim of prison reform should be the prevention of prisoners' deterioration', and this was clearly recognized in *Prisons and the Prisoner* in 1977:

Detention in custody encompasses the whole life of the inmate and must therefore seek to provide for all his basic personal and social needs – physical, spiritual, educational and recreational – if it is to preserve physical well-being, let alone to promote social development. To put it another way, the preservation of personality and the prevention of deterioration call for as high a priority as efforts to bring about the inmate's improvement.[10]

The fact that a custodial sentence may have a deleterious effect on the personality of the individual subjected to it supplies a further reason for using custody as sparingly as possible.

(c) **Doubts about the deterrent effect of custodial sentences**

The effectiveness of a penal sanction has generally been measured by examining the rate of reconvictions in the years after sentence and, despite the drawbacks of this approach, there is not a more satisfactory approach in general penological use. Taking reconvictions as a measure, it has often been said that about three-quarters of those who serve a prison sentence for the first time do not return to prison. This led Cross to argue that it is 'reasonable to suppose that they were deterred by the experience of imprisonment';[11] but it is possible that some of them would not have been reconvicted whatever penal sanction had been applied, especially any first offenders among them, and it is certainly possible that some would not have been reconvicted if they had been subjected to a different penal measure. Nonetheless, it is fair to point out that the first prison sentence does appear to be followed by fewer reconvictions than second and subsequent prison sentences. The reconviction rate (within two years) of adult male prisoners released in 1978 was 50 per cent and it seems probable, although the figures are not given, that fewer of those who had served their first prison sentence were reconvicted than those who had previously served prison sentences. The proportion of young adults released in 1978 from detention centre, borstal and prison who were reconvicted within two years was 66 per cent, and the proportion of reconvictions was higher for borstal and imprisonment (for which offenders generally had more previous convictions) than for detention centres.[12] These findings suggest that the reconviction rate may be affected as much by the age and previous record of the offender than by the nature of the sentence to which he is subjected, so that young offenders or offenders with several previous convictions are more likely to be reconvicted irrespective of the sentence imposed. Research which has attempted to take account of variations in age and previous convictions suggests that imprisonment is followed by slightly more reconvictions than might be expected (except in relation to a small group of first offenders sent to prison, for whom the reconviction rate was comparatively low).[13] The general conclusion is that there is no hard evidence that custodial sentences exert a greater preventive effect on individual offenders than other penal sanctions, if reconvictions are taken as a measure of effectiveness. Of course, even where it does succeed in preventing further offences, it is impossible to say on the available evidence whether that is through reformative treatment in prison or through fear of being sent back to prison.

These, then, are the reasons which have contributed to the spread of the view that custodial sentences should be used as sparingly as possible – growing doubts about the effectiveness of penal institutions to reform or deter most of the offenders they receive, together with a deepening belief that the institutions have a deleterious effect on those offenders. Further arguments may be found in the probable effect on the offender of the stigma of having been in prison, which may make it difficult for him to lead an honest and industrious life on release, and in the recent deterioration of conditions inside English local prisons, serving to increase the impact of incarceration upon inmates. The debate therefore shifts away from reform and individual deterrence towards incapacitation and general deterrence, so that there are some who maintain that custodial sentences may properly be used to incapacitate certain offenders who have shown an unusually high propensity to commit serious offences, and others who maintain that the regular imposition of prison sentences serves as a general deterrent to others. Neither argument is necessarily in conflict with the principle of parsimony in the use of custodial sentences, for the incapacitative and general deterrent arguments are sometimes advanced as reasons for a more selective use of custody. However, those arguments often do militate against the principle of parsimony, and they are considered below in their detailed application to particular lengths of custodial sentences and to imprisonment for particular kinds of offender.

2 The first custodial sentence

Any custodial sentence represents a major incursion into the life of the individual offender, but the first custodial sentence will generally be the most traumatic: quite apart from the deprivations and degradation of a penal institution, he is forcibly separated from his family and friends for the first time, and is subjected to one of society's strongest condemnations, a point which will probably be reflected in the attitude of others towards him. The social consequences may be considerably less significant if the offender already associates with a criminal fraternity where prison is an accepted hazard of life, and the same would apply if his life is in such ruins already that there is little social esteem, self-esteem or individuality to be deprived of.[14] But in general the first custodial sentence may be expected to have a strong psychological and social effect, and it is therefore not surprising that one of the few principles of sentencing which is enshrined in English legislation is that a court should not impose a first custodial sentence on an offender unless it is of opinion that no other method of dealing with him is appropriate.[15]

How many of the custodial population are serving their first custodial sentence? In 1981 some 36,000 adult males were received into English prisons, of whom details were available for some 30,000. Of those, 7,870 were serving their first custodial sentence, i.e. roughly a quarter of those entering prison.[16] The position is slightly different for young offenders. Of those received into detention centres there were no details for 14 per cent, but it was known that 80 per cent had not served a custodial sentence before; for borstals some 35 per cent had not previously served a custodial sentence, and for imprisonment of young adults the figure was as low as 18 per cent (the vast majority having presumably spent time in a detention centre or borstal or both).[17]

Since about a quarter of adult males admitted to prison under sentence are there for the first time, the criteria for imposing the first prison sentence obviously have practical importance. Sentencers often insist that imprisonment is used as a last resort and that they would not send a person to prison unless it was absolutely necessary, but the number of offenders involved confirms the need to scrutinize the criteria used by the courts. When dealing with offenders under 21, different principles come into play: the discipline of a detention centre is sometimes thought to be 'good for' young offenders. This aspect has been emphasized in relation to the 'experimental' regimes based on a 'short, sharp shock' model which have been introduced into a few detention centres since 1980, and it is likely to be crucial now that the Criminal Justice Act 1982 (permitting 3 week orders for detention) is in force. The statistics make it clear that detention in a detention centre is the first custodial sentence for most of those who go there, which makes it vital to examine the reasons for its imposition. Similarly, about a third of those sent to borstal were serving their first custodial sentence, and a number of borstal sentences (probably a minority, but the proportion is not known) were imposed for constructive or therapeutic reasons, in the hope that borstal could change the pattern of the young offender's life. There is little evidence that this kind of change can be effected, and the replacement of borstal by youth custody (by the Criminal Justice Act 1982) does not diminish the need to search for criteria.

(a) The statutory provisions

The principal provision aimed at the first sentence of imprisonment for an adult is section 20 of the Powers of Criminal Courts Act 1973, which reads:

(1) No court shall pass a sentence of imprisonment on a person of or over 21 years of age on whom such a sentence has not previously been passed by a court in any part of the United Kingdom unless the court is of opinion that no other method of dealing with him is appropriate; and for the purpose of determining whether any other method of dealing with any such person is appropriate the court shall obtain and consider information about the circumstances, and shall take into account any information before the court which is relevant to his character and his physical and mental condition;
(2) Where a magistrates' court passes a sentence of imprisonment on any such person as is mentioned in subsection (1) above, the court shall state the reason for its opinion that no other method of dealing with him is appropriate, and cause that reason to be specified in the warrant of commitment and to be entered in the register.

Sub-section (2) incorporates one of the rare requirements for an English sentencer to give reasons for the sentence, but it applies only to magistrates' courts and may in any event be satisfied by a brief reference to the seriousness of the offence. The effect of section 20 as a whole is thought to be minimal:[18] it seems to be treated as a rather general reminder to 'think twice' before imposing a first sentence of imprisonment, and rarely gives rise to detailed discussion in the Court of Appeal about the criteria for a first custodial sentence. It would be possible to give the section a much more vigorous purpose: since the court must be 'of opinion that no other method of dealing with [the offender] is appropriate', it could be argued that the court ought to consider and dismiss each of the non-custodial alternatives, and the suspended sentence, before imposing the first sentence of immediate imprisonment.[19] This approach would not solve the fundamental question of the criteria for the first custodial sentence, but it would at least ensure that full and proper consideration had been given to the various alternatives. The courts have not, however, adopted this interpretation.

A more elaborate attempt to structure the reasoning of sentencers in relation to the first custodial sentence is embodied in section 1(4) of the Criminal Justice Act 1982. A court must not send a young adult offender to detention centre or youth custody

> unless it is of opinion that no other method of dealing with him is appropriate because it appears to the court that he is unable or unwilling to respond to non-custodial penalties or because a custodial sentence is necessary for the protection of the public or because the offence was so serious that a non-custodial sentence cannot be justified.

The court is bound to obtain a social enquiry report before imposing such a sentence (section 2(2)), unless of opinion that such a report is unnecessary in the circumstances (section 2(3)). A magistrates' court must state in open court its reasons for holding that one of the three justifications for a custodial sentence applies, and must record those reasons. Section 1(4) appears to go further towards the structuring of sentencing discretion than most statutory provisions in English law. It contains three heads of justification for imposing a custodial sentence. The third, referring to the seriousness of the offence, seems to import the same problems as those which exist under section 20 of the Powers of Criminal Courts Act, and they are discussed below. The second, referring to the 'protection of the public', may be interpreted either as another allusion to the gravity of the crime or as importing a concept of 'dangerousness' similar to that discussed in Chapter 5.[20] The first, that the offender appears 'unable or unwilling' to respond to non-custodial penalties, apparently adopts the argument that a custodial sentence may be justified merely on the ground that the offender has been reconvicted after experiencing non-custodial measures; and, since the three heads of justification in the sub-section are alternatives, the court need not also be satisfied that the offence is sufficiently serious to justify a custodial sentence. We now turn to a fuller discussion of the possible justifications.

(b) The 'unavoidable' first custodial sentence

What, then, are the contours and the foundations of the policy of regarding a custodial sentence as 'necessary' and 'unavoidable' in certain kinds of case? Norval Morris, having insisted that imprisonment should always be regarded as a last resort and that the sentence should never be greater than is 'deserved' for the crime or crimes of which the offender is convicted, goes on to articulate three 'Pre-conditions to Imprisonment':[21]

A Conviction by jury or bench trial or an acceptable plea of guilty to an offense for which imprisonment is legislatively prescribed.
and
B Imprisonment is the least restrictive (punitive) sanction appropriate in this case because:
either **(i)** any lesser punishment would depreciate the seriousness of the crime(s) committed
or   **(ii)** imprisonment of some who have done what this criminal did is necessary to achieve socially justified deterrent purposes, and the punishment of this offender is an appropriate vehicle to that end,
or   **(iii)** other less restrictive sanctions have been frequently or recently applied to this offender.
and
C Imprisonment is not a punishment which would be seen by current mores as undeserved (excessive) in relation to the last crime or series of crimes.

Precondition A is formally essential: it raises questions about the criteria used by the legislature in deciding to make certain crimes imprisonable. The substance of Precondition B(iii) was strongly critised in Chapter 5;[22] it remains only to emphasize that section 1(4) of the Criminal Justice Act 1982 (set out overleaf) seems to endow it with statutory approval as a reason for depriving a young offender of his liberty. We have seen that in 1981 some 6,500 offenders were given a custodial sentence for the first time. Not all of these would have been sent to prison on reasoning similar to that enshrined in Precondition B(iii), but some would. Precondition C raises a number of difficulties which have been acknowledged from time to time above. How confident can we be about locating 'popular mores', as distinct from the opinions of the mass media or opinions heavily shaped by the mass media?[23] If we can locate them, are they based on a notion of desert linked solely to the amount of harm or damage caused, or do they take account of variations in culpability? If popular notions of desert can be shown to be rather crude, could they be changed by reasoned explanations in sentencing and in wider popular discussion?

Attention here is focused on Preconditions B(i) and (ii). The difficulties with Precondition B(i) are similar to those with C: it rests largely on an assumed definite relationship between the seriousness of cases and the severity of punishment. The level at which the two scales are set must, as was argued earlier, depend on social judgments (or, if we had them, on findings about the effectiveness of sentences):

it is difficult enough to arrive at a scale of the seriousness of cases, but it is virtually impossible to be confident about the level at which the relationship with severity of sentence should be set. It is therefore hardly surprising that the Court of Appeal's judgments in cases which are held to 'call for' imprisonment are not pregnant with attempts to justify their imperative tone. Serious offences of violence and serious sexual offences are obviously to be found in this category, but those descriptions are unhelpful unless there is some yardstick for drawing the distinction between serious and non-serious cases. Rape is a serious offence which will nearly always attract a custodial sentence despite the previous good character of the offender;[24] on the other hand, gross indecency between males is generally treated as not sufficiently serious to require a sentence of imprisonment for a man of good character.[25] Distinctions are more difficult in violent offences because of the varying degrees of injury and methods of causing it. Those offences known as 'glassing', where the offender strikes someone in the face with a glass and causes lacerations, have often been said to require imprisonment[26] – presumably not only because of the seriousness of facial injuries but also in an attempt to create a general deterrent against the use of readily available weapons (e.g. beer glasses) by those in pubs and clubs. Again in *Martin*[27] the Court of Appeal upheld a sentence of 6 months' imprisonment on a first offender convicted of malicious wounding by punching in the eye a man wearing glasses. More generally, the Court has stated that 'senseless' violence is too serious for a non-custodial sentence.[28]

In general, however, there is little doubt that a gap exists between the level of sentences upheld by the Court of Appeal and the lower levels usually imposed in trial courts.[29] It is difficult to establish this specifically in relation to a notion such as 'senseless' violence: the 1979 statistics show that courts imposed immediate custodial sentences for 77 per cent of 'serious woundings' (mostly woundings with intent, contrary to section 18 of the Offences against the Person Act 1861) but only for 15 per cent of 'other woundings' (mostly malicious woundings or assaults occasioning actual bodily harm). To the extent that there is a gap between appellate pronouncements and practical sentencing, and if this does not give rise to public outcry, this tends to undermine the argument that the levels of sentence upheld by the Court of Appeal are necessary from the public point of view, or, to use Norval Morris's phrase, that 'any lesser punishment than that ordained by the Court of Appeal would depreciate the seriousness of the crime.'

What the Court of Appeal regards as the 'inevitability' of custodial sentences in cases of 'senseless' violence might be justified by the centrality of physical integrity to the condition of individuals in society.[30] Whether, as the Court has also stated from time to time,[31] a more-than-trivial assault on a police officer ought to attract a custodial sentence even where the offender is of previous good character is to be doubted: it is right to regard such assaults as more serious, because of the challenge to lawful authority, but it does not follow that the only way to mark this is by passing an immediate custodial sentence. Property offences raise similar problems: where there has been a fraud which was systematic or lucrative or both, several decisions confirm that an immediate prison sentence is 'unavoidable' despite the offender's previous good character. It is not that all these cases are aggravated by breach of trust: they include tax frauds,[32] social security frauds,[33] insurance frauds,[34] abstracting electricity worth £1,000[35] and planned shoplifting.[36] In most of these cases the real or anticipated profit was high, although the Court of Appeal has from time to time upheld a first prison sentence for a planned but relatively unprofitable shoplifting.[37] What emerges powerfully from these decisions is that it is the deliberate flouting of the law for profit which leads the Court to regard an immediate custodial sentence as 'unavoidable'. But does it follow from the fact that such offences are more serious than impulsive offences that a custodial sentence is the only appropriate response?

Then there is the offence of burglary, which accounts single-handed for nearly one-third of the prison population. The Court of Appeal has often held that a residential burglary deserves an immediate custodial sentence, a policy which was evident in *Fagan*[38] where a youth of 18 stole some £1,500 from a house and left the premises in disarray. He had only one minor previous conviction, but the Court of Appeal upheld a borstal sentence. In *Stoakes*[39] Lawton LJ roundly declared that 'even for a person of good character, something in the order of 18 months' imprisonment can be expected for burglary of a dwelling-house.' Residential burglary is regarded as particularly heinous because of the psychological effects on householders,[40] and was excluded (as were 'most offences of serious violence') from the benefit of the reduction in sentencing levels urged in *Begum Bibi*,[41] but burglary of commercial premises is treated more leniently. Thus in *Brown* (1982)[42] a youth of 19 stole property worth some £2,850 from the premises of his employers. The sum was higher than in *Fagan*, and there was a breach of trust, but the presumed psychological effects of residential burglary were absent and the Court of Appeal replaced borstal with a community service order:

> This case is tailor-made for a community service order. The appellant is a first offender – although his position would be the same if he had had a 'light' criminal record – he comes from a stable home with a wife and young child, he has a good work record and a job is available to him. There is apparently genuine remorse and the risk of re-offending is slight.

Once again, however, it can readily be seen from the Criminal Statistics that the vast majority of persons convicted of residential burglary did not receive a custodial sentence. It is true that many of them would have committed less profitable burglaries than that in *Fagan*, although many of those convicted of burglary would have had previous convictions (some 70 per cent of burglars in a Home Office survey had previous convictions)[43] which might dispose a court against a lenient sentence. In the result, it is probable that courts generally under-sentence burglars according to the standards laid down by the Court of Appeal.

The problems, then, are these. The Court of Appeal seems to approve the imposition of a first custodial sentence in certain types of case which would routinely attract non-custodial or suspended sentences. The Crown Court and magistrates' courts impose a first custodial sentence each year on some 7,000 adult males, some 7,500 young adult males, and some 4,750 young persons,[44] and it is not clear on what principles these cases are distinguished from other cases coming before those courts. Clearly *all* courts are not applying the Court of Appeal's decisions or the numbers would be far higher; but we cannot tell whether some courts do adopt the same approach as the Court of Appeal and some do not, whether in fact there are rather different principles which operate widely in trial courts, or whether the decision to impose a first custodial sentence depends largely on the approach to sentencing of the particular judge or bench of magistrates on the day. It is likely that when a sentencer does regard a first custodial sentence as necessary, and the case does not concern an offender with a record of previous offences and non-custodial disposals, the sentencer takes the view that there is no other sentence which symbolizes a sufficient condemnation of the offence from society's point of view. What is the foundation for the views held by sentencers about the expectations of victims and of the public in general? Some victims do indeed call for severe measures to be taken against the person who committed the offence, but the survey of victims by Shapland[45] and the reactions of householders in Maguire's study of residential burglary[46] suggest that victims do not in general feel dissatisfied with the sentences imposed on those who committed the offences against them – even though, according to Shapland's impression, the sentences were relatively lenient. Findings such as these, although they do not cover the whole range of crimes, give some grounds for doubting the refrain of judges (particularly in the Court of Appeal) that a custodial sentence is necessary even for a first offender for certain types of crime in order to retain public support for and confidence in the criminal justice system; those doubts are increased when it is found that those 'unavoidable' custodial sentences are probably not given in many comparable cases which are not taken to appeal.

(c) **The first custodial sentence as a general deterrent**
One justification for a first custodial sentence which refers neither to the individual offender nor to his particular offence is the general deterrent rationale – that a severe sentence is needed to deter others from committing this kind of offence, so that the particular characteristics of this individual case cannot be taken into account. Any claim to mitigation which the offender might otherwise have had is swept aside. This approach to sentencing bears harder on a person who has never been sentenced before than upon someone who has previous convictions, since the former has had no solemn warning about lawbreaking whereas the latter has. Detailed discussion of the justifications for this approach is therefore postponed until section 5 of this chapter, which deals with first offenders. General deterrent sentencing is examined in section 3 below.

(d) **The length of the first custodial sentence**
Recent years have seen the emergence of what has been called the 'clang of the prison gate' theory. An early statement which captures its essence is that of Lawton LJ in *Sargeant:*

> Despite his good character, despite the excellent background from which he comes, very deservedly he has had the humiliation of hearing prison gates closing behind him. We take the view that for men of good character the very fact that prison gates have closed is the main punishment. It does

not necessarily follow that they should remain closed for a long time.[47]

In the mid-1970s came the general movement towards reduction of the level of sentences for 'run-of-the-mill' offences, but the reasoning behind the 'clang of the prison gate' theory is rather more specific:

> The first three months are the worst, and . . . the short sentence on many people as a first sentence may have an equally reformative effect on them and have the effect of preventing them committing crime, just as a longer period of imprisonment would.[48]

A more circumspect statement would be 'that longer sentences offer no more guarantee of reducing criminal propensities than do shorter terms',[49] but in the present context it is more common to find the positive assertion that short terms of incarceration have a greater preventive effect. Few would now accept the reference to the reformative effect of custody, especially as most short terms are served in the overcrowded conditions of local prisons, and the wider assumption is that the first few weeks of custody have such an adverse impact on the offender that he is deterred from committing any further offences which would render him liable to a custodial sentence. The deprivation and degradation which imprisonment often inflicts will probably be felt much more severely by a person who has not served a custodial sentence before. Some might argue that the 'clang of the prison gate' theory is unconvincing, because what makes the first few weeks of a sentence so crushing in their effect on the prisoner is the thought that there are several more weeks or months to be served, and that if the sentence passed by the court is short he may 'grin and bear' a few weeks of torment. This counter-argument is not appealing, since it assumes a great deal of self-assurance in the first-time prisoner, but it points to the paucity of evidence to support the prevailing theory. As the Advisory Council observed, 'it is the first prison sentence in an offender's life which is widely held, *though largely on conjectural grounds*, to have the most traumatic effect.'[50] However, the Advisory Council overlooked the paucity of evidence in a later report and stated the theory firmly as a matter of common sense.[51]

Further support for the 'clang of the prison gate' theory might also be claimed from 'one of the few reliable pieces of criminological knowledge – that many offenders sent to prison for the first time do not subsequently re-offend.'[52] This piece of knowledge might more accurately be described as a prize example of criminological non-sense. It is not that it is untrue. The point is rather that it refers to '*many* offenders sent to prison for the first time' when the unsophisti-cated reader might assume that *most* such offenders do not re-offend: 'many' begs the question, 'how many?', and without an answer to that question it seems inapposite to use the term 'reliable'. Then there is the question of how many offenders given other sentences for the first time do not re-offend. The claim seems to imply that those sent to prison for the first time are less likely to re-offend than offenders who receive another sentence (such as a fine, or a community service order) for the first time. However, it is highly likely that most of those fined for the first time do not re-offend – only 39 per cent of offenders fined for standard list offences were reconvicted of such an offence within 6 years.[53] This second point does not, unlike the first, weaken the Advisory Council's argument, for they were confining themselves to cases where an immediate custodial sentence was regarded by the court as 'unavoidable', but it enters a caution against taking this piece of 'criminological knowledge' too far.

One way in which the theory might be carried too far would be for courts to rely on the supposedly powerful deterrent effect of a first, short custodial sentence as an argument for imposing such sentences in cases where they might otherwise have chosen a non-custodial measure or suspended sentence. Thus, whilst there is no doubt that the average length of prison sentence imposed by the courts has been reduced in recent years (particularly since 1976, but most noticeably in 1980),[54] the statistics also establish that the courts are imposing immediate custodial sentences on a higher proportion of offenders, both under and over 21.[55] This suggests that some judges and magistrates are being drawn towards custodial sentences by the 'clang of the prison gate' theory, a suggestion fortified by the 23 per cent rise in the use of imprisonment by magistrates' courts between 1980 and 1981 (consisting largely of shorter sentences than in the previous year).[56] Several decisions of the Court of Appeal show that the Court is aware of the tendency and has been willing to quash some short custodial sentences and to substitute a fine or other non-custodial measure.[57] In effect, those decisions of the Court apply the spirit of section 20 of the Powers of Criminal Courts Act, but they do so by expressing the view that the cases are not sufficiently serious for a prison sentence rather than by articulating criteria which trial courts can use when deciding on sentence.

For how long should the offender hear the clang of the prison gate? The assumptions which underlie the theory do not yield an optimum length for the first custodial sentence – should it be 2 or 3 weeks (in which case a 1-month sentence would seem appropriate, less remission), or should it be 6 to 8 weeks (in which case, sentences of 2 or 3 months are indicated)? The assumption is that 'the early days' of the first custodial sentence have the greatest effect, and that the offender should not be kept inside so long that he 'acclimatizes himself' to prison life,[58] but there is no accepted view of the periods of time normally involved. In *Doland and Cormack* the Court declared that with a middle-aged first offender 'there is no doubt that the effect of imprisonment is felt in the first month, or the first two months. After that, people get inured to it.'[59] But the Court has not pursued this view consistently, and there is some evidence that it regards sentences of up to 4 months as 'short' (and therefore as not normally long enough for a prisoner to acclimatize himself to the institution). If 4 months were regarded as the upper limit of the short sentence, it would be possible for sentencers to mark differences in gravity among the cases by imposing 1, 2, 3 or 4 months – or to mark those differences more finely if sentences were announced in weeks, as some would prefer – but no such pattern can be found among the Court of Appeal's decisions.[60]

On some occasions, indeed, the Court has introduced some confusion by stating that the 'clang of the prison gate' theory applies to sentences up to 12 months;[61] but on the generally accepted assumptions about the effect of a first custodial sentence, it seems progressively less credible to apply the theory to sentences of 6, 9 or 12 months. There are indeed arguments for using sentences of this length instead of sentences of 2, 3 or 4 years which have traditionally been imposed for certain kinds of offence, as the Court of Appeal has recently recognized in breach of trust cases,[62] but these are not the same as the 'clang of the prison gate' theory and its reliance on the initial impact of imprisonment. It is the difference between the Court's decision in *Upton*[63] that short first prison sentences of 6 months should be made very short, and the decision in *Begum Bibi*[64] that sentencing levels for certain offences of medium gravity could be reduced without a significant loss in preventive effect, and the latter is discussed in its place below.[65]

(e) **Summary**

Although Parliament has clearly provided that a first custodial sentence should not be imposed unless no other method of dealing with the offender is thought appropriate by the court, this is a general prescription which the Court of Appeal has done little to refine in its decisions. Undoubtedly it is difficult to establish comprehensive guidance, but greater discussion of the issues ought to lead to the formulation of some workable propositions. A major difficulty is that courts appear to feel the need for a sentence which will un-ambiguously mark the social gravity of the offence, and appear to dismiss all non-custodial sentences on this basis. To mark the gravity of an assault on a police officer or the gravity of a well-planned acquisitive offence, it is thought necessary to impose a sentence which symbolizes the degree of social condemnation: at present, only an immediate custodial sentence appears to be regarded as an adequate symbol. Another major difficulty is that the Court of Appeal's decisions appear to be out of accord with sentencing practice, so that many (including judges)[66] acknowledge the existence of a gap between the levels of sentence upheld by that Court and the lower levels generally used in the Crown Court and magistrates' courts. Since this gap has not given rise to any general public disquiet (and victims, who know the facts of the offence committed against them, seem not to demand heavier sentences),[67] there must be doubt about the assertion of some courts that the public 'calls for' custodial sentences in certain kinds of case. Even without the 'public opinion' argument, however, some sentencers appear to have been drawn towards a first custodial sentence by the belief that they are exceptionally effective in preventing the offender from re-offending. That is an unfortunate trend, which has gained some colour of official support from observations of the Advisory Council on the Penal System. The tendency of some sentencers to think in those terms is and will become more important in the use of detention centre orders under the Criminal Justice Act 1982: the order will be from 3 weeks to 4 months, which might tempt courts to use a short order where they might otherwise not have imposed a custodial sentence. Some 80 per cent of those received into detention centres have no previous custodial experience, and yet the overall reconviction rate within 2 years of release from detention centres is 67 per cent, which hardly bears out the view that most of those who are sent to detention centres for their first experience of custody do not re-offend. Indeed, that figure might encourage belief in the deleterious effects of penal institutions and sound a needed note of caution to the imposition of any first custodial sentence.

3 Long prison sentences

There are many more sentences of over 4 years' imprisonment passed each year than there used to be. Indeed, sentences of that length formed a higher proportion of all prison sentences imposed in 1977 than in 1967. But this does not mean that the courts are resorting to long sentences with proportionately greater frequency. What happened between 1967 and 1977 was that proportionately fewer offenders received prison sentences, so that although sentences of over 4 years' imprisonment form a greater proportion of all prison sentences, they form approximately the same proportion of sentences of all kinds. There are more, but that is because more people are being convicted. These figures compare 1967 with 1977,[68] since when there has been a slight upturn in the use of imprisonment, but this does not weaken the general point that the courts appear not to be resorting to long sentences at a higher rate than in former years.

The proper use of long prison sentences is, nonetheless, a central issue. Those whose primary concern is the reduction of the custodial population will rightly point out that long sentences make a disproportionately high contribution to that population, since 1 offender serving 4 years is numerically equivalent to as many as 16 offenders serving 3 months: thus the reduction of long custodial sentences is an essential step towards regulating the custodial population. Moreover, long custodial sentences surely require greater moral and social justification than shorter sentences, since the deleterious effect on the offender's personality are likely to be greater with long sentences.

General deterrence is probably the most common justification for long prison sentences advanced by judges, particularly those in the Court of Appeal. Sentences of this length are seen as necessary to deter others from committing like offences. A shorter sentence is not imposed because it is assumed that it would be less effective as a deterrent. Characteristics of the offender which would normally be mitigating factors are accorded less effect in the calculation of sentence than would otherwise be so, for it is assumed that the deterrent effect of the sentence would be impaired if it were shortened for any reason. One might well ask why courts do not increase the levels of sentence further. Existing levels of sentencing manifestly fail to deter serious crimes such as armed robbery, and a crude theory of deterrence suggests that more severe sentences would deter more potential offenders. By not increasing the levels, are the courts not tolerating a certain amount of serious crime? Possibly they are, but they might seek to justify this by reference to limiting principles of retribution, humanity and even economy. The retributivist limitation takes the rather vague form of keeping very long sentences out of the question, so that there can be no increase of 10-year sentences to 20 years if crimes of a particular kind fail to decrease, and then 20 years to 30 years and so on, since this would violate the principle of proportionality. The humanitarian limitation points to the psychologically and socially deleterious effects of imprisonment, effects which seem likely to deepen as sentences become longer. Inasmuch as the judges have not responded to the steadily increasing rate of recorded crime by imposing proportionately more sentences of 5 years, 10 years and more, they may be said to have accepted a possible loss of general deterrence for the sake of stronger considerations of proportionality and humanity.

(a) The mechanics of deterrence

All of this, however, presupposes that there is a relationship of cause and effect between levels of sentences for certain crimes and the incidence of those crimes. The reference above to a 'crude' theory of general deterrence took this relationship for granted. In order to establish such a relationship, various social and psychological facts must be ascertained, although usually their existence is assumed. Let us begin by examining the assumptions as they relate to the crime which attracts the highest number of long sentences each year, for which the judges often give reasons of general deterrence – robbery.[69] Robbery is a broad legal category which covers conduct from the Great Train Robbery down to a push before snatching a handbag; it may be assumed that sentences of more than 4 years are imposed chiefly for planned offences and for lucrative offences of the kind often called 'professional'.[70] What facts, then, must be established in order to show that these kinds of robbery are susceptible to general deterrence through heavy sentencing?[71]

(A) Potential robbers must be persons who, in general, reflect on whether or not to commit the offence, if the aim of the deterrent sentences is to maintain a standing threat to those who would commit such offences. If the aim of general deterrence is not to deter people in the short run so much as to foster a general attitude against robbery in the longer term, the test would be different, but the former aim can be assumed.

(B) Potential robbers must, at the time they are contemplating the offence, have an impression about the level of likely sentences. These impressions may be inaccurate: they may think sentences for robberies of the kind contemplated are lower than they are, or, perhaps as a result of frequent press reporting, they may think that sentences are higher than they really are. It is generally thought that those who have offended in the past will have a more accurate impression of the likely sentence,[72] and this may apply equally to 'professionals' who have not yet been caught. What is important, it must be emphasized, is not the actual level of sentences but the level of sentence which potential offenders believe to be likely at the time they contemplate the offence. The actual level of sentences will only shape the beliefs of potential offenders if publicity and information networks about sentences are adequate; it is beliefs about facts, not unknown facts, which inform the decisions of potential offenders.

(C) Any deterrent effect on a potential robber of the believed level of sentences must not be counter-balanced by other believed probabilities – such as the belief that there is a low probability of detection for the crime (a belief which might relegate the believed severity of the sentence to a minor role); or such as a belief that the effect of parole might or would be to reduce the effective length of sentence (which mitigates the deterrent effect).

(D) Potential robbers must not in general feel that there are other conditions sufficiently strong to pre-dispose them either in favour of offending (e.g. extreme temptation or extreme poverty) or against offending (e.g. automatic criminal bankruptcy on conviction, if that were particularly feared).

(E) Potential offenders must be led, by fear of the believed likely sentence, to desist from robbery and not merely to take greater precautions to avoid detection.

How well, then, might a policy of general deterrent sentencing apply to offences of robbery? It is often assumed that many robberies are committed by persons who plan their crimes, many of whom might fairly be described as professional criminals. Since these offenders probably would contemplate the consequences of their offences, one might start from the assumption that they could be expected to offend less frequently if sentences were higher and more frequently if sentences were lower. Thus the Advisory Council argued that:

> What might be justifiable would be the use of exceptionally long sentences to deal with offenders convicted of extremely lucrative crimes, if there were reason to think that the gains from such crimes were being regarded as sufficient recompense for serving shorter sentences.[73]

To set against this is a probable weakening of the deterrent effect of long sentences by the fact that the official clear-up rate for robbery gives the offender a 3 in 4 chance of avoiding detection. The Criminal Statistics show that in 1981 only 25 per cent of robberies known to the police were cleared up,[74] and the percentage for well-planned 'professional' robberies might even be lower; one might expect many of those who plan lucrative robberies to have a reasonably accurate impression of the risk of avoiding detection. The observations of Sir Leon Radzinowicz twenty years ago are still apposite today:

> If it were proved that the chances of escape were such as to render impunity much more probable than punishment, this would operate as a powerful incentive to the commission of crime, and give grounds for justifiable anxiety. Impunity is itself a cause of crime. It attracts new recruits to the ranks of regular criminals; it encourages first offenders to persevere in crime as a profitable course of activity; and it stimulates daring and initiative among the professional and persistent class. The Cambridge enquiry has gone far in bringing into the open the dark figures in the crime of robbery. The chances of impunity enjoyed by robbers, particularly those who specialise in this offence, are very high indeed and, judging by the data extending over the whole decade, they are getting higher.[75]

There are therefore grounds for believing that the deterrent effect which is inherently probable to result from higher sentences for planned robberies is substantially eroded by the low detection rate, if (as also seems probable) those who plan these lucrative robberies are aware of that detection rate. In contrast, there is unlikely to be a belief that sentences imposed by the courts for robbery will be significantly shortened by parole: the operation of remission may be known, but the published 'Criteria for Selection for Parole' give no encouragement to the prospect of release on parole for those who execute planned robberies,[76] and this is probably known, at least to those with experience of imprisonment.

Since a low detection rate probably weakens the deterrent effect of high sentences for robbery, the essential step in a deterrent strategy for robbery is to increase the (believed) probability of detection. It is often said that certainty of punishment is a more powerful deterrent than the amount of punishment,[77] but to bring about an improvement in the detection of robbery could well either be practically difficult or involve unacceptable extensions of police powers and state surveillance over the lives of individual citizens. If for such reasons it is not considered feasible to improve the believed rate of detection, the next step in a deterrent strategy might be to resort to Bentham's maxim that the severity of punishment should be increased to compensate for any deficiency in its certainty. That might also be considered inappropriate, in the light of the limiting principles of retributivism and humanity which the judges appear to regard as ruling out very long prison sentences.

It would therefore seem to be arguable that Parliament is effectively tolerating some serious crime which could be deterred by increasing police powers and intensifying state surveillance over individuals, and that the courts are effectively tolerating a certain amount of crime which they probably could deter, in that they regard it as unjust and inhumane to impose the extremely long sentences necessary to achieve maximum deterrence. There remain two qualifications, however. First, it seems unlikely that all offenders are susceptible to deterrence – some might go on committing crimes, whatever the chances of detection and likely sentence. The highest aim is therefore maximum deterrence, not total deterrence. Secondly, there is no justification for assuming an ordinal relationship between severity of sentence and volume of crime, even if the chances of detection were relatively high. It is arguable that a significant increase in the levels of sentence would be necessary to produce a noticeable deterrent effect, but that increases and decreases on a moderate scale (e.g. increasing all sentences by 2 years, or reducing all sentences for robbery by 2 years) would have virtually no effect at all. We simply do not know how many more potential robbers would be deterred by a general 2-year increase in all sentences of 5 years or more, and the answer could be that hardly any of those who were not deterred by 5 years are deterred by the thought of 7 years. Until some evidence is produced, it does not seem inherently probable that a certain increase in the level of sentences will lead to a similar or proportional decrease in the rate of offending, or vice versa.

To what extent are these arguments about robbery applicable to other offences for which long sentences are given? The numbers of sentences of more than 4 years (not including 4 years) imposed in 1980 were:[78]

Robbery	278
Serious woundings[79]	92
Rape	90
Burglary and aggravated burglary in a dwelling	78
Drug offences	69
Manslaughter (excluding diminished responsibility)	61
Burglaries other than in a dwelling	52
Arson	32
General fraud	28
Buggery	28
Incest	15
Other woundings	14
Kidnapping	11
Miscellaneous	102

It would be tedious here to consider each of the five deterrence assumptions in relation to each of the offences listed, but it is worth looking in some detail at a type of offence for which the assumptions may well differ from robbery – serious wounding. The difference lies in the fact that few of the robberies which attract long sentences are likely to have been committed impulsively or in response to provocation, whereas a substantial proportion of serious woundings (and also of the 61 manslaughter offences) were probably committed in such circumstances. Some, however, would be committed as deliberately as a robbery. If the offender were a hired attacker, or indeed a person who had considered the risks and consequences of his action, he could be expected to know that the courts generally visit deliberate violence with severe sanctions. But he might also believe that he has a much lower chance of avoiding detection than the robber. There is a high clear-up rate for offences of violence (some 81 per cent for serious woundings in 1980),[80] but this is linked with the very high proportion of offenders who are known to their victims. Serious woundings of strangers carry a much lower risk of detection, as the cases studied by McClintock in 1950 and 1957 showed.[81] As for parole, there is surely little reason to believe that violent offenders will be favoured with early release, although where the serious wounding was 'the one offence of his life' or was committed after drinking, parole is more likely.[82] And, save for the 'professional' man of violence, it is unlikely that increases in punishment would lead violent offenders to take greater care to avoid detection rather than to desist altogether.

(b) **Deterrence and impulsive crimes**

All these speculations are, however, addressed to the problem of the violent offender who deliberates before committing the crime. What effect can high sentences as general deterrents be expected to have upon the frequency of sudden, provoked crimes of impulsive violence? In the view of Lawton LJ:

> So far as deterrence of others is concerned, it is the experience of the courts that deterrent sentences are of little value in respect of offences which are committed on the spur of the moment, either in hot blood or in drink or both. Deterrent sentences may very well be of considerable value where crime is premeditated. Burglars, robbers and users of firearms and weapons may very well be put off by deterrent sentences.[83]

The assumptions in this passage seem similar to those underlying Bentham's view that it is inappropriate to pursue deterrence unless the prospect of punishment could come into the offender's mind in the moments leading up to the offence and could produce an effect on him, 'with respect to the preventing him from engaging in any act of the sort in question'.[84] Bentham was in fact discussing cases which he regarded as 'unmeet for punishment' on the ground that 'punishment must be inefficacious', and it is not necessarily the case that those who commit impulsive acts through anger, rage or drink falling short of complete intoxication have (in Bentham's terms) been temporarily deprived of 'that state of disposition of mind in which the prospect of evils so distant as those which are held forth by the law, has the effect of influencing his conduct.'[85] Indeed, traditional legal doctrine classifies impulsive acts as intentional, on the view that it is sufficient that the offender realized for one fleeting moment what he was doing; and some would add that if there was time for him to realize that, there was also time for the threat of punishment to enter his mind. The argument, then, must be that it may have been possible for the offender to think about the wrongness of his conduct and about its legal consequences, and indeed he may have done so, but that the strong emotions aroused by the circumstances in which he found himself dominated his behaviour. If this suggests that the offender was less responsible for his behaviour than, say, the cool and deliberating offender, it must be set against another view which maintains that stiff punishments aimed at general deterrence might exert an effect on the level of violence:

It is possible that though (as Bentham says) the *threat* of punishment could not have operated on [the offenders], the actual *infliction* of punishment on those persons may secure a higher measure of conformity to law on the part of normal persons than is secured by the admission of excusing conditions.[86]

It will be observed that this view rests on greater conformity to law on the part of 'normal persons': it is not suggesting that impulsively violent offenders will be affected, but that others will. If there is also acceptance of Bentham's view that the infliction of punishment is itself an evil and that the infliction of more punishment than is absolutely necessary is 'so much misery in waste', supporters of this argument must be confident that the general social benefit (in terms of a general reduction in offences of violence) is sufficient to justify the imposition of deterrent sentences on impulsive offenders.

A slightly more attractive argument against low sentences for impulsive violence is that a level of penalties which is seen as emphasizing the great importance of physical safety may have the long-term effect of reinforcing this central social value – by increasing abhorrence of violence and thus strengthening internal and external restraints against it. Although the argument may appear attractive, its empirical basis is uncertain and probably untestable: it would be virtually impossible to separate any influence exerted by the level of sentences passed by the courts, from the myriad social and cultural factors which would also be at play. The argument is clearly bound up with the supposed symbolic effect of sentences and the concept of public opinion, which were subjected to criticism in Chapter 8.[87] The Court of Appeal has striven to resolve the apparent conflict between upholding the value of physical security and giving effect to variations in culpability, through the expedient of reducing a sentence on appeal but declaring that this should not be taken as countenancing or excusing violence. Thus, in suspending a prison sentence for using a knife to wound a husband, the Court of Appeal insisted that this was not to be treated as an indication that it 'looks with complacency upon the use . . . of lethal weapons by one spouse against another. . .'.[88] In a case where the Court also suspended a prison sentence, it stressed that the decision did not indicate 'that husbands who throw corrosive liquid over their wives are not to be treated with gravity'.[89] The Court evidently believes that it is possible, by means of reasoned judgments in this style, both to achieve a long-term general deterrent effect and to mitigate the sentences of less culpable individuals in a way which does not impair that long-term effect. Since the long-term effect depends on the beliefs which are widely held, and depends particularly on the endurance of such beliefs despite the substantial mitigation of some sentences, it becomes crucial that the justifications for substantial mitigation in those cases are widely understood and accepted. Without that widespread appreciation the argument might fail on its own terms, since any deterrent effects of high sentences might be eroded by the knowledge that some lower sentences are passed too. The same might be said of the readiness to grant parole to those who do receive substantial prison sentences for 'once in a lifetime' offences of serious violence.[90]

As a general proposition, it seems fair to assume that sentences intended as general deterrents are likely to have greater success with offenders who plan or deliberate than with impulsive offenders. Deterrent sentences might serve to maintain social abhorrence of violence in the long term, and might in the shorter term lead offenders to stop and think before using violence in at least some situations, but it must be doubted whether impulsive offenders should be subjected to long sentences in order to achieve the social benefit of deterring others. However, so far as empirical support for such propositions is concerned, one must agree with Walker's observation that 'to what extent impulsive acts can be delayed or prevented by deterrents is a matter for research of a kind which has not yet been attempted.'[91]

(c) Exemplary sentences and crime waves

Sometimes the courts rely on a more specific reason for pursuing a policy of general deterrence and imposing long custodial sentences. They believe that a type of offence is unusually prevalent – that there is a 'wave' of such crimes either locally or nationally – and they take the view that it is both appropriate and effective for courts to respond by imposing unusually heavy sentences. Some sections of the judiciary appear to regard exemplary sentences as a valuable expedient, but the difficulty of asserting their effectiveness is formidable.

A preliminary difficulty is that it is often unclear whether the claimed 'crime wave' is taking place, and is likely to continue taking place unless action is taken. The idea of a 'crime wave' is presumably that the number of offences of a particular kind both is higher than normal for the time of year (in this locality) and has increased at a higher rate than other types of offence. It is well known that an increase in the number of offences prosecuted does not necessarily betoken an increase in the number of offences actually committed: the number of offences prosecuted may alter as a result of changes in prosecution policy, fluctuations in the detection rate, more frequent reporting by the public or a deliberate 'drive' by the police. Possibilities such as these must certainly be discounted before a 'crime wave' is proclaimed. In small court centres where a small number of judges have considerable local experience and are in touch with those involved locally in the criminal process, it may be possible to claim with some confidence that there is a wave of a certain type of crime. It is much more difficult in larger court centres and large urban areas. It is virtually impossible at national level to be sure that a crime wave is taking place, although the riots of the summer of 1981 might be put forward as a rare example. The problem is that the assertion of a national crime wave must be supported by national evidence; the most reliable statistics are the number of offences known to the police, which are published months after the event and must be carefully interpreted so as to account for the effect of other changes such as those mentioned earlier; the impressions of other judges, sitting on the same circuit or on other circuits, would be far less complete and again open to careful interpretation, and ought not to be relied upon; and the potential of the newspapers and television for 'creating' a crime wave out of a few notorious cases (and following them with reports of many other crimes which would not normally have received such coverage) should not be underestimated.[92]

Despite these uncertainties, courts do impose exemplary sentences from time to time. Such sentences should generally be no longer than the facts of the offence justify, according to the Court of Appeal, but they are longer than they would otherwise be because no allowance is made for factors which would normally go in mitigation.[93] The major question is whether such sentences are an effective general deterrent and an appropriate response in these circumstances. A brief review of the principal cases cited by English writers should suffice to demonstrate the difficulty of attributing effects to particular causes. In 1958 Salmon J imposed sentences of 4 years' imprisonment on some of the offenders convicted of taking part in the Notting Hill race riots. Trouble of this kind certainly decreased on the streets of Notting Hill (although there were some racial outbreaks in other cities in the following months);[94] but who can assert that it was the sentences imposed by the judge which caused a reduction in the number of offences which would otherwise have taken place? Might it not be the case that the police had arrested and charged the ringleaders, and without them there would be no continuation? Or that increased patrolling of the streets by the police dramatically reduced the opportunity to offend and led people to believe that there was a greater probability of being caught? The Notting Hill case illustrates the formidable difficulties of gathering evidence of the effectiveness of exemplary sentences as short-term deterrents: one can rarely be confident that one is interpreting a sequence of social events correctly, or that there are not other explanations for changes in people's behaviour; and if one devises an experimental situation in which the intrusion of extraneous factors is controlled, the experiment often becomes so far removed from real life that the findings could not confidently be transposed. A graphic illustration of the problem of interpreting sequences of social behaviour is provided by the Birmingham mugging case of *Storey* in 1973.[95] A youth was ordered to be detained for 20 years for his part in the violent robbery of a drunken man, and the sentence was widely publicized, both in Birmingham and in the national newspapers, as an exemplary sentence aimed at deterring others from committing similar offences. Researchers were able to plot the rate of reported robberies in Birmingham and in two other cities during several months before and after the sentence was passed. The monthly figures seem quite unaffected by the sentence in *Storey*: indeed, the rate of reported robberies in Birmingham had begun to rise before the trial and continued to increase before reaching a peak some weeks after the trial.[96] Such an increase goes against the normal assumptions about human behaviour which a deterrence theorist would make. Unless one adopts the hypothesis (unlikely in these circumstances) that more 'muggings' were committed in order that the offenders could attract the notoriety of conviction followed by a spectacular sentence, the only reasonable interpretation is that a whole range of social and personal factors (many of which might not be properly identified or understood) affects the reported rate of offences, and that it is therefore rarely safe to draw firm conclusions.

Exemplary sentences are difficult to justify. We lack the evidence for asserting that they are effective in bringing about a short-term reduction in the rate of a particular crime. They could perhaps be viewed symbolically as a strong reaffirmation of social values in the context of the threat posed by an apparent (though possibly not real) crime wave, but that would be a slender justification for severe sentences which have no probable deterrent effect. Indeed, whether seen in terms of reaffirming social values or in terms of deterring potential offenders, exemplary sentences involve the sacrifice of an individual's liberty for an assumed greater social good, since he receives a longer sentence than would otherwise be considered appropriate, for which the supposed justification lies in the actual or predicted conduct of others. On a rationalistic model of behaviour, it might be argued that if the offender knew that he was risking such a severe sentence when he committed his crime, he might be said to deserve it. Since that condition is usually absent in cases of exemplary sentences, which are typically imposed on the first group of offenders convicted as a result of a supposed crime wave, it seems clear that, in respect of the amount by which the exemplary sentences exceeds the normal sentence, the offender is being used solely as an instrument for the achievement of some wider social good – as a means *only*, and not as an end in himself. This is a course of action which, to say the least, should not be embarked upon without exhaustive searching for alternatives and deep reflection – and even then, some would say, not at all.

4 Prison for 'run-of-the-mill' offences

In the first part of this chapter, it was argued that imprisonment is a sentence which should be used parsimoniously because of growing doubts about the reformative potential of penal institutions, beliefs in the deleterious effects of penal institutions, and doubts about the deterrent effect of custodial sentences. The optimism which was felt in the 1950s and 1960s has gradually ebbed away, to be replaced by a more sceptical view of the constructive potentialities of prison. This has led in recent years to a direct questioning of the levels of sentence typically imposed for 'run-of-the-mill' offences. The argument has been increasingly heard that, whatever the justifications for long sentences for serious offences, it is not necessary to maintain existing levels of custodial sentencing for the large mass of so-called 'run-of-the-mill' offenders who make up such a significant part of the custodial population. The Prison Statistics for 1981 show that some 31 per cent of the sentenced male custodial population had been sentenced for burglary and a further 24 per cent sentenced for theft, handling, fraud or forgery. Thus, well over half the sentenced male population might be regarded as property offenders, subject to the reservation expressed earlier as to whether burglary is properly regarded as a 'property offence' *tout simple*. This compares with some 19 per cent who had been sentenced for offences of violence, 7 per cent for robbery and 4 per cent for sexual offences. Moreover, most of those imprisoned for burglary or for theft, handling etc. had 3 or more previous convictions. Thus, to present the same figures in a different way, some 25 per cent of the entire sentenced male prison population are burglars with 3 or more previous convictions, and a further 18 per cent are thieves, handlers etc. with a similar number of previous convictions.[97] Furthermore, very few of these offenders would receive anything more than a 'run-of-the-mill' sentence: taking *adult* males alone, for example, out of the 36,368 men received after sentence, some 22,877 had been sentenced for burglary, theft, handling etc., and only 3,605 of those were serving more than 18 months (and only 298 over 4 years).[98] The overall impression is therefore that imprisonment is being used for persistent property offenders, with few sentences which could be described as 'long' by English standards. The statistics point to the centrality of arguments about the sentencing of persistent offenders, discussed in Chapter 5, and also to the importance of examining with care the principles used to calculate type and length of sentence for these 'run-of-the-mill' offenders.

What reasoning could be used to attack the alleged need to maintain existing sentencing levels? In their interim report on *The Length of Prison Sentences* in 1977, the Advisory Council on the Penal System reasoned thus:

> Research findings up till now indicate that shorter sentences are no less effective than longer ones. Unless and until there is evidence to the contrary, it will be logical and economical to reduce the length of sentences in the middle and lower ranges. A general lowering of sentence lengths need not disturb the relativity of individual sentences; existing distinctions between different offenders and different offences could still be successfully maintained. Although in our final report we hope to make recommendations for a new system of maximum penalties, at this juncture we wish merely to pose a few simple questions. Are there not cases of two years imprisonment where 18 months, or 15 or even less, might safely be passed, and sentences of 12 months when six months would do just as well? And for the offender going to prison for the first time, should not even a shorter sentence suffice?[99]

The Advisory Council did not merely pose these pointed questions, but went on to advocate that courts should 'stop at the point where a sentence has been decided upon and consider whether a shorter one would not do just as well.' The reasons behind their argument seem to be threefold: efficacy, economy and humanity.

(a) The efficacy argument

The efficacy argument invoked by the Advisory Council is that 'research findings up till now indicate that shorter sentences are no less effective than longer ones.' This is to measure efficacy in terms of individual prevention: by examining reconviction rates of prisoners over a given period (usually 2 years), researchers have concluded that those released from longer terms are not prevented from being reconvicted (either by deterrence or by reform) at a higher rate than those released from shorter prison terms.[100] Such findings could be explained by the suggestion that, even though a longer prison term might constitute a stronger deterrent, it exerts greater deleterious effects on the prisoner's personality too. Whilst long prison terms do not appear to be more efficacious in terms of preventing the individuals from re-offending during the years following release, it might be argued that they certainly are more efficacious in keeping offenders away from society for a longer period. This is what criminologists call an 'incapacitation' argument, and many find its simplicity appealing. Whilst an offender is in prison he cannot be committing offences outside; therefore a longer prison sentence is more efficacious than a shorter one, if viewed in this way.

In fact, calculations of the incapacitative effect of the use of custodial sentences are far from simple. Whilst it is undoubtedly true that an offender who is locked up cannot be committing offences outside, the point only becomes significant if we can be sure that he would have been committing offences if he had been outside. In order to discover that, we need to form an estimate of the rate at which offenders of that kind (i.e. similar offences and number of previous convictions and age) do typically commit their offences. Researchers have found this an extremely difficult matter to assess, with estimated offending rates varying from 1 to over 10 offences per year.[101] It would obviously be wrong to rely on the rate of recorded convictions, since we know that less than half of all reported offences are 'cleared up' and indeed that many offences are never reported in the first place.[102] It may therefore be necessary to rely upon self-report studies in order to estimate the actual rate of offending,[103] and the evidence which they yield does not yet provide us with a reliable estimate.[104] Despite these uncertainties, two Home Office researchers (Brody and Tarling) embarked on a statistical study which aimed to assess the consequences for the crime rate of a reduction in the length of time which prisoners spend in prison. They estimated that if remission on prison sentences were to be increased from one-third to one-half, this would result in a 1.2 per cent increase in the number of convictions recorded in the whole country during a year; and that if the time served by each prisoner were reduced by 4 months (i.e. sentences reduced by 6 months, less remission of one-third), convictions would increase by 1.6 per cent in the year. To set against those low increases in the number of convictions would be significant reductions in the prison population, since the greater remission would reduce by 25 per cent and the shorter sentences by 40 per cent the amount of time which the offenders actually spent in prison.[105]

Why would the total number of convictions only increase by between 1 and 2 per cent if these prisoners were released earlier, according to the two strategies tested? A major reason for this, sometimes overlooked by those who subscribe to the simple incapacitation theory, is that under existing sentencing policy the courts send only a minority of offenders to prison. In 1981, the figures were 18 per cent of adult males and 19 per cent of young adult males given immediate custodial sentences for indictable offences: thus some 81 or 82 per cent of convicted male indictable offenders remain at liberty in the community. It follows that the policy which is chosen for the 18 or 19 per cent is unlikely to have a major effect on the overall conviction rate, since they are responsible for a small part of it only. A possible counter-argument is that those who are sent to prison are likely to be responsible for a disproportionately large amount of crime, and indeed this may be one reason why the courts use custodial sentences for them and non-custodial sentences for others. The basis for the counter-argument cannot, however, be established: although some studies suggest that persons with convictions tend to commit many more undetected offences than persons without convictions, others suggest that imprisoned offenders do not commit (undetected) crimes at a rate higher than others.[106] On balance, this counter-argument provides no substantial reason for doubting Brody and Tarling's conclusion that releasing offenders from prison a few months earlier (whether by imposing shorter sentences or by increased remission) would lead to a very slight increase in the number of convictions overall. But consideration of the counter-argument does draw attention to the frailty of estimates of incapacitation based on recorded convictions: 'no analysis of the preventive effects of imprisonment can be entirely convincing in the absence of notable information about the real extent of crime and responsibility for it.'[107]

Whilst on the subject of incapacitation, it might be argued that we could ensure a greater incapacitative effect by imposing a custodial sentence of 18 months (thus ensuring 12 months' removal from society) on all offenders convicted of indictable offences. Brody and Tarling calculated the effect of such a policy on some 8,000 offenders drawn from two different years, taking the number of principal offences which would have been prevented if each offender had been given an 18-month custodial sentence on previous conviction. They found that between 18 and 26 per cent of the offences would have been prevented by this strategy; for the prison system, however, the result would be an increase of between 4 and 7 times the length of time actually spent in custody by the offenders.[108] Whilst the estimated effect on the prison population would undoubtedly be great, then, the estimate of the incapacitation effect remains subject to the reservations about the hidden number of undetected and unreported crimes. Even if we could be certain of both sets of figures, there would remain a difficult social judgment of whether we accept the cost, pain and felt injustice of mandatory 18-month sentences as the necessary price of reducing convictions (and cost and pain to victims) by up to a quarter, or whether we accept the present level of convictions when it might be possible to prevent up to one-quarter of them by mandatory custodial sentencing.

If the efficacy argument is not supported by evidence that longer custodial sentences have a superior preventive effect to shorter custodial sentences, and if it is agreed that some reduction in the length of prison sentences will have a relatively small effect on the conviction rate and that only an unacceptable policy of mandatory custodial sentencing could achieve a significant incapacitative effect, then the only remaining claims are that the existing level of sentences for run-of-the-mill offences is necessary *either* out of fairness and proportionality *or* in order to achieve denunciation. Many of the relevant points were discussed in the preceding section of this chapter: a lower level of sentences would not be 'unfair' if it preserved proportionality among offences, unless the lower sentences were widely regarded as so paltry that they were an inadequate response to a crime of that gravity; and a lower level of sentences would likewise only be regarded as insufficiently denunciatory if we could be sure about popular conceptions of the existing level and of the appropriate level of sentences, and of whether lower sentences really would depreciate the seriousness of the offence. In conclusion, then, it can be said that the evidence suggests that significant reductions in the length of time spent in custody by offenders could be made without significant increases in the numbers of crimes committed, but that this is merely a suggestion (since it is very difficult to obtain reliable information about actual rates of offending). It raises a strong case for experimentation by reducing the level of sentences for run-of-the-mill offences, and there are many who believe that comparisons with other European countries which have lower imprisonment rates than the English reinforce the view that such a reduction in sentences will not bring social catastrophe.

(b) The economic argument

The second argument is the economic one: the penal system would cost the taxpayer much less if the prison population were reduced, since it is the penal institutions which claim a major share of the funds. This argument might lead to a firm restriction on the numbers incarcerated or to a firm restriction on the conditions to be fulfilled before incarcerating an offender, with the result that the custodial population would be smaller and less of a drain on resources. As the Advisory Council on the Penal System expressed it, however, the argument took a more limited form: 'in the present economic climate, we must take care not to waste money by keeping people in prison unnecessarily long.' The use of 'unnecessarily' is a reference to the efficacy argument: if it is no less effective to imprison fewer people for shorter periods, then the amount by which the present level of imprisonment exceeds that can be regarded as unnecessary expenditure. Once again, we must ask what criterion of efficacy is being used – individual prevention, general deterrence, incapacitation, retribution, denunciation, or some other? It would certainly be wrong, in putting the economic argument, to omit the serious qualifications upon an efficacy argument based on incapacitation. For example, Brody and Tarling conclude that

the general point remains from the evidence that a small amount of increased crime has to be balanced against the real economic and social savings that could be made by quite modest changes in the current use of imprisonment.[109]

The 'evidence', as they point out earlier in their study, is unconvincing: 'no analysis of the preventive effects of imprisonment can be entirely convincing in the absence of notable information about the real extent of crime and responsibility for it.'[110] The point should therefore be put in a much more guarded form. Moreover, even against the incapacitation argument which claims that a significant reduction in lengths of custodial sentence would not bring a significant increase in the crime rate, some might argue that they prefer to see the money spent on penal institutions than suffer a slightly increased risk of being the victim of a crime. Indeed, some go even further and maintain that the level of expenditure on the penal system should be allowed to grow and that other sectors of public expenditure should be more stringently controlled. This, however, is to go against the principle of parsimony. If crime control is the aim, more resources might be put into measures of crime prevention in the community.

(c) The humanitarian argument

The third argument appeals to humanity: 'a general reduction in the length of sentences would ensure that prison sentences were served by smaller numbers in more humane conditions.' There can be no doubt that overcrowding has increased in recent years, and, as buildings have become older and facilities strained, conditions have become extremely unpleasant. The figures for cell-sharing in the table below, demonstrate the trend.[111] There is some research which suggests that sharing a cell may be more humane than being put in a cell alone,[112] but this will depend on how many are sharing and on the conditions they are subjected to: it must surely be highly degrading for three people to be locked for several hours at a time in a cell constructed for one, without toilet facilities and with little circulation of air. This is no mere external value judgment: the Director-General of Prisons has described conditions in local prisons as 'an affront to civilised society',[113] and the Chief Inspector of Prisons has described the conditions in some prisons as 'degrading and brutalising', concluding that 'by no stretch of the imagination can the conditions be regarded as humane or proper. They are unacceptable.'[114]

To some extent, as the Chief Inspector of Prisons noted, the inhumanity of conditions for some prisoners is a matter of choice by the Prison Department: overcrowding is concentrated upon the local prisons, some of which are forced to hold twice or even three times as

Highest numbers of inmates sleeping two or three in a cell

Year	Two or three in a cell	Of which	
		Three in a cell	Two in a cell
1971	14,450	8,238	6,212
1972	13,737	6,609	7,128
1973	12,609	4,221	8,388
1974	14,146	4,122	10,024
1975	15,640	5,298	10,342
1976	16,435	5,709	10,726
1977	15,990	4,950	11,040
1978	16,098	5,082	11,016
1979	16,585	4,833	11,752
1980	17,787	5,847	11,940
1981	16,904	5,610	11,294

many inmates as their certified capacity, whereas it would be possible to spread the load across the whole prison system (which would alleviate the conditions in local prisons but make the conditions in and the management of training prisons less comfortable). If, however, the allocation policy of the Prison Department is treated as a 'constant', unlikely to be altered significantly in the next few years, it can be said that a medium-range custodial sentence of 12 to 18 months in 1980 or 1985 would be much more strenuous, and therefore more of a punishment, than the same sentence in 1970 or 1975. Thus, to keep the actual level of punishment the same the courts would have to reduce lengths of sentence progressively, in step with increases in overcrowding. Similar reasoning was adopted by the Lord Chief Justice in *Upton* (1980) when, referring to the use of custodial sentences for 'non-violent petty offenders', he said, 'Sentencing judges should appreciate that overcrowding in many of the penal establishments in this country is such that a prison sentence, however short, is a very unpleasant experience indeed for the inmates.'[115] Lord Lane used this observation to support his exhortation that, where the court believes that 'there really is no alternative' to an immediate custodial sentence, it should be as short as possible. His argument was not directed at long prison sentences, which are served in training prisons with little or no overcrowding. Strictly speaking it does not apply to those who serve their sentences in open prisons, where there is greater informality and less overcrowding, but they are such a small minority of prisoners, selected by executive decision, that it would be wrong for a court to take account of the possibility that a particular offender might be sent to an open prison rather than serving his whole sentence in a local prison.

(d) **The judicial initiative**

Lord Lane's judgment in the Court of Appeal in *Upton* marked the beginning of a judicial initiative to reduce the level of sentences for run-of-the-mill offences. Lord Lane there referred to 'non-violent petty offenders'; clearly his initiative would have little effect unless the categories of offenders concerned were specified in greater detail, and this he sought to achieve in his judgment in *Begum Bibi*[116] three months later. He began the judgment by stating, as in *Upton*, that the prisons are 'dangerously overcrowded' and that courts must ensure that all sentences are 'as short as possible, consistent only with the duty to protect the interests of the public and to punish and deter the criminal.' The precise import of the duty to which Lord Lane referred is unclear, and it is probably better to regard this part of his preamble as reaffirming the need for judges to take account of factors other than the state of the prisons. The main thrust of the judgment is contained in the three paragraphs which follow.

(i) Many offenders can be dealt with equally justly and effectively by a sentence of six or nine months' imprisonment as by one of 18 months or three years. We have in mind not only the obvious case of the first offender for whom any prison sentence however short may be an adequate punishment and deterrent, but other types of case as well.

Since it may be presumed that this judgment was a carefully prepared text (in contrast with the judgments in most sentencing appeals, which are *ex tempore*), it is fair to look closely at the reasoning of the Lord Chief Justice. The idea that shorter sentences are equally 'effective' for many offenders raises again the question of the criterion of effectiveness; it seems that Lord Lane had in mind preventive efficacy, and was accepting that offenders released from short prison sentences are no more likely to be reconvicted than offenders released from medium-term sentences. The word 'justly' seems to refer to proportionality among offences and offenders, and what Lord Lane proposes in the following paragraphs may be taken as a re-ordering of proportionality. The terms of imprisonment to which *Begum Bibi* was intended to apply are those of 3 years and under, as his first sentence also demonstrates. And, perhaps most significantly of all – though the point should have been developed rather than left hanging – it is clear that the decision is intended to apply to persistent offenders, those with a considerable record of crime.

(ii) The less serious types of factory or shopbreaking; the minor cases of sexual indecency; the more petty frauds where small amounts of money are involved; the fringe participant in more serious crime: all these are examples of cases where the shorter sentence would be appropriate.'

This was the Lord Chief Justice's short list of the types of case which, even if the offender has previous convictions, it is right to think in terms of a sentence of 6 or 9 months where previously the court might have had 18 months or even 3 years in mind. The categories have been somewhat developed by the other cases in which decisions were given on the same day as *Begum Bibi* – some 10 cases, separately reported[117] – and by decisions in the 2 years since then. It is not proposed to embark upon a detailed discussion of these subsequent decisions, for the Lord Chief Justice's third paragraph points the contrast which he was attempting to achieve.

(iii) There are, on the other hand, some offences for which, generally speaking, only the medium or longer sentences will be appropriate. For example, most robberies; most offences involving serious violence; use of a weapon to wound; burglary of private dwelling-houses; planned crime for whole-sale profit; active large-scale trafficking in dangerous drugs. These are only examples. It would be impossible to set out a catalogue of those offences which do and those which do not merit severe treatment. So much will, obviously, depend upon the circumstances of each individual offender and each individual offence. What the Court can and should do is to ask itself whether there is any compelling reason why a short sentence should not be passed. We are not aiming at uniformity of sentence; that would be impossible. We are aiming at uniformity of approach.

The reference to robberies and serious violence suggests that the Court may have been drawing a comparison with the kinds of crime which would attract more than 3 years' imprisonment, and indeed in one of the cases decided on the same day, *Freeman*,[118] the Court did reduce a 4 year sentence for a series of indecent assaults to 1 year. Whilst it might indeed be impossible to set out a catalogue of offences to which the new policy should be applied and those to which they should not be applied, it is perhaps unfortunate that greater guidance was not given on certain questions of general principle. The question of persistent offenders has already been mentioned: Chapter 5 has shown the diversity of possible approaches to the problem of sentencing a persistent offender, and it is clearly vital to custodial sentencing because almost all of those sent to prison have previous convictions and this may well be the factor, rather than the inherent gravity of the crime, which leads a court to impose imprisonment. Again, is Lord Lane suggesting that most burglaries of private dwelling-houses fall into the category for which 'only the medium or longer sentences will be appropriate'? In answer to this question he could surely not take refuge in his proviso that it would depend on each individual offence and offender: if his judgment is to have the greatest effect, it should surely have said something more than it did on burglary. All it suggests is that residential burglary is generally to be viewed more severely than commercial burglary. It cannot have been intended to raise all sentences for residential burglary into the band of 18 months' to 3 years' imprisonment, for this would cause an enormous increase in the prison population – some 22,808 persons were convicted of residential burglary in 1980, of whom 8,757 were given an immediate custodial sentence, and only 1,311 were given sentences of more than 12 months. Nor, as Dr Thomas pointed out at the time,[119] can one of the decisions delivered on the same day as *Begum Bibi* be taken as valuable guidance for sentencers; in *McCann*[120] the Court reduced from 2 years' to 9 months' imprisonment the sentence for a burglary of a shoe shop, imposed upon a man with one previous conviction. Less than two-thirds of adult offenders are given immediate prison sentences for commercial burglary at the Crown Court, and in magistrates' courts it is less than one-third. Moreover, most of the sentences at the Crown Court were for 12 months or less, and those imposed by magistrates' courts necessarily so. And it is probable that many of these imprisoned offenders had longer criminal records and had been involved in more lucrative crimes than this offender. Thus the sentence of 9 months, to which the Court of Appeal reduced the term, was probably higher than trial courts would normally impose. The decision in *McCann* is clear evidence that the Court of Appeal is 'out of touch' with the realities of sentencing practice and may be unable to recognize a trivial case when confronted with one;[121] the case was an unfortunate choice as an illustration of the *Begum Bibi* policy; and, if the reason for not reducing the sentence below 9 months was that this would have been tantamount to an admission that the offender had spent time in custody unnecessarily, the decision must be condemned as an improper way of sparing the blushes of the trial judge.

Since it is recognized that there is a gap between the levels of sentence upheld by the Court of Appeal and the levels used in trial courts, it may be argued, *apropos* of the *Begum Bibi* policy, that 'what must be reduced is the general level of sentences imposed in the courts of first instance, rather than the notional level of sentences approved by the Court of Appeal, in so far as there are differences. If this distinction is not observed, there is a real danger that the present efforts may be counter-productive.'[122] The decision in *McCann* is an example of a failure to observe the distinction.

However, there is some basis for arguing that the *Begum Bibi* declarations have achieved an effect by means of the general impression they have created, and that the publicity attendant on that case itself has had a greater effect than the attempt to illustrate the principles in the 10 judgments delivered in other cases on the same day. That day was 21 July 1980, and the judgment in *Upton* was delivered on 24 April 1980.

According to the annual volumes of *Criminal Statistics*, the average length of prison sentences imposed on males aged 17 and over for indictable offences fell in the magistrates' courts from 3.6 months in early 1980 to 3.4 months in the latter half of 1980 and to 3.1 months in 1981, and in Crown Courts it had already fallen from 20 months to about 18 months in the second quarter of 1980, and it has remained at around 18 months during the remainder of 1980 and the whole of 1981. These slight overall reductions in the average length of prison sentences were not, however, accompanied by any appreciable change in the proportionate use of sentences of immediate imprisonment for indictable offences. Moreover, in neither magistrates' courts nor the Crown Court was the fall in average length of sentence confined to the classes of crime specified in *Upton* (thefts and handlings), and in the Crown Court the decrease in average length of sentence was about 2 months for most offence groups, 'but for sexual offences it was nearer 3 months and for robbery it was about 7 months.'[123] It therefore seems probable that the reductions were not selectively applied by sentencers, as Lord Lane had requested. It appears to have been the general impression created by the Lord Chief Justice's words, rather than the particular examples he gave, which has had this rather small effect on sentencers.

Since the Lord Chief Justice evidently intended his initiative to have a selective effect, it is possible (if the statistics are to be taken at face value) that he would have been better advised to attempt to lay down some general principles of approaching sentence rather than simply listing types of offence. It would probably have been more effective if he had combined the declaration with some discussion of non-custodial alternatives and suspended sentences, so as to give sentencers a more rounded impression of how to approach the various alternatives in these run-of-the-mill cases. However, there has been an attempt more recently to remedy these deficiencies: in *Brown* (1982), with the Lord Chief Justice presiding, the Court gave some guidance on the use of community service orders and seemed to advocate their use for suitable offenders with a 'light' criminal record, even in respect of a commercial burglary of property valued at £2,850 – Dr Thomas, in his commentary, did not miss the opportunity to point to the comparison with *McCann*.[124] More significantly, in *Clarke* the Lord Chief Justice gave guidance on the proper use of the partly suspended sentence and also attempted to discuss its proper relationship to fully suspended sentences and to community service orders.[125] This, surely, is a most fruitful direction for judicial initiatives to take, for it is wrong to consider custodial sentences in complete isolation from the non-custodial alternatives.

(e) Conclusions

The courts appear to have been imposing shorter sentences in what might be called the 'run-of-the-mill' range (i.e. 3 years and under) in recent years. The figures in Table 13 for receptions of adult males into prisons confirm the downward movement.[126] There are good reasons for this. The local prisons, which house most of those serving short and medium sentences, have been and are grossly overcrowded, and considerations of humanity (recognized by Lord Lane in *Upton*) suggest that the periods spent under these conditions should be minimized. There is no evidence that shorter sentences are any less effective, in terms of reconvictions, than longer sentences; and many criminologists would go further and assert that shorter sentences are in fact no less effective. This is sometimes countered by the argument that at least longer sentences have a worthwhile incapacitative effect, but the fact that so few offenders are imprisoned suggests that the incapacitative effect of prison sentences is insignificant in relation to the total volume of crime – though the most accurate statement is that 'no analysis of the preventive effects of imprisonment can be entirely convincing in the absence of notable information about the real extent of crime and responsibility for it.'[127] Study of the statistics certainly affords no justification, however, for maintaining the present level of custodial sentencing for run-of-the-mill offences, and the judiciary have produced some shortening of sentences through two separate initiatives – the 'clang of the prison gate' theory described in part 2(d) above, which applies especially to the first prison sentence, and the *Begum Bibi* guidelines, which appear to have brought about a slight shortening of average sentence length. However, it is doubtful what further effect these initiatives can now have: the *Begum Bibi* decision has been interpreted and refined in a number of subsequent decisions, but there has been no principled treatment of what is surely the most central issue here – the effect of previous convictions on sentence. The failure of the Court of Appeal to deal with the issues raised by persistent offenders (and indeed by multiple offenders) must be remedied if there is to be a further shortening of sentence lengths; and the judges' constant references to what they believe to be the dictates of public opinion also appear to exert a restrictive effect.

Table 13 Receptions of adult males under sentence (excluding fine–defaulters): by sentence length 1973–9 (in percentages)

Sentence length	1973	1974	1975	1976	1977	1978	1979
Up to and including 3 months	13.2	13.6	14.7	16.2	18.8	19.0	20.4
Over 3 months, up to and including 6 months	20.6	20.9	19.8	20.2	20.9	21.5	23.0
Over 6 months, up to and including 18 months	38.7	38.8	38.6	36.9	37.0	36.2	34.2
Over 18 months, up to and including 4 years	23.2	22.5	22.8	22.2	19.3	19.4	18.5
Over 4 years	3.9	3.7	3.7	4.1	3.5	3.5	3.5
Life	0.4	0.5	0.4	0.4	0.5	0.4	0.4
Total	100	100	100	100	100	100	100
Number of receptions	23,607	24,487	27,353	29,089	29,564	29,999	31,023

5 Custodial sentences for first offenders

Whatever difficulties may exist in the interpretation of criminal statistics, one finding which is constantly and rightly reiterated is that the more previous convictions an offender has, the more likely he is to be reconvicted no matter what sentence is imposed upon him. This means that first offenders are most unlikely to be reconvicted – a large-scale Home Office survey showed that only 29 per cent of first offenders were reconvicted within 6 years[128] – and suggests that considerations of efficacy do not militate in favour of a prison sentence for the first offender. Moreover, there is general agreement that the full might of the law should not be brought to bear on first offenders: for example, when the First Offenders Act was passed in 1958, many judges and magistrates took the view that it was unnecessary to have a statutory reminder of the need to use imprisonment as a last resort for the first offender,[129] and in *Begum Bibi* the Lord Chief Justice referred to 'the *obvious* case of the first offender for whom any prison sentence however short may be an adequate punishment and deterrent.' This dictum does not go far enough: since only about 29 per cent of first offenders are reconvicted it might be argued that the experience of being convicted and given *any* sentence seems to exert a strong preventive effect (or, at least, to be followed by a low reconviction rate), and therefore that an immediate custodial sentence cannot be said to be 'necessary' for preventive reasons. Against this, it is sometimes argued that the low reconviction figures for first offenders show how effective and appropriate are the sentences which the courts choose in these cases. That cannot be asserted, however, for not only do we not know whether less severe measures would have been less effective in terms of reconvictions, but it is also inherently probable that it is the experience of prosecution and conviction, rather than the particular sentence imposed, which leads many first offenders to avoid further lawbreaking. The balance is surely in favour of lowering sentences for first offenders still further, in the expectation that little will be lost by way of preventive effect.

First offenders are already, for the most part, treated much more leniently than offenders with a criminal record. Would not a further reduction in sentencing levels for first offenders impair the general deterrent effect of the law? This is one of many questions on deterrence which cannot be answered in the present state of our knowledge about individual attitudes and decision-making. Are we referring to a *type* of offence before which offenders are likely to think of the consequences? If we are, and if sentencing levels are likely to enter their minds at this stage, would offenders with a previous record assume that a lenient sentence upon a first offender gave them a better chance of escaping with a light punishment, or would they take account of the fact that the lenient sentence was specially adjusted to make allowance for the fact that it was a first offence? Or, to press the argument further, is it possible that some individuals who have no previous convictions look upon the lenient sentences handed down to first offenders as evidence that they can count on one 'free' offence before they become liable to a 'real' sentence? The last question seems unlikely to receive an affirmative answer in respect of most types of offence, especially impulsive crimes, but it would be wrong to be completely confident without evidence of the thought-processes typical among those who commit deliberate property offences. As for the effect of a few lenient sentences on the general impression created by high sentences, this is one of the many imponderable questions on deterrence which have arisen in this chapter. It could be argued that if such sentences were presented and understood as sentences applicable to first offenders, they would be viewed separately from the sentences imposed on persistent offenders.

The number of first offenders given an immediate custodial sentence is small in relation to the total numbers received into penal establishments – for adult males in 1981, only 1,369 out of some 30,000 for whom details were available, and for young adults some 2 per cent of those received into prison, some 3 per cent of borstal receptions and some 11 per cent of detention centre receptions.[130] On the other hand, they form a category which (though unlikely to exert a great effect on the overall size of the prison population) require special justification. Since it is difficult to maintain that an immediate custodial sentence is the most effective way of dealing with a first offender, this brings the non-empirical justifications for sentencing policy into sharp focus. Perjury is one of the crimes for which an immediate prison sentence has been said to be 'inevitable' even upon a first offender:

perjury is one of the comparatively few offences which inevitably attract a sentence of imprisonment however good may be the character of the person who commits it, because it totally undermines the whole foundation of the administration of justice. Unless courts can rely on people telling the truth in the witness-box, the administration of justice will become quite impossible.[131]

This was echoed in a later case, where Skinner J added that 'here one has a man of 55, who is extremely unlikely to offend again. In the view of this Court this is a case where the mere fact of imprisonment, the clang of prison gates, is the real punishment.'[132] But why is it so confidently believed that only sentences of immediate imprisonment are sufficient to mark the gravity of the crime? The phrase, 'to mark the gravity', is one frequently used; yet its use in the present context serves only to confirm that the principle of leniency for first offenders gives way to somewhat ineffable concepts of what is symbolically appropriate. The same point arises when it is argued that only immediate imprisonment is sufficient for coinage offences or for assaults on the police. Not only is neither view borne out by the statistics, but it seems that the courts believe that the only means of emphasizing that the crime is more serious than many others is by imposing a sentence of immediate imprisonment.

In an attempt to drive the courts to develop more careful justifications for visiting a first offence with immediate imprisonment, there is a case for introducing a statutory provision that a court should not impose an immediate custodial sentence on any first offender unless there are special reasons for not imposing a non-custodial sentence. Section 1(4) of the Criminal Justice Act 1982 is a step in this direction, but it deals with custodial sentences for *all* young adults,[133] and the effect of a 'special reasons' requirement would be to improve the scrutiny of the particular reasons given by the sentencer when dealing with a first offender. The Court of Appeal would have the opportunity to formulate more detailed principles, for the better guidance of lower courts. A special statutory provision on custodial sentences for first offenders might seem excessive in view of the small number of adult first offenders sent to prison and the availability of the general provision in the 1982 Act for young adults; but the justifications for imposing a custodial sentence upon a first offender must surely be carefully reasoned and open to scrutiny, and for that reason a special provision is the wisest approach.

It is not only true that the offender's previous good character may fail to save him from an immediate custodial sentence for a number of crimes, such as perjury, coinage offences and breach of trust, which cannot be placed in the category of crimes of great gravity; it also appears that first offenders might be subjected to exemplary or general deterrent sentences. The Court of Appeal did declare in *Curran* (1973)[134] that it is wrong for general deterrence to play a dominant role in the calculation of a first prison sentence, but the decision was not followed in *Young* (1973), where the Court upheld an exemplary sentence of 4 years' imprisonment on a first offender.[135] One of the two offenders in the 'mugging' case of *Hall and Brown* (1980) was a first offender, but the Court upheld sentences of 4 years on him and 5 years on his companion (who did have previous convictions). Lord Lane CJ stated:[136]

> The fact remains that this was a brutal, cold-blooded, calculated, violent mugging upon a youth of 17 by two older and more powerful people. This Court has no doubt at all that what was in the judge's mind was to impose a sentence which would act as a deterrent not only to these two, but to all others who were minded to commit this sort of offence. In the judgment of this Court the sentences imposed upon these two men were correct.

Similar observations, based on similar assumptions about crime-reduction, have been made in other cases of 'mugging'[137] and of 'football hooliganism'.[138] Without overlooking the seriousness of the offence committed in *Hall and Brown*, the fact also 'remains' that one of the defendants was a first offender, and that the decision was supported by general deterrent reasoning. Reasoning of this kind is subject to numerous difficulties and qualifications, as we saw above, and it is not known whether leniency for first offenders would impair the deterrent effect and whether people could be so educated that it did not impair it. In the light of all these uncertainties, it seems quite wrong to inflict severe punishment on first offenders in order solely to promote some general social benefit which may or may not result. If the principle of leniency for first offenders is worth anything, it surely ought to be sufficiently strong to prevent them being the subject of general deterrent sentences.

6 Custodial sentences and personal disadvantage

Some offenders are given custodial sentences for reasons connected with their personal disadvantage, and others have their sentences lengthened for this reason. For the 'petty persistent' offender, a prison sentence might be passed simply to give society a rest, even though his lawbreaking proceeds from what is sometimes called 'social in-adequacy'. For the alcoholic or disturbed offender, a custodial sentence may be lengthened to allow time for a course of treatment. For the mentally disordered offender, prison may seem to be the only alternative if the court is informed that the mental hospitals will not accept him. As the May Committee observed: 'As in so many other cases, therefore, prisons pay the penalty for being the resources that are available as opposed to the one that is appropriate in the particular case.'[139] In fact it is the offenders thus imprisoned who 'pay the penalty' – the humanitarian rather than the economic point – but the Committee were rightly emphasizing that the prisons, unlike hospitals and hostels are obliged to admit anyone sent by the courts.

(a) The 'petty persistent' offender

The problem of sentencing those who repeatedly commit offences of the relatively non-serious kind was discussed in Chapter 5, section 6(iii). It need only be added here that, where the repeated offending appears to be connected with rootlessness, homelessness, mental disturbance or an inability to cope with life, imprisonment is being used to cover the lack of sufficient community facilities for such persons. The notion that the relatively short prison sentences handed down for these non-serious offences are noticeably effective in 'giving society a rest' is surely rather weak: at best it is a very short-term relief from one of many such offenders. On moral grounds, it is wrong to subject 'petty' offenders to imprisonment.

(b) Offenders in need of treatment

When a court forms the view that an offender should receive a custodial sentence, and when it is informed that he would benefit from certain treatment which would be available in a particular establishment, the court sometimes imposes a longer sentence than normal, in order to allow sufficient time for the treatment. The Court of Appeal generally disapproves of this course and has been willing to reduce such sentences to a length proportionate to the seriousness of the case; the cases have mostly concerned the treatment of alcoholism. However, the Court of Appeal has been willing to uphold a sentence of borstal training on an offender whose crime was relatively trivial but who appeared to suffer from serious behavioural disturbance, the best-known example being *Coleman* (1976),[140] where a disturbed boy aged 15 was sent to borstal for breaking a small pane of glass. There are many other cases of borstal being used as a rehabilitative measure,[141] but it is to be hoped that this ceases with the replacement of borstal by youth custody in the Criminal Justice Act 1982. In view of the well-grounded doubts about the effectiveness of reformative treatment,[142] it is surely not justified to lengthen a sentence of youth custody beyond what is proportionate to the seriousness of the case. Any efforts at treatment should be made within that period.

(c) The mentally disordered offender

The law provides a number of disposals specifically for the mentally disordered offender: there is the hospital order and the restriction order,[143] and the probation order with a requirement of mental treatment. In recent years, however, the numbers of offenders receiving hospital orders and restriction orders have both declined, as Table 14 shows. Since this decline has occurred at a time when the number of convictions has been increasing, it suggests that a growing number of offenders who would formerly have been sent to hospital by the courts are now being sent to prison. In part this may reflect pessimism about the prospects for treatment, but the principal cause of the decline is probably the restrictive admissions policy now pursued by most mental hospitals. Nursing staff have opposed the admission of 'violent' or 'disruptive' offender-patients.[144] The special hospitals have tended to be full, partly because of their inability to transfer patients to the local hospitals, which operate a restrictive admissions policy. And the much-advocated 'regional secure units', which are supposed to fill the gap between special and local hospitals and to take some of the 'disruptive' patients, are being built extremely slowly.[145]

Table 14

	Total	Hospital orders	Restriction orders
1974	1,011	815	196
1975	1,021	865	156
1976	928	777	151
1977	825	735	90
1978	817	690	127
1979	762	660	102
1980	813	695	118
1981	789	682	107

How are courts to deal with cases where a mentally disordered offender has been convicted of a serious crime, and yet no hospital place can be found for him? It is one thing to declare that the prisons should not be used as 'dustbins for the difficult' where a non-serious offender is concerned;[146] it is quite another thing to maintain the same stance when a serious offence has been committed and the court fears further offences unless the offender is treated. The courts have tended to use imprisonment in such cases, often with a strong condemnation of the health services for their failure to admit an offender who the court has been told requires treatment for mental disorder. This is not 'to do justice to all men', as the Court of Appeal lamented in *Officer* (1976),[147] for prisons – even a prison hospital – can be utterly unsuitable for the mentally disordered.

There is no doubt that the prisons also contain many offenders who are mentally disordered but who were neither sentenced nor recognized as such. Estimates of the number vary: the Prison Department told the May Committee that some 519 mentally disordered people were in the prisons,[148] but a survey of a sample of the prison population in 1972 estimated that about a third of all prisoners could fairly be regarded as psychiatric cases.[149] One-fifth of the prisoners had had either in-patient or out-patient psychiatric treatment at some time, and a group of psychiatrists interviewed a sub-sample of the prisoners and confirmed that about one-third were cases suitable for psychiatric treatment. It is true that in some instances the mental disorder may have been exacerbated or even caused by the experience of imprisonment, but that would be a conclusion which would strengthen the argument in this chapter that custodial sentences have deleterious effects on their recipients, and should therefore be used as sparingly as possible.

(d) Conclusions

A considerable number of people in prison ought properly to be dealt with elsewhere. This is most clearly the case with mentally disordered offenders, although it is not settled whether the true size of the problem is that indicated by prison medical officers (who estimate under a thousand such offenders in the prisons) or the one-third of all prisoners suggested by the survey of the South East prison population. Prison administrators who adopt the more conservative estimate might be tempted to argue that the problem is therefore not a pressing one, because the economic benefit of removing such persons from the prisons is marginal. But that would be another blatant misuse of economic argument: despite the fact that the economic benefits are marginal, the case for removing such offenders from the prison system is strong for humanitarian reasons. It is wrong to regard the problem as less pressing simply because the economic returns would be low.

7 Parole and prison sentences

It has been argued above that the reasons commonly advanced for continuing to impose sentences at the present level are so much open to doubt that sentences ought to be progressively lowered, since this seems unlikely to increase the crime rate and will certainly reduce individual pain (and public expenditure). In effect, this has to some extent been achieved by the parole system which, since 1968, has enabled the release on licence of many prisoners serving sentences of over 18 months. From cautious beginnings the system worked up to a release rate of some 40 per cent of eligible prisoners in the early 1970s, and since the issue of new guidelines in 1975 the rate has increased to over 60 per cent: in 1981, 63.6 per cent of eligible prisoners were released on parole, and the average period of licence was 9 months.[150] On average, fewer than 1 in 10 parolees have been recalled to prison, and so the system provides some evidence that sentences of the lengths imposed by the courts are not generally necessary for the protection of the public and that those sent to prison for over 18 months can often be released early without social catastrophe. Doubters would protest that nearly 40 per cent of those eligible are not released on parole, and that those who are paroled receive supervision so that the figures provide no support for an assertion that shorter sentences, or early release without supervision, would not bring social catastrophe. However, so long as a recall rate of around 10 per cent is regarded as socially acceptable, it is fair to argue that the present rate of early release (i.e. sentence-reduction) has been sufficiently successful to raise questions about the need for the sentences imposed by the courts to be so long.

In order to examine the justifications for having and continuing to have a parole system, it is necessary to consider the criteria upon which the decision to release a prisoner on parole may be reached. One of the primary criteria has always been the predicted likelihood that the prisoner will re-offend. In the early stages of the parole system there was much official reliance on the theory that a prisoner may reach a peak in his training, at which point he might most safely be released and might respond to supervision.[151] The prisoner's behaviour in prison and the satisfactoriness of arrangements for his accommodation and occupation on release have always been and continue to be relevant factors,[152] but the distinct theory of the 'peak in training' has now been supplanted by a statistical calculation of the probability of reconviction of a particular offender.[153] This primary element in the parole decision has always looked to the future, therefore. Another primary element has always looked to the past: it seems that, however low the probability of a prisoner's re-offending may appear to be, he may not be granted parole if it is felt that he has not served a term proportionate to the gravity of the offence he committed. The point is clearly made in the Home Office's *Review of Parole*:

> The Parole Board has taken the view that it may properly make its own assessment of whether the time served has been sufficient penalty for the crime committed; apart from the relationship of the parole decision to the prisoner the Board has in mind that the parole scheme requires the general support of public opinion and this must be an element in the Board's consideration of the particular case.[154]

Thus, whereas the future-regarding element in the parole decision may differ from a traditional sentencing decision, this past-regarding element seems to be a very similar kind of exercise to that performed by the sentencing court. It has been criticized as re-sentencing by an executive body which, apart from its procedural differences from judicial sentencing, accentuates and distorts sentencing differentials by often increasing mitigation and confirming aggravation.[155] According to the published *Criteria for Selection for Parole*, those with a record of violence or of crimes committed for a large reward are unlikely to be released on parole, and it seems that the persistent non-major property offender is not very likely to be paroled unless his 'conduct and attitude' in prison give grounds for hope: these are all types of offender who are unlikely to have received the benefit of any mitigation when the court fixed the length of their sentence. Equally, 'notorious cases of fraud or breach of trust' are likely to have attracted a substantial sentence even though the offender may have been of previous good character, and the Criteria identify these as a group 'for whom early parole will be less clearly justifiable'. On the other hand, the 'one offence of his life' prisoner, having perhaps committed an offence of serious violence, will probably have received a mitigated sentence from the court and is also likely to be paroled; the same applies, in muted form, to the prisoner convicted of violence who is 'young with no or a light record of previous offences'.[156] The general picture, therefore, confirms that those whose sentences are mitigated by the courts are also likely to receive parole, whereas those given long sentences by the courts are much less likely to be paroled. In this way, one could argue, sentencing differentials are widened and careful calculations of proportionality by the courts are subverted. This is a special problem with prisoners serving medium-term sentences: since parole eligibility begins at 12 months or one-third of the sentence, whichever is the longer, all those serving sentences of between 19 months and 3 years become eligible for parole at the same time, i.e. after serving 12 months. If one grants that courts make calculated and reasoned distinctions between sentences of 18 months and 2 years, 2 years and 2½ years, and 2½ years and 3 years, then paroling decisions for these medium-term sentences may be particularly important in their effect on proportionality and on prisoners' feelings of justice. Attempts are made to avoid the obliteration of differentials which were intended to mark the varying culpability among a group of co-defendants,[157] but this removes only the most obvious source of distortion and leaves untouched the broader issue of the structure of sentences between 18 months and 3 years.

One difficult question is the effect of parole decisions on public conceptions of the length of custodial sentences. The above quotation from the Home Office's *Review* places reliance upon 'public opinion', and the English scheme of parole started cautiously because the Government claimed to have 'a fair idea of the reaction of a large sector of public opinion when criminals were seen to be released from prison long before finishing their well-deserved "time" '.[158] But, as we found in Chapter 8,[159] arguments become highly speculative when they turn on the factor referred to as 'public opinion': there is no worthwhile evidence as to the effect of parole on public conceptions of sentence-length.[160] Hood has doubted 'whether the particular length of sentence served by a prisoner released quietly into the community undermines any general deterrent impact the original sentence might have had',[161] but there is no hard evidence. The Parole Board is rightly concerned about the effect of adverse public comment which might result if a paroled offender commits a serious offence whilst on licence, but there is also the further question of whether, in effect, the public is being misled. Hood's reference to the paroled prisoner being 'released quietly into the community' raises the question whether the term of imprisonment publicly imposed by the court is at all intended to preserve the impression that the public is being protected by long prison sentences whilst the parole system in fact facilitates early release in almost two-thirds of medium and long sentences. Some might defend this: the 'law-abiding majority' sleep soundly in their beds on hearing of substantial prison sentences, whilst the parole system saves public money without significantly increasing either public apprehension or the actual risk of being the victim of a crime.[162] Others may condemn any disjunction between what is publicly declared and what is actually done, although that calls into question the one-third remission granted to prisoners at the beginning of their sentence. Indeed, proposals for automatic supervised release of those serving less than 3 years after one-third of their sentence might be even more objectionable on this ground. Apart from the moral issue of perpetuating a gap between declared and actual levels of sentence, however, there is such a confusion over what is to count as 'public opinion', and such a dearth of information about what people in general know and think about such matters as parole, that it is virtually impossible to construct a convincing argument on this ground.

What, then, are the principal justifications for parole? Three reasons for a parole system may be suggested. First, it allows selected offenders serving medium and long terms of imprisonment to be released earlier, under supervision, with an acceptably low risk of re-offending during the licence period. This is not to suggest that parole has a lasting effectiveness, so that former parolees are less likely to be reconvicted within 2 years than those released without parole;[163] but it is more humane to release the offender from prison, and certainly cheaper.

Secondly, parole allows the actual length of a prison sentence to be reduced in the light of changes in the offender's character and circumstances. We have already seen that courts often state that they are passing a lower sentence because of the offender's remorse:[164] if that remorse supervenes only after the offender has actually experienced imprisonment, it may be equally relevant to the offender's future conduct but the court can no longer take it into account. Parole provides the means of achieving this, although at present only for sentences over 19 months. In some cases it has been possible to have the offender's reaction to imprisonment taken into account on appeal, but this has been criticized as a usurpation of the proper function of the Parole Board.[165] If it is granted that such characteristics and circumstances ought to be grounds for mitigation of sentence, then it does seem wrong that mitigation should only be available if those grounds manifest themselves before sentence is passed. However, the only channels for review of sentences provided by English law are the criminal appeal system (which is under great pressure) and the parole system, which at present deals only with sentences over 18 months. The difficulty with conceding this function to the parole system is that it is procedurally inferior to criminal appeals, in that the offender is not represented before the decision-making tribunal; there is also a danger that those in prison who write reports about the offender may not separate remorse from submissiveness.

Thirdly, it has been claimed that parole exerts a 'smoothing effect' on sentences by enabling the Parole Board to 'iron out' disparities which result from similar offenders being given different sentences by different courts. This justification for parole is premised on a despairing view of sentencing and an optimistic view of the parole system, and is probably more applicable to American jurisdictions than to England. Disparity in sentencing should be tackled at root, rather than it being left to an administrative body to review sentences (only those over 18 months); and the multiplicity of Local Review Committees in the parole system, together with the different groupings in which the Parole Board sits, makes it questionable whether parole decision-making is greatly more consistent than sentencing. Parole should surely not be justified as a substitute for an adequate system of criminal appeals.

Parole may therefore be regarded, to a large extent, as a system which can make up for alleged failures in the sentencing system – the failures of the legislature to provide a sentence which includes compulsory supervision on licence and to provide a machinery for judicial review of sentences where there has been a significant change in the offender's character or circumstances, and the failures of the courts as manifested by sentences which are frequently disparate and too long. But we must question how real these failures are, and whether the cure is not worse than the malady. For instance, it would be anathema to most English lawyers to suggest that the defendant should have no right of representation and even no right to present his own plea in mitigation before the court which passes sentence: yet we permit this in the parole system, which may have a substantial effect on the length of time for which the offender is deprived of his liberty, and we do this in the belief that parole is a 'privilege' and that the requirements of natural justice are satisfied if the court has set the maximum period of imprisonment and if the offender is allowed to present his case personally to one member of the Local Review Committee. Moreover, if English courts do make meaningful distinctions between sentences of 18 months, 2 years, 2½ years and 3 years, the effect of parole decisions which give greater weight to certain criteria will be to blur or obliterate the parameters of proportionality. Thus, the factors implicit in an offender's 'previous good character', which lead the court to mitigate his sentence, may be exactly the same as those which suggest that he is a 'good risk' and lead to his early release on parole, so that he receives double mitigation of sentence; the effective gap between him and, say, another offender with several previous convictions is widened. However, to judge sentences solely in terms of proportionality is to ignore the strong effect of mitigation based, in some instances, on a low risk that the offender will re-offend: the next chapter will show that this has a well-established part in the English sentencing system. Both sentencing and parole have many and conflicting objectives. Simply to abolish parole, without more, would increase the prison population by some 3,000 inmates – who, on the evidence of parole, need not be there, in the sense that their early release under supervision will neither create an unacceptable risk of re-offending nor go against public opinion. Any reform which touches the fundamental principles of parole must be part of a wider re-structuring of the sentencing system as a whole.

8 Conclusions

The figures presented in Chapter 1[166] showed that, in the last decade, the prison population increased at a lower rate than convictions for indictable offences. That might be explained by the tendency of the courts to use custodial sentences with proportionately less frequency, or by their use of shorter sentences, or by the effect of increases in the proportion of offenders released on parole. All three factors contribute to the explanation, but in the years since 1974 there has been an increase in the proportionate use of immediate custodial sentences. Thus in 1974 some 15 per cent of adult indictable offenders were sent to prison, and this had increased to 18 per cent by 1981 (the same proportion as 10 years earlier); for young adult males, the percentage given immediate custodial sentences rose from 16 per cent in 1974 to 19 per cent in 1981 (again, the same proportion as 10 years earlier). Taking account of the increase of some 30 per cent in the number of persons convicted of indictable offences, one might therefore expect a substantial increase in the sentenced custodial population between 1971 and 1981; in fact, the increase is around 1 per cent. It therefore appears that the courts are imposing shorter sentences than 10 years ago, but proportionately more custodial sentences than was found necessary in 1974.

The shortening of sentences may reflect the three sources of scepticism outlined at the beginning of this chapter – doubts about the reformative effect of penal institutions, beliefs in the deleterious effects of penal institutions, and doubts about the deterrent effect of custodial sentences. These influences may be discerned, albeit in a diluted form, in the judicial initiative towards the reduction of sentence-lengths for 'run-of-the-mill' offenders, and in the judicial 'clang of the prison gates' principle for the first custodial sentence. However, the 'clang' principle may also have made a major contribution to the proportionate increase in the use of custodial sentences in the last few years. These increases have been chiefly in short sentences, and courts may have been so attracted by the supposedly enhanced effectiveness of a short custodial sentence that they impose it in cases where they might otherwise have suspended the sentence. Another practice, mentioned in Chapter 5,[167] is that courts sometimes pass a longer sentence 'because of an estimated likelihood that the offender will commit or repeat a serious offence'[168] – introducing a covert 'protective' element into the sentence, which is possible within the rather wide ranges upheld by the Court of Appeal.

It is interesting to consider the effect on sentence-lengths and on the custodial population of the time-honoured convention of magistrates pronouncing sentences in months and of judges pronouncing sentences in years and months. In fact, sentencers seem generally to think of custodial sentences in terms of a series of traditional figures: the next sentence up from 4 months is 6 months, with the intermediate term of 5 months being virtually unused; then from 6 months it is usually 9 months, then 12 months, then 18 months, then 2 years, then 3 years, then 4 years, with intermediate lengths being used very rarely. Thus, from 2 years upwards the standard 'increment', necessary to make a 'just noticeable difference' to the length of sentence, seems to be 1 year. As Pease and Sampson observe, 'this one extra unit of seriousness for the sentencer works out at 243 nights locked up for the offender, assuming he is denied parole, and an extra 121 nights assuming he is paroled at the earliest possible date.'[169] This is a vital step towards understanding the way in which sentencing practices produce a given prison population, and it suggests that in medium or long prison sentences there is less regard to each month, let alone each week, of incarceration. However, at a time when sentencers are speaking of reducing some sentence-lengths, that process might be more effective if they use the same increments to decrease as they do to increase.

Whatever the effect of all these practices, the prison population has risen at a lower rate than convictions for indictable offences, and *in a sense* custodial sentences are being more sparingly used. Could it be maintained that the two trends are causally related – that *because* the courts are using custody a little more sparingly, convictions have risen at a relatively high rate? There are surely far too many factors influencing the rate of convictions to attribute its fluctuations to a minor change in sentencing policy. Reporting practices, prosecuting and charging policy may alter; and, more significantly, there is such a welter of personal and social factors (including opportunities for offending, economic hardship and even unemployment) likely to have an effect on rates of offending. It is surely chimerical to argue that a small proportionate decrease in the use of custodial sentences has either consciously or subconsciously entered into and influenced the calculations of those who commit crimes. What we must now ask is whether a more substantial proportionate decrease would influence those calculations so as to bring about a further rise in the rate at which offences are actually committed. Some would rely on a deterrent argument to maintain that crime would increase: however, as we saw in section 3 of this chapter, a detailed examination of the assumptions behind general deterrent sentencing suggests that the conditions necessary for it to work are rarely present. More frequently, a heavy sentence imposed either as a general deterrent or as an exemplary sentence bears severely on the individual offender, with little prospect of short-term social benefit and merely the hope of some longer-term reinforcement of social attitudes against the behaviour concerned. Very large increases in penalties which were perceived as likely to be imposed might well achieve a substantial general deterrent effect, but such increases would undoubtedly be unacceptable. The paradox is, as Beyleveld argues, that

as a general principle the adequacy of our knowledge of deterrence for policy purposes varies inversely with the political morality and feasibility of the proposed deterrence policy. In general, we have good reason to believe that immoral, unimplementable policies would 'work'; rarely reason to believe that more sane and realistic policies will achieve anything. This is quite simply because human behaviour is much more predictable in situations in which freedom of choice is severely limited. If the choice is a clear one between compliance and, for example, certain death, then it is a good bet that a deterrable individual will comply. But to make choices clear and restricted the social milieu must either be extremely repressive or else we require far more knowledge of human behaviour and institutions than we presently possess.[170]

It is therefore arguable that neither a moderate increase in the level of penalties (within the bounds of social acceptability) nor a gradual decrease in the level of penalties would have a significant effect on the conviction rate.[171]

Some would inveigh against a lowering of penalties by relying on the incapacitation argument, yet few appreciate how low is the rate of incapacitation already and how small an effect on the conviction rate[172] a 6-month reduction of all custodial sentences might be expected to have. It might be replied that even a small incapacitation effect is worthwhile, inasmuch as it may protect an innocent victim, but the reply is unhelpful: clearly we could obtain a greater incapacitation effect by sentencing all offenders, or many offenders, to very long custodial sentences but we refrain from such a policy because we find it unacceptable. The incapacitation theorist who wishes to uphold the present level of sentencing must show why the present incapacitation level is the most acceptable one and why he rejects the slightly lower level proposed. Still others might rely on a combined proportionality and denunciation argument, maintaining not merely that severity of sentence should be proportioned to the seriousness of the case (which is not threatened by a progressive lowering of the tariff) but also that sentences should remain at a level which is not inconsistent with public opinion about what is appropriate.[173] The difficulties here are that it is unclear what counts as public opinion; that research suggests that victims themselves tend not to be punitive and tend to envisage sentences lower than those actually imposed; and that the decline in average length of sentence since 1980 seems not to have had an effect on public discussion of crime and punishment.

It is surely correct to start from the premise that, since a custodial sentence is the highest punishment society is prepared to tolerate and since it deprives the individual of that freedom which is fundamental to self-expression, there are positive moral reasons in favour of further reducing the frequency and length of custodial sentences, until and unless it leads to an actual rise in the crime rate which significantly and unacceptably increases the risk of being the victim of a crime. The May Committee noted that most other countries have lower imprisonment rates, and declared that:

Whatever qualifications must be made about how these things are done abroad, it remains the case that Dutch and Scandinavian experience demonstrates that civilised society can coexist with significantly lower sentencing tariffs. Whilst we are as concerned as anyone about giving full weight to the demands of retributive and deterrent justice as well as the need at the very least to keep some kinds of offenders out of circulation for substantial periods, the fact that other advanced societies have achieved an imprisoning balance qualitatively different from ours cannot be set aside.[174]

Since these lower imprisonment rates seem to result mainly from the use of shorter custodial terms,[175] this surely strengthens the case for reducing the level of sentences in England still further.

It should not, however, simply be a matter of progressively lowering the level of sentences. Earlier chapters have indicated a need to reappraise the general principles which lead to shorter and longer sentences within existing practices, and the predominance of persistent offenders among the custodial population shows the importance of this reappraisal. There is wide agreement on the principle that first offenders should be treated leniently and that the first custodial sentence should be as short as possible. Despite the support of sentencers for the former principle, they often seem willing to override it where the offender has committed a crime such as perjury or a breach of trust, for which the court feels that only an immediate custodial sentence will sufficiently symbolize the gravity of deliberately flouting the law. In these cases offenders are being sent to prison, not only because of sentencers' views about the penalty which is symbolically appropriate to the case, but also because either sentencers believe, or they think that the public believe, that the gravity of the offence is of greater symbolic importance than the character of the offender. As is too often the case, agreement about the general principle (leniency for first offenders) means little unless there is agreement on working details and categories. So far as persistent offenders are concerned, it is vital to re-examine the assumptions which underlie the approach to sentencing recidivists. Clearly they cannot claim the mitigation shown to first offenders, but ought not more rigid 'ceilings' to be set for relatively minor property crimes? Is it ever right to impose a custodial sentence on the ground that all other penalties have been tried and have failed?

Beneath the questions raised in the last paragraph lies a conflict between offence-characteristics and offender-characteristics in custodial sentencing. Although it is often generally remarked that the courts impose custodial sentences on a tariff based on the gravity of the offence, offender-characteristics are decisive in quite a few situations. The 'clang of the prison gates' principle is a clear example: the sentence is short because it is the offender's first taste of custody. One cannot say that this is merely the effect of mitigation in taking the sentence to the lowest end of the tariff for the type of offence, unless one also maintains that all 'normal ranges' of penalties were revised downwards on the arrival of the 'clang' principle – which would be equivalent to redefining the question so that it fits the answer. Another example of the influence of offender-characteristics is the principle that the sentence imposed on an offender should not be greatly more severe than the previous sentence if the crimes are of similar gravity: there should be no 'jump' in severity, even if a cumulative approach to sentencing the persistent offender is being adopted.[176] A further example is the use of 'last chance probation' in certain cases where a persistent offender

has undergone various individualized measures such as probation and borstal training,[177] and is now steadily adding terms of imprisonment to his record. Faced with the prospect of his developing into an institutionalized habitual offender, the Court will frequently seek to interrupt the sequence by the use of probation or whatever other measure may offer some reasonable chance of success.[178]

Thus the Court of Appeal has occasionally replaced a substantial custodial sentence with probation where there appears to be an element in the offender's recent history to suggest that he might respond. Even where the Court of Appeal has described a sentence as long as 5 years as correct in principle, it has occasionally seen fit to quash the sentence and replace it with a probation order as a last chance.[179] Decisions such as this provide a dramatic example of the breadth of judicial discretion in sentencing, and of the flexibility of what is for convenience often referred to as the tariff.

The practices evolved by the judges for dealing with what is a small minority of persistent offenders should not, however, be allowed to obscure the major issues of sentencing principles for persistent offenders and the criteria for the first custodial sentence. The recent reduction in the length of detention centre orders to between 3 weeks and 4 months, by the Criminal Justice Act 1982, may well act as an incentive to courts to impose the short 3-week orders where previously they might have imposed a non-custodial sentence or a suspended sentence (suspended sentences have, by the same statute, been abolished for offenders under 21). It is true that section 1(4) of the 1982 Act appears to require the court to justify the custodial sentence upon one of the grounds there stated;[180] pulling in the opposite direction, however, are the suggestions that courts ought to use these shorter custodial sentences on a kind of 'nip in the bud' principle, imposing them towards the start of a criminal career, perhaps after the second or third conviction of a young offender. This, of course, is the absolute opposite of the principle of parsimony in the use of custodial sentences. The assumptions underlying the 'nip in the bud' theory appear to be that, if the court imposes on the young offender a sentence which will make a strong impression and demonstrate the seriousness of lawbreaking, he is more likely to be deterred from re-offending than if he is given a series of non-custodial sentences which he may regard as inconsequential, and which may foster in him the view that lawbreaking is not treated seriously by society. The difficulties of this approach are major, however. First, it ignores the doubts and beliefs outlined at the beginning of this chapter, which have rightly led to a more sparing use of custodial sentences in recent years; or, perhaps, it challenges those doubts and beliefs by arguing that they can be explained by reference to the fact that custodial sentences are often not tried until the offender has proved himself to be a persistent lawbreaker. Even this, however, overlooks the deleterious effects of incarceration: earlier custodial sentences may bring some under the influence of experienced lawbreakers. The second difficulty is what approach to take in sentencing those who have been sent to a detention centre early in their career and then commit a further offence. Does the court then embark on the familiar penal ladder, following detention centre with a low sentence of youth custody, and then imposing longer youth custody sentence on each subsequent conviction? Or does it go back, as it were, to the non-custodial sentences which had not been tried before the offender was sent to detention centre? If it adopts this course, does this not run counter to the argument underlying the 'nip in the bud' theory that most non-custodial sentences are not viewed as serious responses to lawbreaking? There are grave uncertainties inherent in the 'nip in the bud' theory – uncertainties surely too great to allow an experiment with such gross deprivations of liberty as custodial sentences.

Non-custodial sentencing

In Chapter 1 the types of factor which may influence sentencing decisions were tabulated. Four categories were proposed: moving from the general to the particular, these were the demographic features of sentencers, their views on crime and punishment, their views on the principles of sentencing, and their conception of the facts of the case. It was there suggested that views of the principles of sentencing were particularly important. In the previous chapter we examined the principles governing the decision to imprison and the length of imprisonment. If custodial sentences are to be used parsimoniously, then the criteria for non-custodial sentences must be examined. In this chapter we look closely at the aims, effectiveness and use of the various non-custodial measures – at the officially declared aims of these sentences, and at evidence of sentencers' own opinions about them. Each of the measures was explained in broad terms in Chapter 1. Particular attention will be paid in this chapter to probation and community service orders, and to the information and opinions which courts may receive – from the prosecution, the defence, the probation service and others who provide reports. The concluding section examines ways of developing the use of non-custodial measures.

1 Discharges and conditional orders

This section will deal briefly with the absolute discharge, the conditional discharge and binding over: deferment of sentence is discussed separately in section 5. It is known that the absolute discharge is little used in areas where the police choose to caution rather than to prosecute a significant number of suspected offenders, and more widely where the police rarely caution.[1] In some cases in which the court orders an absolute discharge, this is undoubtedly intended to imply criticism that the prosecution was ever brought. In other cases, the sentencer might take the view that the very experience of being prosecuted in open court has been a salutary experience for the offender, and that it is unnecessary to add a punitive order. In still other cases, the sentencer might find that the offender is hardly blameworthy at all – coming close to a full legal defence – and therefore deserves no punishment.

There remains a general issue about the relationship between absolute discharges and the discretion to prosecute. There are legal systems, such as that of West Germany,[2] which require the prosecution of all those against whom there is sufficient evidence. This ensures that any decision relating to the offence and believed offender is taken by a duly constituted court rather than by the police, so that the defendant has an opportunity to challenge any matter with which he disagrees. Against this, it can be argued that no one needs to accept a police caution if he prefers to be prosecuted; that cautioning avoids a court appearance, and this may have both economic benefits (saving time and expense in preparing documents, presenting and hearing the case) and humanitarian benefits to the offender (sparing him the embarrassment and anxiety of court proceedings); and that the coin of social disapproval will be debased if those who have committed trivial or venial offences, or those who have already suffered greatly, are subjected to prosecution along with more serious offenders.

The conditional discharge is an order with more 'bite', in the sense that it empowers the court to impose two sentences if he re-offends during the stated operational period – one sentence for the new offence, and one sentence for the offence which originally led to the imposition of the conditional discharge. In this way, the conditional discharge may be seen as carrying the threat that if the offender fails to avoid conviction during the specified period, he will be dealt with more severely next time. There is thus a marked similarity to the suspended sentence, with the important difference that the penalty for the first offence is already specified when the sentence is suspended but left unspecified in a conditional discharge. The operational period for a conditional discharge may be up to 3 years (compared with 2 years for suspended sentences), and there is the advantage that on reconviction the second court has an unfettered discretion as to what action to take, whereas there is the disadvantage that the vagueness of the implicit threat may lead the offender to be more optimistic than he would be if there was a precise, suspended sentence. It is probable, in view of general sentencing patterns,[3] that the conditional discharge is usually imposed much earlier in the criminal career than a suspended sentence. It is a warning, less clearly focused than the suspended sentence, of what might happen next time. But, since the conviction does not really count if the offender avoids further trouble during the specified period, it could be said to postpone the true sentencing decision in the hope that the problem will go away – which it sometimes does, since some 71 per cent of those who are convicted for the first time are not reconvicted within 6 years, and the same goes for some 46 per cent of those convicted for a second time.[4] Yet the conditional discharge may properly be used later in an offender's criminal career. One obvious case may be where a person commits a non-serious offence after some years free of convictions; and another case of particular importance in times of high unemployment is where the offender would have been subjected to a stiff fine if he had been able to pay – as we saw in Chapter 7, it would violate the principle of equality before the law if such an offender were to receive a suspended sentence, and so the proper course is to impose a conditional discharge (unless a relatively short community service order were thought to be a fair alternative to the fine).[5]

Binding over is similarly conditional, but the specified period may be longer than the 3 years for a conditional discharge, and the conditions may be other than simply avoiding reconviction. Binding over to come up for judgment is similar to deferment of sentence (although the period is not limited to 6 months). Binding over in a fixed sum resembles a suspended fine. Since there are now statutory powers to defer sentence and to order a conditional discharge, it has been argued that it would be 'inappropriate to use the power [to bind over] where a statutory power to the same effect is available, or to use the power in order to exceed the limitations imposed by the statute on the exercise of a particular power.'[6] Moreover, it is lawful for a court to bind over any person involved in the case, including a complainant or other witness who has not been charged with any offence. Although such a person must be given the opportunity to say why he should not be bound over, the power itself runs counter to fundamental principles of criminal justice. There are strong arguments, therefore, for the abolition of the powers to bind over.

2 Fines

From the sentencer's point of view, fines may seem close to the ideal penal measure: they can be adjusted so as to reflect variations in the seriousness of cases and in the ability of offenders to pay, and they are penal in an uncomplicated sense. They do not as such involve incarceration or the threat of it, although the Crown Court may fix a term of imprisonment in default of payment. Nor do fines subject the offender to the elements of control and obligation which form part of probation and community service. The offender is simply deprived of some of his money and, only in that indirect way, of his freedom. In the early 1960s the courts were encouraged to use fines more widely, especially in the place of short custodial sentences. This stemmed partly from a belief that short custodial sentences were ineffective because they gave insufficient time for rehabilitation, and partly from a belief that fines were much less likely than any other penal measure to be followed by reconviction. The rehabilitative argument has now disappeared, and indeed there has been a resurgence of the view that shorter custodial terms are more effective in deterring offenders who have not been in prison before. The basis for the view that the fine is especially effective – a view given much prominence in the first and second editions of the sentencers' handbook, *The Sentence of the Court* – was undermined in an article by Professor Bottoms, who pointed out that the research upon which the finding was based took account of only three factors and left out of account certain factors which might be of central relevance to a court's decision to fine – steady employment record, stable family relations – and, independently, to the probability of reconviction.[7] Fines, in other words, were probably being given to people who were good risks. Nonetheless, it remains true that fines seem to return a relatively low reconviction rate in most studies; and, on account of the factors mentioned at the beginning of this paragraph, they will rightly continue to be widely used.

Some of the theoretical problems arising from the use of fines have already been discussed in Chapter 7. The problem of calculating the amount of financial deprivation requires consideration not only of the gravity of the offence but also of the offender's means: a principle of equal impact was advocated. Deprivation of the profits of lawbreaking is another purpose of financial penalties, whether by means of the fine or of the compensation order. Equality before the law is also a relevant principle, since it is possible that well-to-do offenders may (because of their considerable means) be given substantial financial penalties when poorer offenders would receive a more severe measure. Apart from these issues of principle considered in Chapter 7, there are two further practical issues. First, there is considerable variation in the use of fines in the courts. Tarling found that the proportion of offenders fined in the 30 courts in his survey ranged from 46 to 76 per cent, a variation of 30 per cent which was wider than that for any other penal measure.[8] This may indicate that different magistrates, or at least different benches, hold different views on the merits of the fine as a penal measure. Tarling, however, implies that a more likely explanation would be that the proportion of fines merely reflects the presence or absence of strong views on other kinds of sentence: if a court imposes a relatively high number of custodial and suspended sentences, its fining rate is likely to be lower. In this way, fines appear as a kind of residual measure, and the variation in their use merely as a function of views on other types of sentence. Since the fine is a measure hardly likely to evoke strong views for and against, this view has considerable plausibility.

The second point concerns the enforcement of fines, and this brings a variety of practical and theoretical problems which have, until recently, been somewhat neglected. The principle that fines should be adjusted according to the offender's means is widely accepted; clearly, too, the courts should have some discretion as to the rate at which they order payment, so as to allow for the fact that even a low fine can impinge greatly on an offender at the margin of poverty. What is less clear is whether that discretion ought to be exercised by relatively junior magisterial officers in the local fines and fees office. There is evidence that in some areas they agree a rate of payment which differs from that sanctioned by the court, that in other areas they are less willing to accommodate the offender, and that in some areas the enforcement process is initiated at an earlier stage than in others.[9] There appears to be little principled justification for these differences – certainly they cannot be fully explained as a response to local conditions – and yet they result in the application of different pressures upon offenders in essentially similar positions. In other words, sentencing and enforcement practices have close links which are not widely appreciated. Some might argue that the discretion is usually exercised in favour of the offender, and that if officers in the fines and fees office insisted that the order of the court should be carried out to the letter, the position would be much worse both for offenders and for society. Yet to grant that is not to obviate the need for a more consistent and principled approach to enforcement. The first step is to obtain reliable data on the practices which exist; the second is to decide what approach would be the most fair, and in what circumstances local conditions might be permitted to lead to a variation in practice. Bold words about relating fines to means and preserving equality before the law in sentencing can rapidly be reduced in significance if the actual enforcement of the court's order is not, or not always, responsive to changes in the offender's position.

Another problem in fines enforcement concerns the approach taken to defaulters. Not only is there a variation in the proportionate use of imprisonment for fine defaulters in different courts, but there is also a fundamental difference in the procedure adopted. Some courts have a preference for proceeding by warrant, others by summons – even though research shows that warrants are more effective. Warrants do, however, involve the police, and there may be local organizational reasons why a particular court uses warrants greatly or rarely – which is not to say that those reasons should be accepted as unalterable. Some 17,000 fine defaulters are sent to prison each year, and it is therefore important that further research and further examination of fines enforcement procedures takes place. In a persuasive article,[10] Morgan and Bowles argue that we need systematic knowledge which would provide the answers to five key questions: (i) do different enforcement practices affect rates of fine defaulting? (ii) how does sentencing policy with respect to fines affect rates of defaulting? (iii) what costs are associated with different sentencing and enforcement strategies? (iv) what scope is there for making greater use of enforcement procedures which are already available? and (v) what would be the likely consequences of introducing new procedures? The authors argue that, in the absence of information on these matters, discussion of the broad questions of fining policy – should the economic advantages of the fine, in contributing to the cost of the criminal justice system, lead to its wider use? should so much discretion be left to junior court officers? should imprisonment continue to be available for fine defaulters? how many opportunities, and of what kind, should be given for payment? – is bound to be speculative and not sufficiently constructive. One Home Office study in 1978 gives some basic information on the use of fines in magistrates' courts,[11] but far more information on enforcement procedures is needed if there is to be a worthwhile reappraisal of the place of the fine in the sentencing system. The other issues of principle discussed in chapter 7, such as the introduction of 'day fines', should also form part of this reappraisal.

3 Probation orders

(a) Probation facilities

It was explained earlier that probation is essentially an order of the court, made with the offender's consent, requiring him to submit to the supervision of a probation officer for a specified period between 6 months and 3 years. It is usual to insert into the order the requirements that the offender should be of good behaviour, should keep in touch with the supervising officer and should notify him of any change of address. Apart from interviews between officer and probationer, there may also be participation in one of the increasing range of activities organized either by or in conjunction with the local probation service. Day centres[12] have been introduced in many areas, as a means whereby the probation service can provide group facilities for individuals in need. The centre may be directed at certain types of problem, such as alcoholism, drugs or gambling; or it may simply offer a range of day-time activities such as assistance with reading and writing, and advice. The centres are usually not confined to those convicted by the courts. A supervising officer may suggest to the probationer that he attends a day centre, especially if he has a particular problem with which it might be able to help.

As these developments enable the probation service to offer direct help to some offenders with acute problems, there have been attempts in some areas to persuade sentencers to put on probation certain types of offender who might otherwise receive a custodial sentence, particularly where the offender's bad record appears to stem from a personal problem. The local service may put forward a 'probation package', bringing to the attention of a court which may be considering a custodial sentence the range of facilities upon which probation officers can draw in tackling this offender's problems. Early evaluation of the worthwhileness of these 'multifacility' schemes is inconclusive,[13] and there must be further testing on an experimental scale before their potential for diverting offenders from custody and dealing with their problems can be assessed.

The Criminal Justice Act 1972 introduced day training centres, attendance at which could be made a condition of a probation order. These centres were intended essentially for those offenders who repeatedly commit rather petty crimes and who seem to lack basic social skills and the ability to cope with the demands of modern social life. Four experimental centres were set up, their number was never increased, and no evaluative study was published. The Criminal Justice Act 1982 (Schedule 11) replaces the court's power to require attendance at a day training centre with a wider power to include in a probation order a requirement to attend an approved day centre for up to 60 days.

Residence in an approved hostel can be made a requirement of a probation order, and it has sometimes been claimed that this is a promising alternative to sending an offender to prison.[14] However, the provision of hostel places remains on a relatively small scale; there is evidence that probation officers tend to recommend residence in a hostel on the basis of the offender's characteristics and needs rather than the likelihood that he would otherwise receive a custodial sentence;[15] and some offenders are unwilling to agree to reside in a hostel, perhaps because of the restrictions typically placed on residents, and hostels may decline to take offenders who present particular kinds of problem.[16]

The Criminal Justice Act 1982 (Schedule 11) provides a new power to require a probationer to present himself at a specified place, or to participate in or refrain from participating in specified activities, either for the whole of the probation period or on certain days. It is unclear how courts will use these powers, but the probation service is likely to play a prominent part in developing such conditions, for the new powers may only be exercised after consulting a probation officer and being satisfied about the appropriateness and feasibility of the requirement.

(b) Local variations in the use of probation orders

It is fairly clear that magistrates' courts use probation orders to a greater or lesser extent, and that these variations cannot be fully explained by reference to differences in the age, previous convictions and present offences of the people coming before those courts. Thus Hood's study of 12 magistrates' courts in the period 1951–54 showed that the use of probation varied from 1 per cent to 24 per cent;[17] Tarling's study of 30 magistrates' courts in 1971–75 found that the use of probation varied from 1 per cent to 12 per cent of all sentences, and the indications from his study are that each court maintained a fairly consistent pattern of sentencing over the years.[18] A sentencer's use of probation will probably depend to some extent on his view of its worthwhileness: Hood pointed to the range of opinions among magistrates, from those who were 'probation minded' to those who regarded it as a 'let-off' and therefore inconsequential,[19] and the Oxford pilot study suggests that those who sit in the Crown Court also differ in their opinions about this. Much may depend on the relationship between individual sentencers and probation officers, and between the local bench and the local probation service. In his survey of Canadian magistrates, Hogarth found that those sentencers who relied on probation to a greater extent than their colleagues tended to have 'positive relations with probation officers'.[20] Hood argued that a good relationship between the justices and local probation officers was essential to a frequent use of probation, observing that in the areas where probation was well used there was a relationship of mutual confidence and there was ample opportunity for probation officers and magistrates to meet, either formally or informally.[21]

It has been suggested, for instance by Tarling's study,[22] that the use of probation by the courts is related to the amount of probation resources available in the area. 'Where resources are greater, more social enquiry reports are prepared and more offenders are placed on probation.' Doubts have been cast on the generality of this conclusion by Roberts and Roberts, who show that there is an association between the number of reports and the number of disposals administered by the probation service (i.e. probation and community service orders), but that there is no necessary association between the level of provision of reports and the level of resources.[23] Thus it may be possible for an area with low probation resources to promote a relatively high use of probation, if it can concentrate on increased report-writing and (as other research suggests) on concluding those reports with a reasoned opinion on sentence.[24] The situation should not, however, be depicted solely in terms of probation officers exerting an influence on sentencers; magistrates who sit on local Probation and After-Care Committees are in a position to be influenced by and to influence probation officers and probation policy.

(c) **The decline of probation?**
Until 1978 there was a steady and marked decline in the proportionate use of probation orders for all age-groups. In 1938 more than one-

fifth of adult indictable offenders were placed on probation; since then there has been a decline, so that in 1968 some 7 per cent of male adult offenders and in 1978 some 5 per cent of male adult offenders received probation, and for young adult male offenders the figures were 14 per cent in 1968 and 6 per cent in 1978. Since 1978 there has been a slight upturn in the proportionate use of probation orders, but this does not yet alter the overall impression.

To some extent the decline in probation after 1967 coincided with the introduction of the suspended sentence and, later, of the community service order; it will be recalled that the Advisory Council on the Treatment of Offenders opposed the suspended sentence on the very ground that it would lead to a reduction in the use of probation.[25] But the striking fall in the use of probation for young adult males between 1968 (14 per cent) and 1978 (6 per cent) coincides more exactly with an increase in the use of fines. As we have noted, sentencers were advised in the 1960s that the fine was especially effective in preventing reconviction.[26] Yet the shift from probation to fines may reflect, not so much a belief in the superior efficacy of fines, but either a lack of confidence in the ability of the probation service to deal with the kinds of offenders who now present the greatest problems for the courts, or a belief that probation orders should be reserved for cases of special need. To the extent that there has been a lack of confidence,[27] this may stem partly from the probation service itself: this seems plausible when it is considered that most social enquiry reports contain a recommendation on sentence and about three-quarters of those recommendations are concordant with the court's ultimate decision. Many judges in the Oxford pilot study attributed the decline in probation orders to a reduction in the number of cases in which probation officers recommended them. Indeed, the Central Council of Probation and After-Care Committees advanced a similar explanation in their 1978 paper on the *Diminishing Use of Probation Orders*: 'Officers do not appear to "go for" cases, "pull chestnuts out of the fire" etc., in the same way as the practice of those who built and sustained the service up to very recent years.'[28] Beneath the nostalgic tone of this observation may lie systemic reasons for any withering of the missionary spirit – feelings that the probation service has been given too many other tasks without a corresponding increase in resources, or simply the view that the missionary spirit is likely to meet with a negative response from the courts.

Some of those outside the probation service may applaud the

declining use of probation orders as a proper contraction from the over-use in earlier years: on this view, probation is seen as an intrusive measure, and simple penalties which involve no intervention in the offender's personal life should be preferred unless there are serious personal problems which appear connected with his offending and which might be tackled within the framework of a court order for supervision. Thus, in earlier years probation orders were probably made in cases where a simpler measure (such as a fine or conditional discharge) or a measure involving less personal intervention (such as a suspended sentence or perhaps a community service order) might have been satisfactory. Perhaps probation was, until the publication of Hammond's research in *The Sentence of the Court* in 1964,[29] widely believed to be more effective than a fine or conditional discharge; perhaps it was used in some cases where, had suspended sentences and community service orders been available at the time, it would have been rational to use one of those measures. However, even if it is conceded that there is some substance in this view, it merely suggests that probation was used in some cases where it was not really necessary, and in no way weakens the argument that probation might be more extensively used in cases where custodial sentences are now imposed.

There has been a slight upturn in the proportionate use of probation since 1978: for adult males the percentage increased from 4 to 6 in 1981, and for young adult males it increased from 7 to 8 in 1981. These are, at this stage, relatively short-term fluctuations, but it is noteworthy that they coincide with a rise in the proportionate use of community service orders (thereby countering the argument that community service and probation are necessarily 'in competition') and with decreases in the proportionate use of fines and suspended sentences. The reasons for the upturn may be found partly in the concerted efforts of probation officers and their organizations to promote the probation order and to explain the range of facilities and approaches it has to offer – as one chief probation officer put it, 'to convince the courts that probation is not a sloppy let-off but a constructive, purposeful social work method of dealing with offenders.'[30] Thus in some areas there has been a deliberate policy of making more probation officers attend court, on the assumption that courts are more likely to treat a social enquiry report seriously if the probation officer is present to be questioned about it. The Government's promotion of the probation order as a 'holding measure' may also have had some effect,[31] but it is too early to draw firm conclusions.

(d) Criteria for probation

One consistent finding of sentencing research is that the rate at which a court uses probation is unrelated to its proportionate use of other measures. Hood found 'no direct relationship between the use made of imprisonment and the use made of probation',[32] so that courts with high imprisonment rates did not necessarily use probation less than courts with low imprisonment rates. Tarling's 1975 figures show that 'courts' use of probation was not related to their use of any other disposal'.[33] Roberts and Roberts, examining statistics for magistrates' courts in 1979, remarked upon 'the absence of variation in the use of custody, whatever the use of these probation outcomes' (i.e. probation and community service orders).[34] It has already been suggested that the variation in the use of probation may be connected with sentencers' views about probation and the degree of their contact with the probation service, but in what types of case are orders typically made?

The decision-making process will often begin with a social enquiry report which recommends probation. The reasons for such a recommendation may vary, but three questions about the defendant will be important to a probation officer:

(i)   does he have problems which could be helped by probation?
(ii)   does he acknowledge these problems and wish to change?
(iii)   is he capable of change and of responding to the help offered by probation?[35]

This is to simplify, but an officer may think probation suitable if the answers to these questions are positive, after he has interviewed the defendant and gathered information about him. If the primary criterion is the defendant's need for help from the probation service, then it is clear that some courts are prepared to subordinate such matters as the gravity of the offence and the offender's record to a principle of meeting that need, whereas other courts prefer to use other non-custodial penalties such as the fine and community service order rather than responding to the need by means of a probation order. Courts in the latter group might regard the probation order as lacking penal bite, and might resent their inability to combine it with a fine.[36] Some offenders receive a custodial sentence without ever having experienced probation: they may have been sentenced on previous occasions, without having been recommended for probation or without having come before a relatively probation-minded court. In some courts, probation may sometimes be used as a kind of tariff sentence: Young's study of some 2,000 cases in magistrates' courts included 21 cases in which a probation order was made even though the social enquiry report stated that this would not be an appropriate course[37] – the court apparently wished to deal even-handedly with a group of co-defendants, or to use a measure more demanding than a conditional discharge for someone unable to pay a substantial fine. Even the simple old-fashioned tariff view of probation as 'third in the batting order' after absolute and conditional discharges may gain some support from any contribution it makes to ensuring that offenders are rarely given a custodial sentence before they have experienced probation.

Looking at the question from another angle, we find from the 1981 Probation and After-Care Statistics that 23 per cent of those put on probation had previously received a custodial sentence, and that a further 23 per cent were first offenders. The use of probation for those who have experienced custodial sentences has been encouraged by the Court of Appeal in the few so-called 'last chance probation' cases of persistent offenders in danger of becoming institutionalized,[38] and some of the others may be offenders who have relapsed following a conviction-free 'gap' since their last custodial sentence. It is hard to tell what considerations led to so many first offenders being put on probation – presumably they were seen as individuals with considerable problems, but it is not clear whether their offences were also more serious than those for which discharges or fines were thought appropriate.

To make a probation order may often be said to imply a particular view of the causes of the offence or, at least, a particular view of how to prevent further offending by this individual. Much probation work consists of basic practical assistance in searching for a job, sorting out finances and resolving family difficulties: thus where a person with such problems is put on probation, this testifies to a belief that his lawbreaking was 'caused' by these difficulties or that their resolution may lead him to desist from lawbreaking. The same could be said where the probation order is an attempt to tackle perceived deficiencies in personality and social skills through group work, day centres or other facilities.

(e) **The effectiveness of probation**
There is, as we have seen,[39] much debate about the proper measure

by which to assess the effectiveness of sentences. One might think that, with probation, the room for argument would be less because it is unambiguously a measure which seeks to prevent further offending, so that reconvictions would seem a fair measure. Yet it might be harsh to regard as ineffective a measure which, for example, results in an offender ceasing to commit sex offences even if he continues to commit petty offences of dishonesty; or which, for example, has the consequence that offenders with a history of persistent offending begin to offend less frequently than before.[40] The Court of Appeal could be said to have accepted this point, on the occasions when it has quashed a custodial sentence imposed on someone who has re-offended whilst on probation, substituting a further probation order in view of the general improvement in the offender's behaviour and thus overlooking the lapse.[41] In this way, a probation order might be claimed to 'uphold the law and protect society'[42] even when it does not result in 2 years absolutely free of reconvictions.

If, bearing that qualification in mind, we turn to Hammond's research into the comparative efficacy of sentences, we find that probation orders were followed by proportionately more reconvictions than expected.[43] Hammond made some allowance for variations in age, previous convictions and type of offence, but he took no account of other factors which might well lead the results of probation orders to appear worse (and correspondingly the results of fines to appear better).[44] Similar results emerged from the application of a slightly improved version of Hammond's methodology to 1971 figures by Walker, Farrington and Tucker:[45] probation fared considerably worse than other measures when applied to first offenders (although it appeared to fare better than expected with offenders who had 2, 3 or 4 previous convictions). The argument that first offenders selected for probation may well have a cluster of personal and social problems which would make them 'bad risks' for any sentence seems a plausible explanation for their comparatively high reconviction rates – presumably most first offenders would be discharged or fined, and so those receiving probation may well have had problems of some kind, which would make them worse risks than those receiving other measures. As we saw in Chapter 1, section 5, research which has compared probation with custodial sentences suggests that probation is neither more nor less effective in preventing reconviction than custody. On that basis one might advocate the wider use of probation for offenders who would otherwise receive custodial sentences, but none of the research has been sufficiently rigorous to exclude the possibility that 'better risks' are given probation and 'worse risks' given prison. The 'risk' of reconviction seems determined by the *number* of previous convictions, whilst age and home circumstances are also connected, and these may be much more powerful predictors of reconviction than type of sentence received.

In advocating the probation order as an effective alternative to custodial sentences, the Government has drawn attention to what might be called the 'holding effect' of probation orders. The figures show that 88 per cent of orders for 1 year, 73 per cent of 2-year orders and 67 per cent of 3-year orders are terminated satisfactorily (i.e. without reconviction or revocation for other reasons).[46] Thus, if one were to take a 2-year period from the imposition of a probation order, one could predict that some 27 per cent of probationers would either be reconvicted or have their orders revoked for breach, whereas the remaining 73 per cent would be held in the community without further detected offending. If, by comparison, an offender is sent to prison for 6 months, he will spend some 4 months in custody and will then be returned to the community without supervision (unless he is a young adult offender, for whom there is a short period of statutory after-care). The figures show that some 57 per cent of those imprisoned for such periods are reconvicted within 2 years.[47] It could therefore be claimed that probation gives a better chance of law-abidance during a given 2-year period than a fairly short custodial term. The reply to this would point to the probable differences in the background of the offenders concerned, with the likelihood that those imprisoned had longer criminal records and were for that reason more likely than the probationers to be reconvicted.[48] It is also possible that a fair proportion of those given custodial sentences of this length had previously experienced probation, although that should not debar them from a further such order. The reply is powerful, but not conclusive. We simply do not know how well those given custodial sentences would fare on probation; and, if we seriously regard custodial sentences as a last resort, there is good reason for finding out by actual experiment.[49]

Those sceptical of probation might put another counter-argument which adopts a different concept of effectiveness. Probation, they may say, is not an effective measure because 'action for failure to comply with the conditions of probation orders appears to be taken but rarely.'[50] The order of the court is not duly carried out, and probationers realize this, as do sentencers and some members of the public. Lawson's small study of breach procedures shows that officers sometimes overlook several instances of non-compliance with the terms of the order before bringing breach proceedings;[51] yet he also found that courts tend not to take a punitive approach where the breach does not involve the commission of a further offence. This further finding suggests that the doubters might regard probation as more effective, in these terms, if officers more readily instituted breach proceedings: the court would then play a more significant role in the execution of its own order. Some probation officers would oppose this, regarding some discretion in supervision as essential and arguing that breach proceedings are a last resort and an admission of failure. Yet Lawson also found that the bringing of breach proceedings tends not to worsen relations between officer and probationer. If this is so, it strengthens the case for a reappraisal of the function of breach proceedings and the criteria for instituting them. At present, as with the enforcement of fines, it appears that essential decisions are taken in different ways by different officers, that a justifiable area of discretion may result in unjustifiable differences of approach, and that there may therefore be unwarranted disparity in the way in which individual probationers have their orders enforced.

(f) Probation and the sentencing structure

Although the number of full-time probation officers increased from 3,426 to 5,304 between 1970 and 1979,[52] the service has also been assigned more tasks. Parole supervision came to occupy a significant amount of time in the 1970s, the service has organized and developed community service, it has undertaken the small experiment in day training centres, and has at the same time expanded its own provision of day centres and hostels. Some probation officers would like to see further expansion in community projects of a preventive kind, such as day centres. Although it would be wrong to expect too much of this approach, it is a stark fact that there is an association between unemployment and crime (a Home Office study in 1974 found that 38 per cent of those coming before magistrates' courts were unemployed)[53] and that job-seeking and the constructive use of time have an importance for the penal system. The extent to which the probation service should pursue 'multifacility' schemes raises more contentious issues. Whilst the probation service ought to concern itself with offenders who are drifting into institutions when their offending seems connected with personal or social problems which will not be tackled in prison but which could be tackled if there were facilities in the community, such schemes may demand resources disproportionate to the number of individuals involved and therefore present awkward issues of priority.

It has often been observed that the probation officer is unavoidably in a position of conflict. On the one hand, he is an officer of the court, responsible for carrying out enquiries before sentence and for ensuring the execution of certain orders of the court. On the other hand, he is a social worker trained to assist with the needs and problems of his client. Some officers find the former role uncomfortable at times, and this may explain Lawson's findings of reluctance to institute breach proceedings, the service's opposition to a combined sentence of probation with a fine, and the service's refusal of the power to have a supervisee committed to custody for a short period.[54] How officers approach their work varies. It is not clear how closely English probation practice has ever fitted the model of 'coerced cure', whereby the probation officer defines what his client must do and brings him back to court if he fails. Whether it could completely embrace a 'help' model, whereby the decision to participate in any activity described as 'treatment' is solely that of the probationer, is equally hard to say: some probation officers might think this unwise, and some sentencers might regard it as reducing the probation order to the level of a discharge unless other requirements were stated and enforced. As it is, probation practice appears to stand in the middle, with officers predominantly providing practical assistance with domestic, financial and employment problems which are recognized by both parties.[55]

Although there is evidence that the courts' use of probation is open to influence by the probation service, both directly through social enquiry reports and indirectly through communication and discussions out of court, it is clear that sentencers also have their own views about probation. The Oxford pilot study confirmed that there is some resentment about the statutory restrictions which prevent sentencers from combining probation with other measures: a probation order cannot be combined with a fine, but probation combined with a compensation order is possible, as is probation for one offence and a fine for another (where the court is passing sentence for two or more offences).[56] The Advisory Council on the Penal System reported in favour of combining probation with a fine,[57] but opposition from the probation service ensured that this did not find its way into the 1972 legislation. The combined order might indeed create further conflicts for probation officers between their role as helper or caseworker and their position of authority, but the opposition seems doctrinaire – officers have to cope with offenders who have financial liabilities, often to the court (unpaid fines, compensation orders, etc.), and the combined order might increase the willingness of sentencers to make probation orders. It is also unlawful for a court to impose a suspended sentence either for the same offence or on the same occasion as a probation order.[58] A suspended sentence supervision order may be imposed where a sentence of over 6 months is suspended, a restriction which practically confines the use of this order to the Crown Court. Again, sentencers might argue that if this combination were available, they would have more confidence in both measures.

The difficulty of acceding to these preferences of sentencers, sweeping aside the misgivings of the probation officers about the effect on their relations with clients, is that too many factors are unknown. Would probation orders simply be added to suspended sentences without seeking a special reason for doing so? The suspended sentence restricts the powers of the second court if the probationer re-offends, whereas a probation order *tout simple* leaves a wide discretion. Have we reason to believe that supervised suspended sentences are more often completed successfully than the unsupervised? Would the combined order be an attractive alternative to immediate custodial sentences, or would this not be its purpose? If it were possible to combine a probation order with a fine as a single sentence, instead of which existing measures would the courts use the combined sentence? Again, would it be regarded as a viable alternative to custody, or would courts merely add probation orders to fines?

Further permutations of the probation order have been suggested. An intensive form of probation order, entailing much greater supervision and probation resources, has been tried experimentally. The results showed that it was no more effective in preventing reconvictions than ordinary probation, although individuals with a certain personality might be more effectively treated by intensive supervision.[59] In 1974 the Advisory Council recommended the introduction of a 'supervision and control order' for young adult offenders, which would entail stricter requirements and would empower the supervising officer to apply to the court to have the offender committed to custody for 72 hours as 'a short-term penalty for misbehaviour under supervision or a cooling-off period when a breakdown is feared.'[60] The latter recommendation brought opposition both from the probation service and from those concerned with civil liberties. Another permutation would be to use the probation order as a mechanism for surveillance.[61] This would place emphasis on the formal requirements of the order – regular reporting, notifying change of address, etc. – and would have to be accompanied by an enforcement policy which matched the change in the nature of the order. Any 'treatment' or other activities would be purely voluntary on the part of the probationer, but probation officers would have to apply consistently a rule which specified the circumstances in which an offender in breach of his requirements should be brought back to court. This might be more just, in that each probationer's explanation for breach would be considered in open court, and it might lead some sentencers to take the probation order more seriously, but the probation service might oppose the accentuation of their authoritarian function.

These suggestions for changes in, or additions to, the probation order seem unlikely to lead to any reduction in crime, as by reducing the number of reconvictions, but they have been advanced chiefly as changes which sentencers want. It is arguable whether the preferences of the courts ought to be allowed to prevail, since those preferences may arise from beliefs that existing measures are insufficiently severe, which may in turn be influenced by beliefs about the expectations of the public. The bases of these beliefs is questionable: we do not know what the public believes, or upon what evidence any common beliefs are based; nor do we know what offenders believe, which may also be relevant. In principle it ought to be for the legislature to give some indication of how penal measures should be used. In England, however, where there is frequent reference to whether sentences are 'credible' in the eyes of sentencers and the public, this is far from the position. Indeed, the position might be worsened if any of these variations were introduced by legislation, or any of the restrictions on combined sentences removed. Unless it is agreed how the new measures should fit into the existing pattern of sentencing, and what measures they should displace, such changes would be a recipe for sentencing anarchy. Indeed, any proliferation of alternatives is likely to increase the difficulty of the sentencer's task, and to heighten the need for a clear declaration of policy. As it stands, the probation order is not without ambiguity – should it be regarded solely as a response to the problems of particular offenders, or should it also be promoted as a viable alternative to short and medium custodial sentences? – and so there is much work to be done before legislative changes can be planned.

4 Community service orders

The community service order is an order, to which the offender must consent, by which he is required to perform between 40 and 240 hours' work (as specified) in the community. Community service is organized by the probation service, although the work is usually carried out under the supervision of voluntary workers and others involved in community projects. The court must only make an order if it is satisfied '(i) after considering a report by a probation officer about the offender and his circumstances and, if the court thinks it necessary, hearing a probation officer, that the offender is a suitable person to perform work under such an order; and (ii) that provision can be made under the arrangements for him to do so.'[62]

(a) The use of community service orders

Community service was introduced experimentally in six probation areas in 1972; its extension to all areas was announced by the Government in 1975, and since then the number of orders has grown rapidly. The decision to make community service orders available to all courts seems to have been informed, not by evidence that it had proved particularly effective in preventing reconviction, but by evidence that it was a feasible scheme which the probation service could organize and which the courts would use, and by the continuing optimism and enthusiasm for the idea of work in the community which had led to its swift introduction in 1972, so soon after the Advisory Council's report. In fact, the first study of effectiveness showed that some 44 per cent of those given community service were reconvicted within 1 year of the sentence, which might appear to be a rather high reconviction rate.[63] Nonetheless, the number of orders has increased so that in 1981 some 5 per cent of adult male offenders and some 11 per cent of young adult male offenders received community service orders. In the case of adults, the rise of community service has coincided with a decline in fining; for young adults both community service and probation have increased proportionately in recent years, with a marked decline in fining. The pace of the increase meant that in 1980 the probation service had to cope with 42 per cent more community service orders than in the previous year. None of the empirical studies of sentencing is sufficiently recent to include community service orders, and so information about local variations in its use is relatively sparse.[64]

(b) **Criteria for community service**
What factors should a court take into account when considering a community service order? One might expect the answer to this question to include references to the seriousness of the case, the characteristics of the offender, and the opinion of the probation officer. But there are two difficulties of a fundamental nature which must be considered at the outset, related difficulties which have existed since the measure was first proposed and which have never been resolved. What is the aim or philosophy of community service? How does the order relate to other sentences, particularly custodial sentences? There has always been ambiguity on the first point: the element of hard work presents the order as a punitive yet constructive measure, the element of service to the community presents it as a form of reparation, and the prospect of work alongside volunteers and for the disadvantaged could make it appear as rehabilitative.[65] This ambiguity might have only marginal relevance if it were clear how community service stands in relation to other measures, and for what types of offender it should generally be used, but this is where we meet the second difficulty. The place of the community service order in sentencing has never been established, even in principle. The Advisory Council's extraordinary remark – 'nor do we think it possible to predict what use might be made by the courts of this new form of sentence'[66] – was criticized in an earlier discussion of penal policy-making.[67] The Advisory Council appeared to envisage the use of community service for a wide range of offenders, so that on some occasions it might be 'an adequate alternative to a short custodial sentence', and on other occasions appropriate for 'certain types of traffic offence which do not involve liability to imprisonment.' It might be used 'in cases in which at present a court imposes a fine for want of a better sanction' and, further, 'where it is desired to stiffen probation.'[68] The Government subsequently decided not to allow community service to become a condition of, or to be combined with,

a probation order; it also decided to restrict community service to imprisonable offences, and to increase the maximum from 120 to 240 hours. But even if these decisions were strong evidence of the Government's intention that the order should be seen as a viable alternative to a custodial sentence, there was no clear suggestion that it should be regarded *solely* as an alternative to custody. The Advisory Council took a wider view, and their suggestion (for example) that community service might be appropriate in some cases where a fine formerly seemed the only course remains uncontroverted.

An unusual feature of the legislative framework of the community service order is that a court may not make the order unless it considers a report on the offender by a probation officer. It was argued in relation to probation that the courts' use of the measure depends to a large extent on the initiative, enthusiasm and persuasiveness of the probation service, especially through social enquiry reports; this is likely to be an even more powerful factor in the developing use of community service. Probation officers' opinions about suitability for community service therefore assume considerable importance. Some probation departments have lists of types of offender likely to be suitable for community service; others have lists of characteristics which would probably make the offender unsuitable for community service – lack of fixed address, strong addiction to alcohol or drugs, mental disorder or serious mental disturbance, physical handicap which could not be accommodated in the work schedules, 'offending which involves serious or habitual violence or sexual aberration', total lack of motivation to carry out the order, problems which call for casework, and previous unreliability in reporting.[69] Such an 'unsuitability list' may perform a valuable limiting function, but it offers little assistance with the major problem of identifying suitable cases. In the Home Office study of the six experimental areas, three chief probation officers took the view that community service was solely or primarily an alternative to custody, and the other three regarded it as having a wider use.[70] A survey of other probation officers in these areas found that only 61 per cent expressed views consistent with the policy of their chief officer.[71] The study also found that three-quarters of community service orders followed positive recommendations in social enquiry reports,[72] yet an officer who regards community service primarily as an alternative to custody is likely to recommend it in a rather different, and narrower, set of cases than an officer who takes a wide view of its application. Likewise, to return to the ambiguity in the philosophy of community service, those who regard it as rehabilitative will probably recommend its use in rather different cases from those who regard it as punitive.

The approach of local probation officers may exert an influence in another, less obvious way. Community service schemes differ in the type of work which is available – constructing adventure playgrounds, clearing canals, assisting in hospitals or old people's homes, etc. They also differ in their organization and administration from area to area, as Young found in his research into the use of community service orders in six magistrates' courts situated in five probation areas. He found that 'wide variations exist on many practical issues',[73] and suggested three reasons for this: first, the ambiguity in the aims of the sentence, already noted; secondly, the tradition that each probation officer should use his own judgment, which brings a resistance to uniformity; and thirdly, diversity in local arrangements was encouraged at the experimental stage, and there was no attempt to enforce a particular pattern as community service was extended to all parts of the country. Indeed, the accepted wisdom is that flexibility should be left so as to allow each scheme to adapt to local conditions. But the argument about adapting to local conditions is here, as too often in penal practice, rather overworked and certainly not capable of justifying divergences on such matters as practices of assessment and selection, allowance for travelling time in calculating hours worked, payment of travelling expenses and (as with probation orders) the stage at which breach proceedings are brought against a defaulting offender. Matters such as these, particularly the sensitive issue of default and breach, may well affect the extent to which sentencers 'believe in' community service.

Sentencers, of course, will have their own views about community service. Some will regard it as primarily retributive, others may see it as rehabilitative. Some, perhaps having heard stories about laxity in enforcing orders against defaulters, will share the view of one judge who dismissed it as 'a joke'. As Judge Goldstone wrote recently: 'Perhaps because of this lack of guidance there is a tendency for us all to have our own formula as to the type of offence and offenders suitable for C.S.O.'[74] The early Home Office research found that 'sentencers in many cases seem to regard community service as an alternative to non-custodial measures as much as, or more than, an alternative to custodial sentences.'[75] Young presented a similar picture more vigorously, giving examples of cases from his six courts

402   SENTENCING AND PENAL POLICY

in support of his conclusion that 'the ambiguous location of the community service order in the tariff was reflected in the sentencing practices of the courts studied here.'[76]

This ambiguity has wider consequences in the sentencing system. A court which regards community service primarily as an alternative to custody would presumably give even its shorter orders, say 50 or 100 hours, instead of short custodial sentences. A court which treats it mainly as an extra non-custodial measure might give orders of 100 or 150 hours where it might otherwise have imposed a stiff fine but certainly not custody. 'Insofar as this is the case', writes Pease, 'it introduces one form of inequity into sentencing use.'[77] This inequity may bring further consequences if there is a breach of the order: where the offender appears before a differently-constituted court, the magistrates or judge may take different action according to whether the original order is interpreted as an alternative to custody or merely a non-custodial measure. The second court ought to give the offender credit if he has performed a substantial proportion of the order,[78] but the ambiguity of the original sentence inevitably affects the decision on how to deal with the breach. One way of removing the ambiguity would be to establish a standard scale of community service orders, relating the number of hours to an equivalent custodial or non-custodial measure. Young reports some early and varying local attempts,[79] and these local scales still persist,[80] but this is another issue on which there is no justification for local variation: national consistency should be sought. A detailed proposal is that of Pease, who puts forward two general principles:

The first is that orders of less than 100 hours should be imposed only in cases where the order is not an alternative to an active custodial sentence. The second principle is that 240 hours should be regarded as equivalent to a custodial sentence of not less than one year. Thus the range from 100 to 240 hours would constitute the length of order which could be regarded as equivalent to the range of custodial sentences up to one year. In this way orders between 100 and 135 hours would substitute for prison sentences of up to three months, 135 to 170 hours between three and six months, 171 to 205 between six and nine months, and 206 plus hours sentences of nine to 12 months or more. Since magistrates' courts cannot sentence to periods of more than six months for one offence, one would expect orders made by magistrates' courts to fall within the range 40 to 170 hours, except when more than one offence was involved.[81]

Agreement on a scale of this kind could have only beneficial effects on sentencing: it would be clear to those in court and to later courts how seriously the case was viewed, the offender would have a more accurate notion of the consequences of withholding consent, and long community service orders would be less likely to be recommended and made solely on the basis of the offender's perceived needs. But the establishment of such a scale must be preceded by decisions of principle. Should the smaller numbers of hours be treated as equivalent to non-custodial penalties, or should all orders be alternatives to custodial terms? May a community service order ever be made longer in the belief that this will benefit the offender, when the circumstances of the offence were not of such seriousness?[82] What effect would such a scale have upon the sentencing of young adults, for whom community service orders are much used but for whom it is the fining rate (not the proportion of custodial sentences) which has fallen?[83]

Other issues also call for resolution. Some regard the maximum order of 240 hours as unduly long, arguing that the prospect is so daunting that such orders are likely to lead to despair and breach; on the other hand, long orders are likely to be made on offenders with previous convictions (the Home Office study found that offenders placed on community service had on average three or four previous convictions)[84] who are 'worse risks' in any event. Then there is the vexed question of community service and the unemployed, little discussed in the literature but very much in the minds of some sentencers and, in view of the probability that more than 38 per cent of those sentenced in magistrates' courts are unemployed,[85] of considerable practical importance. The Oxford pilot study suggested that some judges regard community service as inappropriate for unemployed offenders because there is no real punishment in depriving of leisure time someone who has it in abundance: one difficulty with that view is that, since substantial fines are probably impracticable, the sentencer is left with few options and should surely not choose a more severe alternative simply because the offender is unemployed. Other judges regard community service as ideal for the unemployed offender, as it compels him to use his time constructively and might (at least temporarily) remove the boredom and aimlessness which might have led to the crime. Yet Judge Goldstone expresses the view that 'Orders should not be made to encourage the workshy, or to show the idle the error of their ways. They are a penal alternative – not a social reform.'[86] These remarks may be taken as a reference to some unemployed people. Young also found uncertainties in the probation service on how to make arrangements for unemployed offenders to carry out their community service.[87] The differences of opinion among sentencers must surely influence the way in which community service orders are used by the courts.

Guidance from the Court of Appeal has, in fact, been increasing. In 1981 there were at least three reported decisions in which the Court substituted community service for custodial sentences imposed on young burglars,[88] although no general criteria were declared. Then in *Brown* (1982), another case of a youth sent to borstal for burglary, Lord Lane CJ described the case as

tailor-made for a community service order. The appellant was a first offender – although the position would have been the same if he had had a 'light' criminal record – he came from a stable home with a wife and young child, he had a good work record and a job was available to him. There was apparently genuine remorse and the risk of re-offending was slight.[89]

Community service orders need not be limited to cases where there are so many favourable factors: two subsequent decisions suggest that an order should be considered for an offender with a considerable criminal record who commits a relatively serious offence (again, burglary in both cases) after a 'gap' during which he appears to have made efforts to settle down and avoid conviction. In *Lawrence*[90] the sentence of 18 months' imprisonment was reduced to 150 hours' community service and in *Canfield*[91] a sentence of 9 months' imprisonment was reduced to 80 hours' community service, although the precise reductions reflect other factors such as time already spent in custody. In decisions such as these lie the makings of a national scale of equivalence, since in *Lawrence* the Court stated that 190 hours would be the equivalent of 9 to 12 months' imprisonment and that short community service orders should be reserved for cases where there would otherwise be a non-custodial sentence,[92] but the Court has not yet taken that step.

These decisions may at least help to establish the community service order as a credible alternative to short and medium custodial sentences. Indeed, in the judgment which gives guidance to courts on the use of the partly suspended sentence, the Lord Chief Justice stated that, once the court has formed the opinion that a custodial sentence is necessary,

then the court should ask itself secondly this: can we make a community service order as an equivalent to imprisonment, or can we suspend the whole of the sentence? That problem requires very careful consideration. It is easy to slip into a partly suspended sentence because the court does not have the courage of its own convictions. That temptation must be resisted. If it is possible to make a community service order or to suspend the whole of the sentence, then of course that should be done.[93]

Courts must therefore give consideration to a community service order in every case in which they contemplate a custodial sentence of up to 12 months, although the criteria which they should use in deciding for and against such an alternative remain somewhat vague, as do the criteria for preferring a short community service order to a non-custodial sentence. Research suggests that less than one-half of community service orders are made instead of custodial sentences,[94] but that, so far as magistrates' courts are concerned,

courts with a preference for more severe penalties, particularly those involving custody, were less willing to make use of such an entirely new penal measure as the community service order than courts who already made liberal use of non-custodial measures. If this is an accurate indication of wider sentencing trends, then it is likely that any advice that the sentence be used as an alternative to custody is, to the extent that it is heeded, only preaching to the already converted.[95]

The above decisions show that the Court of Appeal now appears to be making an attempt, albeit not yet sharply focused, to preach to the unconverted.

(c) The effectiveness of community service

In terms of reconvictions, there is little evidence about the efficacy of community service orders. Home Office research in the experimental areas showed that 44.2 per cent of those on community service were reconvicted within one year.[96] The possibility that the subsequent offences might have been less serious was tested, but 'no systematic change in the level of seriousness of offences committed after a sentence of community service' was found.[97] No conclusions about the efficacy of community service as compared with other sentences can be drawn from the bald reconviction figure of 44 per cent, and the figure was inherently unlikely to be much lower because most of the offenders concerned were under 25 and the average number of previous convictions was 3 or 4. Each of those factors tends to increase the risk of reconviction,[98] and a concerted attempt to use community service orders more widely for those who would otherwise receive custodial sentences might bring offenders with even more previous convictions. If that were so, then it should surely be enough if the reconviction rate following community service were no worse than that following a custodial term of up to 12 months.

Another sense of effectiveness which gives rise to concern among sentencers is whether the order of the court is effectively enforced. The early Home Office research found that three unsatisfactory failures to attend work appointments would usually lead to breach proceedings, although some areas were more lenient.[99] Young found considerable variation in practice, so that 'some offenders with up to 12 unaccept- able (but not necessarily consecutive) absences had been no more than threatened with breach proceedings.'[100] Apart from the fact that some of the work leaders might be lax in reporting absences, the problems for the probation officer seem similar to those arising on breach of probation. However, as Pease and McWilliams argue,

courts which decided to make community service orders instead of 6 month prison sentences in respect of different offenders will expect the requirements to be enforced equally for each, and social needs should not create major differences in enforcement patterns.[101]

As with probation, therefore, the impression that community service orders are enforced only patchily and inconsistently may affect both their credibility for sentencers and fairness to offenders. Some might argue that the rapid increase in the number of community service orders shows that courts do not regard them with scepticism; the reply is that some sentencers still voice strong doubts about community service, and that if these were overcome its use might increase further.

(d) Community service and the sentencing structure

The proportion of offenders given community service orders in 1982 is probably higher than many in 1972 would reasonably have predicted. Despite the absence of systematic information about its effectiveness in terms of reconviction as compared with other sentences, or about its effectiveness in producing a beneficial change in the outlook and attitudes of those who undergo it, many sentencers appear to find it a useful measure. Yet we have noted evidence that it is used in different proportions and in different types of case in different courts. The statistics suggest that for young adult offenders it is largely being used as an alternative to fines. The Court of Appeal has in recent decisions attempted to establish longer community service orders as a credible alternative to custodial sentences, and it is possible to explain the fact that the proportion of custodial sentences for young adults has not declined during the rise of community service by arguing that custodial sentences might otherwise have shown a substantial increase, although Young's research (carried out in 1976 and 1977) found that 'almost every difference between the community service order and imprisonment indicated that the former was often being used at a lower point in the tariff scale.'[102] The word 'often', however, raises the question of how frequently the order was used instead of custody. This duality in the function of the community service order – longer orders as alternatives to custody, shorter orders as alternatives to non-custodial measures – has its attractions, but it is essential that some consistency is brought into the matter by the establishment of a general scale of equivalences between numbers of hours' community service and numbers of months' custody. In this respect, neither local variations nor variations in individual cases can be justified: there must be a uniform scale. The scale might also enable the legislature to remove the restriction of community service to imprisonable offences. One of the arguments heard during the discussions which preceded the abolition of imprisonment for soliciting by prostitutes was that the abolition would deprive courts of their power to make a community service order. It is unfortunate that abolishing imprisonment for an offence should have this result, and that this consequence may be used as an argument against abolishing imprisonment. Of course there might be difficulties in obtaining consent to community service if a custodial sentence were not an alternative, but some might regard it as a fair option to a stiff fine.[103] Finally, there must be further clarification of the types of offence and offender for whom community service is appropriate, the relevance of unemployment being one major question. It is all very well for the Court of Appeal to urge courts to consider a community service order instead of a custodial sentence; but unless the Court continues to develop the guidance given in recent decisions, sentencers will have insufficient criteria on which to make consistent decisions which conform to the Court's expressed policy.

5 Deferment of sentence

A court has power to defer sentence on an offender until a date up to 6 months later, 'for the purpose of enabling the court to have regard, in determining his sentence, to his conduct after conviction (including, where appropriate, the making by him of reparation for his offence) or to any change in his circumstances.' The court may only exercise this power if the offender consents and if, 'having regard to the nature of

the offence and the character and circumstances of the offender', it is
satisfied that deferment would be 'in the interests of justice'.[104]
Sentence was deferred in some 2 per cent of Crown Court cases and 1
per cent of magistrates' court cases in 1980. The process of deferment
and subsequent sentence raises two issues of fairness to the offender:
he must surely be given precise details of what is expected of him, and
the court which subsequently passes sentence must be accurately
informed both of those details and of his behaviour during the period
of deferment. There is no formal machinery to ensure that the
necessary steps are taken, and the judgments of the Court of Appeal
since the power of deferment was introduced in 1972 illustrate the
pitfalls which trial courts have not always managed to avoid. Clearly
deferment creates an expectation in the offender that if he does as
required he will not receive a custodial sentence: it was therefore held
wrong in *Gilby*[105] to pass a custodial sentence on an offender when the
report upon him was 'not unfavourable'. In *Glossop*[106] it appears that
the requirements upon the offender were neither precise nor recorded,
and that the second court had no report on his conduct during
deferment; the custodial sentence was quashed. In *Fletcher*[107] the
requirements were again imprecise, and the second court seemed to
be influenced, in imposing a borstal sentence, by minor difficulties in
the offender's dealings with the probation officer; the sentence was
quashed.

   In neither *Glossop* nor *Fletcher* were the precise reasons for deferring
sentence apparent: the words of the statute seem to contemplate
either a specific promise to attempt reparation or an imminent change
in the offender's personal circumstances. In practice, not only is there
a social enquiry report in some 90 per cent of all cases where the courts
decide to defer sentence, but about half of the offenders concerned are
already subject to some form of supervision, either under a court
order or on licence from borstal or detention centre.[108] It appears that
only about a third of the recommendations in reports were for
deferment – presumably advancing some reason which related to the
offender's behaviour during the 6 months to come – whereas about 12
per cent of the recommendations were for a custodial sentence.
Corden and Nott suggest, on the basis of their study of deferment, that
it was sometimes 'selected as a means of compromise when the court
was reluctant to follow' a recommendation in favour of some other
sentence.[109] Others have suggested, rather cynically, that deferment
of sentence is sometimes used by part-time judges in the Crown Court

as a means of passing a difficult decision to another judge.

Is the power to defer sentence a worthwhile addition to the range of sentencing options? The Advisory Council on the Penal System regarded deferment as appropriate in a small group of cases:[110] whether it is justifiable to defer sentence in order to see whether the offender pays some compensation is a difficult question, not least because it may lead the court in subsequently passing sentence to breach the principle of equality before the law, discussed in Chapter 7. In practice the power has apparently been used more loosely. Thomas has repeatedly argued that the power of deferment is confusing and unnecessary, and that either a 6-month probation order (if supervision is thought necessary) or a conditional discharge (if supervision is thought unnecessary) should be sufficient.[111] On the other hand, some probation officers support deferment of sentence because it is capable of making specific requirements of the offender within a definite period of time.[112] This may indeed be an advantage which deferment has over the short probation order, so long as the offender is able to cope with such a pressing deadline; but it is not clear whether that advantage justifies a power of deferment which is so procedurally defective as to produce frequent appeals against sentence. If the power is to be retained, it is essential that a fair procedure is established for the process of deferment, and that criteria are established for those cases in which it is appropriate for probation officers to propose, and courts to decide upon, deferment of sentence. Without these improvements, the power will continue to be a cloak for indecision and possibly injustice.

6 Avoiding custody

Some of the most difficult sentencing problems occur on the borderline of custodial and non-custodial measures: the point was made in the context of custodial sentencing in the last chapter, where there was discussion of those statutory provisions, such as section 20 of the Powers of Criminal Courts Act and section 1(4) of the Criminal Justice Act 1982, which are designed to restrict the use of immediate custodial sentences to cases where no other measure is appropriate.[113] Parliament has also attempted other restrictions: section 22(2) of the same Act provides that

A court shall not deal with an offender by means of a suspended sentence unless the case appears to the court to be one in which a sentence of imprisonment would have been appropriate in the absence of any power to suspend such a sentence . . .[114]

There is no corresponding provision for community service orders, which may in certain circumstances be used instead of other non-custodial sentences, but the Court of Appeal has recently established that a community service order should be considered when a court is contemplating a custodial sentence of up to 12 months.[115] In his judgment in *Clarke*, where guidance was given on the partly suspended sentence, Lord Lane CJ seemed to regard community service and suspended sentences as sharing the same 'rung of the penal ladder'. His description of the correct reasoning in these borderline cases has already been quoted, but bears repetition:

> First of all, is this a case where a custodial sentence is really necessary? If it is not, it should pass a non-custodial sentence. But if it is necessary then the court should ask itself secondly this: can we make a community service order as an equivalent to imprisonment, or can we suspend the whole sentence? That problem requires very careful consideration. It is easy to slip into a partly suspended sentence because the court does not have the courage of its own convictions. That temptation must be resisted. If it is possible to make a community service order or to suspend the whole of the sentence, then of course that should be done.[116]

This leaves it unclear how a court should distinguish between community service and a suspended sentence. The latter measure is now unavailable for offenders under 21, whereas community service orders are most widely used for offenders under 25. The main difficulty will therefore arise in relation to offenders in their twenties, and presumably the social enquiry report (where available) will assist by indicating whether the offender is considered suitable for community service. This, however, cannot conceal the fact that a major question of sentencing policy has remained without even an attempt at an authoritative answer for some fifteen years – in what kinds of case is it proper to suspend a prison sentence?

It has long been argued that the statutory scheme, incorporating section 22(2) (quoted above), defies logic. Thomas has argued that, after considering all non-custodial measures and deciding that a custodial sentence is necessary,

> the proper length of the sentence must then be determined, having regard to the gravity of the offence and the mitigation. When this process has been completed, the sentencer may turn his attention to the question of suspension. The difficulty that arises at this point is that if the first two stages have been followed correctly, all factors which are relevant to the sentence should have

been taken into account already. The sentencer must either give double weight to some factors for which he has previously made allowance in calculating the length of the sentence, or search for some new factors which will justify suspension although they are not relevant to the other issues which the sentencer has already considered.[117]

Perhaps the process can be given some meaning if sentencers assume that there are two categories of case – one for which an immediate custodial sentence is 'unavoidable', and one for which full suspension (or community service) may be considered if there are sufficient mitigating factors – although this would not clarify how the court should decide upon the length of a sentence which was to be suspended. If there are two categories of case, how might they be identified? The answer must lie principally with the types of offence for which courts regard an immediate custodial sentence as unavoidable, and these were discussed in the last chapter.[118] In those cases where a court might suspend the sentence, what kinds of factor may lead to this decision? On the basis of Court of Appeal decisions, Thomas has identified three types of case:

the offender who has for the first time committed an offence of substantial gravity, and who fits the image of the 'clang of the gates' offender described above; the offender who has a criminal record, including custodial sentences, in the distant past, but who has gone without conviction for a substantial period of time; and the third category of offender who gets the 'old lag's last chance' in the form of a suspended sentence rather than the probation order which was previously the preferred measure.[119]

The second of these types, the offender with a criminal record who has a 'gap' since his last conviction, bears some similarity to the type of offender suggested for community service in *Lawrence* and in *Canfield*.[120] There are other scattered decisions in which the Court of Appeal has mentioned remorse[121] and good employment record[122] as reasons for suspending a sentence. All the reasons seem little more than familiar mitigating factors, and the decision to suspend may be more influenced by such matters as whether the case falls irretrievably into the 'unavoidable custody' category, whether there is a social enquiry report favourable to the offender or specifically recommending community service, and how the sentencer regards community service orders and suspended sentences as penal measures.

It was suggested earlier that some sentencers find it hard to regard community service orders as a realistic alternative to custody; there can be little doubt that sentencers also vary in their opinions of the suspended sentence. Some may regard it as a non-custodial sentence coupled with a specific threat, others as a mitigated form of custodial sentence, others still as an empty gesture which allows the offender to 'get away with it'.[123] Combining the suspended sentence with a fine may avoid the last objection, although it could raise other objections,[124] but in general it is to be expected that a sentencer's view of the suspended sentence will influence his use of it. Tarling's research in magistrates' courts showed that the proportionate use of the suspended sentence varied from 4 to 16 per cent of cases in different courts: the use of immediate imprisonment varied from 3 to 19 per cent of cases, and courts which favoured custodial sentences also tended to favour suspended sentences.[125] These figures reinforce the argument that, in the absence of clear guidance on the use of sentences, disparity – probably accentuated by the divergent opinions of individual sentencers and of the local bench (in the case of magistrates) – is likely to result.

7 Opinions and information for the sentencer

Before reaching a decision on sentence, the sentencer is likely to receive information and opinion from one or more sources. Information about the offence will come chiefly from the evidence given in a contested trial or from the prosecution statement of facts if there is a guilty plea, and may be supplemented by any evidence heard after conviction, by the plea in mitigation and even by a social enquiry report or medical report. Information and opinions about the offender may also derive from the evidence heard in a contested case, but it will come chiefly from the police antecedents statement, from the plea in mitigation, from a social enquiry report or other reports (where available), and from any evidence heard after conviction. The hearing of evidence after conviction was discussed earlier,[126] and little will be said here about police antecedents statements, about prosecution statements of facts or about medical reports. The section will be focused on social enquiry reports and speeches in mitigation as vehicles of information and opinion for the sentencer.

(a) Police antecedents statements
In broad terms, a police antecedents statement should refer to the age, education, employment and domestic circumstances of the offender, and should contain details of his criminal record (if any).[127] Shapland found that the recommended information about the

offender was not always included in the statements, that practices relating to the reading out of 'spent' convictions varied from court to court, and that it was sometimes difficult to elicit the precise details of the present offence or of any previous offences.[128] The last point arises because, although in theory the police antecedents statement is a proof of the evidence which the officer in the case could give if he were called, it is common for the antecedents to be presented by a court liaison officer. He may be unfamiliar with the details of the case or of the offender's history, and may therefore be unable to give satisfactory answers to questions from the court or from advocates. The legal label of a previous offence may be unhelpful, and the sentence imposed on that occasion susceptible of different interpretations, so that the court may be imperfectly informed on some relevant matters.

(b) Prosecution statements of facts

The prosecution is expected, where there is a guilty plea, to state the facts of the case in court. The defence will probably also refer to the facts in the mitigation speech. If there is a significant conflict between the two versions, the court ought to invite evidence on the point or, at least, it ought not to pass sentence on a more serious view of the facts than that accepted by the defendant.[129] A minority of defendants maintain that they actually plead not guilty despite admitting that they committed the offence charged, solely in order to ensure that the relatively low gravity of the offence and any other mitigating factors are fully brought to the court's attention by sworn evidence.[130] Whilst some defendants believe that the prosecution has given an unjustifiably serious impression of the facts of their case, others acknowlege that the prosecution's statement of facts suffered from inaccuracies which operated in their favour.[131]

In the English system the traditional view is that the prosecution should offer neither an opinion nor even a hint as to sentence. This might be criticized as tending against a balanced approach to criminal justice, since the court hears only opinions and (perhaps in the future) precedents which favour the defendant, in the mitigation speech and social enquiry report. It should surely be open to the prosecution to draw the court's attention to principles of sentencing (found usually in Court of Appeal decisions) which provide guidance for this type of case and this type of offender.[132] This task would require prosecutors to be familiar both with the precedents and with the proper approach to them. It would not require them to 'call for' a particular sentence, as in some North American jurisdictions, nor indeed should they. Some of those who oppose the overt involvement of the prosecution at this stage argue that it might well operate so as to raise sentencing levels, which would run counter to much contemporary sentencing policy. To this there are two replies: first, the opposite occurred in Holland, in the 1950s, where it was the prosecutors who effectively led the courts towards the lower levels of sentence which now obtain in that country;[133] secondly, if the effect of acquainting courts more closely with the sentencing principles laid down by the Court of Appeal were to raise levels of sentences, this would tend to confirm that the Court of Appeal's levels are higher than those current in trial courts or that there is considerable leniency in some courts (leniency according to the established principles of sentencing) which fortuitously benefits some offenders and not others. The Oxford pilot study revealed some concern among judges about 'unjustified leniency', and some of the questions which this raises —could the whole system adopt lower levels of sentence without materially increasing the reconviction rate? is it unjust that only some offenders should benefit from the leniency which is now shown? does this leniency suggest that both the training of judges and the procedure of sentencing require re-thinking? — should be tackled urgently.

(c) Social enquiry reports

Since the Streatfeild Committee in 1961 proclaimed the need for courts to be supplied with comprehensive, reliable and relevant reports, the number of social enquiry reports prepared has increased greatly. It now stands at over 200,000 per year, and the task involves around one-fifth or one-quarter of a probation officer's time. However, the style and content of the reports have been attacked both from outside and from within the probation service, as have the opinions or recommendations put forward in reports, and there remains a crucial ambiguity in the relationship between the probation officer's task in writing the report and the court's task in passing sentence.

The contents of reports vary considerably, as the researches of Perry (1974) and Thorpe (1979) show. What is put into a social enquiry report may depend to some extent on the purpose it is thought to fulfil. One principal purpose is to bring more factual information to the attention of the sentencer: even if the evidence in a contested trial or the prosecution statement of facts on a guilty plea provides sufficient information about the offence itself, the court may need to know more about the offender's attitudes, any personal or other difficulties at the time of the offence, and other surrounding circumstances which might affect an assessment of the offender's culpability. A good illustration of this is *Begum Bibi*,[134] where the social enquiry report explained the Muslim culture which provided the background to the case, and where the Lord Chief Justice quoted extensively from the report in order to support his view of the offender's character and culpability. Another principal purpose of social enquiry reports is to furnish the court with information and opinion which may assist in determining the appropriate sentence. Both these purposes might be said to be shared by the speech in mitigation on behalf of the defendant, and this raises questions about their proper spheres. A further purpose of the social enquiry report is to inform subsequent decisions about the offender, in relation to parole, future sentences and later consultation by other probation officers. This 'future purpose' of reports will not be discussed here, attention being focused on the report as a document before a sentencing court.

The Streatfeild Committee on the Business of the Criminal Courts, one of the very few official committees this century to discuss sentencing practice, declared[135] that 'our cardinal principle throughout is that sentences should be based on reliable, comprehensive information relevant to what the court is seeking to do.' To this end, the social enquiry report should usually include

essential details of the offender's home surroundings and family background; his attitude to the present offence; his attitude and response to previous forms of treatment following any previous convictions; detailed histories about relevant physical and mental conditions; an assessment of personality and character.

To what extent do social enquiry reports conform to these ideals? How comprehensive and reliable is the information commonly presented? Perry (1974) found considerable variations in the content of reports, with some reports omitting family details, others omitting work record, financial position and other basic matters. Of course some selectivity is essential, given the mass of information which an officer may possess[136] or collect, but the criterion of selection ought to be relevance to the court's function in passing sentence, whereas Thorpe found a tendency to omit details which were thought 'too damaging to the recommendation'. From her research it seemed that officers sometimes presented only the information which supported their argument or benefited the defendant.[137] Practices such as these subordinate the information-gathering function of the report to its function of expressing an opinion on sentence. As for the reliability of reports, this has inherent limitations since probation officers often have to take the defendant's word on certain matters and, whilst some reports have to be prepared swiftly, others are completed so long before the trial as to be out of date on certain points when the case is heard.

How reliable and relevant are the opinions or recommendations put forward in reports? It appears that about four-fifths of social enquiry reports include what is termed a 'recommendation', and that in about 70 per cent of cases this accords with the sentence imposed by the court.[138] The Streatfeild Committee considered that the kinds of opinion which probation officers might properly express would be that (a) the defendant is stable and probation is unnecessary; (b) probation has a good chance; (c) probation would be better than custody, which might confirm his criminality; (d) custody would be more suitable; (e) any measure except probation would be appropriate.[139] To express an opinion on some of these courses might seem tendentious, especially in the light of Streatfeild's injunction that the probation officer 'should always take care to confine himself to opinions founded on actual and substantial experience (whether his or that of his colleagues) of the effects of the sentence and should have regard to the results of general research into what sentences achieve.'[140] The Morison Committee were quick to point out that this expected far more of probation officers' opinions than was reasonable, and yet, even though research into the efficacy of penal measures has yielded little in the last twenty years, a Home Office circular of 1974 encourages experienced probation officers to make specific 'recommendations' for or against any of the measures open to the court.[141] A probation officer might be able to assert that an individual needs and is suitable for supervision under a probation order, or is suitable for community service; it is doubtful whether he could predict with any confidence that either measure would be more likely, or no less likely, than any other measure to lead to the individual's reconviction. He could, however, point to the high proportion of 2-year probation orders which are completed without reconviction.[142]

What might be termed the dynamics of social enquiry reports and sentencing are difficult to assert. It is known that probation officers sometimes express an opinion in favour of custody, and it is possible that they do this, less in the belief that this would best satisfy the offender's needs than in recognition (or, to be more precise, in anticipation of the probability) that the court will impose a custodial sentence. Thus the fact that about 70 per cent of 'recommendations' accord with the sentence passed by the court shows a considerable rate of success among probation officers, but it is difficult to say to what extent this is success in persuading sentencers or success in predicting what the court is likely to do. When it is the latter, it is also hard to say whether the officer agrees with the course which he anticipates as probable, or whether he merely endorses it in an attempt to retain the court's respect.[143] Those who tend towards this last view should bear in mind the belief of many sentencers that the decline of probation in the 1970s reflected a reduction in the number of cases in which probation officers recommended it, and that the recent upturn in probation orders seems to stem from the activism of probation officers, partly through social enquiry reports.

The Court of Appeal, however, has taken an inconsistent approach to recommendations in reports. In a line of cases in which Lawton LJ has presided, probation officers have been criticized for making 'unrealistic' recommendations in favour of probation or community service orders for offenders who have committed offences of such gravity that a substantial custodial sentence is considered 'inevitable'.[144] The criticism assumes that part of a probation officer's task in making a recommendation is to have regard to the court's probable view of the gravity of the offence; however, the Streatfeild Committee clearly stated that

opinions of this sort . . . relate to only one of the possible considerations in the court's mind: how to stop the offender from offending again. The court has still to consider the nature of the offence and the public interest, and it has the sole responsibility for the sentence ultimately passed.[145]

Although it may be over-ambitious to expect a sound opinion on 'how to stop the offender from offending again', the probation officer may be able to express his professional judgment that an individual is suitable for and will respond to probation or community service, and opinions of this kind have been welcomed by the Court of Appeal in another line of cases. In *Afzal*[146] the Court, with Ackner LJ presiding, accepted a recommendation of suitability for community service and quashed the sentence of borstal training for residential burglary; in *Coleman*[147] the Court, with the Lord Chief Justice presiding, took exactly the same course. These decisions, together with others on community service orders,[148] are significant not merely because the probation officer's opinion was accepted but also because they show that the boundaries of realism are difficult to plot. Perhaps some sentencers still accept the view of Lawton LJ in *Stoakes* that 'those who commit burglary of dwelling-houses must expect inevitably, in the interests of the public, to be sentenced to a term of immediate imprisonment';[149] if they do, they will dismiss recommendations of the kind accepted in *Afzal* and *Coleman* as 'unrealistic'. Yet the judicial initiative in *Upton* and *Begum Bibi*,[150] combined with the recent judgments in favour of community service orders,[151] suggest that reports which contain clearly-reasoned opinions in favour of non-custodial measures for offenders on the borderland of custody have some chance of success.

What should the probation officer do? His concern is less with the far-away pronouncements of the Court of Appeal than with the probable reaction of his local bench or of the Crown Court judge: it is with them that he must attempt to build a relationship of confidence and trust. They may not respect an officer who appears to recommend non-custodial sentences in serious cases, he may believe that their confidence can be gained if he gives the impression of realism by recognizing the appropriateness of custody in some cases, and so he may fail to recommend a non-custodial sentence in some cases where the court might have been persuaded to consider one. Thus Corden and Nott found that 30 of the 258 recommendations in their sample were in favour of custodial sentences, and yet in all of their cases the court deferred sentence and only 10 of those recommended for custody ultimately received a custodial sentence.[152]

There is, then, a major ambiguity underlying the expression of opinions on sentence in social enquiry reports. If probation officers are to offer an opinion on the offender's needs and likely response, leaving the court (as Streatfeild suggested) to decide whether a more severe sentence is 'called for', this demands complete understanding from sentencers. Otherwise, sentencers will regard these opinions as 'unrealistic' in that they take no account of the gravity of the offence, and this could lead to a lowering of respect for probation officers caused solely by a misunderstanding on the part of sentencers. Some judges still believe that reports ought to take account of the views of the victim and society,[153] and this seems to explain what, it is respectfully submitted, is the error in the judgments of Lawton LJ mentioned above. The proper approach is that laid down in *Mulcahy*: 'the probation officer's duty is to recommend what he or she thinks is most appropriate for the individual, without having regard necessarily to the public consequences.'[154] By these means the courts will be drawn towards consideration of various non-custodial options to which they might not otherwise have given much thought. It should not, however, be assumed that this approach is without its problems, for the criteria of what is 'appropriate for the individual' may vary from perceived needs to predicted response, to likely success, or to mere suitability for a measure such as community service. And the formation of an opinion is not merely a matter of professional judgment but also involves, inevitably, some moral assessments and judgments.[155]

Another purpose of social enquiry reports should be to acquaint sentencers with the range of facilities available in the locality. This task should certainly be approached in other ways too – by encouraging links between sentencers and the probation service, and by ensuring a flow of information about local schemes for offenders – but there is a place, even in a social enquiry report which concludes with an opinion in favour of one particular sentence, for some listing of the available options. Judges and magistrates often express a desire to explore all possibilities before imposing a custodial sentence: providing them with information of the full range of alternatives would assist in a process which, when so many permutations exist (including such measures as deferment, money payment supervision orders and suspended sentence supervision orders), is complex and daunting.

One way of increasing both the courts' awareness of the alternatives and sentencers' confidence in probation officers might be for probation officers to appear more frequently in court to speak to their own reports. Clearly this presents problems of organization and time: the probation service often provides a liaison officer at court, but he will not have written most of the reports presented, and to ensure the attendance at the appropriate hour of the officer who actually wrote the report may be difficult. Nonetheless, McWilliams[156] cogently argues that 'getting probation officers back into court' is an essential first step towards improving mutual confidence, and there is evidence that this would be welcomed by lawyers: Shapland found that 'the majority (54 per cent) of legal representatives and judges interviewed felt that the probation officer preparing the report should attend court to a greater extent than at present.'[157] Some probation officers attribute the recent upturn in probation orders to the presence of more officers in court to speak to their reports. Their attendance could also increase the confidence of sentencers in the judgment of probation officers, provided that the latter were sufficiently trained to create a good impression in an environment dominated by lawyers. Some sentencers would go further and insist that they need to know the results of the order they make in reliance on probation officers' judgment. This in itself is not an unreasonable request, but it would be necessary to ensure that any figures that were compiled were carefully and fairly interpreted. Bald reconviction rates might mislead.

In what types of case ought a social enquiry report to be prepared for the court? The minimum categories are specified by Home Office circular, and (generally) include anyone under 31, anyone who has not served a custodial sentence since the age of 17, any woman and anyone subject to a suspended sentence.[158] There have been strong arguments from the probation service for a more selective approach, enabling energy to be devoted to worthwhile cases rather than expended on cases where a custodial sentence is in little doubt. The difficulty with this has already been pointed out: the Court of Appeal has begun to move away from the notion of custody as 'unavoidable' in quite so many cases and, as Dr Thomas has pointedly asked, 'who can say, in today's changing sentencing conditions, what recommendations are realistic in the sense employed by Lawton LJ and what are not?'[159] The Court of Appeal has, in the decisions advocating community service orders and in *Clarke*,[160] attempted to lead courts away from custodial sentences for crimes such as residential burglary. If lower courts are to move further in that direction, the probation service can assist by using social enquiry reports to point out the alternatives and to assess the defendant's suitability for them.

Not all courts will respond to this prompting, and there will continue to be cases in which an offender is sentenced to custody for the first time without the court receiving a social enquiry report. Even the most demanding of the English statutory provisions – section 2(2) of the Criminal Justice Act 1982, which requires a court to obtain and consider a social enquiry report before imposing a custodial sentence on a young adult offender – is followed by a sub-section which creates an exception if 'in the circumstances of the case, the court is of opinion that it is unnecessary' to obtain a report. The wording of section 20 of the Powers of Criminal Courts Act 1973, dealing with the first custodial sentence for an adult offender, has been amended by section 62 of the Criminal Justice Act 1982 so as to introduce a similar requirement and exception. Previously the Court of Appeal had not insisted on a social enquiry report in these cases.[161] Whether the new provisions will lead to a greater insistence on reports remains to be seen.

Another element in the provision of reports is local variation in practices.[162] In 1977 some probation areas ceased to provide reports routinely in cases where there was a not-guilty plea, arguing that the exercise wasted valuable time when the defendant was acquitted and that in any case it was difficult to discuss matters such as his attitude to the offence when he denied committing it. The Home Office, by means of a circular, quickly reasserted the importance of routine preparation in these cases, although it was recognized that any report would require the defendant's consent and that it might be possible only to prepare a modified report which provided the court with some basic information about his background. Thus the Government still regard as cardinal the Streatfeild principle that sentence should invariably follow conviction at the end of the trial, maintaining that

(a) the public should be able to relate the sentence passed to the offence of which the defendant has been convicted;
(b) if sentence is delayed, the defendant may be subject to unnecessary and considerable inconvenience and suffering, perhaps including avoidable custody; and
(c) if sentence is not passed immediately, there is considerable difficulty in re-assembling all those concerned with the case, and by the time this is possible the facts will not be so fresh in the court's mind.[163]

Consideration (a) is problematic: the extent of the public's interest, and the effect on this of the occasional delay, cannot be confidently stated. Consideration (c) is undoubtedly true, but it must be weighed against any advantage to be gained from the availability of a social enquiry report. Consideration (b) expresses the *dis*advantage to the offender, but there may also be the advantage that a full report prepared after conviction may tell in favour of a non-custodial sentence which he may not otherwise have received. Indeed, Sir Arthur James argued that sentencing would be made 'more efficacious' if there was a requirement, in the case of every offender under 21 and every first offender over that age, 'that sentence be postponed for a period not exceeding six weeks to enable a comprehensive report to be presented to the court.'[164] The benefits of that must remain speculative, but it is important to consider them at a time when economic and bureaucratic reasoning seems to dominate policy-making in this sphere. The Home Office's principal concern in its 1977 circular was 'to secure the efficient administration of the courts and to minimise delays in the process of trial and sentence, particularly insofar as these may entail remands in custody.'[165] The balance of advantage to the defendant in the criminal process may not have been fully explored.

In conclusion, it should be recognized that the uncertainties surrounding social enquiry reports derive from fundamental uncertainties in the sentencing system. It has been claimed that 'there is general agreement with the Streatfeild report that the type of information included in a social inquiry report will be of most use to the court if individualised sentencing, in preference to the tariff system, is decided upon.'[166] Depending on the force of the qualification 'of most use', this appears to mischaracterize the function of reports: to some degree they are informative on matters such as the offender's culpability (in the wide sense discussed in Chapter 4), his family circumstances and his personality,[167] and to some extent they convey information on the range of alternatives and an opinion on the offender's suitability for them or his probable response. It is therefore too narrow to suggest that reports either are or should be of primary relevance in cases where the court has already decided on an order such as probation, community service or deferment; they also have a primary relevance in bringing to the court's attention considerations and possible courses of action which may influence them to shorten a custodial term, to suspend it fully or in part, to fine or even to make some other order. In other words, they do and should set out information and opinions which may lead to a sentence which might not otherwise have been imposed.

A major source of uncertainty is the proper function of recommendations in reports. As we saw earlier, some sentencers fail to appreciate that recommendations relate only to some of the considerations which a court may take into account. It would, however, be preferable if probation officers were to revert to the language of 'opinions' rather than 'recommendations': the latter term is too open to misunderstanding, and probably too concrete as a description of what most probation officers can (and, in cases of 'non-specific recommendations',[168] do) put forward. Other improvements in the form of reports might increase their effect. The avoidance of what sentencers regard as 'jargon' is paramount;[169] anything which goes beyond ordinary usage may even be counter-productive, by turning a sentencer against a probation officer. Shorter reports might also help sentencers (although this might render the reports less useful for the other purposes they serve). A standard lay-out might be beneficial, enabling sentencers to locate particular points and ensuring that probation officers did not omit certain details. Any opinion should nevertheless be reasoned, so that the sentencer is able to assess it properly: this in turn requires the probation officer to be aware of sentencing practice and to invest considerable effort in explaining (where necessary) why he has formed an opinion in favour of a particular order.[170]

Research suggests that reports which carry a concluding recommendation or opinion are more likely to influence sentencing,[171] but this finding raises the question whether such influence is beneficial or not. There is no empirical evidence to suggest that reports lead to more effective sentencing, in terms of sentences which are followed by fewer reconvictions;[172] reports do not appear to lead to a wider use of non-custodial sentences unless they contain an opinion or recommendation;[173] and one experiment suggests that opinions favouring custodial sentences are so frequently followed that, overall, reports do not move courts towards non-custodial disposals.[174] However, recent decisions of the Court of Appeal suggest that a wider use of non-custodial sentences will be assisted if social enquiry reports are available in more 'borderline' custody cases, so that reports might be an engine of change towards goals set by the Court of Appeal and shared by government penal policy. Amidst a sea of uncertainties, this at least is one justification for reports which should command widespread acceptance.

(d) Pleas in mitigation

The speech in mitigation on behalf of a convicted person has come to be taken more seriously in recent years, especially by defence advocates, and the Oxford pilot study suggests that judges often find them more realistic and more helpful than social enquiry reports. Shapland's research into the process of mitigation sheds valuable light on the content and construction of advocates' speeches in mitigation. The group of factors most frequently mentioned in cases in her sample[175] were reasons for the offence (such factors as provocation, suddenness and financial crisis); then the gravity of the offence (especially presenting the offence as a relatively minor manifestation); then the defendant's attitude to the offence (especially contrition, for which the plea of guilty was sometimes the only evidence); then his personal circumstances at the time of the court appearance (especially employment and family circumstances), his future circumstances (continuing support from his family) and his previous record (emphasizing, where possible, the absence of previous convictions or a gap since the last offence). Many of these matters will also be mentioned in the social enquiry report (if there is one) or in the police antecedents statement. To what extent do mitigating speeches fulfil the Streatfeild criteria of providing information which is comprehensive, reliable and relevant? They may well be more comprehensive than social enquiry reports were found to be by Thorpe, inasmuch as the good advocate tends not to omit factors which go against the defendant[176] whereas probation officers sometimes do. Reliability is a difficult question, for the advocate like the probation officer derives most of his information from the defendant himself, although he may revise his views in the light of the evidence emerging during a trial. Nonetheless it has been contended that there is 'wide scope for unchallenged cock-and-bull stories to be put forward in mitigation',[177] alleging some provocation or other misconduct by the victim where the defendant pleads guilty and so no witnesses are in court. Such allegations may unjustly damage the reputation of the victim, and in any event the court ought to call for evidence in order to settle the disputed question of fact.[178] But the relevant point here is that an advocate may simply be doing his duty, and this does not guarantee the veracity of what he says:

> Unless the advocate definitely knows it to be false – for he must not knowingly deceive the court – he must put, as persuasively as he can, whatever explanation his client provides. However honourable the advocate, however much he has earned the confidence of the court, he cannot be regarded as underwriting or guaranteeing the truth of the mitigation which his client alleges . . .[179]

The reliability of mitigation speeches must therefore remain an open question. As for the relevance, one point is that speeches in mitigation are delivered on the day, and so should be much more up-to-date than a social enquiry report or police antecedents statement; another point is that they may be constructed with a better knowledge of what courts in general and this judge or bench in particular believe to be relevant to sentence.

How, then, are speeches in mitigation constructed? Advocates soon come to appreciate that the quality most valued by sentencers is 'realism': a speech which is regarded as realistic is more likely to have an effect than one which seems unrealistic. In general this involves a recognition of the full gravity of the offence and of other factors which tell against the defendant. A common approach which attempts to turn this realism to the defendant's advantage is for the advocate to mention each aggravating factor and immediately to qualify it by reference to a mitigating factor. As Shapland comments,

this would seem to be one effective method of both being seen to be realistic and dealing with the [versions of the] offences given by the prosecution and the police, so turning them to the benefit of the offender.[180]

The good advocate will adapt this approach in the light of his knowledge about the judge or bench, in an attempt to appear as realistic and to be as persuasive as possible. Probation officers in writing social enquiry reports cannot be so persuasive, since they often do not know which judge or group of magistrates will deal with the case; nor will they be 'realistic' in this sense if they adopt the approach recommended by the Streatfeild Committee and endorsed in *Mulcahy* and make no attempt to bring out the aggravating features in the offence. It was suggested above that this is a question of bringing sentencers to understand the function of a social enquiry report.[181] The speech in mitigation has a different function, and should properly deal with all the relevant aspects of offence and offender.

What speeches in mitigation seem to lack is a definitive and authoritative suggestion as to sentence. The practice of advocates is often not to refer to a specific sentence as appropriate for the offender, and usually to go little further than general phrases such as 'taking a lenient course' or 'in need of help'. It also seems unusual for advocates to cite appellate decisions on sentencing as a basis for proposing a particular course. Shapland speculates that it may be ten or twenty years before the practice of not mentioning specific types or lengths of sentence is displaced.[182] This change ought to be brought about more urgently, and one approach would be to encourage the wider citation of precedents. The Court of Appeal gives considerable general and specific guidance and, although its sheer bulk is daunting, the availability of such compendia as Thomas' *Current Sentencing Practice* makes the task manageable. However, the Court of Appeal would need to ensure that its guidance was based on a sound appreciation of existing practice; moreover, advocates would need to learn how to use the decisions, for there are many different factors relevant to sentencing and, as du Parcq LJ remarked on the use of precedent in cases on the law of negligence,

> it is a grave error to suppose that guidance is necessarily to be found in a case where a passenger has fallen through a carriage door-way by referring to all the other cases in the books in which passengers have fallen through carriage door-ways.[183]

Burglary precedents would be relevant in a burglary case, but only in context. There is also guidance on matters of general sentencing policy and the effect of mitigating factors, although guidance on non-custodial sentences remains sparse. If the precedents are to be properly used, and if excessive or indiscriminate citation is to be avoided (as it must), this indicates some reconsideration of the training of barristers and solicitors.

This leads on to an awkward point about lines of mitigation. We have noted that an advocate must put to the court whatever explanation for the offence the defendant advances. If he is to use the precedents too, he would be unwise to construct an argument which has been repeatedly rejected by the Court of Appeal. This point is particularly important in the context of speeches in mitigation on behalf of wealthy persons convicted of moderately serious offences, for there have been numerous appeals recently in cases where the sentencer has been persuaded, as a result of the speech in mitigation, to suspend the sentence of imprisonment which he would otherwise have imposed and to combine this with a substantial fine or compensation order. The Court of Appeal has frequently stated that this is wrong:[184] it enables a rich man to buy his way out of prison when a poorer man would be sent immediately to prison, and this (as argued in Chapter 7) violates the principle of equality before the law. There is little doubt that, despite the appellate decisions, this line of mitigation is still advanced and accepted from time to time. Requiring advocates to pay closer attention to the precedents might contribute to its extinction, although that would be more surely accomplished if the prosecution were also permitted to draw the court's attention to relevant precedents.

Also in relation to the principle of equality before the law, one important finding of Shapland's research is that unrepresented defendants are at a distinct disadvantage at the stage of mitigation. They often lack the ability to select from their life history just those factors which the sentencer regards as relevant, and tend to appear 'unrealistic' by their failure to acknowledge any aggravating features of the offence.[185] The art of successful mitigation seems to be largely a matter of mutual adjustment and anticipation between advocates and courts, between bench and Bar. Anyone unfamiliar with what is expected is likely to take the 'wrong' approach; if the citing of precedents were introduced, unrepresented defendants would be at a greater disadvantage. But these considerations should not prevent efforts to sharpen mitigation speeches; they are powerful arguments for ensuring the wider availability of legal representation and fuller assistance for the unrepresented defendant in court.

(e) Medical reports

Reports on the defendant's mental condition are produced, often after a remand by the court, in a small minority of cases. Gibbens found that there was a medical report in 8.8 per cent of his sample from Inner London magistrates' courts and in 4.5 per cent of his sample from Wessex magistrates' courts,[186] and Shapland found medical reports in some 13 per cent of her cases.[187] Despite this unexpectedly high number of reports, none of the cases in Shapland's sample received a medical disposal, although some received a non-custodial disposal which allowed the continuation of outpatient treatment. It is likely that a number of persons suffering from mental disorder pass through the criminal process without their condition being noticed or taken into account, although probation officers discover some such cases when preparing social enquiry reports.

(f) Conclusions

With information being presented to the court from so many different sources in some cases (the prosecution statement of facts, the police antecedents statement, the social enquiry report, the speech in mitigation and even a medical report), there are obvious dangers of unnecessary duplication and 'information overload'. On the face of it there is little doubt that information is duplicated in some cases. Many basic matters such as previous record, family circumstances and employment situation may be covered by the police antecedents statement, the social enquiry report and the mitigation speech. The only argument for that kind of duplication is that research has shown that none of these is comprehensive, their reliability varies, and some may be out of date. The idea of a single 'court report' incorporating all the basic personal details may be attractive in theory, but it is unclear who would prepare such a report and how they could be made more reliable and up-to-date than existing reports. Another approach might be to reduce the scope of each of the existing sources, by omitting the need for each to present certain details. For example, the gathering of family and employment details for the police antecedents statement must be time-consuming, and often duplicates what is said in mitigation or in a social enquiry report; conversely, one experiment suggests that sentencers look most frequently in a social enquiry report for details of the offender's previous convictions,[188] yet these might be more accurately presented in a police antecedents state-ment, especially if a police officer is able to give evidence about them.[189] However, despite these theoretical possibilities for rational-ization, there are practical difficulties. Social enquiry reports are available only in a proportion of indictable cases – 43 per cent in Shapland's sample;[190] it would be wrong to debar a defendant, either in person or through his advocate, from raising the full range of factors in his favour, even if these have already been mentioned to the court. The scope of the police antecedents statement might be reduced by omitting the personal and family details, but only if it were established that the court would routinely be provided with them from other sources which were no less reliable.

The possibility of what is known as 'information overload' must also be borne in mind. As the number of sentencing options proliferates and the range of information presented to courts in-creases, the Streatfeild Committee's insistence on well-informed sentencing seems to yield to a greater emphasis on the virtue of simplicity. Indeed, sentencers faced with a surfeit of information may tend to select only those items which confirm their own views; so far as that happens,[191] it undermines the whole purpose of providing courts with information. The adoption of a standard form for social enquiry reports might make some contribution to lightening the sentencer's load.

Opinions on sentence come from only two sources, the social enquiry report and the speech in mitigation. Improvements would result if each were more fully reasoned, the social enquiry report explaining the basis for any opinion advanced, and the mitigation speech paying closer attention to the Court of Appeal's principles of sentencing. This might not only improve the quality and cogency of the opinions put forward but might also increase the consistency of sentencing.

8 Developing the use of non-custodial measures

Underlying much of the discussion in this chapter has been the assumption that non-custodial measures should be used more widely, to some extent instead of custodial sentences. No doubt this has been and is government policy, whether we consider the Criminal Justice Act 1967 of the Labour Government (introducing the suspended sentence) or the Criminal Justice Act 1972 of the Conservative Government (introducing the community service order, day training centres and deferment of sentence). Whether this policy makes penological sense depends upon the standpoint adopted. Wider use of non-custodial measures may be seen as a means of minimizing the growth of public expenditure, even reducing it, but there are other possible ways of controlling public expenditure and we must seek arguments for this particular approach. There is the humanitarian argument, that it is generally more humane to leave an individual with his family and (where applicable) his employment than to remove him from society. There is also the effectiveness argument, often presented as the proposition that custodial sentences are no more effective than non-custodial measures. It is more accurate, however, to say that there is little or no reliable evidence for this proposition or its opposite: we do not know that it would be less effective to give every offender a short custodial sentence for his second offence, rather than reserving custody for a later stage in his career.[192] However, if one starts with the moral principle that the infliction of punishment on a member of society requires justification and that greater punishment requires greater justification, the humanitarian and effectiveness arguments support an expansion of the use of non-custodial measures in the stead of custodial sentences. On the other side, there is the argument of general deterrence – that to lower the proportion of offenders given custodial sentences, especially in a system whose inconsistencies may be seen as providing an extra chance of avoiding custody, would be to weaken the general deterrent effect of the criminal law. Once again, however, there is a lack of reliable evidence: we do not know what considerations weigh in the minds of offenders, and there is certainly no international evidence that countries with more punitive sentencing systems have less crime. Indeed, it is difficult to forge a firm link between levels of punishments and levels of crime.

The belief that it is proper to increase the use of non-custodial measures is, however, only one of a number of policy decisions which have to be taken. It is far too easy, for example, to move from the proposition that non-custodial measures have not been shown to be less effective than custodial sentences to the proposition that the use of probation and community service orders should be expanded. This would be to overlook the existence of other non-custodial measures, such as the fine and the conditional discharge, which may be no less effective and which it may therefore be rational to prefer to probation and community service on the principle that the degree of state power exercised over the details of an individual's life should be kept to the minimum.[193] Those who accept such a principle would probably oppose any expansion in the use of probation, whether in its present form or as a more explicitly contractual form of 'surveillance', with help and casework as voluntary 'extras'.[194] On the other hand, to promote the fine as a measure involving no detailed intervention in the individual's life, and which appears to be no less effective than other measures, may import its own difficulties. The fine may, in practice, be used in a way which discriminates in favour of the wealthy and against the poor. The wealthy may avoid immediate custodial sentences through their ability to pay substantial fines, even though the Court of Appeal has declared this improper, or may receive a fine (which they can pay easily) instead of a more intrusive measure such as probation. The poor offender may run the risk of receiving a more severe or more intrusive measure than if he had possessed greater financial resources, although once again the Court of Appeal has declared this improper.[195] Some of this discrimination, which may not be a conscious policy on the part of sentencers and may be suggested to them by the defence advocate, would be eradicated by a 'day fine' system, and some should be eradicated by routine reference to Court of Appeal decisions at the sentencing stage. In view of the practical problems of the fine, only the conditional discharge is left untarnished.

The sheer number of options in non-custodial sentencing, combined with the virtual absence of appellate guidance, leaves courts with difficult choices and inevitably leads to disparity. One way to alleviate the problem might be a drastic reduction in the number of possible sentences to, say, three; and the problem would almost disappear if this reduction were accompanied by the introduction of presumptive sentences. For example, in *Doing Justice* von Hirsch suggests that there should be just two forms of sentence other than imprisonment – 'Warning and Unconditional Release' and 'Intermittent Confinement'. The result of combining this with a presumptive sentencing structure would, according to von Hirsch and his committee, be greater justice: 'The potential benefit done to any one offender under a system of massive discretion is more than offset by the harms done to the vast majority of persons through such a normless scheme.'[196] The benefit would be the elimination of variations in sentencing which discriminate between rich and poor, employed and unemployed, male and female, smartly dressed and scruffily dressed, those with a skilful advocate and those represented less well or not at all.

Many English sentencers would protest that, even if the existing system does produce the occasional injustice on these grounds, a more regimented system would cause even greater injustice – preventing courts from imposing a sentence appropriate to each individual offender and offence. Moreover, it is perfectly possible that English sentencing practices as they now are, disparity and all, are much more lenient overall than any system of guidelines or presumptive sentences which might replace them. Many sentencers maintain that more unduly lenient sentences go uncorrected than severe sentences (which is, of course, partly because there is no right of appeal against sentence by the prosecution), and even the Court of Appeal has occasionally reduced a 'well-merited' sentence of 5 years to probation.[197] The critics who are primarily concerned with the overall severity of sentencing levels are therefore on unsteady ground. The critics whose concern lies with a more principled system must re-examine their principles. The approach put forward in *Doing Justice* 'is one of despair, not hope'.[198] Should probation be discarded, on the view that in either its present or a changed form it involves intervention in the lives of individuals which is unnecessary (in the sense that it is probably no more effective than measures which involve no such intervention)? Many would wish to retain the probation order as a measure which constitutes a serious attempt to assist an offender to tackle personal and social problems which appear connected with his offending: but would they still wish to retain probation if it were shown to be no more effective in terms of reconvictions than other measures? Would they argue that we must retain it, so as to strive for improvements in methods or in screening individuals for suitability for probation? Affirmative answers to these questions prefer hope to despair, and risk disparity and injustice in pursuit of humanity and improved efficacy.

In *Doing Justice* it is conceded that the re-introduction of probation might be contemplated for a defined class of offenders if it were proved that it was particularly successful for them.[199] Yet the point is not followed through, and there would be a difficulty if probation were brought into their presumptive sentencing system. Since they regard it as axiomatic that offenders with the same criminal record who have committed the same offence should be treated equally, probation orders could only be brought in if they were regarded as being on the same level of punitiveness as one of the other available measures – e.g. 1 year's probation might be equivalent to 1 month's 'intermittent confinement'. To argue thus is to assume that offenders share the conception of 'justice' put forward by von Hirsch and his committee, and would not accept a system based on a more sensitive conception of justice – one which emphasized the importance of tackling personal and social difficulties. That is not established: public debate about penal policy rarely comes down to these choices, and neither courts nor any official policy-makers have consistently explained sentences on these grounds – the latter preferring to expound economic arguments in recent years, and the former rarely addressing general issues of policy.

Another problem which is expressly confronted in *Doing Justice* is that of sentencing policy for persistent offenders. The ambivalence of English sentencing practice on this point was noted in Chapter 5, and it is no less important in relation to non-custodial sentencing. Von Hirsch and his committee accept that the penalty should become more severe with each successive offence, but they impose a definite limit of the maximum severity for a particular kind of offence, so that even a person who stole a bottle of wine from a shop for the 50th recorded time, with some 49 similar offences on his criminal record, might not be in danger of receiving a custodial sentence.[200] In English sentencing practice a custodial sentence would be perfectly possible for such an offender, for we have seen the influence of the idea that when non-custodial measures 'fail' a custodial penalty becomes 'unavoidable', and the notion that in English sentencing there is a ceiling (set according to the gravity of the offence) beyond which the sentence may not go is so flexible, and the ceiling sometimes so high, that this apparently restrictive principle exerts only a peripheral influence.

Whether or not the adoption in England of a 'justice' model would be the most desirable course in principle,[201] it seems likely in practice that the framework of the existing system will remain for some years to come. Nonetheless, as the above discussion shows, even a brief acquaintance with the 'justice' movement, either in theory or in its practical application in certain American states, is a reminder of the importance of settling authoritatively some points of principle which have for too long been in a 'normless' state in England. For the foreseeable future, English sentencers are likely to retain their wide discretion under the law, but some steps must be taken urgently to provide guidance on the appropriate use of non-custodial sentences. It should not be assumed that this should be, or ever ought to have been, the function solely of the Court of Appeal. It is a sphere in which the link between penal policy and sentencing policy should be strongly established,[202] and it is one in which those with experience of different aspects of the penal system – probation officers, in particular – should be called upon to make a contribution. Settling principles for non-custodial sentencing is therefore a task which calls for a wide range of expertise and no little skill in co-ordinating and resolving the various views which are likely to be advanced when judges, magistrates, probation officers and government officials are gathered together. There are fundamental questions of policy to be resolved, some of which have been identified earlier. There are also practical questions of implementation to be resolved. A major difficulty is that a precondition of successfully altering a practice is to understand how it now operates at its various levels, and this we do not know.

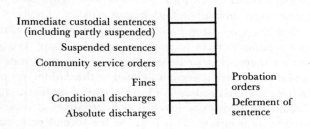

Immediate custodial sentences
(including partly suspended)

Suspended sentences

Community service orders

Fines — Probation orders

Conditional discharges — Deferment of sentence

Absolute discharges

It was noted in Chapter 1 that there is a tendency for offenders to 'graduate' from one non-custodial measure to the next, and thus for courts to use measures in a certain sequence.[203] This lends support to the view that in practice the available measures tend to be treated by sentencers as a kind of 'penal ladder', taking some such form as the Table overleaf.

Writing in 1971, Sparks put forward the analogy of a ladder, observing that there was 'some tendency' for penal measures to be used in this order and also stating, more doubtfully, that the measures 'can obviously be ranked according to severity, by fairly clear criteria.'[204] He reasons that the probability of an offender receiving an immediate custodial sentence increases with each conviction, and concludes:

> To the extent that this is true, the penal system is rather like a ladder, with nominal penalties comprising the bottom rung and imprisonment the top rung: as offenders climb the ladder, i.e. continue to appear before the courts, they receive measures of increasing severity, until they reach the top rung and are sent to prison. To complete the metaphor, we may add that at each rung some offenders 'fall off the ladder,' i.e. are not reconvicted; and that the probability of staying on the ladder increases the further one goes up it. Thus there are many offenders, few of them recidivists, on the lower rungs of the ladder; and a rather smaller number, most of whom are recidivists, at the top rung.

There can be no doubt that the 'ladder' analogy is a fair characterization of the sentencer's reasoning in some cases, especially where an offender persistently commits crimes of moderate gravity and the court places him on the next higher rung of the ladder because his previous sentence 'didn't work'. But there are five respects in which the 'ladder' analogy may be less than perfect.

First, as Sparks himself acknowledged, some measures seem to be regarded as alternatives to others, rather than as separate rungs of the ladder. Although Sparks placed probation orders higher than fines and lower than imprisonment on his 'obvious ranking' of severity, he recognized that 'there is evidence to suggest that fines and probation are in effect separate routes to imprisonment for many types of offender, rather than being successive steps on the same route.'[205] This particular possibility is accommodated in the 'ladder' on page 433 by placing probation orders (and deferment of sentence) apart and aside, allowing them to be invoked as alternatives at whatever stage is thought appropriate. This leads to the second reservation about the 'ladder' analogy: Sparks' assertion that there is a settled ranking of non-custodial measures is difficult to sustain. We have seen that Sparks recognizes that probation orders may form an exception: indeed, the Government has recently attempted to have them regarded also as a kind of 'tariff' measure equivalent to a short term of immediate imprisonment. The rung of the ladder below immediate imprisonment is already rather crowded, however. Not only does the suspended sentence occupy that position, supported by section 22(2) of the Powers of Criminal Courts Act, but it also appears that long community service orders share that rung. The decision in *Clarke* is authority for the proposition that, where a sentencer decides that imprisonment is appropriate in a particular case, he must then ask himself whether a suspended sentence or a community service order would serve the purpose equally well.[206] If this applies to the long community service orders, there remains the question of shorter orders of, say, under 100 hours: are these to be regarded as sharing the same rung as fines, or as more severe or less severe than the fine? The answer might well be that it depends on the magnitude of the fine, an answer which might be refined so as to refer to the impact of the fine on a person with this offender's financial resources. The small survey of magistrates' views carried out by Kapardis and Farrington[207] touches few of these detailed practical problems. Doubt about the 'obviousness' of the ranking of severity must remain.

Thirdly, a doubt must also be entered as to whether most sentencers either consciously or otherwise think of sentences in terms of a ladder. It seems possible that what was said about probation orders by Sparks has a more general application, and that some sentencers tend to act on views about the appropriateness of certain measures for some types of offender and not others, with the result that offenders with similar backgrounds and records might receive successive fines or successive community service orders in one court whereas in another court they might have been given one measure and not the other. There was a definite suggestion from the Oxford pilot study that Crown Court judges tend to think that the analogy of a ladder mischaracterizes the way in which they use sentences: many of them have firm ideas about the suitability of particular measures for certain types of offender or offence. This leads to the fourth reservation, which is that the ladder effect produced nationally by sentencing practice masks considerable variations at local level. Thus Tarling's study of sentencing practice in 30 magistrates' courts showed the following variations in the proportionate use of particular measures.[208]

Table 15 Difference between extreme courts in their percentage use of disposals

Disposal	Minimum use by any court	Maximum use by any court	Difference-range
Discharge	2.2	31.3	29.1
Probation	0.8	12.2	11.4
Fine	45.9	76.1	30.2
Immediate imprisonment	3.1	19.1	16.0
Committal to the Crown Court under s.29	0.7	10.5	9.8
Custodial sentence (imprisonment & committal to the Crown Court)	5.1	22.8	17.7
Suspended sentence	3.7	16.2	12.5

Tarling was unable to show the precise relationship of sentences to the number of previous convictions, but he did show that the variation in sentencing was equally wide when particular offences were considered. Although burglary was the offence most likely, taking all courts together, to result in an immediate custodial sentence (21 per cent of adult offenders) and least likely to attract a fine (37 per cent), the proportion receiving custodial sentences varied between 7 and 47 per cent and the proportion fined between 19 and 62 per cent among the 30 courts. It is sometimes said that crude comparisons of this kind convey a distorted impression, because the proportion of serious cases varies from court to court. Hood found that significant differences remained after account had been taken of differences in age, previous record and offence,[209] but it has been pointed out that those are only three of the possible many factors which courts might take into account, and that in any event it was important to study the different weight assigned to each factor in cases of combination and conflict.[210] Tarling paid attention to differences in offence, age and criminal record, but was unable to give an estimate of the extent to which they accounted for variations.[211] Despite these methodological difficulties, however, both Hood and Tarling formed the strong impression that variations could not be substantially explained by reference to differences in the types of offence and offender coming before the courts. Both writers pointed to local factors, especially the tradition of a particular bench of magistrates.

Fifthly, it is not clear what effect the introduction of a new measure will have on the use of sentences. Sparks argued that, whereas some might have expected the introduction of the suspended sentence to add an extra rung to the ladder, just below imprisonment, this was not its effect, and predictably so. The suspended sentence was not invariably used as a new, extra stage before immediate imprisonment: instead, it was often used in the place of other measures which had previously occupied the rung immediately below imprisonment. This was because courts had previously been urged to use imprisonment only as a last resort, and so tended to use probation orders and stiff fines as a 'last chance' before imprisonment. The introduction of suspended sentences was seen as offering a more fitting 'last chance' before prison, and thus displaced probation and fines to a considerable extent. Sparks' analysis therefore suggests that introducing a new measure does not necessarily lengthen the ladder and thereby push imprisonment one step further up. On the other hand, it may be fair to suggest that in a crude sense courts are likely to use imprisonment less frequently if they have a wide range of non-custodial alternatives than if they have only a few non-custodial measures to choose from. For example, in *Doing Justice* it is proposed that there would be only two measures other than imprisonment – 'Warning and Unconditional Release' and 'Intermittent Custody'. Although there would be a range of alternative periods of intermittent custody, it is quite possible that sentencers would use imprisonment more frequently than if there were several non-custodial alternatives to choose from, especially if sentencers continued to reason that when one measure fails it is appropriate to try a different, more severe measure. Thus the introduction of a measure such as community service might reduce the proportionate use of imprisonment by, as it were, pushing it one rung higher on the ladder. However, prediction of the effect on sentencing practice of introducing each new alternative (or depriving the courts of an alternative which had been used hitherto, such as the recent removal of the power to suspend a custodial sentence upon a young adult offender) depends on accurate knowledge of how sentencers actually do regard and use the various measures available to them.

There is in England little systematic knowledge about the thought-processes of sentencers, particular in the Crown Court. Yet, in the absence of sufficiently extensive guidance on principles of sentencing, it is inevitable that sentencers will consciously or otherwise, develop and act upon principles when dealing with the

problems which confront them. Conceptions of the relative seriousness of offences of low and moderate gravity, the strength of
mitigating factors, the relevance of previous record, the relevance of
previous sentences, and the appropriateness of particular measures
for certain types of offence and offender must inevitably develop on a
local or individual basis, subject only to the occasional sentencing
conference and other informal influences. Benches of magistrates and
individual sentencers (stipendiary magistrates, recorders and judges)
probably slide into a routine, in which they think along certain lines
and perhaps make regular use of only a few of the possible measures.
Occasionally they may be prompted by a social enquiry report or a
particular mitigation speech to consider a different approach, but to a
considerable extent it may be their own conceptions which shape
their approach to sentencing.

What is known about these conceptions, and their effect on
sentencing? Some sentencers and practitioners will have good
knowledge of sentencing in a particular area, and perhaps a fair view
of the differing approaches of certain judges (which is necessary to an
advocate if he is to construct a successful and 'realistic' mitigation); at
the opposite extreme, there is the broad impression given by the
annual statistics of sentences imposed, but there is very little
systematic knowledge of how sentencers approach their task. Studies
of magistrates' courts suggest that variations in sentencing practice
probably cannot be explained by reference to differences in the types
of case coming before the various courts, but there has been little
recent research on the different conceptions and approaches of
magistrates and their clerks. It is inherently likely that there is some
variation of practice among those who sit in the Crown Court, but
research which might (among other things) have shed light on
differences in judicial approaches and the reasons for them was stifled
by the Lord Chief Justice. It must be said, therefore, that the proper
basis for a successful re-appraisal of English sentencing practice –
systematic knowledge of the reasons why sentencers choose one
measure rather than another – is lacking, so that observations on
changes in sentencing policy and their effect on practice must be
tentative.

If one precondition for a re-appraisal of English sentencing practice
is research which will provide systematic knowledge about the
reasons why sentencers take the decisions as they do, another
precondition is the identification and answering of questions of

principle and detail about sentencing policy. There can be little doubt about the importance of settling the ranking of offences, and the relative strength of aggravating and mitigating factors (see Chapter 4). That would also be the first step towards a more uniform and controllable approach to dealing with persistent offenders (see Chapter 5). It would then be important to reconsider the available options – considering such arguments as those against the probation order and the fine mentioned earlier in this section. Possible changes to the form of each sentence should also be considered. Then, and the material in this chapter surely leaves the point in no doubt, it is essential to develop criteria for the use of each measure, and to establish the relationship of each measure to the others. One obvious step is to draw up a national scale for community service orders, relating numbers of hours to lengths of custodial sentence and, at the lower end, to comparable non-custodial sentences. All the guidelines would have to be kept under constant review, and it would be necessary to ensure monitoring of their effects in practice. The beginnings would be tentative and painful, but this is necessary if the system is to become more principled and consistent, and less anarchic than at present.

11

Towards improved understanding and procedures

Whilst Chapters 2 and 3 discussed the legal, procedural and institutional framework of sentencing and penal policy, Chapters 4 to 10 have tackled some of the major issues of principle which arise. In this brief concluding chapter the procedural and institutional framework is reconsidered in the light of the conclusions drawn in earlier chapters. The importance of improving general understanding of the problems of sentencing and penal policy is emphasized – an exercise in communication in which criminologists and the mass media have central roles – and new machinery for the formulation and implementation of policy is advocated. It is not claimed that such formal procedural reforms will be sufficient to engineer the desired change, but they are necessary if the issues of principle are to be resolved consistently and satisfactorily.

1 Improving understanding

The importance within the criminal process of the sentence of the court is beyond doubt: it sets the bounds of State action against the offender, it is a public declaration with various symbolic and general deterrent functions, and to a large extent it determines the extent to which the various resources in the penal system are used. Yet sentencing is one of many stages in the criminal process: it not only affects but is affected by decisions taken at other stages.[1] Thus, for example, the shape of prosecution policy determines the type of cases coming before the courts, and prosecutorial practice determines the approach to selecting charges and the 'statement of facts' given by the prosecution in cases where there is a guilty plea (i.e. the majority of cases). The same might be said of post-sentence decisions relating to the enforcement of fines or probation orders, or parole. Although there are some studies of enforcement decisions and parole decision-making, there is a dearth of knowledge about prosecution policies and practices. Their indubitably close connection with the sentencing process makes prosecutions a vital area for research.

Even more important for present purposes, however, is knowledge about the factors which cause sentencing practices to take the form they do. We have seen that, within the boundaries set by legislation, sentencers have a wide discretion. The appeal system can correct some errors but not errors of undue leniency. The principles laid down by the Court of Appeal are sometimes helpful, sometimes unclear or even contradictory, and sometimes simply absent. There is much latitude for the sentencer, and the factors which enter into the exercise of this discretion ought to be researched and made known. Changes in English sentencing cannot be successfully engineered, within the existing court system, unless the determinative factors are known. Moreover, if penal policy and sentencing practice are to be harnessed together, a working knowledge of the sentencing process is essential. It is apposite to quote, for the third time, the Advisory Council's limp deliverance: 'nor do we think it possible to predict what use might be made by the courts of this new form of sentence' (sc. community service).[2] Even the word 'predict' might carry the connotation of expected accuracy. Until there is systematic research into English sentencing, the arguments will remain at the level of speculation and counter-speculation. Some of the research into magistrates' courts has been quoted here, but there is a notable absence of research into sentencing in the Crown Court. Those who control access to the judges, administrators and practitioners in the Crown Court occupy positions of considerable power. To deny access to researchers who wish to obtain systematic knowledge about sentencing practices, as Lord Lane CJ did in 1981,[3] is to deprive policy-makers, educators and interested citizens of the basic information upon which to evaluate the exercise of this fundamental social and public function.

There is also a need for research into the view of sentencing practice held by members of the public and by offenders. For the latter, it seems that sentencers pay some attention to what they believe to be the attitudes of offenders, and it might be helpful to know to what extent, for example, probation orders and suspended sentences are regarded as 'let-offs' or the threat carried by 'conditional' sentences affects their conduct. Research into public attitudes to (what they believe are) sentencing practices might be informative in some respects, and it would be wrong to neglect the issue of public satisfaction or dissatisfaction with sentencing.[4] However, what passes as public opinion may well be based on incomplete information and imperfect understanding.[5] In some circumstances it is political and practical folly to ignore public opinion. What must be attempted, however, is an improvement in the quality of the inferences publicly drawn from published statistics[6] and from particular sentences.

2 Formulating policies

Improving the degree of general understanding about how the various stages of the criminal process operate and interact is one essential step towards bringing sentencing and penal policy into harmony. A second step is the formulation of acceptable policies, and a third step is to devise means of implementing those policies. The formulation of policies requires an approach at various different levels. General theories have an importance, but the sentencer must deal with the range of problems which confront him. The emphasis in this book has been upon the issues of theory and practice raised by some of the major problems of sentencing. General 'theories of punishment' sometimes deal insensitively with problems which have a significance in their own right (the best example is provided by persistent offenders), often in order to preserve the symmetry of the theory. There are many issues of principle and practice in the middle range, which must be tackled whatever general theory a particular individual, group or legal system subscribes to.

On the general level, two limiting factors which have been much promoted recently in debate over sentencing in England are public opinion and economism. The unreliability of public opinion as a concept has already been asserted. As for economism, there is no doubt that governments have to work within certain constraints of public expenditure, and in principle it may well be proper to choose the less expensive of two penal measures if all other things are equal. Each argument is too frequently overworked, however. The latter point can be met by saying that all other things are rarely equal. The former argument begs the question by priorities among claims for public expenditure. Thus one reaction to the present crisis of overcrowding in English local prisons is that the Government ought to increase its expenditure and build more such prisons, reducing the amount spent in other fields (such as universities or social security payments). Once economic arguments are imported, therefore, general social priorities must be debated. If it is conceded that only a certain amount of money is available for the penal system, however, then the economic constraint forces decisions on priorities. Economic considerations draw attention to the problem and help to indicate the feasibility of possible strategies, but they cannot resolve the issues of priority and principle and may even draw attention away from them.

A major issue of priorities concerns the relative seriousness of types of criminal offence. Sentencers inevitably adopt priorities on this matter. Despite the pronouncements of the Court of Appeal, there are likely to be considerable differences of priority. How could these differences be resolved? To attempt to construct a ranking of types of offence by sentencers or by members of the public would be unsatisfactory, since the rankings might be informed by inaccurate stereotypes of offences. What is needed here is research into the forms which each class of offence takes, into the effects on victims, and (if possible) into the factors which appear to influence its commission in that place, at that time, and in that way. Maguire's research into residential burglary[7] and Levi's work on long firm frauds[8] are two recent examples of research which should enable conceptions of the relative seriousness of offences to be more soundly based. But the results of such research are unlikely to exert much impact upon public conceptions, and the ranking of offences ought therefore to be approached at the level of principle. Fundamental moral issues must be tackled – physical harm must be compared with psychological harm, and with the damaging or loss of property; we must ask to what extent the ranking should be altered to allow for impulsive, unthinking offences and for crimes planned for profit; and to what extent the ranking should be altered if the offender has a substantial criminal record, or if he is a first offender; to what extent it should be altered when an individual is convicted on the same occasion for several offences. Questions of this nature were discussed in Chapters 4, 5 and 6. Possible solutions raise problems of understanding. Thus the popular cry for sentencers to deal more toughly with violent offenders, and the radical criticism that English sentencers value property more highly than life, raise formidable difficulties over the effect on sentence of prior criminal record and of planning and deliberation. If it is accepted that sentencing involves not merely fixing a punishment appropriate to the offence but, more broadly, punishing an individual offender for his offence, then the property offender might well receive a more severe sentence than the violent offender, on the ground that his offence was planned and his record showed persistence. The conflict of middle-range principles at this point is acute, and is further complicated by the issues arising from equality of impact, equality before the law, and the value of ensuring that the criminal process functions smoothly – issues discussed in Chapters 7 and 8.

A further issue of priorities concerns the relative severity and appropriateness of the various penal measures. In terms of penal policy, there is the question whether it is preferable to have few sentencing options or to allow a wide range of alternatives: the answer may depend upon which approach makes the greater contribution to the desired end, which may be the proportionately greater use of non-custodial measures. In practice, 'effectiveness' in terms of reconviction rates has sometimes been accepted as a criterion, but more significant in England is whether a measure is regarded by sentencers as 'credible'. The decision to make community service orders available to all English courts after the initial experimental period was based on the view that they were 'viable' (i.e. would be used by the courts), not on a judgment of effectiveness.[9] The credibility of sentences, particularly when they are put forward as alternatives to immediate custody, is of heightened importance in a system with such a wide sentencing discretion, and with so little appellate guidance, let alone control. It is here that there is the greatest divorce between sentencing practice and penal policy. The divorce is not always the result of sentencers taking a different view of the purpose and proper uses of a measure from that taken by the policy-makers, although this did occur with the suspended sentence.[10] More frequently the cause lies in the failure of penal policy-makers to articulate the precise purpose of making a new measure available, to consider the way in which it might fit into sentencing practice and the measures it would displace, and then to formulate detailed guidance so as to ensure that the desired change is achieved. In England, the absence of guidance of this kind means that policy-makers are left to speculate on the way in which sentencers view the available penal measures[11] – whether as a ladder, and if so in what order of ascendancy, or whether in some other way.

The principal policy decisions relating to sentencing may be listed:

A   What forms of conduct should be criminal offences?

B   Which factors in aggravation should be made the subject of separate offences, and which mitigating factors should be made the subject of defences or qualified defences[12] to criminal liability?

C   In what circumstances should a person against whom there is sufficient evidence not be prosecuted?

D   What orders should be available to courts on conviction?

E   By what criteria should the imposition of those measures in particular cases be determined?

By what body or bodies are these decisions most appropriately taken? The reach of the criminal law (A) has generally been regarded as a question for the legislature, usually following a report from a standing or ad hoc committee on law reform. The judges have to some extent determined this in the past, with their development of common law crimes, but their role is now largely one of interpreting criminal statutes. Questions of aggravation and mitigation (B) have been the subject of less attention from the legislature: although one might expect such issues to form part of the reform of the substantive law, there seems to have been no principled examination of the most appropriate allocation of issues between the tribunal of fact and the sentencer in the English criminal process.[13] What is needed is a set of general principles which can be invoked and, where necessary, applied or departed from when a particular group of offences is being reformed.[14] Questions of prosecution policy (C) have generally been regarded as separate from the reach of the criminal law and from sentencing policy. Indeed, some offences have been defined widely, bringing within the reach of the law a group of cases which ought to be penalized but at the same time capturing others which ought to remain non-criminal. The justification usually advanced for this crude mode of legislating is that prosecutors can be relied upon to exercise their discretion so as to draw the necessary distinctions. There is little empirical evidence of prosecution practices. If the criminal process is to operate consistently and in furtherance of an agreed set of ends, it is necessary to have a set of policies which bring the criteria for prosecution into accord with decision-making on the reach of the criminal law and on sentencing. It therefore follows that there should be a body which is able to consider prosecution policy in relation to these wider issues of sentencing and penal policy.

Decisions on the measures which should be available to sentencers (D) have generally been taken by the legislature, on the basis of committee reports or government White Papers, as modified in the light of representations from interested groups such as magistrates or probation officers. These representations have often led to compromises of a kind which are difficult to avoid in this kind of political system. What has been absent in recent years, however, is either a standing committee (such as the Advisory Council on the Penal System, which ceased to exist in 1979)[15] or at least a forum wherein the various interested groups might be brought together and helped to consider issues in relation to wider questions of penal policy.

The criteria for determining the appropriate sentence in each case (E) have been discussed in detail in this book. Who should settle these criteria? Whereas decisions A, B and D concern general policy, decisions E and C involve both questions of general policy and the individuation of those policies in particular cases. Even those who fully accept the English insistence on a discretion to select the most appropriate sentence for a particular case, because 'the facts of each case are different', surely cannot deny that in assessing the significance of those facts the sentencer will draw upon certain general principles, policies and priorities. These general principles undoubtedly exist, as Chapters 4 to 10 above have demonstrated. For the most part the criteria are left untouched by legislation. The Court of Appeal has in its judgments made attempts to articulate criteria, but it is handicapped by a lop-sided appeal system which means that it hears only certain kinds of case and also, partly as a result, by a lack of knowledge about the problems of sentencing in the lower courts. Now there is no reason of principle, constitutional or otherwise, why the legislature should not lay down general principles of sentencing. Such issues of policy are just what one would expect an elected legislature to resolve. Yet there are practical arguments against allowing a legislature to determine these issues, precisely because its members must have regard to their popularity. First, it is said that legislatures pay too much heed to public outcries, and might raise the level of sentences for a particular crime in response to a few much-publicized cases.[16] This argument, let it be said, seems to concede that public outcries can be irrational, further weakening 'public opinion' as a suitable benchmark in sentencing policy. The argument is also question-begging, for it assumes that legislatures are more prone than judges and magistrates to be influenced by a public outcry. Indeed, there may be a reason for removing policy decisions on sentencing away from both the legislature and the courts. Secondly, there is the argument that legislatures have too little time available for proper consideration of these matters. This is a stronger argument, the more detailed the guidance thought necessary. The shortage of available time in the Court of Appeal is equally an argument against relying on the senior judiciary to provide wide-ranging guidance. In sum, neither Parliament nor the Court of Appeal is well-fitted to formulate guidance for sentencers which deals with the whole range of offences and sentences.

What is needed is a body which can examine and re-examine sentencing practice, can instigate research which will provide systematic knowledge about the reasoning of judges and magistrates, and can then articulate guidance which is both realistic and in keeping with prosecution policy and penal policy. As a first step, a fruitful approach would be to create a Sentencing Council – a proposal which is closely intertwined with the means of formulating guidance and ensuring that it is followed.

3 Implementing the policies

As a practical solution for English sentencing the idea of a complete system of legislative guidelines or presumptive sentence should be rejected: to draft it would present monumental problems, it would take a very long time and it might be too rigid; and, it must be said, picking loopholes in statutes is a time-honoured sport of lawyers and courts, especially when they resent the legislation. On the other hand, we now have a loose and ill-structured system of high maximum penalties for the common offences (e.g. theft, burglary, deception, criminal damage), a wide discretion for sentencers and only patchy guidance from the Court of Appeal, and this urgently needs reform. The aim should be to find a middle way, which builds upon the best of the existing principles and practices whilst improving the system so as to provide sentencers in the Crown Court and in magistrates' courts with fuller and more consistent guidance. My proposal[17] is for a Sentencing Council, chaired by the Lord Chief Justice himself and producing recommendations which would be issued as Practice Directions with the full authority of the Lord Chief Justice. Its membership should draw on persons with considerable experience of the penal system, from magistrates, to a Circuit Judge sitting in second and third tier centres, to a probation officer, a prison governor, a prosecutor, a Home Office official, and an academic. The precise constitution and membership of the Council must remain for further discussion,[18] but it would be essential that there should be a number of sentencers who fairly represent the range of English courts, so as to bring a wider experience than a few senior judges can muster; that it should dilute the influence of any one group which might be so cocksure that it knows what 'public opinion' expects; that it should be capable of developing realistic guidance for sentencing at all levels with the element of co-ordination and overall planning which is now absent.

The work of the Sentencing Council would inevitably involve value judgements. It would be more straightforward to attempt to avoid making judgments by simply adopting the values inherent in existing practice, but if progress is to be made they must be tackled in a systematic fashion now, with the benefit of the appellate decisions and patchy knowledge which we possess, whilst the quest for more systematic knowledge is begun. The English habit of muddling along without being explicit about the priorities and preferences embodied in sentencing practice must be abandoned. Issues such as the sentencing of persistent offenders and multiple offenders and the claim that a guilty plea should be regarded as substantial mitigation are awkward issues which are most comfortably avoided. However, they have to be faced and determined every day by sentencers, usually without much appellate guidance. The Sentencing Council should enable these to be discussed in realistic and constructive terms, with a dialogue between those who are accustomed to passing sentence and those who carry out the sentences. The legislative framework of maximum penalties could remain unchanged, although there is a strong case for reverting to a finer gradation of criminal offences and maximum penalties than has been thought necessary by law reformers and the legislature in recent years.[19] Even with finer gradations, however, the legislature would continue to leave the courts with discretion, and it should be the task of the Sentencing Council to structure that discretion. What the Sentencing Council should aim to produce is sets of declared sentencing ceilings for different grades and types of offence, which have their basis in certain relativities between offences, together with declared principles for use in calculating the precise sentence beneath that ceiling – principles to deal with persistent offenders, multiple offenders, breaches of suspended sentences and so forth. A number of recent judgments of the Court of Appeal adopt an approach which the Practice Directions could develop.[20]

The Practice Directions on different aspects of sentencing could be issued piecemeal, as the work was completed. To establish 'ceilings' for the various forms of each offence is no easy task: it should not merely be a matter of collating statistics on average or 'normal maximum' sentences, using the existing legal classification or even the statistical classification of offences.[21] For the purpose of guiding sentencers, it is necessary to attempt a more detailed and descriptive division of offences, according to prominent factors and known patterns of offending. The available statistics should therefore be considered in conjunction with any guidance laid down by the Court of Appeal, the experience of those on the Council and any general considerations of penal policy. The Council ought to be served by a secretariat composed not only of civil servants but also of academics. The Practice Directions would be subject to review in the light of experience, observations from sentencers and general criticism. One benefit of the publication of Practice Directions would be to stimulate, albeit through the media, public discussion of the problems of sentencing which might be better informed.

Ways must then be found to ensure that what the Practice Directions lay down is translated faithfully into practice. There is, in England, something of a distrust among sentencers towards central direction of any kind. The introduction of a Sentencing Council ought to eliminate this by showing, through its membership and its pronouncements, that it is conversant with the problems faced by sentencers in courts of all kinds. The aim of the Practice Directions would, however, be to structure discretion rather than to eliminate it, and attention must be paid to the effect of the demographic features of sentencers upon their sentencing practices. This suggests further study of influences of the kind discussed in Chapter 1,[22] and renewed attention to the selection and training of those invested with the authority to pass sentence.

The reform of sentencing procedures would also be necessary if the new system were to function properly. At present the procedures fall below what are supposed to be the traditional standards of the English criminal process. Procedures for establishing a precise factual basis for sentencing are still under-developed, so that it is quite possible for an offender to be sentenced on the basis of some further allegation which has not been proved strictly according to the normal standard, 'beyond reasonable doubt';[23] applications for leave to appeal under section 31 of the Criminal Appeal Act 1968 seem to be dealt with in a less-than-fully-principled manner; the citation of the Court of Appeal's decisions on sentencing is extremely rare at first instance, and has even been discouraged in the Court of Appeal on some occasions;[24] and the Court of Appeal does not regularly refer to its own previous decisions on sentencing, a practice which is regarded as integral to the development of the common law, and this has led to inconsistent decisions which can only bewilder the judges and magistrates who are meant to look to the Court of Appeal for guidance.[25] In short, the sentencing process is a disgrace to the common law tradition. Indeed, the absence of a requirement upon sentencers to give reasons and the resistance of certain judges to such a requirement seem to ensure that English sentencing falls below the standards which a court of law should properly attain. The giving of reasons for sentence in open court clearly has a social function, in relation to the different audiences noted in Chapter 8, but it also has a legal function.[26] This function is to justify the sentence in terms of the general principles laid down in the guidance – at present, the judgments of the Court of Appeal, but perhaps in future the Practice Directions generated by the Sentencing Council. It is hardly surprising that reason-giving of this kind is not the normal pattern when the available guidance is patchy and sometimes inconsistent, when advocates are not encouraged to cite precedents, and indeed when the prosecutor is not expected to speak about the sentence. The procedural reforms must therefore be accompanied by changes in professional duties and professional training,[27] and by greater involvement of the prosecution in sentencing. Whether the greater involvement of the prosecution should be carried so far as permitting a prosecution appeal is doubtful in practice, since only a small number of defendants' appeals are able to be heard and judicial manpower should be devoted to these appeals if there is such pressure, but the case for introducing a right of prosecution appeal is compelling in principle.[28]

The question of the role of the prosecution brings the discussion back to the links between sentencing and penal policy in general. The creation of a Sentencing Council is an essential step, but is not sufficient. It would lead to a more systematic and holistic approach to sentencing policy – although this is not to minimize the complexity and profoundness of the issues to be determined – and ought to be combined with the procedural reforms. But sentencing policy should not be treated as a discrete issue: Chapter 3 described its close connection, not only with penal policy but also with prosecution policy and decisions taken at other stages in the criminal process. If it is to be at all accurate to speak of a 'criminal justice *system*', there must be a standing forum for the discussion and creation of policy initiatives. The Home Affairs Committee of the House of Commons, for example, recommended the creation of a National Criminal Policy Committee, with representatives from a wide range of agencies and bodies concerned in the administration of criminal justice, in order 'to construct a comprehensive criminal policy in the light of the most modern administrative knowledge and research findings'.[29] The Government rejected this recommendation in a 58-word sentence which says that when ministers want advice, they will ask for it.[30] This is too high-handed a response. Undoubtedly the Government and civil service do ask persons and bodies for their advice and comment from time to time, not least because it may be politically prudent to do so. But this means that they choose whom to consult and at what stage to do so, and there is no formal mechanism (other than Parliament itself, which is unsatisfactory for this purpose) for raising issues on which they do not choose to consult. This is an unacceptable method of proceeding in a society which aspires to democratic ideals. It also appears to be an unsuccessful method of proceeding, for particular sectional interests continue to have a disproportionate influence upon change. The Home Affairs Committee's ideal of a 'comprehensive criminal policy' must remain the goal, and a system which provides a forum in which to fashion this – and then to communicate with the Sentencing Council – is greatly to be preferred to a system which does not.

NOTES

Chapter 1: An introduction to sentencing

1 Strictly speaking, 'on obtaining information about his character and antecedents' (i.e. leaving out of account the facts of the offence of which he now stands convicted): Magistrates' Courts Act 1980, s. 38

2 Ditchfield, H.O.R.S. no. 37, p. 25.

3 See the discussion of 'stale' offences in Ch. 7, s. 5.

4 Tarling, H.O.R.S. no. 56, pp. 30–2.

5 Ibid., p. 33.

6 See Ch. 7, s. 6.

7 Magistrates' Courts Act 1980, s. 88.

8 Discussed further in Ch. 10, s. 2.

9 See Ch. 10, s. 3.

10 *Trowbridge* [1975] Crim. L.R. 295.

11 The actual provisions are extremely complicated: see Thomas (1982).

12 White Paper, *Young Offenders* (1980), para. 12.

13 Cf. Cross (1981) or, in greater detail, Thomas (1979).

14 Adapted from *Criminal Statistics, England and Wales* 1980 and 1981, Table 2.1. There were minor changes in counting procedures in recent years.

15 Adapted from *Criminal Statistics, England and Wales* 1980, Table 2.14, and 1981, Table 2.16.

16 In addition, some 1,100 indictable offences in 1980 resulted in the conviction of a limited company.

17 Part of Table 5.1 of *Criminal Statistics, England and Wales* 1980 and 1981. The two sets of figures for 1977 and 1978 reflect changes in the recording procedures, and thus make comparisons of earlier and later years rather inexact: this applies also to Tables 5 and 6 below.

18 Table 7.10 from *Criminal Statistics, England and Wales* 1981; see also note 17 above.

19 Ibid., Table 7.12.

20 Adapted from *Prison Statistics 1981*, Table 1.4.

21 Report of the Parole Board 1981.
22 *Prison Statistics 1981*, Table 4.5.
23 For some discussion of symbolism in sentencing, see Ch. 8, s. 1.
24 See Finnis (1972) and Galligan (1981) for detailed explanations.
25 Galligan (1981), p. 157.
26 See Bentham (1789), Ch. XIV, para. 6, and Morris (1974), pp. 59–62.
27 Bentham (1789), Ch. XIII, para. 17.
28 Denunciatory justifications are further discussed in Ch. 8, s. 1.
29 For further discussion, see Cross (1981), pp. 127–43, and Walker (1980), Ch. 2.
30 See Bottoms and Brownsword (1982) for elaboration.
31 Ibid.
32 For further discussion, see Ch. 9, s. 3.
33 Floud and Young (1981), p. 5.
34 Maguire (1982), pp. 138–42; cf. also Shapland (1982).
35 *Observer* (1982), and now Hough and Mayhew, H.O.R.S. no. 76, Ch. 5.
36 Cf. Thomas (1979), p. 235.
37 One attempt was that of Pease *et al.*, H.O.R.S. no. 39, Ch. 4. Cf. also Empey and Ericson (1972).
38 Bottoms (1973).
39 Walker, Farrington and Tucker (1981).
40 For a more detailed and precise discussion of the expectancy method, see Walker (1971); in their 1981 study, Walker, Farrington and Tucker improved the methodology by calculating 'corrected actual reconvictions'.
41 Phillpotts and Lancucki, H.O.R.S. no. 53, p. 16.
42 Softley, H.O.R.S. no. 46.
43 Walker, Farrington and Tucker (1981), p. 360.
44 Bottoms (1973)
45 See Ch. 7, s. 6.
46 Brody, H.O.R.S. no. 35, p. 39.
47 Ibid., p. 37.
48 Folkard, H.O.R.S. no. 36, *Impact*, vol. II. p. 21.
49 See Brody and Tarling, H.O.R.S. no. 64, p. 16, discussed in Ch. 9, s. 4.
50 *Prison Statistics 1981*, Table 8.1.
51 See Beyleveld (1979), Beyleveld (1980), and Walker (1980), Ch. 4.
52 Ross (1973).
53 Chapter 9, s. 3.
54 Harris (1981).
55 Cross (1981).
55a The writer of the leading Scottish work on sentencing, Nicholson

(1981), sits as a sheriff; chapter 10 contains a valuable discussion of general principles.

56 Road Traffic Act 1972, s. 93.

57 *Harrison* (1909) 2 Cr. App. R. 94.

58 *Gumbs* (1926) 19 Cr. App. R. 74.

59 See generally Zellick (1974).

60 Thomas (1979), p. 4.

61 (1980) 71 Cr. App. R. 360.

62 [1982] 1 W.L.R. 1090.

63 See, e.g., *Blick* [1981] Crim. L.R. 507, reviewing a line of precedents on lengths of sentence for incest.

64 [1982] Crim. L.R. 126.

65 As in several recent appeals against short prison sentences; see *Jones, Goodman* and *Pecht* [1981] Crim. L.R. 119–20.

66 *Rees* [1978] Crim. L.R. 298.

67 E.g. *Routley* [1982] Crim. L.R. 383.

68 In *Smith* [1982] Crim. L.R. 469, the Court stated that it had been 'helpfully referred' to three recent decisions which established a change of policy. To similar effect, see *Milne* [1983] (Crim. L.R. 277 and *Ball* [1983] Crim. L.R. 198.

69 See Ch. 10, s. 7.

70 S. 35 Criminal Justice Act 1972.

71 Against which there are strong arguments of principle: see Thomas (1972), Ashworth (1979), Zellick (1979) and King (1979).

72 (1980) 71 Cr. App. R. 360, discussed in Ch. 9, s. 4, and p. 133 below.

73 For sentencing in rape cases, see *Roberts* (1982) 74 Cr. App. R. 242; for sentencing levels for the importation, supply and possession of various drugs, see *Aramah* [1983] Crim. L.R. 271.

74 *Stoakes* [1981] Crim. L.R. 56.

75 (1980) 71 Cr. App. R. 381.

76 *Newsome and Browne* [1970] 2 Q.B. 711.

77 E.g. *French* [1982] Crim. L.R. 380, overruling two previous decisions as *per incuriam* (i.e. as having been reached in ignorance of an earlier decision on the point): see Ch. 6, s. 2.

78 Discussed in Ch. 9, s. 2.

79 E.g. policy in activating suspended sentences (*O'Donnell* [1982] Crim. L.R. 469) and in sentencing so-called 'social nuisances' (*Walsh* [1982] Crim. L.R. 247).

80 Thomas (1979) p. 8.

81 Kapardis and Farrington (1981), p. 114.

82 [1969] 2 Q.B. 29.

83 [1982] 1 W.L.R. 1090.

84 Hood (1962), Tarling, H.O.R.S. no. 56.

85 McConville and Baldwin (1982).
86 Hood (1972), p. 140.
87 Hogarth (1971), p. 211.
88 Cohen (1982).
89 Hood (1972), pp. 140–3.
90 Hogarth (1971), Ch. 13; cf. Hood (1962), Ch. 5, and Hood (1972), p. 141.
91 Hood (1972), p. 145.
92 Hogarth (1971) Chs. 5 to 9; Hood (1972).
93 Morris (1982).
94 See Ch. 9, s. 2.
95 Hogarth (1971), pp. 196–200.
96 Lemon (1974).
97 Hood (1972), p. 99; see the discussion in Ch. 8, s. 1.
98 Hood (1972), p. 141.
99 See Ch. 10, s. 4.
100 See the discussion of the 'penal ladder' approach in Ch. 10, s. 8.
101 Hood (1972), p. 124.
102 Diamond (1981), p. 407.
103 See Hood and Sparks (1970), Ch. 5.
104 See Ch. 10, s. 7.
105 See Editorial, [1980] Crim. L.R. 397.
106 (1980) 71 Cr. App. R. 360; See Ch. 9, s. 4.
107 See Editorial, [1980] Crim. L.R. 397.
108 Speech by Mr Leon Brittan, Minister of State at the Home Office, on 8 October 1980.
109 Ibid.
110 Evidence to the Home Affairs Committee of the House of Commons, on *The Prison System*, Minutes, pp. 221–2 and 250.
111 Ibid.
112 The Attorney-General's statement is summarized at [1980] Crim. L.R. 397ff.
113 The Attorney-General's Guidelines, (1982) 74 Cr. App. R. 302.
114 Cf. the discussion by Tutt (1981).
115 E.g., the Home Secretary's speech to the Leicestershire magistrates in February 1981.

Chapter 2: Judicial independence and discretion in sentencing

1 Jennings (1959), Ch. VIII; cf. the full discussion by Shetreet (1976).
2 Wade and Phillips (1977), p. 44.
3 Jennings (1959), pp. 241–2.
4 Hailsham (1981), p. 240.

5   (1970) 123 C.L.R. 52 at p. 65.
6   Ibid., p. 58; cf. also *Hinds* v. *R.* [1976] 1 All E.R. 353.
7   Stephen (1885), p. 755.
8   A.C.P.S. (1978), para. 317.
9   See s. 2 below.
10 Home Office *Review of Parole 1981*, para. 60.
11 Letter from Lawton LJ to *The Times*.
12 Above, p. 59.
13 See the discussion of parole in Ch. 9, s. 7.
14 Mr Roy Jenkins, Home Secretary, when declining to exercise the prerogative in favour of the 'Shrewsbury pickets' in 1974; H.C. Deb, vol. 883, col. 1788.
15 House of Commons Expenditure Committee (1978), para. 37.
16 Ibid., para. 238.
17 Ibid., para. 32.
18 A.C.P.S. (1977), para. 12.
19 Ibid., para. 16.
20 Ibid., para. 18.
21 Speech on 30 April 1980.
22 Bridge Committee (1978), para. 1.6.
23 Ibid., para. 3.20.
24 Devlin (1979), pp. 52–3.
25 Ibid., p. 44.
26 A.C.P.S. (1978), para. 164.
27 Sir Arthur James (1974), p. 167.
28 Ruggles-Brise (1900).
29 E.g. *Taylor* [1977] 3 All E.R. 627, *Roberts* (1982) 74 Cr. App. R. 242; and *Aramah* [1983] Crim. L.R. 271; see Ch. 1, s. 6.
30 A.C.P.S. (1978), para. 196, discussed in Cross (1981), pp. 209–13.
31 A.C.P.S. (1978), para. 317.
32 For an accessible summary and explanation, see L. T. Wilkins (1980).
33 Australian Law Reform Commission (1980).
34 For an accessible summary, see Tonry (1982).
35 A point emphasized by Thomas (1974), in his excellent essay on legislative techniques.
36 The effect of s. 31 Criminal Justice Act 1982, which allows the court to consider not only the circumstances *since* the suspended sentence was imposed but also the circumstances *in which* it was imposed, is to enable the court now to look at the original and subsequent offences together.
37 See *Lowe* [1964] 2 All E.R. 116, and the discussion in Thomas (1979), pp. 279–80.
38 'In 1947 the number of male young offenders received under

sentence of imprisonment was 2,572; in 1949 it was 1,187.' *Penal Practice in a Changing Society*, Cmd. 645 of 1959, para 29.

39   As Mr M. J. Moriarty, of the Home Office Criminal Policy Department, stated to the House of Commons Expenditure Committee, 'there is not very much evidence that it has greatly affected actual sentencing practice': Minutes of Evidence, vol. III, Q. 1835.

40   See Ch. 9, s. 2.

41   A.C.P.S. (1978), para. 207.

42   Advisory Council (1978), para. 216.

43   (1980) 71 Cr. App. R. 360, above, Ch. 1 s. 6.

44   A.C.P.S. (1978), paras. 312–19.

45   ALRC no. 15, Appendix B, pp. 428–30.

46   See further D. A. Thomas (1977) and M. H. Tonry and N. Morris (1978).

47   This is not to support the Advisory Council's view of the function of statutory maxima; for criticism, see Cross (1981), pp. 41–3.

48   Law Com. no. 29, *Offences of Damage to Property*, para. 13.

49   Criminal Law Revision Committee, 8th Report, *Theft and Related Offences*, para. 11.

50   Criminal Law Revision Committee, 14th Report, para. 3.

51   Criminal Law Revision Committee, Working Paper on Sexual Offences (1980).

52   Ch. 1, s. 9.

53   Criminal Law Revision Committee, 14th Report, para. 152.

54   See s. 4 of this chapter.

55   See Ch. 4, s. 2.

56   See Ch. 4, s. 2.

57   Policy Advisory Committee on Sexual Offences (1981), para. 47.

58   Criminal Law Revision Committee, Working Paper on Sexual Offences (1980), para. 72.

59   See Ch. 4, *passim*.

60   See Ch. 4, s. 2.

61   *Ekwuyasi* [1981] Crim. L.R. 574.

62   *Hudson* (1979) 1 Cr. App. R. (S) 310, *Singh* [1981] Crim. L.R. 724.

63   *Stosiek* [1982] Crim. L.R. 615 and commentary.

64   *Taggart* (1979) 1 Cr. App. R. (S) 144.

65   *Michaels and Skoblo* [1981] Crim. L.R. 725 and commentary, *Milligan* [1982] Crim. L.R. 317, approved in *Ball* [1983] Crim. L.R. 198.

66   *Brown* [1982] Crim. L.R. 53, *Fisher* [1982] Crim. L.R. 191, *Booker* [1982] Crim. L.R. 378 and *Newton* [1983] Crim. L. R. 199.

67   Compare *Anderson* [1977] Crim. L.R. 757 with *French* [1982] Crim. L.R. 380; see also *Rubinstein and Grandison* [1982] Crim. L.R. 614

and commentary.

68 *D.P.P.* v. *Anderson* [1978] 2 All E.R. 512; cf. Ch. 7, s. 1.

69 *Huchison* [1972] 1 All E.R. 936.

70 *Singh and Singh* [1981] Crim. L.R. 509.

71 *Michaels and Skoblo* [1981] Crim. L.R. 725.

72 *Craine* [1981] Crim. L.R. 727.

73 Compare *Russen* [1981] Crim. L.R. 573 with *Connor* [1981] Crim. L.R. 791. *Ayensu* [1982] Crim. L.R. 764 is closer to *Connor*.

74 *Robinson* (1969) 53 Cr. App. R. 314.

75 *Long* [1980] Crim. L.R. 315.

76 *Stosiek* [1982] Crim. L.R. 615.

77 See generally Thomas (1979), pp. 366–72, and Cross (1981), pp. 89–92.

78 Thomas (1982a) pp. 173–4.

79 Ashworth (1979).

80 See Ch. 8, s. 4.

81 (1969) 53 Cr. App.R. 314.

82 *French* [1982] Crim. L.R. 380 and above, at note 52.

Chapter 3: Penal Policy and Sentencing Policy

1 *R* v. *Metropolitan Police Commissioner, ex parte Blackburn* [1968] Q. B.; see generally D. G. T. Williams (1974).

2 Police Act 1964, s. 38.

3 Royal Commission on Criminal Procedure (1981), Ch.7; cf. [1982] Crim. L.R. 626.

4 R. M. Morris (1980), p. 140.

5 Croft (1982), p. 4.

6 E.g. Brody and Tarling, H.O.R.S. no.64, pp. 31–7; see below, Ch. 9, s. 4.

7 Criminal Justice Act 1972, s. 35; for discussion, see Jaconelli (1981).

8 Lord Simon, quoted in A. F. Wilcox (1972), p. 21.

9 Prosecution of Offences Regulations, 1978.

10 See note 3, above.

11 M. J. Moriarty (1977), p. 130.

12 Above, Ch. 2, s. 2.

13 The discussion here is intended to be adequate only for an understanding of the context of sentencing. More detailed treatment may be found in such works as Walker (1971), Hood and Sparks (1970, Chs. 1 and 2) and Bottomley and Coleman (1981).

14 See Ch. 1, s. 3.

15 Hough and Mayhew, H.O.R.S. no. 76; Hood and Sparks (1970, Ch. 1).

16 See Sparks, Genn and Dodd (1977), and cf. *Criminal Statistics* (1979), Introduction, para. 2.2, reporting that victim surveys in 1972 and 1979 suggested that a similar proportion (about half) of domestic burglaries and thefts were reported to the police in each year. But see note 15.

17 See, for example, McCabe and Sutcliffe (1978), p. 38, Zander (1979), p. 205, and Bottomley and Coleman (1981), p. 44.

18 The figure was 9 per cent if cycle thefts were included; for this and a general discussion, see Bottomley and Coleman (1981), Ch. 4.

19 McCabe and Sutcliffe (1978), p. 73.

20 Chatterton, in Borland (1978), Ch. 2, esp. pp. 41–7; cf. Mawby (1980).

21 Further discussed by Walker (1971), Ch. 3, and Bottomley and Coleman (1981), pp. 95–101.

22 Further discussed by Steer (1970) and by Ditchfield (1976).

23 Royal Commission on Criminal Procedure (1981), summarized at [1981] Crim. L.R. 441.

24 Lidstone *et al.* (1980).

25 Shea (1974).

26 See Ch. 2, s. 3, above.

27 Devlin, J., in *Re Beresford* (1952) 36 Cr.App.R.1.

28 *Criminal Statistics* (1978), Introduction, pp. 86–8.

29 See Ch. 8, s. 3.

30 Cornish (1968), p. 181.

31 McCabe and Purves (1974), pp. 53–4.

32 Baldock (1980), pp. 149–50.

33 Australian Law Reform Commission, *Sentencing Federal Offenders* (1980).

34 Mr William Waldegrave MP, in Home Affairs Committee (1981), p. 245.

35 Sir Graham Page MP, ibid., p. 239.

36 *Young Offenders* (1980).

37 Hood (1974a), p. 396.

38 [1969] 2 Q.B. 29.

39 Bottoms (1981), p. 3.

40 Advisory Council on the Treatment of Offenders, *Alternatives to Short-Term Imprisonment* (1957).

41 White Paper, *The Adult Offender* (1965), para. 5.

42 Hall Williams (1970), p. 184–5.

43 See the Home Secretary's Guidelines on Parole of 1975, reproduced in the Home Office's *Review of Parole* (1981), Appendix A; and Home Office Research Study no. 38, *Parole in England and Wales*.

44 A.C.P.S. (1970), para, 33.

45 Wootton (1973), p. 16.
46 A.C.P.S. (1970), para. 72.
47 Now, Powers of Criminal Courts Act 1973, s. 1.
48 'Criminology and Penal Change', Hood (1974a), p. 375.
49 Wootton, in Walker (1977), p. 19; cf. also Wootton (1978), pp. 126–7.
50 Hood, *Tolerance and the Tariff* (1974b), p. 14.
51 Ibid., p. 8.
52 Hood (1974a), p. 142.
53 Ibid.
54 A.C.P.S. (1970), para. 37.
55 Home Office (1972), para. 32.
56 See Ch. 10, s. 5.
57 Ch. 1, s. 3.
58 A.C.P.S. (1977), para. 8.
59 Brody, H.O.R.S. no. 35; see Ch. 1, s. 5.
60 A.C.P.S. (1977), para. 10.
61 H.O.R.S. no. 35, p. 38.
62 [1976] *The Magistrate*, p. 189.
63 See the remark of Mr Waldegrave MP, text at note 34 above.
64 Brody and Tarling, H.O.R.S. no. 64, p. 17.
65 Ibid., p. 18.
66 Speech to National Association of Probation Officers, 17 May 1980.
67 *Prison Statistics, England and Wales*, 1979, p. 80.
68 See Ch. 10, s. 3.
69 See Ch. 9, s. 2.
70 See Ch. 9, s. 2.
71 A.C.P.S. (1977), para. 5.
72 *Review of Criminal Justice Policy*, 1976, p. 5.
73 Which occurred in 1972 and 1977.
74 Conservative Party (1979), p. 19.
75 Home Secretary's speech to Leicestershire Magistrates, 18 February 1980.
76 A.C.P.S. (1977), para. 12.
77 89. A.C.P.S. (1977), para. 14.
78 White Paper, *The Reduction of Pressure on the Prison System* (1980), para. 9, quoting from House of Commons Expenditure Committee (1978), paras, 45 and 48.
79 See Ch. 9, s. 8, and p. 62 above.
80 (1974) 60 Cr.App.R. 74.
81 *Upton* (1980) 71 Cr.App.R. 102 at p. 104.
82 *Bibi* (1980) 71 Cr.App.R. 360, and the decisions reported in that volume at pp. 363–82.

83 [1969] 2 Q.B. 29, above, p. 45.

84 Ch. 10, s. 4.

85 A.C.P.S. (1978), paras. 218–20.

86 The research was to be carried out by a team from the Centre for Criminological Research, University of Oxford; a pilot study of 25 judges was completed.

87 Summarized in Home Office Research Bulletin No. 5 (1978), p. 12.

88 See Ch. 2, s. 2.

89 See Ch. 11, s. 3.

90 In his oral evidence to the House of Commons Home Affairs Committee (1981), p. 240.

91 See The Government Reply to the Fourth Report from the Home Affairs Committee, Session 1980–1 HC 412, *The Prison Service* (Cmnd. 8446 of 1981), p. 21.

Chapter 4: Constructing Culpability

1 Ch. 1, s. 4.

2 Streatfeild Report, para. 262.

3 Hart, (1963), pp. 35–6.

4 Ibid., pp. 36–7.

5 Ch. 8, s. 4.

6 Hart (1968), p. 171.

7 (1975) 61 Cr. App. R. 67, at pp. 90–2.

8 See discussion below, p. 146.

9 See Cross (1981), pp. 176–7, and Ch. 1, s. 6, at note 73.

10 Von Hirsch (1976), p. 69.

11 Ibid., p. 73.

12 Priestley, Fears and Fuller (1977), p. 101.

13 [1977] Crim. L.R. 198; cf. also the conflicting Scottish approaches described by Morris and McIsaac (1978), p. 141.

14 Bentham (1948), p. 312, note 1.

15 Hood (1974b), pp. 7–8.

16 H. Kelsen (1967), p. 36.

17 Ibid., p. 54.

18 Hart (1961), p. 190.

19 See Ch. 8, s. 4.

20 M. Chatterton, in Borland (1976), pp. 26–7.

21 Ibid., p. 27.

22 Below, pp. 167–71.

23 See further Cross (1981), pp. 146–51, although this was written before the decision in *Caldwell* (below).

24 *Caldwell* [1981] 1 All E.R. 961.

25   C.L.R.C. (1980), para. 152.

26   Thomas (1979), pp. 93–9; for a clear example of the differing gravity of planned and spontaneous affrays, see *Annett and Moore* (1980) 2 Cr.App.R. (S) 318.

27   See Bentham (1789), Ch. XI, para. 42.

28   Below, pp. 176–7.

29   Compare Thomas (1979), p. 94 with p. 103.

30   Hadden (1968), pp. 534–5.

31   See Ch. 2, s. 4.

32   C.L.R.C. (1980), para. 120.

33   Thomas (1979), pp. 83–5; cf. *Simpson* (1981) 3 Cr.App.R.(S) 148.

34   *Boyd* (1980) 2 Cr.App.R.(S) 234.

35   See further Ashworth, in Tapper (1981).

36   Cox (1877), p. 97.

37   Ibid.

38   This is not to argue that negligence can never be defended as a ground for criminal liability; the fact that it is not widely used in offences against the person is used as a justification for not bringing negligence into this discussion. Nor is this to argue that a person is necessarily to blame *in proportion to* what he intended or knowingly risked: quite apart from the variations of mental attitudes discussed earlier, other factors (such as the offender's control over the situation) remain to be considered.

39   See Ch. 2, s. 4.

40   See Ch. 2, s. 4.

41   C.L.R.C. (1980), para. 171.

42   See the case of *Hall*, discussed in Thomas (1979), p. 98, where the sentence was reduced because (among other factors) the offender did not realize that his victims were policemen.

43   Cox (1877), pp. 107–8.

44   Criminal Law Commissioners (1839), 4th Report, p. xxi.

45   *Howe* [1978] Crim. L.R. 50 (attack on ticket collectors and upon member of public coming to their assistance).

46   [1976] Crim. L.R. 144.

47   *Dytham* (1979) 69 Cr.App. R. 387.

48   *Guddoy* [1978] Crim. L.R. 366 (housemaster convicted of assaulting mentally subnormal boys in his charge). 'Breach of public trust' is further discussed below, pp. 194–7.

49   [1968] Crim. L.R. at p. 535.

49a   The previous conduct must be duly proved: see pp. 92–4 above.

50   See Thomas (1979), pp. 79–81.

51   Below, p. 167–71.

52   Thomas (1979), pp. 79–81.

53   Harding (1979) 765, at p. 774.

54   Cox (1877), pp. 96–7.
55   *French* [1982] Crim. L.R. 380; the issue is discussed in detail in Ch. 6, at pp. 253–7.
56   Elliott (1957), p. 290, quoting Mr Michael Stewart MP in the House of Commons.
57   C.L.R.C. (1976), para. 109.
58   See Ashworth (1975), Thomas (1979), pp. 76–9 and Wasik (1982).
59   See below, pp. 174–7.
60   Cox (1877), p. 7.
61   See above, p. 151; 'reckless' is used here in the common law, not the *Caldwell*, sense.
62   Butler Report (1975), para. 18.51.
63   Apart from arguments about whether negligence or even strict liability ought to be sufficient for some offences.
64   C.L.R.C. (1980), para. 120.
65   Nagel (1976), p. 140.
66   Hart (1968), p. 152.
67   Ibid., p. 153.
68   Kenny (1978), pp. 32–4.
69   Ibid., p. 44.
70   Hart (1968), p. 153.
71   *Bancroft* [1981] Crim. L.R. 577.
72   West (1973); cf. generally also von Hirsch (1976), esp. Ch. 17.
73   West (1973), p. 191.
74   Mayhew *et al.* (1981).
75   *Clarke* [1982] 1 W.L.R. 1090 at p. 1097.
76   James Committee (1975), para. 84.
77   See below, p. 184.
78   See Ch. 2, s. 4.
79   On which, see p. 173, above.
80   James Committee (1975), para. 92.
81   Ibid.
82   On which, see below, pp. 198–9.
83   Bentham used the term 'secondary consequences', but in a rather different sense: (1789) Ch. XII, paras. 4 and 5.
84   Streatfeild Report, para. 90; *Bibi* (1980) 71 Cr.App.R. 360.
85   E.g. Howard (1981), Clarke and Lewis (1982).
86   Maguire (1980), and Maguire (1982), pp. 129f.
87   See above, s. 2(h).
88   In *Stagg* (1980) 2 Cr.App.R. (S) 53, one of the reasons given by the Court of Appeal for reducing a long sentence for persistent incest was that the daughter/victim appeared to have suffered no permanent emotional damage. If, however, there is a substantial risk of such damage (see Bailey and McCabe (1979), p. 760),

should the offender benefit from its chance non-occurrence?

89 See Ch. 5, pp. 235–9.
90 Levi (1981), Appendix B.
91 Levi (1981).
92 Leigh (1981). Cf. also Hodden (1983).
93 E.g. Hood's 1972 survey of magistrates' rankings.
94 Sellin and Wolfgang (1964).
95 Sparks, Genn and Dodd (1977), Ch. VII; see pp. 182–90 for their discussion of the significance of their own findings.
96 The precise meaning of the phrase 'attached by the law' is unclear: the statutory maximum sentences for the various offences differ from the ranking (e.g. the lowest-ranked offence, theft from shop, carries a maximum penalty of 10 years' imprisonment whereas the assaults ranked 10 and 12 carry much lower maxima), and it is by no means clear that sentencing practice accords with this ranking.
97 Sparks, Genn and Dodd (1977), p. 185.
98 Ibid.
99 Maguire (1982), pp. 138–42.
100 E.g. *Partridge* [1976] Crim. L.R. 641; *Roth* (1980) 2 Cr.App.R. (S) 65; *Macleod* [1982] Crim. L.R. 61.
101 Floud and Young (1981), p. 54.
102 Ibid.
103 See the discussion by Floud and Young (1981), Ch. 1.
104 Lord Elwyn Jones LC, Presidential Address to the Magistrates' Association, [1976] *The Magistrate* 188.
105 Above, pp. 157–9.
106 Above, pp. 162–4.
107 See above, p. 160.
108 Cox (1877), p. 55.
109 *Wooding* [1978] Crim. L.R. 701.
110 Deane (1981).
111 *Usher* (1980) 2 Cr.App.R. (S) 123.
112 Cox (1877), p. 55.
113 (1980) 2 Cr.App.R. (S) 3.
114 'Where the offence of the defendant is difficult to discover or where the offence can be easily carried out', it was held in *Lord* (1979) 1 Cr.App.R. (S) 177 that the usual leniency shown to a first offender might be withheld, in part at least. Cf. also *Regan* [1977] Crim. L.R. 52.
115 See Ch. 1, s. 5.
116 E.g. *Hume* [1973.] Crim. L.R.320.
117 Cf. Trivizas (1981).
118 See pp. 167–71 and 176–7 above.
119 *Principles of Penal Law* (Works, Bowring ed., vol. I), p. 400.

120 A.C.P.S. (1978), para. 164.
121 See Levi (1981) and Maguire (1982).
122 Floud and Young (1981), p. 52.
123 Bentham (1789), Ch. XIV, para. 25.

Chapter 5: Punishing Persistence

1   Radzinowicz and Hood (1980), esp. pp. 1357–68.
2   The quotation is taken from the Home Office circular to Chief Constables about the 1908 Act. See Radzinowicz and Hood (1980) at p. 1371.
3   See Radzinowicz and Hood (1980) at p. 1372.
4   Report of the Departmental Committee on Persistent Offenders (1932), para. 42.
5   See Hammond and Chayen (1963), p. 11.
6   See [1962] 1 All E.R. 671.
7   Advisory Council on the Treatment of Offenders (1963).
8   Hammond and Chayen (1963); West (1963).
9   *The Adult Offender* (1965).
10 Thomas (1979), p. 41.
11 *Queen* [1982] Crim. L.R. 56.
12 [1959] Crim. L.R. 530.
13 [1970] A.C. 642 at p. 650.
14 Von Hirsch (1981), p. 602, altering position slightly from Von Hirsch (1976), p. 85.
15 E.g. *Lalor* [1982] Crim. L.R. 60, a 'first offender' asking for 220 other offences to be taken into consideration.
16 See the discussion in section 6(c) of this chapter.
17 *Williams* (1976), quoted by Thomas (1979), p. 42.
18 See s. 7, below.
19 Report of the Departmental Committee on Persistent Offenders (1932). para. 24.
20 This is not to say that they are *necessarily* more likely to convict: see the report of the L.S.E. Jury Project [1973] Crim. L.R. 208.
21 Report of the Departmental Committee on Persistent Offenders (1932), para. 3.
22 For the history of sentencing theory and practice at this time, see D. A. Thomas (1978) and Radzinowicz and Hood (1979).
23 See particularly Thomas (1978).
24 See Radzinowicz and Hood (1979), pp. 1311–12.
25 (1977) 66 Cr. App. R. 118.
26 See text at note 31, below.
27 (1980) 2 Cr. App. R. (S) 312.
28 Per Lord Widgery CJ, in *Leadley* (1977) 66 Cr. App. R. 118 at

p. 119.

29 Sir Walter Moberly (1968), p. 54.
30 See Radzinowicz and Hood (1979), pp. 1310–11.
31 (1977) 66 Cr. App. R. at p. 119.
32 See Radzinowicz and Hood (1980), p. 1329.
33 *D.P.P.* v. *Ottewell* [1970] A.C. 642 at p. 650.
34 See Ch. 9, s. 2.
35 See Radzinowicz and Hood (1979), p. 1310.
36 See Radzinowicz and Hood (1980), p. 1330.
37 Brody and Tarling, H.O.R.S. no. 64, p. 14, for various projections of a similar kind.
38 Above, note 31.
39 For an attempt to identify special classes of persistent offenders, see below, s. 6.
40 Cf. the category of 'professional criminals', below, s. 6(b).
41 See Radzinowicz and Hood (1980), pp. 1330–1.
42 See Radzinowicz and Hood (1979), pp. 1324–5.
43 Brody and Tarling, H.O.R.S. no. 64, pp. 12–14; below, pp. 348–52.
44 Fairhead, H.O.R.S. no. 66, esp. pp. 47–8.
45 See below, section 6(c).
46 House of Commons (1981), p. 246.
47 Above, at note 27.
48 Morris (1974), p. 79.
49 See Ch. 1, s. 5.
50 See Ch. 9, *passim*.
51 Morris (1974), p. 60.
52 Editorial [1980] Crim. L.R. 1–4.
53 See Ch. 2, s. 3.
54 Von Hirsch (1976), pp. 85–6. His argument is that 'the fact-finding process of the criminal law' is 'crude', but that the possibility of mistaken ascriptions of culpability decreases with successive convictions. On the other hand, is there not the danger of stereotyping or pre-judging a defendant with previous convictions? See above, p. 211.
55 E.g. Fletcher (1978), p. 466.
56 Report of the Departmental Committee on Persistent Offenders (1932), para. 24.
57 Von Hirsch (1981), p. 606–7.
58 Ibid., pp. 602–3.
59 Ibid., p. 616.
60 Ibid.
61 Von Hirsch (1976), pp. 86–7.
62 University of Sydney, Proceedings of the Institute of Criminology

no. 38 (1980), p. 37.

63   The best-known authority is *Brighton* [1963] Crim. L.R. 64. The principle that a suspended sentence need not be fully activated if the breach occurs towards the end of the operational period (e.g. *Kilroy* (1979) 1 Cr. App. R. (S) 179) probably has the same rationale.

64   *Fox* (1980) 2 Cr. App. R. (S) 188; cf. the decisions which suggest that a conviction-free gap may indicate the appropriateness of a community service order instead of a custodial sentence: *Lawrence* [1982] Crim. L.R. 377 and *Canfield* [1982] Crim. L.R. 460. See below, Ch. 10. s. 4.

65   See Ch. 2, s. 4.

66   Cf. Twentieth Century Fund Task Force (1976), p. 41.

67   See Ch. 9, pp. 343–6.

68   [1959] Crim. L.R. 530; above, p. 000.

69   Report of the Departmental Committee on Persistent Offenders (1932), para. 21.

70   [1979] Crim. L.R. 262.

71   [1979] Crim. L.R. 263.

72   Thomas (1979), p. 150.

73   See the discussion in Ch. 4, s. 4.

74   A.C.P.S. (1978), para. 217.

75   Ibid., para. 204.

76   (1980) 2 Cr. App. R. (S) 35.

77   Floud and Young (1981).

78   See the July 1982 issue of the *British Journal of Criminology*, *passim*.

79   Cf. Floud and Young (1981), Ch. 1, and above, Ch. 4, s. 2.

80   Bottoms and Brownsword (1982).

81   A.C.P.S. (1978), para. 207.

82   Ibid., para. 198.

83   Floud and Young (1981), pp. 118–19.

84   Radzinowicz and Hood (1981).

85   See Ch. 2, s. 3.

86   See Table 11, in Ch. 1, s. 5(b).

87   Floud and Young (1981), Appendix C.

88   Walker (1982), p. 277, argues that we can predict future 'violence', but that includes conduct from minor assaults upwards.

89   Floud and Young (1981), p. 49.

90   Ibid., p. 111.

91   *Hodgson* (1967) 52. Cr. App. R. 113.

92   Cross (1981), pp. 49-50; cf. *Hay* [1983] Crim. L.R. 276.

93   Brody and Tarling, H.O.R.S. no. 64, p. 33.

94   Ibid., pp. 33–4.

95   A.C.P.S. (1978), Ch. 11.

96 Floud and Young (1981), p. 86.

97 (1981) 3 Cr. App. R. (S) 144.

98 [1982] Crim. L.R. 316; cf. also *Chadbund* [1983] Crim. L.R. 48.

99 Bottoms and Brownsword (1982) accept that protective sentences might be justified in cases of 'vivid danger'.

100 Report of the Departmental Committee on Prisons (1895), p. 335.

101 Radzinowicz and Hood (1980), p. 1354.

102 Ibid., p. 1360.

103 Ibid., p. 1371.

104 Above, p. 207.

105 See the historical sketch above, s. 1.

106 A.C.P.S. (1978), para. 207.

107 A.C.P.S. (1978), para. 204.

108 (1980) 2 Cr. App. R. (S) 191; see also *Dowling* (1981) 3 Cr. App. R. (S) 7.

109 E.g. J. A. Mack (1975) and M. McIntosh (1975), for discussions of the slightly different category of organized crime; cf. Maguire (1982), pp. 64, 65 and 81, for discussion of 'professionalism' in burglary.

110 See Ch. 9, s. 3.

111 *Crick* [1982] Crim. L.R. 129, on the possession of elaborate machinery for forging coins.

112 Fairhead, H.O.R.S. no. 66.

113 Ibid., p. 2.

114 (1975) 61 Cr. App. R. 320.

115 Fairhead, H.O.R.S. no. 66, pp. 47–8; this kind of incapacitative reasoning was also advanced by the Court of Appeal when dealing with the persistent shoplifter in *Gilbertson* (1980) 2 Cr. App. R. (S) 312.

116 The decisions are discussed in Cross (1981), p. 58; cf. now *O'Donnell* [1982] Crim. L.R. 469.

117 Bottoms (1981), p. 6.

118 A.C.P.S. (1977), para. 14.

119 See Ch. 9, at pp. 330–3.

120 Von Hirsch (1981), p. 603, quoted at p. 223 above.

121 Bottoms (1981), p. 18.

122 '. . . those given the suspended sentence will, like those given any sentence, be broadly divisible into three categories: those likely to re-offend (regardless of the penalty imposed), those likely not to re-offend (regardless of penalty), and those in a middle range of probability' (Bottoms (1981), p. 18).

123 Unreported, see Thomas (1979), p. 235.

124 Ibid.

125 Unreported, see Thomas (1979), p. 235.

126 Bottoms (1981), pp. 19–20.
127 See Ch. 9, s. 8.
128 This is the effect of Part I of the Criminal Justice Act 1982.

Chapter 6: Multiple Offenders

1 E.g. Lawton LJ in *Ambrose* (1973) 57 Cr. App. R. 538.
2 Cf. [1980] Crim. L.R. at p. 400.
3 *Broad* (1979) 68 Cr. App. R. 281.
4 Cf. above, pp. 92–4.
5 *D.P.P.* v. *Anderson* [1978] 2 All E.R. 512; on this question and the related sentencing problems, see generally Cross (1981), pp. 87–92.
6 Thomas (1979), p. 55.
7 Ibid., n. 12.
8 If the burglary was charged under s. 9(1) (a) rather than s. 9(1) (b) of the Theft Act 1968.
9 Burglary contrary to s. 9(1)(b) includes the infliction of grievous bodily harm, but no lesser form of violence. Aggravated burglary (s. 10) concerns the carrying, not the use, of weapons.
10 Thomas (1979), p. 54; a similar set of issues arises on the determination of whether multiple charges 'form or are a part of a series of offences of the same or similar character', and so may be tried together (Indictment Rules, r. 9); see discussion in Archbold (1982), paras. 1.75–1.77.
11 Thomas (1979), p. 54.
12 Ibid., p. 55.
13 [1973] Crim. L.R. 642.
14 Thomas (1979), p. 55, n. 5.
15 (1972) 56 Cr. App. R. 594.
16 (1979) 1 Cr. App. R. (S) 166.
17 [1981] Crim. L.R. 346.
18 [1982] Crim. L.R. 380, with eloquent commentary by D. A. Thomas.
19 Ch. 4, s. 2.
20 (1972) 56 Cr. App. R. 298.
21 Thomas (1979), p. 54.
22 A.C.P.S. (1978), para. 218.
23 Thomas (1979), p. 56.
24 Ibid., p. 58.
25 Above, ch. 4, s. 5.
26 Sellin and Wolfgang (1978), Introduction; see above, pp. 189–90.
27 Pease *et al.* (1974).
28 Thomas (1979), p. 58.

29   (1965) 4 C.C.C. 289.

30   (1975) 61 Cr. App. R. 67.

31   Above, p. 142.

32   (1975) 61 Cr. App. R. at pp. 91–2.

33   Thomas (1979), p. 59.

34   [1962] 2 Q.B. 377.

35   There is an ambiguity here: does the 'normal bracket' refer to burglaries, residential burglaries, or residential burglaries of the particular kind committed (e.g. without violence, and with amounts less than £1,000)? It is difficult, as Thomas himself recognizes, to identify 'normal brackets' for burglary: Thomas (1979), pp. 147–51.

36   A.C.P.S. (1978), para 219.

37   Discussed in Ch. 9, s. 2.

38   For an illustration, see *Hamilton* (1980) 2 Cr. App. R. (S) 229.

39   See *Kemp* (1979) 69 Cr. App. R. 350; the question of general deterrent sentencing is examined in Ch. 9, s. 3.

40   [1976] Crim. L.R. 694; the sentencing of 'dangerous' offenders is discussed in Ch. 5, s. 6(i).

41   [1978] Crim. L.R. 574.

42   See Ch. 5, s. 6(i).

43   [1981] Crim. L.R. 265.

44   *Britten* [1969] 1 All E.R. 517.

45   See *Young* [1973] Crim. L.R. 575, and *Millen* (1980) 2 Cr. App. R. (S) at p. 360; cf. Ch. 8, s. 3.

46   See notes 39 and 40 above, and text thereat.

Chapter 7: Two Principles of Equality

1   Gross (1979), p. 446.

2   Bentham (1789) Ch. VI, para. 6, note 1.

3   Ibid., para. 6.

4   Ibid., para. 43.

5   Ibid., para. 44.

6   [1981] Crim. L.R. 272.

7   By rule 43 of the Prison Rules, a prison governor is empowered to segregate an inmate for his own protection. See the discussion in the text below.

8   *Jones* (1980) 2 Cr. App. R. (S) 134.

9   Cf. Moody and Tombs (1982), Ch. 4, p. 66.

10   Walker (1980), p. 123.

11   The Court was strongly sympathetic to this view in *Holmes* (1979) 1 Cr. App. R. (S) 233 and *Weeks*, ibid., p. 239, both sex cases, but in *Kirby*, ibid., p. 214, a case of an informer, the Court held that

this was a matter for the Parole Board and not for the sentencer.
12   Bentham (1789), Ch. XIV, para. 14.
13   For the corollary of increasing a fine for the very wealthy offender and lengthening imprisonment for the hardened 'gaol-bird', see below, p. 296.
14   Walker (1980), p. 81.
15   Gross (1979), p. 455.
16   See Ch. 1, sections 4 and 5.
17   E.g., see Thomas (1979), pp. 211–13.
18   L. Taylor (1976), p. 12; some support for these class differences may be found in Table 3 of Farrington and Bennett (1981), p. 130.
19   Von Hirsch (1976), p. 90.
20   Cf. Cross (1981), pp. 189–90.
21   Bottoms (1981), p. 18.
22   Cf. Bottoms (1973); reconviction rates do depend to some extent on enforcement policies, however (see Ch. I, s. 5(b)), and those policies may be affected by bias towards some sections of the community and away from other sections.
23   Jardine *et al.* (1983).
24   (1953) 37 Cr. App. R. 125.
25   E.g. *Copley* (1979) 1 Cr. App. R. (S) 55.
26   See s. 5(a), below.
27   See Chapter 10, s. 7(d).
28   Compare the massive fines and suspended sentences in *Milbern and Simon* [1981] Crim. L.R. 511, with immediate prison sentences for shoplifting and D.H.S.S. fraud: see note 40 below.
29   E.g. *Hanbury*, discussed below at pp. 290–1.
30   E.g. *Sisodia* (1979) 1 Cr. App. R. (S) 291.
31   [1981] Crim. L.R. 59; to the same effect is *Roe* [1982] Crim. L.R. 57.
32   [1981] Crim. L.R. 59.
33   (1980) 2 Cr. App. R. (S) 284.
34   Thomas at [1982] Crim. L.R. 57–8.
35   Wilcox (1972), pp. 66–8.
36   See the discussion by Walker (1980), pp. 132–4.
37   [1982] Crim. L.R. 53; also *Stanbury* [1981] Crim. L.R. 845.
38   [1975] Crim. L.R. 113; to similar effect, see *Reeves* (1972) 56 Cr. App. R. 366, and *Ball* [1982] Crim. L.R. 131.
39   [1980] Crim. L.R. 191; cf. *French* [1977] Crim. L.R. 116, where a suspended sentence was upheld on apparently similar reasoning, although it was stated that a sentence of immediate imprisonment *would* have been appropriate, and argued that a suspended sentence would cause less hardship than a fine.
40   It might also be noted that when dealing with cases of tax evasion

courts seem willing to contemplate a relatively short term of imprisonment combined with a substantial fine (e.g. *Hodkinson* [1981] Crim. L.R. 117, *Ford* [1981] Crim. L.R. 352), a course not usually possible where the offence is D.H.S.S. fraud and the offender poorer (e.g. *Boyle* [1981] Crim. L.R. 350).

41   Some would contend (as in *French*, note 39 above) that a suspended sentence is less severe than a fine; that is arguable where an offender has no previous convictions (since he is unlikely to be reconvicted during the operational period), but the fact remains that if the offender is reconvicted during the operational period (which is more likely if he has previous convictions) the second court is likely to have to activate the suspended sentence and send him to prison – its choice is restricted.

42   See Thomas (1979), p. 321; one year is the maximum period for community service.

43   A.C.P.S. (1970), para. 18.

44   One attempt to justify what is here dismissed as a 'crude conception' is the argument of the Chicago Economic School that penalties should reflect the true economic cost of offences. All offenders, rich or poor, should be required to pay for the costs of their offending, and this will have the proper deterrent effect; see Posner (1977), pp. 163–78.

45   Cf. A.C.P.S. (1970), para. 20 and Appendix B.

46   A.C.P.S. (1970), para. 19.

47   *The Reduction of Pressure on the Prison System*, Cmnd. 7948 of 1980, pp. 4–5.

48   *Report of Interdepartmental Working Party on Road Traffic Law*, H.M.S.O. 1981.

49   (1980) 2 Cr. App. R. (S) 315.

50   [1981] *The Magistrate*, p. 152.

51   Thomas (1970), p. 221, repeated at [1981] Crim. L.R. 191.

52   (1979) 1 Cr. App. R. (S) 243 at p. 245.

53   Above, p. 278.

54   A.C.P.S. (1970), para. 18.

55   The argument is less clear-cut than it may appear, because the fines are for loitering or soliciting for the purpose of prostitution, whilst the money is earned from the act of prostitution (which is not a criminal offence). Fines for soliciting may lead prostitutes to adopt lawful methods of attracting clients. By s. 71 of the Criminal Justice Act 1982, imprisonment for soliciting was abolished.

56   Cf. A.C.P.S. (1978), para. 204, referring to professional offenders by whom 'the gains from such crimes were being regarded as sufficient recompense for serving shorter sentences.'

57   Hart (1968), p. 5.

58 The complexity of this notion will not be explored here; cf. Galligan, in Tapper (1981), p. 155, and above, Ch. 1, s. 4.
59 See Cross (1981), pp. 64–6.
60 Cf. *Forsythe* (1980) 2 Cr. App. R. (S) 15.
61 See *Agius* [1979] Crim. L.R. 672, *Colton* [1981] Crim. L.R. 58.
62 Hodgson Committee on Forfeiture, set up in 1980 by the Howard League.
63 As the Court remarked in *Ford* [1981] Crim. L.R. 352.
64 Criminal Justice Act 1982, s. 67; this raises issues about punishment and compensation which are not pursued here.
65 Walker (1980), p. 122; the Court of Appeal has distinguished between co-defendants aged 39 and 22 on the ground that 'there is a world of difference in the responsibility to be attached to two men of these very different ages'. *Turner* (1976), quoted by Thomas (1979), p. 68, n. 1.
66 Above, s. 6(b).
67 Quotations from the decisions cited by Thomas (1979) at pp. 50–2 show that the Court of Appeal *says* that remorse is to be inferred from a guilty plea; see further, Ch. 8, s. 4.
68 E.g. *Barbery* (1975) 62 Cr. App. R. 248, where the offender's hand was severed during the affray in which he participated, and the Court of Appeal reduced the sentence.
69 Wilcox (1972), pp. 86–7..
70 See Ch. 8, s. 2
71 Von Hirsch (1976), p. 122.
72 Thomas (1979), pp. 64–71.

Chapter 8: Symbolism, Moral Accounting and the Smooth Running of the System

1 White (1971).
1a Shapland (1981), pp. 138–9.
2 Spreutels (1980).
3 Walker (1981), pp. 117f.
4 Feinberg (1965).
5 Royal Commission on Capital Punishment (1953), pp. 17–18.
6 Pease and Sampson (1977).
7 Durkheim (1969).
8 See Ch. 1, s. 4.
9 Walker (1981), p. 71.
10 Hart (1963), p. 58.
11 Cf. the quotation from Gross, in Ch. 7, s. 1, above.
12 Walker (1981), p. 114.
13 See the cases discussed at p. 342 below.

14 (1980) 2 Cr. App. R. (S) 348.
15 See Ch. 1 s. 4 (a) and (b).
16 (1980) 2 Cr. App. R. (S) 184.
17 E.g. *Robinson* (1980) 2 Cr. App. R. (S) 348, above, p. 304.
18 Walker (1980) p. 124.
19 See Ch. 10, s. 7.
20 Walker (1980), p. 125.
21 See Ch. 10, s. 7.
22 (1980) 2 Cr. App. R. (S) 38 at p. 39.
23 (1980) 2 Cr. App. R. (S) 110.
24 *Harper* [1967] 3 All E.R. 618n.
25 *Spinks* (1980) 2 Cr. App. R. (S) 335.
26 See s. 4, below.
27 Ch. 4, s. 2.
28 Cross (1981), pp. 194–5.
29 E.g. *Lowe* (1977) 66 Cr. App. R. 122.
30 66 Cr. App. R. at p. 125.
31 *De Haan* [1968] 2 Q.B. 108.
32 E.g. *Wigley* [1978] Crim. L.R. 635; *Whybrew* [1979] Crim. L.R. 599.
33 Above, note 27.
34 *Davis* (1980) 2 Cr. App. R. (S) 168.
35 Per Lawton LJ in *Davis* (1980) 2 Cr. App. R. (S) at p. 170.
36 Baldwin and McConville (1978), p. 119.
37 [1980] Crim. L.R. 445.
38 *Davis* [1979] Crim. L.R. 327.
39 In *Boyd* (1980) 2 Cr. App. R. (S) 234, the Court of Appeal reduced by one-third a sentence which had been imposed without taking account of the guilty plea.
40 Baldwin and McConville (1979), pp. 121–5.
41 [1980] Crim. L.R. 59.
42 [1980] Crim. L.R. 60.
43 [1970] 2 Q.B. 321.
44 Cf. *Davis* [1979] Crim. L.R. 327, where the judge had intimated that he would reward a guilty plea with a discount of 20 to 30 per cent, yet the Court of Appeal was satisfied that the defendant was not 'deprived of that complete freedom of choice of plea which is essential'.
45 Bottoms and McClean (1976), and Baldwin and McConville (1977).
46 Cf. Baldwin and McConville (1977), p. 108.
47 Cf. Wolchover (1981) and Cohen (1981).
48 *Ibrahim* v. *R* [1914] A.C. 599.
49 Shapland (1982); Hough and Mayhew, H.O.R.S. no. 76, ch. 5.
50 Miers (1978), Wasik (1978).

51   Von Hirsch (1976), p. 73.

Chapter 9: Custodial Sentencing

1   For discussion, see M. Ignatieff (1977) and R. Cross (1971).
2   Morris (1974), pp. 61ff.
3   See Ch. 5, s. 3(d).
4   Cmnd. 645 of 1959, para. 47.
5   Cmnd. 4214 of 1969, para. 134.
6   *Prisons and the Prisoner* (1977), para. 17.
7   May Committee (1979), para. 4.26.
8   See, for example, the studies summarized by Hood and Sparks (1970), Ch. 8.
9   Cross (1971), p. 85.
10   *Prisons and the Prisoner*, para. 16.
11   Cross (1971), p. 101.
12   *Prison Statistics 1981* Table 8(b).
13   Walker, Farrington and Tucker (1981), discussed in Ch. 1, s. 5.
14   Martin and Webster (1971), p. 215.
15   Sections 19 and 20 Powers of Criminal Courts Act 1973, discussed below.
16   *Prison Statistics 1981*, Table 4.3.
17   Ibid., Table 3(d).
18   As stated by a senior Home Office representative to the House of Commons Expenditure Committee; see 15th Report, *The Reduction of Pressure on the Prison System* H.C. 662, Session 1977–8, Minutes of Evidence, vol. III, Q.1835
19   This argument is advanced, and the detailed application of the section is discussed, by Ashworth (1977).
20   Chapter 5, s. 6.
21   Morris (1974) p. 60.
22   See Ch. 5, s. 3(d).
23   See Ch. 7, s. 1.
24   See, e.g., *Anker* (1980) 2 Cr. App. R. (S) 76.
25   E.g. *Morgan and Docherty* [1979] Crim. L.R. 60, *Clayton* [1981] Crim. L.R. 425.
26   E.g. *Evans* [1980] Crim. L.R. 64.
27   [1981] Crim. L.R. 427.
28   Ashworth (1977), pp. 666–7.
29   See Ch. 1, s. 6.
30   See Ch. 4, s. 2.
31   E.g. *McKenlay* (1979) 1 Cr. App. R. (S) 161.
32   *Thornhill* [1981] Crim. L.R. 350.
33   *Boyle* [1981] Crim. L.R. 116.

34   *Ruelle* [1981] Crim. L.R. 425.

35   *Wright* [1982] Crim. L.R. 52.

36   *Roth* (1980) 2 Cr. App. R. (S) 65.

37   Compare *Partridge* [1976] Crim. L.R. 641 and *Finnigan* [1978] Crim. L.R. 441 with *McGrae* [1981] Crim. L.R. 426 and *Macleod* [1982] Crim. L.R. 61.

38   [1981] Crim. L.R. 844.

39   [1981] Crim. L.R. 56.

40   See Ch. 4, s. 4.

41   (1980) 71 Cr. App. R. 360, discussed in s. 4(d) of this chapter.

42   [1982] Crim. L.R. 126, fully discussed in the context of the use of community service orders in Ch. 10, s. 4.

43   Phillpotts and Lancucki, H.O.R.S. no. 53, Table 2.3.

44   Calculated from the Prison Statistics 1979, Tables 4.3, 3(b) and 3(d).

45   Shapland (1982). Cf. Hough and Mayhew, H.O.R.S. no. 76, ch. 5.

46   Maguire (1982).

47   (1974) 60 Cr. App. R. at p. 77.

48   Mark Carlisle MP, speaking on the Criminal Justice Bill in 1967: H.C. Deb, vol. 751, col. 807.

49   Brody, H.O.R.S. no. 35, p. 16.

50   A.C.P.S. (1977), para. 10.

51   A.C.P.S. (1978), para. 281.

52   A.C.P.S. (1978), para. 282.

53   Phillpotts and Lancucki, H.O.R.S. no. 53, Table 3.2.

54   See s. 4(d), below.

55   *The Criminal Statistics, England and Wales* 1981 show that between 1974 and 1980 the proportion of male young adults given immediate custodial sentences for indictable offences rose from 16 per cent to 19 per cent (Table 7.10), and of male adults from 15 per cent to 18 per cent (Table 7.12).

56   *Prison Statistics 1981*, Table 1(c).

57   E.g. *Jones, Goodman, and Pecht* [1981] Crim. L.R. 119–20 and *McRae* [1981] Crim. L.R. 428.

58   A.C.P.S. (1978), para. 281.

59   [1981] Crim. L.R. 657.

60   Cf. *Satterthwaite* [1981] Crim. L.R. 658 (3 months); *Turnbull* [1981] Crim. L.R. 653 (4 months); *Wright* [1982] Crim. L.R. 52; with *Hough* [1980] Crim. L.R. 662 (28 days) and *Wilson* [1980] Crim. L.R. 663 (2 months).

61   E.g. *Smedley* [1981] Crim. L.R. 575.

62   *Jacob* [1982] Crim. L.R. 135.

63   (1980) 71 Cr. App. R. 102.

64   (1980) 71 Cr. App. R. 360.

65   Section 4(d).
66   McLean (1980), Introduction; see Ch. 1, s. 6, above.
67   Cf. the research cited at notes 45 and 46 above.
68   See the discussion by Baldock (1980).
69   Robbery is thus characterized by Thomas, (1970), p. 9 and (1979) p. 14.
70   Cf. McClintock and Gibson (1961), Chs. VIII and IX.
71   See Beyleveld (1979), and Walker (1980), Ch. 4
72   Beyleveld (1979), p. 140.
73   A.C.P.S. (1978), para. 204.
74   See Table 2 above, in Ch. 1, s. 3.
75   Foreword to McClintock and Gibson (1961), p. xi.
76   *Review of Parole* (1981), Appendix A, paras. 21(c), 24 and 25.
77   The proposition receives qualified support from Beyleveld (1979), pp. 137–8.
78   Taken from *Criminal Statistics, England and Wales* 1980.
79   The category of 'serious woundings' consists mainly of woundings 'with intent', contrary to s. 18 of the Offences against the Person Act 1861; the category of 'other woundings' includes malicious woundings (s. 20) and assaults occasioning actual bodily harm (s. 47).
80   *Criminal Statistics, England and Wales* 1980, Table 2.4.
81   McClintock (1963), p. 80.
82   *Review of Parole* (1981), Appendix A, paras. 21, 28 and 29.
83   (1974) 60 Cr. App. R. 74.
84   Bentham (1789), Ch. XIII, para. 9.
85   Ibid.
86   Hart (1968), p. 19.
87   Ch. 8, s. 1.
88   See Thomas (1979), p. 93n.
89   Ibid.
90   See note 82 above, and text thereat.
91   Walker (1980), p. 69.
92   Cohen (1967); see the discussion by Sheriff Nicholson (1981), pp. 210–11.
93   See Thomas (1979), pp. 35–7.
94   See [1958] Crim. L.R. 709; Popkess (1960) on the subsequent riots in Nottingham; and for discussion Cross (1981), pp. 186–8.
95   (1973) 57 Cr. App. R. 340.
96   Baxter and Nuttall (1975).
97   *Prison Statistics 1981,* Table 1.9.
98   Ibid., Table 4.2.
99   A.C.P.S. (1977), para. 14.
100 Brody, H.O.R.S. no. 35, pp. 14–16.

101   Brody and Tarling, H.O.R.S. no. 64, pp. 9–10.

102   See Ch. 3, s. 2.

103   See Ch. 3, s. 2.

104   Brody and Tarling, H.O.R.S. no. 64, p. 9.

105   Ibid., H.O.R.S. no. 64, p. 17; see Ch. 1, s. 5(c).

106   Ibid., p. 18; the studies showing a higher rate of undetected offending for those with convictions tend to have persons under 21 as subjects.

107   Ibid., p. 18.

108   Ibid., pp. 14.

109   Ibid., p. 35.

110   Ibid., p. 18.

111   *Report on the Work of the Prison Department* 1981, p. 11, Table 3.

112   Emery (1973).

113   *Report on the Work of the Prison Department* 1980, para. 11.

114   Report of H.M. Chief Inspector of Prisons 1981, p. 19.

115   (1980) 71 Cr. App. R. 102.

116   (1980) 71 Cr. App. R. 360.

117   See (1980) 71 Cr. App. R. 363 *et seq.*, and the commentaries of D. A. Thomas at [1980] Crim. L.R. 732–740.

118   (1980) 71 Cr. App. R. 366.

119   [1980] Crim. L.R. 735.

120   (1980) 71 Cr. App. R. 381.

121   See the discussion in Ch. 1, s. 6, above, at pp. 41–2.

122   [1980] Crim. L.R. 733 (D. A. Thomas).

123   *Criminal Statistics, England and Wales* 1981, paras. 7.22 to 7.26.

124   [1982] Crim. L.R. 125; see Ch. 10, s. 4.

125   [1982] 1 W.L.R. 1090, discussed in Ch. 10, s. 4.

126   *Prison Statistics 1979*, Table 4(a).

127   Brody and Tarling, H.O.R.S. no. 64, p. 18.

128   Phillpotts and Lancucki, H.O.R.S. no. 53, Table 3.2.

129   See Ashworth (1977).

130   *Prison Statistics 1981*, Tables 4.3 and 3(b).

131   *Ellahi* (1979) 1 Cr. App. R. (S) 164; see above, p. 308.

132   *Feldman* (1981) 3 Cr. App. R. (S) 20.

133   See s. 2(a) of this chapter.

134   (1973) 57 Cr. App. R. 945 at p. 948.

135   [1973] Crim. L. R. 585.

136   (1980) 2 Cr. App. R. (S) 333.

137   *Morgan* (1979) 1 Cr. App. R. (S) 356.

138   *Stevenson* [1980] Crim. L.R. 65.

139   May Report (1979), para. 3.48.

140   (1976) Cr. App. R. 124.

141   Thomas (1979), pp. 12, 69 and 262ff.

142 Cf. Hood (1965); Gunn *et al.* (1978), pp. 205–8.
143 Mental Health Act 1983, sections 37 and 41, (replacing sections 60 and 65 of the Mental Health Act 1959).
144 *Review of the Mental Health Act 1959* (1978), Ch. 5.
145 Cf. the strictures of the May Committee (1979), para. 3.43.
146 *Clarke* (1975) 61 Cr. App. R. 320.
147 [1976] Crim. L.R. 698; cf. also *McFarlane* (1975) 60 Cr. App. R. 320.
148 May Report (1979), para. 3.39, commenting that the figure was 'a matter of dispute'.
149 Gunn *et al.* (1978), Ch. 11.
150 Report of the Parole Board 1981, para. 28.
151 *The Adult Offender* (1965), para. 5.
152 *Review of Parole* (1981), Appendix A, paras. 8–17.
153 Nuttall *et al.*, H.O.R.S. no. 38.
154 At para. 62. On development of parole, see Morgan (1983).
155 Hood (1974c).
156 *Review of Parole* (1981) Appx. A, paras. 21–31.
157 Hood (1974c), p. 9.
158 Home Office, *Review of Parole*, para. 21.
159 See Ch. 8, s. 1.
160 See Hood (1975), Walker (1975).
161 Hood (1974c) p. 7.
162 See Ch. 8, s. 1, and Bentham (1789), Ch. XV, 9.
163 Nuttall *et al.*, H.O.R.S. no. 38, Ch. 6, found a small difference in two-year reconviction rates, perhaps suggesting a 'treatment effect'.
164 See Ch. 7, s. 7.
165 See Ch. 7, s. 5.
166 See Ch. 1, s. 3.
167 See Ch. 5, s. 6.
168 Floud and Young (1981), pp. 82–6.
169 Pease and Sampson (1977), p. 61.
170 Beyleveld (1979), p. 147.
171 The reference must properly be to the conviction rate and not to the actual crime rate, about which we know too little; see notes 102–4 above and text thereat.
172 Ibid.
173 See Ch. 8, s. 1.
174 May Report (1979), para. 3.64.
175 Fitzmaurice and Pease (1982).
176 See Thomas (1979), p. 137 for an example.
177 This refers to one of the two purposes formerly served by a borstal sentence – as a 'rehabilitative' measure for an offender, rather than

as a sentence proportionate to the gravity of his offence: see Thomas (1979), pp. 18–19 for examples, and above, p. 364.
178 Thomas (1979), p. 20.
179 Ibid.
180 Discussed in section 2(a) of this chapter, at pp. 325–6.

Chapter 10: Non-Custodial Sentencing

1 Ditchfield, H.O.R.S. no. 36.
2 See K. C. Davis (1969).
3 Phillpotts and Lancucki, H.O.R.S. no. 53, pp. 8–9.
4 Ibid. p. 16.
5 See below, s. 4, on community service orders.
6 Thomas (1979), p. 230.
7 Bottoms (1973).
8 Tarling, H.O.R.S. no. 56, p. 9.
9 For a general survey and suggested reforms, see the Howe Report (1981); for a critical empirical survey, see Morgan and Bowles (1983).
10 Morgan and Bowles (1981).
11 Softley, H.O.R.S. no. 46; cf. also Softley and Moxon (1982).
12 See Burney (1980) for description and discussion.
13 Crow, Pease and Hillary (1980).
14 Cf. A.C.P.S. (1970), paras. 194–5.
15 H.O.R.S. no. 52, pp. 20–1.
16 Ibid.
17 Hood (1962), p. 87.
18 Tarling, H.O.R.S. no. 56, Ch. 2.
19 Hood (1962), p. 90.
20 Hogarth (1970), p. 353.
21 Hood (1962), pp. 95–6.
22 Tarling, H.O.R.S. no. 56, pp. 20–1.
23 Roberts and Roberts (1982), pp. 80–3.
24 See s. 7(c) below.
25 See Ch. 3, s. 3.
26 Above, s. 2.
27 On which, generally, see McWilliams (1981).
28 C.C.P.A.C.C. (1978), para. 13.
29 *The Sentence of the Court* (1964), Appendix VI.
30 Mathieson (1982).
31 Below, s. 3(e).
32 Hood (1962), p. 87.
33 Tarling, H.O.R.S. no. 56, p. 11.
34 Roberts and Roberts (1982), p. 79.

35   Mathieson (1982).
36   See below, s. 3(f).
37   Young (1979), p. 81.
38   Thomas (1979), pp. 20–2.
39   Above, Ch. 1, s. 5.
40   Burney (1980), p. 53, discussing the results of day centres.
41   See above, p. 245.
42   *Sentence of the Court* (1978), para. 52.
43   *Sentence of the Court* (1964), Appendix VI.
44   Bottoms (1973).
45   Walker, Farrington and Tucker (1981), discussed in Ch. 1, s. 5.
46   Probation and After-Care Statistics 1981, Table 2.11.
47   *Prison Statistics* 1979 Table 8.1; of prisoners released from sentence of over 6 months but less than 18 months, some 50 per cent are reconvicted within 2 years.
48   Cf. Lawson (1980), showing that probationers brought to court for breach had more previous convictions than other probationers.
49   Cf. the Hampshire experiment, briefly reported by Home Office Research Bulletin no. 13, p. 37.
50   Central Council of Probation and After-Care Committees (1978), para. 15.
51   Lawson (1978).
52   McWilliams (1982).
53   Softley, H.O.R.S. no. 46, p. 6.
54   See below, p. 397.
55   See the small study by Willis (1981).
56   *Bainbridge* (1979) 1 Cr. App. R. (S) 36.
57   A.C.P.S. (1970), Ch. 8.
58   S. 22(3) P.C.C.A. 1973.
59   Folkard, H.O.R.S. 36 (the *Impact* study).
60   A.C.P.S. (1974), para. 284.
61   Bottoms and McWilliams (1979).
62   S. 14(2)(b) P.C.C.A. 1973.
63   Pease *et al.*, H.O.R.S. no. 39, Ch. 3.
64   Cf. the discussion below of Young's findings in five areas.
65   A.C.P.S. (1970), para. 33.
66   A.C.P.S. (1970), para. 37.
67   Ch. 3, s. 3 at p. 123.
68   A.C.P.S. (1970), paras. 37–8.
69   Young (1979), pp. 131–2.
70   Pease *et al.*, H.O.R.S. no. 29, Ch. 5.
71   Pease (1978), p. 271.
72   Pease et al., H.O.R.S. no. 29, Ch. 3.
73   Young (1979), p. 68.

74   Goldstone (1982), p. 71; since then, a little judicial guidance has emerged, see below, pp. 404–5.

75   Pease *et al.*, H.O.R.S. no. 29, p. 34.

76   Young (1979), p. 127.

77   Pease (1978), p. 272.

78   *Paisley* (1979) 1 Cr. App. R. (S) 196.

79   Young (1979), p. 127.

80   The recommended scale for Cheshire is printed at [1982] *The Magistrate* 73.

81   Pease (1978), p. 273.

82   Young (1979), p. 130, found some such cases.

83   It might be argued that the advent of community service has prevented the proportion of custodial sentences for young adults from rising substantially.

84   Pease *et al.*, H.O.R.S. no. 29, Ch. 4.

85   Softley, H.O.R.S. no. 46, p. 7, at a time of lower unemployment than the present (1974). Cf. now Jardine, Moore and Pease (1983).

86   Goldstone (1982) at p. 72; the judge's lecture was published for the benefit of magistrates.

87   Young (1979), p. 65.

88   *Afzal* [1981] Crim. L.R. 505, *Coleman* [1981] Crim. L.R. 721, *Stanbury* [1981] Crim. L.R. 845.

89   [1982] Crim. L.R. 126.

90   [1982] Crim. L.R. 377.

91   [1982] Crim. L.R. 460.

92   This roughly accords with the scale recommended in Cheshire; see [1982] *The Magistrate* 73.

93   *Clarke* [1982] 1 W.L.R. 1090, at 1095.

94   Pease *et al.*, H.O.R.S. no. 39, Ch. 2.

95   Young (1979), pp. 101–2.

96   Pease *et al.*, H.O.R.S. no. 39, p. 15.

97   Ibid., Ch. 4.

98   See Ch. 1, s. 5.

99   Pease *et al.*, H.O.R.S. no. 29, Ch. 4.

100   Young (1979), p. 67.

101   Pease and McWilliams (1980), p. 113.

102   Young (1979), p. 116.

103   A.C.P.S. (1970), para. 37.

104   S.1.P.C.C.A. 1973, slightly amended by s. 63 of the Criminal Justice Act 1982.

105   (1975) 61 Cr. App. R. 112.

106   [1982] Crim. L.R. 245.

107   [1982] Crim. L.R. 462.

108   Corden and Nott (1980), p. 362.

109 Ibid., p. 363.
110 A.C.P.S. (1970) Ch. 4; see Ch. 1, s. 2.
111 E.g. [1979] Crim. L.R. 259, [1982] Crim. L.R. 463.
112 Cf. letter at [1979] Crim. L.R. 608.
113 Ch. 9, at pp. 324–6.
114 This enacts the so-called *O'Keefe* rule; see *O'Keefe* [1969] 2 Q.B. 29.
115 See above, s. 4(b), p. 404.
116 [1982] 1 W.L.R. 1090 at p. 1095.
117 Thomas (1979), pp. 244–5.
118 Ch. 9, s. 2.
119 Thomas (1982b), p. 289.
120 Above, p. 404.
121 *Whitfield* [1975] Crim. L.R. 400.
122 *Leigh* (1970) 54 Cr. App. R. 169.
123 See generally Bottoms (1981).
124 Cf. Bottoms (1979), p. 440.
125 Tarling, H.O.R.S. no. 56, Ch. 2.
126 Ch. 2, s. 4.
127 Practice Direction [1966] 2 All E.R. 929.
128 Shapland (1981), pp. 123–30.
129 See Ch. 2, s. 4.
130 Bottoms and McClean (1976), pp. 113 and 131.
131 Baldwin and McConville (1978), pp. 545–6.
132 Cf. Thomas (1972) and Ashworth (1979).
133 Downes (1982).
134 (1980) 71 Cr. App. R. 360, discussed in Ch. 9, s. 4.
135 Streatfeild (1960), para. 336.
136 Perry (1974) found that 64 per cent of reports were written on individuals already known to the probation service; Thorpe (H.O.R.S. no. 48, p. 19) found a lower proportion.
137 Thorpe, H.O.R.S. no. 48, p. 16 and pp. 34–5.
138 The findings of various studies are collated by Thorpe, op. cit., p. 11.
139 Streatfeild (1960), para. 345.
140 Ibid., para. 342.
141 H.O.C. 194/74.
142 See section 3(e) above.
143 Cf. Davies (1974).
144 E.g. *Blowers* [1977] Crim. L.R. 51; *Smith and Woollard* [1978] Crim. L.R. 758; *James* [1982] Crim. L.R. 59.
145 Streatfeild Report, para. 346.
146 [1981] Crim. L.R. 505.
147 [1981] Crim. L.R. 721.

148   Above, s. 4(b).

149   [1981] Crim. L.R. 56.

150   Ch. 9, s. 4.

151   Above, s. 4(b).

152   Corden and Nott (1980), pp. 363-4.

153   Shapland (1981), p. 133.

154   Quoted at [1978] Crim. L.R. 759.

155   Raynor (1980).

156   McWilliams (1981).

157   Shapland (1981), p. 134.

158   See H.O.C. 59/1971.

159   [1982] Crim. L.R. 60.

160   See above, pp. 404-5.

161   *Ampleford* (1975) 61 Cr. App. R. 325 and *Peter* [1975] Crim. L.R. 593, discussed by Ashworth (1977) at p. 663.

162   Thorpe, H.O.R.S. no. 48, p. 31.

163   H.O.C. no. 118/1977, para. 7.

164   James (1974), p. 171.

165   H.O.C. no. 118/1977, para. 4.

166   Thorpe, H.O.R.S. no. 48, p. 12.

167   Ibid., p. 28.

168   Thorpe. H.O.R.S. no. 48, p. 26.

169   Burney (1979), p. 169.

170   Roberts and Roberts (1982), p. 89.

171   Hine, Pease and McWilliams (1978).

172   Thorpe, H.O.R.S. no. 48, p. 10.

173   Ibid., p. 26.

174   Hine, Pease and McWilliams (1978).

175   Shapland (1981), Ch. 3.

176   See below, p. 425.

177   Brayshaw (1982).

178   See Ch. 2, s. 4.

179   Brayshaw (1982), p. 79.

180   Shapland (1981), p. 82.

181   Above, p. 418.

182   Shapland (1981), p. 84.

183   *Easson* v. *L.N.E.R.* [1944] K.B. 421 at p. 426.

184   See the authorities discussed in Ch. 7, s. 4.

185   Shapland (1981), pp. 82, 120, 145.

186   Gibbens *et al.* (1977).

187   Shapland (1981), p. 134.

188   Thorpe, H.O.R.S. no. 48, p. 32.

189   See s. 7(a) above.

190   Shapland (1981), p. 131.

191   Cf. Hogarth (1970), Ch. 14.
192   See Ch. 1, s. 5, and p. 378.
193   Cf. Cohen (1979) and the concept of the 'punitive city'.
194   Cf. Bottoms and McWilliams (1979); Haxby (1978).
195   See Ch. 7, s. 4.
196   Von Hirsch (1976), Introduction, p. xxxv.
197   E.g. *Heather* (1979) 1 Cr. App. R. (S) 139.
198   Von Hirsch (1976), Introduction, p. xxxix.
199   Ibid., p. 127.
200   Ibid., p. 133.
201   Cf. Thomas (1982).
202   See Ch. 11, below.
203   See Ch. 1, s. 7.
204   Sparks (1971), p. 397.
205   Sparks (1971), p. 397.
206   [1982] 1 W.L.R. 1090, above, p. 410.
207   Kapardis and Farrington (1981), p. 114, discussed in Ch. 1, s. 7.
208   Tarling, H.O.R.S. no. 56, p. 9.
209   Hood (1962), Ch. 3.
210   Sparks (1965).
211   Tarling, H.O.R.S. no. 56, p. 10.

Chapter 11: Towards Improved Understanding and Procedures

1   See Ch. 3, *passim.*
2   A.C.P.S. (1970), para. 37; see Ch. 3, s. 3.
3   The research was to be carried out by a team from the Centre for Criminological Research, University of Oxford. See Preface, above.
4   Clarke and Sinclair (1974). The published results of the first *British Crime Survey* (Hough and Mayhew, H.O.R.S. no. 76) seem rather general on this point.
5   See Ch. 1, s. 5 and Ch. 8, s. 1.
6   This is not to suggest that there is a single correct inference; there are, however, inferences which are manifestly incorrect or are highly improbable in view of certain unstated factors.
7   Maguire (1982).
8   Levi (1981).
9   See Ch. 10, s. 4.
10   See Ch. 3, s. 3.
11   See Ch. 1, s. 4 and Ch. 10, s. 8.
12   A qualified defence reduces the crime from one category to a lesser category, e.g. provocation reduces murder to manslaughter.
13   See Wasik (1983).

14   Cf. Ch. 2, s. 3.

15   See Ch. 3, s. 4.

16   For American experience of this, see von Hirsch (1982), pp. 167–9.

17   This draws upon my Noel Buxton lecture in October 1982; see Ashworth (1983).

18   See the proposal of the Australian Law Reform Commission (1981), p. 270 and Ch. 11.

19   See Ch. 2, s. 3.

20   See the 'guideline' judgments, discussed at pp. 40 and 78.

21   Cf. A.C.P.S. (1978), para. 164.

22   See Ch. 1, s. 8.

23   See Ch. 2, s. 5.

24   E.g. *Rees* [1978] Crim. L.R. 298; *Routley* [1982] Crim. L.R. 383.

25   See Ch. 1, s. 6.

26   There are considerable practical problems with the requirement to give reasons. Where the sentencers number two or more (such as a judge sitting with two magistrates in the Crown Court), some agreed set of reasons should be announced. Where the sentencers are a bench of lay magistrates, they ought to be advised by a justices' clerk. It is arguable that reason-giving is vital, particularly where a custodial sentence or indeed any substantial deprivation of liberty or money is to be imposed, but the practical problems (see Shapland (1981), pp. 137–8) need further discussion.

27   See Ch. 10, s. 7.

28   See Thomas (1972), Ashworth (1979), Zellick (1979).

29   Home Affairs Committee (1981).

30   *The Government Reply to the Fourth Report from the Home Affairs Committee, The Prison Service* (1981).

BIBLIOGRAPHY

A.C.P.S., *see* Advisory Council on the Penal System.

Advisory Council on the Penal System (1970), *Non-Custodial and Semi-Custodial Penalties*, H.M.S.O.

Advisory Council on the Penal System (1974), *Young Adult Offenders*, H.M.S.O.

Advisory Council on the Penal System (1977), *The Length of Prison Sentences*, H.M.S.O.

Advisory Council on the Penal System (1978), *Sentences of Imprisonment: a Review of Maximum Penalties*, H.M.S.O.

Advisory Council on the Treatment of Offenders (1957), *Alternatives to Short Terms of Imprisonment*, H.M.S.O.

Archbold (1982), *Criminal Pleading, Evidence and Practice*, 41st edn., Sweet & Maxwell.

Arnold, T. (1969), 'Law as Symbolism', in Aubert, V. (ed.), *Sociology of Law*, Penguin.

Ashworth, A. J. (1975), 'Sentencing in Provocation Cases', *Crim. L.R.*, 553.

Ashworth, A. J. (1977), 'Justifying the First Prison Sentence', *Crim. L. R.*, 661.

Ashworth, A. J. (1979), 'Prosecution and Procedure in Criminal Justice', *Crim. L.R.*, 480.

Ashworth, A. J. (1981), 'The Elasticity of Mens Rea' in Tapper (1981).

Ashworth, A. J. (1983), 'Reducing the Prison Population in the 1980s: the Need for Sentencing Reform', in *A Prison System for the Eighties and Beyond*, NACRO.

Australian Law Reform Commission (1980), *Sentencing of Federal Offenders*, 15th Report (Interim), Canberra.

Bailey, V. and McCabe, S. (1979), 'Reform of the Law of Incest'. *Crim. L.R.*, 749.

Baldock, J. C. (1980), 'Why the Prison Population has Grown Larger and Younger', *Howard J.*, 142.

Baldwin, J. and McConville, M. (1977), *Negotiated Justice*, Martin Robertson.

Baldwin, J. and McConville, M. (1978a), 'The Influence of the Sentencing Discount in Inducing Guilty Pleas', in Baldwin and Bottomley (ed.), *Criminal Justice: Selected Readings*, Martin Robertson.

Baldwin, J. and McConville, M. (1978b), 'Sentencing Problems Raised by Guilty Pleas', *Modern L.R.*, 544.

Baxter, R. and Nuttall, C. (1975), 'Severe Sentences: No Deterrent to Crime?', *New Society*, 11–13.

Bentham, J. (1789), *Principles of Morals and Legislation*; edition by Hart and Burns, University of London Press, 1970.

Beyleveld, D. (1979a), 'Deterrence Research as a Basis for Deterrence Policies', *Howard J.*, 135.

Beyleveld, D. (1979b), 'Identifying, Explaining and Predicting Deterrence', *B.J. Crim.*, 205.

Bottomley, A. K. and Coleman, C. (1981), *Understanding Crime Rates*, Saxon House.

Bottoms, A. E. (1973), 'The Efficacy of the Fine', *Crim. L.R.*, 534.

Bottoms, A. E. (1979), 'The Advisory Council and the Suspended Sentence', *Crim. L.R.*, 437.

Bottoms, A. E. (1981), 'The Suspended Sentence in England, 1967–78', *B.J. Crim.*, 1.

Bottoms, A. E. and Brownsword, R. (1982), 'The Dangerousness Debate after the Floud Report', *B.J. Crim.*, 229.

Bottoms, A. E. and McClean, J. D. (1976), *Defendants in the Criminal Process*, Routledge.

Bottoms, A. E. and McWilliams, W. (1979), 'A Non-Treatment Paradigm for Probation', *B.J.S.W.*, 159.

Brayshaw, A. J. (1982), 'Guilty, But . . .', *The Magistrate*, 79.

Bridge, Lord (1978), *Report of the Working Party on Judicial Studies and Information*, H.M.S.O.

Brody, S., *The Effectiveness of Sentencing*, Home Office Research Study no. 35, H.M.S.O., 1975.

Brody, S. and Tarling, R., *Taking Offenders out of Circulation*, Home Office Research Study no. 64, H.M.S.O., 1981.

Burney, E. (1980), *A Chance to Change*, Howard League for Penal Reform.

Butler, Lord (1975), *Report of the Committee on Mentally Abnormal Offenders*, Cmnd. 6244, H.M.S.O.

Central Council of Probation and After-Care Committees (1978), 'The Diminishing Use of Probation Orders', Mimeo.

Chatterton, M. (1976), 'The Social Contexts of Violence', in Borland, M. (ed.) *Violence in the Family*, Manchester University Press.

Clarke, A. H. and Lewis, M. J. (1982), 'Fear of Crime Among the Elderly', *B.J. Crim.*, 49.

Clarke, R. V. G. and Sinclair, I. (1974), 'Towards More Effective Treatment Evaluation', in *Collected Studies in Criminological Research*, vol. XII, Council of Europe.

Cohen, M. (1981), 'Challenging Police Evidence of Interviews', *Crim. L. R.*, 523.

Cohen, P. (1982), 'Born to Judge', *L. A. G. Bulletin*, 8.

Cohen, S. (1967), 'Mods, Rockers and the Rest: Community Reaction to Juvenile Delinquency', *Howard J.*, 121.

Corden, J. and Nott, D. (1980), 'The Power to Defer Sentence', *B.J. Crim.*, 358.

Cornish, W. (1968), *The Jury*, Allen Lane.

Cox, E. (1877), *The Principles of Punishment*.

Criminal Law Revision Committee, 8th Report, *Theft and Related Offences*, Cmnd. 2977, H.M.S.O., 1966.

Criminal Law Revision Committee, 14th Report, *Offences Against the Person*, Cmnd. 7844, H.M.S.O., 1980.

Criminal law Revision Committee, Working Paper, Sexual Offences, H.M.S.O., 1980.

Croft, J. (1982), 'Planning', *Home Office Research Bulletin* no. 14.

Cross, R. (1971), *Punishment, Prison and the Public*, Sweet & Maxwell.

Cross, R. (1981), *English Sentencing System*, 3rd edn., Butterworths.

Crow, I. *et al.* (1980), *The Manchester and Wiltshire Multifacility Schemes*, N.A.C.R.O.

Davies, M. (1974), 'Social Enquiry for the Courts', *B.J. Crim.*, 18.

Davis, K. C. (1969), *Discretionary Justice*, Louisiana State U.P.

Deane, K. D. (1981), 'Tax Evasion, Criminality and Sentencing the Tax Offender', *B.J. Crim.*, 47.

Departmental Committee on Persistent Offenders (1932), (Chairman, Dove-Wilson).

Devlin, P. (1979), *The Judge*, Oxford University Press.

Diamond, S. S. (1981), 'Exploring Sources of Sentence Disparity' in Sales, B. D. (ed.), *The Trial Process*, Plenum Press, New York.

Ditchfield, J., *Police Cautioning in England and Wales*, Home Office Research Study no. 37, H.M.S.O. 1977.

Downes, D. (1982), 'The Origins and Consequences of Dutch Penal Policy', *B.J. Crim.*, 325.

Durkheim, E., (1969), 'Types of Law in relation to types of Social Solidarity', in Aubert, V. (ed.) *Sociology of Law*, Penguin.

Elliott, D. W. (1957), 'The Homicide Act 1957', *Crim. L.R.*, 290.

Empey, L. T. and Ericson, M. L. (1972), *The Provo Experiment*, Lexington Books.

Fairhead, S., *Persistent Petty Offenders*, Home Office Research Study no. 66, 1981.

Farrington, D. P. and Bennett, T. (1981), 'Police Cautioning of Juveniles in London', *B.J. Crim.*, 123.

Feinberg, J. (1965), 'The Expressive Function of Punishment', *The Monist*, vol. 49, p. 397.

Finnis, J. (1972), 'Meaning and Ambiguity in Punishment and in Penology', *Osgoode Hall L.J.*, 265.

Fitzmaurice, C. and Pease, K. (1982), 146 *Justice of the Peace* 575.

Fletcher, G. (1978), *Rethinking Criminal Law*, Little, Brown & Co.

Floud, J. and Young, W. (1981), *Dangerousness and Criminal Justice*, Heinemann.

Folkard, M. S., *Impact*, Volume II, Home Office Research Study no. 36, H.M.S.O., 1975.

Galligan, D. (1981), 'The Return to Retribution', in Tapper (1981).

Gibbens, T. C. N. *et al.* (1977), *Medical Remands in the Criminal Court*, Oxford University Press.

Glazebrook, P. R. (ed.) (1978), *Reshaping Criminal Law*, Sweet & Maxwell.

Goldstone, Judge (1982), 'From the Crown Court: a Fresh Look at Community Service Orders', *The Magistrate*, 71.

Gross, H. (1979), *A Theory of Criminal Justice*, Oxford University Press.

Gunn, J. *et al.* (1978), *Psychiatric Aspects of Imprisonment*, Academic Press.

Hadden, T. (1968), 'Offences of Violence: the Law and the Facts', *Crim. L.R.*

Hodden, T. (1983), 'Fraud in the City', *Crim. L.R.* (July).

Hailsham, Lord (1981), *see* Home Affairs Committee (1981).

Hall Williams, J. E. (1970), *The English Penal System in Transition*, Butterworths.

Hammond, W. H. and Chayen, E. (1963), *Persistent Offenders*, H.M.S.O.

Harding, R. (1979), 'Firearms Use in Crime', *Crim. L.R.*, 765.

Harris, B. T. (1981), *The Criminal Jurisdiction of Magistrates*, 7th edn., Barry Rose.

Hart, H. L. A. (1961), *The Concept of Law*, Oxford University Press.

Hart, H. L. A. (1963), *Law, Liberty and Morality*, Oxford University Press.

Hart, H. L. A. (1968), *Punishment and Responsibility*, Oxford University Press.

Haward, L. (1981), 'Psychological Consequences of Being a Victim of Crime', in Lloyd-Bostock, S. (ed.), *Law and Psychology*, S.S.R.C., Centre for Socio-Legal Studies, Oxford.

Haxby, D. (1978), *Probation: a Changing Service*, Constable.

Hine, J., Pease, K. and McWilliams, W. (1978), 'Recommendations, Social Information and Sentencing', *Howard J.*

Hogarth, J. (1971), *Sentencing as a Human Process*, University of Toronto Press.

Home Affairs Committee (1981), *The Prison Service*, H.C. Paper 412.1, H.M.S.O.

Home Office (1972), *A Guide to the Criminal Justice Act 1972*, Home Office.

Hood, R. (1962), *Sentencing in Magistrates' Courts*, Heinemann.

Hood, R. (1965), *Borstal Re-assessed*, Heinemann.

Hood, R. (1972), *Sentencing the Motoring Offender*, Heinemann.

Hood, R. (ed.) (1974a), *Crime, Criminology and Public Policy*, Heinemann.

Hood, R. (1974b), *Tolerance and the Tariff*, N.A.C.R.O. Paper No. 11.

Hood, R. (1974c), 'Some Fundamental Dilemmas of the English Parole System and a Suggestion for an Alternative Structure, in D. A. Thomas (ed.) *Parole: its Implications for the Criminal Justice and Penal System*, Institute of Criminology, Cambridge.

Hood, R. (1975), 'The Case Against Executive Control Over Time in Custody', *Crim. L.R.*, 545.

Hood, R. and Sparks, R. (1970), *Key Issues in Criminology*, Hutchinson.

Hough, M., and Mayhew, P. (1983) *The British Crime Survey*, Home Office Research Study no. 76, H.M.S.O.

House of Commons Expenditure Committee (1978), *The Reduction of Pressure on the Prison System*, H.M.S.O.

Ignatieff, M. (1977), *A Just Measure of Pain*, Macmillan.

Interdepartmental Working Party on Road Traffic Law, H.M.S.O., 1981.

Jaconelli, J. (1981), 'Attorney-General's References – A Problematic Device', *Crim. L.R.*, 543.

James, Sir A. (1974), 'A Judicial Note', in Hood (1974a).

James Committee (1975), Report of the Committee on the Distribution of Criminal Business Between the Crown Court and Magistrates' Courts, Cmnd. 6323, H.M.S.O.

Jardine, E. *et al.* (1983), 'Community Service Orders, Employment and the Tariff', *Crim. L.R.*, 17.

Jennings, W. I. (1959), *The Law and the Constitution*, University of London Press.

Karpardis, A. and Farrington, D. P. (1981), 'An Experimental Study of Sentencing by Magistrates', *Law and Human Behaviour*, 107.

Kelsen, H. (1967), *The Pure Theory of Law*, University of California Press.

Kenny, A. (1978), *Freewill and Responsibility*, Oxford University Press.

King, M. (1979), 'The Role of Prosecuting Counsel on Sentencing – What About Magistrates' Courts?', *Crim. L.R.*, 775.

Law Comm. no. 29 *Offences of Damage to Property*, H.M.S.O. 1970.

Lawson, C. (1978), *The Probation Officer as Prosecutor*, Institute of Criminology, Cambridge.

Leigh, L. H. (1981), *The Control of Commercial Fraud*, Heinemann.

Lemon, N. (1974), 'Training, Personality and Attitude as Determinants of Magistrates' Sentencing', *B.J. Crim.*, 34.

Levi, M. (1981), *The Phantom Capitalists*, Heinemann.

Lidstone, K. *et al.* (1980), *Prosecutions by Non-Police Agencies*, Royal Commission on Criminal Procedure Research Study no. 10, H.M.S.O.

McCabe, S. and Purves, R. (1972), *By-Passing the Jury*, Oxford University Penal Research Unit.

McCabe, S. and Sutcliffe, F. (1978), *Defining Crime*, Oxford University Centre for Criminological Research.

McClintock, F. H. (1963), *Crimes of Violence*, Heinemann.

McClintock, F. H. and Gibson, E. (1960), *Robbery in London*, Heinemann.

McConville, M. and Baldwin, J. (1982), 'The Influence of Race on Sentencing in England', *Crim. L.R.*, 652.

McIntosh, M. (1975), *The Organisation of Crime*, Macmillan.

McLean, I. (1980), *Crown Court: Patterns of Sentencing*, Barry Rose.

McWilliams, W. (1981), 'The Probation Officer at Court: from Friend to Acquaintance', *Howard J.*, 97.

McWilliams, W. (1982), 'A Reply', *Howard J.*, 116.

Mack, J. A. (1975), *The Crime Industry*, Saxon House.

Maguire, M. (1980), 'The Impact of Burglary upon Victims', *B.J. Crim.*, 261.

Maguire, M. (1982), *Burglary in a Dwelling*, Heinemann.

Martin, J. P. and Webster, D. (1971), *The Social Consequences of Conviction*, Heinemann.

Mawby, R. I. (1978), 'A Note on Domestic Disputes Reported to the Police', *Howard J.*, 160.

May Committee (1979), *Report of the Committee of Inquiry into the United Kingdom Prison Services*, Cmnd. 7673, H.M.S.O.

Miers, D., (1978) *Responses to Victimization*, Professional Books.

Moberly, Sir W. (1968), *The Ethics of Punishment*, Faber.

Morgan, N. (1983), 'The Shaping of Parole in England and Wales', *Crim. L.R.*, 173.

Morgan, R. and Bowles, R. (1981), 'Fines: the Case for Review', *Crim. L.R.*, 203.

Morgan, R. and Bowles, R. (1983), 'Fines: Where Does Sentencing End and Enforcement Begin?', *Crim. L.R.*, 78.

Moriarty, M. (1977), 'The Policy-Making Process: how it is seen from the Home Office', in Walker and Giller (1977).

Morris, A. and McIsaac, M. (1978), *Juvenile Justice?*, Heinemann.

Morris, D. (1982), 'It Is My View . . .', *The Magistrate*, 113.

Morris, N. (1974), *The Future of Imprisonment*, Chicago University Press.

Morris, R. M. (1980), 'Home Office Crime Policy Planning: Six years On', *Howard J.*, 135.

Nagel, T. (1976), 'Moral Luck', *Proceedings of the Aristotelian Society (Supplement)*, 137.

Nicholson, C. G. B. (1981) *Law and Practice of Sentencing in Scotland*, Green and Son.

Nuttall, C. *et al.*, *Parole in England and Wales*, Home Office Research Study no. 38, H.M.S.O., 1977.

Pease, K. (1978), 'Community Service and the Tariff', *Crim. L.R.*, 269.

Pease, K. and McWilliams, W. (1980), *Community Service by Order*, Scottish Academic Press.

Pease, K. and Sampson, M. (1977), 'Doing Time and Marking Time', *Howard J.*, 59.

Pease, K. *et al.* (1974), 'The Development of a Scale of Offence Seriousness', *International Journal of Criminology and Penology*.

Pease, K. *et al.*, *Community Service Orders*, Home Office Research Study no. 29, H.M.S.O., 1975.

Pease, K. *et al.*, *Community Service Assessed in 1976*, Home Office Research Study no. 39, H.M.S.O., 1976.

Perry, F. (1974), *Information for the Court*, Institute of Criminology, Cambridge.

Phillpotts, G. J. O. and Lancucki, L. B., *Previous Convictions, Sentence and Reconviction*, Home Office Research Study no. 53, H.M.S.O., 1979.

Policy Advisory Committee on Sexual Offences (1981), *Report on the Age of Consent in Relation to Sexual Offences*, Cmnd. 8216, H.M.S.O.

Popkess, A. (1960), 'Racial Disturbances in Nottingham', *Crim. L.R.*, 673.

Posner, R. (1977), *Economic Analysis of Law*, Little Brown.

Priestley, P., Fears, D. and Fuller, R. (1977), *Justice for Juveniles*, Routledge.

Radzinowicz, Sir L. and Hood, R. (1979), 'Judicial Discretion and Sentencing Standards: Victorian Attempts to Solve a Perennial Problem', *University of Pennsylvania L.R.*, 1288.

Radzinowicz, Sir L. and Hood, R. (1980), 'Incapacitating the Habitual Criminal: The English Experience', *Michigan L.R.*, 1305.

Roberts, J. and Roberts, C. (1982), 'Social Enquiry Reports and Sentencing', *Howard J.*, 76.

Ross, L. (1973), 'Law, Science and Accidents: the British Road Safety Act of 1967', *Journal of Legal Studies*, 1.

Royal Commission on Capital Punishment (1953), Report, Cmnd. 8932, H.M.S.O.

Royal Commission on Criminal Procedure, Report, Cmnd. 8092, H.M.S.O., 1981.

Ruggles-Brise, E. (1901), *Report to the Secretary of State for the Home Department on the Proceedings of the Fifth and Sixth International Penitentiary Congress*, Cd. 573, H.M.S.O.

Sellin, T. and Wolfgang, M. (1964), *The Measurement of Delinquency*.

Shapland, J. M. (1981), *Between Conviction and Sentence*, Routledge.

Shapland, J. M. (1982), 'The Victim in the Criminal Justice System', *Home Office Research Bulletin* no. 14, 21.

Shetreet, S. (1976), *Judges on Trial*, North Holland.

Softley, P., *Fines in Magistrates' Courts*, Home Office Research Study no. 46, H.M.S.O., 1977.

Sparks, R. (1965), 'Sentencing by Magistrates – Some Facts of Life', *Sociological Review Monograph*, no. 9, 71.

Sparks, R. (1971), 'The Use of Suspended Sentences', *Crim. L.R.*, 384.

Sparks, R., Genn, H. and Dodd, D. J. (1977), *Surveying Victims*, Wiley.

Spreutels, J. (1980), 'Giving Reasons for Sentence in the Crown Court', *Crim. L.R.*, 486.

Steer, D. (1970), *Police Cautions*, University of Oxford Penal Research Unit.

Stephen, J. F. (1885), 'Sentencing', 17, *The Nineteenth Century*, 755.

Streatfeild, Mr Justice (1961), *Report of the Interdepartmental Committee on the Business of the Criminal Courts*, Cmnd. 1289, H.M.S.O.

Sydney University (1980), Proceedings of the Institute of Criminology no. 38, *Alternatives to Imprisonment*.

Tapper, C. (ed.) (1981), *Crime, Proof and Punishment*, Butterworths.

Tarling, R., *Sentencing Practice in Magistrates' Courts*, Home Office Research Study no. 56, H.M.S.O., 1980.

Taylor, L. *et al.* (1979), *In Whose Best Interests?*, The Cobden Trust.

Thomas, D. A. (1972), 'Increasing Sentences on Appeal – the Case for a Re-examination', *Crim. L.R.*, 288.

Thomas, D. A. (1974), 'The Control of Discretion in the Administration of Criminal Justice', in Hood (1974a).

Thomas, D. A. (1977), *Equity in Sentencing*, Albany, New York.

Thomas, D. A. (1978), *Constraints on Judgement*, Institute of Criminology, Cambridge.

Thomas, D. A. (1979), *Principles of Sentencing*, Heinemann, 2nd edn.

Thomas, D. A. (1982a), 'Sentencing – Some Unresolved Legal Issues', in Oxner, S. (ed.), *Criminal Justice*, Carswell, Canada.

Thomas D. A. (1982b), 'The Partly Suspended Sentence', *Crim. L.R.*, 288.

Thorpe, J., *Social Inquiry Reports: A Survey*, Home Office Research Study no. 48, H.M.S.O., 1978.

Tonry, M. (1982), 'More Sentencing Reform in America', *Crim. L.R.*, 157.

Tonry, M. and Morris, N. (1978), 'Sentencing Reform in America', in Glazebrook (1978).

Trivizas, E. (1981), 'Sentencing the "Football Hooligan" ', *B.J. Crim.*, 342.

Tutt, N. (1981), 'A Decade of Policy', *B.J. Crim.*, 246.

Twentieth Century Fund Task Force on Criminal Sentencing (1976), *Fair and Certain Punishment*, New York.

von Hirsch, A. (1976), *Doing Justice*, Hill and Wang.

von Hirsch, A. (1981), 'Desert and Previous Convictions in Sentencing', *Minnesota L.R.*, 591.

von Hirsch, A. (1982), 'Constructing Guidelines for Sentencing', *Hamline L.R.*, 164.

Wade, E. C. S. and Phillips, G. (1977), *Constitutional Law*, Longman.

Walker, N. D. (1971), *Crimes, Courts and Figures*, Penguin.

Walker, N. D. (1975), 'Release by Executive Discretion: a Defence', *Crim. L.R.*, 540.

Walker, N. D. (1980), *Punishment, Danger and Stigma*, Blackwell.

Walker, N. D. (1981), 'The Ultimate Justification', in Tapper (1981).

Walker, N. D. (1982), 'Unscientific, Unwise, Unprofitable or Unjust?', *B.J. Crim.*, 276.

Walker, N. D. and Giller, H. (1977), *Penal Policy-Making in England*, Institute of Criminology, Cambridge.

Walker, N. D., Farrington, D. P. and Tucker, G. (1981), 'Reconviction Rates of Adult Males after Different Sentences', *B.J. Crim.*, 357.

Wasik, M. (1982), 'Domestic Violence and Cumulative Provocation', *Crim. L.R.*, 29.

Wasik, M. (1983), 'Excuses at the Sentencing Stage', *Crim. L.R. (July)*.

West, D. J. (1963), *The Habitual Prisoner*, Heinemann.

West, D. J. (1973), *Who Becomes Delinquent?*, Heinemann.

White, S. (1971), 'Homilies in Sentencing' *Crim. L.R.*, 690.

White Paper, *The Reduction of Pressure on the Prison System*, Cmnd. 7948, H.M.S.O., 1980.

White Paper, *Young Offenders*, Cmnd. 8045, H.M.S.O., 1980.

Wilcox, A. F. (1972), *The Decision to Prosecute*, Butterworths.

Wilkins, L. T. (1980), 'Sentencing Guidelines to Reduce Disparity', *Crim. L.R.*, 201.

Williams, D. G. T. (1974), 'The Accountability of the Police', in Hood (1974a).

Willis, A. (1981), 'Social Welfare and Social Control: a Survey of Young Men on Probation', *Home Office Research Bulletin* no. 11, 27.

Wolchover, D. (1981), 'Cross Examination of the Accused', *Crim. L.R.*, 312.

Wootton, B. (1973), 'Community Service Orders', *Crim. L.R.*, 16.

Wootton, B. (1978), *Crime and the Penal System*, Allen & Unwin.

Young, W. (1979), *Community Service Orders*, Heinemann.

Zander, M. (1979), 'The Investigation of Crime: a Survey of Cases Tried at the Old Bailey', *Crim. L.R.*, 203.

Zellick, G. (1974), 'Precedent in the Court of Appeal, Criminal Division', *Crim. L.R.*, 222.

Zellick, G. (1979), 'The Role of Prosecuting Counsel in Sentencing', *Crim. L.R.*, 493.

INDEX